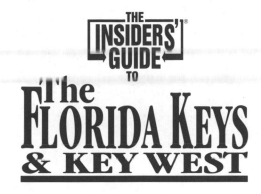

THE
INSIDERS' ®
GUIDE
TO

The
FLORIDA KEYS
& KEY WEST

THE INSIDERS' GUIDE

TO

The FLORIDA KEYS & KEY WEST

by
Victoria Shearer
&
Janet Ware

The Insiders' Guide®
An imprint of Falcon® Publishing Inc.
A Landmark Communications company
P.O. Box 1718
Helena, MT 59624
(800) 582-2665
www.insiders.com

Sales and Marketing: Falcon Publishing, Inc.
P.O. Box 1718
Helena, MT 59624
(800) 582-2665
www.falconguide.com

Advertising: Falcon Publishing, Inc.
150 W. Brambleton Ave.
Norfolk, VA 23510
(757) 446-2933
rwalsh@infi.net

•

FIRST EDITION
1st printing

•

Copyright ©1998
by Falcon Publishing, Inc.

•

Printed in Canada

•

Publications from *The Insiders' Guide*® series are available at special discounts for bulk
purchases for sales promotions, premiums or fundraisings. Special editions, including
personalized covers, can be created in large quantities for special needs.
For more information, please contact Falcon Publishing.

ISBN 1-57380-091-0

Preface

Remember well the black-and-white world you leave behind. When you arrive in the Florida Keys, life suddenly turns to Technicolor, and it doesn't take a twister to lead you to the lush Emerald City of Oz that is ours and yours to share. Settle yourself in. Take Toto along too.

Nowhere else on earth is there an Eden such as ours, where all are admitted freely and via so many varied means. Ours is the land of dreamers, doers and do-si-doers; of train makers, treasure trovers and time-honored tranquility. There are no munchkins along the yellow brick road that unites each of our magical isles and then appends us to the mainland. In the Florida Keys, everyone and everything is larger than life.

Look closely, and the enigmatic view from afar becomes as lucid as the crystalline waters of the Atlantic and the Gulf of Mexico that envelop us. From coconut palms to cormorants, you'll see that we are more than the Duval Street party scene in Key West. We are angelfish and anemones, gorgonians and groupers, lobsters and lizardfish, sponges and stone crabs. We're a thriving city of marine creatures commuting daily from North America's only barrier reef, 5 miles offshore, to sweeping underwater meadows of turtlegrass nearshore where we forage and feed.

By day, we are the golden sun that rises over the ocean, glows brightly and then, in ardent shades of red, dips ever-so-gently into the Gulf horizon. As darkness enfolds the Florida Keys, we are a cornucopia of stars that seem to gleam more brilliantly here in our endless skies than anywhere else.

We are a necklace of tiny, fossilized pearl islands tenuously strung together by 42 majestic bridges and the dream of one man, Henry Morrison Flagler. We're divers and diesel mechanics, anglers and archaeologists, sailors and salvagers, cruisers and commercial fishermen, boaters and bartenders, gunk-holers and guides, restaurateurs and real estate agents, hoteliers and hostesses. And our heart is in the sea.

In countless ways we are history. We're the ghosts of Spanish conquistadors, Native American Calusas, Bahamian fishermen and Cuban cigar makers. We're the bones of ships tortured so greatly on the reef that we forever rest in a watery offshore graveyard. We're pirates, smugglers, wreckers, spongers and turtlers. We've built boats, lighthouses and wharfs, even a bat tower. We've survived without fresh water and in hurricane gales, amid clouds of mosquitoes and through Indian massacres. We're no strangers to courage.

We are hardwood hammocks, tropical pinelands and mangrove islets. Unique in the universe, we are diminutive Key deer, sour Key limes and endangered Key Largo woodrats. We are nesting great white herons, communal white pelicans, showy roseate spoonbills. Creatures great and small, we are bonefish and billfish, sharks and stingrays, sea turtles, manatees and dolphins. And, because we vigilantly guard our copious treasures, we are The Florida Keys Wild Bird Center, Reef Relief, The Turtle Hospital, The Nature Conservancy and Bay Watch. At last we have a brain.

We are the 81,000 full- and part-time Florida Keys citizens: men, women and children of all races, religions and sexual preferences. Rich, poor and somewhere in between, each of us sports similar T-shirts, shorts and baseball caps. We bear genuine, unpretentious smiles, seeking little more than the harmony needed to fully render a place called Paradise.

Whether you mistakenly believe that you lack a heart . . . a brain . . . the nerve . . . you're sure to unearth it all, along with a deeply enriched spirit, on your journey through the mysteries, rich history and legends of the Florida Keys. Experience all the marvels of this awe-inspiring Oz. You'll never want to click your ruby slippers, sandals or bare feet — or board a plane, boat or automobile — longing for home. One visit is, after all, what led so very many of us to become Insiders. Welcome to this side of the rainbow. We are the Florida Keys.

About the Authors

Victoria Shearer

Victoria Shearer traversed more than the Atlantic Ocean when she settled in Paradise five years ago. Yin met yang. After traipsing through the British Isles, the European continent, the Middle East and the Far East from her two-year temporary base in gray, cloudy London, she relocated to the Florida Keys. Far from the culture shock she expected, life in these pearlescent islands threw open the window to the sun, the sea and the wonderment of nature. No stranger to the wonders of the world, Vicki found that the Keys reign in a class by themselves.

A University of Wisconsin graduate, Vicki jumped into the world of advertising with both feet, writing copy extolling the multiple virtues of products ranging from paper napkins to mail-order beach tents. Her career ran the gamut of most facets of the print industry. Once empty-nested, she combined editing skills with a healthy appetite, bloodletting the pages as copy editor at *COOK'S Magazine*. Her European sojourn kindled the fire of her passions, travel and food, about which she now writes experientially for newspapers and magazines across the nation.

Now living, loving and writing from her home on Duck Key, Vicki shares the cherished bounty of the Keys with her husband, Bob, and her visiting adult children, Kristen, Brian and Lisa, and granddaughter, Bethany.

Janet Ware

A burning desire to never shovel snow again led Janet Ware to make her permanent home in Key West. She came to the southernmost city from Champaign, Illinois, where she had lived for 15 years working as a publicist for an ad agency specializing in travel promotion, for a Girl Scout Council and for a publisher of books on health and fitness. A native of Michigan, Janet is a graduate of the University of Missouri School of Journalism and a former newspaper reporter.

Janet's work in travel marketing and as a freelance travel writer took her all over the world, but never to the Florida Keys — until 1991. She fell in love at first sight with Key West, returning twice more for extended vacations before moving here in 1995. At the suggestion of a friend, she took up bartending to make money for the move and to ensure that she'd have a job once she arrived.

Now, Janet leads a double life — writer by day, bartender by night. Her mornings are spent writing promotional copy and working on her novel, a romance set in the Florida Keys. Five nights a week, she bartends at a seaside resort, mixing Margaritas and offering advice to tourists. The rest of the time, she plays tourist herself — sunbathing, snorkeling or simply exploring Key West on foot. For Janet, who made her dream of living on an island in the sun come true, writing this book has been a labor of love.

Acknowledgments

Victoria Shearer

The Beatles said it all when they crooned, "I get by with a little help from my friends," and mine rank right up there on the Top 40. To my best friend and life partner, my husband, Bob, thank you for undying patience, encouragement and support; great grilled tuna, swordfish and shrimp during the pre-deadline weeks "down under"; and for translating a lifetime of Florida Keys angling experience for me so that we may all catch the magic of the sport. To my dear friends Wayne and Mary Moccia, thank you for sharing your expansive knowledge of the Keys' cruising waters and for divulging your secret hideaways and favorite dive locations. I am grateful for all those evenings you donated to my cause to read behind my endeavors so I could get my facts and lingo right. And thanks for unlimited check-out from your personal Florida Keys library and slide collection. To Barbara and Dick Marlin, thanks for all the good camping tips and the read-behind. To Bill Beardsley, hearty thanks for your great sidebar on the Florida Keys Fly-Fishing School. Nothing beats personal experience. To James Hankins, Frankie Wilson and Joe Winter, thanks for the fishing photo ops and all those Insider angling and lobstering tips. To the Lunch Bunch — Mary, Gail, Judy, Loraine, Joan, Rose, Mary Lou — culinary medals of the year to you all for visiting a different restaurant every week, my choice, and critiquing your food. And a special thank you to Jay Yates for his Insider insights into the culinary scene of Key West. To Marilyn Beardsley goes appreciation for leads on duplicate bridge tournaments. To John Ghee, Dick Adler and the Everglades houseboat gang, thanks for the green flash, the sunset scale and all the giggles. To Suzanne and John Tobey and Vivienne and Frank Afshari, my four favorite houseguests, I promise I won't drag you around the Keys on my research junkets anymore. Your laughter and support kept me going. To my many friends on Duck Key — you know who you are — thank you for all the unsolicited tips and Insider info that you dropped in my mailbox and, most importantly, for never failing to ask, "How's it going?" I am truly blessed. My appreciation to Beth Storie and Eileen Myers at Insiders' Guides for constant good humor and support. Thanks and apologies to my all-grown-up children — Kristen, Brian, Lisa — to my mother June and to Mom and Dad Shearer, for their patient understanding of my deadline-oriented life. Love and kisses to my new granddaughter, Bethany Dianne. And finally, to my co-author Janet Ware, thanks for rowing your end of the boat. We crossed the finish line in record time. Good job, Insiders. Thanks for the memories.

Janet Ware

Like most people who love to travel, I've consulted and collected my share of guidebooks over the years. But I never gave serious thought to what goes into putting one together . . . until now. Updating this *Insiders' Guide®* has been one tough, exacting assignment. And although I'm listed as a co-author, the real kudos for this task should go to my partner in crime, Vicki Shearer. Without her solid foundation of thorough research and just plain good writing in the first edition, this new and improved version would simply not have been possible. I feel privileged to have worked alongside her. Of course, every good writer needs a good editor and, luckily, I found one of those, too. Thanks to Eileen Myers at Insiders for fine-tuning my copy and always making sure I stayed on time and on track. I owe a debt of gratitude, too, to the folks who staff the various Chambers of Commerce throughout the Keys as well as the many sources too numerous to name who helped me update a wealth of facts and figures. I came to know many of you only as voices over the phone, but your patience and always-friendly attitudes, even in the face of my persistent questions, never ceased to amaze me. Thanks are also owed to my much younger co-workers at Marriott's Casa Marina, who were a constant source of information about the latest hot spots and happenings in and around Key West, and to my best friend, Linda Zimnicki, who came from Chicago to spend what should have been a restful vacation and was forced instead to run hither and yon helping me play tourist. Finally, a special thanks to three people whose influence on my life and career helped me get where I am today: Richard Newman, who taught me the travel promotion business; Barry Barker, from whom I first heard about the wonders of the Florida Keys; and Nancy Camp, who not only accompanied me on my first visit to Key West but suggested a source of income — bartending — that has served me well ever since. And last but not least to my brothers, Dave and Bruce, who, when I said I was leaving a perfectly good job in Illinois to move to the Florida Keys without one, never questioned my sanity. They simply noted my address, then bought plane tickets and paid me a visit. Thanks! I love you all.

Table of Contents

Directory of Maps

The Florida Keys

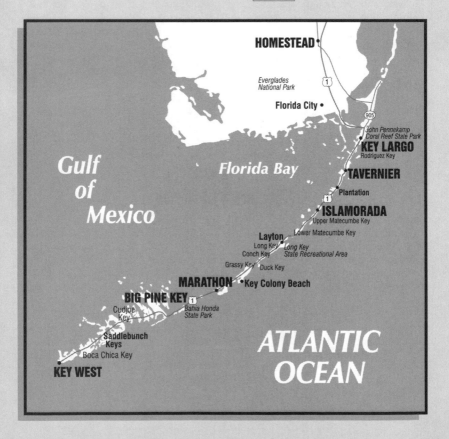

HOMESTEAD •

Everglades National Park

Florida City •

$U.S. 1$

905

John Pennekamp Coral Reef State Park

KEY LARGO
Rodriguez Key

Gulf of Mexico

Florida Bay

TAVERNIER

Plantation

ISLAMORADA
Upper Matecumbe Key

Lower Matecumbe Key

Layton
Long Key   *Long Key State Recreational Area*
Conch Key
Grassy Key   Duck Key

MARATHON   • Key Colony Beach

BIG PINE KEY
Cudjoe Key   *Bahia Honda State Park*

Saddlebunch Keys
Boca Chica Key

KEY WEST

ATLANTIC OCEAN

Key West and The Lower Keys

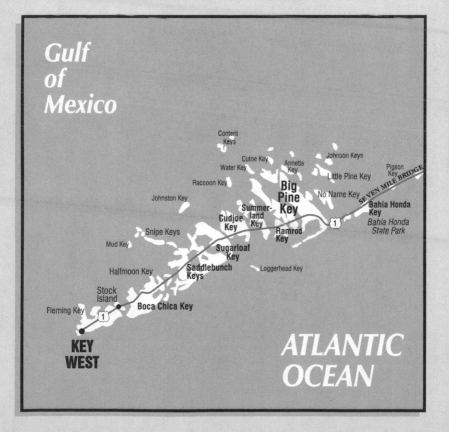

Gulf of Mexico

Content Keys

Cutoe Key

Water Key

Annette Key

Johnson Keys

Little Pine Key

Pigeon Key

Raccoon Key

Big Pine Key

No Name Key

SEVEN MILE BRIDGE

Johnston Key

Summer-land Key

Bahia Honda Key

Cudjoe Key

Ramrod Key

Bahia Honda State Park

Snipe Keys

Sugarloaf Key

Mud Key

Saddlebunch Keys

Halfmoon Key

Loggerhead Key

Stock Island

Fleming Key

Boca Chica Key

KEY WEST

ATLANTIC OCEAN

Marathon and The Middle Keys

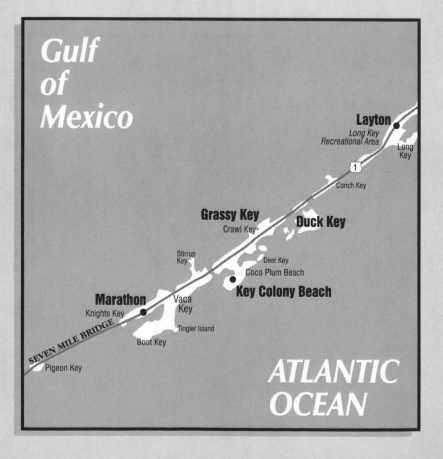

Gulf
of
Mexico

Layton
Long Key
Recreational Area
Long
Key

1

Conch Key

Grassy Key
Crawl Key

Duck Key

Stirrup
Key

Deer Key
Coco Plum Beach

Marathon
Knights Key

Vaca
Key

Key Colony Beach

Tingler Island

SEVEN MILE BRIDGE

Boot Key

Pigeon Key

ATLANTIC
OCEAN

Key Largo and The Upper Keys

HOMESTEAD

Biscayne Bay

Cardsound Toll Road

Florida City

1

905

John Pennekamp
Coral Reef State Park

KEY LARGO

Eagle
Key

Nest
Keys

End Key

Club
Key

Hussett
Key

Rudriguez Key

Buttonwood
Keys

Florida Bay

Stake Key

Bob Allen Keys

TAVERNIER

Panhandle
Key

Crab Keys

Plantation

Windley Key

Barnes Key

Shell Key

ISLAMORADA

Lignumvitae Key

Upper Matecumbe Key

**ATLANTIC
OCEAN**

1

Lower Matecumbe Key

Layton

Long Key

Long Key
State Recreation Area

Key West

Gulf of Mexico

Stock Island

Blue Lagoon

N. Roosevelt Blvd

Northside Dr.

Dredgers Key Rd.

Duck Ave.

Donald Ave.

14th St.

11th St.

Kennedy Dr.

13th St.

Rivera St.

Bay of Florida

Key West International Airport

FLEMING KEY

7th St.

5A

A1A

MacMillan Dr.

Mustin St.

Whiting Ave.

Palm Ave.

S. Roosevelt Blvd.

1st St.

George St.

Flagler Ave.

Smathers Beach

White St.

Bertha St.

Mallory Square

Caroline St.

Eaton St.

Fleming St.

Southard St.

Truman Ave.

United St.

South St.

Reynolds St.

A1A

Rest Beach

Simonton St.

Duval St.

Whitehead St.

Emma St.

Fort St.

Virginia St.

Amelia St.

Higgs Beach

Southernmost Beach

Southernmost Point of the Continental U.S.

Fort Zachary Taylor State Park

Harry S. Truman U. S. Naval Station Annex

ATLANTIC OCEAN

How to Use This Book

Here at the southernmost tip of the continental United States, the serpentine Overseas Highway fuses many of our 800-plus islands with ligaments of vaulted bridges and concrete connective tissue. This Key chain of coral wonderment is but a pleasure dome for its heart and soul, however, for the pulsating beat and the vital spirit of the Florida Keys undulates beneath the surface of its all-encompassing waters.

Ours is a marriage of land and sea. To merely introduce you to the topside society of the Florida Keys would neglect the flamboyant and fascinating communities living below. This guide lifts the curtain, bringing the many facets of our watery stage to life. We treat you to our unique geology and colorful history.

We introduce you to the flora and fauna of the habitats of our tropical ecosystem. And we take you where you've never been before — fishing, diving and boating in our waters.

We'll help you sate your appetite with listings of restaurants, seafood markets and specialty food shops. We'll show you where the action is with the rundown on attractions, recreation sites, festivals and special events and nightlife of the Keys. We'll offer myriad alternatives for you to rest your weary head: hotels, motels, inns, guesthouses and condominiums; campgrounds; even resort marinas and anchoring-out spots for your motor or sailing yacht. Landlubber or seafarer, everything you need to know is in *The Insiders' Guide® to the Florida Keys and Key West*.

Keys-Speak Glossary

backcountry — shallow seagrass meadows and mangrove islet waters of Florida Bay.

bayside — anything on the opposite coast from the Atlantic; i.e. Florida Bay in the Upper Keys, the Gulf of Mexico in the Middle and Lower Keys.

Close-up

bight — a body of water bounded by a bend or curve in the shore; several are found in Key West.

bluewater — deep, offshore waters of the Atlantic Ocean.

chickee — an open-sided, thatched-roof hut commonly found near the water's edge that is used as shelter from the sun.

Conch — a descendant of the original Bahamians that settled the Keys; a person born in the Florida Keys.

freshwater Conch — a person who has lived in the Florida Keys for at least seven years.

conch — meat of a marine mollusk used in chowder and fritters; once a staple in the diet of early Conchs and Keys-dwelling Native Americans, now an endangered species that may not be harvested in the Keys.

Croakies — band for securing sunglasses around your head so they don't fall overboard.

'cuda — slang for barracuda.

flats — shallow, nearshore waters of the Atlantic.

gunk-hole — to explore the shallow, nearshore waters and mangrove islets in a shallow draft craft in search of bird life and marine species.

hammock — an elevated piece of bedrock covered with a hardwood tropical forest.

hammock — a woven lounger strung between two palm trees.

oceanside — anything on the Atlantic coast of the Keys.

Paradise — The Florida Keys.

The Rock — Slang for the Florida Keys, usually uttered by locals heading for Miami to shop or party, i.e., "Getting off the Rock."

To navigate this book, begin with the assumption you are traveling "down the Keys," that is, from Key Largo to Key West. We have organized our information by descending mile marker. Mile markers are those small green signs with white numbers you'll see posted at the sides of the Overseas Highway. We have designated mile marker addresses as either oceanside (on your left as you travel down the Keys) or bayside (on your right as you go toward Key West). At Key West, which is MM 0, locations will be stated using street names.

Most chapters have three parts. A general preface to the subject matter acquaints you with aspects of the topic common to all areas of the Florida Keys. This is fol-lowed by specifics for the Upper Keys (MM 106 on Key Largo to MM 70 on Long Key), Middle Keys (MM 70 to MM 39 on Ohio Key) and the Lower Keys (MM 39 to Stock Island). The final section will give you the scoop on Stock Island and Key West, the entrance to which is actually about MM 3, although such appellations are not used in Key West.

When making phone calls from outside the area, note that the area code in the Florida Keys is 305. The Florida Keys is divided into calling areas, or scopes. You may call within a scope by using only seven digits. To dial Florida Keys numbers outside a calling scope you will need to first dial 1-305 and then the seven digits. Such calls made with BellSouth

service, as well as some calls made to area code 305 in Miami, incur a flat 25¢ rate, regardless of how long you talk. Calls with other carriers, such as MCI or AT&T, may be charged differently.

The following calling scopes require only seven-digit numbers:

Key West — from Key West to Sugarloaf Key.

Sugarloaf Key — from Big Pine Key to Key West.

Big Pine Key — from Marathon to Sugarloaf Key.

Marathon — from Big Pine Key to Islamorada.

Islamorada — from Key Largo to Marathon.

Key Largo — from Islamorada to North Key Largo.

North Key Largo — to Key Largo.

Throughout all the chapters we have sprinkled Insiders' Tips, extracted from those in the know with a little arm-twisting. You'll find enlightening Close-ups chock-full of information on everything from a recipe for Key lime pie to how to make yellowtail chum balls. And, just so you will be sure to understand the language, we have included a glossary of Keys-speak.

You hold in your hand a passport to the Florida Keys. We help you hit the road, explore the sea and speak the language of the natives. Locals call this Paradise. Judge for yourself.

We introduce you to the flora and fauna of the habitats of our tropical ecosystem. And we take you where you've never been before — fishing, diving and boating in our waters.

Gateway to the Keys

The rural areas of Homestead and Florida City, home to alligators, airboat rides, agriculture and achievement, are known as the Gateway to the Florida Keys.

Residents of these two south Dade County cities are courageous and industrious individuals, continuously demonstrating resilience in the wake of peril. To date, four mighty hurricanes have altered their region's history. Andrew, the most recent, roared across South Florida in August 1992 with 150 mph winds, causing some $30 billion in damage and leaving an estimated 160,000 homeless. Almost immediately, the residents of south Dade County resolved to rejuvenate their community, and they have remarkably succeeded.

Today, with two of nature's most splendid showpieces and the opening of the multimillion dollar motorsports complex in November 1995, Homestead and Florida City draw more than a million tourists each year. Riveted by the glory of Everglades and Biscayne National Parks and the thrill of NASCAR racing, visitors find ample reason to pause at "The Gateway" before continuing on to the Florida Keys and Key West.

First settled by the Tequesta and Calusa Indian tribes some 11,000 years ago, South Dade County was later inhabited by Creeks and Muskogees, or Seminoles (meaning "separatists"). In 1830, many Seminoles were forced west to Oklahoma along the

Completely covered in flaming orange blossoms in the spring the royal poinciana trees regally dress the Keys.

Several research facilities in the Keys conduct on-going dolphin behavior studies.

Trail of Tears. Those who remained in South Dade either lost their lives or barely managed to endure the tragic Seminole Wars. Ultimately, survivors found refuge within the area now designated as Everglades National Park. Their descendants continue to reside there.

Had it not been for the Florida Keys and Key West — and Henry Flagler's effort to extend the Florida East Coast Railway to this country's southernmost city — Homestead and Florida City might not be what they are today. Railway officials laid out a town toward the end of the mainland; workers settled in, and a station house and water plant were built. These workers recommended naming the town Homestead, and Flaglor approved. He sent a tomato farmer to the area south of Homestead, and the town founded by this farmer became known as Detroit. Engineer William Krome directed construction of the railway, and Krome Avenue, which parallels U.S. Highway 1 through the two cities, was named for him.

The marl lands (marl is calcitic mud beneath the water of the Everglades) near Detroit had already spurred a growth in farming. Portions of the Everglades had been drained, crops were harvested and, at last, the railroad station provided a means of shipping produce north. When the railway to Key West was completed in 1912, it provided easier access to the Florida Keys and a means of receiving fresh water. Property values in this new agricultural community began to skyrocket. In 1914, residents of Detroit incorporated and renamed their new city Florida City. Ten years later, the residents of Homestead incorporated their city. In 1926, a powerful hurricane prompted an exodus of many area residents, and the great Labor Day hurricane of 1935

came along and destroyed Flagler's Key West extension of the railway (see our Historical Evolution chapter).

The "Gateway" population dwindled.

It wasn't until 1942 that Homestead and Florida City began to experience a rebirth. The Army Air Corps established Homestead Army Air Field as a training base on the site of what had been a county-owned airfield used by Pan American Ferries Inc., and it became one of the largest military installations in the nation. Home to approximately 25,000 military personnel, civilian employees and dependents as well as its own hospital, bank, post office, library, nursery, preschool, barber shops and more, the field eventually became an official military base, pumping $450 million annually into the local economy.

Following World War II and yet another hurricane in 1945, the base closed, reopened and then closed again. In 1979, the Pentagon transferred 25 percent of its military personnel from South Dade to other bases, and retail businesses and housing in Homestead and Florida City suffered immeasurably. Later, the facility reopened as a tactical air command and training base, but it never again funneled the amount of money into these communities it once did.

The south Dade County economy today relies heavily on agriculture. Fruits and vegetables for many tables throughout the United States are grown in this area, and nurseries and landscaping operations are big business here as well, providing Northerners with a chance to have their own real tropical plants.

Tourism has also become a major player in the economy, as the area boasts NASCAR racing, two beautiful, huge national parks and close proximity to the Florida Keys.

This fragile strand of coral beads, which arcs southwest from the U.S. mainland to within 100 miles of Cuba, has endured for eons at the mercy of the elements.

Historical Evolution

The saga of the Keys, like the livelihoods of its inhabitants, tethers itself first, foremost and forever to the sea. Our fragile strand of coral beads, which arcs southwest from the U.S. mainland to within 100 miles of Cuba, has endured for eons at the mercy of the elements. Nature determined, more than man ever did, the course of our history. That is, until one man accomplished what natural forces could not: the coupling of the islands to each other and to the mainland United States.

We will chronicle the Florida Keys, therefore, as a manmade triptych, highlighting the eras before, during and after Henry Flagler's Florida East Coast Railroad Extension refashioned the subsequent history of the region.

Prologue

Native Americans and the Spanish

The earliest recorded evidence of a Native American population in the Keys is thought to be around 800 A.D., when maritime Indians populated the islands. Kitchen middens, or mounds of fish and sea-turtle bones and conch shells, can be found throughout the Keys. Archaeologists believe that although ancient villages may have existed thousands of years before this time, the rising sea level of the present Holocene Epoch (see our Paradise Found chapter) has buried these settlements beneath the ocean.

Historians do not agree as to which tribes of Native Americans inhabited the Florida Keys in the ensuing centuries. The Tequestas, Calusas, Matecumbes, Caribbean Island tribes and Seminoles from the mainland are all mentioned, although no archaeological evidence is conclusive. Widely accepted, however, is the notion that the Native Americans were sea-farers by necessity and initially friendly to the white men they encountered.

Ponce de Leon garnered the credit for naming the Florida Keys Los Martires in 1513 during his exploration of the Gulf of Mexico. Legend maintains that the string of rock islands looked to him like suffering martyrs from his vantage point at sea. The Spanish took interest in the Native Americans of Los Martires in the centuries that followed, but had no desire to seize their rocky islands. Priests from Havana attempted to convert the Native Americans to Catholicism, not in an attempt to save their souls but to teach them to be friendly to the crews of the Spanish ships and to hate the French and English, Spain's enemies who also were attempting to explore the New World. Spain's overriding interest in the Florida Keys at this time simply was to protect their fleet of treasure ships voyaging past its shores en route from Mexico and Cuba to the mother country.

The Gulf Stream: Treasure Highway

Long before the Overseas Highway became the main road of the Florida Keys, another highway controlled the islands' destiny: the great, blue river-in-the-Atlantic — the Gulf Stream. (The warm water of the Gulf Stream, the temperature of which varies greatly from surrounding waters, flows in a northerly direction between the Keys and Cuba, up the northeast coast of the United States and then turns toward the east where it crosses the Atlantic Ocean to the European continent.) Conquistadors, explorers and adventurers capitalized on the pulsing clockwise current (2 to 4 knots) to carry them swiftly back to Europe, where they unloaded the harvested riches of the New World at the feet of greedy monarchs.

The Spanish were the first to send their treasure-laden ships on this precarious route past our island chain, which is protected from the ocean's fury by a barrier coral reef (see our Diving and Snorkeling chapter). The Gulf Stream, which is not a definitive channel, winds an uneven course about 45 miles wide just outside the reef. Bad weather or bad judgment dashed the hopes, dreams and cargo of hundreds of ships against this unforgiving coral graveyard.

It was the Native Americans who initially took advantage of this unexpected shipwrecked bounty, but salvaging became big business in the Keys with the arrival of the Bahamian Conchs (see "Wrecking Industry" in this chapter). The passing ships inspired piracy from many nations, particularly the English who lurked in the cuts and channels between the islands waiting to raid the ships' caches of gold and silver.

www.insiders.com

See this and many other **Insiders' Guide®** destinations online — in their entirety.

Visit us today!

The Native Americans learned the ways of the Europeans, trading with the Spanish in Havana by means of large oceangoing canoes, pirating English ships and free-diving to salvage the cargo of their wrecked vessels. Falling ill with the white man's diseases greatly reduced Native American numbers. In 1763 Spain gave Florida to England in exchange for Cuba. At this time, the last of the indigenous Native American families fled to Havana, fearing retribution for the cruelty to which they subjected the British sailors who had been dashed upon the reef and stranded without recourse.

The Bahamians

By the early 1700s, a group of white settlers from the Bahamas had begun active trading with Havana. Their ancestors, religious dissenters from England, had originally settled on Eleuthera and the Great Abaco Islands in the Bahamas in the 1600s. Experienced seamen and fishermen, these Bahamians harvested the waters of the Florida Keys, selling their catch in Havana. (The word "key" is believed to derive from the English word "cay," which in turn is a corruption of the Spanish "cayo," all meaning "island.") The Keys were considered the pantry of Havana, for our waters supplied Cuba with green-turtle meat, conch, fish and crawfish. The Bahamians traded their catch for knives, rope, spices and other much-needed supplies, which they took back to the Bahamas.

When the English took over Florida in 1763, they placed the waters near the Florida Keys off-limits to residents of the Bahamas, which upset the trade balance between the Bahamas and Havana. This inconvenience was short-lived, however, because Spain regained Florida in 1783, and trade between the Bahamas and Cuba returned to normal. There was some settlement of the Keys by the English during this interval, but colonization of Key West did not begin in earnest until 1821, when Spain ceded Florida to the United States. Before 1821 Key West was just a watering stop for ships traveling the Gulf Stream route from the Gulf to the Atlantic.

A new edict insisting that only U.S. residents could engage in the now lucrative wrecking operations off the Florida Keys spurred many Bahamian families to emigrate to the settlement of Key West. Many dismantled their entire houses and transported them to our southernmost city (see the Architecture Close-up in our Attractions chapter). Some settlers were freed black slaves, dumped throughout the Bahamian islands by the English as they

---

INSIDERS' TIP

Widows' walks atop Key West buildings, long said to be the spots where lonely sea captains' wives watched for their husbands' arrivals, were actually the lookout spots from which islanders awaited sightings of shipwrecks in the waters off the reef. "Wreck ashore," was heralded when a ship went aground, inciting a frenzy of people to the wharf to watch the wreckers race to the floundering ship.

Photo: Victoria Shearer

Anchors such as this one at East Martello Museum in Key West
are reminders of ancient ships that wrecked on the coral reef.

were released from captured slave traders. Ship owners and captains of merchant ships moved to Key West to be close to the trade lanes.

British Bahamians were known as Conchs for three legendary reasons: First, a prolific amount of conch flourished in the waters of the Bahamas, and the meat from the conical shells was a staple in the Bahamian diet. Second, it is believed that as a means of early communication, the Bahamian islanders blew into queen conch shells, creating a distinctive wailing cry that could be heard a great distance. Third, during the American Revolution of 1776, Tory sympathizers escaped to the Bahamas, where they supposedly said, "We'd rather eat conchs than go to war." Only descendants of the original Conchs who settled the Florida Keys may be so called legitimately, although today the word Conch generally refers to anyone born in the Florida Keys.

Key West

A time-honored story persists that warring tribes of mainland Seminoles and island Calusas had one final battle on the southernmost island of our chain of keys. Spanish conquictadors purportedly found the island strewn with bleached bones of the Native Americans and called the key Cayo Hueso, (pronounced KY-o WAY-so) or "island of bones." Bahamian settlers pronounced the Spanish name as Key West.

Settled long before the other keys in the chain, Key West was very much a maritime frontier town by the 1820s, booming with sea-driven industries. Ships sailing out of Key West Harbor set across the Florida Straits to Havana, their holds filled with fish, sea turtles and sponges harvested the length of the Keys. A lively fishing trade with Cuba continued into the 1870s. The melting pot of Key West included seamen from many cultures: black Bahamians, West Indian blacks, Spanish Cubans and white Bahamians of English descent.

Key West was incorporated in 1828. Within 10 years it was the largest and wealthiest city in the territory of Florida, even though it could only be reached by ship, a geographic fact of life that continued until Henry Flagler's Florida East Coast Railroad Extension was finished in 1912. But it was the very waters isolating Key West from the rest of the world that contributed to its wealth.

Piracy

When the United States gained possession of Florida and the Florida Keys in 1821, the island of Key West took on a strategic importance as a U.S. naval base. Deemed a safe, convenient and extensive harbor by Lt. Matthew Perry, who was assigned to secure the island for the United States, Key West became the base of operations to fight the piracy ravaging the trading vessels traveling the Gulf Stream superhighway and those heading through the Gulf of Mexico to New Orleans. English, French and Dutch buccaneers had threatened the Spanish treasure galleons in the 18th century. In the early days of the 1800s, Spanish pirates, based mainly in Cuba, hid among the islands of the Keys and preyed on all nations, especially the United States. Using schooners with centerboards that drew only 4 to 5 feet of water, the pirate ships dipped in and out of the shallow cuts and channels to avoid capture.

In 1830 Commodore David Porter was sent to Key West to head up an anti-piracy fleet and wipe out the sea-jacking from the region. Commandeering barge-style vessels equipped with oars, Porter and his crews were able to follow the sea dogs into the shallow waters and overtake them. After 1830 the area was safe from banditry once again.

The Wrecking Industry

Where the Gulf Stream was once the sea highway carrying the Spanish treasure galleons back to Europe, the 18th and 19th centuries saw the route traversed in the opposite direction by trading vessels sailing from New England ports to the French and British islands of the West Indies and the Antilles. The ships hugged the shoreward edge of the Gulf Stream so as not to have to run against its strong northerly currents. They often ran aground on the reef, giving birth to a lucrative wrecking industry that salvaged silks, satins, lace, leather, crystal, china, silver, furniture, wine, whiskey and more.

After the United States took possession of Florida in 1821, Key West became an official wrecking and salvage station for the federal government, which sought to regulate and cash in on the lucrative trade that until this time was going to Nassau or Havana. Salvage masters had to get a license from a district court judge, proving that they and their salvage vessels were free of fraud. By 1854 wrecking was a widely practiced profession in the Keys. Fleets of schooners patrolled the Keys from Biscayne to the Dry Tortugas. First they would assist the shipwrecked sailors then try to save the ship (there was no Coast Guard in those days).

Unlike early unregulated times, the wreckers couldn't just lay claim to the ship's cargo for themselves. They were paid off in shares of the bounty. During peak wrecking years, 1850 to 1860, nearly one ship a week hit the reefs, some with cargo valued in the millions of dollars.

Although by 1826 some of the reefs along the length of the Keys were marked by lighthouses or light ships, most remained treacherous and claimed many cargoes, particularly in the Upper Keys where the Gulf Stream meanders close to the reef. Stories have endured throughout the years that some of the more

---

INSIDERS' TIP

During Prohibition in the 1920s, rum running became a cottage industry in the Florida Keys. Runners secured liquor in Cuba or the Bahamas, staying in international waters out of U.S. jurisdiction, while small boats spirited the drink in the dead of night back to shore. They hid the contraband in the mangroves (see our Paradise Found chapter).

Uniden Products are the Wave of the Future!

1. Purchase this Uniden product and the LOST IN SPACE™ video from October 6, 1998 to March 30, 1999.

2. Return this completed form with your original "Lost in Space" video sales receipt, your original Uniden sales receipt and the UPC bar code from the Uniden carton (make an additional copy of receipts and bar code for your records.) Circle the item and purchase price on your receipt.

3. All claims must be postmarked no later than March 30, 1999 and received by Apirl 15, 1999.

Mail to: **UNIDEN AMERICA CORPORATION**
ATTN: MARKETING DEPARTMENT
RE: LOST IN SPACE MAIL-IN REBATE
4700 AMON CARTER BLVD.
FORT WORTH, TEXAS 76155

NAME _____

ADDRESS _____

CITY _____ STATE _____ ZIP _____

DATE OF UNIDEN PURCHASE _____ DATE OF VIDEO PURCHASE _____

Uniden

enterprising and unscrupulous wreckers even changed or removed navigational markers or flashed lights in imitation of a light ship to lure an unsuspecting vessel to its demise on a shallow shoal so they could salvage the cargo. The construction of additional lighthouses along the reef in the mid-1800s improved navigation to the point that the wrecking industry gradually faded away by the end of the 19th century.

Sponging

Sponging developed quickly in the Keys after the area became part of the United States, maturing into a commercially important industry by 1850.

Initially, sponge harvesting was accomplished from a dinghy: One man sculled while the other looked through a glass-bottomed bucket. The spotter held a long pole with a small, three-pronged rake on one end used to impale the sponge and bring it into the boat. On shore, the sponges were laid on the ground to dry in the sun so that the living animal within would dehydrate and die. The sponges then were soaked for a week and pounded on a rock or beaten with a stick to remove a blackish covering. Cleaned of weeds, washed and hung to dry in bunches, the sponges were displayed for sale.

Cubans, Greeks and Conchs harvested the sponges as fast and furiously as they could, with little regard for how the supply would be maintained, and it inevitably began to diminish. The Greeks began diving deeper waters for the sponges, much in demand on the world market by 1900, and eventually moved to the west coast of Florida at Tarpon Springs, where the sponging was more bountiful.

By 1940 a blight wiped out all but about 10 percent of the Keys' sponge population. Although sponges again grow in our waters, commercial sponging is no longer a viable industry as synthetic sponges have absorbed the market.

Cubans and the Cigar Industry

Cuba, closer to Key West than Miami is, has always played a role in the historical evolution of the Keys. Cuban fishermen long frequented the bountiful Keys waters, and in the 19th century Cuban emigres brought new life and new industry to Key West. William H. Wall built a small cigar factory in the 1830s on Key West's Front Street. It was not until a year after the Cuban Revolution of 1868, when a prominent Cuban by the name of Señor Vicente Martinez Ybor moved his cigar-making factory to Key West from Havana, that the new era of cigar manufacturing began in earnest.

Ybor was followed by E.H. Gato and a dozen or so other cigar-making companies. And an influx of Cuban immigrant cigar workers "washed ashore," joining the melting pot in Key West. Tobacco arrived in bales from Havana, and production grew until factories numbered 161, catapulting Key West to the rank of cigar-making capital of the United States. Though the manufacturers moved their businesses to Key West to escape high Cuban tariffs and the cigar-makers union, the unions reestablished themselves in Key West by 1879, and troubles began anew.

The industry continued to flourish in Key West until its peak in 1890, when the city of Tampa offered the cigar manufacturers lower taxes if they would move to the Gulf Coast swamplands, an area now called Ybor City. With this incentive, the cigar-making industry left the Keys, but many of the Cuban people stayed, creating a steady Latin influence on Key West that has endured to this day.

The Salt Industry

Early settlers of Key West and Duck Key manufactured sea salt beginning in the 1830s, using natural salt-pond basins on both islands. Salt was essential for preserving food in those days because there was no refrigeration. Cut off from tidal circulation except during storms, the salt ponds were flooded with seawater and then allowed to evaporate. The resulting salt crystals were harvested.

Capricious weather often flooded the salt ponds with fresh water, ruining the salty "crop." By 1876 the salt industry no longer existed in the Keys. The destructive forces of repeated hurricanes made the industry economically unfeasible.

Homesteading the Keys

Bahamians also homesteaded other Keys in the early 19th century, settling in small family groups to farm the thin soil. Familiar with cultivating the unique land of limestone islands, the Bahamians worked at farming pineapples, Key limes and sapodillas, called "sours and dillies."

Indian Key is thought to be the first real settlement in the Upper Keys. By 1834 it had docks, a post office, shops and a mansion belonging to the island's owner, Jacob Housman. It became the governmental seat of Dade County for a time, but attacks from mainland Native Americans proved an insurmountable problem for this little key (see our Attractions chapter). Through the ensuing decades, Bahamian farmers homesteaded on Key Vaca, Upper Matecumbe, Newport (Key Largo), Tavernier and Planter. By 1891 the area that is now Harry Harris Park in Key Largo had a post office, school, church and five farms (see our Attractions chapter).

The census on any of these keys varied widely over the course of the century, and little is known as to why. For instance, Key Vaca had 200 settlers in 1840, according to Dr. Perrine of Indian Key, but by 1866, a U.S. census revealed an unexplained population of zero for Key Vaca.

Flagler's Folly: The Florida East Coast Railroad Extension

The dream of one man changed the isolation of the Florida Keys for all time. Native New Yorker Henry Flagler, born in 1830 and educated only to the 8th grade, established the Standard Oil Company with John D. Rockefeller in 1870 and became a wealthy, well-respected businessman. In 1885 he purchased a short-line railroad between Jacksonville and St. Augustine and began extending the rails southward toward Miami, then only a small settlement.

Flagler's vision of his railroad project went beyond Miami, however. He wanted to connect the mainland with the deep port of Key West, a booming city of more than 10,000 people, in anticipation of the growing shipping commerce he thought would be generated by the opening of the Panama Canal in the early years of the 20th century. He may even have set his sights on eventually connecting Key West with Cuba.

The railroad extended to Homestead, at the gateway to the Keys, by 1904. The year 1905 saw the commencement of what many perceived as an old man's folly: a railroad constructed across 128 miles of rock islands and open water, under the most non-idyllic conditions imaginable, by men and materials that had to be imported from all over the world. Steamships brought fabricated steel from Pennsylvania, cement from Germany and Belgium for use as concrete supports below the water line, cement from New York state for abovewater concrete, sand and gravel from the Chesapeake, crushed rock from the Hudson Valley, timbers and pilings from Florida and Georgia and provisions from Chicago. Barges carried fresh water from Miami to the construction sites. Nothing was indigenous to the Keys except the mosquitoes and the sand flies.

By 1908 the first segment, from Homestead to Marathon, was completed, and Marathon became a boom town. Ships brought their cargoes of Cuban pineapples and limes here, where they were loaded onto railway cars and sent north. (The railroad turnaround was at the present site of Knight's Key campground.) Railroad workers used Pigeon Key (see our Attractions chapter) as a base for further railway construction.

The 7-mile "water gap" between Marathon and Bahia Honda took some engineering prowess to overcome, and the completion of the project was severely hampered by several devastating hurricanes in 1909 and 1910. But on January 22, 1912, Henry Flagler, by then age 82, finally rode his dream from Homestead to Key West, across 42 stretches of sea, over 17 miles of concrete viaducts and concrete-and-steel bridges, over 20 miles of filled causeways and ultimately traversing 128 miles from island to island to the fruition of his vision. He entered Key West that day a hero. He died the following year probably never knowing that his flight of fancy changed the course of the Florida Keys forever.

Flagler's railroad, called the Key West Extension, made Key West America's largest deepwater port on the Atlantic Coast south of Norfolk, Virginia. Trade with the Caribbean increased, and Key West flourished for 23 years, recovering from the loss of the sponge and cigar industries.

The railroad stop on Key Largo was called Tavernier, and it developed into a trading center for the Upper Keys. Pineapple farming faltered in Key Largo and Plantation Key from a combination of tapping out the nourishment in the thin soil and market competition from the shiploads of Cuban pineapples transported by railway car from the docks of Key West to the mainland. The railroad company built a fishing camp on Long Key that attracted sportfishing aficionados from all over, including writer Zane Grey, a camp regular. Real estate boomed for a time, as people came to the Keys to homestead. The Florida East Coast Railroad Company completed construction of Key West's first official tourist hotel, the Casa Marina, in 1921. La Concha was built in 1928.

In 1923 Monroe County appropriated funds to construct a road paralleling the railroad. The bumpy rock road crossed Card Sound with a long area of fill and a wooden bridge. Half a dozen humpback bridges crossed the creeks and cuts on Key Largo. Extending the length of Key Largo, the road continued over Plantation Key, Windley Key and Upper Matecumbe. At the southern end of our island chain, a narrow, 32-mile road connected Key West with No Name Key off Big Pine Key. A car ferry service provided the waterway link between the two sections of roadway by 1930, which traversed what we now call the Upper and Lower Keys.

Still, the journey across this 128-mile stretch from Homestead to Key West proved a rugged, dusty, insect-ridden, costly, all-day affair, and tourism did not flourish as hoped and expected. Fresh water remained a coveted, scarce resource in the Florida Keys. Cisterns saved the funneled rainwater, which was parsimoniously meted out. Salt water was used whenever possible, and wash days were also always bath days. Hardly a tourist mecca, this.

The Great Depression delivered a near-fatal blow to the Florida Keys with a one-two punch. The cigar industry had moved to Tampa, sponging went to Tarpon Springs and lighthouses had put an end to wrecking long before. The population of Key West dropped from 22,000 to 12,000. By 1934, 80 percent of the city's residents relied on government assistance. The Federal Emergency Relief Administration stepped in and commenced development and promotion of Key West as a magnet for increased tourism in the Keys.

To that end, developers began building bridges to connect the watery cavities between the Middle Keys to each other and to the two sections of finished roadway. A "bonus army" of World War I veterans was employed to accomplish this momentous task. However, in 1935 Mother Nature reasserted her authority and once again charted the destiny of our islands. On Labor Day, what today we would call a Category Five hurricane hit the Upper and Middle Keys, destroying much of Flagler's Railroad. Hurricane Georges, the most recent hurricane to strike the Keys head-on, came ashore at Key West on September 25, 1998. With sustained winds of 105 mph, this strong category-two hurricane wreaked havoc from one end of the Keys to the other. No lives were lost; however, property damage was significant, particularly in the 15-mile stretch between Big Pine and Sugarloaf Keys.

Epilogue

In the late 1930s, the U.S. Navy, stationed in Key West, began construction of an 18-inch pipeline that carried fresh water from wells in Homestead to Key West. The naval presence in Key West grew with the beginning of World War II, when antisubmarine patrols began surveillance of surrounding waters. The Navy also improved the highway to better accommodate the transfer of supplies for its military installation. The Card Sound Road was bypassed. The new road, which followed the old railroad bed, now is known as the "18-mile stretch." By 1942, the Keys enjoyed fresh water and electricity service, and the Overseas Highway (U.S. Highway 1) officially opened in 1944, ushering in a new era of development that continues to this day.

After World War II, the Florida Keys became more and more popular as a sportfishing destination, and fishing camps dotted the shores from the Upper Keys to Key West. Still a rather remote, primitive spot to visit, the Florida Keys nevertheless continued to evolve into a desirable tourist terminus, and Key West burgeoned as a port of call. Also contributing to Key West's rebirth was the discovery of pink gold: shrimp. Fishermen who had caught a shark in the waters between Key West and the Dry Tortugas found the fish's stomach filled with large pink shrimp. This led to the discovery of a bountiful shrimping area off the Tortugas, and the "Key West Pinks" shrimping industry spawned in the Florida Keys. It is still a viable occupation as far up the Keys as Marathon.

From 1978 to 1983 the old rail-bed conversion bridges were retired. Modern concrete structures, some four lanes wide, now span our waters. Most mind-boggling as an engineering feat is the seemingly endless Seven Mile Bridge, which connects the once insurmountable watery gap between Marathon and Bahia Honda Key. Many of the old bridges have been recycled as fishing piers, but others still stand, abandoned and obsolete alongside their successors, crumbling reminders of the Keys' not-so-distant past.

By the 1980s the Florida Keys had emerged as a tourist-driven economy. Tourism remains the major industry of the Keys today, with fishing, scuba diving, boating and the attractions of Key West topping the list of popular agendas.

Of growing concern as the 21st century approaches is the effect the influx of visitors will ultimately have on the delicate balance of habitats within the tropical ecosystem of the Florida Keys (see our Paradise Found chapter). The jury is still out: Will man or Mother Nature determine the postscript for Paradise?

The Military in Key West

The position of Key West on the Straits of Florida allowed protection of American sea commerce in any war in the Western Hemisphere, for vessels heading to all Gulf ports historically had to go through here. During the Civil War, more ships were stationed in Key West than in any other port in the United States, and historians feel the result of the war may have been different if the island had not been occupied by Union forces. Even though most of Key West was sympathetic to the Confederacy, Union forces stationed at Key West's Fort Taylor and at Fort Jefferson in the Dry Tortugas were considered essential in the capture of the Confederate blockade runners heading for Southern ports from Havana. Key

Photo: Victoria Shearer

Part of the remains of Flagler's railroad, this trestle is visible from Bahia Honda and the Overseas Highway.

West remained in the hands of the federal government for the entire war.

The forts acted as coaling stations during this conflict and were so employed again in the Spanish-American War (1898), when every available vessel was again dispatched to Key West along with a flotilla of newspaper boats filled with war correspondents. The USS *Maine* made Key West her home port before she met her demise in Cuba in this conflict.

During World War I, with protection of the Panama Canal of paramount importance, the U.O. government stationed a submarine and naval aviation training base in our southernmost city. The base expanded in World War II, when blimps scouted for German U-boats preying on tankers and freighters in the shipping lanes off the Florida Keys. A mine field (removed in 1944) was planted north and west of Smith Shoal, and it also claimed four non-German vessels that accidentally entered the area (see Key West dive sites in our Diving and Snorkeling chapter).

Today, a U.S. Naval Air Station is still maintained in Key West at Boca Chica. The station hosts many tenant commands, including Fighter Squadron VF-45 and the Naval Security Group, which provides communications support to U.S. forces. The Key West Tactical Aircrew Combat Training System (TACTS), popularized by the movie *Top Gun*, trains aircrews in tactical air warfare without using live ammunition. In addition to a number of other tenant commands, the Key West Naval Air Station hosts official activities of the U.S. Coast Guard, Air Force and Army.

Rafts to Freedom

With the onset of the Cuban Revolution in 1959, when Fidel Castro took over that country, large numbers of Cubans chose to emigrate to the United States, many settling in the Florida Keys. In spring of 1980 Castro allowed an unprecedented 125,000 people to leave Cuba en masse. Called the Mariel Boat Lift, the immigrants landed in Key West from April through September of that year. Many continued on to Miami, where they settled in Little Havana.

Cuban refugees have continued to escape Castro's brand of communism on small homemade rafts, drifting to our shores until the mid '90s when the U.S./Cuban immigration policy changed. Political asylum is no longer a guaranteed option for these immigrants, even if they triumph over suppression in their homeland and the turbulence of their sea voyage.

To be in the Florida Keys is to become one with Nature, for the Keys offer unparalleled opportunities to be in direct daily contact with her substantial bounty.

Paradise Found

The Florida Keys . . . from the sea we came and to it we shall return. Make no mistake, the sea is in charge here and always has been.

About 100,000 years ago during the Sangamon Interglacial period of the Pleistocene Epoch, the Florida Keys flourished under the waters of the Atlantic Ocean as a string of living coral patch reefs at the edge of the continental shelf. Deposits of oöids (small calcareous spheres) accumulated on the lower portion of the reef. Sea level was some 25 feet higher than it is today. But with the onset of the last glacial period, the Wisconsin, the oceans receded and the sea dropped more than 150 feet.

The reef emerged as a land mass, exposing the corals and oöids to the atmosphere, rain and pounding surf. The onslaught of the elements killed the corals, and the fossil remnants cemented themselves together, creating coral bedrock. This bedrock, called Key Largo limestone, now comprises the basis of the Upper and Middle Keys from Soldier Key near Miami to Big Pine Key. When the waters receded, the oöids also compacted into rock called oölite. Now referred to as Miami oölite, this rock forms the foundation of the Lower Keys and Key West, cut through by tidal channels from the Gulf of Mexico to the Florida Straits. At the lowest sea level of the Wisconsin period, Florida Bay and Hawk Channel unfolded as dry land.

About 15,000 years ago the climate began to warm, and sea levels rose again. This present interglacial period is called the Holocene Epoch. As the sea once again claimed portions of the coral bedrock, living corals attached themselves to the limestone and began to grow anew. These growths now form the living coral reef tract that presently extends, submerged 4 to 5 miles offshore, from Fowey Rocks to the Dry Tortugas

(see our Diving and Snorkeling chapter). The higher elevations of bedrock became isolated above sea level, a sparkling chain of islands dividing the seas.

The fluctuation of the sea has determined the fate of the coral islands we call the Florida Keys throughout the ages and will dictate its future as well. Put into simple perspective, sea level has been rising for the past 15,000 years, and the rate appears to be increasing due to the long-range effects of global warming. Just imagine: A 6-foot rise in sea level would eliminate all of the Lower and Middle Keys except Key West. The Upper Keys, being somewhat higher, would escape extinction for a time. But if sea level increases by 15 feet, the string of islands known as the Florida Keys will be reduced to a couple of tiny islets, and the majority of Paradise will be lost once again to the sea.

To be in the Florida Keys is to become one with Nature, for the Keys offer unparalleled opportunities to be in direct daily contact with her substantial bounty. From the moment you crest the first of the 42 bridges now spanning our islands and feel the vast power of the surrounding seas, you'll know what we mean. Gaze down on our string of coral pearls from the air and the Keys look insignificant juxtaposed against the encompassing Atlantic Ocean and Gulf of Mexico.

Insiders' Guides® to other locales will introduce you to the lay of the land. But to gain an understanding of our world, which we reverently refer to as Paradise, you must be forearmed with the scope of our waters, for all things revolve around the sea here. We will acquaint you with our climate, weather and the multiple interrelated habitats of our tropical ecosystem — the only such ecosystem in the continental United States.

The word "tropical" generally refers to plants and animals living in the latitudes between the Tropic of Cancer in the Northern Hemisphere and the Tropic of Capricorn in the Southern Hemisphere. The Florida Keys are somewhat north of the Tropic of Cancer, but the warming influence of the nearby Gulf Stream assures us the benefits of a tropical climate. Our natural flora grows nowhere else in North America, and the combination of our eight interrelated habitats and the creatures dwelling therein are truly unique. Come, join us for a sneak preview of Paradise. We're one of a kind — here, there or anywhere.

Habitats of the Florida Keys

The Land

Hardwood Hammocks

When the coral reef emerged from the sea many eons ago and calcified into limestone bedrock, floating debris accumulated on it, decomposed and gradually evolved into a thin layer of soil. Seeds from the hardwood forests of the Yucatan, Honduras, Nicaragua, South America and the Caribbean Islands were carried to the Florida Keys by the winds of hurricanes, the currents of the Gulf Stream, migrating birds and eventually even by humans. Thus, the vegetation of the Florida Keys is more common to the tropical Caribbean Basin than to the adjoining temperate areas of mainland Florida.

Found throughout the Keys, these West Indian tropical hardwood hammocks nurture highly diverse communities of rare flora and fauna — more than 200 species — some found nowhere else in the United States. The hammocks (originally an Indian word meaning "shady place") also shelter a variety of endangered species.

Most of the hardwood hammocks of the Keys were cleared years ago to supply the wood for ship and home building and to clear the land for planting pineapples or citrus as a commercial venture. But several good examples of West Indian hardwood hammocks still flourish in the Keys. The largest contiguous hammock in the continental United States is on North Key Largo. Known as the Key Largo Hammock State Botanical Site, it encompasses 2,700 acres. You will find a virgin hardwood hammock on Lignumvitae Key, which is preserved as a state botanical site. You can access the island only by boat. State park naturalists offer guided tours of the hammock. The Crane Point Hammock in Marathon offers self-guided tours (see our Attractions chapter). You'll find other stands of hardwood hammocks sprinkled about the Keys.

A hardwood hammock has a layered structure much like other forests, with a tall overstory, a midstory and an understory. Many of the trees and plants will be unfamiliar to you, and some carry with them a colorful past. In the next paragraphs we describe four of our hammocks' more infamous residents: lignum vitae, gumbo limbo, Jamaica dogwood and poisonwood trees.

Probably the most sought-after tree in

INSIDERS' TIP

It is illegal to harass, harm or kill manatees, which are protected by the Marine Mammal Protection Act of 1972, the Endangered Species Act of 1973 and the Florida Manatee Sanctuary Act of 1978. The state of Florida has established cautionary and regulatory speed zones to protect the manatee in its habitat. Observe all manatee speed zones. Proceed slowly and with caution. If you see a manatee, take a photograph but don't touch. Penalties incurred for violating state and federal manatee protection laws include heavy fines and imprisonment.

Sunrise, Sunset

In the Florida Keys we justifiably lay claim to the most spectacular sun awakenings and finales in the universe. Anglers rise early enough to witness the brilliant fireball burn its way out of the ocean, its igneous shafts dramatically piercing the clouds overhead. Divers relish the midday sun's intense rays, which light up the ocean waters like a torch, illuminating the colorful corals below. Sun bathers lie prone on pool decks and manmade beaches, soaking the solar rays, storing up some much-needed vitamin D.

But our sunsets take center stage in the twilight hours. Visitors and residents alike jockey for an unobstructed vantage point from which to watch the smoldering orange ball ooze into the sea like a sphere of molten lava. Flotillas of small boats drift anchorless in the Gulf waters . . . waiting. Travelers pull their autos off the Overseas Highway and stand at the water's edge, their awestruck attention riveted on the setting sun. Key West even has a daily sunset celebration ceremony at Mallory Square complete with fire eaters, jugglers and Keys characters of every shape and description.

If you are vigilant, you may see the green flash, a brilliant, emerald-colored spark of light that occasionally appears just as the sun melts into the sea. The rare sighting lasts only a second or less and has inspired legends the world over. According to Usha Lee McFarling of the *Boston Globe*, "The green color results from the refraction, or bending, that sunlight undergoes as it passes through the thick layers of atmosphere near the horizon. Blue and green wavelengths of light are refracted the most, just like in a prism, so the setting sun appears to have a very thin blue-green fringe on its top edge. This fringe is hidden by the glare from the rest of the sun until all but the last of the sun's rim is blocked by the horizon."

To see the green flash you must have a sharply defined horizon in the West. In the Florida Keys the sun sets over the Gulf of Mexico. The day must be clear, and the brilliant yellow sun must meet the horizon through a cloudless sky.

— continued on next page

Photo: Victoria Shearer

Rate our famous sunset with the Ghee Whiz sunset rating scale.

Although sighting a green flash is a singular phenomenon akin to spotting a comet or a shooting star, every sunset is reason for celebration in the Florida Keys. So allow us to share with you our little known and much guarded 10-point secret rating scale for the ceremonial Keys sunset watch:

The Ghee-Whiz
Sunset Rating Chart

Score five points if the sun sets at all because that means you are alive. Add:
- one point for pre-glow (reflection of sun and streaks across the water).
- one point if you see the bottom of the sun touch the horizon.
- one point if the top of the sun touches the horizon.
- one point for an afterglow (the sky turns pastel colors).
- one point for the company you keep while you are watching the sunset.

Score a bonus point if a sailboat, bird or cloud moves in front of the sun as it sets. Sighting of the green flash is an automatic 10.

---

the virgin hammock was the lignum vitae (Latin for "wood of life"). It is so valuable, heavily harvested and slow-growing that it now tops the endangered list. Most visible today sprinkled throughout the hardwood hammock on Lignumvitae Key, the tree has a resin content of 30 percent. The wood cannot be kiln-dried or glued because of the gum content of this resin, called guaiac gum. Lignum vitae was used in the hinges and locks on the Erie Canal, which have been functioning now for more than 100 years. Mythical tales surround the tree: Old texts suggest lignum vitae, often called the "holy wood," was the tree referred to in the Biblical Garden of Eden and was used to fashion the holy grail.

Bold and brazen, the gumbo limbo trees, often reaching 40 feet, cop the moniker "tourist trees" because their reddish, peeling bark brings to mind sunburned visitors to our islands. The tree hides a checkered past. In early times, settlers stripped off a piece of bark from the gumbo limbo, revealing the tree's gluelike oozing sap. When birds landed on this particular branch, they stuck tight and could not fly away. Gathered by the human predators, the birds were sold for 5¢ each to the Cuban cigar industry for the entertainment of the cigar rollers. Florida law forbids this practice of bird capture today. On a more respectable note, the resin from the gumbo limbo was once used in the manufacture of varnish.

Also contributing to antics on the wrong side of the law is the Jamaica dogwood tree, called the fish poison tree. The roots, twigs, leaves and gray-green scaly bark were used to stupefy fish and aid in their capture. When ground into a sawdust chum and placed in the shoreline waters, the vegetation emitted a chemical similar to an invertebrate poison that paralyzed the gills of the fish, affected their air bladders and caused them to float to the surface where they were easily harvested.

Belonging to the same family as poison ivy, the poisonwood tree masquerades as a beautiful, harmless canopy but contains a poisonous sap that causes severe dermatitis in humans. Native Americans of the Keys used to tie their captives beneath the foliage of the 30-foot poisonwood tree. When it rained, the fresh water passing through the leaves carried the urushiol oils with every drop, causing a raging rash and slow torture.

Beneath the wide awning of the overstory, the smaller trees of the midstory flourish with less drama. Many of the trees bear fruits favored by the feathered tenants of the hardwood hammock habitat.

A dense understory of plants, shrubs and vines adapts to the shady conditions on the hammock floor. And wild flowers must reach for the sky under the shady foliage top-hat of the hammock, often turning into creeping vines.

Joining the Key raccoon, the Key cotton mouse, opossums, gray squirrels and an assortment of migratory birds amid the flora of the hammocks is the Key Largo woodrat, an endangered species that looks more like a big-eared Disney mouse than a London sewer rat. This 16-inch-long rodent, found only in the hammocks of North Key Largo, has been dubbed a "pack rat," because it likes to collect empty shells, aluminum pop-top tabs and the colorful rings from plastic milk bottles.

The Pinelands

Pinelands in the Lower Florida Keys differ from the vast forests you may have seen in other areas of the United States. Adapting to growing conditions atop Miami oölite with limited fresh water, the tall, spindly trees are small in girth and sparsely foliated. Primarily found on Big Pine Key, these South Florida slash pines mingle with an understory of silver palms and brittle thatch palms, both of which are rare outside the Keys and protected under the Preservation of the Native Flora of Florida Act. Among the 7,500 protected acres in the Lower Keys, other pinelands grace No Name Key, Little Pine Key, Cudjoe Key, Sugarloaf Key and Summerland Key.

The most famous pineland resident in the Lower Keys is undoubtedly the Key deer, a subspecies of the Virginia white-tailed deer, found nowhere else in the world. These tiny deer, each about the size of a large dog, attempt to coexist with human inhabitants who have taken over much of the unpreserved woodlands of the Lower Keys. However, the diminutive animals frequently venture out of the woods and onto the Overseas Highway, where they are often struck and killed by vehicles. For that reason, speed limits through Big Pine Key are reduced (45 mph daylight, 35 mph nighttime) and strictly enforced by law enforcement officials.

In 1957 the National Key Deer Refuge was established in Big Pine Key to ensure a sheltered natural habitat for the endangered species. About 250 to 300 Key deer exist in the Lower Keys today. The Key deer feed on red and black mangroves, thatch palms and a variety of native berries. While they can tolerate small quantities of salt in brackish water, fresh water is essential to their survival. No official records document the origin of the Key deer in the Florida Keys, but it is widely believed they migrated from the mainland as white-tailed deer when the seas receded in the Wisconsin Glacial Period. When sea level rose again during the present interglacial epoch, the deer were trapped in their pineland habitat. Over time their diminutive stature evolved as an adaptation to their sparsely vegetated environment.

The Shoreline

Mangrove Habitats

Called the island builders, mangroves comprise the predominant shoreline plant community of the Florida Keys, protecting the land mass from erosion. Able to establish itself on the coral underwater bedrock or in the sand, the mangrove's root structure traps, holds and stabilizes sediments. Over time the infant mangrove habitats establish small islets such as those you'll see peppering Florida Bay and the oceanside nearshore waters. Mangrove habitats bordering the Keys filter upland runoff, maintaining the water quality of our seas.

The leaf litter that falls from the red mangroves decomposes in the tangle of its prop roots, forming a critical base in the food chain that supports the myriad species of the marine community inhabiting shoreline waters. Important as a breeding ground and nursery for juvenile spiny lobster, pink shrimp, snook, mullet, tarpon and mangrove snapper, the mangroves also shelter these sea creatures from their predators. (See our Diving and Snorkeling chapter and our Fishing chapter for more on the fascinating underwater creatures living here.)

Great rookeries of wading and shore birds

INSIDERS' TIP

Do not feed the Key deer. Deer accustomed to being hand-fed lose their natural fear of humans and venture into areas that put them at risk, such as busy highways and residential subdivisions.

Photo: Victoria Shearer

The great white heron is found only in the tropical ecosystem.

roost and nest on the canopy of broad leaves of the mangrove habitats, creating a virtual aviary in every uninhabited islet (see the Gunk-holing Close-up in this chapter for our bird-watching primer). Three kinds of mangroves thrive in the Florida Keys. The distinctive high-arching prop roots of the red mangrove enable the plants to exchange gases and absorb oxygen from the seawater. Long, pencil-like seed pods, called propagules, develop during the summer and drop off the mangroves in the autumn, floating upright hither and yon with the tides. Eventually snagged on a branch or caught against a rock, the seedling establishes itself by growing prop roots, and a key is born.

The black mangrove, with dark, scaly bark, grows in the high-tide zone. The white mangrove, smallest of the three species, looks like a shrub with broad, flat oval leaves and grows above the high-tide line along with stands of buttonwood trees.

Sand Beach Habitats

Most of the islands of the Florida Keys have a limestone rock shoreline, but Long Key, Bahia Honda Key and small portions of the shoreline of Lower Matecumbe have beaches of sand consisting not of quartz but of tiny fossils. These minuscule remains of calcareous, lime-secreting marine plants and animals are broken down by wave action upon the sea bottom. Only keys that have a break in the offshore reef line or are near a deep tidal channel receive enough sediment to build a natural beach. Fronted in most cases by beds of seagrass, the Keys beaches always have a "weed line" on shore made up of remnants of turtle grass, manatee grass or sargassum weed washed up with the tide.

The natural beaches of the Keys don't have

sand dunes but rather more bermlike mounds. Sea oats grow in the sand, helping to hold the particles together. State law mandates that you may not pick sea oats at any time.

The Sea

Seagrass Habitats

In the shallow nearshore waters of the ocean or Florida Bay, sediments build up on the limestone bedrock sea bottom, supporting a variety of seagrasses that perform an integral function in our tropical ecosystem. Seagrasses grow entirely under water, one of the few flowering plants to do so. Most prevalent of the seagrasses in the Florida Keys are the sweeping meadows of turtle grass, which have interlocking root systems that burrow as deep as 5 feet into the sediment. The wide, flat blades, often more than 12 inches long, break the force of the waves and slow current velocity.

The turtle grass traps marine sediments and silt carried in and out on the tides, allowing them to settle to the bottom. This natural filtration system clarifies the water and enhances coral growth in the nearby reef habitat. The sunken pastures of turtle grass and the less-abundant shoal grass and manatee grass, which have rounded leaves and weaker root systems, become very dense, providing food and shelter for marine life at all levels of the food chain. (See our Fishing chapter for more on the species dwelling within.)

More than 80 species of resident and migratory coastal birds forage the seagrasses, feeding on fish and invertebrates of the habitat (see the Gunk-holing Close-up in this chapter for our bird-watching primer).

Boat propellers and personal watercraft can easily scar the shallow turtle grass meadows, effectively destroying that portion of the habitat. These scars do not heal over because the seagrass will not grow back. The drastic reduction in fresh water from the Everglades also threatens the seagrass habitat, for it is believed to have contributed to the recent seagrass die-off in Florida Bay. Because of its pivotal position among the habitats, ill health of the turtle grass meadows will ultimately affect the entire Florida Keys ecosystem.

Hardbottom Habitats

Wave action and tidal currents sweep the limestone bedrock of the nearshore sea-bottom habitats nearly clean, permitting no sediment buildup. Algae, sponges, gorgonian corals and stony corals attach themselves directly to the bedrock. The most common sponge you will see from your small skiff or while snorkeling in these waters is the loggerhead sponge, a barrel-shaped sponge easily identified by the dark holes in its upper surface.

Snapping shrimp often make their homes within the sponges; they make a popping sound with their large snapping claw to repel predators.

More seaward of the nearshore waters, colonies of soft corals dominant the underwater hardbottom landscape. A feathery fairyland blooms like a backstage theater costume room.

Also calling the hardbottom habitat home, the tentacled anemones peacefully coexist with conchs and tulip snails, the spiral-striped spindle-shaped mollusks. The much sought-after stone crabs and juvenile spiny lobsters try to stay out of sight here (see our Diving and Snorkeling chapter). Boat wakes, anchor damage and collection of sea creatures by divers and snorkelers threaten the hardbottom habitats.

Coral Reef

Extending 200 miles, from Fowey Rocks near Miami to the Dry Tortugas, our living coral reef habitat — the only one in the continental United States — is a national treasure. The reef, composed of the limestone remains of colonies of individual animals called polyps, plays host to an unbelievable assortment of marine creatures, fish and vegetation (see our Diving and Snorkeling chapter and our Fish-

ing chapter). The coral reef habitat, together with the mangrove and seagrass habitats, is the breeding ground for 70 percent of the commercial fishing industry's catch.

This wave-resistant barrier, which protects the seagrass meadows from erosion and heavy sedimentation, is particularly beautiful off the Upper Keys. The land mass of Key Largo shields the coral habitat from changing water temperatures and sediments that emanate from Florida Bay through the tidal channels of the Middle and Lower Keys. Though it rigidly protects the shoreline of the Florida Keys from tropical storms, the coral reef itself is a fragile habitat. Field studies since 1984 have indicated some coral die-off and the sometimes-fatal bleaching or discoloration of the corals in select areas of the Keys' barrier reef. Excessive nutrients in the water due to land-based pollution will degrade water quality and foster the growth of algal blooms, which screen the sunlight, robbing the coral of oxygen necessary for healthy development.

Humans constitute one of the reef's most destructive threats. Anchor damage, boat groundings and snorkelers and divers touching, collecting or stepping on the delicate organisms can cause injury and certain death to the reef.

Bare-Mud and Sand-Bottom Habitats

Along the barrier reef, skeletons of reef plants and animals form areas of open, bare-sand sea bottom, inhabited by species of algae, sea urchins, snails, clams and worms that serve as the food train for visiting starfish, conch and finfish. Similar belts or patches of bare-mud bottom habitats, both oceanside and in Florida Bay, support a like assemblage of marine creatures. Joining this group are burrowing shrimp, whose tunneled dwellings leave telltale mounds in the mud.

Weather and Climate

The mild tropical climate of the Florida Keys reigns without equal in the United States. Neither frost, nor ice, nor sleet, nor snow visit our islands. In fact, Key West is the only city in the continental United States below the frost line.

Temperature

The proximity of the Keys to the Gulf Stream in the Straits of Florida and the tempering effects of the Gulf of Mexico guarantee that average winter temperatures vary little more than 14 degrees from those of the summer months. Average year-round temperature is about 75 degrees. Cold, dry air moving down from the north in the winter is greatly modified by the Gulf waters over which it passes. And southeasterly trade winds and fresh sea breezes keep summer temperatures from ever reaching the triple-digit inferno experienced by the Florida mainland. The different rate at which the water and land heat and cool causes thermal currents that air-condition the Keys.

Rainfall

The Florida Keys experiences two seasons: wet and dry. From November through April, the sun shines abundantly and less than 25 percent of the year's precipitation falls, usually associated with a cold front in the dead of winter. May through October is the rainy season, when nearly three-quarters of our annual rainfall occurs during brief daily showers or thunderstorms. But these percentages are deceiving; our climate is really quite dry. Average rainfall in the winter is less than 2 inches a month; summer months see closer to 4 to 5 inches of rain.

Hurricanes

The piper must be paid for this idyllic climate, and hurricanes have always been a key ingredient in our tropical mix. The potentially deadly weather systems move westerly off the African coast during hurricane season (officially June 1 to November 30 but most prevalent in August and September) and generally turn northward near the Lesser Antilles islands, often heading our way.

Hurricanes have been harassing visitors to our shores for centuries. In 1622, at least five ships of the Spanish Tierra Firma Fleet wrecked as a result of a hurricane west of the Dry Tortugas. One of the most famous of these ships, the *Atocha*, was discovered and salvaged just over a decade ago by Mel Fisher (see Mel Fisher Museum in our Attractions chapter). The New Spain Armada suffered a fatal blow by a hurricane in 1733, when 17 of 21 galleons struck the reefs of the Upper Keys, spewing treasure cargo amid the coral.

Key West suffered a devastating hurricane in 1835, but the hurricane of 1846 is considered the city's most severe. Its residents pluckily rebuilt after these hurricanes and through the repeated hammerings of 1909, 1910, 1914 and 1919. On Labor Day 1935, a Category Five hurricane tore through the Upper Keys and Lower Matecumbe, totally destroying the area, including Flagler's Florida East Coast Railroad. Five hundred people lost their lives in the high winds and 7-foot tidal surge in Lower Matecumbe alone. Experts estimate that the Labor Day hurricane packed winds of between 200 and 250 miles per hour. By comparison, Hurricane Andrew's winds, which hit the Miami area in 1992, peaked at an intensity of 175 miles per hour.

On August 29, 1960, an African storm caused an airplane crash near Dakar, Senegal, Africa, killing 63 people. Three days later this storm system was officially named Donna by the National Hurricane Center, which was formed in 1955 in Miami. By September 9, Donna's eye, which stretched 21 miles wide, passed over the region, bringing horrendous winds that effectively leveled the area from Marathon to Lower Matecumbe. Tides in Marathon were more than 9 feet high, and the surge in Upper Matecumbe topped 13 feet. Tea Table Bridge washed out; the freshwater pipeline broke in six places, and electricity was out. Donna ranks among the 10 most destructive storms in U.S. history.

Hurricane Betsy looped back from its move up the coast of Florida to strike the Upper Keys in 1965, causing significant damage. The most recent official hurricane to hit the Keys was Hurricane Floyd on October 12, 1987. It suddenly changed course and made a minimal appearance here.

Visitors to the Florida Keys during hurricane season should heed official warnings to evacuate our islands in the event of a potential hurricane. Because we have only one main artery, the Overseas Highway, linking our islands to the mainland, it takes 22 to 26 hours of crawling, bumper-to-bumper traffic to clear residents

Gunk-Holing

Rachel Carson may have said it all in *The Edge of the Sea*: "I doubt that anyone can travel the length of the Florida Keys without having communicated to his mind a sense of the uniqueness of this land of sky and water and scattered mangrove-covered islands."

Nowhere will you be more aware of our quintessence than when you are gunk-holing. Here in the Florida Keys, gunk-holing simply means slipping off land in a small dinghy, canoe, sea kayak or shallow-draft skiff equipped with a push pole and tranquilly gliding through our shallow, inshore, mangrove-lined waters in search of sightings of indigenous birds and aquatic creatures.

Though the dedication to spotting feathered friends may be referred to as birding or bird-watching in some areas of the country, here in the Keys another whole arena of fascinating marine creatures presents itself in the shallow waters of our flats. You can easily gunk-hole on your own without a guide, or you can sign up for a guided eco-tour (see our Recreation chapter).

Hundreds of virgin mangrove islets sprinkle the inshore waters of the inhabited Keys, often serving as giant rookeries for shorebirds and wading birds who are attracted to the abundant chow wagon beneath the waters' surface. Look to our Recreation chapter for information on renting a kayak, canoe or small skiff. See our Attractions chapter for descriptions of the wildlife refuges of the Florida Keys, many of which encompass myriad out-islands. And most importantly, read on for a primer of the most frequently encountered species on a gunk-holing expedition in our tropical ecosystem.

Nature's Aviary

When gunk-holing around the mangrove islets in search of wild bird life, be sensitive to the presence of nesting birds. Do not anchor within 200 feet of an island, and keep noise to a minimum so as not to frighten the birds. If you do happen to flush a bird from its nest, move away from the nest area so that the bird will swiftly return to guard its young.

Here are several species you can expect to spot:

Brown Pelican — Some say the brown pelican's mouth can hold more than its stomach can, but this common resident of the Florida Keys will push this theory to the limit given half a chance. The brown pelican will dive from 20 to 30 feet above the sea, entering the water like a competing Olympian and scoring with a freshly caught fish every time. You'll see these cute, personality-packed fish-beggars everywhere, especially hanging out at fishing marinas. Look for them on their favorite gravity-defying perches atop mangroves or feathery Australian pines.

American White Pelican — With a wingspan of 10 feet, the white pelican is more than a bird of a different color. These winter visitors to the Florida Keys (they are frequently spotted in Montana in the summer months) live a much different lifestyle than their brown cousins. Completely white except for black-tipped wings and long yellow beaks, white pelicans live together in flocks in the uninhabited wild of the backcountry keys. The white pelicans, far from the panhandling ways of the browns, are cooperative feeders, congregating as a team on the water's surface and herding fish into an ever-narrowing circle where the group will dine. Look for white pelicans at Little Arsenecker or Sandy Keys in the Upper Keys backcountry.

— continued on next page

Photo: Victoria Shearer

Fun in the sun gunkholing by dinghy in shallow nearshore waters.

Cormorant — Cormorants by the thousands inhabit rookeries in the mangroves of the unpeopled islands. These large-bodied, hook-billed black birds, consummate fish-catchers all, will launch themselves in attempted flight at the first inkling of an approaching gunk-holer, often hitting the water in a brief belly-flop before gaining momentum to become airborne. Like the lesser-seen anhinga, or water turkey (more prevalent in the Everglades), the cormorant's plumage becomes waterlogged, which facilitates diving and swimming skills in its endless search for fish. You'll often see the birds perched on poles and buoy markers, wings outstretched in a drying maneuver. Cormorants swim with only their necks and heads visible above the water.

Snowy Egrets and Great Egrets — Plume hunters nearly eradicated the egret population at the turn of the century, for the birds' magnificent snow-white aigrettes were high fashion in the millinery industry. The egrets achieve their feathery plumage only in breeding season, so it was easy for the hunters to kill the birds in their nests. Both snowy and great egrets thrive once again in the Florida Keys. Distinguished from their cousins, the great white herons, which also grace the shorelines of the Keys, the white egrets have black legs with yellow feet and black bills. Though both egrets display magnificent white plumage, the snowy egret is about half the size of the great egret.

Great White Heron — Formerly considered a separate species from the great blue heron encountered in many parts of the United States, what we commonly call the great white heron is actually the white "morph," or color phase, of the great blue. Found only in the tropical ecosystem, this large white heron, more than 4 feet tall, is not as fearful of humans as other species, and is often seen in backyards and other inhabited areas. You'll be able to tell a great white heron from a great egret because the heron has long yellow legs and a yellow beak. The heron still-hunts for its food: Standing stiffly at full-alert, the heron stalks a prey of fish, frogs or lizards; it then stabs the prey with its beak, flips the prize whole into its narrow throat and swallows it in one long neck-expanding gulp. Herons and egrets build their lofty stick nests atop the mangroves of remote rookery keys.

Roseate Spoonbill — A rare sighting in the Florida Keys, the roseate spoonbill, or

— continued on next page

pink curlew, is more common in the upper Florida Bay near Flamingo in Everglades National Park. Like the Great White Heron, it also was slaughtered to near extinction in the early 1900s for its brilliant pink plumage, which was used for ladies' hats. The roseate spoonbill moves its large spatulate bill from side to side underwater in the shallows, searching for minnows and small aquatic creatures. This distinctive bird is decked out like a vaudeville dancer: Its pink body is accented by an orange tail, a bare greenish head, bright-red shoulder and chest patches and a black-ringed neck.

White Ibis — Common in the Florida Keys, the white-plumed ibis bears black-tipped wings, most apparent when spread in flight, a distinctive scarlet, down-curved bill and red legs. You'll often see young ibises, which are brown, in a flock of their white brethren, searching for aquatic insects, crabs, shrimp and small snakes. The ibis was once worshiped in Egypt as a bird-headed god, and the Pharaohs were buried alongside a mummified ibis. Killing an ibis for any other purpose was an offense punishable by death.

Osprey — The high wooden, platform-topped poles you may see along the Overseas Highway have been erected for the osprey, which builds its bulky nest atop, laying three eggs out of harm's way each breeding season. Look up when trying to spot these fish-eating birds in the wild as well, for their nests will be constructed on the very pinnacles of the trees. Resembling a bald eagle, the osprey can be distinguished by a black streak behind each eye.

Magnificent Frigatebird — The graceful, effortless flight of the frigatebird, or man-o-war bird, often heralds fish below, for this coastal forager is constantly on the lookout for finned pleasures. Often known to harass other sea birds until they drop their catch, the piratical frigatebird catches the spoils midair. Having a wingspan greater than 7 feet, the frigatebird inflates its throat sac and floats on air currents, its deeply forked, scissorlike tail a distinctive sight.

American Bald Eagle — Once endangered nearly to the point of extinction, the American bald eagles have made a recovery all across the United States due to preservation efforts. Look for the bald eagle's distinctive white head and tail high in the mangroves of uninhabited keys in Florida Bay, where they build their nests. Fish dominates their diet, and it is not uncommon for the bald eagle to steal the catch of a neighboring osprey.

Nature's Aquarium

As you gunk-hole through our shallow seagrass, mud, sand and hardbottom habitats surrounding mangrove areas of our uninhabited keys, you may observe life below the surface of the water. Be sure to wear polarized sunglasses and proceed in a shallow-draft craft.

Starfish — Commonly adorning the sandy bottom areas or seagrass meadows of the shallow waters are the cushion sea stars, often referred to as starfish. These heavy-bodied, orange-brown creatures with five thick starlike arms don't look alive, but they are.

Sponges — See "Hardbottom Habitats" in this chapter for a description of sponges you'll see growing on the sea floor.

Sting Ray — This unusual creature, shaped like a diamond or disk, often lies motionless on the bottom, partially buried in the sand. The ray has eyes and breathing holes on its top side, with its mouth positioned on the under side to feed off the sea floor. When frightened, the sting ray will swim away, its huge, winglike fins flapping in gentle undulation.

Horseshoe Crab — You'll quickly spot the distinctive spikelike tail and smooth, horseshoe-shaped body shell of this 300-million-year-old species as the crab forages the seagrass habitat for algal organisms.

— continued on next page

Sea Turtle — Keep a close lookout for the small head of the giant sea turtle as it pops out of the water for a breath of air. Loggerheads can remain submerged for as long as three hours. Green turtles, once commonplace here but overharvested for use in soup, for steaks, in cosmetic oils and for leather, are rarely encountered today. The sea turtles' front appendages have evolved into flippers.

Manatee — On a lucky day, you may catch a rare glimpse of the timid West Indian manatee, or sea cow, a docile aquatic mammal that likes to graze on the turtle-grass flats. The brownish-gray manatee has armlike flippers, a broad spoonlike tail and an adorable wrinkled face. It can grow to 15 feet long, weighing-in at nearly a ton. Protected as an endangered species, the manatee often rolls on the water's surface for air and cannot swim rapidly enough to avoid collision with oncoming boaters, a constant source of peril. (See Insiders' Tip in this chapter for regulatory information.)

Bottle-Nosed Dolphin — A more frequent sight on a gunk-holing excursion is that of the bottle-nosed dolphins, which you probably remember as the "Flipper" performers of marine parks. Seen in free-swimming pods in open waters, the graceful dolphins undulate through the waves with rhythmic regularity, sometimes curious enough to approach your boat.

Fish of the Flats — Alert attention to underwater movements in the seagrass of the flats may net you a sighting of a baby black-tip or bonnethead shark, a nurse shark, barracuda, bonefish and more. See The Flats section of our Fishing chapter for descriptions of the finned treasures lurking beneath the shallows.

---

and visitors out of the Florida Keys. Officials warn that storm-watching during a hurricane is not a diversion to be considered here. A sizable hurricane will cut all services in the Keys and communications to the outside world.

Protectors of Paradise

The natural wonders that make up the Florida Keys have good friends in the following organizations, which oversee efforts to protect the region's environment as best they can.

Florida Keys National Marine Sanctuary

In 1990, President George Bush signed into law the Florida Keys National Marine Sanctuary and Protection Act, designed to protect our spectacular marine ecosystem. The resulting Florida Keys National Marine Sanctuary encompasses 2,800 square nautical miles, incorporating within its boundaries the previously formed Key Largo National Marine Sanctuary (1975) and the Looe Key National Marine Sanctuary (1981). The Florida Keys National Marine Sanctuary engulfs all of the Florida Keys, including the Marquesas Keys and the Dry Tortugas, and surrounding waters. In an effort to provide a secure habitat for the marine flora and fauna that make the Florida Keys so special, the Protection Act immediately prohibited oil drilling within the sanctuary and created an "area to be avoided" (ATBA) for large ships in our waters.

Through access restrictions and activity regulations in select areas of the Florida Keys National Marine Sanctuary, ecologists hope that sensitive areas of the ecosystem will be protected, that areas of high ecological importance will evolve naturally with minimal human contact and that those areas representing a variety of habitats will be sustained. This zoning program will be monitored for revision

INSIDERS' TIP

Don't feed gulls, pelicans or shorebirds. They are more likely to become entangled in fishing line if they learn that anglers are a source of fresh fish food.

every five years. (See our Boating chapter for more information on specific regulations and restrictions.) For more information, call the Florida Keys National Marine Sanctuary offices at (305) 743-2437.

Florida Keys Initiative

The Florida Keys Initiative of The Nature Conservancy, launched in 1987, focuses on issues affecting the health and well-being of our tropical ecosystem, particularly the coral reef and Florida Bay, the rock pinelands of Big Pine Key and the tropical hardwood hammocks of North Key Largo. The stated mission of this nonprofit group is to preserve the plants, animals and natural communities of these habitats. To this end, they, along with federal and state agencies, work to acquire critical acreage for preservation and long-term management. Among their many conservation programs are the conch replenishing endeavor and the Florida Bay Watch.

Florida Bay Watch

The Florida Bay Watch volunteer program, coordinated by The Nature Conservancy, trains citizens of the Keys to monitor water quality and algae blooms in Florida Bay. Water quality in the bay has been deteriorating for some time, evidenced by increased algae blooms and seagrass die-off. Fishing guides and tour-boat operators join other concerned locals to compile research used in the ongoing efforts of The Nature Conservancy, the Florida Marine Research Institute and Florida International University. More than 100 trained volunteers collect water samples and other raw data relating to the algae blooms, fish kills and sponge die-offs in the 1,000-square-mile bay. They also monitor water quality along docks and in canals. If you are interested in joining the Florida Bay Watch, call (305) 743-2437.

Conch Replenishing Program

Many years ago, the queen conch grew abundantly on the ocean's floor, a staple in the diets of Native Americans and the Keys'

early settlers, those Bahamians called Conchs. Commercial overharvesting, however, depleted the resource dramatically, and by 1986 all conch harvesting in state and federal waters, commercial or recreational, was banned. The conch population, expected to regenerate, did not recover.

In 1995, a program was launched to aid the conch rehabilitation process. Hatchery-raised juveniles, nurtured at the Conch Research Laboratory at the Keys Marine Laboratory on Long Key, are tagged prior to release so that their movements can be monitored. Volunteer boat captains transport volunteer divers, all trained and coordinated by The Nature Conservancy, to sites chosen by the Florida Marine Research Institute, which supervises the hand-planting of the conch in seagrass and hardbottom rubble communities. For more information or to volunteer for the ongoing program, call The Nature Conservancy, (305) 743-2437.

Reef Relief

Reef Relief, a Key West-based nonprofit group of volunteers founded in 1986, works toward the preservation and protection of the coral reef habitat of the Florida Keys. The group has installed and maintains more than 100 mooring buoys, which, when used properly, eliminate anchor damage at the reef.

Another part of Reef Relief's mission is public awareness and education regarding the living coral reef habitat. To this end, each year the organization sponsors a cleanup campaign that attracts hundreds of volunteers. They comb shorelines and out-islands and dive the reef, collecting trash and storm-driven debris. For more information, call or visit the Reef Relief Environmental Education Center, 201 William Street, Key West, (305) 294-3100.

The Turtle Hospital

The grounds of the Hidden Harbor Motel — MM 48.5, Bayside, Marathon (see our Accommodations chapter) — shelter the famed Turtle Hospital, a turtle rapid-care center and recovery room run as a labor of love by Richie Moretti since 1984. The reptilian effort, which is financially supported in total by the income generated from Hidden Harbor Motel, has drawn the attention and cooperation of the University of Florida.

Local veterinarians volunteer their time, performing complicated turtle surgery on fibropapilloma tumors, impactions and shell fractures caused by hit-and-run boating injuries. Fisherman's Hospital donates surgical supplies and offers complimentary X-ray readings and MRIs. After surgery, the turtles are moved to the recovery room, the property's original saltwater pool.

More than 5,000 school children visit the Turtle Hospital every year, learning about the fascinating reptilian order Chelonia. Moretti does not allow the public access to the Turtle Hospital. However, guests at Hidden Harbor are among the privileged few invited to tour the turtle recovery room at will, often assisting with a rescue at sea or a dash in the Turtle Hospital ambulance.

The Marathon Airport, midway in the Florida Keys, is an FAA-certified facility that makes Flagler's railway journey seem a bad dream.

Getting Here, Getting Around

You are headed for the Florida Keys. Whether you travel by land, by sea or by air, you must conform to some strict, uncompromising standards that your travel agent may have neglected to tell you.

"Ha!" you say.

"Ah, but true," say we.

First, remove your socks. You won't need them here. Don your shorts. They are de rigueur. Slip on those shades. How else can you see? And reset your watch. The pace is slower here; you're on Keys time now.

Things really are different here. Our single main street stretches 126 miles — from Florida City to Key West — and deadends at the sea. Our 42 bridges span the kissing waters of the Atlantic Ocean and the Gulf of Mexico. And our Keys communities resound as distinctively as the ivories of a piano (see our Key West section in this chapter for information on transportation options in that city).

So come on down. We're playing your song.

The Florida Keys

By Air

Commercial Flights

Marathon Airport
MM 52 Bayside, Marathon
• **(305) 743-2155**

Icarus has landed. The Marathon Airport is an FAA-certified facility that makes Flagler's railway journey seem a bad dream. This modern, state-of-the-art operation offers you the option of flying directly to the middle of the Keys, where you can rent a car and arrive at your island of choice without the wear-and-tear of driving from Miami or Fort Lauderdale. Ask your travel agent about through-fares from your home city to Marathon. Often they are only a few dollars more than a round-trip fare to Miami.

The $7.5 million, 20,000-square-foot building opened opened in February 1995. The tropical architecture in the new structure and the utilization of the talents of local artists in its interior design led the Federal Department of Transportation and the National Endowment for the Arts to award Marathon Airport the 1995 Design for Transportation Award. Don't miss the ceiling fans fashioned from fishing rods and strung canvas.

One carrier offers flights here:

• **American Eagle**, (800) 433-7300, connects with American Airlines and other major carriers in Miami.

Flights are often overbooked during peak seasons, especially January and February, so be sure to arrive early to check in for your flight. The number of flights offered per day is greatly reduced during the summer months.

Avis, Budget and Enterprise rental cars are available at the airport. Make reservations for a vehicle in advance whenever possible (see our By Land section in this chapter). Taxis stand by in front of the airport awaiting each flight.

Other Commercial Options

and Jet A fuel. Jet charter service is available to most locations.

Miami International Airport
LeJeune Rd., Miami • (305) 876-7000

An international airport offering flights on most major airline carriers, Miami International Airport is accessible from either Interstate 95 or Florida's Turnpike via Fla. Highway 836 and LeJeune Road. You can rent a car (see the listing in this chapter for 800 numbers) and drive the distance to the Keys. Miami to Key Largo is approximately 60 miles; to Islamorada, 80 miles; to Marathon, 115 miles; to Big Pine, 130 miles; to Key West, 160 miles.

Fort Lauderdale-Hollywood International Airport
Interstate 595-East, Fort Lauderdale
• (954) 359-1200

Smaller than Miami International, this airport off Interstate 595 offers fewer flight options but is hassle-free compared to Miami's. To drive to the Keys from Fort Lauderdale-Hollywood International Airport, follow signs to Florida's Turnpike via Interstate 595. Driving from the Fort Lauderdale-Hollywood International Airport, will add about 45 more minutes to your total trip.

Private Aircraft

Paradise Aviation
MM 52 Bayside, Marathon
• (305) 743-4222 • Pilots: ARINC 131.45

Paradise Aviation is a flight-based operation at the east end of the Marathon Airport runway. If you wish to land your private aircraft or jet in Marathon, call Marathon UNICOM on frequency 122.8. Paradise Aviation will issue a wind and a runway advisory. After you land, they will contact you by tail number and advise you where to tie down. No landing fee is charged, but it will cost you from $7 to $20 to tie down at Paradise Aviation for the night, depending on the size of your aircraft. Paradise Aviation offers both 100 low-lead (LL) fuel

Grantair Service Inc.
MM 52 Bayside, Marathon
• (305) 743-1995

Located at the west end of Marathon Airport, Grantair Service Inc. is a flight-based operation that caters to general aviation and light aircraft. It offers a maintenance facility on premises and sells 100 low-lead fuel. Tie downs cost $10 per night or $60 per month. You can earn a single or twin engine, sea plane or instrument license at Grantair's flight school, then rent either a Cessna 152 or a Cessna 172. Grantair also offers sightseeing tours of the Middle Keys and the reef.

By Sea

Visit the Florida Keys as the pirates and buccaneers did before you — by sea. Revel in the beauty of these sea pearls, strung together by the wisp of the Overseas Highway. Your perspective of the Keys will be different when viewed from our waters. Navigate your motor or sailing craft through the Intracoastal Waterway, which extends from Miami through Card Sound and Barnes Sound and down the length of the Keys in the Florida Bay/Gulf of Mexico. Or parallel the oceanside shores following Hawk Channel, a well-marked route protected by the reef. For comprehensive information on arriving and vacationing on your pleasure craft, see our Cruising chapter.

By Land

The Overseas Highway tethers our islands to the mainland like a long umbilical cord. Addresses along this common main street are issued by mile markers, designated as MM. Commencing with MM 126 in Florida City and culminating with MM 0 in Key West, small green markers with white numbers are posted every mile.

The Overseas Highway actually curves and drifts toward the southwest, rendering it all but impossible to refer to directions as "north

Photo: Monroe County Tourist Development Council

Getting here and getting around means crossing some of the 42 bridges that connect our string of islands. This is the longest of them all — the magnificent Seven Mile Bridge.

to here" or "south to there." Here in the Keys everything is grounded by a mile marker, and you'll note that we orient most of the addresses we give in this book by mile marker.

As you head toward Key West, mile marker numbers descend in order. Any place on the right side of the road bordering Florida Bay or the Gulf of Mexico is referred to as bayside. The opposite side of the road, bordering the Atlantic Ocean, is therefore called oceanside. So, addresses on the Overseas Highway will usually be referred to by both mile marker number and a bayside or oceanside distinction.

The old saying, "All roads lead to the sea," could very well have been written about the Keys. The occasional side street you might encounter on one of our wider islands — such as Key Largo, Marathon or Big Pine Key — will terminate at the bay, the Gulf or the ocean after only a few blocks.

One dangerous stretch of road calls for diligence from drivers. From Florida City at MM 126 to Key Largo at MM 106, a two-lane, 20-mile section of U.S. Highway 1 monotonously rolls through barren-looking sawgrass prairie. This paved purgatory is statistically so treacherous that government leaders are considering having the road widened to four lanes. Be patient and cautious. Although brief passing lanes are interspersed throughout the stretch, the flat, straight road incites reckless, lead-footed or impatient drivers to pass slower-moving vehicles.

INSIDERS' TIP

Directions from Miami International Airport via Florida's Turnpike: Take LeJeune Road south to Fla. Highway 836 W. As you approach the ramp for Fla. 836 W., get in the right-hand lane. Be aware, however, that a frontage-road access just before the Fla. 836 W. sign and arrow often lures confused first-timers into turning too soon. The ramp is actually just after the Fla. 836 W. sign and arrow. Follow Fla. 836 W. to Florida's Turnpike South, Homestead. Continue on Florida's Turnpike until it ends in Florida City at U.S. Highway 1. Continue south on U.S. 1 to the Keys.

Rental Cars

Public transportation in the Keys (except for Key West) is practically nil. You really need a car to get around. Most rental car companies are based in Marathon. Some pick up and deliver vehicles. Reserve your automobile before you arrive in the Keys — availability in peak seasons is often limited — at one of the following agencies:

Avis Rent A Car
MM 52 Bayside, Marathon Airport
• **(305) 743-5428, (800) 331-1212**

Avis offers pickup and delivery in Marathon from Coco Plum to the Seven Mile Bridge only.

Budget Car & Truck Rental
MM 52 Bayside, Marathon Airport
• **(305) 743-3998, (800) 527-0700**

Budget picks up and delivers within Marathon only.

Enterprise Rent-A-Car
MM 100.2 Oceanside, Key Largo
• **(305) 451-3998, (800) 325-8007**
MM 52 Bayside, Marathon
• **(305) 289-7630, (800) 325-8007**

Enterprise has locations serving the Keys from top to bottom, including Key West (see subsequent listing). The Key Largo office offers pickup and delivery of vehicles from Key Largo to MM 70, Fiesta Key. The Marathon Enterprise office is in the Marathon Airport terminal. This office will pick up or deliver your rental car as far up the Keys as MM 70 or as far down the Keys as Little Palm Island.

Taxi Service

If you don't have your own automobile or haven't rented a car for the duration of your visit, you may find yourself in need of ground transportation within the Keys. Be aware that the fare could get pricey (sometimes approaching the cost of a daily rental vehicle), especially if you are traveling any distance. But if you need a lift call one of the following:

• In the Upper Keys, **Tavernier Taxi**, (305) 664-7527, or **Mom's Taxi**, (305) 852-7999.

• In the Middle Keys (Marathon), **Action Express Taxi**, (305) 743-6800, or **Cheapo Taxi**, (305) 743-7420.

• In the Lower Keys, **Courtesy Taxi and Delivery**, (305) 872-9314, or **Big Pine Taxi**, (305) 872-0577.

Limousine and Airport Shuttle Service

In the event you are stranded without transportation to either of the mainland airports, alternative transportation is available.

Go Tours Airport Shuttle
MM 54 Oceanside, Marathon
• **(305) 743-9876, (800) 689-3304**

This airport shuttle operates 24 hours a day, seven days a week, transporting travelers from anywhere in the Keys to Miami International or Fort Lauderdale-Hollywood International Airport. Based at the Holiday Inn in Marathon, Go Tours picks up customers at all Keys resorts as well as private homes. Following are examples of daytime fares to Miami International: from Marathon, $39.90; from Big Pine, $49.90; and from Key West, $49.90. Nighttime fares will be higher.

INSIDERS' TIP

Card Sound Road (County Route 905A) forks off U.S. Highway 1 just south of Florida City and provides an alternative to the sometimes dangerous primary route to the Keys. The picturesque, less-traveled road (also two lanes with no passing lane) traverses a toll bridge ($1) that passes between Card Sound and Barnes Sound. This route will put you north of Key Largo, near the Ocean Reef Club. At the T-junction with County Route 905, turn right and follow the road until it merges with U.S. 1 (Overseas Highway) in Key Largo.

Call for reservations 24 to 48 hours in advance. Go Tours also offers bus charters and island tour packages.

Luxury Limousine of the Florida Keys, Inc.
Ocean Reef Club, North Key Largo
• (305) 367-2329, (305) 664-2524

Four super-stretch limos seating up to 10 passengers, smaller limos, Lincoln towncars and minivans are available from Luxury Limousine for private transportation anywhere between Key West and West Palm Beach. Price is quoted per trip, one way. For example, Key West to Miami International Airport is $300; from the Middle Keys, $175; Upper Keys, $125. Advance reservation is required.

Bus Service

Greyhound Bus Lines
Adam Arnold Annex, Key West International Airport, 3491 S. Roosevelt Blvd., Key West • (305) 296-9072, (800) 231-2222, Intra-Keys (800) 410-5397

Greyhound bridges the gap in mass ground transit from Key West to Miami and beyond. Greyhound departs the Key West depot, which is housed in the Adam Arnold Annex at the airport, four times a day, seven days a week at 7:30 and 10:15 AM and 12:30 and 5:45 PM, bound for Miami International Airport, the Miami Amtrak station and downtown Miami. Four of the Greyhound stops in the Keys sell tickets: Big Pine Motel, Big Pine, MM 30.7 Bayside; Chamber of Commerce, MM 53 Bayside, Marathon (tickets only, pickup spot is at Marathon Airport, MM 52); Burger King, Islamorada, MM 83.5 Oceanside; and Howard Johnson Hotel, Key Largo, MM 102 Bayside.

Additional boarding locations are sprinkled along the Overseas Highway, marked by signs with the Greyhound logo. They are at at the corner of Caroline and Grinnell streets, site of the Park N' Ride lot in Key West; Boca Chica, MM 7; Big Coppitt, MM 10.6; Sugar Loaf, MM 17; Cudjoe Key, MM 22; Ramrod Key, MM 27.8; Marathon Airport, MM 52; Layton, MM 69; Islamorada, MM 82.5; and Tavernier, MM 92. The bus also stops at MM 126 in Florida City.

The trip will take 4 hours, 20 minutes from Key West to Miami International by Greyhound Bus. Fares to Miami International Airport depend on embarking and disembarking sites. For example, the fare per person from Key West is $30 one way or $57 round trip. Discounts are offered for multiple riders. Commuter rates are also available. Greyhound schedules and fares are subject to change. Be sure to confirm your specific travel arrangements when purchasing tickets.

Key West

Key West, the southernmost point in the continental United States, slumbers closer to Havana than it does to Miami — when it sleeps, that is, which is not all that often. In Keys-speak, this is where the action is.

Although nearly 25,000 people make Key West their home, this island still retains a small-town charm. The quaint Old Town area remains essentially a charming, foliage-canopied grid of streets lined with gingerbread-trimmed frame structures that evoke a succession of bygone eras and a cache of simmering secrets. This area, by the way, boasts the largest collection of frame structures in a National Register Historic District of any city in Florida — nearly 3,000 — and some architectural elements that are found nowhere else in the world.

The Mid Town area is predominantly residential. New Town takes in the shopping centers and fast food and hotel chains along N. Roosevelt Boulevard on the Gulf side and across the island to the airport and beaches along S. Roosevelt Boulevard on the Atlantic side.

Old Town, destination of choice for most visitors to Key West, is accessed from the Overseas Highway by either N. Roosevelt Boulevard (U.S. Highway 1) to Truman Avenue or S. Roosevelt Boulevard (A1A) along the beach to White Street. From White Street, Southard Street runs one way toward the heart of Old Town. Fleming Street is one way leading the opposite direction.

Old Town is anchored by Duval Street, which has been dubbed the longest street in the world because it runs from the Atlantic to the Gulf of Mexico. It is actually only a little more than a mile long. Although finding your way around Key West is not difficult, the narrow, often one-way streets — combined with a proliferation of tourist-driven rental cars and scooters in peak seasons — can make driving around this island both frustrating and time-consuming. Old Town is best explored on foot or by bicycle.

Key West provides public bus service and several other unique modes of transportation, which we describe in this section.

By Air

Commercial Flights

Key West International Airport
3491 S. Roosevelt Blvd., Key West
• (305) 296-5439

Although Key West is the Florida destination of choice for thousands of visitors each year, do not expect to arrive here via commercial jetliner. Air service to this island in the sun is of the commuter variety. The planes are small, and flights are often overbooked during peak seasons, especially in January and February, so be sure to arrive early to check in for your flight.

Avis, Budget, Dollar and Hertz rental cars are available at the airport terminal (see subsequent listings in our Rental Cars section). Whenever possible, make reservations for your vehicle in advance. Taxis stand by in front of the airport awaiting each flight and many hotels offer complimentary shuttle service.

Commercial flights into and out of Key West are provided by the following airlines:

•**American Eagle (American Airlines)**, (800) 433-7300 — American Eagle offers connecting service to a multitude of American Airlines flights via Miami.

•**Cape Air**, (800) 352-0714 — Cape Air provides scheduled service between Key West and southwest Florida airports in Naples and Fort Myers and also Fort Lauderdale.

•**Delta Air Lines**, (800) 354-9822 — Comair, the Delta Connection, offers service between Key West and Orlando. In Orlando, you can pick up any number of connecting flights on Delta Airlines.

•**Continental Connection**, operated by

Gulfstream International Airlines, (800) 992-8532 — Gulfstream provides feeder service to Key West for both Continental Airlines and United Airlines. Flights from Key West connect through Miami, Tampa, Orlando and Fort Lauderdale.

•**USAir Express**, (800) 428-4322 — USAir Express offers flights from Key West to Jacksonville, Miami, Tampa, Orlando and Fort Lauderdale, where you can connect with many USAir — and, in some cases, even British Airways — flights.

Private Aircraft

Island City Flying Service
3471 S. Roosevelt Blvd., Key West
• (305) 296-5422

Island City Flying Service is a flight-based operation at the Key West International Airport. If you want to land your private aircraft or jet in Key West, call Island City UNICOM on frequency 122.95. There is no reserved parking — you may take any available space you see on the ramp. No landing fee is charged, but overnight tie-down fees are assessed depending on the size of your aircraft: $7 for single engine; $10 for twin; $25 for turbo with no fuel purchase (the tie-down rate for turbo craft is reduced with fuel purchase).

Island City Flying Service offers both 100 low-lead (LL) fuel and Jet A fuel and rents life vests and life rafts as required by law for flying to the Bahamas or the Caribbean. Flight instruction is available.

By Sea

Long a bustling port, Key West harbor is still busy — full of commercial traffic, tourist-filled tour boats and visiting cruise ships. If you choose to navigate your motor or sailing craft to Key West from the Atlantic, come in through the main ship channel, which is marked "S.E. Channel" on the charts. From the Gulf take the N.W. Channel until it intersects with the main ship channel. You can anchor out in protected areas of the harbor or put into one of the comprehensive Key West marinas (see our Cruising chapter).

By Land

Rental Cars

All of the nationally advertised names in the rental car business maintain locations in Key West. Several have lots at the airport, and many will even pick up and deliver your rental vehicle directly to your hotel. Inquire when you make your reservation. And speaking of reservations, it is always wise to phone ahead to reserve your car especially during peak travel periods.

The following companies offer rental vehicles:

•**Alamo Rent A Car**, 2834 N. Roosevelt Boulevard, Key West, (305) 294-6675, (800) 327-9633.

•**Avis Rent A Car**, Key West International Airport, 3491 S. Roosevelt Boulevard, Key West, (305) 296-8744, (800) 831-2847.

•**Budget Car & Truck Rental**, Key West International Airport, 3491 S. Roosevelt Boulevard, Key West, (305) 294-8868, (800) 527-0700.

•**Dollar Rent A Car**, Key West International Airport, 3491 S. Roosevelt Boulevard, (305) 296-9921, (800) 800-4000.

•**Enterprise Rent-A-Car**, 3031 N. Roosevelt Boulevard (in Howard Johnson Hotel), Key West, (305) 292-0220, (800) 325-8007.

•**Hertz Rent A Car**, Key West International Airport, 3491 S. Roosevelt Boulevard, Key West, (305) 294-1039, (800) 654-3131.

•**Value Rent-A-Car**, 2516 N. Roosevelt Boulevard, Key West, (305) 296-7733, (800) 468-2583.

In most cases, you will need a credit card to rent a car from any of the nationally advertised rental car agencies listed above. However, the following locally owned and operated auto rental agencies will accept cash: **Island Car & Truck Rental**, 2826 N. Roosevelt Boulevard, Key West, (305) 295-7368; and **Tropical Rent-A-Car**, 1300 Duval Street, Key West, (305) 294-8136.

Taxi and Limousine Service

Taxis are plentiful, reliable and relatively inexpensive in Key West. You will find several at the airport awaiting each flight. Or, you can call one of the following companies directly for door-to-door service: **A Airport Cab Company**, (305) 292-1111; **Five 6's Cab Company**, (305) 296-6666 or (305) 296-1800; or **Friendly Cab Company**, (305) 292-0000 or (305) 295-5555.

Limousine companies offer a variety of services. Some will take you all the way to Miami if you like, and others cater specifically to groups. Prices and services vary so do call around and compare. The following options are available to Key West visitors: **Action Express Limousine**, (305) 743-6800; **Airport Limousine Van Service**, (305) 294-5678; **Eggs Transport, Inc.**, (305) 744-4496; **Go Tours**, (305) 743-9876, (800) 875-4555; **Island Coaches**, (305) 296-4800, (800) 539-7386; and **Luxury Limousine of the Florida Keys**, (305) 664-0601, (800) 664-0124.

Bus Service

Greyhound Bus Lines
Adam Arnold Annex, Key West International Airport, 3491 S. Roosevelt Blvd., Key West • (305) 296-9072, (800) 231-2222

See our Keys section for comprehensive information on schedules for Greyhound bus service to Miami International Airport. Buses make multiple stops between Key West and the top of the Keys. The weekday fare per person from Key West to Miami International is $30 one way or $57 for a round trip; fares are slightly higher Friday through Sunday. Schedules and fares are subject to change so be sure to confirm your travel arrangements when purchasing tickets.

INSIDERS' TIP

To see the best of Key West, we strongly recommend renting a bike or walking. This small island is perfect for bicycles. See our Recreation chapter.

Photo: Monroe County Tourist Development Council

Boating through narrow waterways, around shallow
waters and near the reef requires careful navigation.

City of Key West Department of Transportation

627 Palm Ave., Key West
• (305) 292-8160

Two public transport city buses circle the island of Key West — one clockwise, the other counterclockwise. The two vehicles travel basically the same route with one exception: The Mallory Square Schedule sends the bus down Duval Street to Truman, then takes a circuitous counterclockwise route back to the point of origination; the Old Town Schedule takes in Bahama Village via Emma and Angela streets before heading out on a clockwise circuit. Although this may sound confusing, the buses in Key West are actually quite easy to use. You cannot get lost since whatever bus you take will eventually return to the stop where you boarded it.

The buses, which run from Stock Island to Mallory Square, incorporating the airport, East Martello Museum and stops at all the major hotels and condominiums along S. Roosevelt Boulevard, make their rounds once an hour except on weekdays during peak times (before and after school hours: 7:05 to 9:05 AM and 3:05 to 6:05 PM), when service is offered every half-hour. Buses begin running at 6:05 AM and continue until 10:30 PM. The Sunday schedule is altered slightly: The buses stop only once an hour during peak times, and the hours are shorter — 9:15 AM to 7:15 PM.

Fare is 75¢ for adults. Children younger than 5 ride free with a paying adult. Senior citizens pay 35¢, but they must first obtain an identification card for $2 at the Port and Transit Authority office; address is listed above. Students also may ride for 35¢ if they display their school ID card upon boarding. You are asked to have exact fare because drivers do not carry change. Monthly passes and bus schedules are available at the PATA office ($20 for adults, $12 for senior citizens and $12 for students).

Alternative Transportation

Trolley Tour

Old Town Trolley Tours of Key West

Key West Welcome Center, 3840 N. Roosevelt Blvd., Key West
• (305) 296-6688

Listen to a narrative of historic Key West on this continuous loop tour, learning as you go. Although this transportation option is promoted and sold as a 90-minute tour, you can hop on and off the trolley as many times per day as you wish. It's one hassle-free way to shop, dine or take in the myriad attractions Key West has to offer.

You can park your car free at either the Key West Welcome Center or the Adventure Scooter rental at 1910 N. Roosevelt Boulevard, where you can buy tickets and board the trolley. Both these locations are readily accessible as you enter Key West (bear right as you come into Key West from Stock Island). Then grab a trolley and let your conductor spirit you around Key West. You can disembark at Mallory Square, Key West Hand Print Fashions & Fabrics, Holiday Inn La Concha, Angela Street Depot (corner of Angela and Duval), Old Town Trolley Carbarn (Adventure Scooter), Fairfield Inn, Ramada Inn, EconoLodge, Key West Welcome Center, Key Ambassador, East Martello Fort Museum, Sheraton Suites, Casa Marina and the Southernmost Point Trolley Stop. Trolleys stop at each location every 30 minutes.

Cost of the trolley tour is $16 per day for adults and teens, $7 for children ages 4 through 12. Children 3 and younger ride free.

Note: The Conch Trains that you see chugging around town are bona fide touring vehicles; you cannot get on and off a Conch

---

INSIDERS' TIP

Holiday weekends can make getting onto the Keys a traveler's nightmare. We suggest flying into Marathon or Key West and renting a car.

Train at will. See our Attractions chapter for further information on this and other tours.

Passenger Ferry Service

Curry Princess
Historic Key West Bight, 201 William St., Key West • (305) 293-1999

Key West is a tiny island and what better way to get from one side of it to the other than by boat? That's just what *Curry Princess* owner Bruce Amsterdam thought when he purchased the old Rum Runner party boat and transformed it into a passenger ferry vessel.

From its dockside home at the Historic Key West Bight, the Curry Princess now beckons visitors to put away their car keys and traverse Paradise by water. Billed as "your car's vacation," this 60-foot, 155-passenger historic vessel carries tourists from Key West Bight on the Gulf side of the island to the Casa Marina on the Atlantic side, with a stop in between at the Hilton Resort and Marina nestled beside Mallory Square.

The *Curry Princess* operates daily from noon to one hour past sunset, and $10 buys a full-day pass with unlimited re-boarding privileges; children younger than 12 ride free. Free shuttle service to the boat is available for those not staying at or near one of the ferry docks.

Special Transportation Services

Conch Commute
3108 Riviera Dr., Key West • (305) 296-0131

Need to get your child to a dance class? Soccer practice? Just home from school every Tuesday afternoon? Call Conch Commute. Based in Key West, Conch Commute began in 1996 by offering parents in the Lower Keys a way to get their kids to regular appointments and/or occasional activities when they couldn't do the driving themselves. This door-to-door service was later expanded to include transportation for seniors who had no way to run errands or get to doctor's appointments on their own. Today, two vans travel around Key West and as far up the Keys as Big Pine carrying senior citizens and kids wherever they need to go. The service is similar to a taxi except

that it requires slightly more notice; parents and seniors are asked to register in advance, indicating their transportation needs and whom to contact in the event of an emergency. Prices vary depending on the distance and regularity of the commute. And just in case you want to check on the exact whereabouts of your child or grandma and grandpa, each van is equipped with a cell phone.

Pedal Cabs

Hail a pedal cab if you'd like an Old World-type transport around Key West. These bicycle-driven, open-air, two-seater passenger carts weave in and out of traffic on Duval Street and in the surrounding historic district. Your pedal-pumping guide will point out the sights for $1 per minute, with discounts generally given for journeys of 30 minutes or more. Be sure to negotiate the price before you set off so there won't be any surprises on either side.

Just like a taxicab, your pedal-cab can transport you to a destination that you specify. However, most pedal-cab drivers are also willing to do any kind of tour you like — tours of restaurants, bars, historic sites and architectural wanderings. Pedal-cabs make regular journeys up and down Duval Street; the best way to secure a ride is to simply flag one down. But if you can't hail a pedal-cab, feel free to call **Perfect Pedicab** at (305) 292-0077 to reserve a vehicle.

Bicycle, Moped and Scooter Rentals

Key West is the perfect place to explore by bicycle or moped, although we wouldn't recommend riding in the Mallory Square/lower Duval Street area or along N. Roosevelt Boulevard, which are heavily congested with people, automobiles and delivery trucks. Many places rent a choice of either mopeds or bicycles by the hour, day, overnight or week. Some rentals provide a backpack, and some may include a helmet in the rental price. Expect to pay around $5 for eight hours of bicycle rental.

Mopeds or scooters swing a wider range, varying from $10 to $30 per day. Some companies consider a daily moped rental to be 24 hours rather than eight hours. Inquire when you call. Some moped rental agencies even rent double scooters that seat two; it is illegal to carry a passenger on any other kind. The following Key West companies rent a full range of vehicles — bicycles, mopeds and/or scooters: **Adventure Scooter & Bicycle Rentals**, 2900 N. Roosevelt Boulevard (and nine other locations), (305) 293-9933; **The Bicycle Center**, 523 Truman Avenue, (305) 294-4556; **Moped Hospital**, 601 Truman Avenue, (305) 296-3344; **Pirate Scooter**, 401 Southard Street, (305) 295-0000; **Scooter Safari**, 3706 N. Roosevelt Boulevard, (305) 294-4420; and **Tropical Scooter Rentals**, 1300 Duval Street, (304) 294-8136.

In addition, the city has several bike-only rental outlets. For a complete listing of these, check the Yellow Pages under Bicycles.

A few words of caution about two-wheeled transportation: Bicycle, moped and scooter riders are subject to the same traffic laws as those who operate four-wheeled vehicles. That means you must have lights at night, obey all traffic signals and signs, stay off the sidewalks and travel in the correct direction on one-way streets. Keep in mind, too, that you operate these vehicles at your own risk. In a collision with a car, a scooter or moped almost always loses. If you wreck your rental scooter, you will be personally liable for the damages. The rental agents are not required to offer insurance. They are, however, required to provide instruction and to offer helmets. Even so, the hospital emergency room on Stock Island sees an average of two scooter accidents per day. And that doesn't account for the drivers who simply pick themselves up off the street and carry on. Words to the wise: Be careful!

Foot Power

Strolling Key West is a great way to work off the pounds you'll be packing on by grazing the tempting kiosks, juice bars, ice-cream shops, restaurants and, of course, bars of Key West. The sidewalk-lined streets in Old Town often front little-known lanes where unusual shops or galleries hide beneath ancient foliage. You'll miss these — and much of the mystery and charm of this southernmost city — if you don't get out of your car and walk a bit.

You can explore on your own or take advantage of one of the many guided tours that are available (see our Attractions chapter for several options). Perhaps the best-documented self-guided walking tour of Key West has been compiled by Sharon Wells. Her *Walking & Biking Guide to Historic Key West* is free for the asking at the Key West Chamber of Commerce (open 8:30 AM to 5 PM daily) in Old Mallory Square. You can also find copies at several shops around town. Wells guides you along 10 routes, identifying the buildings of architectural or historical significance you will pass along the way.

While at the Chamber, you may also want to pick up a copy of the Pelican Path map/brochure. Originated by the Old Island Restoration Foundation, the Pelican Path is a self-guided walking tour that takes you past some of Key West's most historically and architecturally significant buildings.

Parking

Ask any local if there's a downside to living in Paradise and he or she will almost always complain about parking problems. There are simply too many cars in Old Town Key West and too few places to put them. And because the permanent population of this tiny island keeps growing and most visitors either arrive by car or rent a vehicle when they get here, the parking problem isn't going away any time soon.

Patrons of the shops and restaurants in Duval Square (1075 Duval Street) will find free parking available in an adjacent lot accessed from Simonton Street. Free parking for patrons of some Duval Street restaurants, shops and bars may also be available in designated lots off either Whitehead or Simonton Streets, both of which run parallel to Duval. Metered curbside parking is, of course, available on several downtown streets, including Duval, Whitehead and Simonton, as well as along most of the streets that intersect them. Special curbside parking areas are designated for scooters and mopeds; do not leave vehicles on the sidewalk.

In the past, tourists who wanted to avoid feeding meters and didn't mind a little extra walk could simply secure a free curbside parking spot in the many residential Old Town neighborhoods several blocks off Duval. No more. In an effort to appease Key West residents who complained about having to park several blocks from their homes because tourists had taken their curbside spots, the city of Key West inaugurated a resident parking program in early 1998. We're sorry to say it's not very visitor-friendly.

Here's how parking in residential Old Town now works: Curbside spots along many Old Town streets have been ruled off with white paint and marked with the large yellow letters "RP." In order to park your vehicle in one of these spots, your car must display either a Monroe County license plate or a residential parking permit (available for $5 from the City of Key West with proof of residence). If you park in one of the "RP" spaces and your car does not show the proper proof of residence, you may return to find it gone. Your "illegally parked" vehicle will have likely been towed to the city's impound lot on Stock Island. To retrieve it, you will have to have cash (about $75) — no checks or credit cards are accepted.

When it comes to parking in Key West, the bottom line for nonresidents is this: If you want to be right in the thick of things, you will either have to feed a meter or pay to park in a lot. The meters cost $1 per hour, and they run until midnight daily, including Sundays and holidays. Meter maids (and men) regularly patrol the streets of Key West, and tickets are liberally distributed. All-day parking is available for more reasonable prices at several privately owned lots on either side of Duval Street; watch for the lot attendants holding cardboard signs. You might also consider one of the convenient parking facilities described below.

In all cases, we recommend that you lock your car and either carry your valuables or

stow them out of sight, preferably before you park. Key West is a relatively safe place. However, leaving your video camera in plain view on the front seat of your rental car or stuffing your purse in the trunk just as you leave your car unattended is an open invitation to thievery.

Keep in mind that none of the parking lots described below accepts RVs, nor are you allowed to park your RV on a public street in Key West. During the day, you may park your vehicle on Barracuda Pier at Garrison Bight, off N. Roosevelt Boulevard, or on the bridle path across from Smathers Beach on S. Roosevelt Boulevard. Do not park in any of the beachside spaces at Smathers, however; S. Roosevelt is considered a city street, and your vehicle may be towed. After 11 PM, you must park your RV on private property, in a licensed RV park or campground. For additional information about RV parking in Key West, call (305) 292-PARK.

Whatever kind of vehicle you drive, be sure to park only in designated areas, pay attention to the signs and never, never park alongside a yellow curb. If the sign says that unauthorized vehicles will be towed, believe it. And tempting as those empty spots in the post office lot on Whitehead Street may be, don't even think about leaving your car in one all day. They are for post office customers only. After 5 PM, however, the post office lot becomes a public parking lot and you may park your vehicle here for a fee.

Hilton Parking Garage
231 Front St., Key West • (305) 296-9296

At the end of Front Street, just past the lobby area of the Hilton Hotel, this public parking garage can accommodate 400 cars and offers 24-hour security. Rates are $2 per hour with a maximum cost of $16 in a 24-hour period.

Mallory Square Parking Lot
Corner of Wall and Front Sts., Key West • (305) 292-8158

This parking lot abuts the cruise ship dock off Wall Street in the Mallory Square area and is convenient to all the west-end attractions and the sunset celebration. It has, however, recently been reduced in size to accommo-

Photo: Wayne Moccia

The first sight of the massive brick fortress of Fort Jefferson, guarding the pristine Dry Tortugas, is breathtaking.

date the newly remodeled and enlarged Mallory Square so parking space is limited. Rates run $2 per hour. The lot is open from 8 AM until midnight.

Key West Park N' Ride
300 Grinnell St., Key West • (305) 293-6426

Key West's newest attraction, the award-winning Park N' Ride offers a chance to find one of 250 covered parking spaces at a reasonable rate any time, day or night. For 50¢ an hour ($3 maximum), you can park and then ride one of the shuttles to the downtown area several blocks away. To qualify for this slightly reduced rate, your ticket must be validated by the shuttle driver. For only 75¢ an hour ($6 maximum), avail yourself of the opportunity to walk the quiet streets of Key West. If your stay will be longer, choose the monthly option: For $50, receive unlimited parking for 30 days. An attendant is on duty from 7 AM until 11 PM.

Key West Bight Caroline Street Lot
Corner of Caroline and Margaret Sts., Key West • (305) 293-8309

Adjacent to the attractions at Key West's Historic Seaport, this open-air lot offers full-day parking for $10. If you just need to run a quick errand, you can park free for the first 20 minutes; each additional 20 minutes costs 50¢. Caution: This lot closes at 11 PM; if you arrive later, you won't be able to retrieve your car until the next morning.

Join us on a culinary tour of the Florida Keys, where the sea meets the land with a gustatory bang and nary a whimper.

Restaurants

Surrounded by water, the Florida Keys yields a bounty that easily could qualify as the eighth wonder of the world, We confidently can boast that nowhere else in the continental United States — oh, why not say it, the universe even — will you find fresher, more innovatively prepared fish and seafood than in our restaurants.

Be sure to sample our special natural resources, served any way you like. We import a few raw materials in the feather and flesh categories as well, so your palate will be truly well-rounded.

For preparing your own fare, see our Seafood Markets and Specialty Foods chapter.

Enjoy the relaxed atmosphere of our restaurants, where even the most upscale dining carries a laid-back apparel code. Be it a roadside cafe or a resort dining room, you need dress no more formally than "Keys casual," typically an ensemble of shirt and shorts, shoes or sandals. Men may leave their sports jackets at home, and don't even think about bringing a suit to the Keys unless it is the swimming variety. The same code applies to women as well; we don't discriminate here. The occasional restaurant, such as Cheeca Lodge or Little Palm Island affords you the chance to dress up a bit more if you like — long slacks for the gentlemen, perhaps an island-style dress for the ladies. But the choice is yours. As we keep saying, "Things really are different down here."

The appearance of a restaurant's decor doesn't hold to the strict expectations of other parts of the country either. You'll find that the most unassuming hole-in-the-wall cafe, diner or bistro may serve the best food in town. Don't drive by. Some of our culinary treasures are hidden away off the beaten track. We'll help you find them.

You may find our specialties, from fish to fowl, a trifle confusing. We will translate the Keys-speak. Join us on a culinary tour of the Florida Keys, where the sea meets the land with a gustatory bang and nary a whimper. We have organized the restaurants of the Keys from Key Largo to Big Coppitt Key by descending mile marker and have noted their locations oceanside or bayside. In the Key West section, we offer a cuisine-oriented arrangement with restaurants listed alphabetically.

Free, on-site parking is available at virtually all our recommended establishments in the Upper, Middle and Lower Keys. However, most restaurants in Key West do not have on-site parking. Most restaurants suggest reservations during the high season. Those that require advanced booking year-round will be noted, as will those that do not take reservations.

Many restaurants serve limited alcoholic beverages. You may infer that unless we specify that an establishment offers a full-service bar — usually the larger restaurants or resort facilities — only beer and wine will be served.

Accessibility for the physically challenged varies greatly in restaurants throughout the Keys. While many of our establishments are ground-level and some second-story locations within large resorts may have elevators, steps sometimes must be negotiated and some bathrooms may be too tiny to accommodate a wheelchair. If this is of particular concern to you, be sure to call the restaurants to see exactly what arrangements might be made to fit your needs.

Unless otherwise specified, you may assume that our recommended restaurants are air-conditioned. Those that provide outdoor seating or accessibility by sea will be highlighted. Children are generally welcome in Florida Keys restaurants. The odd exceptions or age restrictions will be stated.

The dollar-sign price code indicated in each restaurant listing (see gray box) will help you gauge the cost of your dining experience. Each code category is based on dinner for two, without starters, dessert, alcoholic beverages, tax or tip. Some of our restaurants include soup or a house salad with an entree; at others, entrees are strictly a la carte. Most of our restaurants accept major credit cards but rarely a personal check. If plastic is not acknowledged, we alert you in advance so you won't be caught short of cash.

Price Code

$	Less than $25
$$	$25 to $40
$$$	$41 to $55
$$$$	More than $55

The Florida Keys

Upper Keys

Crack'd Conch
$$ • MM 105 Oceanside, Key Largo
• (305) 451-0732

Inside this 1930s Conch house is some of the finest seafood in all the Florida Keys. Patrons sit on benches set at unadorned wood tables with paper placemats and napkins; outdoor dining is offered within a screened backyard patio. But don't let the Keysy simplicity fool you. The imaginative cuisine of the Crack'd Conch will not disappoint.

The restaurant began as a fishing camp with sleeping bunks and facilities for storing and smoking fish; then it was converted to a chicken-to-go establishment. Since the 1970s it has been known as the Crack'd Conch, and the Peterson family has now owned and operated it for more than 15 years . . . from all

appearances with a hearty sense of humor. They note in the menu: "This establishment is run by a very close staff and family . . . close to broke, close to insanity and close to killing each other!"

Chowders here are rich, creamy and filled with chunks of shellfish; conch salad contains just enough spice to give it the right kick. The seafood platter, broiled or fried and consisting of shrimp, scallops, conch and catch-of-the-day, is a hefty enough portion to feed two. Fried 'gator tails are the most popular appetizer and dinner. Crack'd Conch serves wine and carries more than 100 labels of beer.

The restaurant is open for lunch and dinner every day except Wednesday. Reservations are not accepted. In addition to cash, traveler's checks or credit cards, Crack'd Conch will accept "gold, pirate treasure or the keys to expensive sports cars" as payment for your dining adventure.

Italian Fisherman
$$ • MM 104 Bayside, Key Largo
• (305) 451-4471

Guarding the entry to this Italian seafood establishment is La Pescatore and his *la rezza del mare* (translation: the fisherman with fishing net). Beyond the statue is an open dining room filled with white Italianate tables, candlelit in the evening, which overlooks Blackwater Sound and the restaurant's docks. Ceiling fans enhance the coastal breezes. Feel free to bring your swimsuit along, for Italian Fisherman also offers patrons the opportunity to take a dip in its Olympic-size pool.

Owned by John Baiamonte, a New Jersey native of Sicilian ancestry, the Italian Fisherman has been a Key Largo institution for 17 years, specializing in southern-style Italian cooking. Pastas, pizzas, sandwiches and salads are reasonably priced, and you can also dine on steak, veal, chicken or seafood platters if you so desire. The specialty of the house

INSIDERS' TIP

Want to sample the fish you caught today? Many Keys restaurants will be happy to prepare your catch — along with some side dishes, like potatoes, corn on the cob and coleslaw. Phone around for availability and prices.

is Linguine Marechiaro, a cioppino-style combination of scallops, shrimp, mussels and cubed catch-of-the-day served in a white wine, olive oil and marinara sauce over linguine.

Spacious and open to sweeping views of Florida Bay by day, the Italian Fisherman offers spectacular sunset vistas as well. Its dock is brightly lit at night, and patrons head there to feed an abundance of visiting catfish. The Italian Fisherman has a full-service tiki bar. The restaurant is open every day but Monday for lunch and dinner. The restaurant is boat-accessible.

Sundowners on the Bay
$$ • MM 104 Bayside, Key Largo
• (305) 451-4502

One of Key Largo's most popular places to enjoy the sunset, this open and airy — yet cozy and intimate — establishment overlooks the azure expanse of Blackwater Sound. Customary appetizers — cracked conch, stuffed mushrooms and mozzarella sticks — are best, and the burgers and fish sandwiches can't be beat. If you prefer a more elaborate meal, choose from an assortment of steaks and seafood offerings. Yellowtail specials are always winners, as are the kabobs.

All tables are set with fresh flowers for evening dining. A large bar, adjoining the indoor dining area, is available for dinner service as well, and busy evenings tend to run on the loud side. The patio and deck afford more privacy. Sundowners offers a full bar and is open for lunch and dinner. Reservations are recommended. The restaurant is accessible by boat.

Señor Frijoles
$ • MM 103.9 Bayside, Key Largo
• (305) 451-1592

Don your sombrero for a taste of Mexico by the sea — Keys style. Señor Frijoles nestles on Florida Bay next to Sundowners and offers the usual chicken or beef Tex-Mex fare — burritos, chalupas, chimichangas, tacos, enchiladas, fajitas, nachos — as well as some jazzed-up Conch Republic versions made with the Keys local seafood and catches of the day. And you don't have to look for Jimmy Buffett to find Margaritaville. Señor Frijoles offers nine different Margaritas as well as a potpourri of other tropical libations and Mexican beers with which you can toast the fabulous Keys sunset. Señor Frijoles is boat accessible. It is open for lunch and dinner daily.

Manny's Authentic Key Lime Pie

This recipe creates the best Key lime pie in the Florida Keys, say Insiders whose taste buds have thoroughly researched the subject. Our thanks to Manny, from Manny & Isa's Kitchen in Islamorada (see our listing in this chapter) for sharing his trade secrets with us.

1 14-ounce can Eagle Brand condensed milk
4 large eggs or 6 medium eggs
4 ounces Key lime juice
1 pie crust, baked and cooled
½ cup sugar
¼ teaspoon cream of tartar

Close-up

Separate egg yolks and put aside whites to make meringue. Slightly beat yolks; add condensed milk and mix together. Add Key lime juice and mix again. Pour into baked, cooled pie crust. (If you are using fresh Key lime juice, the pie will set without refrigerating. If you are using bottled Key lime juice, you must refrigerate the pie until set.) To make meringue, beat egg whites until medium peaks form. Add cream of tartar and continue to beat. Slowly add sugar and continue beating until the mixture is stiff. Preheat the oven to 375 degrees. Spread the meringue over the pie, sealing it to the crust. Bake until meringue is golden brown. Refrigerate Key lime pie until cold. Serve to applause.

Gus' Grille

$$ • MM 103.8 Bayside, Marriott Key Largo Bay Beach Resort, Key Largo • (305) 453-0000

Gus' seafood-inspired menu mixes Asian, Latin American and traditional American cuisine to create a style referred to by the chef as Floribbean. Grilled dolphin is served with Asian mango and papaya salsa and exotic greens tossed with a jalapeno vinaigrette dressing and a side of fried rice noodles. Equally popular is yellowtail snapper with an almond crust, topped with avocado, orange and chive sweet-butter sauce. Food is prepared before your eyes in an open kitchen, an up-market grill-style presentation reminiscent of a tony trattoria.

Unobstructed views of the Florida Bay and the famous Keys sunset are available from virtually every seat in the house. Booths line the window walls of the light and airy dining room; outdoor patio dining is also available.

Open daily for breakfast, lunch and dinner, Gus' has handicapped-accessible facilities and an elevator. You can dock your boat at the Marriott while you enjoy your meal at Gus', but reservations for both slips and tables are recommended here.

Num Thai Restaurant & Sushi Bar

$$ • MM 103.2 Oceanside, Key Largo • (305) 451-5955

If your taste for Asian food hovers around Thailand or Japan, Num Thai can offer you the best of both worlds: spicy Thai curries and noodle dishes or sushi, sashimi and traditional Japanese dishes. The fresh bright restaurant basks in the glow of deep-teal colored walls covered with Asian accents. Three tatami tables, which seat two to four people, complement the wood laminate tables peppering the interior. A sushi bar affords one and all the opportunity to watch the masters at work. Japanese offerings include temaki, cone-shaped hand rolls; hosomaki, medium rolls cut into bite-sized pieces; a wide assortment of sushi, by the piece or in dinner combos; and tempura. Or, enjoy Thai satays; spicy beef salad; seafood, chicken or beef curries; or shrimp, gin-

gered with basil or fired with chili paste. Pad Thai proves to be a hefty portion.

Open for lunch Monday through Friday and dinner every day, Num Thai accepts reservations for parties of more than five. American and Oriental beers, wine, plum wine and sake all are offered.

The Quay Key Largo

$$$ • MM 102.5 Bayside, Key Largo • (305) 451-0943

The Quay Key Largo is the type of place where you can spend the entire day. Perched on Florida Bay, the restaurant guarantees every patron in the main dining room a water view. Diners also can enjoy the swimming pool, personal watercraft rentals, boat excursions and the restaurant's more casual venue, Dockside Grill.

www.insiders.com

See this and many other **Insiders' Guide®** destinations online — in their entirety.

Visit us today!

Whereas the outdoor Dockside Grill offers lunch, dinner and happy hour, the main dining room of The Quay features candlelit mahogany tables surrounded by tropical flowers, plants and trees. The dining room has banquet facilities and is open for dinner only. Both have full bars. Head to Dockside for burgers and fish sandwiches. In the dining room, you can enjoy seafood, steak and pasta specialties such as yellowtail stuffed with crabmeat and topped with shrimp in a béarnaise sauce, grouper or dolphin Florentine and grouper or yellowtail almondine. New York strip steak, filet mignon, and surf and turf are popular with beef eaters. Broiled twin tails of lobster or live Maine lobsters are available at market prices.

The Quay is accessible by boat. Reservations are recommended for the main dining room. Early-bird specials are served in the main dining room from 4 to 6 PM and include complete dinners (entree, soup, salad, coffee or tea and dessert) at reduced prices. The Quay and Dockside Grill are open daily.

The Fish House

$$$ • MM 102.4 Oceanside, Key Largo • (305) 451-4665

The Fish House puts on no pretenses. The scent of freshly prepared seafood alone is enough to lure patrons into this establishment bedecked with fish nets, mounted fish and buoys galore. Part seafood market and part restaurant (see our Seafood Markets and Specialty Foods chapter), The Fish House offers indoor dining and the option of patio dining on picnic benches and tables within a screened porch. Chowders are so thick you can eat them with a fork; seafood entrees are served broiled, blackened, fried or française. One of the most popular Fish House dishes is pan-seared catch-of-the-day (especially yellowtail) with a lemon-butter sherry sauce. Specials allow the chef to experiment even further with imaginative medleys that include shrimp, lobster and scallops topped with mushrooms and served in a spicy Key lime sauce. No matter which entree you order, be prepared to request a doggy bag.

The Fish House serves beer and wine and is open for lunch and dinner daily. Reservations are not accepted, and activity teems most every evening.

Makoto Japanese Restaurant

$$ • MM 101.6 Oceanside, Key Largo
• (305) 451-7083

Behind the incongruous screaming yellow awning, a touch of the Orient awaits your taste buds. At this Japanese restaurant you're on a Makoto roll, which also happens to be the name of the house specialty: salmon, cream cheese and scallions rolled with rice into a seaweed wrapping, deep fried and served with teriyaki sauce. Shrimp and chicken tempura also are favorites, and you'll find traditional Japanese teriyaki sautées, from simple shrimp to soft-shell crab to barbecued eel. All the sweetest sushi specialties are offered, including salmon, yellowtail, shrimp and more.

If sushi or sashimi isn't your fancy, dine, instead, in the hibachi room, where chefs will cook teppanyaki selections before your nose. Steak, shrimp, chicken, scallops, even tuna or salmon steak. Flambé? No problem. Makoto's selection of beer and wine includes American and Canadian favorites along with Sakoro, sake and plum wine.

The restaurant serves lunch and dinner daily except Monday when it opens at 5 PM for dinner only. Reservations for large parties are suggested.

Tower of Pizza

$ • MM 100.5, Key Largo
• (305) 451-1461
$ • MM 81.5, Islamorada
• (305) 664-8216

Each Tower of Pizza has a different owner, and the specialties are equally unique. The Key Largo restaurant features antipasto, Greek salads and pizzas baked in a brick oven. Sauces and doughs are homemade, and cheeses are fresh. Our favorite is the thick-crust round Sicilian variety. Delivery is free with an $8 minimum order from MM 94 to MM 107.

At Tower of Pizza in Islamorada, the specialty is gourmet pizza, with toppings such as artichoke hearts, feta cheese and pesto, and white pizza. Its Sicilian is equally tasty.

Both Towers are open every day for lunch and dinner.

Frank Keys Cafe

$$$ • MM 100.2 Oceanside, Key Largo
• (305) 453-0310

For fine Florida Keys dining, Frank Keys Cafe, set off the main highway amid burgeoning foliage and somewhat tricky to uncover, is well worth a couple of trips around the block. Situated in a natural hardwood hammock, the restaurant was built in 1994, designed as a replica of a Victorian Conch-style home — peachy-pink stucco with a white wraparound porch and lots of gingerbread trim. Both on the veranda and in the dimly lit pastel interior dining room, the tables are appointed with white linen cloths, fresh flowers and flickering candles. Ceiling fans revolve overhead. Despite the traffic sounds on the nearby Overseas Highway, outdoor dining is romantic because lush tropical gardens surround Frank Keys Cafe.

The specialties here are steaks, seafood, rack of lamb and imaginative pasta dishes. Wowing the palate are specials such as filet mignon served on a bed of spinach with Portobello mushrooms, brandy sauce and mashed-potato accents or pistachio-encrusted grouper with black bean salsa.

Frank Keys Cafe is open daily for dinner only. To find Frank Keys Cafe, look for the large sign with white lights on the Overseas Highway and turn toward the ocean.

Dining al fresco at water's edge lends island ambiance
to the adventure of eating in the Florida Keys.

Coconuts Restaurant & Lounge
**$$ • MM 100 Oceanside, Marina del Mar
Resort, 528 Caribbean Dr., Key Largo
• (305) 453-9794**

This vibrant outdoor restaurant sits cornered between Key Largo Harbor and the swimming pool of Marina del Mar Resort & Marina. Ceiling fans cool patrons seated at wood tables decorated with conch shell centerpieces. Coconuts' Portobello mushrooms stuffed with crabmeat and topped with béarnaise sauce provide a tasty start to any meal, and seafood platters prepared blackened, grilled, broiled or fried are especially popular. So too is the restaurant's namesake: coconut shrimp with Malibu rum sauce. A raw bar, open seasonally, features stone crab claws, shrimp, oysters and clams.

After dinner, head for Coconuts' indoor nightclub and dance the night away, or sit back and enjoy the live entertainment (see

our Nightlife chapter). The establishment has a full bar and offers weekday happy hours from 5 to 7 PM. Coconuts is boat-accessible. Reservations are accepted for parties of more than nine. To reach Coconuts, head toward the ocean on Laguna at MM 100; the restaurant is about a quarter-mile in on the left.

Jim & Val's Tugboat Restaurant
**$ • MM 100 Oceanside, Seagate Blvd.
and Ocean Dr., Key Largo
• (305) 453-9010**

Jim and Val Mayfield purchased the restaurant, once known as the original Tugboat Annie's, in 1993. Renamed Jim & Val's Tugboat Restaurant, this unassuming little dining establishment is a favorite with area locals.

A campy cartoon tugboat adorns the white facade of Jim and Val's place, which is tucked away from the fray off the Overseas Highway. The menu is limited, but specials abound. On any given evening, you may find jumbo stuffed mushrooms with crabmeat and hollandaise, smoked fish dip or stuffed jalapenos served as appetizers; fried whole snapper or Jamaican jerked yellowtail fillets or blackened grouper may be offered as an entree. Jim & Val's is known for its consistent offering of cracked (pounded, breaded and fried) conch.

The decor here is simple, casual and outdoorsy. You can opt to sit indoors in a small air-conditioned dining room, on an airy screened porch or outside under a canopy of tropical hardwoods. Reservations are accepted.

To reach Jim & Val's Tugboat Restaurant, which is open for lunch and dinner seven days a week and for breakfast on weekends, turn toward the ocean on Ocean Bay Drive and continue about a half-mile; the restaurant is on the left, on the corner of Seagate Boulevard.

Snook's Bayside Restaurant
$$$ • MM 99.9 Bayside, Key Largo
• (305) 453-3799

Exquisitely nestled amid towering palms at the very edge of Florida Bay, Snook's hides away down a narrow, winding driveway off the Overseas Highway. Virtually every seat in the house affords a view of the water, be it from the elegant pink, teal and white indoor dining room — fronted by a glass window wall — or on the patio deck suspended over the bay. Expect linen cloths and napkins, fresh flowers and candlelight — not always an ambiance found accompanying great food in the Keys. And great food it is.

Catch-of-the-day or Snook's signature fish, yellowtail snapper, is served blackened, broiled, fried, sautéed, almondine, tropical style (covered with exotic fruits and melon liqueur) or grenoblaise (with lemon butter and capers). You'll find Scallops Bayside wrapped in prosciutto with gorgonzola cream sauce over tomato and eggplant raviolis. Beefeaters can choose their steaks prepared several ways. Chicken lovers appreciate Snook's hazelnut

chicken, which is served with Frangelico in an orange-thyme sauce.

Snook's pastry chef prepares all breads and desserts, which challenge the waistline with decadence: crème brûlée with Jack Daniels, tiramisu, bread pudding or sinfully chocolate cake.

Two full bars are on premises, one sporting a pounded copper top, and an extensive wine list includes more than 175 selections from all over the world. Snook's offers live entertainment nightly in season and on weekends during the off-season. The restaurant is open for lunch and dinner Monday through Saturday; brunch is served on Sundays. Snook's is boat-accessible.

Cafe Largo
$$ • MM 99.5 Bayside, Key Largo
• (305) 451-4885

Florida Keys history includes tales of Bluebeard and Black Caesar, but at Cafe Largo the legendary Redbeard has made his mark — in the airbrushed wall murals featuring local scenery, that is. Bistro tables atop terracotta tile floors evoke a continental flair in Cafe Largo's charming interior— a mix of stark white, hunter green and peach.

Providing no less a spectacular diversion from the decor are the house specialties, a vast array of pasta, chicken, veal and eggplant dishes as well as individual hand-tossed pizzas. Fresh fish and seafood offerings round out the diverse menu.

The restaurant has a full bar. It is open every day for dinner only; reservations for large parties during high season are recommended.

Bayside Grille
$$ • MM 99.5 Bayside, Key Largo
• (305) 451-3380

Situated at the end of a winding drive behind Cafe Largo and perched on the very edge of Florida Bay, Bayside Grille commands one of the most premier waterfront vistas in the

INSIDERS' TIP

Believe it or not, in a town like Key West that rocks until well into the wee hours, late-night dining is hard to come by. With few exceptions, most restaurants do not serve past 11 PM. As a rule of thumb: Eat early, party late.

Keys. Small, casual and bistro-ish, Bayside Grille sports a dozen or so tables, fronted by pocketing glass doors, enabling all diners to drink in the shimmering blue sea while partaking of a palate-tingling selection of food and beverages. Garlic mussels join forces with clams casino, fried calamari and Cajun clams as appetizers. Seafood reigns here, but landlubbers will also find a good selection of beef, chicken and lamb entrees.

Bayside offers libations from a full bar. The restaurant serves lunch and dinner daily.

Anthony's Italian Restaurant & Lounge
$ • MM 97.5 in the median, Key Largo • (305) 853-1177

According to owner Anthony Colarusso, a native New Yorker, he was the first restaurateur to introduce South Floridians to the calzone and Sicilian pizza. Today, Colarusso offers these items and more, including veal francese, Marsala and parmigiana; scungilli; fried calamari; and frutta del mar, a seafood combination of scallops, shrimp, mussels and clams served over a bed of linguine. Hot and cold appetizers, sandwiches and a solid selection of pasta dishes and Italian specialties fill out the menu.

Colarusso makes his own doughs and sauces using recipes his mother followed when he was a child. Anthony's is open for lunch and dinner. Reservations are not accepted.

Harriette's
$, no credit cards • MM 95.7 Bayside, Key Largo • (305) 852-8689

This popular roadside diner-style restaurant started in 1948 as a homemade ice cream parlor. In seven years it went through 10 owners. Then in 1982 preschool teacher Harriette Mattson came along. Honing in on customer satisfaction, the chef and owner offers reasonably priced home-style meals in a simple setting. Tables and chairs surround counter dining; local arts and crafts on consignment provide the decor.

Harriette's specialty: ensuring that no guest leaves the restaurant hungry. Open only for breakfast and lunch, Harriette's serves filling omelets, oversize homemade biscuits with sausage gravy, burgers and hot and cold sandwiches. The restaurant caters primarily to a repeat local crowd, so lunch specials change daily. Forget Caribbean or gourmet seafood specials: at Harriette's, it's meat loaf, pork chops, stuffed peppers, roast pork, chicken and dumplings.

The longtime waitstaff here knows many of the customers by name. Harriette stays in the kitchen, doing what she does best: producing the satisfying meals that keep 'em coming back. Harriette's is open seven days a week. Reservations are not accepted.

Snappers Waterfront Saloon & Raw Bar
$$ • MM 94.5 Oceanside, 139 Seaside Ave., Key Largo • (305) 852-5956

The best part of Snappers is sitting out on the deck near the water overlooking Snappers Marina . . . next to the food, that is, which is Old Florida and Bahamian cuisine at its best. You can graze on conch fritters, gator bites and stuffed jalapenos, or the "reel meals," selections from our sizable Florida Keys piscatory pantry — Grouper Dakota, which is coated with toasted almonds and Parmesan, or "Big Reds" Snapper, which is served with Cayo Largo sauce. Choose from a well-developed raw bar or ceviche or settle for the more pedestrian landlubbers fare — steaks, chicken or burgers. Snappers also offers a children's menu.

Weekends feature live entertainment. The restaurant is boat-accessible. Reservations are accepted.

The Copper Kettle
$ • MM 91.8 Oceanside, Tavernier • (305) 852-4113

Margaret Thompson, owner of the historic Tavernier Hotel (see our Accommodations chapter), offers a dining room with an English country ambiance — lace curtains, floral drapes, an antique hutch, Edwardian chaise longue and intimate bar — on the former site of the Old Tavernier Restaurant (see separate listing). Paintings lining the walls were done by Thompson herself.

Dine inside or out along the backyard garden. The menu features local cuisine that combines Thompson's European background with her newfound island home. You'll find such comfort food as meat loaf, baked macaroni and cheese and spinach pie, or more exotic offerings such as Cajun honey rum shrimp, seafood stuffed mahi-mahi or chicken Neptune. The island chowder at Copper Kettle is an award-winning secret recipe that marries New England-style seafood chowder and Caribbean conch chowder.

The Copper Kettle is open for breakfast, lunch and dinner. Reservations are recommended on weekends.

Craig's Restaurant
$$ • MM 90.5 Bayside, Tavernier
• (305) 852-9424

A 1977 graduate of the Culinary Institute in Hyde Park, New York, who honed his skills at Plantation Yacht Harbor and the Pilot House Restaurant, Craig Belcher opened his own establishment in 1981 with his signature sandwich, which he bills "World Famous Fish Sandwich."

A simply appointed diner-style restaurant with an all-day menu, Craig's sates every palate, be it down-home or gourmet. Specialties of the chef include Fish Tropical (grouper or dolphin sautéed with bananas, pineapples, oranges and strawberries and topped with sliced almonds) and Fish Seminole (baked grouper or dolphin with sautéed shrimp and mushrooms, scallops, scallions, tomatoes and hearts of palm in lemon-butter sauce). The Jon Chicken Sandwich, a grilled chicken breast with Dijon mustard, Cajun seasoning, melted cheese, grilled onions, grilled mushrooms and bacon, puts a little pep in the ubiquitous poulet.

Open seven days a week, Craig's does not accept reservations.

Old Tavernier Restaurant
$$ • MM 90.1 Oceanside, Tavernier
• (305) 852-6012

One of the Upper Keys' most popular establishments, Old Tavernier specializes in Italian cuisine with a continental flair.

Its beginnings date back to 1988, when the restaurant occupied the site of The Copper Kettle. Loyal, satisfied patrons have followed the restaurant's every move. Diners enjoy traditional pasta favorites: pasta primavera, angel hair marinara, baked ziti, fettuccine Alfredo and eggplant, chicken and veal

parmigiana. Or, they opt for a culinary adventure with yellowtail Provençale (pan-sautéed and served with fresh tomatoes, button mushrooms, scallions, garlic, white wine/lemon butter sauce and fresh basil); cioppino (fresh seafood stewed in a zesty tomato sauce with white wine and served over fettuccine); grill-seared Greek rack of lamb rubbed with kosher salt and oregano in a lemon glaze; or yellowtail with a toasted almond-banana-berry-rum glaze.

Guests have the option of dining indoors, where white linen tablecloths are aglow with candles and watercolor sailboat scenes dot the walls, or outdoors on a balcony overlooking a canal. Old Tavernier has a full bar and is open daily for dinner only. The restaurant is boat-accessible. Reservations are recommended.

Marker 88
$$$ • MM 88 Bayside, Islamorada
• (305) 852-9315

An Islamorada culinary landmark for decades, Marker 88 combines bayside ambiance with innovative preparation of the Keys' freshest bounty. Established in 1978 by German-born, Swiss-trained Andre Mueller, Marker 88 is popular with presidents — such as George Bush — and local patrons alike.

Marker 88's cuisine is legendary. Fish Rangoon, a sautéed catch-of-the-day, is served with banana, papaya, pineapple, mango, currant jelly and cinnamon butter; steak Madagascar, a New York strip, is topped with sliced tomato, hearts of palm and béarnaise sauce and is encircled in a brown demi-glace sauce.

Dessert is no less lavish. Key Lime Baked Alaska towers with layers of ice cream and Key lime filling encircled in meringue.

As sophisticated as the Marker 88 menu may be, decor here is charmingly Keys rustic: Wood tables are made of hatch covers lifted from boats. Tiffany lighting provides a soothing romantic setting, and views of Florida Bay abound. Marker 88 is surrounded by heavy tropical vegetation, and rambling docks, and a deck laden with wood outdoor tables and chairs, beckons for a pre-dinner sunset libation or a starlit after-dinner drink.

Marker 88 offers a children's menu with

basic dishes such as fried shrimp in small portions. The boat-accessible restaurant maintains a full bar and is open for dinner every day but Monday. Reservations are recommended.

Jammers Grill Room & Party Pub
$ • MM 86.7 Oceanside, Islamorada
• (305) 852-8786

If you like your food hot, hot, hot, you'll find it at Jammers. Wings here suit any number of tastes and temperatures, starting with sweet and sour, barbecue and Cajun and moving on to medium, hot and nuclear with every pepper known or unknown to man. Even conch chowder is prepared with a spicy red base so tempting that one Miami resident travels 60-plus miles to buy it by the gallon. For more "mild" tastes, burgers come in plain, cheese and club (a.k.a. the garbage burger) with Swiss and American cheese, bacon, turkey, ham, lettuce, tomato and onion. Baby-back ribs in homemade barbecue sauce are cooked so slowly that the meat practically falls right off the bone. A Beach Brats menu for children younger than 10 includes burgers, beach dogs and grilled cheese sandwiches.

Jammers bustles with Generation Xers. Female waitstaff are outfitted in cut-off T-shirts and short shorts (Jammers once was a part of the Clearwater, Florida, Melons chain.) The full bar here features a signature drink called "The Jammer Slammer": a concoction of Bacardi Black, orange juice, pineapple and coconut milk.

Weekends at Jammers feature live music. The restaurant is open for lunch and dinner daily but does not accept reservations.

Horizon Restaurant & Lounge
$$ • MM 84 Oceanside, Holiday Isle Resorts, Islamorada • (305) 664-2321

Holiday Isle is hoppin', and Horizon lets you see it all from greater heights. The sixth-floor interior has a semiformal ambiance in mauve, teal and coral completely surrounded by windows to allow views of the Atlantic. Among Horizon's seafood specialties are Catch Florasian, catch-of-the-day poached in Asian hot and sour broth and served with Oriental vegetables, or Catch Islamorada, fresh fish encased in an onion crust, broiled and

served with mango and black bean salsa. You'll find a selection of meats, poultry, soups, salads and pastas, and a "lite bites menu" is served in the lounge only from 2 PM to closing. A children's menu includes burgers, spaghetti, chicken fingers and fried shrimp.

Open for breakfast, lunch and dinner daily, Horizon has a full bar and wine list featuring everything from Copper Ridge and Turning Leaf to Moët & Chandon, Taittinger and Dom Perignon. The restaurant is boat-accessible, and reservations are recommended. Live music is offered on weekends.

Coral Grill
$$ • MM 83.5 Bayside, Islamorada
• (305) 664-4803

Coral Grill is actually two restaurants in one: On the first floor, menu service includes all-you-can-eat soup, salad and dessert bars; there's a full buffet offered on the second floor. The concentration in both places is food, food and lots more food.

The menu's 50 items include prime rib, filet mignon, tender sirloin tips and surf and turf. House specialties focus on the catch-of-the-day prepared française, spicy blackened or Matecumbe (sautéed with scallions, black olives, mushrooms and roasted red peppers); and the Long Boat (beer-battered fish with a Key lime-nut butter sauce).

The buffet upstairs is a balance of hot and cold fresh and imported items such as Dungeness crab, Alaskan snow crab legs, prime rib, steamed and fried shrimp, baked grouper in wine and butter, fried dolphin fingers, smoked fish and 40 varieties of salads. Special hot entrees, such as barbecued ribs, roast turkey and Szechwan beef, are added to the buffet each day.

Children 3 and younger eat for free at the Coral Grill. The buffet is half-price for children ages 4 to 11, and a children's menu downstairs features hot dogs, hamburgers, fried shrimp and grilled cheese.

Coral Grill is open for dinner from Tuesday through Saturday and from noon to 9 PM on Sunday. Early-bird specials are offered from noon to 3 PM Sunday and from 4:30 to 6 PM the other days. Smoking and nonsmoking sections are designated. Reservations are not accepted.

Ziggie's Conch Restaurant
$$ • MM 83.5 Bayside, Islamorada
• (305) 664-3391

If you walked into Ziggie's Conch unaware of its reputation in Islamorada as a first-class eatery, you might wonder what the fuss is all about. But the Formica-topped diner-style tables, carpetless floors, and a we've-been-here-a-long-time decor is just a guise. The fuss, my friends, comes from the talents in the kitchen where for decades Ziggie's has been creating some of the finest cuisine in the Keys. The waitstaff will take your drink orders and ask if you'd like to hear the specials. Say "yes"! And you'd better pay attention, because the lengthy list of dishes you will hear described in mouth-watering detail sounds like a who's who — or a what's what — at the Culinary Institute.

Traditional favorites, those tried-and-trues popular for years, are rich and still loaded with all that good stuff the tabloids say you shouldn't have anymore — butter, cream, eggs. Oysters come stuffed a half-dozen ways. The fresh fish concoctions defy description. Insiders love their yellowtail prepared meunière, almondine or veronique. And call ahead to request Lobster English. It is not always a canted special but quite often the chef will make it just for you. Plain grilled fish soars off the charts here too. And the chef will prepare your catch if you like.

Ziggie's Conch is open for dinner nightly,

except Wednesday. Reservations are accepted. Each year Ziggie's closes the day after Labor Day and reopens the Friday before the beginning of stone crab season in mid-October.

Bentley's Restaurant
$$ • MM 82.8 Oceanside, Islamorada
• (305) 664-9094

At Bentley's Restaurant, the names of the dishes will intrigue your mind and ignite your taste buds. And the portions guarantee that you don't go home hungry. Try the Outtahand Lobster or Sensational Shrimp, immodestly superlative, but right on the gustatory mark. And the surf and turf, half a stuffed lobster, fish or crab plus a petite filet mignon, grants the best of both worlds. We know you've had dolphin before, but ever tried it "in the weeds" (on a bed of creamed spinach)?

Bentley's raw bar is popular with the happy-hour crowd (see our Nightlife chapter). The restaurant is open daily for lunch and dinner. Reservations are suggested for dinner.

Sloop's Seagrill
$ • MM 82.7 Bayside, Islamorada
• (305) 664-4442

The most recent addition to Islamorada's burgeoning restaurant scene, Sloop's Seagrill combines a quirky Keys ambiance with a stellar all-day menu of imaginative offerings. The muted gold and salmon walls of Sloop's are strewn with fish nets, life rings, waterskis, oars, fish skeletons and potpourri of artfully arranged lobster traps and buoys. The building itself, which was once Perry's, received a complete face-lift in 1998, so that the final result is fresh, new and revitalized.

There is something for everyone on Sloop's menu, from sandwiches such as salmon BLT or a smoked salmon wrap to a fine selection of imaginative appetizers, salads, soups and entrees.

Lorelei Restaurant, Cabana Bar and Grand Slam Lounge
$$$, restaurant; $, bar and lounge
MM 82 Bayside, Islamorada
• (305) 664-4656

The legend of Lorelei — a nymph of the Rhine — maintains that her sweet, lyrical singing lured sailors to shipwreck on a rock. Today's Lorelei lures you to a primo perch on the very edge of the Florida Bay, where you'll relish breakfast, lunch and dinner daily as well as those other munching hours in between. Come by boat, if you like, for the Lorelei also maintains a marina where you'll be able to rub shoulders with some of the Keys' renowned fishing guides.

The Cabana Bar breaks the day starting at 7 AM and serves a casual lunch menu from 11 AM until 9 PM. Look for Cabana Madness, a giant platter of Buffalo wings, conch fritters, zucchini and cheese sticks, quarter-pound steamed shrimp, and a cluster of snow crab and smoked fish slices. Also a winner is the sesame noodle and spicy chicken salad, topped with a spicy peanut sauce. If shrimp is your fancy try Bahamian palm coconut shrimp, tangy and sweet with orange horseradish sauce.

Or opt to dine at the air-conditioned Lorelei Restaurant, where an expansive menu makes a gustatory decision a difficult task. The catch-of-the-day can be enjoyed six different ways, or try Shrimp Madness, offering seven preparations for shrimp. Mix it up with a combination platter of shrimp, fish, scallops, conch and crab

cakes — fried or blackened if you like. Landlubbers will find steaks, chicken and pasta.

The Lorelei Restaurant is open daily for dinner. Early-bird specials are offered from 5 to 6 PM. In addition to the Cabana Bar, the air-conditioned Grand Slam Lounge serves lunch until 3 PM. Reservations are not taken at the Cabana Bar.

Atlantic's Edge and Ocean Terrace Grill
$$$, restaurant; $$, grill • MM 82
Oceanside, Cheeca Lodge, Islamorada
• (305) 664-4651

Chef Dawn Sieber, a University of Miami alumna who obtained her culinary degree in Maryland, has been with Cheeca Lodge since the resort was reopened by Coastal Hotel Group in 1988 (see Accommodations). So successful is Sieber that she was invited to act as a guest chef for Julia Child's 80th birthday in Boston. Among her specialties: spicy orange shrimp with passionfire, dark rum, cilantro black bean fritter and cilantro oil; Florida snapper pan-seared with an onion crust and served over braised Roma tomatoes and baby artichoke hearts in a warm balsamic vinaigrette sauce; and dolphin baked in filo and served with sautéed spinach in a balsamic glaze.

The Cheeca children's menu is the result of consultations with local Plantation Key elementary school children; it includes all their favorites, such as pizza, chicken fingers, fish fingers, popcorn shrimp and a child-size filet mignon. A dessert highlight is "The Dirt Cup" — chocolate pudding with crumbled Oreo cookies topped with a candy gummy worm.

The indoor dining atmosphere at Atlantic's Edge features casual elegance — beige linen tablecloths, crystal goblets and bud vases — highlighted by a panoramic view of the Atlantic through floor-to-ceiling glass walls.

Cheeca's Ocean Terrace Grill offers indoor and outdoor dining with a more casual menu that includes everything from burgers and fish sandwiches, salads and soups to full dinners such as snapper with Creole shrimp sauce or

---

INSIDERS' TIP

In the off-season, many restaurants limit their hours; some even close altogether. To avoid disappointment, phone ahead.

penne pasta with chorizo, Manchego cheese and guajillo butter sauce.

Atlantic Edge is open for dinner nightly, offering libation from a full bar. The restaurant offers a Sunday brunch from 10 AM to 3 PM from Thanksgiving until June. Reservations are recommended on weekends. The Ocean Terrace Grill is open for breakfast, lunch and dinner daily during the high season, breakfast and lunch only in the off-season.

Woody's Saloon & Restaurant
$ • MM 82 Bayside, Islamorada
• (305) 664-4335

Don't let Big Dick and the Extenders (see our Nightlife chapter), the well-known entertainment here, take your attention away from what's really best about Woody's: the restaurant's hand-tossed Chicago style pizza. It's incredibly thin and tasty, made from the freshest of products, and quite a unique combination of them. Woody's Hawaiian pizza is topped with ham and pineapple. He also offers a jalapeno pizza, a fresh garlic pizza, a hamburger pizza and more. Among the local favorites here is the BLT pizza topped with — you guessed it — bacon, lettuce and tomatoes. Woody's satisfies from dinnertime into the not-so-wee hours (4 AM!) daily with a last call for pizza at 3:30 AM. Dine in and take-out service is available.

Grove Park Cafe
$$ • MM 81.7 Oceanside, Old Highway, Islamorada • (305) 664-0116

Entering the gingerbread-trimmed Conch cottage of Grove Park Cafe is like stepping into a life-size dollhouse. A palette of pastels adorns the cloudlike ceiling and walls — peach, seafoam green, yellow, lavender and pink — offsetting the restaurant's charming offbeat decor. An eclectic assortment of memorabilia and antique bric-a-brac is sprinkled all around. Each of the three small dining rooms exudes its own distinctive personality.

Grove Park Cafe offers meat, chicken and seafood entrees with a tropical flair. Among the chef's specialties is yellowtail macadamia, a boneless yellowtail fillet encrusted with crushed macadamia nuts and topped with a tropical salsa of mangoes, bell peppers, onions and tomatoes. Roast duck arrives crispy, accom-

panied by a tangy orange sauce; rack of lamb tingles with rosemary, nestled around a mountain of garlicky mashed potatoes. Pasta Florentine and Grove Park's crab cakes are perennial favorites, and children's and vegetarian dishes are made to order. Early-bird menus are available at various times of the year.

Grove Park Cafe is open for lunch and dinner every day except Sunday. Reservations are recommended for large parties.

Manny & Isa's Kitchen
$ • MM 81.6 Oceanside, Islamorada
• (305) 664-5019

Cuban cooking at its finest is the treat in store for you in Manny & Isa's Kitchen, the tiny, unassuming, one-room restaurant on the old U.S. Highway 1 in Islamorada. You'll find traditional favorites such as picadillo and ropa vieja, palomilla steak, black beans and rice, but you can enjoy steaks, chicken and chops here too. Selections from the sea include lobster or shrimp enchilado, bite-size pieces of seafood served in a hot or delicate Spanish sauce. The special Cuban dinner, Spanish paella (minimum two people) requires advance notice. Isa's renowned salad dressing is yummy, but the pièce de résistance here is Manny's Key lime pie. Residents come from as far as Marathon to pick up one of Manny's famous pies. The meringue-laden treats are usually out of the oven by 11 AM. Visitors have been known to carry Manny's creations by airplane all the way back to New York City. Manny was kind enough to share his secret recipe with us, so whether you go back to Tucson, Tulsa or Timbuktu, you'll always be able to have an Insiders' taste of the Keys (see Manny's Key Lime Pie recipe in this chapter).

You'll find sangria, beer and wine here to accompany your dinner. Manny & Isa's is open every day except Tuesday for lunch and dinner.

Islamorada Fish Company Restaurant and Bakery
$ • MM 81.6 Bayside, Islamorada
• (305) 664-8363

Not to be confused with its sister down the road, Islamorada Fish Company Restaurant and Bakery, open daily, is actually mainly a bakery (opens at 6 AM) and a popular breakfast spot, although it also serves lunch and dinner daily.

You'll find light fare, such as soups, sandwiches and salads, offered all day in this small, simple cafe. Dinner augments the classic seafood selections with chef's specials: Shrimp or chicken morada heat up the palate with Cajun spices; tuna or steak au poivre is served seared with pink, green and black peppercorns. (See our Seafood Markets and Specialty Foods chapter for more information.)

Morada Bay
$ • MM 81.6 Bayside, Islamorada
• **(305) 664-0604**

A stellar addition to the Purple Isle's lineup, the new Morada Bay in Islamorada delivers a tapas-type selection of eclectic dishes in the most seductive of atmospheres. Beginning with the bark-chip parking lot and continuing past a huge copper urn filled with bougainvillea petals, then down the cobblestone brick entrance under a thatched roof canopy, Morada Bay neglects no detail of ambiance. A wide expanse of sandy beach (imported from the Bahamas) peppered with pastel beach tables and Adirondack chairs fronts the gentle waters of Florida Bay. Curving palms and tiki torches complete the outdoor illusions. Indoors, a handful of funky painted pine tables sit under a vaulted whitewashed ceiling, shadowed by an imposing bar that is flanked by shiny teak stools. The white Key West-style restaurant building itself sparkles with raspberry shutters and periwinkle trim. Design detailing on light fixtures, wall sconces and artistic renderings is exquisite.

And the food at Morada Bay is as imaginatively designed as the decor. Caribbean kabobs of beef or chicken with a jerked rum glaze, tuna tartar, stuffed Anaheim chili, Thai ribs and house-cured salmon and asparagus shine from the tapas menu. And the four designer salad creations — Mediterranean, Sunshine, Morada Bay and Caesar — tempt even the most ardent meat-and-potatoes lovers. Burgers, fish sandwiches and fajitas will fully satisfy the less adventuresome palate, but the Portobello burger should not be missed; it is a grilled mushroom served atop Morada Bay's signature bread with a topping of grilled red onions, warm spinach, roasted garlic alioli and herbed goat cheese. If you prefer a traditional dining entree instead of the wonderful array of light noshes, any of Morada Bay's fresh fish selections — all imaginatively prepared — will more than satisfy your taste for the sea. To finish you off, Morada Bay saves some calorie-loaded ammunition — Turtle Tower, an Oreo crust with tropical chocolate ganache, caramel, vanilla and cinnamon ice cream with chocolate and vanilla sauce; mango white chocolate crème brûlée; or a tropical sorbet medley featuring homemade Indian mango, Key lime and wildberry served a la martini. Morada Bay is open for lunch and dinner daily.

Islamorada Fish Company
$ • MM 81.5 Bayside, Islamorada
• **(305) 664-9271**

Islamorada Fish Company, primarily a seafood market that opens at 8 AM, also serves lunch and dinner daily until 9 PM. You'll find fish so fresh it almost jumps out of the water onto your plate. Tables are set on a cement peninsula behind the market, surrounded by the waters of Florida Bay (or alternately there are a few in a screened porch in the market). Extremely picturesque — fishermen's white rubber boots dry upended on the posts of the pier —you'll see herons and egrets, pelicans and other beggars perched on the roof of the market or waiting patiently outside the door of the fish-cleaning room for a free tidbit. This is the perfect place for a light meal on a fine day. The seafood offerings please one and all. (See our

---

INSIDERS' TIP

Visitors to the Florida Keys often overlook Cuban cuisine because they think it is the same as Mexican or Spanish. It is not. Cuban food features hearty pork, beef and chicken that has been marinated, breaded and grilled. Most meals are served with yellow rice, black beans and fried plantains and, of course, crispy Cuban bread.

Photo: Victoria Shearer

Morada Bay imported sand from the Bahamas to create this islandy watering hole in Islamorada.

Seafood Markets and Specialty Foods chapter for more information.)

Green Turtle Inn
$$ • MM 81.1 Oceanside, Islamorada
• (305) 664-9031

Generations of Keys vacationers have flocked to the Green Turtle Inn since its inception in 1947, for this place is a historic landmark, both officially and in the hearts — and stomachs — of all who have eaten here. Until a few years ago, the Green Turtle Cannery and Seafood Market operated across the Overseas Highway. But, unlike yesteryear, today the turtle soup and consomme now served at the Green Turtle Inn must be made with tortoise meat imported from Nicaragua and the Cayman Islands; our sea turtles are endangered and illegal to harvest.

The menu at the darkly lit Green Turtle is extensive, and the chef creates nightly specials as well. You'll find a great conch chowder or cracked conch here and fresh, fresh fish, as you might expect. A traditional catch-of-the-day favorite prepared à la Roxie (named after one of the original owners) is broiled and covered with tomatoes and onions. Landlubbers can order steak, chops, chicken or prime rib of beef if they wish. The Green Turtle is open for lunch and dinner daily except Monday.

Uncle's Restaurant
$$ • MM 81 Oceanside, Islamorada
• (305) 664-4402

Mexican tiles, ceiling fans, stained glass, candlelit tables, stereo music and original paintings of Keys flora and fauna set the stage for fine dining at Uncle's. And if you'd prefer to sit under the stars, Uncle's will accommodate, for it also serves dinner at tables sprinkled on an outdoor deck.

Sporting cuisine with a decidedly Mediterranean flair, Uncle's offers fresh local fish, shrimp, mussels and little-neck clams for those who love seafood. Veal aficionados will find Marsala, parmigiana, saltimbocca, piccata or française preparations as well as hefty veal chops. Appetizers include roasted garlic, fried calamari, steamed mussels or clams, roasted red peppers or a Greek salad. If your tastes run to fowl, you'll enjoy the grilled quail. Many entrees are served with a side of pasta, which is topped with a savory-sweet marinara sauce that is one of the best around.

A children's menu is available. Uncle's offers a full bar and is open daily for dinner only. Reservations are suggested on weekends.

Dino's of Islamorada Ristorante Italiano

$, family dining; $$, fine dining • MM 81 Oceanside, Islamorada • (305) 664-0727

Dino's covers all culinary bases with dual restaurants: Both are distinctively designed, both authentically Italian, both under one roof.

The family dining side of Dino's is an upscale pizza parlor, offering individual gourmet pies topped with an inspiring array of ingredients. We particularly relish the pizza con legumi, which comes out of the brick pizza oven loaded with grilled, fresh vegetables and topped with low-fat mozzarella and basil. You can watch the masters stretch, twirl and toss the pizza dough before they add your favorite ingredients. You'll also find a wide selection of dinner-size salads, from spinach, Cobb or grilled chicken to Italian, Greek or the quintessential mozzarella alla Caprese.

The dining room itself sparkles with pale pink stucco walls, a pastel tile floor and light wood-paneled walls. You may also dine outdoors on a covered deck. Evenings find an array of pasta and seafood specials on offer. In addition to beer and wine, Dino's family side makes a wickedly good homemade sangria. The family dining room is open for lunch and dinner.

When the mood hits to dine in style, with fine Italian cuisine and a candlelit romantic setting, you'll want to try the fine dining room at Dino's. Linen tablecloths over lace underskirts set the stage for china and crystal settings and sprays of fresh flowers at tables flanked by upholstered, black-lacquer armchairs. The walls are painted with murals, floors are carpeted, and chandeliers and recessed fixtures softly light the room. Muted opera music or show tunes emanate from the speaker system.

Complimentary garlic knots and tomato bruscetta start the unhurried meal here, followed by an exquisite selection of antipasti and soups. Pasta e fagioli scores high with our taste buds, as do the clams and mussels in white-wine sauce, fried mozzarella and a delicately delicious carpaccio. The entree selection is extensive, ranging from an assortment of traditional preparations for poultry and veal to some truly unusual combinations such as salmon with vodka, cream and grapefruit juice, which melts in your mouth. You'll find seafood and fresh local fish as well as a good selection of pasta dishes, such as spicy ziti arrabiata, gnocchi della mamma and manicotti Romani. And just when you think you can't possibly put away any more food, around comes the dessert cart, loaded with such diet busters as tiramisu, napoleans and the mysterious "Whatchamacallit," which, of course, everyone wants to try. Complimentary fritas, dusted with powdered sugar, accompany coffee, cappuccino or espresso. Oooh, yumm, get out that treadmill.

Dino's is a family affair. The Morra familia came from Rome in 1996, and you'll find Luciano, Dino, Antonio and mama too, all involved in the execution of the creative dining options of both rooms. The fine dining room is open for dinner only. Both sides of Dino's are closed on Tuesdays.

Lazy Days Oceanfront Bar & Seafood Grill

$$ • MM 79.9 Oceanside, Islamorada • (305) 664-5256

Lazy Days provides the ideal setting for kicking back, gazing over the sparkling blue Atlantic and dining on a revolving selection of seafood offerings. The elevated plantation-style building with a turquoise roof, French doors and a wraparound balcony is, indeed, designed for lazy days, for it perches directly on the shoreline of the ocean. During the winter season all doors are open, and Bahama fans circulate the fresh ocean air inside and out. The dining room is enhanced by brass hangings and rich tropical foliage, including towering palms in the center of the floor that stretch to the vaulted ceiling. Outdoors, diners are shaded by the roof overhang.

Seafood aficionados will love the Caribbean bouillabaisse, a menage of shrimp, clams, scallops, mussels and fish basking in a saffron-lobster broth. Perennially popular is the dolphin with tropical fruit salsa, which is served with a mango rum sauce. Or try the Mediterranean dolphin, which is finished with roasted shallots, garlic, shiitake mushrooms, Roma tomatoes and fresh basil.

The restaurant's walnut, brass-trimmed bar with granite top serves up some of the best frozen drinks around, including a signature Mango Bango with rum. California, French, Italian and German wines are available, and an extensive beer list boasts about 40 imports.

Lazy Days serves lunch and dinner every day but Monday. The restaurant is closed Mondays and Tuesdays during the summer. Children's dishes are made to order. Lazy Days is accessible to boats with a 2- to 3-foot draft.

Papa Joe's Landmark Restaurant
$$ • MM 79.7 Bayside, Islamorada
• (305) 664-8109

Built in 1937, Papa Joe's is a historic landmark and the site of Islamorada's very first fishing tournament. The restaurant has a no-nonsense, no-frills ambiance that is perennially popular with visiting anglers and locals alike.

Papa Joe's is a fish house specializing in lobster and catches of the day. Try the yellowtail Maria, which is coated with crushed pecans and served over roasted pepper chipotle. If you've had a lucky day fishing, Papa Joe's will cook your catch any way you like it. Steaks, prime rib, chicken and veal dishes are available for the landlubber.

Closed Tuesdays and open for lunch and dinner all other days, Papa Joe's is boat-accessible through the on-premises marina. The

restaurant maintains a full bar. A waiting list takes the place of reservations; when you call, you're put at the top of the waiting list.

Little Italy
$$ • MM 68.5 Bayside, Layton, Long Key
• (305) 664-4472

If good, hearty Italian cooking is what you're after, Little Italy rates a hearty *molto buono*. This family-style restaurant offers an extensive menu of pasta, veal, chicken and seafood dishes and a selection of steaks for red meat lovers. Favored by locals who appreciate the huge portions, Little Italy garners particular accolades for its veal Parmesan and linguine with red clam sauce. And save up those calories for Mermaid's Delight, a savory concoction of scallops layered with crabmeat stuffing topped with shrimp.

Little Italy is open for breakfast, lunch and dinner seven days a week. It offers libation from a full-service bar. The cuisine of Little Italy is mirrored at its sister restaurant, the Key Colony Inn in Key Colony Beach, MM 54 (see separate listing in this chapter). Reservations are recommended, especially in season.

Middle Keys

Hawk's Cay Resort
$, Cantina; $, Palm Terrace; $$ Puerto Cayo; $$$, WatersEdge • MM 61
Oceanside, Duck Key • (305) 743-7000

Poolside dining at the Cantina is relaxed and casual with an assortment of noshes, soups, salads and sandwiches along with tropical drink specialties from the full-service bar. The Cantina serves light bites daily, from 11 AM onwards. Closing time varies from day to day, so call ahead before planning on supper here.

The high-ceilinged rotunda room of Palm Terrace offers a sumptuous breakfast buffet each morning until 10:30 AM (Sunday until 11

AM). Fresh tropical fruits, freshly baked pastries, hot items and an omelet station start your day in a hearty way. Palm Terrace allows you to partake of a continental buffet if you wish to eat lighter fare. You also may order à la carte. Palm Terrace is open seven days a week for breakfast only.

Porto Cayo offers an Italian alternative to the dining options of Hawk's Cay. The relaxed service of the Mediterranean-style dining room brings you an eclectic selection of dishes certain to sate any appetite. Enjoy soups such as ribollita, minestrone, conch chowder or vongole zuppa (clam soup with roasted garlic and tomato). Create your own pizza or pasta from a laundry list of tempting ingredients. Or opt to order a more substantial meal, such as veal parmigiana, swordfish Florentine, blackened snapper or Bistecca alla Griglia (beef tenderloin with a three-peppercorn brandy sauce). Porto Cayo has a full-service bar. The restaurant is open for dinner only, and the evenings it's open vary, depending upon the number of bookings in the hotel. Call ahead; reservations are suggested.

Flanking the Hawk's Cay Marina, WatersEdge provides the option of dining on the casual open-air porch or indoors in air-conditioned comfort. Most diners prefer to dine amidst the light tropical breezes. Nightly specials center on fresh local fish prepared many ways, but you can always choose among blackened, grilled or sautéed. Available in season, the stuffed Florida lobster is one of the best you'll find in the Keys. Barbecued ribs and chicken are other perennial favorites. Prime rib is a specialty on Wednesdays, grilled tuna on Mondays. The soup and salad bar is included with all dinner entrees. WatersEdge serves dinner nightly. If you plan to come by boat, be sure to call the marina in advance to secure a slip (see our Cruising chapter).

Grassy Key Dairy Bar
$$ • MM 58.5 Oceanside, Grassy Key
• (305) 743-3816

Gone are the two giant ice cream cones along the oceanside of the Overseas Highway in Grassy Key that for decades marked the spot of an unpretentious dining treasure favored by locals and visitors alike: the Dairy Bar. No El Niño meltdown this. A collision with a couple of out-of-control drivers took out these historic monuments to great food. But, not to worry, the Dairy Bar still serves up some of the best "vittles" in the Middle Keys.

Owned and operated by the Eigner family and once actually a dairy bar serving ice cream creations, the Dairy Bar's extensive menu reflects the considerable self-taught culinary talents of owners/chefs Johnny and George Eigner. Their renditions of yellowtail almondine, wasabi dolphin and lobster Marsala are legendary, and you can still savor a melt-in-your-mouth filet mignon for less than a ten spot. Be sure to try the Johnny's Salad. Tuesday night is Mexican night, when the brothers cook up a south-of-the border flair, and Saturday features chicken and dumplings. October is always German Oktoberfest month, when the chefs — who hail from Wisconsin — bring on the sausages, Wiener schnitzel and kraut. All seasons find Johnny and George developing new creations and taste sensations for a changing rota of tempting daily specials.

Grassy Key Dairy Bar serves lunch and dinner Tuesday through Saturday. Reservations are suggested. The Dairy Bar is closed for the month of September.

Gallagher's "Little Gourmet" Restaurant
$$$ • MM 57.5 Oceanside, Grassy Key
• (305) 289-0454

Something of an institution in these parts, Gallagher's attracts fans from the length of the Middle Keys and beyond. Maybe it is the four kinds of freshly baked breads served with a pitcher of warm honey that attracts them. It could be the homemade salad dressings; the blue cheese is so thick you can stand a spoon upright in it. All agree that Gallagher's serves great steaks, which come topped with a leaning tower of chunky fried onion rings. The Crab Imperial packs a gratin full of lump crabmeat. And the grilled catch-of-the-day topped with artichoke hearts wins rave reviews. The chef offers tastes of his featured curry so you can have it as heavily spiced as you like.

Popular for dinner and limited in seating, Gallagher's suggests you make reservations in all seasons. The restaurant is closed on Wednesdays; during the summer Gallagher's is closed Tuesdays as well. The restaurant closes completely for the months of September and October.

Ocean Landing

$$ • MM 54 Oceanside, on the causeway, Key Colony Beach • (305) 289-0141

"Keys casual" marks the ambiance at Ocean Landing, which, has changed ownership and name three times in three years. But still perched canalside along the water in Key Colony Beach and consistently offering great waterside Keys atmosphere, the restaurant continues to offer light luncheon fare on picnic tables along the water and more upscale dining indoors in the evening. A selection of fresh seafood such as blackened tuna or braised grouper in tomato-saffron-wine broth competes with roast duck or roast pork loin, barbecue ribs or chicken, or clams over linguine.

You can motor to Ocean Landing by small boat if you wish. Ocean Landing is open every day but Monday for lunch and dinner.

Key Colony Inn

$$ • MM 54 Oceanside, 700 West Ocean Dr., Key Colony Beach • (305) 743-0100

Owned and operated by Harry and Donna Kirchner, who also run Little Italy on Long Key (MM 68.5), the Key Colony Inn in Key Colony Beach is a favorite haunt of residents and visitors alike. Besides the varied menu selections of Italian-style pasta, veal and chicken dishes, Key Colony Inn offers innovative presentations of Florida Keys seafood, steaks and interesting daily specials. Diners agree, portions here are large; you'll get a lot of bang for your buck.

If dinner conversation is important, request a corner table, which may be a bit quieter. (Ceiling acoustics in Key Colony Inn do not filter the noise of a room full of chattering diners.) Or, if the weather is fine, and it usually is, sit outside on the covered veranda. The restaurant features a full-service bar and offers a children's menu. Take-out is available upon request. Key Colony Inn is open for lunch and dinner seven days a week. This place is always packed, lunch or dinner. Reservations are suggested all year long.

The Quay

$$$ • MM 54 Bayside, Marathon • (305) 289-1810

Three cavernous air-conditioned dining rooms and an outdoor palm-speckled patio bustle with diners, for the perpetually popular Quay packs them in. The Quay has snagged a prime piece of waterfront aside the Gulf of Mexico so sunsets and starlight create a romantic ambiance here.

The restaurant sports an eight-page menu, one of the most extensive in these parts, and you can find fish, seafood, pasta and a good offering of hoofed selections prepared in many different ways. Particular favorites are snapper, dolphin or grouper Casa Quay, Rangoon or Lorenzo. Shrimp scampi à la Quay rates as a winner too. You'll find alligator or frogs' legs on this diverse menu. The tropical drinks are fun too: Sample a Marathon Yellow Bird or a Hemingway's Paradise from the selections offered at its full-service bar.

The Quay draws a good-sized early-bird crowd from 4 to 6 PM. You can come here by boat and dock at the Quay pier if you like. The Quay serves lunch and dinner daily. Reservations are suggested, especially in high season.

The Island Restaurant

$ • MM 54 Bayside, Marathon • (305) 743-4191

Perched on a narrow spit of land jutting out into the Gulf of Mexico, 1998's popular addition to the Marathon restaurant scene is The Island Restaurant. Owned and operated by Gregg and Cindy Chapman, who also run Shucker's (see listing in this chapter), The Island provides one of the most scenic sunset spots in the Middle Keys, and some doggone great food to boot. Whether you feel like a Margarita and some nachos, a grilled grouper sandwich, a bowl of conch chowder or a more substantial meal, The Island doesn't disappoint. Try the chef's salad which, unlike its ubiquitous cousins elsewhere, is loaded with shrimp, grilled chicken, faux crab and two types of shredded cheese. Not a cold cut in sight. Order a hot seafood wrap, a trendy favorite, or be treated to a number of daily specials, usually seafood.

Tables are of the picnic or patio varieties, super casual. Kids enjoy beach toys in the sandy open-air terrain. And occasionally the beat picks up with live entertainment. You can come to The Island Restaurant in a shallow draft boat and dock alongside the action. The Island is open from 11 AM to midnight daily. You'll be able to take a seaplane tour from the end of the Island's point if you'd like a soaring adventure to accompany your nosh and libation.

Don Pedro Restaurant
$ • MM 53.5 Oceanside, Marathon
• (305) 743-5247

Savor the fine cuisine of our neighbor to the south, Cuba, at Don Pedro's. This storefront cafe offers a tasty, whole-fried yellowtail snapper; ropa vieja (which means "old rags"), a shredded flank steak simmered in tomato sauce with bell pepper, garlic and onion; and churrasco, Argentinian steak. Be sure to try yucca, a vegetable similar to a potato, and caldo gallego (garbanzo bean soup). All the *especialidades Cubanas* are served with yellow rice, black beans, sweet plantains (a member of the banana family) and Cuban bread. Top off your meal with a traditional Cuban dessert, flan de leche (egg custard) or arroz con leche (rice pudding Cuban style). Select cafe con leche when you order coffee, for Cuban coffee is very strong, like espresso. Don Pedro's also serves a tasty homemade sangria. All menu prices include sales tax.

Don Pedro Restaurant serves dinner Tuesday through Sunday in high season. During the summer it is closed Sundays and Mondays.

Wooden Spoon
$, no credit cards • MM 51 Oceanside, Marathon • (305) 743-7469

Start your day with freshly squeezed orange juice at the Wooden Spoon, one of Marathon's most popular breakfast spots. This small cafe bustles with good service and good cheer. The pink walls are adorned with a photo collection of local regulars, and wood spoons hang everywhere you look. Besides an extensive menu of normal breakfast fare, you'll find omelets 10 different ways (with egg substitutes if you like), blueberry or banana pancakes, corned beef hash and polish sausage. The Wooden Spoon is open for lunch daily.

Box lunches for take-out include two sandwiches, a boiled egg, fruit and a brownie. During the winter season it is not unusual to see a line out front awaiting entry to the Wooden Spoon for breakfast, as it doesn't take reservations. The Wooden Spoon opens at 6 AM and serves until 1:30 PM on weekdays, 1 PM on weekends.

Village Cafe
$ • MM 50.5 Bayside, Gulfside Village, Marathon • (305) 743-9090

Generous portions and tasty Italian pasta and pizza entrees distinguish the extensive menu of the Village Cafe, a bustling place at breakfast, lunch or dinner. Murals of scenes from Venice to Rome grace the walls of this trattoria, a vision of white-latticed simplicity that doubled in size in 1998. Village Cafe now offers separate smoking and nonsmoking dining rooms, as well as a posh service bar offering a complete selection of libations. The outstanding pizza at the Village shines amid a number of perennial pasta favorites: ziti with broccoli, blue crab with spaghetti in red sauce, penne with fresh tomato and basil, and gnocchi. You'll find the traditional Italian renditions for veal, chicken and seafood, as well as a changing rota of daily specials that pique the appetite.

Village Cafe is open for all three meals from Monday through Saturday. Sundays it serves a breakfast buffet until 2 PM and then reopens at 5 PM for a dinner buffet.

Panda House
$ • MM 50.5 Bayside, Marathon • (305) 743-3417

Enormous wall murals of wild horses and the Great Wall of China set the stage for the dimly lit Panda House, Marathon's popular Chinese restaurant specializing in Mandarin and Szechuan cuisine. Diners sit upon black lacquered chairs at tables covered in white linen at this quiet, subdued place. Panda House offers Keys renditions of the standard Chinese dishes and features a few chef's specialties as well, such as Tangerine Beef, which is deep fried with tangerine rind and hot peppers; Happy Family, an exotic combination of lobster, shrimp, chicken, pork, ham, mushrooms, snow peas and vegetables; and Lake

Tung Ting Shrimp, large shrimp sautéed with vegetables and served with a special Panda House seafood sauce. Diet dishes, which are served without salt, sugar, cornstarch or MSG, are available. The lunch buffet, which is all you can eat, is popular at midday.

Panda House is open daily for lunch and dinner. Free delivery for take-out orders of $10 minimum is available in a 5-mile radius.

Marathon Pizza & Pasta
$ • MM 50.5 Oceanside, Publix Shopping Center, Marathon • (305) 743-9338

Marathon's newest pizza establishment, MP&P has already received accolades for its specialty pizzas. Such unusual offerings as Chicken & Bacon Club; Black Bean, Tomato and Onion; Surf & Turf; Chicken & Ham Dijon; or Nick's Stuffed Pizza, leaves you asking, "This is pizza?" Choose your favorite pasta, then pick the sauce you want from the eight classics on offer. Or you can opt for one of Marathon Pizza & Pastas hot or cold sandwiches, calzones or stromboli. Diners sit at tables covered with red-and-white checked cloths while they watch the pizza creation in the open kitchen.

Open from midday to late evening daily, MP&P offers free delivery in Marathon.

53rd Street Dock & Deli
$ • MM 50.3 Oceanside, 71 53rd St., Marathon • (305) 743-0500

Though this tiny restaurant/delicatessen does actually sit alongside a Marathon canal, it isn't vital to maintaining its quirky island charm. The brightly painted interior re-creates the dockside experience — in air-conditioned indoor comfort. You really need to visually take in all the decorative details here before you ever glance at the menu. Let the illusion take you: The floor of Dock & Deli is painted as a dock, with sharks and manatees swimming alongside. Twinkling lights ornament artificial palm trees. The screaming-yellow ice cream parlor-style counter is lined with blue and silver stools. Tables, chairs and accent furniture are eclectically painted, and bright buoys and Caribbean dolls hang over the edge of an actual boat that is suspended from the ceiling. Local art adorns the walls, and there's even a mermaid on the back door.

Once you're sated with funky island ambiance, order a sandwich, salad or soup, along with a side or two. The portions are enormous. You may want to sample a few selections and share. Whatever you do, though, try the Cuban sandwich; it is one of our favorites. And save room for ice cream; it's the old-fashioned kind. The Dock & Deli is open every day except Sunday from 10 AM to 6 PM.

Herbie's
$, no credit cards • MM 50 Bayside, Marathon • (305) 743-6373

Ask anyone; Herbie's is classic Keys. This roadhouse-style watering hole — a simple two rooms and a porch with a large bar area and picnic tables — attracts a loyal contingent of locals and snowbirds alike. The conch chowder is packed with conch and chunks of potato. You can order fried shrimp, clam, oyster or fish baskets or platters, or opt for burgers, dogs and conch sandwiches. And you'll find country-style lemonade and sweetened tea, two old-time beverage selections not readily encountered this far south.

Wednesday is Hump Day at Herbie's, and the joint is jumping from 6 to 10 PM with music and dancing and $1 drafts. Herbie's is open for lunch and dinner daily. The restaurant is not air-conditioned and does not accept reservations.

Barracuda Grill
$$ • MM 49.5 Bayside, Marathon • (305) 743-3314

Imaginative preparation and presentation showcase the entrees at the Barracuda Grill, a small, bustling place in the heart of Marathon. Chef/owners Jan and Lance Hill invest their considerable talents in an exquisite selection of culinary offerings, assuring that Barracuda Grill retains its coveted place in the hearts — and tummies — of locals and visitors alike. Tantalizing repeat stars of the menu are the char-grilled veal chops, roasted rack of lamb with a saute of porto Portobellos, and the stellar Bahamian conch cakes, which are served with a Key lime-honey-mustard sauce.

A changing menu of the chefs' creative interpretations rivals the old favorites: Ralph's Tuna — grilled rare with sauce au poivre — and the grilled yellowfin tuna — served rare on a bed of seaweed salad with wasabi drizzle — draw raves from seafood lovers. The broth of the Littleneck Clams appetizer is so tasty it fairly dictates that you mop it up with lots of bread. And Jack's Really Red Hot Calamari — named after the Hill's baby son Jack — packs a popular wallop thanks to a healthy dose of Barracuda Bite hot sauce. The sauce is a secret recipe bottled in Barracuda Grill's kitchen; you may buy it by the bottle at the restaurant. Rumor has it sales of Barracuda Bite will finance baby Jack's college education. Barracuda Grill also maintains an extensive wine list.

Barracuda's is open for dinner Monday through Saturday. Reservations are never required, but this popular spot fills up quickly, especially in high season.

Takara
$$ • MM 49.5, Bayside, Marathon • (305) 743-0505

Nimble fingers at this Japanese restaurant and sushi bar fashion hosomaki, temaki and nigiri (that's sushi to those of you who haven't sampled the Asian delicacies) and a wide assortment of sashimi. Here in the Florida Keys you are assured that the raw fish is fresh, right off the boat. And if you prefer your food cooked, Takara creates a tasty teriyaki ranging from chicken or steak to lobster or salmon. The tempura is crispy, and you can treat your-self to the traditional Japanese sukiyaki or katsu. For the sushi lover — or a large group — Takara artistically divines an ornate "sushi boat" chock-full of a wide assortment of sushi and sashimi. Remember to go easy on the wasabi.

Takara is open for lunch Monday through Friday and dinner seven days a week during the season but is closed on Sundays during the summer.

The Stuffed Pig
$, no credit cards • MM 49 Bayside, Marathon • (305) 743-4059

During high season mornings, you'll see a line of hungry diners outdoors reading newspapers and patiently awaiting admittance to the inner sanctum of The Stuffed Pig. This popular cafe packs 'em in for hearty country breakfasts. Try the Pig's Breakfast: two eggs, two pancakes, two sausages, two slices of bacon, potatoes and toast. Or a Pig's Omelet, a four-egg wonder with the works. You'll find grits-and-grunts, which includes fish, two eggs, potatoes and toast. And, of course, country-fried steak or gravy and biscuits. If you adhere to less porcine standards, the veggie-and-egg-substitute omelet will hold the cholesterol.

The Stuffed Pig also serves lunch, with tasty barbecue and daily specials. Anglers can get box lunches to take with them on the boat.

Photo: Cheeca Lodge

Dining at Atlantic's Edge in Islamorada offers a panoramic ocean view.

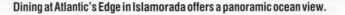

The Stuffed Pig is open Monday through Saturday at the crack of dawn (5 AM; an hour later on Sunday). No reservations are accepted.

Angler's

$ • MM 48.5 Bayside, Faro Blanco Marine Resort Bayside, Marathon
• (305) 743-9018

This percolating lounge atop the swimming pool deck at Faro Blanco Resort serves a delightfully laid-back lunch inside or out. Besides a bar-menu selection of burgers, grilled fish sandwiches, salads, soups and self-avowed "mishmash," lunchtime means a few chef's specials such as sautéed yellowtail with fruit salsa or blackened dolphin with spinach ravioli.

Angler's, featuring a full-service bar, is open seven days a week and serves until 9:30 PM every day but Monday, when the kitchen closes at 3 PM. The beat at Angler's picks up in the evening with live entertainment. A short flight of stairs must be climbed to reach the elevator.

Kelsey's

$$$ • MM 48.5 Bayside, Faro Blanco Marine Resort Bayside, Marathon
• (305) 743-9018

You can enjoy consistently fine dining and attentive service at the upscale Kelsey's in the Faro Blanco Marine Resort Bayside. The sprawling dining rooms accommodate many diners, but reservations are still suggested in all seasons. The walls of the main dining room and bar area are adorned with canoe paddles or oars inscribed with the monikers of boats that cruise the Middle Keys waters. Winner of culinary awards for its cuisine, Kelsey's has an extensive menu that covers the spectrum from oysters Moscow and seafood bisque to stuffed lobster, tournedos Oscar, veal piccatta, Caribbean chicken and Chateaubriand for two. If you bring your own catch, Kelsey's will prepare it for you almondine, pan-fried, blackened or grilled. Kelsey's will finish you off with sweet indulgences difficult to pass up: chocolate macadamia pie, banana-pecan delight or raspberry cheesecake. A children's menu is available.

The restaurant is open for dinner every evening except Monday.

Crocodiles On The Water

$ • MM 48 Oceanside, 1415 15th St., Faro Blanco Marine Resort Oceanside, Marathon • (305) 743-9018

For relaxed dining on the waterfront at Sister's Creek, Crocodiles can't be beat. Sit indoors at a booth or at a picnic table on the deck overlooking the canals and boat slips of Faro Blanco oceanside.

The eclectic menu offers something for everyone. From coconut shrimp, fried calamari and conch fritters to baked brie, potato-skin soup and barbecued oysters, you can nosh away or just whet your appetite for a more substantial entree. Catch of the day, shrimp or scallops — blackened, broiled, fried or grilled — competes with potato-crusted grouper and marinated tuna steak. Hawaiian chicken, jerk pork and grilled ribeye or filet mignon duel for applause with house specialties such as chicken chimichangas, black beans and rice and three-mushroom pizza. Crocodiles has a limited kids' menu.

Crocodiles, at the end of 15th Street, serves dinner seven nights a week all year and opens for lunch from December 15 until May 1. It offers selections from a full-service bar. No reservations are accepted.

Upper Crust Pizza

$ • MM 48 Oceanside, Marathon
• (305) 743-7100

Pizza is the name of the game here, and some pizza it is: thick crust, loaded with goodies and larger than your average pies. Insiders love the deluxe. The pizzas are available with whole wheat crust if you prefer. Daily specials, hot subs on homemade rolls and a selection of veggie sandwiches guarantee you can sate your appetite for less than a fiver.

Upper Crust, a small storefront pizza cafe, is open for lunch and dinner Monday through Friday and for dinner only on Saturday and Sunday. Though a perennially popular spot, reservations are not necessary. Take-out service is available.

Shucker's Raw Bar & Grill

$$ • MM 47.5 Oceanside, 725 11th St., Marathon • (305) 743-8686

Tucked on Sister's Creek at the entrance to Boot Key Harbor by water and at the end of 11th

Street by land, Shucker's affords a pelican's-eye view of the sunset from its expansive dining deck. While indoor, air-conditioned seating is available, most diners prefer to sit outside along the water, at least during the winter season. The large menu is Keys eclectic, offering everything from burgers, conch chowder and grilled fish sandwiches to full dinners with a bevy of seafood, beef, chicken or pasta dishes. Of particular note is the chef's salad, chock-full of crabmeat, shrimp, grilled chicken strips and cheese, instead of the usual cold-cut fare.

The atmosphere is casual and congenial, the service generally prompt and unpretentious. Adjacent to Marathon Marina, Shucker's has a number of boat slips available so you can arrive by sea if you like. Shucker's is open every day for lunch and dinner. No reservations are accepted during high season, but you can call for reservations during the off-season. You can enjoy libation from a full-service bar.

Latigo Dinner Cruise
$$$$ • MM 47.5 Oceanside, Marathon Marina, 11th St., Marathon
• (305) 289-1066

Cruise into the sunset aboard a 56-foot power yacht for a private dinner cruise in our sparkling waters. Ken and Val Waine, your hosts aboard the Latigo, pamper you with attention down to the last detail. You'll enjoy hors d'oeuvres such as cheese pinwheels, artichoke dip or smoked salmon canapés and sip your choice of beer, wine or chilled champagne while you watch the famed Florida Keys sunset from a comfortable location in sheltered waters.

Then the Waines will prepare and serve your dinner entrees, your choice of filet mignon, grilled dolphin with garlic butter or mesquite-grilled, boneless chicken breast. Your meal will include salad, bread, mixed vegetable and rice pilaf or a baked potato. And you'll top off the evening with coffee and dessert — Key lime pie or German chocolate cake.

Latigo takes only private parties on their four-hour dinner cruise, so whether you are a couple or a group of friends, you'll not be thrown together with strangers.

For ultimate pampering, you may also book the yacht for a private bed and breakfast cruise, which includes the sunset dinner; an evening's lodging in the master stateroom, anchored out; full or continental breakfast; and a morning snorkeling excursion to the reef. The bed and breakfast cruise is $159 per person. (See our Accommodations chapter.)

Porky's Bayside
$, no credit cards • MM 47.5 Bayside, Marathon • (305) 289-2065

You wouldn't guess to look at Porky's from the vantage point of the Overseas Highway that this tiny open-air restaurant offers casual, waterfront dining. On a canal inlet across from a picturesque setting of lobster traps stacked on the commercial fishing docks, Porky's is known for great barbecue . . . among other things. Touted as "Swinin' and Dinin'," Porky's is decked out with skull-and-crossbones banners and lobster buoys hanging from the ceiling and condiment servers made from glued-together coconut-shell halves on the tables.

Blackened conch on Caesar salad rates an A+, as do the barbecue ribs, pork and beef. Don't miss the baked beans. Porky's will smoke your catch if you like.

Porky's serves lunch and dinner every day beginning at 11 AM. Only reservations for large parties are accepted. Porky's will treat you to a free sunset cruise to Fanny Key and the Seven Mile Bridge aboard a pontoon boat; availability is first-come, first-served.

Lower Keys

Montego Bay Food and Spirits
$$ • MM 30.2 Bayside • (305) 872-3009

A welcome addition to the restaurants of Big Pine Key, Montego Bay offers a taste of

---

INSIDERS' TIP

Remember, the dolphin you see offered on the menu is not the cute bottle-nose variety that cavorts in our seas. You will be ordering dolphin fish, commonly marketed outside the Keys as mahi-mahi.

the islands in a cozy atmosphere. Grab a casual lunch or a bite to eat in the lounge or at the bar, where you can sip a rum punch at the same time. If you dare, delve into dinner and choose from seafood, steaks, veal or chicken dishes. Opt for a stuffed shrimp special or seafood Alfredo if it is offered. Montego Bay is open seven days a week, and reservations are only necessary if you have a large party.

No Name Pub
$ • MM 31 Bayside, N. Watson Blvd., Big Pine Key • (305) 872-9115

This funky one-of-a-kind establishment bills itself as "a nice place . . . if you can find it." And you might not find it without a little inside knowledge. The No Name Pub, an old, gray weathered building that looks like a house in a residential neighborhood, is marked by two ancient boards nailed together with No Name Pub painted in small, red letters. Easy to miss. And N. Watson Boulevard is off the beaten track too. Turn right at the traffic light at MM 31 in Big Pine (the only light from Marathon to Stock Island) onto Key Deer Boulevard. Proceed to Watson Boulevard and take another right. At the fork in the road, bear left heading toward No Name Key. Go over a humpback bridge and past a subdivision. Just before the No Name Bridge over Bogie Channel, the pub will be on your left, all but hidden under a canopy of large trees.

Although the pizza is a star culinary attraction at No Name Pub, the decor and local Keys characters distinguish it from other pizza establishments. The interior is literally wallpapered with dollar bills autographed by diners of years past. A pool table at the far end of the compact restaurant/pub attracts locals and visitors alike. Above the bar a stuffed deer head is mounted, adorned with twinkling white lights and bearing the cryptic sign: "Biggest Key Deer On Record — Shot at No Name 2/18/90." Key deer are a protected species in the Florida Keys.

Be sure to scope out the bar stools; no two of them stand at the same height. Those too short for the bar have four-by-four blocks of wood nailed to the bottoms of their legs. Problem solved. The famous pizza is deep dish and arrives at your picnic table steaming hot; let it cool a bit to avoid burning your palate. You'll taste a jolt of oregano, and the

cheese is so thick it will drip down your chin with every bite. Yummm! Enjoy the outdoor bar and seating too.

No Name Pub is open seven days a week for lunch and dinner from lunchtime until "whenever."

The Sandbar
$ • MM 28.5 Bayside, Barry Ave., Little Torch Key • (305) 872-9989

Perched 14-feet-high on stilts overlooking Big Pine Channel, the multi-windowed pavilion-style Sandbar serves as a gathering place as well as a restaurant. An all-day, all-night bar menu runs the gamut: fried conch and calamari; quesadillas, nachos and stuffed jalapenos; New Orleans-style muffaletta; and fresh catch-of-the day. The Sandbar will even cook your catch.

Casual and unhurried during the day, evenings bring a changing rota of specialties. Monday is Heart Healthy; Tuesday, Jamaican; Wednesday, Home Cooking; Thursday, Mexican; Friday, Seafood with a Difference; and Saturday and Sunday, Prime Rib. Each month The Sandbar celebrates with a Full Moon Party and bashes for other events such as the Kentucky Derby and Valentine's Day. You'll find pool tables aplenty and enjoy free refills of soft drinks. Watch out, though. The check delivers a bit of a snap. It arrives in a mousetrap!

The Sandbar is open daily from 11 AM to 11 PM and does not take reservations. An elevator is available for those who may have difficulty negotiating the stairs.

Little Palm Island
$$$$ • MM 28.5 Oceanside, Little Torch Key • (305) 872-2551

Dining at Little Palm Island is pure magic . . . romance with a capital R. You step into a fairy tale the moment you check in at the mainland substation on Little Torch Key to await the launch *Escape*, which will spirit you to the island. The 15-minute boat ride to Little Palm Island simply heightens the anticipation. As you arrive at the island's dock, you'll spot the Great House nestled amid towering coconut palms bedecked in twinkling white lights. Once a rustic, fishing camp retreat, the Great House now houses Little Palm Island's world-renowned restaurant.

You may dine beneath the stars under a palm tree, at water's edge alongside the beach, on the outside wood deck, in the covered open-air porch or indoors in air-conditioned comfort. Wherever you choose to partake of Little Palm's gourmet repast, you will be pampered with exquisite food and prompt, unobtrusive service. Swiss-born chef Michel Reymond has garnered myriad awards for his creative cuisine, which Little Palm Island describes as "an exciting blend of classic and nouvelle French cooking with the new American genre, often embellished with the flavors of the Caribbean and the Orient." Insiders know this translates into the meal of a lifetime.

Little Palm Island's dining room is open to the public for lunch and dinner daily. Sundays a tropical buffet-style brunch from 11:30 AM to 2:30 PM replaces the luncheon offerings. Thursday night is Gourmet Night, which features a preset seven-course menu that changes weekly.

Little Palm offers libations from a full-service bar and maintains an extensive wine list. Reservations are a must. The launch leaves the Little Torch Key substation for luncheon dining at 11:30 AM, 12:30 and 1:30 PM; for dinner at 6:30 and 8:30 PM. You will be seated immediately upon disembarking. You may come to Little Palm Island on your own boat, but be sure to make slip reservations in advance (see our Cruising chapter). Children must be 12 or older to dine at the Little Palm Island dining room.

Boondocks
$ • MM 27.5 Bayside, Ramrod Key • (305) 872-0022

The appearance of this happening place can be deceiving from the Overseas Highway. The expansive, open-air informal restaurant/bar that is Boondocks sits under a massive, thatched roof surrounded by palm trees. A casual, nosh-style menu ranges from steamed shrimp and clams on the half shell to conch fritters and chowder, hot wings and fried oysters. You'll find the de rigueur burgers and dogs plus some innovative toppings for Caesar salads and imaginative presentations for the catch-of-the-day. The Maryland-style crab cakes are particularly good. Boondocks has a kiddie menu.

On Sunday evenings, Boondocks has a live band in an outside band shell for dancing under the stars. Boondocks is open for lunch and dinner daily and does not accept reservations.

Monte's Restaurant and Fish Market
$, no credit cards • MM 25 Bayside, Summerland Key • (305) 745-3731

Don't let the picnic tables and paper plates fool you. Insiders know that Monte's is a great place for fresh fish in the Lower Keys. The small open-air restaurant area adjoins the seafood market (see our Seafood Markets and Specialty Foods chapter) and is almost always packed, with long lines outside. During the season you have the best chance of securing a table quickly between 2 and 4 PM.

You can overdose on the plethora of difficult-to-resist seafood selections: oysters, clams, mussels, Louisiana crawfish, shrimp, Florida lobster, stone crab claws, conch or locally caught fish, grilled or fried. Try the super seafood basket where you'll get a taste of them all. Top off your meal with Key lime tart or chocolate nut pie.

Monte's is open seven days a week for lunch and dinner. No reservations are accepted.

Raimondo's Ristorante Italiano
$$ • MM 21 Oceanside, 457 Drost Dr., Cudjoe Gardens, Cudjoe Key • (305) 745-9999

The striking forest-green-and-white color scheme of Raimondo's sets the stage for a fine Italian-style dining experience. From the green swags softening the windows to the ribboned green-and-white tile on the floors, the light, airy feeling reverberates throughout the restaurant and out onto a dining patio amid palms and scheffleras.

Decor aside, the food makes the biggest splash at Raimondo's. Appetizers include a tasty bruschetta and caponata, a sweet-savory concoction of eggplant, capers, black olives and tomatoes that is Raimondo's secret recipe. Among the stellar entree offerings are carpaccio di manzo, thinly sliced raw beef tenderloin topped with a mustard vinaigrette; pollo Amalfi, chicken scaloppine sautéed in white wine, topped with fresh diced tomato and mozzarella; and calamari al quazzetto, fresh diced tomato, baby shrimp, mussels, clams and calamari over crostini or, for an extra charge, linguine. The chef creates enticing specials nightly.

During the season, Raimondo's Ristorante Italiano is open for dinner seven days a week and serves lunch every day except Sunday. During the summer it is open for dinner only, every day except Tuesday. Brunch is served on Sundays year round. To find Raimondo's, turn at the Sheriff's Substation at MM 21 on the Overseas Highway.

Mangrove Mama's Restaurant
$$ • MM 20 Bayside, Sugarloaf Key
• (305) 745-3030

Everyone agrees Mangrove Mama's is special. This brightly colored Caribbean-style roadhouse secrets a rustic old garden in the back where you can nosh or dine amid the banana trees. The old chairs are painted in a barrage of drizzled primary colors; ceramic fish sculptures adorn the walls. Bright tropical tablecloths cover the simple tables, and painted buoys hang from the trees and suspend from the rafters.

Shrimp gets scampified, tempura-ed, stuffed with crabmeat or coconut-ed at Mangrove Mama's, and ribs, scallops, chicken, steaks and fresh fish march to a different drummer here too.

Mangrove Mama's pulsates with live entertainment on Friday and Saturday evenings and features reggae on Sundays. Mangrove Mama's serves lunch and dinner daily. Indoor dining is now air-conditioned. In addition to a full-service bar, Mangrove Mama's has an extensive wine list. Reservations are suggested during high season.

Bobalu's Southern Cafe
$ • MM 10 Bayside, Big Coppitt Key
• (305) 296-1664

Appearances can be deceiving. Bobalu's may look a little shabby on the outside; the food and portions are anything but. The cuisine at Bobalu's Southern Cafe is home-style, hearty Southern offerings, from authentic fried chicken to okra and turnip greens. This is also a family affair, run by dad Bob, mom Lu and

the rest of the family. Family style also means reasonably priced, and if inexpensive hearty food is what you're looking for, then look no more for you are home. The place is famous enough to garner intense loyalty in many locals, as well as Key West's favorite native son, Jimmy Buffett, who mentions the Cafe in his book *Where is Joe Merchant?* Bobalu's is open daily for lunch and dinner.

Key West

Called the most successful melting pot in the United States, Key West has a vibrant spirit that sparkles nowhere more brilliantly than in its cuisine. With restaurants as diverse and creative as a miniature Manhattan, Key West reflects the enduring ethnic traditions of generations past as well as cutting-edge composition and presentation most evident in major cosmopolitan cities worldwide. Add to all this gustatory wonder a dash of plain old Key West party and pizzazz, and you have a combination that is difficult to beat — anywhere! You can graze the sidewalk cafes of Duval Street or drink and nosh at Key West's panoply of saloons. Sit beneath a canopy of poinciana trees, sample the upscale '90s cuisine, or eat your way around the world, never leaving our southernmost city.

But while it's tough to find a bad meal in Key West, it isn't tough to find an expensive one. When it comes to dining out, our small town leans toward big-city prices. Even a simple hamburger can be costly here. But hey — you're on vacation. Just sit back, relax, enjoy!

Whatever your pleasure, remember this is still the Keys. Dress code is always Keys casual; just make sure you wear a shirt and shoes with your shorts, and you're dressed for any occasion.

Key West has more than 150 restaurants, some say the most per capita in the United States. Many line the famed Duval Street; others are tucked away down tree-lined alleys or in unassuming residential-looking buildings. We will not highlight the national restaurant chains, most of which are in the newer sections of Key West along N. Roosevelt Boulevard, because you are probably already familiar with their offerings. But we will assist you in finding those treasures known to locals — Insiders who keep their collective culinary finger on the pulse of the restaurant scene in Key West.

Our restaurants, like our people, defy easy classification. But we have divided the establishments into four categories to help you choose your dining preference: Key West Classics, those inimitable restaurants you won't want to miss; Surf and Turf, primarily casually presented, simply prepared red meat and seafood; Island Eclectic, upscale gourmet dining of the modern-American or new-American cuisine genre, created with a tropical flair; and The Melting Pot, a potpourri of diverse ethnic offerings that spirit your taste buds to the corners of the globe — The Americas, South of the Border, The Continent, The Far East and Intercontinental. Restaurants are listed in alphabetical order in each category.

You will find that reservation policies vary in Key West, establishment by establishment. The more upscale the restaurant, the more likely you will need a reservation, especially in high season. We mention each restaurant's reservation policy in its description.

Unlike those in the rest of the Keys, most Key West restaurants maintain full-service bars. We will highlight those that serve beer and wine only. On-site parking is a rarity among our recommended restaurants, most of which are in Old Town where land is at a premium. In most cases you will need to park curbside on one of Key West's side streets or in a municipal or private lot (see our Getting Around chapter).

Unless stated otherwise, you may assume that restaurants are air-conditioned. Major credit cards are widely accepted, but personal checks are not. And there is no restriction as to children dining in most establishments. Because restaurants in Key West's Old Town are often situated in 19th-century frame buildings that were formerly houses, accessibility for the physically challenged varies greatly. Sometimes steps must be negotiated, some bathrooms may be too tiny to accommodate a wheelchair, and separate nonsmoking sections may not always be available. If any of these anomalies are of particular concern to you, be sure to call the establishment to see

exactly what arrangements might be made to fit your needs.

Our price code (see gray box) mirrors that of the rest of the Florida Keys and is based upon dinner for two, without starters, dessert, alcoholic beverages, tax or tip.

Price Code

$	Less than $25
$$	$25 to $40
$$$	$40 to $55
$$$$	More than $55

Key West Classics

Blue Heaven
$$ • 729 Thomas St., Key West • (305) 296-8666

The word is out without so much as a cock's crow: Blue Heaven — at various times a bordello, a pool hall, a railroad water tower, a cockfighting arena, a boxing ring (frequented by Papa Hemingway himself) and an ice cream parlor — is now a popular restaurant with a rich history. Owned by brothers Richard and Dan Hatch, this throwback to the hippie era offers Caribbean and vegetarian cuisine in an unhampered island setting. Situated in historic Bahama Village, Blue Heaven's ambiance is as legendary as its cuisine. Roosters, hens and chicks strut in the distance and all around the picnic tables that fill Blue Heaven's backyard; so do the resident kitties. Jimmy Buffett's 1995 song, "Blue Heaven Rendezvous," was inspired by this diamond in the rough.

Indeed the magic is alive and well at Blue Heaven, where patrons enjoy specialties such as jerk chicken, Caribbean shrimp and locally caught seafood entrees. Vegetable roulade is a light and pleasing appetizer, and burgers are made with tofu, no beef. Sunday brunch at Blue Heaven, with diverse preparations of eggs, waffles and pancakes — including the famous beer-batter and pecan varieties — draws crowds that line themselves up 'round the corner. Shrimp and grits are a highlight of brunch.

Live entertainment is offered most nights at Blue Heaven. When you visit, step upstairs to the Bordello, now an art gallery touching on styles from primitive to the offbeat (see our Arts and Culture chapter). Reservations are not accepted. The restaurant, which once served only beer and wine, now has a full liquor license. It's open seven days a week for breakfast, lunch and dinner.

Camille's Restaurant
$$ • 703½ Duval St., Key West
• (305) 296-4811

Ask Key West residents where you should eat, especially for breakfast, and they'll send you to Camille's. The menu at this eclectic local favorite features a wide array of gourmet breakfast, lunch and dinner specials, and the reasonably priced menu changes daily and nightly. Stone crab clawmeat cakes are grilled and served with spiced rum-mango sauce. Full rack of lamb is a hefty portion of seven to eight pieces, grilled and cooked to order and served with garlic-oregano marinade or raspberry coulis. Weekend breakfast at Camille's is a particular treat, with pecan waffles fluffy and sweet, and as many as five styles of eggs Benedict. Sample Black Angus filet mignon or Norwegian smoked salmon. And for lunch, the homemade chicken salad sandwich is always a delicious choice.

In the People's Choice Awards sponsored annually by WKRY Key 93.5 FM, Camille's almost always garners Best Breakfast, Best Lunch and Best Dining on a Budget. The restaurant is owned by Denise Chelekis, who is the former catering manager to Donald Trump, and Denise's husband, Michael, once a sound system director for Atlantic City's Golden Nugget Casino. Camille's serves only the freshest ingredients.

Beer and wine are offered, and the ambiance is so friendly that tourists are treated like locals. At Camille's, you'll find patrons so moved by Beatles songs on the CD player that they often join in a rendition of "I Wanna Hold Your Hand." Camille's, which has seating for 42, does not accept reservations; expect a wait — especially for breakfast. Camille's is open every day for breakfast and lunch; dinner is served Tuesday through Saturday.

The Deli Restaurant
$ • 531 Truman Ave., Key West
• (305) 294-1464

Enter through the double portals of The Deli Restaurant, each of which sports a giant seahorse-shaped window, and you will be welcomed home.

This family-run restaurant has been greeting Key West locals with good cheer and affordable home-style cookin' since 1950. The Deli Restaurant received a face-lift in 1995, when more windows were added. Giant stained-glass tropical reef fish now dangle in front of the windows. Established by John and Joan Bernreuter as a corner delicatessen where Aunt Mamie and John's grandmother, Poppy, made the salads, The Deli Restaurant today serves up generations of vintage Conch dishes under the supervision of Bobby Bernreuter. Try roast turkey (the real thing) or fried chicken, franks and beans or sugar-cured ham, roast beef or pork. You'll find Key West shrimp or yellowtail grilled or fried and conch chowder made from the secret family recipe. Allow some room for dessert, because Toll House cookie pie, apple crumb pie or sweet potato pie will bring on a wave of nostalgia.

The Deli Restaurant is open for breakfast all day and serves a wide selection of sandwiches as well. Beer and wine are available. The Deli Restaurant serves breakfast, lunch and dinner without reservations. It's closed on Tuesdays and Wednesdays.

Dennis Pharmacy
$ • 1229 Simonton St., Key West
• (305) 294-1577

This no-nonsense establishment is reputedly the restaurant that inspired Jimmy Buffett's song "Cheeseburger in Paradise." To the left of its entrance is a pharmacy; to

---

INSIDERS' TIP

Take advantage of early-bird specials at any of our restaurants bordering the Gulf of Mexico or Florida Bay and watch the spectacular Florida Keys sunset while you dine at bargain prices.

its right, an old-fashioned, brightly lit lunchroom with two horseshoe-shaped counters and white metal tables and chairs with turquoise vinyl upholstery. To add a homier feel to the place, owners Emilio and David Alea recently have added tablecloths. This facility, which sits on the site of a former grocery store, was converted in 1962 to a pharmacy with a soda fountain and sandwich counter. In the 1970s the Aleas expanded the menu to include full meals.

Hearty cuisine is the star here. Dennis Pharmacy specializes in American food with a Latin flair. On the regular menu are breaded steaks and pork chops, fried shrimp, sandwiches and burgers. The palomino steak and grilled chicken and dolphin sandwiches are particularly popular, and daily specials include ropa vieja, roast pork, roast chicken, corned beef and cabbage, meat loaf and Spanish beef stew. Homemade soups are offered each day; chili is served once a week. Beer, wine and soft drinks are available, as is a *real*, old-fashioned, thick and flavorful, chocolate malt.

Dennis Pharmacy is open seven days a week for breakfast, lunch and early dinner. Off-street parking is available, and reservations are not accepted.

Harpoon Harry's
$ • 832 Caroline St., Key West
• (305) 294-8744

Harpooned and hanging from the ceilings of this hometown-style diner is everything — including the kitchen sink. Across from Land's End Marina on the site of what was a small hospital turned barber shop, Harpoon Harry's combines Tiffany lighting fixtures with old roller skates, sleds and carousel horses. Framed advertisements recall the days of Lucky Strike cigarettes, Mennen Toilet Powder, knee-highs and antique cars; the restaurant's movie star wall boasts Elvis, Sophia and Lucy and Desi. A case contains a collection of Mickey Mouse glasses, which are probably worth a fortune.

It is, in fact, this original decor that drew The Travel Channel to Harpoon Harry's in 1995. Restaurateur Ronald Heck is the creative genius responsible for it. The owner of Michigan's Lighthouse Inn, Heck informed his Midwestern employees and patrons of the interior design plans he had for his new estab-

lishment, and they came bearing all sorts of amusements.

The luncheon menu at Harpoon Harry's is much less eccentric than the decor: meat loaf or roast turkey with mashed potatoes, breaded veal cutlets, homemade chicken pot pie and melt-in-your-mouth roasted pork chops with gravy. Breakfast is highlighted by Harry's Special: eggs, sausage, bacon, ham, toast and jelly served with home fries or grits. Two counters and booths and tables are available. Beer is the alcoholic beverage of the house.

Harpoon Harry's is open daily for breakfast and lunch. It closes at 2 PM. Reservations are not accepted.

Hog's Breath Saloon
$ • 400 Front St., Key West
• (305) 296-4222

The name of this establishment may not be appealing, but its fish sandwiches — blackened or grilled with lemon — are. They're served up by the ton. Built to resemble an authentic surfer bar, Hog's Breath features lots of wood, including an African mahogany bar at which some guests are fortunate enough to land a seat. Mounted fish and surfboards hang from the walls, along with active water-related photographs. Not surprisingly, owner Jerry Dorminy of Alabama is a watersports enthusiast. He originally established a Hog's Breath Saloon in Fort Walton Beach, Florida, in 1976, as a place where he and his friends could retreat after a day of fishing and sailing.

In 1988 Dorminy opened Hog's Breath Key West. Here, nautical charts of Caribbean waters are lacquered into wood tables, and patrons dine indoors or outside on a brick patio from which large trees sprout. In addition to the fish sandwich, Hog's Breath's smoked fish dolphin dip and raw bar with oysters, shrimp and stone crabs (in season) are extremely popular.

The restaurant's full-service bar features the medium-bodied Hog's Breath beer, brewed in the Midwest and now served at all four of Dorminy's locations, including those in Cancun and New Orleans. In case you were wondering, the name of the joint comes from an old saying of Dorminy's grandmother, that "bad breath is better than no breath at all."

The restaurant is open for lunch and din-

Photo: Victoria Shearer

The palm-fringed Gulf of Mexico is a perfect backdrop to your Keys meal.

ner, and live bands play folk rock, rock, blues and jazz throughout the day and evening. Happy hour is 5 to 7 PM daily. Reservations are not accepted.

Jimmy Buffett's Margaritaville Cafe
$ • 500 Duval St., Key West
• (305) 292-1435

Lunch really could last forever at Jimmy Buffett's Margaritaville Cafe, and patrons who steer here quite often remain throughout much of the day, regardless of whether or not they have amended their carnivorous habits. Margaritas are de rigueur, but bartenders also serve up the performer's personal favorite: a Cajun martini infusion of Smirnoff vodka and potent jalapeno and Scotch bonnet peppers. "Parrothead" and other island music sounds in the background, and decorations include oversize props from stage settings of Buffett tours, including stuffed iguanas from "Off to See the Lizard," a mock-up version of his seaplane, a flying goose, and a big warm bun and a huge hunk of meat. The fixin's — lettuce and tomato, Heinz-57 and french fried potatoes — are not forgotten.

In 1985, Buffett opened a store at the city's Land's End Village. Two years later he decided that he also wanted a cafe, and he opened this establishment in the heart of downtown Key West. The casual and friendly Margaritaville, he feels, combines his great love for music and food, both of which satisfy the soul. He has since opened a second cafe in New Orleans.

Specialties of the house include Cheeseburgers in Paradise, fresh fish platters and sandwiches and fried Key West shrimp baskets.

Margaritaville is open for lunch and dinner daily. Live music is offered nightly, beginning at 10:30 PM. Reservations are not accepted, but those on the waiting list may shop for souvenirs in Buffett's adjacent store.

Kelly's Caribbean Bar & Grill
$$ • 303 Whitehead St., Key West
• (305) 293-8484

Actress Kelly McGillis owns this Caribbean restaurant on the site of the original Pan American World Airways offices. In 1927, Pan Am launched its first international air service from Key West, when mail was flown from the island's Meacham Field to Havana. The following year, Pan Am began providing passenger service to Havana.

A display of early photographs and memorabilia of Pan Am service from Key West line the elegant violet and blue library room on the first floor. Clever decorating details fit the theme: When you dine in the front room of the first floor, you settle your tail feathers into old airplane seats, some of which offer views of a triangular bar designed to resemble the wing of a plane; ceiling fans in the first-floor lounge (known as the Crash Room Bar) are miniature reproductions of an airplane motor.

Outdoor dining is available on a stone patio with gardens. On the second floor, Kelly's Clipper Club Lounge invites patrons to relax in an open-air gazebo-style setting.

Among the house specialties here are barbecued pork with fresh mango salsa, whole yellowtail snapper with tomato-basil vinaigrette sauce, plantain-encrusted fresh fish of the day with Scotch bonnet and bird pepper sauce and Jamaican jerk chicken with a tamarind sauce.

Kelly's Caribbean Bar & Grill also is home to the Southernmost Brewery, which whips up an all-natural selection including Key West Golden Ale, Havana Red Ale, Southern Clipper wheat beer and Black Bart's Root Beer.

The restaurant is open for lunch and dinner seven days a week. Reservations are accepted for parties of more than six. Key West hotel guests receive preferred seating.

Paradise Cafe
$, no credit cards • 1000 Eaton St., Key West • (305) 296-5001

The sign outside reads "home of the island legend monster sandwich." Indeed. It would be tough to find a bigger, better sandwich anywhere in Key West. Choose from 14 lunchtime varieties — everything from ham and cheese, sliced turkey and hot Italian beef to chicken salad, tuna salad and BBQ pork — all made to order on Cuban bread with the fixin's you select. Paradise Cafe also serves up breakfast sandwiches — hearty combinations of egg, cheese, ham and/or steak, on Cuban bread, of course.

Nothing on the menu here costs more than $5. Eat in, take out or phone ahead for delivery. Paradise Cafe is open daily for breakfast and lunch.

Pepe's Cafe & Steak House
$$ • 806 Caroline St., Key West
• (305) 294-7192

Billed as the "Eldest Eating House in the Florida Keys, established 1909," Pepe's is as beloved to Conchs and Key Westers as the Mallory Square sunset celebration. In the old commercial waterfront area of Old Town, Pepe's touts its Analachicola Bay oysters, when available, as among its specialties: raw, baked, Florentine, Mexican or Rudi-style. But you will find a bit of the hoof available at Pepe's as well: New York strip steaks at 8, 12 and 15 ounces, filet mignon, pork chops, even barbecue. And Pepe's burgers sound as intriguing as they taste: White Collar Burger, Blue Collar Burger, Slit Ray Burger and patty melt. Be sure to try a Margarita here (the lime juice is squeezed fresh) and, for dessert, the brownie pie, served warm with ice cream — ask for Cuban coffee flavor instead of vanilla. Mmmmm! Pepe's serves early (mainly breakfast, 6:30 AM to noon), late (primarily dinner, after 4:30 PM to closing) and in between, predominantly oysters, soups and sandwiches.

One thing is for certain, no matter when you visit Pepe's, you will not leave hungry. And don't forget: Pepe's gives free pickles to pregnant women! The restaurant is open every day. Patio dining is also available. Reservations are not accepted.

Turtle Kraals Waterfront Seafood Grill and Bar
$ • 1 Land's End Village, Key West
• (305) 294-2640

Offering Southwestern food with a definite seafood influence, Turtle Kraals occu-

pies the site of a former turtle cannery, thus the name which essentially means "turtle pen." Turtle Kraals has an immense affection for wildlife, which is evidenced by the large saltwater enclosure behind the restaurant, where many kinds of injured sea life recover. Watch the wildlife in the pen from the back deck overlooking the water as you dine on a stuffed shrimp, fish and scallop burrito with rice and beans or a seafood combo. Turtle Kraals offers a huge selection of beer, and a full bar is available as well. Watch for specialty nights such as Taco Tuesday, with 99 ̃¢ chicken tacos. Turtle Kraals is open daily for lunch and dinner.

Yo Mama's House of Ribs
$ • 411 Petronia St., Key West
• (305) 295-0805

This tiny little restaurant tucked halfway down Petronia between Duval and Whitehead is so unpretentious, some of the locals haven't even discovered it yet. But once you sample the cooking at Yo Mama's, we guarantee you'll be back again. And again.

No glitz or glamour here. Just the best lip-smackin', mouth-waterin', up-to-your elbows-in-barbecue-sauce ribs this side of Texas. The plates and napkins (you'll need lots of those) are paper, the silverware is plastic. But what Yo Mama's lacks in ambiance, it more than makes up for in good food and reasonable prices. The rib dinner goes for less than $8; a full rack of ribs is $19.95. Fried chicken and pork dinners are under $5 each. All dinners include coleslaw and one additional side — baked beans, potato salad, french fries or corn on the cob. Yo Mama's has a full array of sandwiches, too, as well as wings, conch fritters and conch salad. Canned beer and sodas are available.

The restaurant is open daily for lunch and dinner. But come early if you plan to dine in — Yo Mama's only has six tables; take-out is available.

Surf and Turf

Crab House Seafood Restaurant
$$ • 2001 S. Roosevelt Blvd., Key West
• (305) 294-1370

Within the Sheraton Suites Key West Resort, the Crab House offers authentic New England-style dining in a nautical atmosphere appointed with mounted fish, crab and lobster traps, buoys and netting. Specialties of the house include the Maryland Blue Crab Platter, with 3 pounds of crab steamed and seasoned in Old Bay, and broiled or fried crab cakes made with 85 percent jumbo lump crabmeat.

Unlike most other Crab Houses throughout the country, this establishment does not offer a seafood bar or a live lobster tank on display. It does, however, offer full breakfast, an all-you-can-eat breakfast buffet with omelet station and outdoor poolside dining among tropical gardens. Off-street parking is available within the Sheraton lot. Reservations are accepted only for hotel guests. The Crab House is open every day for breakfast, lunch and dinner.

Duffy's Steak & Lobster House
$$ • 1007 Simonton St., Key West
• (305) 296-4900

The beginnings of this structure date back to the late 1890s, but it wasn't until 1948 that the building actually became Duffy's Tavern. Today, the interior has been updated with deep-green paint and the original glass block set off by neon lighting. Bulky wood booths, a wood floor and high ceilings lend a rustic atmosphere. The entertainment is found through abundant windows, for Duffy's sits on a busy corner at Simonton and Truman that proves ideal for people-watching.

Owned by Timothy Ryan, proprietor of Cafe des Artistes (see separate restaurant listing in this chapter) next door, Duffy's specializes in prime rib, steaks and lobster. All dishes are simply prepared and served with a salad, freshly baked bread and a choice of potato. We recommend the "smashed" option — twice-baked redskin potatoes with chives, cheese and bacon. Daily specials, such as angel-hair pasta with Gulf shrimp in a bro-

chette béarnaise sauce or chicken San Bernardino, a breaded breast of chicken sautéed and covered in eggplant and mozzarella in a tomato-basil sauce satisfy more intricate taste buds.

Lunch and dinner are served here daily. Reservations are not accepted.

Half Shell Raw Bar
$$ • 231 Margaret St., Key West
• (305) 294-7496

When Half Shell Raw Bar's owners opened this seafood establishment in 1980, they dotted the all-wood walls with amusing license plates. Today, these same walls are literally covered with plates donated by customers, and many a spare is stored out of view.

Always consistent at Half Shell Raw Bar is its fresh seafood served on the casual, open-air waterfront. Set on the historic Key West Bight, or harbor, the restaurant is known for its oysters, clams, crabs and local seafood simply prepared, reasonably priced and served with plastic silverware on paper plates at picnic tables. Half Shell carries stone crabs in season and Maine lobster. Its full bar offers beer, wine and frozen drinks.

Patrons may opt for outdoor dining on either a waterfront deck or a patio. Reservations are accepted for parties of more than six. Half Shell Raw Bar is open for lunch and dinner. Off-street parking is abundant.

Martha's Steaks & Seafood
$$$ • 3591 S. Roosevelt Blvd., Key West
• (305) 294-3466

The panoramic vista of the Atlantic Ocean is but a precursor to the aged, certified Black Angus beef and fresh native seafood starring nightly at Martha's. Prime rib is a specialty of the house, joining a stellar array of steaks, calves liver, lamb tenderloin and roast duck entrees. You'll find yellowtail grenoblaise, blackened swordfish and nut-crusted grouper among the selections. Florida lobster and stone crabs in season round out the menu. Enjoy fancy island drinks while you listen to nightly piano music.

Once a bowling alley, Martha's, which has the same owners as Benihana's next door, offers early-bird specials for entrees ordered between 5:30 and 6 PM. Reservations are suggested in all seasons. Martha's is open for dinner seven days a week.

Rusty Anchor Restaurant
$$ • MM 5 Oceanside, 5510 Third Ave., Stock Island • (305) 294-5369

Weigh anchor for a satisfying seafood meal at the Rusty Anchor, a casual seafood haven for the piscatorially inclined. You won't find fresher fish and seafood anywhere, for in the back of the Rusty Anchor is a commercial seafood market that supplies many of Key West's restaurants. The fish, lobsters, shrimp and stone crab claws are delivered right from the boat (see our Seafood Markets and Specialty Foods chapter). The restaurant exudes a casual nautical atmosphere punctuated by rope-edged tables, wood buoys, nautical art prints and photographs of the fishing fleets of old Key West. A 400-plus pound marlin is mounted at one end of the dining room, and a couple 15-pound lobsters grace the other walls.

Lunch and dinner are simply prepared. The saltwater fish is caught daily in the Key West area and generally is served broiled or fried. Try the teriyaki-grilled tuna sandwich on Cuban bread if it is offered as a special. You can nosh on conch fritters or slurp chowder, peel steamed shrimp or nibble a salad. If seafood is not your favorite, Rusty Anchor also serves burgers, steaks and ribs. Food is presented picnic-style on plastic plates, drinks in plastic cups, beer out of the can.

Open Monday through Saturday, the Rusty Anchor does not require reservations. It's a great place to bring the kids.

Seven Fish
$$ • 632 Olivia St. at the corner of Elizabeth St., Key West • (305) 296-2777

Don't be fooled by the name. Although the seafood here is excellent, this restaurant has much more to recommend it. In addition to the freshest fish, the menu includes grilled chicken, meat loaf with mashed potatoes and a New York strip steak cooked the way you like it and served with roasted red skins on the side. Salads — three-cheese Caesar or mixed greens with balsamic vinegar, roasted red pepper and goat cheese — are available in two sizes.

And for an additional charge, you can add grilled chicken or a crab cake to your greens if you like.

The environment at Seven Fish is cozy and friendly, the food flavorful and inexpensive. Nothing on the menu here tops $20. On the downside, Seven Fish is small — go early or you may have to wait — and the tables are quite close together. But don't worry about inhaling any secondhand smoke from the table next door: Seven Fish is smoke free; there isn't an ashtray in the place. The restaurant is open nightly 0 to 10 PM except Tuesdays. That's when the staff goes fishing.

Island Eclectic

Bagatelle
$$$ • 115 Duval St., Key West • (305) 296-6609

Incongruous amid the tourist trappings of lower Duval, Bagatelle sits reservedly amid the fray, adding a touch of class to the surroundings. Situated on two floors of a gracious old Key West home, Bagatelle serves fresh local ingredients with island inventiveness. Try the grilled Portobello mushroom or the Bahamian conch steak for something different. Or allow a salad made with hearts of palm or escargot Martinique to foreshadow grilled fresh tuna or snapper Rangoon, which is served with tropical fruit.

Wraparound balconies on both levels afford outdoor dining, or you may choose to dine indoors where the decor favors that of a first-rate art gallery. Bagatelle is a premier spot from which to view the Fantasy Fest parade (see our Annual Events chapter). An extravagant seafood buffet is offered that evening, and a dinner reservation secures you a seat for the entire night. You receive a Bagatelle wristband so you may come and go as you like, partying the night away on Duval Street. Reservations for the evening of Fantasy Fest should be made well in advance of the event, even up to a year.

Bagatelle serves lunch and dinner daily. Reservations are suggested for dinner in all seasons at this popular restaurant, but at least a day in advance in high season.

Café Solé
$$ • 1029 Southard St., Key West
• (305) 294-0230

This charming little restaurant sits out of the way of the hustle and bustle of downtown Key West, so you might have a little trouble finding it. If you find Southard Street, you are halfway there; just wander the wrong way up Southard until you come to Frances Street. Look to the left and you will see this great little French-Caribbean eatery offering gourmet seafood, lamb and even ostrich.

The most popular dishes here are probably the seafood ones, like Grouper Romanesco, with a sauce consisting of tomatoes, hazelnuts, roasted red peppers and garlic. Café Solé only seats 60 diners, so reservations are highly recommended. The cafe is open for dinner only, starting at 6 PM, and is closed on Wednesdays.

Latitudes Beach Cafe
$$$ • Sunset Key, 245 Front St.,
Key West • (305) 294-4313

When you think of dining seaside somewhere on a secluded island, this is the kind of place that comes to mind. Just five minutes across the water from the hustle and bustle of Mallory Square, Latitudes might just as well be half a world away. It is that peaceful, that serene. And, as near as we can tell, still largely undiscovered. Granted, it takes some planning to get here. You have to make a reservation, and you have to board a boat. But if what you seek is a quiet evening escape from the craziness of Key West, dinner at Latitudes on Sunset Key is well worth the effort.

The cuisine here could best be described as eclectic. Dinner entrees include the likes of charbroiled yellowtail snapper topped with fresh crab, pan-fried tequila-soaked chicken breast served with Key lime Margarita sauce, beef tenderloin stuffed with cornmeal-coated oysters, and Jamaican jerk chicken with guava glaze and sweet potato-plantain mash. Latitudes also serves breakfast and lunch. A full bar offers exotic frozen island drinks as well as beer and wine.

Sunset Key is a private island, half of which is devoted to guest cottages, the other to pricey waterfront homes (see our Accommodations and Real Estate chapters for additional information). Island access is thus largely limited to residents. Launches for Sunset Key leave regularly throughout the day from the pier at the Hilton Resort and Marina on Front Street. If you are not living or staying on the island, you must make a reservation for your meal at Latitudes with the Hilton concierge to secure a boarding pass.

Louie's Backyard
$$$$ • 700 Waddell Ave., Key West
• (305) 294-1061

An enduring favorite among locals and visitors alike, Louie's Backyard combines island manor house ambiance with cutting-edge cuisine. And though the exquisitely prepared, complex combination of ingredients that marks Louie's is often imitated elsewhere in Key West, this restaurant continues to shine. A sweeping veranda, for outdoor dining, overlooks Louie's "backyard," which is actually a prime piece of Atlantic oceanfront property. Indoors, the pale lavender-blue walls showcase the finely appointed tables. In the '70s this spot was a favorite with next-door neighbor Jimmy Buffett, who often played for his supper.

Dinner entrees span the globe, with fresh local seafood garnering center stage. An equally innovative cuisine is offered on the lunch menu for half the price of evening dining. Try the Bahamian conch chowder with bird-pepper hot sauce or a wilted spinach salad with grilled shiitake mushrooms and warm, roasted garlic vinaigrette. The wild mushroom Caesar salad is topped with seared beef tenderloin and steak tartare. And you can savor your grilled catch-of-the-day with tropical fruit salsa as you gaze out over the azure water. Top off lunch or dinner with a Key lime tart (like a light Key lime pie) or a Key lime cheesecake (more like a mousse).

Louie's Backyard serves lunch and dinner daily, except from Labor Day to Columbus Day, when it's open for dinner only. Reservations are recommended in all seasons but especially in winter and on weekends. The Afterdeck outdoor oceanside bar is open all day and into the wee hours (see our Nightlife chapter).

Mangoes
$$ • 700 Duval St., Key West
• (305) 292-4606

Patrons enjoy one of the best views of Duval Street at Mangoes, where fresh Caribbean-style seafood is served in an outdoor, corner cafe setting of white umbrella-covered tables. Indoor dining is equally sophisticated, with candlelight and fresh flowers on every table and original artwork lining the walls.

Open daily for lunch, dinner and late-night pizza (cooked in a wood-fired oven), Mangoes' specialties include pan-seared yellowtail snapper with passion fruit, on the sweet side, and a lobster, scallops and shrimp dish known as gueddengo, served with a slightly spicy tomato sauce. Reservations are accepted during peak season for parties of more than five.

Cafe Marquesa
$$$ • 600 Fleming St., Key West
• (305) 292-1244

Golden walls covered with paintings, pastel tile floors, large mirrors and a panoramic country-kitchen mural set the scene for one of the finest dining encounters in Key West. Long a front-runner in the panoply of establishments plying to please your palate, Cafe Marquesa remains a consistent winner.

Gracing the white linen tablecloths is an eclectic assortment of innovative dishes: spicy Jamaican barbecued prawns, honey-bourbon-cured pork loin with apple-onion chutney, seared yellowfin tuna with salsa verde and grilled lamb chops with roasted banana-papaya compote.

Cafe Marquesa, reminiscent of a European brasserie, is a nonsmoking restaurant. Reservations are highly recommended in all seasons. Cafe Marquesa serves dinner nightly.

Square One
$$$ • 1075 Duval St., Key West
• (305) 296-4300

Enjoy a touch of class and a bit of craziness, Manhattan-style, at Square One, a ca-sually sophisticated uptown bistro in Duval Square. Two enormous tropical floral murals flank the walls, offsetting the highly polished wood of other areas. The green carpet is mirrored in the green-rimmed chargers, which sit upon white linen tablecloths in the rich-looking dining room.

Diners are treated to light piano music as they sample Square One's considerable creative offerings. You may wish to try roast rack of lamb, seasoned with whole grain mustard, honey shallot confit and minted Bordelaise. Or perhaps you'd like Square One's signature sautéed sea scallops served on a bed of poached spinach with a mustard cream sauce. If lighter fare appeals, warm, peppered duck salad on mixed greens with roasted Holland peppers and mango vinaigrette may sate your palate. And there is always a chef's choice pasta selection and other daily specialties.

Square One offers the option of outdoor dining in the tree-lined courtyard. Ample free parking is available in the adjoining lot accessed from Simonton Street. Square One serves dinner nightly, 365 days a year. Reservations are always highly recommended.

Rooftop Cafe
$$$ • 310 Front St., Key West
• (305) 294-2042

High amid the treetops, Rooftop Cafe looks down on the tourist mecca along Front Street near Mallory Square. And although the restaurant bustles with dining activity, the atmosphere remains unhurried and removed from the fray. Diners may sit on a second-floor balcony, which extends on two sides of the building, under the canopy of ancient leafy trees. Inside, ceiling fans mounted on the white vaulted ceiling gently move the air about the open-air pavilion-style dining room. Philodendron trails from overhead and dwarf bougainvillea trees dot the floor. Oilcloth in a modern-art barrage of primary colors covers the tables.

The cuisine, innovative in both composition and presentation, combines local piscatory resources with an international flair. Dinner creations include sautéed pepper tiger tuna, a tuna steak with black pepper and sesame seeds served with soy-wasabi sauce and mung sprouts; savory shrimps, Key West pinks marinated in shallots, herbs and oil, then grilled and served on roasted corn and fennel risotto; shellfish lasagna, a chef's selection of seafood under a blanket of lemon-pepper pasta served on a lobster and oregano coulis. Luncheon selections transcend the norm as well, including the "very veggie" sandwich and conch steaks diced and marinated in lemon and lime with veggies and avocado.

Rooftop Cafe is open seven days a week for breakfast, lunch and dinner. Reservations are strongly suggested for dinner in all seasons, especially at sunset.

Melting Pot

The Americas

Garden Cafe
$ • American • 310 Duval St., Key West • (305) 294-2991

Jewelry makers, glass blowers and artists surround visitors to the Garden Cafe, which offers exclusively outdoor seating on an elevated concrete platform. Views include busy Duval Street or more private and shady courtyard gardens. Situated next to the Porter mansion, c. 1880s, this establishment serves one of Key West's biggest and best burgers; also on the menu is a wide variety of homemade vegetarian fare, including Caesar salads and vegetable soups. Tropical and Asian chicken salads satisfy light meat eaters, and specials such as a grilled organic tofu sandwich with roasted peppers are offered daily. Homemade ice cream and brownies are dessert options.

Garden Cafe is open daily for breakfast, lunch and dinner; Mondays the restaurant closes early, about 7 PM. Beer, wine and frozen Margaritas, daiquiris and piña coladas are available. Reservations are not accepted.

Gato Gordo Cafe
$$ • Tex-Mex • 404 Southard St., Key West • (305) 294-0888

Perhaps most intriguing about Gato Gordo is its name, which is Spanish for "fat cat," especially amusing considering its close location to the Green Parrot Bar. This Tex-Mex establishment's owner, Lupe Flores, was formerly a partner in Key West's popular Pancho and Lefty's.

Both of the restaurant's two interior rooms are painted in Southwestern designs of red, black, purple, seafoam and terra cotta accented by paintings, painted tiles and other works of local artists. Dine outside in the garden, where you can't help but notice the large mural in which a local artist portrays a group of fat cats passed out (quite possibly from one of Gato Gordo's Margaritas). The restaurant is noted for carrying the island's widest selection of tequila; its 46-ounce Margarita is equivalent to five of those you'd find in most other Key West establishments. Enjoy this hefty drink at the outside bar for a real Key West Tex-Mex treat.

As hefty but not as potent as the Margaritas are Gato Gordo's deluxe nachos appetizer, steeped in tomatoes, onions, black olives, Monterey Jack and Colby cheeses and sliced jalapeno peppers and baked with a rich mole sauce. Add beef, chili or chicken on top, and even the fattest of cats can share this dish as a meal. Fajita specials offered daily are equally popular.

The decor is fun, beginning with the front door covered with geckos and chili peppers; the ceiling in the smoking room is painted as a reflection of the sky. Out on the tiled alameda, the real, smokeless sky is covered by a tent. Gato Gordo serves lunch and dinner daily. During peak season, reservations are accepted only for parties of more than five.

Mo's Restaurant
$, no credit cards • French-Canadian • 1116 White St., Key West • (305) 296-8955

Locals know that for good, modestly priced food, Mo's is the place to go. In fact, originally the restaurant was called Mo's to Go, for it sold only take-out items. Now the small (fewer than 30 seats), white clapboard eatery offers an interesting menu with a strong French influence. Run by a French-Canadian brother-sister team, Mo's seafood lasagna, variety of quiches and casseroles and garlic- and spinach-stuffed leg of lamb receive raves from regulars and critics alike. Look for the smilin' moustached garlic that denotes Mo's Restaurant. It foretells of palate pleasers to come.

Mo's serves beer, wine and homemade sangria. The restaurant serves lunch and dinner from 11 AM onward, Tuesday through Saturday during the season; it is closed in summer. Reservations are not accepted.

South of the Border

B's Restaurant
$, no credit cards • Cuban • 1500 Bertha St., Key West • (305) 296-3140

Hola, and welcome to the simple homestyle restaurant of Cuban émigré Dortha Cubria, affectionately known as "B." For 15 years, Señora B has been doling out generous portions of roast pork, fresh fillet of grouper and grilled top sirloin steak, each served either with beans, rice and plantains or french fries and salad.

B's Restaurant is open daily for breakfast, lunch and dinner. It offers beer, wine and soft drinks in smoking and nonsmoking rooms with dark, paneled walls and red tablecloths.

Beware that "B" also stands for busy, and reservations are accepted only for parties of more than five. Off-street parking is available.

Chico's Cantina
$$ • Mexican • MM 4.5 Oceanside, Stock Island • (305) 296-4714

Sit among giant cacti, Mexican tapestries and a selection of south-of-the-border folk art at Chico's Cantina, a perennial favorite for Mexican cuisine. This small cantina — only 12 tables — knocks itself out with the freshest ingredients fashioned into off-the-charts homemade Mexican dishes. The food at Chico's is not your ordinary Mexican fare. Complimentary salsa is prepared with fresh tomatoes, onions and peppers, creating the perfect balance between sweet and sassy. The salsa is so popular among locals that the restaurant sells the stuff in bulk. The sizzling fajitas — with a choice of vegetarian, chicken, beef, chicken-and-beef combo, shrimp or shrimp-and-beef combo — are accompanied by fresh vegetables, cooked just until crispy. And the fish adobado grilled in corn husks packs just the right spicy zing. Daily specials usually highlight local seafood such as yellowtail.

Chile peppers rule the roost at Chico's

Cantina. Not only is their subtle presence notable in the cuisine, but their icons appear on the curtains, as lights around the windows, even on ceramic pots. Chico's serves the same menu for both lunch and dinner. It's open every day except Monday. Beer and wine are served; take-out is available.

El Siboney
$, no credit cards • Cuban • 900 Catherine St., Key West • (305) 296-4184

A cascade of bilingual chatter washes over the enthusiastic diners at El Siboney, an informal restaurant specializing in Cuban cuisine. El Siboney is a Cuban Indian, and artwork depicting the El Siboney adorns the white walls of the restaurant. Red vinyl covers the simple cafe chairs, and your cutlery is served in a white paper bag. The food is top drawer all the way, though. Hot, buttery Cuban bread is whisked to your table, and then begins the difficult decision of which taste-tempting delicacy to order. Portions are enormous at El Siboney; the same menu is offered at lunch or dinner.

We recommend one of the combination platters, especially if trying Cuban cuisine is a new experience for you: A platter of roast pork, black beans and yellow rice, and cassava is served heaped with raw onions. The pork melts in the mouth. Or try the roast pork accompanied with yucca and tamale; sounds similar, tastes totally different. You'll find a myriad of Cuban twists with beef, including the popular ropa vieja (shredded beef) and boliche (Cuban pot roast). Crab, shrimp and chicken all get the wonderful Cuban garlic treatment, and you can choose paella for two persons. You can order an array of sandwiches or sides of tamale, yucca, black beans, plantanos and tostones. Wash it all down with homemade sangria, beer or house wines, and try rice pudding, flan or natilla for dessert if you are able.

El Siboney is closed on Sunday.

Jose's Cantina
$ • Cuban • 800 White St., Key West • (305) 296-4366

Step inside this little neighborhood diner and you might believe you'd just walked in from the streets of Havana. The owners are Cuban and so are most of the customers. But even if

Restaurants in the Florida Keys serve up a variety of palate-pleasers.

you don't speak Spanish, you're sure to receive a hearty *bienvenida* (welcome) here. The menus are in English, the waitstaff is bilingual, and the food is plentiful, delicious and cheap.

Jose's has one of the best Cuban mixes on the island — that's a sandwich combination of ham and shredded pork on Cuban bread with lettuce, tomato, mayo, mustard, onions and pickles. The dinners — Cuban variations on chicken, pork and beef — come with the traditional black beans, yellow rice and plantains. Beer, wine and homemade sangria are available.

Jose's is open for breakfast, lunch and dinner, seven days a week, 365 days a year — yes, even Christmas. This restaurant is very small and, judging from the lack of parking spaces in the surrounding neighborhood at 8 AM, high noon and 7 PM, quite popular. To avoid the congestion, plan to arrive a little ahead or well after peak dining periods. Reservations are not accepted.

The Continent

Alexander's Cafe
$ • Italian • 509 Southard St., Key West • (305) 294-5777

A casually intimate cafe with wood-paneled walls, open kitchen, red ceilings and soft track lighting, Alexander's carries nearly every pasta dish imaginable. Here you will find pasta primavera, pasta with garlic and olive oil, pasta marinara, spaghetti Bolognese, spinach pesto ravioli and pasta carbonara. Among the local favorites are chicken Marsala and garlic shrimp pasta. The tomato-basil pizza at Alexander's is among the best in Key West, and specials, such as blackened dolphin, are available daily.

The restaurant seats 50 and accepts reservations only for parties of more than five. Lunch and dinner are served daily.

Antonia's Restaurant
$$ • Italian • 615 Duval St., Key West
• (305) 294-6565

Stroll by this Northern Italian restaurant on any afternoon, and you can watch pasta in the making along the marble window-front table. Stringy mozzarella also is made fresh on-premises. Established in 1979 and named for owner Antonia Berto, Antonia's burned to the ground 16 years later as a result of arson, along with a string of neighboring buildings. After 10 months, the restaurant reopened, displaying the same elegant wood floors and walls, upholstered banahoo, candlelit tables, recessed lighting and small wood bar. Equally spectacular is Antonia's food prepared by Berto's husband, chef Phillip Smith — particularly the grilled fillet of beef tenderloin Rossini, served with mushrooms, brandy and cream; the pan-seared yellowtail braised with watercress, endive, radicchio and white wine; and the linguine Cousteau with a variety of shellfish and fresh tomatoes.

Virtually all the restaurant's veal dishes are popular, and even with all these spectacular entrees, patrons simply cannot pass up the homemade desserts. Tiramisu features layers of lady fingers dipped in espresso, filled with rich mascarpone cheese sauce and topped with grated dark Belgian chocolate. Antonia's flourless chocolate-and-walnut tart is topped with warm chocolate sauce and whipped cream, and Tuscany's well-known grandmother's torte is a baked pastry cream served with toasted almonds. Crème brûlée is always a taste tempter, and this dessert's specials are made with chocolate and mocha. Bellisimo!

Antonia's maintains an extensive Northern Italian and American wine list. The restaurant is open daily for dinner only.

Banana Cafe
$$$ • French • 1211 Duval St., Key West
• (305) 294-7227

Settle into this quiet open-air bistro, and choose from more than 40 breakfast and lunch crepes. The exterior of Banana Cafe resembles a quaint Caribbean cottage; the airy interior says "French bistro," with pinkish pine wood, artistic black-and-white photography, ceiling fans and a small piano bar. Dining also is offered on the front balcony or along the side on a wood deck shaded by large tropical trees.

Thin, pancake-like crepes are stuffed with veggies, fish and meat, and they are designated either sweet or savory. The most desirable crepe among patrons is the ratatouille, overflowing with sautéed eggplant, zucchini, peppers, extra-virgin olive oil and garlic and topped with a fried egg sunny-side up. Also on the menu are salads, sandwiches and daily specials.

Dinner also is served throughout the winter season, and meals are complemented by soft drinks, beer and a nice selection of wines. Reservations are recommended on weekend evenings when entertainment is offered.

Cafe Bianco
$$ • Italian • 917 Duval St., Key West
• (305) 296-7837

Indoors or out in the romantically lit garden, Cafe Bianco (formerly the Lighthouse Cafe) serves up homemade multicolored pasta with a flair. Diners can savor the delicacies of homemade lasagna alla Bolognese and manicotti alla ricotta magra as well as linguine, penne or cappellini prepared al pomodoro (tomato sauce), ragu (meat sauce), frutti di mare (shrimp, calamari, mussels, scallops and fresh local fish), or fra diavolo (spicy tomato sauce with assorted seafood). Beer and selections from a varied wine list are offered.

Credit cards are accepted with a $20 minimum. Cafe Bianco is open daily for lunch and dinner during the winter season, dinner only in the summer. Reservations are suggested in all seasons.

Café des Artistes
$$$$ • French • 1007 Simonton St., Key West • (305) 294-7100

This enduring tropical French establishment has won awards and accolades from *Gourmet*, *Bon Appetit* and *Wine Spectator* magazines, and the recognition is well-deserved. At Cafe des Artistes, chef Andrew Berman's creativity culminates in lobster with passion fruit sauce, raspberry duck and shrimp in pumpkin broth. One of his finest treasures is yellowtail Atocha, snapper sautéed in tarragon butter with shrimp and scallops. Specials are available nightly.

Each of two dining rooms has a distinctive character. Exquisite as the food, the decor at Cafe des Artistes features wainscoting, lace curtains, subdued lighting and local acrylic, watercolor and oil paintings. Fresh flowers decorate every table.

Dining is available seasonally on the outdoor patio. This establishment's extensive wine list features some of the best of the vineyards of France and California. Cafe des Artistes is open every day for dinner. Reservations are recommended.

Finnegan's Wake Irish Pub & Eatery
$ • Irish • 320 Grinnell St., Key West • (305) 293-0222

No need to kiss the Blarney stone at Finnegan's Wake, whose staff guarantees this is one wake you won't want to miss. This Irish pub and eatery sails your spirit across the Big Pond, as you toast the legend of the miraculous resurrection of mythical Tim Finnegan. Try authentically Irish fare: bangers and mash (sausages and mashed potatoes, to those of you not wearing the green), shepherd's pie, corned beef and cabbage, Mrs. Finnegan's Irish stew, potato pancakes or the Dublin pot pie. Lip-smacking lovely is the Irish potato-leek soup, a house specialty, thick and chunky and served with grated cheddar, chopped scallions and bacon. And be sure to try a black and tan — half Guinness, half lager — or a pint of bottled cider.

Like any good Irish wake, the merriment goes on all day and into the wee hours. Finnegan's Wake is open from lunchtime until 4 AM (serving dinner until 10:30 PM, bar menu until 3 AM). Patio dining is available. Reservations will be honored at Finnegan's Wake but usually are not necessary. Wednesday through Saturday enjoy live Irish music.

La Trattoria Venezia
$$ • Italian • 524 Duval St., Key West • (305) 296-1075

This upscale SoHo-style New York bistro rates as a Key West treasure. A romantic taste of old Italy favored by locals, visitors and Keys residents from as far away as Key Largo, La Trattoria Venezia redefines the traditional pasta, veal, chicken, lamb and seafood dishes

of the mother country. The sophisticated decor — linen cloths top intimate tables encircled with black lacquer-style chairs — belies the fact that you are a stone's throw from the sidewalks of busy Duval Street.

Try agnello alla grigfin (lamb with rosemary) or spaghetti alla pescatore, topped with a bounty of seafood. Penne arrabbiata delivers a bit of a bite, and rigatoni al ragu does not disappoint. The insalata mista will transport your taste buds to Venice for sure. La Trattoria Venezia serves dinner nightly. Reservations are suggested, especially in high season.

Mangia Mangia
$$ • Italian • 900 Southard St., Key West • (305) 294-2469

Off the main drag but definitely on the right track is the pasta lovers' nirvana, Mangia Mangia. Meaning "eat, eat" in Italian, Mangia Mangia bestows a passel of homemade fresh pasta and finely seasoned sauces that would excite even Marco Polo's palate. The paneled interior of the storefront trattoria at the corner of Southard and Margaret streets showcases Caribbean-style artwork.

The chefs work their macaroni magic in plain view. You can always order the basic sauces — marinara, Alfredo, pesto and seafood — but, for something out of the ordinary, try picadillo pasta (black bean pasta shells with a Cuban-inspired sauce). The daily specials will prove difficult to pass up.

Mangia Mangia does not allow smoking inside the air-conditioned restaurant. Diners wishing to smoke may sit in a brick patio area outside, where the tables are surrounded by palm trees. Mangia Mangia serves dinner daily. It does not take reservations and advises you to come before 7 PM to avoid a wait. You can enjoy selections from Mangia Mangia's extensive wine list. Beer also is served.

Martin's Cafe Restaurant
$$ • German • Corner of Fleming and Grinnell Sts., Key West • (305) 296-1183

Put on your *lederhosen*, for Martin's treats you to German cuisine with an island flair. Situated next door to the Eden House, Martin's expansive menu all but guarantees *guten appetit*. Begin with pilze à la Martin, toasted bread rounds topped with sautéed mushrooms and herb garlic butter. You'll find classic German dishes such as pepper steak, sauerbraten with spaetzle and red cabbage, and Wiener schnitzel, but Martin's also prepares island seafood creations à la *deutsch*. Grouper Dijon arrives on a bed of champagne kraut with rosemary potatoes. Sea scallops wunderbar is baked with spinach encased in puff pastry and is served with a Riesling sauce. Choose from a large selection of fine German wines and beers.

Martin's Cafe Restaurant serves dinner Tuesday through Sunday and offers Sunday brunch. Reservations are suggested.

The Far East

Benihana Japanese Steaks and Seafood
$$$ • Japanese • 3591 S. Roosevelt Blvd., Key West • (305) 294-6400

If ever you have been to Benihana, you know that this is not the place for a quiet, romantic evening at a corner table. Rather, tepan chefs entertain as many as eight guests per table with skillful cooking on grill-like tables and salt-and-pepper sideshows. Tepan training at Benihana takes three to six months, depending upon each chef's ability to "cook a table." Chefs come from a variety of backgrounds and offer different antics. Some are, like Benihana founder Rocky Aoki, more entertaining than others. This particular establishment does not offer sushi. Privately owned, it features the standard beef and seafood combination dinners amid original Japanese artwork and oceanfront views. The snapper at Benihana is locally caught (calamari, shrimp, lobster and scallops are imported).

Dinner is served nightly.

Dim Sum
$$ • Chinese • 613 Duval St., Key West • (305) 294-6230

Head through an alley off Duval Street, and you will be pleasantly surprised by the interior architecture of Dim Sum: all white walls with etched-wood window trims, sconces dimly aglow, Bali batik tables with candles and fresh flowers and framed photographs that recount the owner's travels to Asia. Dim Sum's à la carte menu carries these travels into the tummy with specialties such as duck in Chinese black bean sauce, whole-fried yellowtail snapper and coconut shrimp in red curry sauce. The signature dish here is Dragon Hot Noodles, stir-fried noodles combined with vegetables and fish and spiced with a fiery pepper sauce. Daily specials may include grilled salmon in red curry sauce or fish tempura over mixed greens with sliced avocado and tomato with a miso mustard sauce.

Open daily for dinner only, Dim Sum serves beer and wine. Off-street parking is available behind the building. Reservations are recommended during high season weekends.

Dynasty Chinese Restaurant
$ • Chinese • 918 Duval St., Key West • (305) 294-2943

Red, black and white colors dominate the interior of this traditional Szechwan and Cantonese restaurant. One of four establishments throughout the country owned by the Chow family of Hong Kong, Dynasty has been in business in Key West for eight years. Spicy dishes such as Szechwan shrimp, chicken and lobster and Kung Pao chicken are most in demand; more mild offerings include honey-garlic chicken and Peking duck served with thin pancakes for wrapping and sauces for dipping. Daily combination specials, such as grouper fillet with Szechwan sauce, come with steamed rice and vegetables, a choice of soup and an egg roll.

Outdoor dining is offered on a patio surrounded by plants and palms, and music from the Orient sounds from speakers. Dynasty serves beer and wine and is open daily for lunch and dinner. Reservations are recommended.

Kyushu Japanese Restaurant
$$ • Japanese • 921 Truman Ave., Key West • (305) 294-2995

Take off your shoes: Kyushu provides an authentic Japanese dining experience in tatami rooms, or individual low-to-the-ground tables and benches secluded by bamboo screens. As a courtesy, your Asian waitress removes her slippers in unison with you. The open entranceway at Kyushu takes patrons out of Key West and into an exotic garden with a bridged pond and views of royal poinciana trees. Handpainted Japanese sheets stretch from floor to ceiling, and saltwater aquariums, fresh flowers and Japanese paintings of geisha women are found throughout. Crepe-paper box lights add soft lighting.

The menu includes sashimi, sushi rolls, tempura, katsu and stir-fry and teriyaki dishes. An extensive selection of sushi — including eel, conch, octopus, yellowtail, tuna and snapper — is most popular, and patrons are offered the option of dining at the informal sushi bar.

Like Yo Saké (see separate restaurant listing in this chapter), Kyushu is owned by the Nippon Sogo corporation. The full-service bar features sake and plum wine, along with Japanese beers such as Sapporo, Kirin and Asahi. Off-street parking is available at the restaurant lot on Packer Street. Reservations are recommended during high season; Kyushu is open for lunch Monday through Saturday and for dinner seven nights a week.

Origami Japanese Restaurant
$$ • Japanese • 1075 Duval St., Key West • (305) 294-0092

The stark, white decor of Origami provides a backdrop for the brightly colored tropical fish adorning the walls. And like the Japanese art of folding paper into decorative or representational forms — origami — the restaurant fashions fresh, local seafood into exquisite sushi and sashimi. Rumor has it that the dragon roll must not be missed. Origami also offers traditional Japanese cuisine, such as teriyaki, chicken katsu, steak yakiniku and tempura.

Sit at the cafe-style tables or at the sushi bar and watch the masters at work. Origami is situated in Duval Square. Free parking is available in the adjoining lot off Simonton Street. Origami is open for dinner every day except Sunday. From December through May it is open for lunch also. Smoking is not permitted inside, but smokers may sit in Origami's lovely outdoor seating area. Beer, wine and sake are served. Reservations are suggested in high season.

Siam House
$$ • Thai • 829 Simonton St., Key West • (305) 292-0302

Owner Suriya Siripant of Bangkok has combined imported sculptures, woodwork and paintings from Thailand with genuine Thai food. His luncheon buffet, offered along with menu fare each day but Sunday, features a selection of six items including curry and sautéed beef, chicken and pork, noodles and fried rice. Specialties such as curry lobster and roast duck are offered in a variety of spice levels.

Reservations at Siam House are recommended during high season. The restaurant serves beer and wine. Siam House is open for dinner seven days a week.

Thai Cuisine
$ • Thai • 513 Greene St., Key West • (305) 294-9424

Screaming banana-yellow walls bathe the tiny interior of Thai Cuisine with a cheerful glow. And the salubrious cuisine of Thailand tingles your palate with the afterglow of Thai curries. Thai curry is a fiery Southeast Asian stew that's not even a kissing cousin to the bland Indian-style powder we Americans associate with the moniker. Thai curry is actually a cooking method, not an ingredient. Together with spices, herbs and aromatic vegetables, hot chile peppers are ground into a dry paste that infuses Thai curries with heat and passion. At the same time, coconut milk, fish sauce, sugar and Kaffir lime leaves — ubiquitous to every variation of Thai red and green curry — confuse the palate with a riot of sweet and sour sensory stimuli.

For another traditional delight, try Pad Thai, spicy rice noodles sautéed with shrimp, chicken, egg, ground peanuts, scallions and bean sprouts. The portions are enormous. Enjoy a selection of Thai and Japanese beers, house wines, plum wine and sake. Outdoor seating is available in the evening. Thai Cuisine serves lunch Monday through Friday and

INSIDERS' TIP

Some Key West restaurants offer a discount to locals upon proof of residency.

is open for dinner every night. Take-out is available, and Thai Cuisine offers free delivery in Key West.

Yo Saké
$$ • Japanese • 722 Duval St., Key West • (305) 294-2288

The cozy cocoon of Yo Saké sates the wandering palate with an array of sushi and sashimi and imaginative variations on traditional Japanese cuisine. Tasty miso soup or a soup-of-the-day, such as snapper vegetable, clears the taste buds for the pleasurable assault to follow. Crispy salads with portions enough for two are dressed with a light peanut dressing or a soy and sesame seed combination. Entrees of chicken, pork, beef or seafood are presented in teriyaki or ginger sauce, soy-garlic sauce or curry, orange-garlic or ginger-sesame sauce. Particularly delightful is the yaki udon, or fire-breathing noodles, prepared mild to hot with your choice of shrimp, chicken or vegetables.

Yo Saké will seat you at one of its tatami tables if you request, which are in the main room of the restaurant where smoking is allowed. You may also book a private tatami room, each of which will accommodate six persons, for a traditional Japanese dining experience. Wall partitions can be removed to seat a party of up to 12 if desired. Smoking is not permitted in the private tatami rooms. Yo Saké also has outdoor seating in an intimate courtyard garden setting. The restaurant serves dinner nightly. Reservations are suggested in high season.

Intercontinental

Alice's on Duval
$$$ • 1114 Duval St., Key West • (305) 292-4888

"Eclectic" means to select from various doctrines, methods and styles. Alice's rightly bills itself as "eclectic cuisine." What it essentially comes down to is that, no matter what your hankering, you will find your ideal match for dinner at this upscale establishment located on the corner of Duval and Amelia streets. Homestyle but far from bland meat loaf with mashed potatoes is offered alongside a full French rack of lamb. Ethnic cuisine is in evidence, from the far reaches of the world, like Vietnam and Thailand, to just around the corner, from Cuba. Alice's is open seven days a week in the high season, and reservations are strongly recommended.

Cafe Karumba!
$$ • 1215 Duval St., Key West • (305) 296-2644

Cafe Karumba! boasts more than 50 different kinds of rum that can blend together in a limitless variety of drinks. Once your thirst is quenched, don't forget the great cuisine offered here. Choose from a mostly Caribbean menu offering spicy island selections. If spicy isn't your favorite, Cafe Karumba! also offers Italian pastas, grilled fish and seafood, Cuban specials and three different preparations of tender conch. Reservations are recommended, but not necessary. Cafe Karumba! is open seven days a week.

When you stop at one of
our many seafood
markets, you will
undoubtedly meet the
three royal families of
our tropical waters:
snapper, grouper
and dolphin.

Seafood Markets and Specialty Foods

Here in the Florida Keys, we think our fish is pretty special. It's certainly the freshest — sometimes only minutes from line to linen. Its pedigree is elite; most species are not marketed outside South Florida. And the abounding variety of innovative culinary presentations are astounding. Visitors to the Florida Keys, accustomed back home to choosing among cod, halibut, haddock, swordfish or tuna, are often overwhelmed when confronted with the bountiful selections from our underwater treasure trove.

When you stop at one of our many seafood markets, you will undoubtedly meet the three royal families of our tropical waters: snapper, grouper and dolphin. The moist, sweet snapper dynasty most often is represented by the famed yellowtail or the equally desirous mangrove or mutton snapper. The firm, mild-flavored grouper clan, member of the sea bass family, competes in popularity with the large-flaked and sweetly moist dolphin fish (not to be confused with the porpoise dolphin, which is a mammal).

You won't want to miss our Florida lobster, a delicacy any way you look at it (see Diving for Lobster in the Diving and Snorkeling chapter). And, if you have never tasted a stone crab claw, you are in for a treat (see the Close-up in this chapter). To round out your palate, we have provided you with a rundown of delicatessens and shops selling specialty foods.

We have listed our recommended seafood markets and specialty food shops by mile marker (MM) from the top of the Keys in Key Largo to Big Coppitt in the Lower Keys and Stock Island at the gateway to Key West. Key West businesses are listed in alphabetical order.

Most places remain open until at least 5 PM, with the exception of bakeries, which usually open early and close in the early afternoon. During high season, December through April, many of these markets and stores extend their hours. The off-season often brings abbreviated hours, so you may want to call before you shop.

The Florida Keys

Upper Keys

Dockside Cakes Bakery & Deli
MM 103 Bayside, Key Largo
• **(305) 451-7060**

You won't lose any weight indulging here, but it's definitely worth it. All cakes, breads, pastries, muffins and bagels are made on the premises, and they taste as good as they smell. Enjoy a potpourri of deli sandwiches or freshly brewed hazelnut, French vanilla, Irish cream or chocolate almond coffee too. Dockside Cakes also caters deli and breakfast platters.

The Fish House Restaurant & Seafood Market
MM 102.4 Oceanside, Key Largo
• **(305) 451-4665**

Parking is at a premium at this popular seafood restaurant/market combo, but pull in anyway; you'll be amply rewarded for your efforts at this unassuming wood cottage. On any given day, a selection of four to eight fresh local catches feature fillets and steaks, including wahoo, dolphin, shark and cobia. A variety of snapper and deepwater grouper also is available, depending upon the spawning season. In season (October 15 through May 15), The Fish Market carries stone crab claws. Amberjack and kingfish are smoked, and Florida lobster, Indian River littleneck clams and Apalachicola oysters almost always are abundant. In season, lobster is fresh; off-season, you can buy frozen tails.

Heading north along the Overseas Highway, The Fish House is just past the Tradewinds Plaza shopping center. Be alert! White Christmas lights surround its casual sign, but drive too fast and you are sure to pass it by.

www.insiders.com

See this and many other **Insiders' Guide®** destinations online — in their entirety.

Visit us today!

Key Largo Fisheries
MM 99.5 Oceanside, 1313 Ocean Bay Dr., Key Largo • (305) 451-3782

Commercial fisherman Jack Hill opened Key Largo Fisheries in 1972 in order to sell his catch out of a single location. As more fishermen began bringing their catches to Jack's place, he expanded the store and hired employees. Today, the family-run Key Largo Fisheries works with 30 boats, employs a staff of 35 and ships wholesale to more than 500 clients throughout the country. They also offer retail sales at the store and via overnight delivery. At Key Largo Fisheries, customers will find choice seafood, including snapper, grouper, shrimp and, in season, Florida lobster and stone crab claws. Conch here is imported from the Bahamas and the Turks and Caicos islands.

Remedy's Health Foods
MM 99.5 Oceanside, Key Largo • (305) 451-2160

If your idea of a pick-me-up requires vitamins, herbs and healthful foods, you'll find all this plus berries, dried fruit-and-nut mixes and more at this health-food store. The shop stocks food supplements, herb cheese and protein supplements as well as a wide range of natural products for face and body — soaps, shampoos, conditioners, toothpastes, moisturizers and face creams.

Chad's Deli & Bakery
MM 92.3 Bayside, Tavernier
• (305) 853-5566

Fresh, bright and clean, Chad's offers a mouth-watering assortment of pastries and breads as well as custom sandwiches, salads and soups. Coca-Cola memorabilia adorns the deli's walls. And judging from the volume of hungry locals popping in for a bite, Chad's special brand of chow satisfies the palate and keeps 'em coming back for more.

Sunshine Supermarket
MM 91.8 Oceanside, Tavernier • (305) 852-7216

There isn't a Tavernier resident who doesn't know about the rotisserie chicken and Cubano bread at the Sunshine Supermarket. Local businesses, families, holiday hosts and excursionists often purchase as many as six chickens at a time. So warm and supple is the fresh-baked bread that few customers can leave the store without taking a bite of it.

The store, owned and operated by the Tomas family, serves 400 chickens per day during high season and bakes 800 loaves of bread daily. The secret to the tasty poultry, which is cooked only with salt, no marinades or spices, is the continuous self-basting as the chickens rotate.

Also available at Sunshine Supermarket is fresh roast pork, ribs, yellow rice and black beans and rice, all at reasonable prices. Mojo sauce — a Cuban concoction of oil, vinegar, garlic and other spices — soaks into the pork and is available for chicken upon request; the store sells bottles of it.

INSIDERS' TIP

The eyes of a fresh whole fish should protrude and be bright, full and clear. As the fish becomes stale and ages, the eyes often turn pink and become cloudy and sunken.

Florida Keys Payfair
MM 90 Bayside, Plantation Key
• (305) 852-5492

Established in 1961 by the Hack family, Payfair was at one time virtually the only grocery store in town. So reliable is the quality and service of the store that many customers have continued to patronize it despite an influx of other shopping options. The full-service meat department here carries USDA choice aged meats cut to order upon request. The butcher is on premises at all times, offering sirloin steaks bone-in and -out, porterhouse, rib eye, New York strips, ground chuck and ground beef. If you ask, he will grind round and sirloin too. Payfair carries fresh poultry and assorted Boar's Head and Thumann's lunch meats.

Over the years, this family-run business has added gourmet spices and dressings as its customers demand them. It carries fresh, refrigerated produce and a variety of ethnic foods not found in larger supermarkets.

Flagler Café
MM 88.5 Oceanside, Plantation Key
• (305) 852-3354

The bright yellow interior of the tiny Flagler Café serves as a cheerful backdrop for a giant painting of (what else?) Flagler's railroad (see our Historical Evolution chapter). And the bright smiles of the help here are but a forerunner of a selection of deli sandwiches, salads, chili, soup-of-the-day. Known for its hot roast beef sandwich, Flagler's bridges the hunger gap.

Made to Order Cafe & Bakery
MM 86.7 Oceanside, Islamorada
• (305) 852-2600

A peek at the sandwich board listing in this specialty food market, which perches in the courtyard boardwalk of Treasure Village, will tweak your taste buds for sure. Such creative sandwich offerings as sun-dried fajitas, Havana chick or grilled brie with avocado, bacon and tomato will vie for your attention with an equally toothsome salad selection such as jerk chicken, Caesar salad or tortellini with sun-dried tomatoes and artichoke hearts. Or, enjoy a selection of creative wraps: Cuban, Mardi Gras, Italian, American Barbecue, or Asian Pepper Steak. Tempting as well are the jumbo muffins — banana chip, very-berry, pumpkin spice, sunshine, Key lime or carrot. But the pièce de résistance is the dessert case, where meringue shaped like a court jester's hat covers Key lime pies, and such offerings as Chocolate Sin and Hummingbird Cake pique both curiosity and tummy rumblings. You can find an assortment of dried gourmet pastas, sauces and marinades here. Made to Order also caters private functions.

Henry's Bakery & Gourmet Pizza Shop
MM 82.8 Oceanside, Islamorada
• (305) 664-4030

Ummmm. It is tough to pick out a pizza from Henry's — the choices are so unusual and palate pleasing. How about saltimbocca pizza? Or California Bird, a concoction of avocado, turkey, tomatoes, onions and mozzarella? Or Sublime Pie — I'm not kidding — shrimp or Florida lobster with roasted bell peppers and sundried tomatoes. Just in case pizza doesn't float your boat, pick from a large selection of salads, sandwiches, pastas, and soups. Eat in or take out. Free delivery is offered from MM 74 to MM 88 for a minimum order of $8.

Islamorada Fish Company Restaurant and Bakery
MM 81.6 Bayside, Islamorada
• (305) 664-8363

On a good Sunday, this bakery/restaurant sells 200 of its oversize cinnamon rolls. Topped with cream-cheese icing, the buns are undoubtedly one of the local favorites. Also available are "gooey" or sticky buns, bagels, muffins, scones and croissants. Cakes and pies prove a variety of uses for the famous Key lime. Here you will find Key lime cake and pie and Key lime cheesecake. Fresh-baked breads include banana and mango, all-grain and Bimini — a light, low-cholesterol white bread. Full breakfast, lunch and dinner are served daily (see our Restaurants chapter).

Islamorada Fish Company
MM 81.5 Bayside, Islamorada
• (305) 664-9271

This Islamorada favorite carries fresh local catches including dolphin, Florida lobster, grouper, snapper, swordfish, stone crab claws, blue crab, Key West pink shrimp and tuna. Conch here is offered either ground or in steaks and is flown in fresh and frozen from the Turks and Caicos islands. Sea and bay scallops come from Boston, oysters from Apalachicola, and the market carries clams and mussels. Islamorada Fish Company has a sister bakery that sells freshly baked breads in a small deli area; you can also purchase homemade mustard, tartar and cocktail sauces at Islamorada Fish Company.

If you prefer to dine in this charming seafood market ambiance, the store has a full-service restaurant (see our Restaurants chapter). Its fried grouper sandwich is an award winner.

The Trading Post
MM 81.5 Bayside, Islamorada
• **(305) 664-2571**
Established in 1966, this epicurean shop began as a grocery store stocked with the basics, and it did a brisk business in barbecued chicken. Today owners Jim and Betsy Mooney have increased the inventory tenfold, carrying extensive deli choices and gourmet items, including spices, seasonings and sauces, and fine imported and domestic wines, salads and fresh produce. The Mooneys still serve chicken, but they now prepare their poultry roasted, broasted, fried and seasoned with lemon and garlic. The store also offers customized catering.

Meats are outstanding here. You can choose from an extensive selection of prime cuts, and your meat can be cut to order by the on-site butcher. Poultry is shipped in fresh.

Lobster Walk
MM 74.5 Bayside, Lower Matecumbe
• **(305) 664-2353**
Lobster Walk is a wholesaler, retailer and live-lobster exporter that carries yellowtail, tuna, Key West pink shrimp and other daily catches supplied by 50 local fishing operations. You can get stone crab claws in season and Apalachicola oysters, mussels, clams, softshell crabs and conch from the Turks and Caicos. If, after heading home from the Florida Keys, you would like to continue dining on fresh local seafood, you may order by mail

from Lobster Walk's mail-order catalog for 24-hour delivery.

Middle Keys

Nichols Seafood of Conch Key Inc.
MM 63 Bayside, Conch Key
• **(305) 289-0900**
Nichols Seafood is a family affair, and Beth, Gary and "Dad" Nichols are on hand to greet you. A large selection of fresh whole yellowtail and fillets of grouper and dolphin are usually available. You'll also find lobsters and stone crab claws in season. For something different, try the smoked lobster tail and amberjack smoked in applewood.

Duck Key Emporium
MM 61 Oceanside, 294 Duck Key Dr., Duck Key • **(305) 743-2299**
Whether you want breakfast or sandwiches to take on your fishing charter or you need to stock up on provisions for your motor or sailing yacht anchored at neighboring Hawk's Cay Marina, the Duck Key Emporium delicatessen can fit the bill. Famous for its home-cooked dinners, which change daily, the Emporium also keeps a supply of frozen T-bone and New York strip steaks in the freezer. A selection of beer, wine and soft drinks is available. You'll enjoy the Emporium's Key lime pie and Key lime cheesecake. Enjoy your repast outdoors: An expansive deck out back features umbrella-shaded tables with a tranquil view of the boat basin of Duck Key Marina.

Owned by Laurie Tencelski since the summer of 1997, the Duck Key Emporium sports some new features while retaining all the tried-and-trues. Fresh bakery goods — pastries, doughnuts, muffins, desserts — are available daily, and a selection of homemade salads now graces the deli case. Catering for private functions is also available.

Martha's Caribbean Cupboard and Dangerous John Hubert's Hot Sauces & Cigars
MM 54 Bayside, Quay Village, Marathon
• **(305) 743-9299**
A visit to Martha Smith and John Hubert Bynum's place is just plain fun. Nestled in a

Florida Stone Crab Claws

Now, you Yankees can brag about your blue crabs, and you West Coasters may boast of Dungeness. But here in the Florida Keys we crow about crab claws like none other — those of the Florida stone crabs.

The stone crabs, large nonswimming crabs found in deep holes and under rocks in the waters surrounding the Keys, have the unusual ability to release their legs or pincers if caught or when experiencing extreme changes in temperature. The separation always occurs at one of the joints to protect the crab from further injury. What is particularly unique about this situation is that the stone crab regenerates the severed appendage, a feat it can accomplish three or four times during its lifetime.

Close-up

The stone crab's two claws serve distinct purposes: The largest claw, or crusher, is used to hold food and fight predators. The smaller claw, known as the ripper, acts as a scissor for cutting food.

The crabs are harvested commercially in the Florida Keys with baited traps. One or both of the crab's claws are removed (it greatly improves the crab's chances of survival if only one claw is taken). The forearm must measure at least 2¾ inches to harvest it legally. The live stone crabs must then be returned to the water, where in 18 months a new claw will have grown to legal size. It is illegal in the state of Florida to harvest whole stone crabs. They are one of our precious resources.

The Florida stone crab possesses the unique ability to lose one of its claws and regenerate.

A stone crab claw has a hard, heavy, porcelain-like shell with a black-tipped pincer. Seafood markets sell stone crab claws fully cooked. When cooked, the meat inside the shell is sweet and firm-textured. A mild sweet odor indicates freshness.

The shells must be cracked before serving. If you plan to eat your stone crab claws within an hour of purchase, have the seafood market crack them for you. It is not recommended that you crack the claws until you are ready to eat them. If you crack the claws yourself, lightly tap the crockery-like shells with a hammer, a small wooden mallet (available at seafood markets) or the back of a tablespoon. The shells also will crack like a fine china teacup if you hit one claw against the other. Pick the meat from the shell using a small cocktail fork and serve with mustard sauce (cold claws) or with clarified butter (re-steamed claws).

Stone crab claws are in season from October 15 until May 15. They do not freeze particularly well, but most seafood markets listed in this chapter will ship iced, fresh stone crab claws anywhere in the United States.

funky little two-room shop in the Quay Village complex, next to the popular Quay restaurant, the shop features a potpourri of specialty cigars mingling with unusual kitchen gifts and gourmet foods. At center stage, however, is the wildly eclectic selection of hysterically named hot sauces, many of which occupy a round tasting table in the middle of the room. Giggle over Velvet Elvis, a hot sauce that boasts, " . . . makes any dish a hunka, hunka burnin' love." Velvet Elvis comes with a tape by the same name, made by John Bartus, a local musician who performs on Saturday evenings at the Key Colony Inn in Marathon. Treat your libido to Endorphin Rush, Total Insanity or Hot Buns at the Beach. The Ultimate Burn is a super-hot concoction with a label that sports a woman in a bikini, with a scratch-off halter top. A close inspection of some of the bottles reveals that some customers "just looking" were also "just scratching." And in case spicy isn't your bag, check out the chocolate body paint. The label says it is good on ice cream, too.

Captain's Three
MM 54 Oceanside, Coco Plum Blvd., Marathon • (305) 289-1131, (800) 869-3474

Captain's Three maintains its own fishing, crabbing and lobstering crews, guaranteeing the freshest catches of the day. The shop always has plenty of Key West shrimp that have not been dipped in preservatives. Black grouper is a specialty at Captain's Three, and the staff will special-order oysters and cherrystone clams for you if you have a hankering for paella. Be sure to try the homemade cocktail sauce. Captain's Three is closed May through July.

Island City Fish Market & Eatery
MM 53 Oceanside, Marathon • (305) 743-9196

Stop in at Island City for shrimp, stone crab, conch and catch-of-the-day, which you can buy whole or filleted. The market will ship a taste of our islands home for you if you like. Or, if you can't wait for a bite of our succulent seafood, pop into the eatery for a fry-up — fish, oysters, clams, calamari, shrimp, even conch fritters.

Produce Express
MM 52.5 Oceanside, Marathon • (305) 743-9131

Sweet, ripe fruits and veggies at bargain prices distinguish Produce Express. You'll always find great tomatoes, melons, pineapples and sugar snap peas, as well as mixed baby greens and baby spinach, hydro-washed and ready to toss. For those who like to "put up" their produce by canning or making jam, Produce Express offers specials on overly ripe veggies and fruits.

Leigh Ann's Coffee House
MM 52 Oceanside, Marathon • (305) 743-2001

This popular new addition to the Marathon nosh scene is quaintly closeted in a pale peach-and-white Key West-style building on the Overseas Highway. With French doors flung open wide, tiled floors, tropical plants, an eclectic array of rustic furniture and Keys art, this is coffeehouse à la Keys. Chic, clean and packed with personality, Leigh's Ann's food is pretty good too. Homemade soups rival sandwiches on bagels, croissants and sub rolls. Specials are made in small batches to assure freshness. You can get an upscale pizza and a selection of salads as well. And don't forget the coffee. Choose among cappucino, mocha coolers, muddy mocha or macchiato . . . if you can.

Food for Thought
MM 51 Bayside, Gulfside Village, Marathon • (305) 743-3297

If you are in the market for health-food products, you'll find them tucked in Food for

Thought, a shop that is also half bookstore. It carries wheat-free, fat-free and sugar-free staples, organic foods, vitamins and homeopathic remedies. Pick up your favorite novel or magazine in the book section to treat your mind as well.

Marathon Liquors & Deli
MM 49.5 Oceanside, Marathon
• **(305) 743-6350**

Well, all the liquors, wines and beers are here, all right, but it's the deli that will make you salivate. "Gourmet" is the much-cliched word that comes to mind, but when you browse the aisles of porcini mushroom penne, tomato-basil linguine, Rollantine Alfredo, pasta Raphael and Grand Marnier liqueur cake, you'll see what we mean. There are pâtés, sausages, smoked salmon, oils, vinegars, mustards, fresh fruits, fresh vegetables and homemade soups. Breakfast includes apple-cinnamon or raisin scones, bagels and freshly baked bread.

Lunch showcases a different deli sandwich each day, such as hot meatball or Italian sausage and peppers. And if you don't feel like fixing dinner, rotisserie-cooked whole chickens, barbecued ribs, an assortment of hot veggies and a Key lime pie can make it to your table faster than you can say Chef Boyardee.

The Garden Gourmet
MM 49.5 Oceanside, Marathon Plaza, Marathon • (305) 289-9425

The stellar selection of produce at The Garden Gourmet costs a little more, but it's definitely worth it. Three times a week, owner Jose Palomino travels to Miami where he hand-chooses produce from the International Market. All produce sold at the International Market is received within 48 hours of shipping and is vine-ripened or tree-ripened, never picked green. Jose and his wife, Teddy Thompson, think you can tell the difference, and so do we.

A trip down the aisles of Garden Gourmet is like a visit to the United Nations: Guatemalan leeks, Israeli tomatoes, Costa Rican pineapples, Holland peppers, Chilean pears. The United States is represented as well: California greens and Driscoll strawberries,

Texas watermelons, Pennsylvania Portobello mushrooms. Garden Gourmet guarantees everything it sells, which also includes a few things in the decadent category: sinfully chocolate truffles, apple brown Betty, cappuccino mousse and cakes and pastries made by a bona fide pastry chef formerly from Little Palm Island. Custom orders are accepted.

You can eat a healthy lunch if you order one of the special made-to-order salad plates or veggie wraps, or drink your fruit-of-the-day with an all-fruit smoothie (no ice added). Garden Gourmet also offers freshly squeezed juices — orange, tangerine, grapefruit or grape. And they make a great cappucino.

Millis Seafood
MM 48 Oceanside, 210 20th St. and Boot Key Rd., Marathon
• **(305) 743-5445**

Shrimp is a great deal at Millis, which often has multiple-pound specials. Much of the seafood here is local, but the store routinely stocks some special items as well. You can find Caicos tenderized or ground conch, smoked fish, Wakefield crabmeat stuffing, ready-to-cook hush puppies, oysters from Galveston Bay and frog legs from Bangladesh.

Captain Cliff's Seafood Market Inc.
MM 47.5 Oceanside, 1350 Oceanview Ave., Marathon • (305) 743-1900

Fresh Key West pinks with heads — and tails, of course — are served with a sense of humor at Captain Cliff's. These shrimp, caught by the market's own shrimp boat out of Stock Island, are a specialty offered at this Marathon seafood market. Cooking shrimp before they are beheaded enhances the flavor, we are told. Captain Cliff's will pack and ship any of its select fish, lobsters and stone crab claws. The market also carries Florida golden crab, a nonswimming deepwater crab of the south Atlantic and Gulf of Mexico waters that tastes like Dungeness crab. Captain Cliff's sells a selection of bottled sauces, rice mixtures and smoked-fish dip. If you'd like to whip up one of Florida Keys' seafood specialties yourself, ask for recipes.

To find Captain Cliff's, turn oceanside at 15th Street.

Lower Keys

Good Food Conspiracy
MM 30 Oceanside, Big Pine Key
• (305) 872-3945

A full assortment of health foods, homeopathic remedies, vitamins, organic poultry and organically grown produce is offered at the Good Food Conspiracy. If you browse the shelves you'll find interesting specialty items such as mangrove honey and Immunitea. The store also stocks a contingent of Oriental specialty foods, which are difficult to come by in the Keys. Part of the Conspiracy is a juice and sandwich bar, which features an "outgoing menu." You could try a carrot colada or a glass of wheat-grass juice, but you may want to overdose on fruit instead. Try the banana, strawberry, blueberry, papaya, cantaloupe, pineapple, peach smoothie. You may even want to have an "Everything Sandwich" to go with your drink: tuna, avocado, cheese, cashews, mixed veggies and sprouts. Whew!

Monte's Restaurant and Fish Market
MM 25 Bayside, Summerland Key
• (305) 745-3731

Locals in the Lower Keys love Monte's for fresh seafood. Besides local snapper, grouper and dolphin, you can find imported Caicos conch (tenderized or ground steaks) and spicy Louisiana crayfish. Monte's will ship any of its inventory for you overnight or ice it for the rest of your journey up or down the Keys. You may eat a selection of Monte's seafood bounty in the adjoining restaurant if you wish (see our Restaurants chapter).

E Fish and Seafood
MM 22.5 Oceanside, Cudjoe Key
• (305) 745-3887

Shelves and shelves of marinades and seafood sauces will inspire you to try your culinary skills in a new creation when you stop in at E Fish. The very complete fish and seafood selection lets you choose between the usual Keys finfish (grouper, snapper and dolphin) and golden crab, stone crab claws, lobsters, blue crabs, oysters and mussels. For an unusual twist on the grill or in pasta, try the seafood sausage — fish mousse with lobster and scallops in a sausage casing.

Nut House Corporation of Key West
MM 10 Bayside, Big Coppitt Key
• (305) 292-8688

You can really mix it up with the nuts at this little shop full of bizarre baskets, snappy sauces and kitschy kernels. The Nut House will concoct gift creations for all your friends, pulling together any number of shop specialties. With a papier-mache banana leaf or lizard or maybe a cat box or an alligator as a base, select your favorite nuts: Duval Crawl, Hemingway Bar Mix, Wreckers Mix or Key West Trail Mix, to name a few. Mix in some Key Lime Taffy, Keys Krunch, Flamingo Fruit Mix and a few Fantasy Balls, and you've about got all the fruits and nuts on your Christmas list covered. The Nut House will send mail orders.

Key West

You really could eat yourself to death in Key West and come back in another life to do it again. Willingly. The edible choices are surpassed only by the individuality of the people here at MM 0. Nosh your way up and down our famed Duval Street, where close to a zillion coffee bars and juice bars compete with ice cream stands and sweets shops. Or eat in one of our palate-wise restaurants (see our Restaurants chapter). But if you're eating in tonight or tomorrow, you'll want to know what we know: the out-of-the-way shops that help you make Martha Stewart look like an also-ran.

INSIDERS' TIP

Fresh fish has practically no odor at all. The fishy odor becomes more pronounced with time. If you notice a strong disagreeable odor when making your purchase, the fish is not fresh.

Photo: James DiLoreto

Fresh seafood can be enjoyed at some seafood markets, or take the catch-of-the-day home and cook it yourself.

Cafe Europa
1075 Duval St., Duval Square, Key West
• (305) 294-3443

A little taste of the continent awaits you at this charming cafe, where you will most likely overhear several foreign languages from the customers seated at the outdoor tables. Offering mostly German fare and bakery products, Cafe Europa is open for breakfast, lunch and dinner. But it will probably be the baked goods that lure you in. The smell of croissants, Linzer tortes, Danish pastries, cookies and assorted breads fresh from the oven is sure to attract your attention any time of day. For foot-weary travelers, this cafe offers a bonus — free parking. The entrance to the lot is off Simonton Street.

Cole's Peace
930-A Eaton St., Key West
• (305) 292-6511

Bread is the specialty at this tiny European-style bakery, but not just any bread, mind you. These are artisan loaves — each one based on an Old World recipe, handcrafted and baked from scratch. All of the mixing, kneading, rising, shaping and baking are done right on the premises, and every loaf, from sourdough to focaccia, is a work of art. The stock changes daily and with the season. You're apt to find pumpernickel in winter or whole grain laced with mangoes when the fruits are ripe. Housed in the old Salgado Brothers' Market at the corner of Eaton and Grinnell, the bakery is easy to find.

The good smells wafting from the open doors are sure to entice you in.

The Cook's Bazaar
516 Fleming St., Key West
• (305) 296-6656

Tucked amid an eclectic display of gourmet cooking accessories, barrels of exotic coffee beans from all over the world tickle your olfactories in this compact shop. Unusual teas, candies, oils, chutneys and mustards tempt the connoisseur, but the best find is Lighthouse Gourmet Flamingo and Palm Pasta — dried pasta shaped as pink flamingos and green palm trees. Only in the Keys!

Croissants de France
816 Duval St., Key West • (305) 294-2624

If you repressed the calorie count, you could sit here all morning and evening munching French creations and watching the characters stroll Duval. Fifteen types of croissants — cream cheese, coconut, feta, spinach and others — join forces with chocolate eclairs, Key lime mousse and a family of rich pastries. A wide selection of crunchy French breads provides a conscience salvo. The adjoining cafe serves breakfast and lunch, but you can sip cappuccino or latte from the espresso bar anytime.

Flamingo Crossing
1107 Duval St., Key West
• (305) 296-6124

A favorite with locals and visitors alike, Flamingo Crossing is *the* place to pause for refreshment as you make your way up and down Duval. Fresh homemade ice cream is the business here, and you can choose from such flavors as Cuban coffee, raspberry cappuccino, coconut, pina colada, Key lime, passion fruit or green tea, among many others. Or try the ice cream called guanabana/sour sop — two names for the same tasty, delicate fruit. Flamingo Crossing also makes its own sorbet and yogurt. If you're just in the mood for a thirst quencher, try a Key limeade. This tangy concoction will gear you up for a walk all the way from the Gulf to the Atlantic.

Flora & Flipp on Fleming
811 Fleming St., Key West
• (305) 296-1050

Don't be fooled by appearances. This unassuming little neighborhood deli attracts everyone from the movers and shakers of Key West (the mayor is a regular customer) to tourists who just happen on it. Why? Because these folks really know how to make a sandwich. There's a special concoction on the menu each day, but you can enjoy our favorite, the Very Veggie, anytime. The sandwich has avocado, tomato, leaf lettuce, daikon, watercress, beets and red onion with tamari dressing on Cuban bread; it's presented like a gift — wrapped in floral wrapping paper and topped with a candy kiss.

To give your repast the respect it deserves, walk one block up Fleming toward Duval to the brick patio garden beside the pale pink Monroe County Library and sit on a park bench under the palms.

Independent Fisheries
6475-F Second St., Stock Island
• (305) 292-7785

This wholesale fish and seafood operation maintains a small retail counter in the warehouse area of Stock Island. You'll find a selection of fresh locally caught fish, Key West shrimp, stone crab claws and Florida lobster tails.

INSIDERS' TIP

The skin of the grouper is tough, so the fish does not lend itself to cooking whole or as an unskinned fillet. The most important factor to note when buying grouper is the size of the natural fillet. As the fish grow older and larger, their flesh may get tougher and less flavorful. Giants such as the Warsaw grouper (300 to 750 pounds) usually end up as chowder. Those 25 to 50 pounds are best cut up in fingers and fried. Look for grouper in the 2- to 20-pound range for all other preparations.

Heavenly Ham
925 Toppino Dr., Key West
• (305) 292-6444

Off North Roosevelt just past Searstown and First State Bank, Heavenly Ham has a misleading name. Inside the unimposing exterior lies a store that looks just the way you would love your pantry to look. Exotic breads, crackers, pasta, platters, gift tins, gourmet vinegars, sauces of all kinds and baked goods fill this airy country store. More than 60 kinds of whole-bean coffees fill your senses with their aroma. And then there are the meats: whole hams, rib eye, filet mignon, turkey and roast beef are among the choices. Luckily, Heavenly Ham does double time as a deli. Let these folks prepare a platter full of appetizers, a whole country dinner or just a box lunch order for you. You'll be glad you did.

Key West Candy Company
817 Duval St., Key West • (305) 293-8508

Become a kid again — or become your kid's sweet-tooth fairy — with a visit to this old-fashioned candy store. All those wonderful little candies of every shape, size and color sit in covered bins just waiting for copious consumption. Make your selection from chocolates to Gummi Bears to Jelly-Bellies and beyond. Sold by the piece or the pound, these treats will take you back in time. Key West Candy Company will ship anywhere in the United States, so your friends and family back home can nourish their sweet tooth as well.

Key West Key Lime Pie Company
701 Caroline St., Key West
• (305) 294-6567

Key lime pie, a Florida Keys tradition, is the primary business at this Old Town company, established in 1985. Each handmade, 9-inch pie (also sold by the slice) is frozen, literally melting in your mouth, bite by bite. The company will ship the pies anywhere in the continental United States overnight or provide you with a frozen travel pack, so you can take a pie on the road with you or back home by airplane. If Key lime pie isn't your style, treat yourself to an ice cream cone. Cuban coffee and coconut are among the flavorful choices.

Key West Key Lime Shoppe
200 Elizabeth St., Key West
• (305) 296-0806, (800) 376-0806

Key lime yourself into the next century at this little store on the corner of Elizabeth and Greene streets. Everything is made with Key lime juice, including oils, cookies, candy kisses, salad dressings, juice concentrate, pie filling and sweets of all sorts. Go for it.

Klitenick & Katz Bagel Bakery & Delicatessen
2796 N. Roosevelt Blvd., Overseas Market, Key West • (305) 294-3354
914 Duval St., Key West • (305) 294-0067

If not for the palm trees outside the door of this full-service restaurant/deli in the Overseas Market, you'd swear you just walked in from the streets of New York or Chicago. Here, the hot corned beef and pastrami sandwiches are sliced thin and piled high in traditional deli style, the bagels are baked fresh daily and the cans of Dr. Brown's black cherry and cream sodas are icy cold. You can carry out such delicacies as chopped liver, potato knishes, smoked whitefish and kosher franks, along with the bagels and an array of flavored cream cheeses sold by the pound. Try our favorite — the everything bagel "schmeered" with smoked-salmon cream cheese. Breakfast, lunch and dinner are served at tables along one side and at the counter. Deli platters and catering services are also available.

The Duval Street site is a take-out venue only, offering a slightly more limited menu plus free delivery seven days a week to any Old Town address.

Peppers of Key West
291 Front St., Clinton Square Market, Key West • (305) 295-9333

At Peppers, which bills itself as "the hottest spot on the island," chili peppers are the name of the game. More than 300 types of hot sauces already grace the shelves at this establishment in Clinton Square Market, and more arrive from all over every day. Peppers always has a basket of chips and a few open bottles at the front counter so you can have a taste, if you dare. In addition, the folks here will open any bottle in the store if you ask for a sample. Try our favorite — Tahiti Joe's Garlic Hot Sauce — or get a bottle of the best-selling Ring of Fire Hot Sauce. You'll find Key West S.O.B. hot sauces here as well as oils and vinegars and prepared sauces such as pad Thai and sweet-and-sour ginger. Chile pepper memorabilia of all kinds decorates this upbeat store — even Christmas lights! And be sure to look around the neighborhood for the chili pepper car. It belongs to one of the owners and can usually be found parked near Clinton Square.

Pusser's West Indies Candy Company
810 Duval St., Key West • (305) 292-1496

This little shop is evocative of a rustic old mill, with one big exception: The old barrels strewn all over the place are full of jellybeans and saltwater taffy. One corner of the room is off-limits to wandering customers, because it's where they make the fudge. You may see huge bars of fudge cooling on a big metal table. Several other taste-tempting treats are made on the premises including cookies, Key lime pie bars (chocolate-covered pies), coconut patties and rum balls. A selection of spices and sauces is also offered. This store will make custom-decorated gift packages full of all your favorites.

Rusty Anchor Fisheries
5510 Third Ave., Stock Island
• (305) 296-2893

Where's the fish? A little Insider help is needed to negotiate for fish at this place, known to locals as having the freshest at the best prices. The fish market is directly behind Rusty Anchor Restaurant, which is on Fifth Avenue (see our Restaurants chapter), although no sign on Third Avenue indicates the fishmonger's presence. Your safest bet is to enter the restaurant and look for brown double doors at the far end of the room. Exit through these portals, and you will find yourself outside, directly in front of a fish-cleaning building. Ask for Jimmy, who will be about the grounds or in his trailer office. Find out what his catch of the day is, and then it's "Let's make a deal!" Rusty Anchor is known for some of the best prices on jumbo stone crab claws and colossal shrimp ("under 15s"). Alternately, but not as much fun, you can call Jimmy and get the daily fish report by telephone.

Sloppy Joe's Candy and Coffee Co.
291 Front St., Clinton Square Market, Key West • (305) 293-0309

As you walk through the Clinton Square Market down by Mallory Square, you won't be able to pass by this place without stopping because the aroma of freshly baked chocolate chip cookies is overwhelmingly irresistible. Each one of these sweet monsters is a half-pound of yum. You can watch an aproned candy maker prepare fudge atop a marble slab table at one side of this old-fashioned, brick-walled cubbyhole. Taster plates top the counters, more than tempting a nibble of rocky road, Key lime or maple/pecan fudge or almond and macadamia brittle. Coffee is a specialty here, too. The freshly roasted beans — priced dearly at $12.95 to $23.95 per pound — are never more than 10 days old and, we must admit, pass the taste test with high marks.

The candy and coffee company pays a licensing fee for the use of Sloppy Joe's name and icon, most familiarly seen on the marquee above the famous bar on Duval Street.

Stock Island Lobster Co.
6639 Maloney Ave., Stock Island
• (305) 296-5844

This wholesale fishery and lobstering operation doesn't have a showcase retail shop, but it will sell to the general public. Call for prices and availability of the catch of the day (sold as whole fish only), stone crab claws and whole Florida lobsters in season.

INSIDERS' TIP

Shucked oysters are plump and have a natural creamy color and clear liquid. There should be no more than 10 percent liquid, by weight, when shucked oysters are purchased in a container.

Sugar Apple
917 Simonton St., Key West
• **(305) 292-0043**

The largest health-food store in the Florida Keys, Sugar Apple stocks organic and hard-to-find groceries, vitamins, beauty aids, homeopathic remedies, books and herbs. A juice bar and deli serves up sandwiches, smoothies, specials and teas. Therapeutic ball chimes are among the most popular items sold here.

Waterfront Market
201 William St., Key West
• **(305) 296-0778**

The serious cooking aficionado and the robust eater will have a ball in this market, recently relocated to the Caroline Street side of the Historic Keywest Seaport. Browsing the shelves reminds us of perusing an international library. All the weird, difficult-to-find ingredients for Japanese, Thai, Chinese or even Middle Eastern dishes dress the shelves here, often scrutinized by Key West's top professional chefs. A dried-bean emporium showcases bins of baby limas, black beans, pintos and even black-eyed peas. A similar rice case offers sushi rice, hard red, winter wheat and bulgur (and those are just the ones we recognize).

Besides a complete fish market, bakery, deli, coffee-bean center and produce counter, this market stocks some of the best bottled fat-free dressings and marinades we've found anywhere, even off the Rock. Be sure to stop at the juice bar to drink your vitamins before you leave.

Come promenade our pubs, bars and nightclubs from Key Largo to Key West.

Nightlife

In the Florida Keys, what to do after our famous sun sets is a choice as individualistic as our residents and visitors.

But for those revelers who like to party until the wee hours, we take you on a club crawl, tavern tromp, saloon slog — call it what you like. Come promenade our pubs, bars and nightclubs from Key Largo to Sugarloaf Key. Then read on in our Key West section, where a night on the town redefines the cliché.

Bars are open later the farther down you go, with many establishments in Key West open until 4 AM. Taverns and pubs in the Upper and Middle Keys are more likely to close between midnight and 2 AM.

We encourage you to have fun and enjoy our casual Keys pubs, but keep in mind that the DUI limit here is .08, less than other states. Remember, too, that driving-under-the-influence laws apply to all vehicles — scooters and bikes included. So if you drink, don't drive. Or pedal. Take a cab or take along a designated driver.

You'll find the majority of these places open seven nights a week. Exceptions are noted.

The Florida Keys

Upper Keys

Caribbean Club
MM 104 Bayside, Key Largo
• (305) 451-9970

Bogie and Bacall discovered each other at the Caribbean Club in the 1948 film classic Key Largo. What you'll find today is a dark, brooding bar where the barely visible walls are loaded with movie memorabilia. Caribbean Club offers live music Friday, Saturday and Sunday; it's open every night. Designated drivers receive free soft drinks.

Breezer's Tiki Bar
MM 103.8 Bayside, Marriott Bay Beach Resort, Key Largo • (305) 453-0000

Breezer's is an elegant, elevated gazebo-sheltered bar overlooking the showy property and wondrous waters of the Marriott Key Largo Bay Beach Resort. This fantasy island setting provides the perfect backdrop for the accompanying live island-style music on Fridays and Saturdays. Having a drink here is soothing to the soul.

Coconuts Restaurant & Lounge
MM 100 Oceanside, Marina del Mar Resort & Marina, 528 Caribbean Dr., Key Largo • (305) 453-9794

A perennial nightclub favorite with a percolating dance floor, Coconuts has theme nights that keep 'em coming: Monday, disco night; Tuesday, blues; Wednesday, ladies' night, with free drinks to all females from 9 to 11 PM; Thursday, Friday and Saturday, live top-40 dance bands; and Sunday, karaoke. See our Restaurants chapter for dining options here.

Holiday Inn Key Largo Resort & Marina
MM 100 Oceanside, Key Largo
• (305) 451-2121

You'll discover a couple of options at the Holiday Inn Key Largo. Bogie's Cafe has a piano lounge where you can enjoy the tinkling of the ivories. Picking up the pace a bit with live music Thursday through Saturday, a mix of reggae, rock and bop attracts an equal mingling of locals and tourists to the outdoor tiki bar.

Zappie's Bar & Tackle
MM 99.2 Bayside, Key Largo
• **(305) 451-0531**

Offering "live music and live bait," Zappie's seeks a new and unexplored niche in Key Largo nightlife. Formerly a bait and tackle shop only, this establishment is about as Keys funky as it gets, with tin roofs inside and the atmosphere of Everglades City and, well, a tackle shop. Beer and wine only are served. Live music is offered Thursdays through Saturdays.

www.insiders.com

See this and many other **Insiders' Guide®** destinations online — in their entirety.

Visit us today!

Snappers Waterfront Saloon & Raw Bar
MM 94.5 Oceanside, Key Largo
• **(305) 852-5956**

Snappers oozes Keys atmosphere, especially on the cypress-and-palm-frond chickees on the outside waterside deck. Menu items are innovative (see our Restaurants chapter), and patrons enjoy live entertainment on the weekends.

Dockside Lounge
MM 87 Bayside, Plantation Yacht Harbor Resort & Marina, Plantation Key
• **(305) 852-2381**

The Dockside Lounge, referred to fondly as "PYH" by locals who consider it the pulse of their community, offers jazz and blues. Its dance floor beckons all comers on the weekends. The outdoor Lagoon Saloon at Plantation Yacht Harbor rocks at sunset on the weekends with live entertainment as well.

Jammers Grill Room & Party Pub
MM 86.7 Oceanside, Plantation Key
• **(305) 852-8786**

A bellowing jukebox, 14 satellite televisions (including one with a large screen) and a female waitstaff dressed in midriff tops and hot-pink hot pants attract a young, upbeat crowd, especially on weekends when a DJ spins the platters. See our Restaurants chapter for Jammers' tasty menu entrees.

Hog Heaven Sports Bar
MM 85.3 Oceanside, Islamorada
• **(305) 664-9669**

The congenial outdoor saloon of Hog Heaven Sports Bar sits unassumingly on the waterfront. You can consume yourself with televised sports, talk with the locals or head to the point, where a chickee yields seclusion that may foster romance. As you might expect, the pork here is heavenly.

Ocean View Sports Bar
MM 84.5 Oceanside, Islamorada
• **(305) 664-8052**

Known locally as the OV lounge, Ocean View is owned by former Pittsburgh Steeler Gary Dunn and former L.A. Ram Dennis Harrah. Following football is a passion here.

Holiday Isle Resorts & Marina
MM 84 Oceanside, Islamorada
• **(305) 664-2321**

No two ways about it: Ask anyone where the action is around here and, day or night, the answer undoubtedly will be Holiday Isle. With two beaches and a panoply of outdoor restaurants and bars, Holiday Isle buzzes with activity. You can nosh at the Wreck Bar, Raw Bar, Beach Bar or Bimini Treats, enjoy steel drums at Kokomo's or catch the Polynesian show at the Tiki Bar. Come evening, live music at the Tiki Bar raises the adrenaline, and dancers gyrate until the wee hours. Holiday Isle often hosts weekend special events ranging from charity luaus to bikini and body-building contests to Fourth of July fireworks and Halloween costume parties (see our Annual Events chapter).

INSIDERS' TIP

Most Florida Keys watering holes have a happy hour, which often coincides with the sunset celebration.

After the Beach Boys released the song "Kokomo," travelers to the Florida Keys looked all over for the fictitious place. Holiday Isle provided for their needs.

Lorelei Cabana Bar
MM 82 Bayside, Islamorada
• (305) 664-4338

Winning "The People's Choice Award" for the best view of the sunset six years running, Lorelei's outdoor Cabana Bar offers live entertainment seven nights a week, beginning at sunset and continuing by starlight. The bar is a laid-back, waterside watering hole and lunch spot all day long, and the views of Florida Bay cannot be beat. See our Restaurants chapter for dining options here.

Bentley's Raw Bar
MM 82.8 Oceanside, Islamorada
• (305) 664-9094

The upstairs bar at Bentley's Restaurant is small and intimate but usually bustling with a happy-hour crowd and those waiting for a table at this popular eatery (see our Restaurants chapter). Noshing on fresh raw bar offerings brings to mind an after-work Manhattan crowd, but there isn't a power suit or necktie in sight.

Woody's Saloon & Restaurant
MM 82 Bayside, Islamorada
• (305) 664-4335

Woody's Chicago-style pizza is great, but this saloon's claim to fame just has to be its regular entertainment offering: Big Dick and the Extenders. A suggestive play on words, Big Dick is most certainly a tall man, and his schtick — making rude fun of members of the audience — makes Howard Stern look like a choir boy. The Extenders do play some music, but the audience-participation dirty joke contest allows Dick, who wears a very big top hat, to sharpen his barbs. Sit in the back unless you have a thick skin or a penchant for verbal abuse. Oh, and having said that, there is always a line waiting outside for the privilege of admission to Woody's.

Middle Keys

WatersEdge
MM 61 Oceanside, Hawk's Cay Resort & Marina, Duck Key • (305) 743-7000

A large dance floor heats up the action with live entertainment on Friday and Saturday nights, but the rest of the week this local watering hole, just off the Hawk's Cay Marina, finds guides, island residents and hotel guests trading fish stories. The bar area fronts the popular family-style restaurant, also called WatersEdge (see our Restaurants chapter).

Dockside Lounge
MM 53 Oceanside, 35 Sombrero Rd., Sombrero Marina, Marathon • (305) 743-0000

The dock rocks during Sunday night jam sessions, when bands from throughout Florida showcase their talents. This laid-back, open-air harborside lounge is a hub for Boot Key liveaboards, who ride dinghies to shore and park their bicycles and cars nearby. Live entertainment is offered nightly at Dockside.

Gary's Pub & Billiards
MM 49 Oceanside, Marathon • (305) 743-0622

Gary's took over the nightlife scene in Marathon with a quick eight-ball in the corner pocket. This billiard parlor cum public house draws a diverse crowd, all happy to partake of libations aside the long mahogany bar, shoot pool or OD on sporting events televised simultaneously on all of Gary's 25 television screens. Hot hors d'oeuvres are offered during happy hour. An electronic sobriety test can tell whether or not you should take a taxi home.

Angler's Lounge
MM 48 Bayside, Faro Blanco Resort & Marina, Marathon • (305) 743-9018

Live entertainment sets the stage at Angler's, a popular nightspot amid the Faro Blanco Resort. Situated topside of Kelsey's Restaurant, adjacent to the resort's swimming pool, Angler's concocts island drinks such as the Pink Cadillac, Mud Ball and Goombay Smash. Be sure to try the Australian ring-toss game or a round of darts between sets. (See our Restaurants chapter for Angler's lunchtime offerings.)

Lower Keys

No Name Pub
MM 31 Bayside, N. Watson Blvd., Big Pine Key • (305) 872-9115

Wallpapered with dollar bills and full of good cheer and local color, No Name Pub is a must-do, night or day (see our Restaurants chapter for menu offerings and directions). Off the beaten path about as far as you can go in Big Pine, this small saloon sports a funky bar and a pool table.

The Sandbar
MM 28.5 Bayside, Barry Ave., Little Torch Key • (305) 872-9989

High on stilt legs above the Big Pine Channel of the Gulf, The Sandbar's pavilion-like interior beckons Lower Keys wassailers. Party bashes celebrating the full moon, Valentine's Day, the Kentucky Derby and more compete with myriad pool tables and an enormous bar. An all-day, all-night menu will satisfy any hunger pangs (see our Restaurants chapter).

Boondocks
MM 27.5 Bayside, Ramrod Key • (305) 872-0022

This open-air, thatched-roof gathering place, surrounded by copious plantings of coconut palms and cooled by Bahama fans, offers a light-bite menu from lunchtime to bedtime. Built in 1989 by Miccosukee Indians who specialize in palm thatching, the casual bar bursts with activity: televised sports, billiards and horseshoes. On Monday night, women can drink two for one, and on Sunday evenings outdoor live entertainment draws a crowd of locals to the starlit dance floor. Boondocks serves beer and wine only.

Mangrove Mama's
MM 20 Bayside, Sugarloaf Key
• (305) 745-3030

Something of an institution in the Lower Keys, Mangrove Mama's grooves on Friday and Saturday nights, when the Caribbean-style roadhouse restaurant puts away the good china and pulsates with live entertainment. Sundays feature the famed reggae fest, and as they say, "the joint is jumpin'." Space is limited here, so be sure to plan ahead so you aren't disappointed. Reservations are suggested for dining (see our Restaurants chapter for dining options.)

Key West

Key West lays claim to more bars per capita than anywhere else in the United States. With many bars open seven days a week until 4 AM, this tiny island lives up to its slightly eccentric reputation. The intrepid traveler will want to experience some of these establishments via an age-old tradition called the "Duval Crawl." This journey simply entails sampling wares from one place, then moving along to the next.

We have presented here some of the highlights of such a crawl. We start at the Atlantic end of Duval Street, where the pubs are more sparse, and move toward the Gulf of Mexico, where the kegs flow freely. Note: We do not recommend trying to take in every establishment listed here in one night, but if you do try, please take a taxi when you finish (see our Getting Here, Getting Around chapter).

Of course, not all the bars in Key West are on Duval Street. We have also included a section called Local Favorites — Key West classics that are a little more off the beaten path but definitely worth checking out. Cheers!

The Quintessential Duval Crawl

801 Bourbon Bar
801 Duval St., Key West • (305) 294-4737

With a clientele consisting of primarily gay patrons and tourists, the 801 offers a first-floor bar with billiards. A second floor offers live entertainment with drag shows nightly.

Bourbon Street Pub
724 Duval St., Key West • (305) 296-1992

Live entertainment at the predominantly gay Bourbon Street includes bands, drag shows, comedians and, on weekends, male dancers. Key West's only VJ plays tunes, mixing videos with songs for dancing. The emphasis here is on high-energy dance music. Happy hour is noon to 8 PM daily, and Friday is the Drag Your Ass to Bourbon Street party, when all bartenders dress in drag and the bar sees its largest crowd of the week.

Diva's
711 Duval St., Key West • (305) 292-8500

There's never a cover charge at this, Key West's newest and most popular dance club, where the music is loud and the action doesn't really get started until well past 10 PM. The club attracts a varied clientele, but is largely frequented by gay revelers. Happy hour runs from noon to 8 PM. Stop in for a drink and be sure to stay for the show — drag queens strut their stuff on stage here nightly.

Green Parrot
601 Whitehead St., Key West
• (305) 294-6133

Not exactly on Duval Street, but close enough and so quintessentially Key West, the Green Parrot rates a stop on any Duval Crawl. Frequented primarily by locals since its inception in the 1970s, this eclectic bar is housed in an 1890s-era building a half-block off Duval down Southard Street. Walls are adorned with unusual oversize portraits and a wall mural of the Garden of Eden. Weekends feature local and national bands playing blues and zydeco, and the large dance floor is usually crowded. The bar also sports video games, billiard tables, darts, a pinball machine and a jukebox.

One Saloon
524 Duval St., Key West • (305) 296-8118

Dimly lit and intimate, One Saloon features exotic male dancers nightly. This primarily gay nightclub has three bars, a disc jockey, dance floor and billiards. One Saloon is accessed through a side entrance at Appelrouth Lane.

Mulcahy's Tavern
509½ Duval St., Key West
• (305) 295-8797

Stop in at this popular locals' watering hole for a little taste of Dublin on Duval. Guinness is the drink of choice here, and on the menu you'll find plenty of mouthwatering Irish fare. Live bands are featured on Friday and Saturday nights.

Jimmy Buffett's Margaritaville Cafe
500 Duval St., Key West • (305) 292-1435

Yes, the big man himself does play here once in a while, as do some of the Coral Reefers, such as Fingers Taylor and Peter Mayer, and bands that have opened for Jimmy on tour. Props from past concerts decorate the walls and ceiling. Beginning at 10:30 each night and continuing well into the wee hours, a variety of bands and solo artists perform everything from rock 'n' roll to reggae to rhythm and blues. Margaritas are just one of the many frozen drinks offered at the air-conditioned yet open-air bar. An adjacent store sells Buffett clothing, recordings, books and memorabilia (see our Restaurants chapter).

Celebrities at La Concha Hotel
430 Duval St., Key West • (305) 296-2991

With its art deco styling and classic glassware, this glitzy, ground-floor hotel bar has a 1920s New York feel. But when the doors are open onto bustling Duval, you'll know you're definitely in 1990s Key West. Grab a spot at the bar or at one of the linen-covered cocktail tables for the nightly entertainment — jazz, blues and, if you're lucky, perhaps even The Fabulous Spectrelles, an all-girl singing trio straight out of the '60s.

Hard Rock Cafe
313 Duval St., Key West • (305) 293-0230

A world-renowned classic, Hard Rock Cafe joined the Conch Republic in the summer of 1996. Situated in a renovated, three-story, Conch-style house on Duval Street, Hard Rock Cafe Key West celebrates historic Key West,

the preservation of the Florida Keys' fragile environment and, of course, rock 'n' roll. This 235-seat Hard Rock marks the 57th location worldwide. It is open seven days a week and serves up all-American fare.

Fat Tuesday
305 Duval St., Key West • (305) 296-9373

Stop in at Fat Tuesday and choose from one of 26 flavors of frozen drinks, including Margaritas, pina coladas, 190 Octane and rum runners. Our favorite is the Pain in the Ass, a combination pina colada and rum runner. The motto here is "One daiquiri, two daiquiri, three daiquiri, floor," and you can even buy a T-shirt that says it.

Bull and Whistle
280 Duval St., Key West • (305) 296-4545

This local favorite is actually three bars in one. The Bull is downstairs and features live music in an open-air setting. The Whistle is upstairs and offers pool and video games, along with a great view of Duval Street from the balcony. The Garden of Eden, on the very top, has a great view of Key West . . . and more. It's the only clothing-optional roof garden in town.

Rumrunners/Hideaway/Upstarez/ Channel Zero
218 Duval St., Key West • (305) 294-1017

This entertainment complex has something for everyone. Rumrunners offers reggae nightly; the Hideaway presents live alternative rock; Upstarez features live adult entertainment; and Channel Zero caters to the classic rock crowd.

Durty Harry's/Rick's/Angelina's Pizzeria/Red Garter Saloon
208 Duval St.

Owner Mark Rossi offers four nightspots in one complex. Durty Harry's Bar, (305) 296-5513, features acoustic guitars and karaoke in a first-floor, sports bar setting. Rick's Bar, (305) 296-4890, is an all-mirror, second-floor discotheque. Angelina's Pizzeria, (305) 296-3600, satisfies late-night cravings, and the Red Garter Saloon, (305) 296-4964, is a mirror-and-brass adult club. Pick your pleasure.

Captain Tony's Saloon
428 Greene St., Key West
• (305) 294-1838

Just a half-block off Duval, this watering hole is the site of Key West's first hanging tree, still in evidence inside the bar. Captain Tony's is the original location of Sloppy Joe's. Once owned by Capt. Tony Tarracino, a friend of Jimmy Buffett and a former Key West mayor, the saloon features walls concealed by undies and business cards. Live entertainment is offered nightly.

Sloppy Joe's Bar
201 Duval St., Key West • (305) 294-5717

It's no wonder this was Hemingway's favorite watering hole. The upbeat atmosphere of Sloppy Joe's is contagious. The bar opened in 1933 on the site of what is now Captain Tony's Saloon. In 1937 it moved to its current location. Some say that Hemingway did some writing in the back rooms of the bar and kept a few of his manuscripts locked up here. Photos of Hemingway line the walls. Live entertainment is offered from noon to 2 AM daily except Monday, when entertainment is replaced at 9 PM with a "Moon Dance," with free T-shirts awarded winners of the dance contest. Among the brews offered here is Sloppy Joe's beer, which is brewed by Coors. A gift shop sells T-shirts, boxer shorts, hats and other souvenirs with the Sloppy Joe's logo.

Around the corner and upstairs, you'll find Sloppy Joe's Speak Easy, an intimate little cigar bar where the specialty of the house is a chilled martini and a more genteel atmosphere. The Speak Easy is open daily, noon to 4 AM. Look for the entrance on Greene Street, between Sloppy Joe's Food and Bar.

Hog's Breath Saloon
400 Front St., Key West • (305) 292-2032

"The Hog," as locals know this place, features an open-air mahogany bar surrounded by watersports-related memorabilia, including mounted fish and surfboards. You can try the medium-bodied Hog's Breath beer and sample one of the saloon's famed fish sandwiches. The restaurant (see our Restaurants chapter) is open for lunch and dinner. Live bands play rock, folk rock, blues and jazz throughout the day and well into the evening. You can purchase T-shirts, hats and sundry other items emblazoned with the saloon's slogan: "Hog's Breath is better than no breath at all."

Planet Hollywood
108 Duval St., Key West • (305) 295-0003

Planet Hollywood puts Key West on the international music map with a new location on Duval Street, joining such worldly locales as Cancun, Maui, New York City and many more. One of a growing number of these themed restaurants owned by Sylvester Stallone, Bruce Willis and others, Planet Hollywood Key West is worth a stop. Head for the bar for some cocktails, or have yourself some rocking good American food. Reservations are not necessary. Planet Hollywood is open seven days a week.

Pier House Resort
1 Duval St., Key West • (305) 296-4600

Pier House offers a little something for everyone. The view of the famous Key West sunset is great from here, and in high season the indoor-outdoor Havana Docks offers calypso entertainment with dancing on weekend evenings. Or settle in and enjoy the piano bar in the dimly lit Wine Galley. The tiny Chart Room Bar, which is filled with peanut shells, is a favorite locals' hangout.

INSIDERS' TIP

If you plan to imbibe, be sure to carry ID. Anyone who looks under 30 will likely be carded, especially in Key West, where underage spring breakers try their best each year to circumvent the law. (They rarely succeed, by the way.)

Local Favorites

Isle. Enjoy live Irish music Wednesday through Saturday.

The Afterdeck Bar at Louie's Backyard
700 Waddell Ave., Key West
• (305) 294-1061

The deck is large and right on the water. And we do mean right on the water. One false step, a few cocktails too many and . . . splash! Service is friendly and courteous, and the setting is exactly what you were thinking of when you first thought of coming to the Florida Keys. The adjoining restaurant is one of Key West's finest (see our Restaurants chapter under Louie's Backyard).

Atlantic Shores Resort
510 South St., Key West • (305) 296-2491

The weekly tea dance at Atlantic Shores — Key West's own version of Miami's South Beach-style art deco joints — draws Sunday night partyers in droves. A poolside disc jockey plays dance tunes, and a wait staff serves cocktails. The pool area at Atlantic Shores is clothing optional and tends to be mostly frequented by gays. On Thursday nights, Atlantic Shores also shows artistic independent and foreign films not found at the big cinemas as well as some popular recent flicks you may have missed; call for details.

Finnegan's Wake Irish Pub & Eatery
320 Grinnell St., Key West
• (305) 293-0222

Exactly like a good Irish public house ought to be, Finnegan's keeps the merriment going until nearly dawn (4 AM) and is among a mere handful of Key West establishments serving food into the wee hours (see our Restaurants chapter). You're sure to find your Guinness here, and you can even down a Black and Tan. Order one an' the barkeep will think ye just returned from the Emerald

Flagler's Steakhouse and Lounge
Marriott's Casa Marina, 1500 Reynolds St., Key West • (305) 296-3535

Live music kicks off nightly beginning at 9 PM. Dance to the dulcet vocal sounds of Carmen Rodriguez Thursday through Saturday or catch Lonnie Jacobson on the bass with his friends on keyboard, sax and percussion Sunday through Wednesday. The Monday-night jam sessions with Lonnie and friends are especially popular.

Key West Bar and Grill and Down Under Sports Bar
1970 N. Roosevelt Blvd., Key West
• (305) 294-1970

This is two bars in one. Upstairs is the Key West Bar and Grill, where you can order a tasty, fresh-grilled fish sandwich and a beer to accompany. Downstairs is Down Under, the "bar with balls." Free pool and popcorn draw the locals back time and again.

PT's Late Night Bar & Grill
920 Caroline St., Key West
• (305) 296-4245

This local gathering spot offers billiards, darts, trivia games and the opportunity to catch up with friends over a variety of homestyle meals or drinks. The pot roast here is legendary. Televised sports provide most of the entertainment, but PT's hosts a late-night "Bars Party" the first Monday of each month, when Key West bar and restaurant employees receive free food and happy-hour drink prices. Live bands occasionally perform.

Schooner Wharf Bar
202 William St., Key West
• (305) 292-9520

Dockside at the Historic Key West Bight is the open-air, thatched-palm Schooner

Wharf, which bills itself as "the last little bit of old Key West." The place offers outdoor thatched-umbrella tables, a covered bar, grill and indoor games, including billiards and darts. Live jazz, rhythm and blues and island music are featured each Thursday through Saturday night. Wednesday at the Wharf is ladies' night.

Stick and Stein Sports Rock Cafe
Key Plaza Shopping Center, 2922 N. Roosevelt Blvd., Key West
• **(305) 296-3352**

With pool tables galore, air hockey, darts, video and pinball games, Stick and Stein earns its reputation as the biggest sports bar in Key West. Watch the game of your choice on one of the many big-screen TVs, or just hunker down for a drink at one of the three bars. If your appetite beckons, satisfy it with some classic bar food.

Sun Sun Pavilions and Raw Bar
Marriott's Casa Marina, 1500 Reynolds St., Key West • (305) 296-3535

Tucked beside the ocean on the grounds of the Casa Marina, this combination tiki bar and open-air restaurant offers one of the best pina coladas on the island. Singer/guitarist Joel Nelson has played this seaside venue for more than a decade. Some guests return here year after year just to hear him play his original compositions as well as those made famous by the likes of Jimmy Buffett, James Taylor and Van Morrison.

Turtle Kraals Waterfront Seafood Grill and Bar
1 Lands End Village, Key West
• **(305) 294-2640**

The lounge portion of this turtle cannery-turned-restaurant rocks throughout the evening, offering live entertainment and billiard tables in an open-air, waterfront setting (see our Restaurants chapter). Turtle Kraals' full bar is known for its frozen Margaritas, microbrewed beers and imported beers on tap. Blues bands perform each Wednesday through Saturday. Happy hour is 4 to 6:30 PM with 99¢ tacos and 33¢ oysters available on Tuesdays. For a great view of the wharf, climb up to TK's new upstairs bar. It opens daily at 3 PM.

Whether the accommodations are large, small or somewhere in-between, all of our guest properties exude a casual, barefoot ambiance.

Accommodations

From luxury resorts to little-known hideaways, the Florida Keys' myriad accommodations suit every vacation fantasy and budget.

What began in the 1930s as a small assortment of fishing camps experienced a renaissance after World War II ended. Henry Flagler's railroad and the creation of the Overseas Highway had made our islands more accessible, but residents still relied on cisterns for fresh water until water lines were installed to service the Key West naval base during World War II. The availability of fresh water made our region a more civilized and desirable vacation destination, and, by the 1950s and 1960s when motoring became a popular means of travel, hotels and motels sprang up all over our islands.

Location and Amenities

Like our Conchs — those of us born in the Keys — and Keys characters — those of us who were not — accommodations in the Florida Keys are highly individualistic. Most are situated on the Florida Bay, the Gulf of Mexico or the Atlantic Ocean. We commonly refer to the Atlantic as "oceanside." For simplicity's sake in this chapter, we refer to the bayside and gulfside as "bayside."

You can enjoy swimming and watersports in either the bay or the ocean. Expect to find our coastline waters calmer than those you may have encountered in the rest of South Florida. The waters of the Gulf of Mexico and Florida Bay cover shallow seagrass flats, and the barrier reef, some 4 to 5 miles offshore in the Atlantic, breaks the surf, thereby keeping waters inside the reef from 1 to 3 feet most of the time. The oceanside coastline is also fronted with shallow flats in places. The interruption of wave action by the coral reef dictates that the Florida Keys does not have an abundance of natural beaches. Most of our beaches are man-made and unsupervised.

Oceanside accommodations offer exotic sunrises and proximity to dive sites, oceanside flats and bluewater locations for sportfishing. Water access is generally deeper on the ocean side than in the bay, affording boaters and sailors more options. Bayside lodgings can boast of our spectacular Keys sunsets, which sink into the placid skinny waters of the Gulf like a meltdown of molten lava. Some hotels, motels, resorts and inns sit alongside inland canals or marina basins, and many of our waterfront facilities are accessible by boat.

Many of our small mom-and-pop motels you will see lining the Overseas Highway were primarily built in the 1950s and 1960s as fishing camps. These facilities offer basic, affordable rooms and efficiencies, some with screened patios. Mom-and-pop motels often draw cost-conscious families, last-minute travelers, anglers and scuba divers — those active, outdoorsy types seeking nothing more than a bed and a shower. These motels have a high return rate.

Also individually owned, but often with more expansive waterfront properties and recreational amenities, are facilities that offer a potpourri of accommodation options, ranging from sleeping rooms to efficiencies to multiple-bedroom apartments, often within one diverse property. Many sleeping rooms provide mini-refrigerators and have balconies, while efficiencies offer abbreviated kitchens as well. Suites, villas and cottages will allow you the space to spread out a bit and to cook a meal or two "at home" when the mood hits. They usually have a sleeper sofa in the living space and a full kitchen. These accommodations often maintain freshwater swimming pools, hot tubs and guest laundry facilities. If they don't offer on-premises watersports, these recreational activities are almost always located nearby. Since all of these properties have evolved over the decades with a multitude of owners, ask whether your accommodations have been updated recently. Most owners renovate when the budget allows, so some rooms or cottages may be more desirable than others.

Our large comprehensive resorts offer all the amenities of a mom-and-pop facility and then some. From fitness to child-care centers and concierge to room services, these hotels cater to families and honeymooners, business travelers and sports en-thusiasts, power players and movie stars. You'll find tennis courts and watersports, fishing char-ters and dive excursions. Some offer optional con-ference rooms or a vari-ety of travel/sport packages. Couples often opt for romantic weddings and honeymoons amid our tropical breezes, lush foliage, crystal seas and magnificent sunsets.

And when spring break rolls around, col-lege students throughout the country flood our hotels, beaches, tiki bars and nightspots.

Whether the accommodations are large, small or somewhere in-between, all of our guest properties exude a casual, barefoot am-biance. To one degree or another, all bestow the uninterrupted escape for which the Florida Keys has always been known.

Rate Information

Rate structures for Keys lodgings vary nearly as much as the accommodations them-selves, but you can draw a few generaliza-tions. Rates fluctuate by season and depend largely upon the size of the accommodation and its proximity to the water.

High season (December through April) supports the highest rates. High-season rates usually prevail during sport lobster sea-son in July (a near-holiday in the Keys; see our Diving chapter), Fantasy Fest in the au-tumn (our southernmost decadent version of Mardi Gras; see our Annual Events chap-ter) and most national holiday weekends. You must make reservations well in advance of your visit during any of these times. Many facilities fully book available accommoda-tions one year in advance for high season and the holidays.

A second season commences in May and continues through the summer months, attract-ing vacationers seeking to escape the steamy heat of the rest of Florida and the deep South. Rates during this period are generally slightly less than high season.

Low season is September and October, bringing a savings of about 20 percent off high-season rates. Some facilities maintain low-season rates into November as well.

Rates for motel or sleeping rooms, which typically hold two double beds, are based on single or double oc-cupancy. Additional guests are charged a supplementary fee, but motels impose a maximum occupancy for each room.

Children younger than 13 frequently are permitted to stay for free when accompanied by an adult. Cribs and cots often are provided at no charge or at a minimal additional cost.

Condominiums, villas and cottages gen-erally establish a weekly rate per unit, but many also offer a three- or four-night pack-age as well, which is priced per night. Ac-commodations of like stature will command differing prices, depending upon how close they are to the waterfront and what kind of view they offer.

If you prefer accommodations overlook-ing the bay or ocean, ask for a bayfront or oceanfront room. Sometimes waterfront means a canal or lagoon. Be sure to query. Water view does not necessarily mean that your room will be on or facing the water, but as a general rule, water view is less expen-sive and provides at least a glimpse of the bay or ocean. Garden views and non-water-front accommodations, often just a short walk to water's edge, are priced even lower.

We suggest you shop around for exact daily or weekly rates and vacancies. Be sure to ask if the facility offers any discounted rates. Sometimes you can luck into a short-term dis-count or sport package that will be just what you are seeking.

In all cases, rates are expressed for the high season. Prices for motel or sleeping room facilities are figured on a double-occu-

Photo: Cheeca Lodge

Many Keys accommodations offer both swimming pools and ocean or gulf frontage.

pancy average rate per night. Villas, efficiencies and condominium units, which generally establish rates per unit rather than per person, will be quoted as such. And even though these units traditionally are rented by the week, we have computed our code on an average daily rate so that you can compare apples with apples.

It is not uncommon to find accommodations that run the gamut of several price code categories all at the same place. The code will indicate if you can expect a range of space and pocketbook possibilities. (Accommodations in Key West generally are more expensive than the rest of the Keys, therefore we have established separate pricing keys for Key West accommodations.)

Price codes are figured without additional fees, such as room service and calls, and without the 11.5 percent room tax. Our recommended accommodations accept major credit cards unless otherwise specified.

Price-Code Key

$	$55 to $95
$$	$96 to $150
$$$	$151 to $250
$$$$	$251 and higher

Reservation and Cancellation Policies

Typically, you confirm your room by holding it with a major credit card. If you do not have a major credit card, you may often hold a room with an advance check or money order. The balance — always paid with a credit card, traveler's checks or cash — will be collected either upon check-in or checkout. Be aware that cancellation policies vary.

If you do not cancel your room within a property's specified advance time, you will likely be charged a sizable fee whether or not you arrive. And when you pay for a room upon check-in, most facilities do not provide refunds or credits if you pay for more days than you are able to stay.

During high season and special events, our facilities almost always are full. You might benefit from a no-show on a walk-in basis late at night, but we suggest reserving and confirming dates, accommodations and prices three to six months in advance. More desirable facilities fill up most rapidly, and special events sometimes require one year advance planning.

To avoid potential complications, be sure to inquire about all details of your accommodations when making reservations and confirmations. Obtain a confirmation number and the full name of the reservationist who assists you.

If you are planning to arrive at one of our resort marinas by sailing or motor yacht, be sure to read our Cruising chapter first. Dockage space for transient cruisers is at a premium at these desirable establishments and is often booked a year in advance during high season. Be sure to ascertain water depth and size restrictions of the marina before you venture here in your vessel. Many of our recommended accommodations offer marina facilities where you may bring your own trailered boat and, for a small daily fee, secure dockage of your craft for the duration of your stay. The boat basins of these facilities are usually not as deep as the resort marinas that accommodate large vessels and therefore are more suitable for shallow-draft boats. Those accommodations offering accessibility by boat have been noted throughout.

Check-in time typically is after 2 PM, and checkout is between 10 and 11 AM. Some facilities levy an extra charge if you occupy your room after checkout time. But, in some cases, the management is prepared to keep your luggage safe while you soak in a few extra rays before catching that flight home. They may even have a room designated for you to shower and change before you leave. It is always better to inquire than to ignore posted checkout times.

In this chapter, we escort you through some of the Florida Keys' more outstanding facilities. Our selections are based on attributes of rooms, service, location, property and/or overall ambiance. Listed by descending mile marker number beginning with Key Largo in the Upper Keys and heading down the Keys to Big Coppitt, these facilities encompass a wide assortment of styles and rates. In the Key West section, we switch to alphabetical order; we also provide a separate section of inns and guest houses in our southernmost city, with a corresponding pricing code for those accommodations.

The Florida Keys

Upper Keys

At the top of the Keys, Key Largo, home of John Pennekamp Coral Reef State Park, bustles with an energetic crowd of divers and snorkelers in all seasons. The orientation here is definitely geared toward the underwater treasures of the coral reef that lies just 4 miles offshore. Many motels and resorts in this area offer dive and snorkel packages.

The settlement of Tavernier stretches from Key Largo to Plantation Key, or from about MM 94 to MM 88. This quiet area is known for its historic qualities. Dubbed the Sportfishing Capital of the World, Islamorada, which stretches from Plantation Key to Lower Matecumbe Key, is renowned for its contingent of talented gamefishing guides (see our Fishing chapter) as well as prestigious fishing tournaments. Islamorada incorporated in 1998.

INSIDERS' TIP

For information about accommodations in Key West — whether you're looking for a quaint guesthouse or a full-service resort — call the Key West Information Center at (305) 292-5000. The service is free.

The Blackfin Resort
Motel & Marina

4½ Acres Situated on the Gulf of Mexico
40 Newly Renovated Rooms
Restaurant • Bar • Marina

4650 Overseas Highway, Marathon, FL 33050

(305) 743-2393   **800-548-KEYS**   Fax (305) 743-6417

The Upper Keys pulsates with tiki bars and watering holes as well as an array of fine restaurants (see our Restaurants and Nightlife chapters). Generation Xers head for a popular nearby party spot known as Holiday Isle. Excursions to historic Indian Key and Lignumvitae Key and daytrips to Theater of the Sea, which offers dolphin and sea lion shows and allows guests to swim with the dolphins, rate high on the list of things to do for families and sports enthusiasts alike (see our Attractions chapter).

Amy Slate's Amoray Dive Resort
$$-$$$ • MM 104 Bayside, Key Largo
• (305) 451-3595, (800) 426-6729

About 80 percent of the guests at Amy Slate's Amoray Dive Resort are divers. An eclectic collection of plantation-style villas springs to life daily as the undersea enthusiasts rustle about, eager to embark on the resort's 45-foot *Amoray Diver* for the half-hour ride to John Pennekamp Coral Reef State Park (see our Diving and Snorkeling and Recreation chapters).

Amy Slate's Amoray owes its name in part to *People* magazine. The publication sent a writer to Key Largo to cover an Amy Slate underwater wedding "crashed" by a moray eel, and thus coined the term "That's Amoray."

The rooms here, renovated in 1996, are named after tropical fish. Varying in size, amenities and price, the rooms range from the standard motel variety to small apartments with full kitchens. The accommodations all have ceiling fans and feature tile floors, queen-size beds and day beds. Two-story, two-bedroom, two-bath duplexes accommodate as many as eight guests; they offer full kitchens and screened porches with personal hammocks. Some accommodations afford partial water views.

A pool and Jacuzzi front Florida Bay, and a bayfront sun deck and small sandy area at the water's edge sport a picnic table, barbecue grill and hammock, allowing for off-property swimming, snorkeling and fishing. Continental breakfast is included in the room rate. Boat slips are available.

Kelly's on the Bay
$$ • MM 104.2 Bayside, Key Largo
• (305) 451-1622, (800) 226-0415

Well known as a dedicated dive resort, Kelly's is a 1950s-style island-Caribbean motel. Constantly updated, the rooms feature tile floors, bright window treatments, wicker furnishings and eclectic wall hangings. Efficiencies feature refrigerators, stoves and sinks.

Part of the Kelly's operation is Aqua Nuts Dive Center. Two 46-foot dive boats transport guests to underwater sites within John Pennekamp Coral Reef State Park (see our Diving and Snorkeling chapter). Guests enjoy

Kelly's heated pool, situated to take full advantage of the spectacular sunsets over Florida Bay. Complimentary kayaks are available to explore a small adjacent cove.

Kelly's provides a complimentary full "divers" breakfast to all guests. These facilities are boat-accessible.

Marriott Key Largo Bay Beach Resort
$$$-$$$$ • MM 103.8 Bayside, Key Largo
• (305) 453-0000, (800) 932-9332

Bayside sunset views and a primo location near John Pennekamp Coral Reef State Park mark only two of a multitude of pluses at the Marriott Key Largo Bay Beach Resort. The 153 hotel rooms of this Key West-style resort vary in view (bayview and deluxe bayview cost more) but all include a room safe, mini-bar, pay-per-view in addition to free cable television, hair dryer and coffee maker. All but 20 have patios.

Rooms are equipped with voice mail and a data port. For more spacious quarters but more dearly priced, each of 23 suites —1,000 square feet apiece — has a full kitchen, a full bathroom, a queen-size sleeper sofa in the living room and two other bedrooms, one with a king-size bed and one with two doubles. Wraparound patios provide panoramic views of Florida Bay and its famed sunsets. For the royal treatment, the resort also offers one 1,400-square-foot penthouse suite, which, in addition to the amenities of the other suites, features a Roman tub in the master bedroom as well as a bath-and-a-half.

Treat yourself to libation or dining at one of Marriott Key Largo Bay's restaurants or bars — Gus' Grille (see our Restaurants chapter); Breezer's Tiki Bar & Grille (see our Nightlife chapter); or Flipper's Pool Bar, aside the pool, hot tub and beach area. The beat heats up on weekend evenings with late-night live entertainment at Gus' After Dark nightclub.

The resort also features a fitness area with state-of-the-art equipment and offers a full-service European-style health spa as well as therapeutic sea-breeze-kissed massage in a private open-air tiki hut. A nine-hole "putting challenge" golf course, "hot clock" basketball, table bowling, Ping-Pong, horseshoes and Velcro target toss stand ready to amuse you. Marriott

Key Largo Bay Beach Resort also has a tennis court. A boutique shop in the lobby called By the Way will lure the shopaholics. It's A Dive provides on-premises watersports selections ranging from diving, snorkeling, parasailing and glass-bottom boat excursions to boat or personal watercraft rentals.

Fishing charters can be booked through the hotel as well. Guests receive unlimited passage aboard the *Sun Cruz* casino boat (see our Recreation chapter). Boat dockage is available for guests' vessels at no extra charge. Marriott also offers a full activities program for children ages 5 to 15.

Jules' Undersea Lodge
$$$$ • MM 103.2 Oceanside,
Transylvania Ave., Key Largo
• (305) 451-2353

If you prefer a room under the water rather than beside it, head on down — way down — to the gem of a dive known as Jules' Undersea Lodge in Key Largo. About 30 feet beneath the surface of the Emerald Lagoon at Key Largo Undersea Park, Jules' serves as a research habitat and as the world's only underwater hotel.

Talk about a great view of the water!

Guests scuba dive in order to reach the lodge, which resembles a submarine resting on the sea bottom. Baggage is carried in watertight cases by bellhops. The two-bedroom air-conditioned suite is equipped with hot showers, TV and VCR, a stereo system, a telephone, VHF and radio and a living room and galley. The radio and intercom are monitored 24 hours a day. Room service is available.

In 1972 a biologist built the lodge as an undersea research laboratory. Later, he converted it to an underwater hotel. Cables connect the lodge to headquarters at the lagoon's surface, whereby fresh water, electricity, communications and compressed air are transmitted. NASA has often used the lodge to study the effects of extended space travel, and famous Key West treasure salvager Mel Fisher spent his 30th wedding anniversary here.

Key Largo Undersea Park arranges underwater weddings and caters to underwater honeymoons. Guests who are not certified divers must take an introductory course with an instructor at an additional cost. Accommodations include diving, lodging and meals. A choice of package options is available.

To find Jules' Undersea Lodge, turn on Transylvania Avenue toward the ocean and follow the signs to the carved mermaid entrance gate of Key Largo Undersea Park.

Largo Lodge
$$ • MM 102 Bayside, Key Largo
• (305) 451-0424

A secluded, romantic, rain-forest setting greets you at this old-island-style adults-only hideaway. At Largo Lodge, a collection of three rustic duplex cottages is nestled among lush, tropical gardens overflowing with bromeliads, orchids and trickling water fountains. A quiet and spacious sandy pier faces the waters of Florida Bay, where you can relax and read, swim, picnic or simply worship the sun. And you may meet one of the contingent of wild birds that frequents the premises.

Each one of the lodge's six ground-level concrete block-style units features one bedroom, a living/dining combination, full kitchen, terrazzo floors with area rugs, open-beamed cathedral ceilings with fans and French doors opening to spacious screened patios. Bedrooms feature two double beds; some units have sleeper sofas, and rollaways are provided. The private, tiled baths — still authentically '50s — are old but functional. Maximum capacity in each unit is four occupants.

Largo Lodge's owner, Harriet Stokes, collects ceramic memorabilia from the 1940s and 1950s, which you'll see decorating the rooms. Boat dockage is available, but you should launch your boat at a public ramp (see our Boating chapter) and bring it around to Largo Lodge, because the lush tropical plantings make it difficult to maneuver a trailer.

Marina Del Mar Resort and Marina
$$-$$$$ • MM 100 Oceanside, Key Largo
• (305) 451-4107, (800) 451-3483
Marina Del Mar Bayside Resort
$$-$$$$ • MM 99.5 Bayside, Key Largo
• (305) 451-4450

Two expansive Marina Del Mar facilities serve two distinct sets of travelers.

The West Indies-style Marina Del Mar Bayside Resort, set back from the Overseas Highway, overlooks the Florida Bay and attracts those seeking a private beach, sunset views and backcountry fishing. The bayside facility also offers a freshwater swimming pool, sun deck and volleyball court.

The contemporary Marina Del Mar Resort and Marina, on a quiet, dead-end street along an ocean-fed canal and boat basin, draws an active boating, fishing and diving crowd.

The rooms of both facilities are bright and modern with tile floors, ceiling fans, white wicker furnishings and bold tropical accents and feature king-size beds or two doubles. Some also have whirlpool tubs, complete kitchens and private waterfront balconies. All are equipped with ironing boards and irons. Both facilities offer complimentary continental breakfast and room service; restaurants and attractions are nearby.

Guests at either hotel may take advantage of the unique properties and services of both facilities. Deep-sea charter fishing boats are docked behind the Resort and Marina (see our Fishing chapter). This hotel also maintains two tennis courts and a small fitness room with Nautilus equipment.

Overlooking the Resort and Marina's heated freshwater swimming pool, complete with cedar sun deck and hot tub, is Coconuts, a casual indoor/outdoor restaurant (see our Restaurants and Nightlife chapters). Coconuts features a raw bar and serves lunch and dinner throughout the week; the place heats up with live entertainment nightly.

INSIDERS' TIP

The following Florida Keys chambers of commerce can provide information about most area accommodations: Key Largo, MM 106 Bayside, (305) 451-1414, (800) 822-1088; Islamorada, MM 82.5 Bayside, (305) 664-4503, (800) 322-5397; Marathon, MM 53.5 Bayside, (305) 743-5417, (800) 262-7284; Lower Keys, MM 31, Oceanside, (305) 872-2411, (800) 872-3722.

The resort's marina attracts long-term and transient cruisers (see our Cruising chapter). A snorkeling excursion vessel and a glass-bottom tour boat, which both offer daily trips to the coral reefs, are berthed here as well. Next door are Club Nautico powerboat rentals and a full service dive center that offers resort and open-water diving instruction and certification.

Holiday Inn Sunspree® Resort
$$$ • MM 100 Oceanside, Key Largo
• (305) 451-2121, (800) 843-5397

If action is what you seek on your vacation, the 132-room Holiday Inn, situated on a busy boat basin, bustles with activity from dawn until dark. You'll find charters for snorkeling, diving, fishing, sunset cruises and sailing excursions and even a Las Vegas-style gambling boat emanating from the docks that run between the Holiday and its sister hotel, the Ramada Ltd. (see separate listing). Together they compose the Key Largo Resorts.

Bogie's Cafe offers indoor or outdoor dining for breakfast, lunch or dinner. Complimentary coffee is available in the bar at 6 AM, and the tiki bar serves light fare all day while live music percolates poolside on weekend evenings. You'll find a small "marketessen" in the lobby for sandwiches, pastries, juice, soda and water on-the-go.

Rooms at the Holiday Inn face lush tropical gardens or the harbor, and the colorful appointments in each room reflect the flora that flourishes outside the tinted glass doors. Rooms feature all-new bathrooms, king-size beds, floor-to-ceiling beveled mirrors and great vacation amenities such as coffee makers, hair dryers, mini-refrigerators, ironing boards and irons, cable TV with HBO guest choice movies, and voice mail.

Palm trees, frangipani and bougainvillea weave a foliage trail between the two heated pools and the Jacuzzi, and chickees and tropical waterfalls pepper the property. Docked canalside at the Holiday Inn are two famous boats: the original *African Queen* from the legendary movie of the same name and the *Thayer IV* from the motion picture *On Golden Pond*.

The Holiday Inn maintains a fitness room, a children's playground and a changing rota of children's activities. Guests receive complimentary passes for the casino cruise.

Ramada Ltd.
$$ • MM 99.7 Oceanside, Key Largo
• (305) 451-3939, (800) 843-5397

Sister hotel to Key Largo Resorts hotel Holiday Inn, the Ramada exudes a quieter, more laid-back ambiance. Reciprocal privileges exist between the two facilities, so guests may enjoy dining at or room service from Bogie's Cafe as well as all the chartered action.

The 88 rooms and five Jacuzzi suites of this boutique hotel have all the same amenities as the Holiday Inn (see the previous listing) and are decorated in island rattan. The spacious rooms have king-size, queen-size or two double beds; some also have sleeper sofas. Each room opens onto a private patio or balcony. The king suites feature two bathrooms, two televisions and a Jacuzzi bath as well as a shower and a private sun deck. The Ramada wraps around a small, private kidney-shaped swimming pool. All room rates include a complimentary continental breakfast and tickets for the casino cruise.

Port Largo Villas
$$$ • MM 100 Oceanside, 417 Bahia Ave., Key Largo • (305) 451-4847

This upscale timeshare resort offers nightly and weekly rentals with all the comforts of home. Each of Port Largo's six buildings contains four units, two on the first floor and two on the second. All are two-bedroom, two-bathroom villas with more than 1,500 square feet of living space and wraparound patios or decks.

Features include large, full kitchens with washer/dryers, master baths with whirlpool tubs and ceiling fans. Furnishings mix dark wood, bamboo and wicker with pastel floral prints. With a queen-size bed in the master bedroom, two singles in the second bedroom and two sleeper-sofas in the living room, each unit accommodates as many as six guests.

Port Largo's extensive, manicured property offers two swimming pools, volleyball, basketball, table tennis, shuffleboard and croquet. Tennis, dining and entertainment are available at the adjacent Marina Del Mar Resort and Marina (see directions in an earlier listing), and diving, snorkeling, fishing and boating excursions are nearby. A $20-per-day

surcharge is added to all rates during major holiday periods. Port Largo Villas is accessible by boat.

Sunset Cove Motel
$-$$ • MM 99.5 Bayside, Key Largo
• (305) 451-0705

Camels, elephants, lions, tigers and leopards lurk on the grounds of the Sunset Cove Motel, incongruously poised between the nine scattered sleeping rooms and the 10 freestanding cottages. Don't worry, they are only life-size painted statues of the African beasts, remnants of a former owner's travels and hobbies. All the units at Sunset Cove are individually decorated, with a variety of bedding options, tile floors and futons. The cottages also have full kitchens.

At the top of the property is Diver's Den, actually three separate rooms with private baths that can open up, one to another, to accommodate a group as large as 13. Popular with dive clubs, Diver's Den also has a kitchen and allows a cohesive group a home-like atmosphere with plenty of sleeping space.

Down at the sandy beach on Florida Bay, a fleet of paddleboats, canoes and kayaks awaits your leg or arm power. The beach is peppered with lounge chairs and barbecue grills if your idea of recreation is more reclined. Jamaican chairs under thatched chickees create an island ambiance. Guests are welcome

to use Sunset Cove's boat ramp, and boat dockage for vessels up to 20-feet in length is available at no extra charge.

Hungry Pelican Motel
$ • MM 99.3 Bayside, Key Largo
• (305) 451-3576

Murals of manatees, pelicans and wading birds decorate the outside walls of the one-story buildings at Hungry Pelican, which are linked by masses of burgeoning bougainvillea. The motel's 20 units are grouped two to four in a building. A variety of bedding options is available, ranging from one or two doubles, a double and a queen, or one queen-size bed. Each unit is air-conditioned and has a small refrigerator, private bathroom with a shower and tile floors; some have kitchens as well. A duplex unit by the water features two queen-size beds and screened porch on one side and one queen-size bed, a kitchen and screened porch on the other. The units cannot be connected.

Situated on Florida Bay, Hungry Pelican has two fishing piers. You'll be able to swim or snorkel between the piers, but the facility does not have a swimming pool. You may launch your boat from Hungry Pelican's boat ramp, and dockage for small boats is available for an extra fee. Use of a paddleboat and canoe is complimentary. Continental breakfast is offered daily. The property sports a large chickee for lounging, and barbecue pits are scattered about.

Kona Kai Resort
$$-$$$$ • MM 98 Bayside, Key Largo
• (305) 852-7200, (800) 365-7829

Lost in a cluster of mom-and-pop motels toward the southern end of Key Largo sits a truly intimate gem known as Kona Kai. Four years ago owners/operators Joe Harris and Ronnie Farina, young "retired" NBC-TV executives, purchased this unoccupied residence-turned-fishing camp and began converting it into the small, quiet concierge-style resort hermitage that it is today. Near the facility's tennis court, the owners have planted an exotic tropical fruit garden of lichees, guava, starfruit, sapote, Florida pistachios and more. Guests are free to help themselves to samplings of the tropical fruits.

Gardens throughout the 2-acre property of winding walkways showcase 20 varieties of palm trees and 50 varieties of hibiscus, plus heliconia and birds-of-paradise. The owners collect and plant rare and endangered species of flora. An elevated freshwater swimming pool and a hot tub are accented by wood decking and a thatched-palm chickee; a glass-block wall shelters a saltwater pond with a waterfall. Lounge chairs, picnic tables, barbecue grills, a hammock and a fiberglass Ping-Pong table sit close to Kona Kai's white sand beach, which is guarded by a stone alligator. You'll be able to snorkel, swim and fish off a platform at the end of a dock, and a paddleboat, kayak and other water "toys" are available free of charge.

Kona Kai's nine cottage-style suites have been completely renovated with flair and style, with attention to every detail. All suites feature a queen-size bed or two doubles, ceiling fans, tile baths and floors, glass-block showers, antiques and eclectic design accents. Many also have full-size sofa/sleeper futons, and some units have full kitchens. Those without kitchens have small refrigerators and coffee mak-

ers. Each room is named after a tropical fruit, and in keeping with this theme, Harris and Farina place fruit-scented soaps and skin lotion in each bathroom. Just look for the corresponding icon on the tile under the outside lantern to your room. Rooms, some of which are connected, offer either courtyard or full waterfront views.

Opened in 1997, a small, lovely fine art gallery exhibits the work of South Florida artists such as Clyde Butcher (see our Arts and Culture chapter). Many of the original paintings from the gallery are hung in the individual guest suites as well and can be purchased. An outdoor dive station with rinse and soak tanks, an outdoor shower and open-air lattice lockers are just down the walkway. Kona Kai can accommodate five boats with up to a 2-foot draft.

Westin Beach Resort Key Largo
$$$-$$$$ • MM 97 Bayside, Key Largo
• (305) 852-5553, (800) 539-5274

Formerly the Sheraton Key Largo and now under new ownership, the Westin Beach Resort Key Largo sparkles with $4 million in renovations, which were completed in March 1998. Orchids, bromeliads, towering palms and gas torches set the stage for tropical ambiance in this four-story, tin-roofed enclave, painted in shades of beige and featuring walls of windows. The three-story open lobby showcases a Mexican-tile floor, mahogany and rattan furnishings, a coral encased elevator and open-air walkways.

Probably the most unique aspect of the Westin Beach Resort is its 2,000-foot boardwalk nature trail, which stretches virtually the full length of the hotel through a protected hardwood hammock. In one direction, hikers may head for a lighted gazebo area and dock for views of the sunset. Or, they may hike

INSIDERS' TIP

Florida Keys Visitor Assistance Program, (800) 771-5397, is available around the clock for problems you encounter en route to our islands or during your stay. The program has multilingual operators who have instant access to computerized maps and can offer directions to lost motorists. They are equipped to provide on-the-spot translation services and information on nearby medical facilities, automotive services and more.

through mangroves and view environmentally protected exotic flora and fauna. In 1998, the Westin labeled the predominant species of trees in the hammock and prepared an annotated map for guests so that they might further enjoy the nature trail.

In the resort's pool area, which is tucked amid the hardwood hammock, water cascades into the resort's family and adult-only pools over mounds of bougainvillea-lined coral rock. A large hot tub is surrounded by colorful mural-covered walls. A nearby bar and grill provide creative gustatory comforts. Bayside, the Westin boasts an intimate sandy beach, a waterside tiki bar/grill and a dive and watersports concession (see our Recreation chapter).

The Westin Beach Resort Key Largo offers more than 8,000 square feet of conference space; it also has fitness facilities, a gift boutique, a full-service unisex salon, two lighted tennis courts and a game room. In addition to the tiki bar/grills near the pools and beach, the resort offers several on-premises dining options: Cafe Key Largo serves breakfast, lunch and dinner; Treetops offers fine evening dining from its third-floor perch amid the leafy tops of giant gumbo limbo trees; and Parrots Lounge provides libations at its tapas bar daily. Don't miss the Sunday champagne brunch on the cafe balcony overlooking the bay.

Two hundred recently renovated guest accommodations at the Westin include standard and standard-deluxe bay-view, island-view or trail-view rooms and Jacuzzi suites. All rooms have full marble baths, safes and refreshment centers. Standard rooms are comfortably sized with a choice of one king-size bed or two queen-size beds, and each features a sleeper sofa. Double the size of a standard room, the Jacuzzi suite features a wet bar, mini-refrigerator, queen-size sleeper sofa and long, private balconies with sweeping waterfront views. A partition divides the living and sleeping areas, where a large Jacuzzi tub, dressing room and connecting bathroom invite guests to pamper themselves.

The Westin Beach Resort Key Largo's Keys Kids Club offers full-day hiking, swimming and arts and crafts programs for child guests (see our Kidstuff chapter.) And boaters will enjoy the 21-slip docking facilities at no extra charge.

Ocean Pointe Suite Resort

$$$ • MM 92.5 Oceanside, 500 Burton Dr., Tavernier • (305) 853-3000, (800) 882-9464

Directly on the Atlantic Ocean, this tropical contemporary three-story, all-suite stilt condominium complex boasts 240 units with gingerbread-trimmed balconies facing the water. One- and two-bedroom suites at Ocean Pointe are individually owned, so decor varies, but, for the most part, expect to find tropical prints with wicker and rattan furnishings. About 150 units are in the rental program; virtually all have been freshened with a full or partial facelift in 1998.

Space and amenities are all generous at Ocean Pointe: One-bedroom suites offer master bedrooms with queen-size beds, full baths with oversize hot tubs and living rooms with sleeper sofas, allowing the unit to sleep as many as four; two-bedroom suites include two full baths, and each features a queen-size bed in the master bedroom and two twins in the second, sleeping as many as six. The suites feature full kitchens with microwaves and coffee makers as well as washers and dryers.

Just outside your door are nature walks, barbecue grills, picnic areas and lighted tennis courts. The 70-acre property also has a playground, a boat ramp, a marina and a man-made white-sand beach with a volleyball net. If you feel like a light bite, head for the outdoor cabana club. Or, work up an appetite in Ocean Pointe's Junior Olympic-size swimming pool. Kayak and canoe rentals also are available. With such a comprehensive array of activities to enjoy, Ocean Pointe attracts families from all over the world and provides an attractive honeymoon package. Some lucky residents live here year round.

To reach Ocean Pointe, head toward the ocean at Burton Drive (MM 92.5) where signs lead to Harry Harris Park. Follow Burton Drive about a quarter-mile, turn right into the Ocean Pointe complex and pass the guard house. Signs will guide you to the manager's office.

Bay Breeze Motel

$$ • MM 92.5 Bayside, 160 Sterling Road, Tavernier • (305) 852-5248, (800) 937-5650

Reincarnated as the Bay Breeze Motel, the former Vaughn Villas on the shores of

Photo: Little Palm Island

Little Palm Island is more like the South Seas than South Florida.

Florida Bay now sparkle with the effects of a complete make-over. Owned by Bill and Bonnie Coffin since December 1996, the Bay Breeze offers 15 units, all with full kitchens for self-catering convenience, living rooms with double futons, king-size or two twin beds and terrazzo or tile floors. Freshly painted inside and out, the one-bedroom efficiencies and Caribbean cottages are tropically furnished with hunter green upholstery on rattan and wicker. A riot of flora — birds of paradise and banana leaves — adorn the brightly printed swag curtains and matching throw pillows. The Caribbean cottages sport Dade pine beamed ceilings. The beds in these bungalows are surrounded with mosquito netting for an island feeling. Barbecue grills are strategically placed for each unit's use and also grace the beach area.

Completed in 1998 is a sparkling poolside garden suite, an all-in-one tiled great-room featuring a queen-size bed; kitchen with breakfast bar, cooktop and microwave; glass-walled bathroom and decks overlooking the beach, pool, banana trees and tropical foliage.

Bay Breeze Motel enjoys 3 acres of primo bayfront property, planted with palms and bougainvillea and featuring a large beach area peppered with chaise lounges, Adirondack beach chairs and hammocks. Bay Breeze maintains two boat ramps and a 100-foot dock. Boat dockage and use of the boat ramp is available to guests at no extra charge.

Unique to this property is a special feature of Florida Bay called the "deep hole," where depths drop dramatically to 20 feet right off shore. A coral rock ledge shelters lobsters and starfish, and a regiment of sergeant-major fish keep company with mangrove snappers and parrot fish. This assortment of marine life as well as a sunken Haitian raft makes for dynamic snorkeling.

Guests enjoy complimentary use of a rowboat, paddleboat and bicycles during their stay at Bay Breeze. Day breaks here with a complimentary breakfast as well. A new freshwater swimming pool is due for completion by the end of 1998.

To find Bay Breeze Motel, turn onto Sterling Road at MM 92.5 and proceed toward Florida Bay.

Tavernier Hotel
$-$$ • MM 91.8 Oceanside, Tavernier
• (305) 852-4131

Gracing Tavernier since 1928, the historic building now sheltering the Tavernier Hotel withstood the ravages of the hurricane of 1935 (see our Historical Evolution chapter). The pale-pink building contains 17 simple sleeping rooms. A variety of bedding options is offered, but all rooms are decorated in hot pinks and pastels and sport lacy curtains and comforters, all in all exuding an English bed and breakfast ambiance that reflects the owner's British roots.

While the reasonably priced accommodations here are basic but spiffy, the facility also provides a small fitness center and a laundry. A hot tub nestles amid lush greenery out back. The popular Copper Kettle Restaurant, next door and under the same ownership as the hotel (see our Restaurants chapter), provides breakfast, lunch and dinner a stone's throw from the hotel.

Lookout Lodge Resort
$-$$ • MM 88 Bayside, Islamorada
• (305) 852-9915, (800) 870-1772

Situated next to Marker 88, one of the Upper Keys' most distinguished restaurants (see our Restaurants chapter), Lookout Lodge is a pleasant, private and moderately priced motel of Spanish-influenced architecture. Owned by former shipwreck diver Michael Sheen and his wife, Angie, the two-story facility is strewn with portholes, anchors and other items pulled from wrecks off the North Carolina coast.

The resort's nine rooms come in four styles: studios with one double and one twin-size bed; studios with two double beds and a patio; and one- and two-bedroom suites. Suites each include a queen-size sleeper sofa. Cribs, side rails and rollaway beds are provided at no additional cost. All have kitchenettes, tile floors

INSIDERS' TIP

For child-friendly resorts at a glance, see our Kidstuff chapter.

and baths, voice-mail telephones and ceiling fans. Three afford full water views. A limited number of small pets is allowed.

Steps lead from the resort's raised man-made beach to the bay for swimming and snorkeling, and the property features gas grills, picnic tables, a thatched-palm chickee and lounge chairs. Dock space is free but limited and must be reserved in advance. A dive/snorkel boat on premises takes guests to the reef.

One night's prepayment with a major credit card is required to reserve a room at the Lookout Lodge, and two weeks' advance cancellation is required.

Plantation Yacht Harbor Resort & Marina
$-$$ • MM 87 Bayside, Islamorada
• (305) 852-2381, (800) 356-3215

Wide-open spaces and sweeping sunset views of Florida Bay distinguish the vast grounds of Plantation Yacht Harbor. Each of the four ranch-style concrete buildings here contains eight spacious units with either king-size beds or two double beds. Pale pastel spreads and white Formica furnishings lend an airy feel; some sunken sitting areas offer partial bay views, and some are furnished with sleeper sofas. Most units have patios.

Especially popular are the four new floating suites — actually floating homes permanently tethered at the Plantation Yacht Harbor Marina (see our Cruising chapter). Rented daily, weekly or monthly, the floating suites provide a vacation alternative: a real taste of sleeping on a yacht, Onassis style. The three two-bedroom floating suites and the one three-bedroom unit are all air-conditioned and have king-size or queen-size beds. They each sport a full kitchen, a spacious living area with bay windows and one bathroom (head) with shower. You'll

enjoy the panoramic views of Florida Bay and our famous sunsets from decks fore and aft as well as from the top deck.

Guests will find a freshwater swimming pool, basketball courts, two lighted tennis courts, a restaurant, a beach with a tiki bar, a grill and a watersports concession on premises. Happy hour, breakfast buffets and live entertainment are offered regularly. A dive shop offers certification and trips to reefs and wrecks. Boats can be docked at the marina.

Tropical Reef Resort
$-$$$$ • MM 85 Oceanside, Islamorada
• (305) 664-8881, (800) 887-3373

Here is an eclectic tropical mix that thoroughly captivates children and adults alike: A sculpted dolphin spouts water into a kiddie pool; a wood walking bridge leads to a miniature peninsula; a large sandy playground entices kids with a merry-go-round and climbing platforms; and thatched-palm chickees and hibiscus are everywhere, bordering winding walkways and more than 100 yards of white-sand man-made beach.

A potpourri of divergent accommodations ranges from motel rooms in a one-story orange building to large ground-level one- and two-bedroom villas with such names as Seagull Cove and Porpoise Place. A full gamut of bedding options is on offer at Tropical Reef Resort. Extra-deluxe motel rooms feature a refrigerator, while the spacious studios, villas and studio/villa combos have full kitchens. Some rooms connect; many afford a partial water view. Children younger than 13 stay free, and cribs and rollaway beds are available.

Outdoor facilities and activities abound at Tropical Reef Resort. The resort has its own basketball court, two shuffleboard courts, two hot tubs and three freshwater swimming pools. A dive shop offers dive excursions, tiki tours

and sunset cruises. An eco-tour/snorkeling combination cruise includes exploration of historic Indian Key. Tropical Reef has a boat ramp, and trailer space can be secured for a fee. Stays of one week or more earn a 10-percent discount, and cancellations require seven days' advance notice.

Pelican Cove Resort
$$$-$$$$ • MM 84.5 Oceanside, Islamorada • (305) 664-4435, (800) 445-4690

This aesthetically pleasing, well-designed, plantation-style facility truly considers the needs and desires of its visitors. Constructed in concrete with a tin roof and Bahamian shutters, Pelican Cove's jagged shape assures an ocean view from every room.

The hotel offers a choice of standard rooms, efficiencies or one-bedroom hot tub suites, each with its own balcony. Efficiencies and suites have full-size, full modern kitchens with curved breakfast bars and either two queen-size beds or a queen-size bed and sleeper sofa. Hotel rooms are furnished with one or two queen-size beds,

and are equipped with mini-refrigerators and coffee makers. Some hotel rooms and suites connect, and all units feature bold floral comforters and striking emerald-green carpeting.

Pelican Cove rests a short hike from action-packed Holiday Isle. If what you seek is tranquility, request a room on the northeast side of the building.

Behind the resort, steps connect the raised man-made beach to the ocean, where dredging for a once used quarry has caused waters to run 30 feet deep. A freshwater swimming pool with sun deck, an outdoor cabana bar and cafe, a poolside hot tub, a volleyball net, playground and watersports concession all front the beach.

Complimentary coffee and juice are offered in Pelican Cove's office 24 hours a day and a complimentary continental breakfast is served daily. Children younger than 17 stay free at Pelican Cove. Sandbox toys for children are available in the office.

Limited boat dockage is available to guests at an additional fee. Reservations must be made in advance. Pelican Cove offers meet-

INSIDERS' TIP

Few hotels and resorts offer free local telephone calls from rooms. To avoid surprises when you check out, inquire about local and long-distance charges when you check in.

ing and conference space aboard a 770-square-foot houseboat that is permanently moored in the marina.

Holiday Isle Resorts
$$-$$$$ • MM 84 Oceanside, Islamorada • (305) 664-2321, (800) 327-7070

Justifiably garnering its reputation as the Party Capital of the Keys, Holiday Isle is a bustling, happening place (see our Cruising, Restaurants, Nightlife and Annual Events chapters). Four separate hotel facilities operate under the Holiday Isle umbrella: Howard Johnson's and Holiday Isle are on premises; El Capitan and Harbor Lights Motel are a short distance away. Holiday Isle is a pulsating entertainment complex favored by Generation Xers — a mass of indoor and outdoor restaurants, boardwalk shopping, thatched-palm chickees, white-sand beach and a full-service marina with a charter fishing fleet and watersports facilities.

Rooms within the Howard Johnson and Holiday Isle hotels are similar, but Holiday Isle offers direct oceanfront views and spacious suites. Howard Johnson's partial water-view rooms are this facility's most desirable. Comfortable guest rooms in both facilities are furnished with two double beds or a single king-size bed and are decorated with Southwestern and tropical accents. All have tile baths.

El Capitan, a small cottage-style complex to the north of HoJo, is a collection of quiet beachfront wood-paneled cottages with full kitchens and sliding glass doors. The 13 cottages vary in size and decor. The oceanside Harbor Lights offers 11 rooms with a variety of bedding options and 22 efficiencies that also sport kitchenettes. Considered a part of Holiday Isle, El Capitan and Harbor Lights are quiet enough that guests can catch up on some R&R but close enough to the action that they need only walk a few steps to partake of the never-ending festivities.

Chesapeake Resort
$$-$$$$ • MM 83.5 Oceanside, Islamorada • (305) 664-4662, (800) 338-3395

Once known as Al Lucky's Whale Harbor Spa, the elegant Chesapeake Resort, owned and operated by the Sandry family, hugs the Atlantic on 6½ acres of lushly landscaped grounds. Expanded and completely renovated into a pristine three-story, 65-unit resort, Chesapeake now sports two heated pools, a hot tub, tennis courts, on-site laundry facilities and an outdoor gym as well as a 700-foot sunning beach and a saltwater lagoon.

Rooms come in 16 styles, from the garden-view standard to villas and oceanfront suites. All are exquisitely adorned in pale greens, peaches and pinks, pickled bamboo and faux-stone furnishings and have tile floors. Some connecting rooms combine to provide 1,000 square feet of living space. Suites and villas offer full kitchens and have balconies or screened porches. The higher-priced units also feature whirlpool bathtubs, king-size beds, queen-size living room sleepers, two televisions and wet bars. The one- and two-bedroom suites even have a Jacuzzi in the bedroom.

Fishing, snorkeling, diving and parasailing excursions can be booked on premises as well as sunset cruises. You can rent kayaks and powerboats of up to 33 feet. Chesapeake also provides a boat ramp and boat dockage.

Chesapeake provides a playground for children, who can stay for free if they are younger than 13.

Cheeca Lodge
$$$$ • MM 82 Oceanside, Islamorada • (305) 664-4651, (800) 327-2888

Majestically sprawling amid 27 manicured, tropical acres with more than 1,100 feet of beachfront, Cheeca Lodge creates a vacation enclave you may never want to vacate. Follow the winding drive through splashes of bougainvillea beneath towering coconut palms, stroll across the courtyard between an avenue of

Holiday Isle Resorts and Marina
84001 Overseas Hwy Islamorada Fl Keys
1-800-327-7070   305-664-2321

date palms and enter an island lobby alive with tropical birds, bromeliads and potted palms. This elegant main building, tiled with Key Largo limestone and peppered with stone pillars, houses the famed Atlantic's Edge Restaurant as well as the casually laid-back Ocean Terrace Grill (see our Restaurants chapter). The Light Tackle Lounge, which offers cocktails and light fare, is wallpapered with photos of celebrity anglers, including former President George Bush, for Cheeca hosts many a prestigious fishing tournament in the Florida Keys (see our Fishing chapter).

All 203 spacious guest rooms and one- or two-bedroom suites and villas were completely renovated in 1998. Tropical themes and colors reflect the sun and the sea of the Florida Keys. The bamboo and wicker furniture has been revitalized, and comfortable armchairs with ottomans have been added. From bathtubs to bedspreads, carpeting to wall coverings, everything is sparkling. All units feature ceiling fans, mini-bars and televisions with videocassette players. Tennis Villas, Golf Villas, Lake Villas and Ocean Villas also offer full kitchens.

Five hot tubs are sprinkled around the property, tucked privately amid lush tropical foliage. Many rooms have balconies that look out over the ocean or across the grounds of the resort; some units have screened porches.

Focused on fishing, families and the envi-

ronment, Cheeca Lodge offers an overflowing cache of recreational options. A saltwater lagoon is stocked with tropical fish for easy on-site snorkeling. A fishing pier juts out into the ocean where guests can dock boats with up to a 3-foot draft or just drop a line and try their luck. Two pools grace the premises, a freshwater option to the sand beach and seductively salty Atlantic.

Guests enjoy Cheeca's par 3, nine-hole golf course, designed by Jack Nicklaus, and six Hard-tru tennis courts. Nature trails wind throughout the property. Cheeca also maintains a full-service dive center, Caribbean Water Sports (see our Recreation chapter), and offers water toys such as Hobie Cats and Hobie Waves.

The award-winning children's club, Camp Cheeca, keeps the kids occupied with specially designed, environmentally inspired activities (see our Kidstuff chapter).

The Moorings
$$$-$$$$ • MM 81.5 Oceanside, 123 Beach Rd., Islamorada • (305) 664-4708

If the Florida Keys is considered Paradise, then The Moorings is our Utopia: Cottages and homes are cast throughout miles of ivory sand; hammocks laze between majestic palms; winding, floral-lined trails emit the essence of gardenia; and canoes and skiffs appear as if guests washed ashore, never again yearning for more than they have right here. On the site of a former coconut plantation, The Moorings maintains a low profile and is The Very Best-Kept Secret among our islands.

French proprietor Hubert (pronounced u-BEAR) Baudoin and his large and friendly Newfoundland reside in what was once this plantation owner's stately oceanfront home. Guests have their choice of five completely refurbished mid-1930s to 1960s cottages, four new Conch-style oceanfront homes with porches and seven charming two-story homes overlooking the swimming pool and tennis court. All are bright white with Bahamian shutters and trimmed in Caribbean colors; they're named after some of Islamorada's pioneers. With the exception of a two-bedroom oceanfront cottage, all refurbished units are rented by the night; the fifth cottage and the fully equipped homes are available only by the week.

Use of windsurfers and kayaks is free, and barbecue grills, a volleyball net, thatched-roof gazebo and citrus trees add to the accommodating surroundings.

Older cottages feature Dade County pine, and newer units have plantation-style porches, tin roofs and cypress paneled interior walls. Sizes range from one to three bedrooms and one to 3½ baths. Home and cottages feature African fabrics, all-cotton sheets and towels, down comforters and wicker and rattan furnishings. Kitchens are fully equipped, and baths in the newer units feature handpainted tiles, oversized soaking tubs and shower stalls. Ceiling fans are standard throughout accommodations at The Moorings.

Kon-Tiki Resort
$-$$$ • MM 81 Bayside, Islamorada • (305) 664-4702

Kon-Tiki's pebbled walkways, private patios and cottages consistently attract anglers and families alike. The resort's quiet, U-shaped property boasts a shuffleboard court, a chickee, pier, private beach on Florida Bay,

park benches and a brick barbecue. The primary attraction here, though, is the saltwater pond stocked with all sorts of tropical fish. Guests are invited to don snorkel and mask and take an underwater look-see.

Accommodations feature bright, clean and comfortable motel units, fully equipped efficiencies and one-bedroom apartments, most of which have private patios or screened porches. Two-bedroom, two-bath apartments and three-bedroom, three-bath villas, priced according to size, accommodate as many as six.

Kon-Tiki offers a freshwater heated pool and a boat ramp and dockage for vessels up to 24 feet long at no extra charge.

Hampton Inn & Suites
$$$-$$$$ • MM 80, Oceanside, Islamorada • (305) 664-0073, (800) 426-7866

A welcome addition to Islamorada hosteleries in January 1997, the Hampton Inn & Suites adds a touch of class to the Atlantic shores. Situated directly at ocean's edge, the hotel offers 59 suites, 16 standard rooms and four handicapped-accessible rooms with vistas of our endless sparkling sea.

Suites feature one or two bedrooms, one or two baths, sleeper sofas in the living rooms and full kitchens (coffee and popcorn are supplied every day). Satellite television with HBO and pay-per-view movies entertains in each unit; suites have two televisions, which are equipped with VCRs. Fresh and new, the furnishings of the Hampton Inn reflect island ambiance with fabrics of pastels and teal amid light rattan.

The common lobby area of the Hampton sports a fishing theme — giant mounted dolphin, wahoo and tarpon; carved wood piscatory reliefs; bronze gamefish sculptures. Tables and comfy chairs flank a keystone fireplace, which is more decorative than functional given the balmy Keys weather. A complimentary continental breakfast is served here from 6 to 10 AM daily.

Outside, guests enjoy a heated pool and

INSIDERS' TIP

See our Healthcare chapter for listings of veterinarians who will board your pet.

spa, tiki bar and palm-laden, sandy sunning area. A dock jutting out into the Atlantic affords boat dockage for small vessels; depths fall to a scant 18 inches at low tide. You'll find a complete selection of watersports on premises from WaterWorld Activities Inc., which offers snorkel or dive excursions, parasailing and backcountry fishing, as well as rentals of 17-foot powerboats, pontoon boats, Sun Kats, kayaks and bicycles.

Breezy Palms Resort
$-$$$ • MM 80 Oceanside, Islamorada
• (305) 664-2361

Quaint coral buildings with turquoise doors and trim, shake roofs and screened porches mark Breezy Palms Resort, a cozy place nestled on 320 feet of oceanfront. The brightly wallpapered motel rooms, efficiencies, apartments and cottages are clean, spacious and well-appointed, featuring rattan furniture and colorful island floral prints.

Chickees and copious coconut palms pepper the property, which sits directly on the Atlantic Ocean and sports a sandy beach as well as a freshwater pool. A brick barbecue, picnic table and volleyball net add to the amenities; dockage is available for an additional fee. No straight inboards or personal watercraft, such as Jet Skis or Waverunners, are permitted.

Breezy Palms is accessible by boat. Children younger than 13 stay free.

Matecumbe Resort
$$ • MM 76.3 Oceanside, Islamorada
• (305) 664-8801

The sprawling Matecumbe Resort — 32 fully equipped apartments in four two-story buildings -- provides the perfect family vacation setup. The reasonably priced, constantly updated units, which range from one- or two-bedrooms to efficiencies, all have complete kitchens. A range of bedding options is available (doubles, queens, kings), and baths are modernized with fresh tile and appointments. Units vary in decor and layout, but all sport bright tropical pastels and have some sort of eat-in dining arrangement. Televisions with cable hookup are standard.

The grounds feature a heated freshwater pool and a man-made beach adorned with chaise lounges and chickees. A sand volleyball court, horseshoes and shuffleboard provide adult entertainment while two children's play areas beckon the kiddies. The expanses of mature trees and curving coconut palms are peppered with grills and picnic tables.

Matecumbe Resort offers the use of its boat ramp to guests and provides free boat dockage as well as boat rentals. Bicycles are available to guests for a $100 refundable deposit.

White Gate Court
$-$$$ • MM 76 Bayside, Islamorada
• (305) 664-4136

A touch of understated European elegance marks the newly restored villas and bungalows at White Gate Court, situated on 3 acres abutting the placid Gulf of Mexico. These 1940s-era Conch cottages survived the hurricane of 1961 and decades of neglect before receiving tender loving care from owner Suzanne Orias DeCargnelli, a native of Hungary who spent many years in South America. Painted cheerful yellow and white inside and out, the seven private units — completed in 1997 — exude a rustic Old World charm. The spacious interiors sport rough plastered walls; fresh tile and lightly stained wood-plank floors; fully equipped, stylistically European white kitchens; and sparkling modern bathrooms. Beds are covered with exquisite individualized quilts in shades of green. All units have covered porches and outdoor tables and chairs. Some even have rope hammocks.

White iron gates guard this tropical hermitage, fronting a long, narrow driveway lined with palm trees, oleanders and white coach lamps. Lounge chairs pepper a 200-foot white sand beach where guests enjoy swimming and snorkeling in the sandy-bottom Gulf; White Gate Court does not choose to have a pool. A finger dock stretches into the water for fishing, and tiki torches and barbecue grills are available for an evening cookout. A guest laundry also is provided.

Tropic Aire Resort Motel
$-$$ • MM 75.8 Bayside, Islamorada
• (305) 664-4989

If there is any question as to why this small motel promotes itself as "Almost Heaven," the reason becomes apparent with one step inside the rooms: Many are painted stark white

Photo: Hawk's Cay

Sand-belted lagoons such as this one at Hawk's Cay offer shallow, protected saltwater swimming.

CORAL BAY Resort

Mile Marker 75.5
75690 Overseas Highway
Islamorada, FL 33036
305-664-5568

"The Keys the way they used to be"

Five acres of lush tropical landscape surround this beautiful resort located directly on the crystal clear waters of the Gulf of Mexico. Nestled among brightly colored hibiscus and bougainvillea sit spacious cottages with lazyday covered porches, each styled after an historic Keys home. With so much to do and so little pressure to do anything, the Coral Bay Resort is perfect for couples as well as families.

Sandy Beach • Heated Freshwater Pool
Tidal Pool • Fishing Pier
Ramp/Boat Dockage

---

with white tile, white wicker and white wood-beamed ceilings. The motel makes a fine choice for those who enjoy clean, relaxed comfort at a value.

Don't let this facility's understated exterior mislead you: One- and two-story adjacent units come in an assortment of styles and sizes and overlook a parklike setting of picnic tables, grills and large shade trees. A volleyball court and a coral barbecue grill sit near the man-made beach and swim area.

Tropic Aire has a lighted fishing pier and fish-cleaning station. It is accessible by boat.

Topsider Resort
$$$ • MM 75.5 Bayside, Islamorada
• (305) 664-8031, (800) 262-9874

The 20 octagonal, elevated time-share villas at Topsider Resort flank a wood boardwalk that marches from the secluded parking lot to the crystalline waters of the Gulf of Mexico. Ablaze with gumbo limbos, crotons and bougainvillea, the grounds of the Topsider effect a rain forest mystique, even though the resort itself is right off the Overseas Highway.

Units are identical in layout, and all but five have been recently remodeled. Each features two bedrooms, two baths, a dining area, living room and full kitchen. Ceiling fans, washer and dryer and ground-level storage are standard.

Guests at Topsider Resort enjoy an el-

evated pool and spa, a tennis court, children's swings and slides, grills, picnic tables and bayfront wood lounges for sunning on the sandy lagoonside beach. Free boat dockage is available on Topsider's long pier. Minimum stay here is three nights, but most guests opt for a week's sabbatical.

Coral Bay Resort
$-$$ MM 75.5 Bayside, Islamorada
• (305) 664-5568

Formerly known as the Gamefish Resort, this bayfront property received a total facelift in 1997, compliments of new owners Selby and Michele Blair. The totally rejuvenated Coral Bay Resort's three motel rooms, eleven efficiencies and two villa suites are secreted away in white-trimmed, pastel pink, air-conditioned Conch-style cottages, each with a lazy-days front porch. Each unit is distinguished by a painted icon, creating a virtual school of tropical fish.

The fresh interior furnishings sparkle with light furniture, pastel fabrics and tile floors. A selection of South Florida art adorns the walls, supplied by an Orlando art gallery. A variety of bedding options is available. The efficiencies feature full kitchens, and each villa suite also provides a living area with a sleeper sofa.

You'll enjoy Coral Bay's new heated pool as well as a sandy beach on the Gulf of Mexico that is peppered with lounges and chickees. Fishing and snorkeling off the U-shaped dock and 14-foot tidal pool are excellent. The pier itself has built-in seating and a fish-cleaning station. Guests can dock their own vessels for free or use the resort's paddleboat for exploration. Waters beyond the dock are illuminated at night so the seaside fun doesn't have to end at sunset.

One thing that hasn't changed at Coral Bay is the lush tropical ambiance created by mature plantings of yesteryear. You'll find a bougainvillea two stories high, and palms and indigenous hardwood trees pepper the property. Love birds roost in a gigantic bird cage that has been constructed around a real tree. The casual elegance of this resort, coupled with Coral Bay's dedication to the carefree simplicity of "the Keys the way they used to be," ensures a relaxing holiday.

Caloosa Cove
Resort Condominium
$$$ • MM 73.8 Oceanside, Islamorada • (305) 664-8811

An irregularly shaped condominium complex set apart from civilization on a large parcel of prime oceanfront property, Caloosa Cove offers 30 spacious, light and bright efficiencies and one-bedroom suites. Suites offer eat-in kitchens, spacious bedrooms, and living rooms with sofa beds; each efficiency is a large one-room unit with an eat-in kitchen, queen-size bed and loveseat. All are decorated with tropical rattans and pastels. Every unit is fronted by a covered deck that looks directly at the Atlantic.

Caloosa Cove's large irregular-shaped pool, surrounded by extensive wood decking and thatched-palm chickees, sits directly on the ocean's edge, affording endless vistas of the beyond. The grounds encompassing the coral-laden exterior of Caloosa Cove burgeon with mature tropical plantings.

Activities and amenities on condo premises include shuffleboard and basketball courts, a barbecue area, lighted tennis courts, a full-service marina, fishing charters and boat and bicycle rentals. The nearby Safari Lounge serves your choice of cocktails.

Middle Keys

The Middle Keys, known locally as the "heart of the Keys," stretch from the Long Key

Bridge to the Seven Mile Bridge. Conch, Duck and Grassy Keys lead the way to the string of bridge-connected islands known as Marathon.

Basing your accommodations in the Middle Keys offers some distinct advantages. The Marathon airport offers you the option of flying directly to the Keys instead of driving from the mainland. The barrier reef sheltering the prolific fishing waters of the Atlantic supports a plethora of marine life and harbors a number of primo shipwrecks for divers (see our Diving and Snorkeling chapter). Fishing in the Middle Keys rivals that of the famed Islamorada, a well-kept secret. From flats to backcountry, bluewater to bridges, you won't hear too many tales of the "one that got away" here (see our Fishing chapter).

Marathon offers two golf courses: the nine-hole Key Colony Beach public course and the 18-hole private Sombrero Country Club. Sombrero honors reciprocal privileges from other golf clubs in the United States (see our Recreation chapter). Active, ongoing tennis programs with drills, round-robins and lessons are available at Hawk's Cay Resort on Duck Key and at Sombrero Resort (a separate facility from the Sombrero Country Club) in Marathon to all players regardless of where they are staying.

Marathon has a movie theater too (cinemas are few and far between in the Keys). This quirky little theater, which shows first-run movies that change weekly, seats viewers in movable, swivel, barrel chairs that surround small round tables designed to hold your popcorn and soda. (See our Recreation chapter for details of golf, tennis, movie theaters and more.)

The Dolphin Research Center on Grassy Key is a must-do regardless of where your accommodations might be. And, in Marathon, Tropical Crane Point Hammock will captivate the whole family, as will historic Pigeon Key, at the end of a length of the old Seven Mile Bridge accessed at MM 47 (see our Attractions chapter). Sombrero Beach in Marathon, a very nice man-made public beach, provides endless ocean vistas to all.

Needless to say, like the rest of the Keys, this whole area is packed with recreational water options from party fishing boats and glass-bottom reef excursions to personal watercraft and sea kayak rentals. Parasailing and ultralight rides are available here as well (see our Recreation chapter).

The pace is less tiki-bar frenetic here than in the Upper Keys. The sidewalk rolls up at a relatively early hour. But this area will appeal to families with children as well as serious anglers and divers who, after a day on or under the water, relish a relaxing dinner at one of the many topnotch restaurants and then a nocturnal refueling of energy for whatever tomorrow may bring.

Lime Tree Bay Resort
$$-$$$ • MM 68 Bayside, Layton
• (305) 664-4740,
(800) 723-4519

Wiggle your toes as you laze in one of the string hammocks tied among the copious palms surrounding Lime Tree Bay Resort. Perched on the shores of Florida Bay, this resort — which features a variety of overnight options — tucks chickees and lounge chairs amid lush tropical vegetation so that your escape from the workaday world is complete. An elevated freshwater pool and heated hot tub extend over a wood boardwalk at water's edge. Accommodations range from waterfront motel-style rooms and efficiencies to one- and two-bedroom apartments. All rooms have been renovated, including the two-bedroom tree-house and bayview apartments.

Watersports are offered by an on-premises concessionaire, including diving, snorkeling and sunset excursions and boat and Waverunner rentals. Bicycles also are available for rent. Guests may dock their own boats at no extra charge (up to 28 feet, 3-foot draft at low tide). But Lime Tree Bay has no boat ramp, so boats must be launched at nearby Seabird Marina near Fiesta Key. Shuffleboard, a horseshoe pit and one tennis court stand ready in case you feel like a little exercise. Children younger than 8 stay free.

Adjacent to the property is a popular Italian restaurant, Little Italy (see our Restaurants chapter) and the Roseate Spoonbill Restaurant, which is open daily for breakfast and lunch.

Conch Key Cottages
$$-$$$$ • MM 62.3 Oceanside, Little Conch Key • (305) 289-1377,
(800) 330-1577

Step back in time as you drive across the narrow causeway from the Overseas Highway into Keys past. Lovingly restored beyond their former grandeur, the pastel, gingerbread-trimmed Conch Key Cottages — like an upended basket of Easter eggs — reflect the upbeat, zany personalities of owners Wayne Byrnes and Ron Wilson. Each cottage — bright, fresh and full of crisp, tropical cottons — is as unique as the conch shells for which they're named.

The wood-paneled Coquina, resting at water's edge, provides king-size beds in each of its two voluminous bedrooms. A walled patio with a hot tub and gas grill maximizes your privacy, and the sizable well-equipped kitchen — complete with a set of Fiesta ware — might even entice you to cook during your holiday. The largest cottage, the King's Crown, is about 1,200 square feet of living space, with a king-size bed in one bedroom and two queen-size beds in the other, plus a living room, dining room, kitchen and 1½ baths. The Whelk, Queen and Fighting Conch cottages each fringe the living/dining/kitchen combo room with a queen-size bedroom, one bathroom and a massive, screened porch overlooking a primo bonefish flat. These one-bedroom oceanfront units received full facelifts in 1998, complete with new kitchens and baths. The honeymoon cottage, the Baby Conch, miniaturizes the features of the others, but the custom-painted lamps and specially made furnishings mirror the details of its more capacious relatives.

Three all-new cottages — Periwinkle, Seahorse and Horse Conch — were constructed in 1997. Grabbing a coveted ocean view, these two-bedroom, two-bath units feature full kitchens, living and dining areas, two

---

cable televisions (one with VCR) and every amenity imaginable for a luxurious vacation stay.

A small freshwater swimming pool nestles amid towering palms, and eight varieties of bananas hang at the ready for guest consumption. Plantings reflect the owners' philosophy of growing old-fashioned vegetation that attracts birds and butterflies. Burgeoning bushes of golden dewdrop — a mass of purple flowers and yellow berries growing concurrently — does just that. The butterflies like the nectar of the flowers; the birds crave the berries.

Conch Key Cottages maintains a boat ramp and marina that can accommodate an 8-foot draft. Guests may dock their vessels at no extra charge. So you are sure to bring those freshly caught snappers to the table, there is a fish-cleaning station complete with water and electricity.

Hawk's Cay Resort
$$$-$$$$ • MM 61 Oceanside, Duck Key
• (305) 743-7000, (800) 432-2242

Step through the pink portico of Hawk's Cay to the strains of a disembodied steel drum. A pith-helmeted doorman sporting a riotously colored shirt bids you welcome. Mount the steps to the tiled veranda, its Bahama fans slowly stirring the subtropical air over the wicker settees. Pass into the palm-filled lobby and out the other side to . . . the West Indies? Like Alice passing through the looking glass, you will adjust your perspective, slow down, kick back and recharge your batteries at this rambling Caribbean-style resort. Gracious yet low key, opulent but subdued, Hawk's Cay's 60-acre facility encompasses one of the five islands of the Duck Key configuration.

Accommodations in the inn building include standard rooms with two full-size beds; the larger captain's suites, each with a king-size bed and a sleeper sofa in a separate seating area; and the huge penthouse suites with two bedrooms, 1½ baths, a living room, dining room and private rooftop sun deck with hot tub. All rooms have balconies, mini-refrigerators and coffee makers.

The Villas at Hawk's Cay, completed in 1998, offer guests the option of their own self-contained vacation homes. These two-story Key West-style abodes all offer full kitchens,

living rooms, covered porches, washers and dryers, ceiling fans and televisions with VCRs. The Conch and the smaller Bungalow units feature two bedrooms and two baths. The more spacious Cottages offer two bedrooms, a den and 2½ baths. The 22 older Marina Villas each have two bedrooms and two baths. All are individually owned and decorated, but all are enhanced with light and bright tropical Keys furnishings.

Unique to this Keys property is the saltwater lagoon, belted by a man-made, sandy beach, which borders the canal entrance to Hawk's Cay Marina boat basin (see our Cruising chapter).

When you've had enough of doing nothing at all — lazing around the lagoon, the freshwater family or adults-only pools or the hot tub — check out the diversions. Observe the ongoing dolphin discovery program at Dolphin Connection (see our Attractions chapter). Scuba dive the reef and Coffin's Patch with Abyss Dive Center, which is adjacent to the Ship's Store at the marina. Take the glass-bottom *Osprey's* morning boat trip or afternoon snorkeling trip. Book a fishing charter or sunset sailing cruise, parasail or gunk-hole with a local naturalist on an eco-tour through the backcountry waters (see our Fishing, Recreation, Boating and Paradise Found chapters). Or swing your racket in the tennis garden, participating in lessons, round-robins or just whacking returns at the ball machine.

The four popular restaurants on premises whet any appetite: Palm Terrace for breakfast; Cantina for poolside light bites; Porto Cayo for eclectic Italian; and the WatersEdge for steaks and seafood (see our Restaurants chapter). Children fare equally well at Hawk's Cay. The Island Adventure Club guarantees that Mom, Dad and the kids all find a holiday wonderland (see our Kidstuff chapter).

Flamingo Inn
$ • MM 59.5 Bayside, Grassy Key
• (305) 289-1478, (800) 439-1478

Accommodations within this roadside motel are a pleasant surprise. bright, spotless standard units with a variety of bedding options and efficiencies with double and queen-size beds, microwaves, full kitchens and full refrigerators. Some units are tiled, some are

A Caribbean Vacation in the Heart of the Florida Keys.

A Caribbean-styled resort on a private island in the Florida Keys. Hawk's Cay offers 176 guest rooms and suites. 200 new two-bedroom villas. Enjoy four restaurants, water activities, 2 pools (one is adult-only), a lagoon, exclusive interactive dolphin program, tennis, marina and golf access. Call 800-432-2242 for reservations. If you're outside the U.S. call 305-743-7000.

Hawk's Cay Resort
In The Heart Of The Florida Keys.

INN • VILLAS • CLUB • MARINA

61 Hawk's Cay Blvd., Duck Key, FL 33050 • www.hawkscay.com

carpeted, and larger efficiencies offer a combination of both. All rooms have coffee makers and are decorated with floral prints and drawback curtains.

An elevated freshwater all-ceramic-tile swimming pool is on-premises. Flamingo Inn offers guests use of its boat ramp a short distance away down a private road. There is plenty of space to park boat trailers at the motel.

Rainbow Bend Resort
$$-$$$ • MM 58 Oceanside, Grassy Key
• (305) 289-1505, (800) 929-1505

Fire up a 15-foot Boston Whaler and head for the flats, for at Rainbow Bend each day of your stay entitles you to four free boating hours. If you'd rather sail, a Sunfish awaits. Prefer a canoe? Paddle away. Stretched across 2½ acres of palm-speckled oceanfront beach, Rainbow Bend presents a mixed bag of accommodations, ranging from large sleeping rooms and efficiencies to oceanfront one- and two-bedroom suites.

Relax under chickees on the lounges and Adirondack chairs that pepper the beach. If fresh water appeals to you, dip into the large pool and hot tub that edge the property. A long, wood pier extends into the shallow ocean waters, where you can drop a line or dock your own small watercraft for the duration of your stay.

Small pets are allowed for an additional fee.

The Hideaway Restaurant, which overlooks the beach, offers lunch and dinner. A complimentary breakfast is served here each morning.

The White Sands Inn
$-$$ • MM 57.5 Oceanside, Grassy Key
• (305) 743-5285

So far the best-kept secret on Grassy Key, news of The White Sands Inn is hereby "out of the bag." Hugging a prime piece of direct ocean frontage, The White Sands Inn — formerly Golden Grouper — has been lovingly refurbished by Dennis and Lavina Conroy, a young couple formerly from Jacksonville, Florida. Opened in December 1997, the pale pink and white inn houses seven one-room units — four efficiencies and three sleeping rooms. All units are freshly painted, have new tile floors, remodeled bathrooms, two queen-size beds and crisp, new bedding. All are air-conditioned, and some sport ceiling fans as well. Efficiencies feature fully equipped kitchens, but even the sleeping rooms are fitted with mini-refrigerators, coffee makers and microwaves so you can self-cater if you wish.

The White Sands Inn nestles amid towering coconut palms, banana trees, bottle-brush bushes and lush manicured vegetation. A giant hammock is strung between two such curving palms at waters' edge, where the Conroys have imported sparkling white sand to form a beach. Grills are available, and a large picnic table rests under a thatched chickee. The ambiance at this intimate hideaway is casual and friendly, due in large part to the unflagging enthusiasm of its owners.

A long curved pier stretches out into the ocean, where two kayaks, a rowboat and a paddleboat are docked for free use by guests. At low tide, the nearshore waters abutting The White Sands Inn recedes forming a natural sandy beach. You can walk for miles along the sandy flats. And rumor has it that bonefish lurk at the edge of the flat.

The White Sands Inn has a boat ramp which guests may use at no charge. Mooring buoys are also available, but keep in mind that the shallow water becomes sand beach at low tide.

Royal Plum Club
$$-$$$, no credit cards • (305) MM 54.5 Oceanside, 133 Coco Plum Dr., Marathon • (305) 289-1102

The garden angel bids, "May all your weeds be wildflowers," in the parklike plantings surrounding the Royal Plum Club vacation apartments. Meander along stone paths and wood boardwalks that wind amid a cascade of orchids hanging from every tree. Sitting directly on a 200-foot private beach on the ocean, this property looks like a piece of the Caribbean.

The spacious, well-appointed units with one, two or three bedrooms offer full kitchens and all linens. All overlook either the subtropical gardens or the heated swimming pool

flanking the Atlantic. If you get restless soaking up the sun and surf, play tennis on Royal Plum's regulation court.

Reservations require a one-week minimum stay.

Coco Plum Beach Villas
$$-$$$, no credit cards • (305) MM 54.5 Oceanside, 133 Coco Plum Dr., Marathon • (305) 289-1102

This four-story stark-white block building — composed of 16 two-bedroom, two-bath condominium villas — neighbors the Royal Plum Club on Coco Plum Beach but offers none of the tropical ambiance. Don't let the lack of vegetation put you off, however. The panoramic ocean view from an elevated swimming pool bordering the private sandy beach will ease those city cares in no time.

The self-catering 1,500-square-foot apartments, each complete with washer and dryer, provide all the essentials for a vacation in Paradise. All units are individually owned, but reservations are handled through the Royal Plum Club.

Reservations require a one-week minimum.

Cocoplum Beach and Tennis Club
$$$-$$$$ • MM 54.5 Oceanside, 109 Coco Plum Dr., Marathon • (305) 743-0240, (800) 228-1587

If you want quiet, quiet, quiet, find the illusive Cocoplum Beach and Tennis Club. Hiding among a stand of mature coconut palms and girdled by sea grape hedges, pigmy date palms and Key lime trees, the pod of 20 three-story "mushrooms" at Cocoplum bestows true island ambiance. The endless ocean stretches to tomorrow, ribboned in a blue-to-green prism like paint chips on a color chart.

Each octagonal villa — ringed with sliding doors to a wraparound deck and screened porch — houses two bedrooms, two baths, a family room with sleeper sofa, wet bar, TV with a VCR, a complete kitchen, dining room, washer and dryer. In 1998 all units were updated with new carpeting and drapes.

Loll by the anvil-shaped swimming pool or pop into a green-and-white-striped cabana on the beach. The hot tub awaits your tired muscles after a few hours of spirited tennis or beach volleyball. Or just fold yourself into one of the many secluded hammocks and take a snooze.

Reservations require a three-night minimum and a full week for Christmas and New Year's. Prices vary by proximity to the ocean.

Howard Johnson Resort
$$$ • MM 54 Oceanside, Marathon • (305) 743-8550, (800) 321-3496

Even though this Howard Johnson facility conforms to the expected motel block construction, lush vegetation creates a tropical feeling you won't find in Kansas.

The rooms are clean and modern, decorated in island rattan. Most rooms have two double beds, but guests have the option of a room with a king-size bed. Every room has a small patio or balcony, each shaded by a personal palm tree.

Children stay for free and enjoy volleyball, a giant sandbox and the pool. You can rent personal watercraft or paddleboats from a private concession on the property. Grills and picnic tables sit on a sandy area overlooking a picturesque cove so you can cook your catch-of-the-day. Or stop at Denny's Restaurant, connected to the motel's lobby, for a quick bite.

Holiday Inn
$$ • MM 54 Oceanside, Marathon • (305) 289-0222, (800) 224-5053

If you fancy staying near watersports action, this Holiday Inn caters to your whims. Kiosks along the tidal basin bordering the motel tender boat rentals, personal watercraft, pontoon boats and fishing charters, and Abyss Pro Dive Center gets you wet with snorkeling/dive trips to the reef (see our Diving chapter).

The rooms — spotless and spacious — commingle the pastels so popular in the tropics. Twelve suites and some standard rooms look out over the marina. Suites and rooms with queen-size beds also contain a sleeper sofa; standard rooms have two double beds.

The tiki bar, which heats up with live entertainment in the late afternoon, is next to the two heated swimming pools — one for adults, one for children.

Children stay for free at the Holiday Inn and, if they are younger than 13, they eat for free as well in the on-premises Royal Pelican

Restaurant and Pub. Holiday Inn honors AARP and other rate discounts.

Sea Isle Condominiums
$$ • MM 54 Oceanside, 1101 W. Ocean Dr., Key Colony Beach • (305) 743-0173

The sandy beach and ocean views distinguish this 29-unit condo resort. Three tri-level, white buildings, one behind another, line Sea Isle's narrow strip of Key Colony Beach. Built in the late '60s and individually owned and decorated, the furnishings of these spacious two-bedroom, two-bath apartments swing widely between styles of ensuing decades. Many were freshened with new ceilings, carpeting or air conditioners in 1998.

Nevertheless, all necessities for a sun-filled, fun-filled vacation are provided: a freshwater, heated swimming pool, shuffleboard, gas grills and picnic tables, lounge chairs and chickees. Stroll down Key Colony's "condo lane" to the public golf course and tennis courts or head into Marathon for a selection of boating, fishing and diving activities (see chapters devoted to those subjects).

Reservations require a one-week minimum.

Continental Inn
$$-$$$ • MM 54 Oceanside, 1121 W. Ocean Dr., Key Colony Beach • (305) 289-0101, (800) 443-7352

Don your mask, fins and snorkel because a small, rocky formation at the edge of Continental Inn's beach supports an aquarium of marine life. Located on the coveted sandy stretch of Key Colony Beach, this condominium resort, with its white stone balustrade, looks faintly Mediterranean. Gulls and terns dart about the lobster-trap buoys hanging from the three oceanfront chickees as guests drink in the limitless vistas of the Atlantic.

These individually owned, simply decorated, one-bedroom efficiencies flank a large, heated swimming pool. A small kitchen/dining/sitting area adjoins each bedroom and bathroom unit. Two, two-bedroom apartments, each of which has a full living room with a sofa and a full eat-in kitchen, provide more spacious quarters for up to four people.

You can play the links at the nearby public golf course, head for the tennis courts or take your kids to a nice playground (see our Recreation chapter). Continental Inn is the only condominium resort on Key Colony Beach to accept walk-ins and offer nightly rates. No boats or trailers are allowed.

Key Colony Beach Motel
$ • MM 54 Oceanside, 441 E. Ocean Dr., Key Colony Beach • (305) 289-0411

Sitting proudly on the oceanside Key Colony Beach, often called "condo row," the modest Key Colony Beach Motel provides simply furnished rooms, each featuring two double beds and a refrigerator, and a primo location. A lovely, palm-lined, sandy beach fronts this two-story, white motel, which also has a heated swimming pool that was refurbished in 1998. Stone tables covered with thatched chickees pepper an oceanfront patio. Sky-blue, mini-Adirondack chairs line the beach so all you need here is a towel, some sunscreen and a good book.

Bonefish Bay Motel
$-$$ • MM 53.5 Oceanside, Marathon • (305) 289-0565, (800) 336-0565

Offering a range of homey accommodations from sleeping rooms with two double beds to one-bedroom apartments, guests at Bonefish Bay enjoy the added luxury of the motel's boat ramp and canalside dockage (3-foot draft) at no extra charge. The motel's location just above Vaca Cut ensures easy boat access to our ocean waters.

Added in 1997 are four units, formerly the caretaker's residence. The renovated facilities include two efficiencies, which feature two double beds, private bath and kitchenette, and two large apartments, each with one bedroom, a full kitchen, living and dining areas and private bath. The apartments can be connected if desired.

A mature landscape of coconut palms frames the unheated raised-deck swimming pool. Now distinctively painted white with screaming yellow trim, Bonefish Bay began its days as a 1950s fishing camp. Guests are treated to free use of bicycles and may use the private Cabana Club beach on Key Colony Beach for a small charge. There is a three-night minimum during high season.

In 1998 Bonefish Bay moved its office to a prominent position on Overseas Highway. The motel now sells bait and tackle as well as basic boating supplies for the convenience of their guests.

Coral Lagoon Resort
$-$$ • MM 53.5 Oceanside, Marathon • (305) 289-0121

The 18 duplex-cottage efficiencies of Coral Lagoon Resort — swaddled in trailing purple and red bougainvillea — flank a quiet, dead-end, deep-water canal. Each unit opens onto a private, canal-side wood deck, where you can lounge in a Pawleys Island hammock strung between the posts of your own private canvas-covered chickee. Dock your boat (up to 30 feet) at the palm-lined bulkhead in front of your room for easy access out Vaca Cut to the ocean.

The units vary in size, but each one features a compact living room, dining area and kitchen as well as a king-size bed or two twins. Most have a sleeper sofa. Each duplex shares a barbecue grill. Many units received new ceramic tile floors in 1998.

Complimentary use of tennis rackets, fishing equipment and a built-in wall safe add an extra touch of hospitality. In addition to enjoying the Coral Lagoon's swimming pool, guests may use the oceanside beach at the Key Colony Beach Club for a small fee.

Seascape
$$-$$$ • MM 51 Oceanside, 1075 75th St., Marathon • (305) 743-6455, (800) 332-7327

It is a family affair at Seascape, a 5-acre oceanfront resort reminiscent of a small exclusive European country-house hotel. Built as a stone-faced private home in 1953, Seascape offers nine refurbished units uniquely reflecting the talents of the owners, Sarah and Bill Stites.

Sarah, an artist whose canvas-filled studio intrigues her guests, has painted stylized tropical fish on the headboards of each bed. African prints dominate the custom-made bedding, and her colossal modern-art creations grace the walls. Books featuring Bill's photography casually adorn the arty barn-board common room, where morning will greet you with a buffet of specialty coffees, tropical fruits and freshly baked muffins. Each evening at 6 PM, complimentary wine and hors d'oeuvres magically appear as Brazilian or Hawaiian slide-guitar music softly whispers through the room.

You will notice small, gracious touches everywhere: a seashell basket of mango soap, sun block and shampoo in each bathroom; thick, luxurious towels; fresh fruit and flowers in every room; and a backyard herb garden for the guests' use.

Seascape has several efficiency units, and, although the other rooms are not equipped with full kitchens, all have small refrigerators. Gas grills, outdoor tables and chairs nest in the shaded gardens in case you care to stay in and cook your own dinner. Purple passion flowers bloom along the white picket fence surrounding the gated swimming pool that hugs the ocean edge.

You can even arrive at Seascape by boat. A deep channel leads to the U-shaped bulkhead that accommodates craft drawing up to 5 feet. Enjoy exploring the saltwater flats in one of Seascape's complimentary kayaks.

To find Seascape, turn on 76th Street toward the ocean and follow the signs.

Seahorse Motel
$ • MM 51 Bayside, Marathon
• (305) 743-6571, (800) 874-1115

You can't miss the hot-pink doors and trim of the Seahorse Motel, a freshly refurbished roadside lodging offering perky, clean, affordable accommodations to cost-conscious travelers. The basic motel-style rooms sport two double beds; some also have a sleeper sofas and mini-refrigerators. Efficiency units have full kitchens. A plugged canal borders the back of the property affording dockage for your boat for an additional fee. Rooms with sliding glass doors open onto canalside patios or overlook the central swimming pool and playground. Gas grills and picnic tables are scattered about the premises.

The Reef Resort
$$-$$$ • MM 50.5 Bayside, Marathon
• (305) 743-7900

As you drive through Marathon, you may spot a cluster of beige spaceships hugging Florida Bay. No, the aliens have not landed. These 22 octagonal villas, suspended on a one-story "landing" shaft, actually provide a luxurious Keys getaway.

Photo: Victoria Shearer

Canalfront bungalows, like these at Coral Lagoon in Marathon, offer the opportunity to moor your boat in front of your unit.

Each villa features the same floor plan — two bedrooms, two baths, a full kitchen and living room with sleeper sofa. The open ceiling vaults around a spoked, central fulcrum. Lushly landscaped grounds surrounding the two newly resurfaced tennis courts belie the fact that The Reef Resort borders the Overseas Highway.

Bicycles, canoes, paddleboats and rowboats are available at no extra charge for guests who can tear themselves away from the freshwater pool. Picnic tables, grills and chickees on the waterfront inspire a cookout at sunset. The Reef Resort's marina offers dockage for your boat of 25 feet or less (5-foot draft at low tide).

Minimum stay at the Reef Resort is four nights.

Sombrero Resort & Lighthouse Marina
$-$$$ • MM 50 Oceanside, 19 Sombrero Blvd., Marathon • (305) 743-2250, (800) 433-8660

Flanking Boot Key Harbor and an adjoining inland canal, Sombrero Resort & Lighthouse Marina offers efficiencies and condominium accommodations with all the amenities of a resort. This destination resort, located in the heart of Marathon between the Overseas Highway and the oceanfront Sombrero Beach, allows you to be within steps of all the action, yet bathed in a laid-back and relaxing atmosphere.

The 121 suites are situated in two three-story, white buildings with covered parking beneath (first-come, first-served). A typical one-bedroom condominium is light, bright, modern and clean, featuring a living room with sleeper sofa, dining area, kitchen, bedroom with a king-size bed and a full bathroom with shower. Some units have two double beds. Connecting doors may be opened between units if desired. Waterview suites received a complete facelift in 1998, now sporting fresh paint and new furnishings. Garden view units also were painted and revitalized with new bedspreads. Complimentary morning coffee is served daily in the lobby.

A keystone deck surrounds the large swimming pool, complete with tiki bar for that midafternoon tropical libation. A game room, also poolside, will amuse the kids with billiards, table soccer and video arcade games. You'll be able to improve your tennis on the four lighted courts under the expert tutelage of Tim Wonderlin. Lessons, round-robins and group drills are scheduled on a regular basis.

Sombrero Resort maintains a marina and a boat ramp. Guests may launch their boats at Sombrero's ramp and secure dockage at one of the slips for an additional fee per day based on availability. Boats and trailers may be kept in the parking lot. The active angler will enjoy the marina's fish-cleaning station and the ready availability of crushed and block ice.

Meeting, conference and banquet rooms are available at Sombrero Resort. And the on-premises Chef's Restaurant offers family dining.

Banana Bay Resort & Marina
$-$$$ • MM 49.5 Bayside, Marathon • (305) 743-3500, (800) 226-2621

Ozzie and Harriet, two blue-crowned conures, raucously squawk from their screened aviary as you register at Banana Bay, the Caribbean plantation-style resort tucked on 10 acres aside Florida Bay. The two residential areas — Island House and Marina Bay House — are only seven years old, an oddity in the Middle Keys. Decked out in the prerequisite Keys teals and peaches, the spacious rooms feature upscale island-style rattan furnishings and Bahama shutters. The grounds, however, are ancient: gnarled trunks of massive royal poinciana trees, 20-foot traveler's palms and mature bird-of-paradise plants. And don't miss the bananas, 15 varieties tucked between towering scheffleras and gumbo limbos, papayas and staggering banyan trees.

INSIDERS' TIP

Most comprehensive dive centers will help you put together an accommodations/dive package, saving you both time and money. See our Diving and Snorkeling chapter for details.

A resident hawk makes regular passes at the small goldfish pond, hoping for an unsuspecting appetizer.

Don't let this quiet island charm fool you. There is plenty to do besides loll by the L-shaped swimming pool or soak in the hot tub. Banana Bay offers an on-premises playland: tennis, parasailing, sea kayaking, windsurfing or rentals of personal watercraft, sailboats and powerboats from Rick's Watercraft Rentals. You can even book an excursion to the reef to snorkel or dive.

Just when you think you can't take any more, Hoot Mon Sail Charters sets off from Banana Bay's marina dock for a sunset champagne cruise (see our Boating and Recreation chapters). The sand-floored tiki bar burned to the ground in 1998, but Banana Bay plans to have the structure rebuilt and bumping and grinding with live entertainment on weekends by the end of the year. Banana Cabana Restaurant, on premises, is conveniently open for lunch and dinner daily. A complimentary continental buffet breaks the day poolside each morning.

Banana Bay offers popular island wedding packages, including a choice of romantic settings for the ceremony. For Banana Bay Sailing School, refer to our Boating chapter.

Marathon Key Beach Club
$$-$$$ • MM 49.5 Bayside, Marathon
• (305) 743-6522

All the comforts of home await you at the Marathon Key Beach Club, where you are greeted with a cackling "Hi!" by Buddy, the resident macaw. Each of these 1,300-square-foot timeshare condominiums features two bedrooms, two baths, a living room with queen-size sleeper sofa, dining alcove, a complete kitchen and washer and dryer. A screened porch off the Berber-carpeted living room nestles in a canopy of mature trees on the shores of Florida Bay.

Gas grills and picnic tables are sprinkled throughout the property. Guests at Marathon Key Beach Club share all the facilities of the adjoining Banana Bay Resort (see separate listing in this chapter), including pool, hot tub, tennis, marina, sandy beach, sunset tiki bar and Banana Cabana Restaurant.

Reservations require a three-night minimum.

The Blackfin Resort
$-$$$ • MM 49.5 Bayside
• (305) 743-2393, (800) 548-5397

Joining the ranks of Marathon's hostelries, The Blackfin Resort — formerly The Hurricane Resort — received tender loving care and a complete refurbishment in 1997. All 35 units have new paint, carpeting, beds and spreads in tropical florals, furniture and drapes and have private baths. Accommodations fall into a number of comfortable, affordable configurations: 16 doubles, each of which features a queen-size bed and small sitting area; eight singles, which are smaller rooms than the doubles, but still are equipped with queen-size beds; and two king rooms, which have king-size beds and loveseats. Some mini-refrigerators are available for these rooms.

For those who like the option of self-catering, The Blackfin Resort maintains six cozy single efficiencies (queen-size bedrooms with kitchenettes), comfortable for two adults; two large efficiencies, each of which features a large kitchen and dining area and two queen-size beds (sleeps five people comfortably with addition of a complimentary rollaway bed); and one very large two-bedroom apartment, a 1,600-square-foot unit that offers a separate kitchen and dining room, two baths and a porch.

The Blackfin Resort sits upon 4½ acres abutting the Gulf of Mexico. The grounds are peppered with poinciana, gumbo limbo and strangler fig trees and curving coconut palms. Stone paths wind through gardens of tropical flora. On a remote point of land at the end of the marina marked by a miniature lighthouse, guests enjoy a 600-foot man-made sandy beach, which is sprinkled with lounge chairs, picnic tables, barbecue grills and a thatched chickee. A freshwater pool overlooks the Gulf. The placid waters of the Gulf shelter a potpourri of angelfish, snappers, parrotfish and sergeant-major fish, a virtual aquarium for anglers and snorkelers.

A large marina accommodates guests' vessels at no extra charge. The resort lies just 2 nautical miles from the Seven Mile Bridge for easy access to the Atlantic for fishing or diving. Benches and a fish cleaning station at the marina are well-utilized by anglers. Personal watercraft and kayak rentals are available on premises.

Hidden Harbor Motel
$ • MM 48.5 Bayside, Marathon
• (305) 743-5376, (800) 362-3495

If you're looking for a clean and simple room plus boat dockage and a spectacular view of the bayside sunset, this is the place. The 21 reasonably priced rooms of 52-year-old Hidden Harbor each supply two double beds, a two-burner hot plate, a small refrigerator and a full bath.

New in 1998 is the Honeymoon Cottage, a one-bedroom hideaway near the Gulf that features a full kitchen, living room and bath. Decorated in island rattan and tropical florals, the cottage rents for $175 per night in high season; a three-night minimum is required.

Guests enjoy a freshwater swimming pool and may dock their small boats at no additional charge. Hidden Harbor maintains a video rental facility on premises.

Hidden within this unassuming motel property, far from the madding crowd percolating up and down the Overseas Highway, nurtures a special secret: Hidden Harbor is also the home of the renowned Turtle Hospital. Guests at the motel are among the privileged few invited to tour the hospital, where they are treated to a slide show about the turtle recovery program. At 5 PM every day, registered guests can watch as volunteers feed the turtles and disperse their medications at the saltwater turtle recovery room. (see our Paradise Found chapter).

Blue Waters Motel
$-$$ • MM 48.5 Bayside, Marathon
• (305) 743-4832

You'll enjoy a Mediterranean feeling here at Blue Waters Motel, for the white stucco buildings, gray tile roofs and bright, turquoise-blue doors evoke visions of Greece. Two banks of motel units, some with efficiency kitchens, flank the parking lot. The rooms feature two double beds or a king-size bed. Rooms were renovated with new tile floors in 1997.

A raised swimming pool affords a view of a small boat basin on the Gulf where guests may dock their boats for a small additional charge per day. Check out the wood double-bench swing that nestles under a huge octopus-like cactus. The swing sports a table between the two seats, where several people

can glide the afternoon away, playing checkers or cards or just dreaming.

The toll-free reservations-only number is (800) 222-4832.

Faro Blanco Marine Resort
$-$$$ • MM 48 Bayside, Marathon
• (305) 743-9018, (800) 759-3276

Straddling the Overseas Highway, Faro Blanco Marine Resort fronts both the Atlantic and the Gulf of Mexico with a potpourri of lodging alternatives. Forty years ago Jim Kelsey (who no longer owns the resort) bought the original 32 bayside fishing-camp cottages, now updated but still retaining a rustic Conch feeling. Neighboring the cottages, twin towers of 16 individually owned two- and three-bedroom condominiums (each 2,000 square feet) are equipped for rental with all the amenities. Access to the tennis courts within this secured property is granted only to guests staying at the condos.

Perhaps the most recognized lighthouse in the Middle Keys, Faro Blanco's working navigational structure lights up the bayside marina. You may stay in either of the two upper-level apartments or book deep-sea and backcountry charters in the lower level outfitters (see our Fishing chapter). An Olympic-size swimming pool adjoins Angler's Lounge, which purrs at lunchtime and pulses the night away with entertainment and dancing. Kelsey's Restaurant, below Angler's, wines and dines with upscale continental cuisine (see our Restaurants chapter). A free shuttle service transports you to Faro Blanco Oceanside.

Not a landlubber? Stay on one of Faro Blanco's permanently moored houseboats. These floating staterooms and efficiencies won't make you seasick. They are stabilized to go only up and down with the tide. The decor is contemporary, and the houseboats feature private decks with fabulous views. For a small additional charge, you can lash your own craft (up to 25 feet) to the houseboat dock.

Rent small boats and personal watercraft on premises or take sailing lessons from Annapolis Sailing School (see our Boating chapter). Crocodile's On The Water, another Faro Blanco restaurant, pleases the palate with a casual offering of seafood, steaks and salads (see our Restaurants chapter).

Latigo Bed and Breakfast Cruise
$$$$ • MM 47.5 Oceanside, 11th St., Marathon Marina, Marathon
• **(305) 289-1066**

Sample the lifestyle of the rich and famous aboard the 56-foot yacht *Latigo*, where captains Ken and Val Waine will pamper you and spirit you away for a bed-and-breakfast cruise or a multi-day sojourn into "the beyond." The *Latigo* features a spacious main salon, a king-size master bedroom aft and a double and two singles forward; it carries a maximum of six passengers. You'll enjoy gourmet repasts prepared by Val in the galley.

Prices range from $159 per person for an overnight bed and breakfast cruise to a $5,600 flat rate per week. Or, the Waines will customize a charter for you anywhere in the Florida Keys, the Dry Tortugas, the Florida West Coast or the Bahamas. The Waines also cater to sunset wedding ceremonies and bed-and-breakfast weddings. (See our Restaurants chapter for information on *Latigo's* dinner and sunset cruises.)

To find the yacht, turn on 11th Street toward the ocean at MM 47.5. Drive past Shucker's restaurant and look for slip 73 on the right.

Lower Keys

The Lower Keys, sleepier and less densely populated than the Middle or Upper Keys, distinguish themselves with acres and acres of shallow-water turtle grass flats and copious uninhabited mangrove out-islands. This is a gunkholing bonanza. The Lower Keys are surrounded by the Great White Heron National Wildlife Refuge, a large area in the Gulf of Mexico encompassing tiny keys from East Bahia Honda Key to the Content Keys to Cayo Agua and the Bay Keys. Big Pine Key is the home of the National Key Deer Refuge, a preserved area of wilderness sheltering our diminutive Key deer. See our Paradise Found chapter for details.

Fishing is outstanding here, though ocean access is more limited (see our Fishing chapter). The Lower Keys can also boast of the Looe Key National Marine Sanctuary, one of the best snorkeling and diving reefs in the world (see our Diving chapter).

Accommodations are scattered through-

out the Lower Keys, where campgrounds tend to predominate (see our Campgrounds chapter if you'd like to camp in the area). Most of the accommodations started as fishing camps decades ago and have been updated to varying degrees. Several wonderful bed-and-breakfast inns are tucked away on a little-known oceanfront road, offering seclusion, privacy and limitless vistas of the sea.

Crowning the assets of Lower Keys accommodations is Little Palm Island, a premier resort that rules in a class by itself. Whatever your lodging choice in the sanctuaries of the Lower Keys, your close proximity to Key West more than makes up for any tourist attractions or nightlife that may be lacking here.

Barnacle Bed & Breakfast
$$ • 1557 Long Beach Dr., Big Pine Key
• **(305) 872-3298, (800) 465-9100**

Isolated from the clot of autos percolating down the Overseas Highway toward Key West, the Barnacle Bed & Breakfast lolls on a serene stretch of beach on an elbow of oölite extending into the Atlantic. Constructed as three rotated, star-shaped levels, the Barnacle is a study in contradictions.

The generous Tarpon and Dolphin rooms on the second level, with two queen-size beds per room, open to a foliage-filled atrium that houses the hot tub. Comfortably furnished with ceiling fans, a sofa, television, table and chairs, the atrium serves as a common room. Guests meet here each morning for a complimentary breakfast buffet. The Blue Heron cottage perches in an outbuilding, its stained-glass windows lending a romantic perspective. Both the Blue Heron and the Ocean room (which nearly rests on the sand) have kitchens, living rooms, private entrances and patios. In stark contrast to the laid-back tropical surroundings, art deco dominates every guest room. Each ceiling radiates a different color, and tile designs pervade the bathrooms.

A circular stairway crawls to the crow's nest, where you can recline on lounge chairs to soak up the sun. Or perhaps you'd like to roll into one of the many hammocks strung between palms around the property.

Owners Tim and Jane Marquis provide a catamaran, a paddleboat, bicycles and snorkeling gear, so you need not drive back into the fray. Barbecue grills are a nice touch for those wishing to fire up the barbie. Children younger than 16 are not permitted. Smoking is permitted only outside the guest rooms.

Finding Long Beach Road is a little dicey: Turn left at Big Pine Fishing Lodge, MM 33 Oceanside, and proceed about 2 miles.

Casa Grande Bed & Breakfast
$, no credit cards • MM 33 Oceanside, 1619 Long Beach Dr., Big Pine Key
• (305) 872-2878

The architecture of this mission-style hacienda harkens back to the roots of the Spanish conquistadors who once settled in the Keys. The second of a trio of bed and breakfast inns along oceanfront Long Beach Drive, Casa Grande exudes a reserved, almost mystical, charm. Owner Kathleen Threlkeld recycled the foyer light fixture and stained glass from a demolished church in New York City; from Maryland she salvaged the clanking old mission bell on the red tile roof.

All three airy bedrooms with combination louvered and paneled doors feature both Bahama fans and individually controlled central air conditioning. Queen-size beds and private baths grace the nicely appointed rooms, and each is equipped with a small refrigerator, television and sofa. You can watch television by the seldom-needed fireplace in the common room or hop into the hot tub on the deck. The hostess serves a full breakfast at 8:30 AM daily in the garden patio. Bicycles, windsurfers and snorkeling equipment afford you a little exercise if you are between books.

If you'd like to bring your boat, Casa Grande's canal will accommodate craft up to 26 feet in length. Children are not allowed at Casa Grande. There is a two-night minimum and reservations are essential.

To find Long Beach Road, turn left at Big Pine Fishing Lodge, MM 33 Oceanside, and proceed about 2 miles.

Deer Run Bed & Breakfast
$$, no credit cards • MM 33 Oceanside, Long Beach Dr., Big Pine Key
• (305) 872-2015

The diminutive Key deer really do have the run of this Florida cracker-style home, for they stroll the grounds like boarded guests. Owner Sue Abbott met the herd 12 years ago when she first bought the property, and they've remained fast friends ever since. Staying at Deer Run is akin to vacationing in a nature preserve. Self-proclaimed the "Mother Teresa of wildlife," Abbott hand-raises macaws, and 5-year-old Miss Mango and 6-year-old Wally Brown join Tarp and Lola and a half-dozen others in a wild cacophony. Count Dracula, one of several revered cats at Deer Run, stalks the wild game, who pay him nevermind.

If you love animals and eccentricity, the three diverse units at Deer Run emanate a homey folksy appeal. A complimentary bottle of private-label Deer Run California wine awaits your private tasting. Two of the three rooms have a private entry and bath. A king-size bed fills the lower level oceanfront room, which sports a large, screened porch. A small, affordable room-without-a-view is accessed from the side yard. And in the upper level of the main house, a queen-size bed distinguishes the oceanfront third bedroom, the bathroom facilities of which are the conventional hallway variety.

A sign at the door of Deer Run admonishes, "Please remove your shoes." Instructions in the antiques-filled common room relate, "Breakfast on the veranda at 8:30 AM," "Do not feed the deer" and "P.S., the birds bite!" The peaceful beach, only 50 feet beyond the raised hot tub, fronts a productive bonefish flat. After you've visited with the animals, wade out and spot a tailing fish.

Deer Run caters to adults. Smoking is not permitted. A three-night minimum is required on holidays. Payment must be made in cash or traveler's checks. (To find Long Beach Road, turn left at Big Pine Fishing Lodge, MM 33, and proceed about 2 miles.)

Canal Cottage
$ • MM 30.5 Bayside, Big Pine Key
• (305) 872-3881

You won't find this old-style weathered-wood stilt cottage on your own. Tucked back in a residential area of Big Pine on a shady canal, the modern yet rustic duplex units of Canal Cottage offer a quaint alternative to the older motels of the Lower Keys. Bahamian shutters made of metal louvers salvaged from old buildings in Key West frame the many windows.

As in days of yore, Canal Cottage relies on ceiling fans and island breezes instead of air conditioning. The facility consists of two two-story units sitting side by side; each is a completely furnished one-bedroom apartment connected by a long porch overlooking the canal and separated by a breezeway. Both units have queen-size beds on the second floor and opening skylights. Each apartment has a single bath opening into the bedroom. A wood divider can be removed if two couples wish to rent both duplex units of Canal Cottage.

Grills and bicycles are provided, and guests may swim and play tennis at the Indian Mounds Racquet and Swim Club on Sugarloaf Key. You may dock your boat of up to 25 feet in the canal in front of the cottage.

Reservations require a two-night minimum. Weekly rates are available.

Old Wooden Bridge Fishing Camp
$, no credit cards • MM 30.5 Bayside, 1791 Bogie Dr., Big Pine Key • (305) 872-2241

Old-timers love this historic bastion of another era that hugs the shores of the Bogie Channel. Things haven't changed much since men training at No Name Key for duty in the Bay of Pigs invasion used to come over to drop a line, have a beer or play some cards. Owner Jim Oettle still deals a few hands with his regulars on the oilcloth covered table in the bait and tackle shop. The 13 one- and two-bedroom cottages have been updated to a mid-1950s style.

There are no amenities of modern life here, so leave your dreams of faxing, swimming in chlorine and watching soaps behind. Be sure to book early and plan on paying a deposit with a check or cash.

Parmer's Place
$-$$$ • MM 28.5 Bayside, 565 Barry Ave., Little Torch Key • (305) 872-2157

Started as a fishing camp in the 1930s and owned by Frank and Ardith Parmer for 24 years, Parmer's Place is something of an institution in the Lower Keys. The 43 units in 13 buildings sprinkled over the 5-acre property have copped the monikers of the fish, birds and flora populating the Florida Keys.

From the Grunt, Hibiscus and Flamingo to the Permit, Spoonbill and Jasmine, the homey '60s-style units differ widely in both size and amenities. Small, medium and large motel rooms, standard and small efficiencies, cottages and one- and two-bedroom apartments, are all clean and simple.

Fronting Big Pine Channel, Parmer's offers boat dockage at a small additional fee, but there is no beach. A free-form swimming pool ringed by red ixora anchors the center of the property. You'll need to use a pay phone to call the office, and you must pick up after yourself or pay a fee for maid service. But you can always stoke up the barbie and cook your room's namesake for dinner if you're staying in the Snapper, Wahoo or Cobia rooms. A complimentary continental breakfast is served daily. One partially handicapped-accessible unit is available.

Dolphin Marina Resort at Little Palm Village
$-$$$ • MM 28.5 Oceanside, Little Torch Key • (305) 872-2685, (800) 553-0308

If snorkeling, diving, fishing and boating top your agenda of must-do activities, consider staying in the bustling Dolphin Marina Resort, which became a Noble House Resort in 1997. Canals border two sides of the peninsular marina, and an almost-a-beach shoreline on Newfound Harbor forms the third. A variety of diverse suites speckles the property, most with two bedrooms, one bath, a completely equipped kitchen, a living area and a screened porch or patio.

Book a charter at the docks to fish the bluewater or the backcountry, or rent a motor boat for a day or half-day and explore the neighboring waters yourself (see our Boating chapter). Marina staff are very helpful in plotting a waterway route to rookery out-islands and sand spits. A bait store, fuel dock and ship's store cater your provisioning needs.

Little Palm Island
$$$$ • MM 28.5 Oceanside, Little Torch Key • (305) 872-2524, (800) 343-8567

Superlatives fall short when describing Little Palm Island because this tiny slice of Paradise soars off the charts. An exquisite resort encapsulated on its own 5-acre island 3 miles offshore from Little Torch Key, Little Palm is the centerpiece of the jeweled necklace of the Florida Keys.

Fourteen thatched-roof villas, reminiscent of the South Pacific, shelter Little Palm's privileged guests. One-bedroom suites (two under each thatch) pamper you with opulence: a cozy sitting room, complete with a stocked mini-bar and coffee maker; a separate bedroom with a king-size bed romantically draped in mosquito netting; a Guatemalan lounger and a polished wicker writing desk; a lavish dressing room with vanity and a luxurious Mexican-tile bathroom sporting an indoor whirlpool and privately fenced outdoor shower. A full-service spa provides massages, facials, pedicures, manicures and body treatments, either in your suite or in the bathhouse.

The island restores your soul as well. Television sets, telephones and alarm clocks are banned, ensuring your escape from reality. Curving coconut palms and flourishing flora pepper the grounds surrounding the villas. At Little Palm Island, you can elevate doing nothing at all to an art form. The unhurried pace encourages serious lounging aside the free-form pool, atop the crystal sand beach or enveloped in a two-person hammock.

When you've unwound at last and you're ready to function vertically once again, the island offers a cornucopia of diversions. Play with Little Palm's complimentary toys — windsurfers, day sailers, kayaks, canoes, sailboats and snorkeling and fishing equipment. Rent a pontoon boat or a nifty Sun-Kat motorized lounge chair and gunk-hole around the surrounding miniature mangrove islets. Dive Looe Key National Marine Sanctuary or hire a backcountry guide and fish for tarpon, permit or bonefish. Head offshore with a sportfishing captain and catch that marlin, or set sail on the *Chimera* for a sunset or moonlight cruise. And if you are really adventurous (and your pocketbook is limitless), Little Palm will shuttle you to a deserted island by seaplane for a tropical tryst.

Access to Little Palm Island is provided from its mainland substation at Little Torch Key. The aptly named launch, *Escape*, ferries you and your worldly possessions to this very civilized outpost. Meals are taken in the outstanding gourmet dining room (see our Restaurants chapter). Choose one of two plans while on the island: The Modified Meal Plan

(most popular option) provides a choice of any two meals per day; the Full Meal Plan supplies breakfast, lunch and dinner.

Once a fishing camp called Little Munson Island, this quiet hermitage hosted the nation's movers and shakers, such as presidents Roosevelt, Truman, Kennedy and Nixon. Little Palm Island still attracts a tony clientele. Such notables as Vice President Al and Second Lady Tipper Gore and Joan Lunden, formerly of *Good Morning America*, found the lifestyle irresistible.

Little Palm Island and its restaurant garner myriad awards and accolades from rating services and publications all over the world, consistently ranking in the top 10. But Insiders know Little Palm Island is No. 1 in the Florida Keys. Children younger than 16 are not permitted.

Sugarloaf Lodge
$-$$ • MM 17 Bayside, Sugarloaf Key • (305) 745-3211

For 25 years, Sugar, a gray Atlantic bottle-nosed dolphin, held court in her private lagoon here at Sugarloaf Lodge. Sadly, Sugar died of natural causes in the summer of 1997. Although gone in body, Sugar is still very much in evidence, as you might expect since she spent most of her 32 years at this fascinating resort.

Built in the early 1960s, Sugarloaf Lodge retains the best of the era, due in no small measure to the personable attentions of Lloyd and Miriam Good, owners for more than 25 years. The 55 motel-style sleeping rooms all have direct water views of either Sugarloaf Bay or the marina canal. Though the furniture is a little dated, drapes and spreads are crisp and bright, and gigantic wall murals of local flora and fauna lend an artsy allure.

Sugarloaf Lodge is at the periphery of the Great White Heron National Wildlife Refuge. Egrets and herons and their shoestring relatives visit Sugarloaf Lodge on a regular basis. Just beyond the croton-bordered west-wing guest rooms lies the Sugarloaf Dolphin Sanctuary, a release and retirement facility for previously captive dolphins that is run by the Goods' son, Lloyd III.

When you feel like a little exercise, play tennis at one of the Lodge's two courts, swim in the freshwater pool, putt a round of miniature golf or compete at shuffleboard. Equipment for these diversions and a lending library

Cigar-worker cottages accented with lush foliage have
been revamped for a peaceful accommodation option.

are available in the Lodge reception lobby. Sugarloaf Lodge leases some of its property to outside suppliers, thereby providing guests with nearby pertinent essentials: a marina, bank, country store and gas station.

The Goods are back in the restaurant business too. They again manage the on-premises Sugarloaf Lodge restaurant, which they unsatisfactorily leased out during the past several years. Captain Chuck spins the platters for dancing '60s-style each Friday and Saturday in the restaurant's Pirates Lounge. But to qualify as a serious loafer, you must take the time to sample Sugarloaf's famed strawberry daiquiri (the original!) at the tiki bar. Sip slowly as you watch the equally famous sunset melt into Sugarloaf Bay.

Caribbean Village
$-$$ • MM 10.7 Bayside, Big Coppitt Key • (305) 296-9542

Each evening, tiki lights illuminate the white-trimmed pastel clapboards of the Key West-style Caribbean Village. Units range from an inexpensive sleeping room with an outside bath to a much grander floating unit, popular with wedding parties, that can open to five rooms. Some feature an efficiency kitchen in addition to a sleeping room and bath and have a metal spiral staircase that can connect the lower quarters to another unit above.

Only 10 miles from Key West, Caribbean Village offers the best of both worlds: It is close to the action but quiet and away from the fray.

Key West

This diverse, charming, historic and romantic city is considered one of the nation's top travel destinations. Key West's accommodations range from the comfort of a standard motel room to the luxury of a private suite in a historic inn. In this section, we escort you through a variety of facilities. Our selections are based on attributes of rooms, service, location and overall ambiance, and all facilities have air conditioning, cable television and telephones unless stated otherwise.

Daily rates for the high-season (mid- to late December through early to mid-April) for double-occupancy are categorized in the Price Code. Because many facilities offer a variety of accommodations within one property, we have provided a range, the first to indicate the rate for a typical room and the second for more complex units, such as apartments and suites. Prices indicated in the key do not include the 11.5 percent room tax, room service or added fees for phone calls, rollaway bed and crib rentals and other incidentals. In most cases, an additional per-person charge is levied when occupancy exceeds two. Off-season rates are typically lower, and in some cases dramatically less.

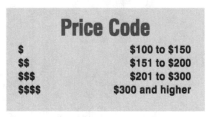

Price Code

$	$100 to $150
$$	$151 to $200
$$$	$201 to $300
$$$$	$300 and higher

Motels, Hotels and Resorts

Motels often cater to families, Europeans, last-minute travelers, spring breakers and active, outdoorsy types. Count celebrities among those who enjoy our full-service resorts. While filming the movie *True Lies* in the Florida Keys, Arnold Schwarzenegger chose The Pier House; *Good Morning America* host Charles Gibson and former co-host Joan Lunden stayed at the Key West Hyatt. Couples often opt for romantic weddings and honeymoons at hotels that offer tropical breezes, lush foliage, crystal seas and magnificent sunsets. And when spring break rolls around, college students throughout the country head for Key West's less expensive hotels, motels and chains.

Hotels, motels and resorts on this island tend to be so pricey that it is difficult to find a room for less than $100 during the high season (mid- to late December through early to mid-April). During Fantasy Fest (see our Annual Events chapter) in October and Christmas week, rates jump even higher.

Some chains and individually owned motels along N. Roosevelt Boulevard offer waterfront accommodations. Near the city's shopping centers and fast food restaurants in New Town, they are somewhat removed from the charm of the city's historic district, the hustle and bustle of Duval Street and public beaches.

Motels

Best Western Hibiscus Motel
$-$$ • 1313 Simonton St., Key West
• (305) 294-3763, (800) 972-5100

As Best Westerns go, this independently owned affiliate is small and understated. It is also one of few chains or franchises within Key West's historic Old Town. Of concrete-block construction, the Hibiscus has 61 units, including standard rooms and five one-bedroom efficiencies.

Standard rooms are relatively large with two queen-size beds, while efficiencies offer separate bedrooms and kitchens. Decor is bright and clean in a mainly blue color scheme and features wood furnishings, carpeting and coordinating wallpaper and bedspread patterns. All units overlook either the motel's heated swimming pool and hot tub or the street and a variety of palms. Bicycles are available for rent, and cribs cost an additional $5 per night. Four people can share a room at the given rate.

Blue Lagoon
$-$$ • 3101 N. Roosevelt Blvd., Key West
• (305) 296-1043

Most of the 72 rooms in this one- and two-story complex are furnished either with one queen-size or two double beds; six have king-

size beds. First-floor rooms have tile floors, and upstairs rooms are carpeted. Cedar furnishings and walls provide a rustic appeal. Some rooms offer full water views.

Blue Lagoon has a swimming pool and a cement sun deck facing the Gulf, and along the motel's small beach are watersport rentals for personal watercraft, fishing boats, parasailing and pontoon boats. Parking is outside your door. Rates are based on double occupancy, with each additional guest costing $10 per night. Cots also are an additional $10 per night.

Comfort Inn at Key West
$-$$ • 3824 N. Roosevelt Blvd., Key West
• (305) 294-3773, (800) 228-5150

Guests at the two-story Comfort Inn have a choice of 100 rooms housed in three buildings. Options include a room with two double beds or a few larger rooms with king-size beds. The rooms are carpeted and have comfortable furnishings; rollaways are provided upon request to a limited number of rooms. Smoking and nonsmoking rooms are available as are handicapped-accessible facilities.

The motel is less than a half-mile from the Stock Island Bridge and is across the street from the Gulf of Mexico. Rooms face either the pool or the parking lot. Those on the second floor share a common balcony.

The motel offers complimentary continental breakfast and maintains a large outdoor swimming pool surrounded by concrete decking. Scooter rentals are on-premises, and public transportation is available. Complimentary hot and cold beverages are served in the lobby throughout the day.

Children younger than 17 stay free.

Comfort Inn proprietors also own Econo Lodge (see listing in this section) next door, where a poolside tiki bar, 24-hour restaurant, dance club and coin-operated laundry are available.

Econo Lodge Resort of Key West
$-$$ • 3820 N. Roosevelt Blvd., Key West
• (305) 294-5511, (800) 766-7584

Next door to the Comfort Inn (see listing in this section) is the six-story Econo Lodge, offering 145 rooms with two double beds or a king-size bed. Suites and efficiencies also are available. The honeymoon suite, with king-size bed, Jacuzzi bathtub and living room with mini-fridge, microwave, coffee maker and stove, has a private balcony with a view of the city and of the Gulf of Mexico across the street. Most other rooms face either the city or the Gulf.

On premises at Econo Lodge are an outdoor swimming pool, a tiki bar, dance club, 24-hour Denny's restaurant and coin-operated laundry. Guests receive discount coupons for on-premises scooter rentals. Public transportation is easily accessed from here, and front desk personnel will assist you with sightseeing and sporting excursions.

Handicapped-accessible facilities and smoking and nonsmoking rooms are available. Children younger than 17 stay free.

Fairfield Inn by Marriott
$-$$ • 2400 N. Roosevelt Blvd., Key West • (305) 296-5700, (800) 228-2800

Fairfield Inn's easygoing prices and comfortable, well-kept facilities make this one of Key West's popular choices with vacationers. The motel offers 100 standard rooms and 32 suites throughout three two-story buildings. Standard rooms primarily are furnished with two double beds; suites with varying amenities, including kitchens or kitchenettes and king-size beds, are other options.

Completely remodeled in 1994, Fairfield Inn offers contemporary furnishings and attractive decor. On premises are two swimming pools, gas grills, a tiki bar, a volleyball court and guest laundry facilities. A separate concessionaire offers on-premises scooter rentals.

Complimentary continental breakfast is offered daily, and covered parking spaces are available. The inn has smoking and nonsmoking rooms.

The Santa Maria Motel
$-$$ • 1401 Simonton St., Key West • (305) 296-5678, (800) 821-5397

This 50-unit one- and two-story motel has one of the city's few lap swimming pools; the pool features a tiled ship motif and is surrounded by stone. Sadly, the Santa Maria's gourmet restaurant closed in 1997; however, the motel is within walking distance of several eateries.

Rooms are categorized as economy, with a double bed or two twin beds; deluxe, larger

than the economy room, with two double or one king-size bed; one-bedroom efficiency, which has a double and single bed, two studio beds, a dinette set and a small kitchen; and deluxe efficiency, without a kitchen or dividing walls but instead offering white-brick dividers and a mirrored dressing area with wash basin.

All units are carpeted and have basic wood furnishings set against pastel colors and tropical prints. Deluxe rooms have private balconies overlooking gardens. All deluxe efficiencies have private balconies overlooking the pool; one-bedroom efficiencies face the courtyard.

A particularly appealing feature of the Santa Maria is its location: two blocks to Key West's popular Southernmost Point (see our Attractions chapter) and near stores, restaurants, beaches and Duval Street. Set in Key West's historic preservation district, the facility experiences a high return rate of visitors. Off-street parking is provided outside your door.

South Beach Oceanfront Motel
$-$$ • 508 South St., Key West • (305) 296-5611, (800) 354-4455

Built in the 1950s and renovated in 1992, this two-story 47-unit motel sits on a peninsula overlooking the water. As waterfront properties go, it provides an incredible value, with 90 percent of its rooms offering a full ocean view. Carpeted rooms appointed in florals and pastels primarily feature king-size and double beds, and all rooms have safes. Balconies overlook the beachfront bay from six rooms, and three of these have kitchenettes.

South Beach also has an Olympic-size swimming pool, a tanning pier leading to the Atlantic and an on-site dive concierge. The motel offers limited parking, but its owners and managers also operate the Southernmost Motel (see listing in this section), which provides additional spaces.

Southernmost Motel in the USA
$-$$ • 1319 Duval St., Key West • (305) 296-6577, (800) 354-4455

Gingerbread architectural detail, native flora and pavement all come together at Southernmost Motel, if only to remind visitors that they have reached an eclectic city on an island. Situated just across from South Beach,

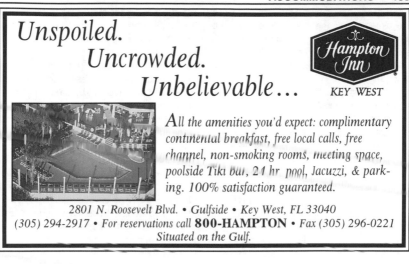
Southernmost's six buildings are surrounded by ample parking and are trimmed with exotic plants, flowers and trees. One of the motel's two swimming pools sits in the center of the parking lot, concealed by lush greenery and a wall. The main pool, surrounded by decking, and a hot tub are in the courtyard. Each pool has its own outdoor bar.

Rooms have either two double beds or a king- or queen-size bed; some rooms include sleeper sofas. A large room with two double beds and a kitchen serves as the facility's one and only efficiency. Some rooms have private balconies.

Scooter and bicycle rentals are on premises, and concierge services are available. A tiki bar on the property serves light bites for breakfast and lunch. Southernmost Motel is handicapped-accessible and offers smoking and nonsmoking rooms. Children younger than 18 stay free.

Hotels

Best Western
Key Ambassador Resort
$$ • 3755 S. Roosevelt Blvd., Key West
• (305) 296-3500, (800) 432-4315

The Best Western Key Ambassador Resort consists of a cluster of two-story buildings scattered throughout 7 acres of profuse tropical gardens punctuated by palm trees and hibiscus across from the Atlantic Ocean. All 100

units have pleasant views of either the garden, the harbor, the pool or the ocean.

Rooms are decorated in "Key West tropical" — light wood furnishings and floral bedspreads and drapes — and the walls are hung with the works of local artists. Floors are a combination of tile and pastel carpeting, and guests have a choice of two double beds or a king-size bed. Each unit is equipped with mini-refrigerator and has its own private balcony.

Central to Best Western Key Ambassador and overlooking the ocean is an elevated (heated in winter) swimming pool with a sun deck. A small bar and grill sits beside it. For do-it-yourselfers, a cookout area offers barbecue grills and outdoor tables and chairs. Other amenities include guest laundry facilities and a daily complimentary continental breakfast.

From Best Western Key Ambassador it's a 15-minute walk to Smathers Beach and 2 miles to historic Old Town. Scooter rentals are available next door; children younger than 10 stay free at the resort.

Hampton Inn
$$-$$$ • 2801 N. Roosevelt Blvd., Key West • (305) 294-2917, (800) 395-1634

The L-shaped design of Hampton Inn provides bay-view rooms in back of the building; Gulf-view and garden-view rooms are also available. All 157 rooms are carpeted, with king-size beds or two double beds and all-wood decor. All rooms are the same size with the exception of the one-bedroom hot-tub suite, which has a king-size bed, two televisions, a stereo system, a mini-refrigerator, a sleeper sofa and an oversize bath with glass-block shower.

The swimming pool and hot tub are open 24 hours a day, and lunch and full outdoor bar service is provided in a nearby tiki hut. Hampton Inn's gazebo overlooks the bay, providing a quiet alternative to Mallory Square for sunset viewing. Parking spaces under the hotel are available, and a full parking lot is in front of the building.

Also on-premises are a gift shop and personal watercraft, bicycle and scooter rentals. A complimentary continental breakfast buffet, including toast, muffins and cereals, is offered daily in the lobby. Local telephone calls also are free, and guests may request discount passes to a nearby fitness facility.

At the Hampton Inn, rates vary according to the room's view and the size of the bed you select. Rooms with king-size beds are slightly more expensive than those with double beds. Weekend rates, too, are higher. Rates are assigned on a per-room basis, however, so rooms with two doubles sleep as many as four, while rooms with king-size beds can accommodate as many as three.

Rollaways cost $15 per day and mini-refrigerators, $10 per day; use of cribs is free. Hampton Inn also maintains designated pet rooms, with guests paying $20 per night per pet. The Hampton Inn guarantees guest satisfaction; if you're not satisfied, your night's stay is free.

Holiday Inn La Concha
$-$$ • **430 Duval St., Key West**
• **(305) 296-2991, (800) 745-2191**

Not your typical Holiday Inn, the La Concha offers visitors the opportunity to step back into a rich past while enjoying all of the amenities of the present. Built as the Hotel La Concha in 1926, the seven-story facility remains the tallest building in the city. At the time the hotel was built, Key West's accommodations were limited, and La Concha's owners spent more than $800,000 to construct and furnish their facility. Room rates were $3 per night, and an additional 35¢ would buy guests a steak dinner. During the 1930s Hotel La Concha, then known as the Key West Colonial,

was the setting for numerous banquets. In 1945 legendary jazz musician Louis Armstrong performed a benefit concert here.

Today, marble, stone and frosted glass in the hotel's angular lobby suggest art-deco influences; paddle fans cool a glass-enclosed atrium; a self-playing piano sounds by the lounge; black-and-white photographs of the original hotel and its view line the lobby walls; and a halogen lamp hangs from the lobby's vaulted ceiling. Some of Hotel La Concha's original furnishings are scattered throughout the facility.

Old World-style furnishings and accessories adorn each of the hotel's 160 rooms and 10 suites, all of which offer either one king-size or two double beds. Lace curtains and pleated print shades frame views of the city; bedside lamps with fringed shades provide ample reading light. Period armoires conceal 25-inch color televisions with Nintendo games. Room service is available throughout the day and evening. Parking is free.

Within the hotel are two restaurants that offer everything from sports-bar fare and entertainment to elegant fine dining. You'll also find two gift shops, an outdoor spa, swimming pool and lounge on the premises. The top floor provides meeting space, and a sunset bar is open to the public. The wraparound terrace is an ideal place to view both the sunset and boaters on the water.

Pelican Landing Resort & Marina
$-$$$$ • **915 Eisenhower Dr., Key West**
• **(305) 296-7583, (800) 527-8108**

You've found your home away from home in the inconspicuous gulfside Pelican Landing, a concrete-block condominium and marina complex with an on-site manager. Among the 32 units, guests are offered a choice of standard rooms with two double beds or one, two-or three-bedroom suites. All accommodations are decorated according to the taste of their individual owners.

Suites have balconies overlooking the marina, and those on the fourth (top) floor are duplex-style with either loft bedrooms or two enclosed second-story bedrooms. Large sliding glass doors with vertical blinds lead to furnished balconies, and all suites have washer/dryers. Suites have king-size beds in the master bedroom, two double beds in the second and third bedrooms and queen-size sleeper sofas. Some suites have hot tubs. A one-bedroom penthouse suite is among the most romantic.

Pelican Landing's heated swimming pool is surrounded by a sun deck. Gas barbecue grills and a fish-cleaning station are available for guests. The facility is boat-accessible by powerboat only because a fixed bridge offers only an 18-foot clearance. All guests have off-street parking. Charter fishing boats are just across the dock.

Full-Service Resorts

Hyatt Key West
$$$-$$$$ • 601 Front St., Key West
• (305) 296-9900, (800) 554-9288

Fronting on the Gulf of Mexico, the five-story Hyatt Key West is a three-building, 120-unit complex of standard rooms, junior suites and standard suites, all with sliding glass doors and private balconies. Rooms overlook the city, pool or Gulf of Mexico.

Fully carpeted except for tile entranceways, standard rooms generally face the city and have one king-size or two double beds, fully-stocked mini-bars, hair dryers, coffee makers, irons and ironing boards. Some have ceiling fans, and bathrobes are provided upon request. A variety of suites feature panoramic views of the Gulf.

Junior suites (L-shaped with a small sitting area and no dividing walls) and standard suites (one-bedroom units with a door separating the bedroom from the living area) are all fully tiled and boast the same amenities as standard rooms. Junior suites also have whirlpool tubs. Furnishings all are primarily light oak accented by wicker and rattan; bed coverings and draperies are done in tropical prints. Wall hangings feature colorful local and Caribbean scenes.

Hyatt maintains an outdoor swimming pool and hot tub, three restaurants, a small health club, two dive boats, a charter fishing boat and a 68-foot sailing yacht for afternoon snorkeling and early-evening sunset sails. Also available are watersport rentals, scooter and bike rentals, and the hotel has a small private beach.

A three-tier sun deck overlooks the beach, and the resort's own Nick's Bar & Grill is a great place to enjoy the sunset. Concierge and room service and laundry valet are available, as is a resident masseuse, who will provide a massage in your room at an additional cost.

The Hyatt has smoking and nonsmoking rooms and handicapped-accessible facilities. Children younger than 10 stay free. Pets are prohibited. The resort offers special packages throughout the year, so inquire when you call to make reservations. Rates are based on double occupancy, and the charge is $45 per night for each additional person.

Key West Hilton Resort and Marina
$$$-$$$$ • 245 Front St., Key West
• (305) 294-4000

The newest of all Key West resorts, the bayfront Hilton was designed so all rooms provide views of either the pool, the bay or the marina (see our Cruising chapter) and its surrounding waters. Guests here also are provided launch service to a relatively secluded public beach at Sunset Key (see separate listing).

The two buildings that make up the Key West Hilton have 178 rooms; one structure has only nonsmoking rooms. The three-story building overlooks the marina; the other, a four-story structure, sits adjacent to Mallory Square (see our Attractions chapter). Situated in historic Old Town near the old customs house, the Hilton and its grounds are surrounded by brick walkways. Sliding glass doors framed by wooden shutters open onto private terraces. Textured interior walls

---

INSIDERS' TIP

Dade County pine is a dense, termite-resistant species of the slash pine family. The unusual amount of resins in the wood makes it very hard and heavy, unlike most pines. It was a popular lumber source in the early years of the Keys. A drawback: It's extremely difficult to drive a nail through Dade County pine.

boast sconces; floors feature stone tiles. Bleached oak and stone furnishings and handpainted walls welcome visitors to the hotel lobby.

On premises are a swimming pool, hot tub and sun deck area, fitness facilities, a restaurant offering indoor and outdoor dining and a sunset deck and lounge. Meeting space is available for large groups.

Marriott's Reach Resort
$$$-$$$$ • 1435 Simonton St., Key West • (305) 296-5000, (800) 874-4118 in Fla., (800) 626-0777 in continental U.S.

Splendor by the sea is what visitors to the Marriott's Reach Resort will discover. The resort boasts the only natural sand beach on the island of Key West. A gracious ambiance — and a complimentary rum punch — greet guests at an island-type get-acquainted check-in every afternoon.

All 149 units within the resort feature Spanish-tile floors and soothing tones of creams, purples, teals and oranges, combining a Caribbean twist with Southwestern appeal. Print drapes and bedspreads pull all of these colors together. Standard rooms, junior suites and one-bedroom executive suites offer either island or ocean views. Standard rooms have either one queen-size bed or two double beds, and those with queen-size beds also have queen-size sleeper sofas.

Junior suites are large, L-shape studios with queen- or king-size beds and queen-size sleeper sofas. King-size beds and pullout sleeper sofas are standard in all executive suites. Each room at the Reach Resort has a ceiling fan, balcony, wet bar, mini-bar, hair dryer, terry-cloth robes, iron and ironing board. Complimentary coffee is offered each morning in the lobby.

The resort has an outdoor swimming pool, hot tub and full watersports concession for rafts, parasailing, personal watercraft rentals and more. The Sandbar, a casual poolside bar and restaurant, provides full daytime service at the pool and the beach, and the more formal Ocean View, featuring steaks and seafood, is open for breakfast, lunch and dinner. An on-premises gift shop carries a wide variety of items, and a salon offers haircuts, colorings, facials and body wraps. Enjoy a mas-

sage beneath an outdoor gazebo or in the privacy of your room, or head for the fitness center with sauna and steam room.

Room service, valet laundry service and concierge services are available, along with complimentary transportation to and from Key West International Airport.

Tennis facilities at the neighboring Marriott's Casa Marina are open to all guests, as are the Casa's magnificent beach and two pools (see separate listing). Use of rollaways and cribs are free, and children younger than 13 stay free. Rates are based on double occupancy, and each additional person is charged $35 per night. Pets are not allowed. RV campers do not fit under the resort's enclosed parking garage. Smoking and nonsmoking rooms and handicapped-accessible facilities are provided upon request.

Marriott's Casa Marina Resort
$$$-$$$$ • 1500 Reynolds St., Key West • (305) 296-3535, (800) 235-4837 in Fla., (800) 626-0777 in continental U.S.

Construction of the Casa Marina Hotel dates back to 1918, after railroad magnate Henry Flagler had envisioned a resort hotel for wealthy snowbirds. Made of poured concrete and featuring walls 12 to 22 inches thick, the hotel has hosted prominent guests including the late professional baseball star Lou Gehrig and President Harry Truman.

The original structure is one of three buildings that now compose the resort, and its Old World-style lobby is lined with old photos of Flagler, Gehrig, Truman and others. Lobby walls, floors and columns are made of Dade County pine, and an expansive mahogany front desk with marble top accommodates seven check-in terminals.

The Casa Marina's three- and four-story buildings are set on the Atlantic Ocean, offering a total of 311 standard rooms and suites. Rates increase from the standard non-ocean view to the standard ocean view and from non-ocean view suites to ocean-view suites. Standard rooms hold two double beds or one king-size bed. Each suite has a king-size bed in the bedroom and a double sleeper sofa in the living room. All suites have sliding glass doors and private balconies. Floors are carpeted, and

rooms have stocked mini-bars, cotton robes, hair dryers, irons and ironing boards. Suites also have two televisions, mini-refrigerators and ceiling fans.

Two restaurants, one indoor and the other outdoor, serve everything from burgers, salads and sandwiches to steaks and seafood; the Casa's Sunday brunch, which is served on the terrace overlooking the ocean, is legendary. The Casa Marina also has two swimming pools, one of which is lap-size and the other designated for, but not restricted to, children. Both pools and a hot tub are surrounded by a concrete sun deck with ramps leading to the resort's private beach. The pools and hot tub are open 24 hours a day.

A concession stand rents scooters, bicycles, personal watercraft and Hobie Cats. Parasailing, sunset cruises and fishing, snorkeling and diving excursions can also be arranged through this concession. On the premises is a fitness facility with dry or wet sauna, and masseuse services are offered on a large

lawn beneath magnificent palm trees or in the privacy of your room.

Three hard-surface tennis courts on the property are lighted, and equipment and lessons are available. The Casa Marina offers concierge services, valet laundry and complimentary shuttle service to and from Key West International Airport. On slow evenings, the shuttle provides free transportation downtown; more often, a taxi company provides this same service at a discounted rate.

Room service is available 24 hours. Smoking and nonsmoking rooms are available, and cribs and cots are free.

Casa Marina rates are structured on a per-room basis, so as many as five guests can share the cost. Children younger than 19 stay free when accompanied by an adult. Marriott's Casa Marina offers organized activities for children, free of charge (see our Kidstuff chapter). The resort is handicapped-accessible, and off-street parking is provided at no charge.

Ocean Key House
Suites Resort & Marina
$$$-$$$$ • Zero Duval St., Key West
• (305) 296-7701, (800) 328-9815

This is a large resort with an intimate flavor. From their rooms and balconies, Ocean Key House guests can see the water, our famous sunsets and offbeat Mallory Square entertainers, all without the hassle of crowds.

Among the 100 units in this five-story resort are guest rooms and one- and two-bedroom, two-bath suites furnished with laminated wood and other lightweight furnishings. Ceiling fans are standard. Guest rooms all feature tiled floors and one queen-size bed. Kitchens and living rooms in all suites are tiled, and bedrooms are carpeted. Other features include oversize baths and private hot tubs, kitchens, living rooms with sleeper sofas and private balconies.

One-bedroom suites have either a king-size bed or two queens. Two-bedroom units have a king-size bed in the master bedroom and either two twin beds or one queen-size bed in the second bedroom. All suites have hair dryers in the master bedroom, and all units offer guests thick terry-cloth robes.

Penthouse suites, the most expensive units in the facility, feature full kitchens with microwaves and washers and dryers.

On premises are three bars, a swimming pool, deli and raw bar and a marina with fishing, snorkeling and dive charter boats and a glass-bottom tour boat. A highlight of Ocean Key House is its sunset pier overlooking both the harbor and Mallory Square (see our Attractions chapter). Other amenities include valet laundry, room service and concierge service. The hotel honors requests for nonsmoking rooms. Children younger than 18 stay free when accompanied by an adult. Pets are not allowed. Ocean Key House does not provide cots. Cribs are provided free upon request.

Pier House
Resort & Caribbean Spa
$$$-$$$$ • One Duval St., Key West
• (305) 296-4600, (800) 327-8340

Portions of the Pier House are on the grounds of Key West's former Porter Dock Company and Aeromarine Airways Inc., two companies that played significant roles in the city's illustrious shipping days. The Pier House offers luxurious, tropically appointed standard rooms with one king-size bed or two double beds and views of the Gulf, the swimming pool or the city.

Rooms overlooking the pool and the Gulf have sliding glass doors and private balconies, and those facing the water may look out on topless sunbathers along a portion of the resort's private beach. Standard in all rooms are mini-bars, coffee makers and hair dryers. A magnificent owner's suite has recently been made available.

Lush tropical foliage and brick paving surround the swimming pool and outdoor hot tub. The resort's beach and a secluded island glisten in the distance.

The Pier House is noted for its full-service spa, which offers fitness facilities, facials, massages and hair and nail care. Room service is available and a concierge will arrange for additional needs.

Off-street parking is abundant. Rates are based on double occupancy; each additional person is charged $35 per night. Children younger than 17 stay free when accompanied by an adult. Pets are not permitted.

INSIDERS' TIP

Do you notice a malodorous smell as you travel along certain mangrove-lined stretches of the Overseas Highway? Leaf litter that remains caught in the prop roots of the red mangroves decomposes into sediment that often forms into peat. When the peat is exposed to the sun at low tide, its sulfur content oxidizes and a rotten egg smell is noticeable.

Sheraton Suites Key West
$$$-$$$$ • 2001 South Roosevelt Blvd., Key West • (305) 292-9800, (800) 452-3224

Situated across from Smathers Beach, the Conch-style three-story, 180-unit Sheraton is a luxurious all-suite facility built around an expansive concrete sun deck and a swimming pool. Suites here are decorated in relaxing tropical teals, peaches and lavenders and are furnished in colorful wicker. Walls feature bright Caribbean-colored borders; floors are carpeted, and rooms are furnished with refrigerators and wet bars, mini-bars, microwaves and coffee makers. Most offer king-size beds and whirlpool tubs, and those facing the pool and ocean have sliding glass doors leading to furnished balconies. Suites have irons and ironing boards, built-in hair dryers and two televisions — one in the bedroom and another in the living room. Central courtyard gardens feature a mix of palms and flowering plants.

The Crab House restaurant offers food and drinks at its full-service poolside tiki bar; the restaurant also provides a poolside happy hour and room service from 7 AM to midnight. A hot tub by the pool accommodates eight, and lounge chairs and pool towels are provided. Sheraton Suites employs bellhops and offers guests complimentary shuttle service to and from Key West International Airport as well as hourly transportation to Mallory Square (see our Attractions chapter) between 10 AM and 10 PM. The staff at the guest activities desk will assist you in planning fishing and diving excursions, restaurant bookings and more. On the premises are a fitness center, 1,100 square feet of banquet meeting space and a gift shop. Guest laundry facilities are available, and off-street parking is plentiful. Children have a very special time at Sheraton Suites' Coral Reef Kids Club (see our Kidstuff chapter).

Sunset Key Guest Cottages
$$$-$$$$ • 245 Front St., Key West • (305) 292-5300, (888) 477-7786

Billed as the ultimate island hideaway, the guest cottages at Sunset Key are an extension of the Key West Hilton Resort and Marina, tucked away directly across the harbor from the main hotel, overlooking Mallory Square. Access is strictly by private launch, which operates 24 hours a day between Sunset Key and the Hilton marina.

Nestled amid swaying palms and lush flowering hibiscus, the cottages offer an opportunity to truly get away from the hustle and bustle of Duval Street, yet still enjoy the heart of Key West. You may come and go from Sunset Key at will, of course, but you truly never have to leave at all. The emphasis here is on privacy and service; if whatever you require is not on the island, rest assured that it can be delivered post-haste from Key West.

Cottages feature either a beachfront, ocean view or garden view, with beachfront being the most expensive. Rates are structured on a per-cottage basis and up to six guests may share a single cottage. Interiors feature separate living and dining areas and bedrooms with either double or king-size beds; every bedroom has its own bath stocked with hair dryer, bathrobes and plush, oversized towels. The decor has a distinctly Caribbean flavor — ceramic tile floors, pastel accents, ceiling fans, and comfortable, casual, whitewashed furnishings. Every cottage features a CD player, state-of-the-art stereo system and VCR.

Airy living rooms open onto private verandas, and kitchens are fully stocked with select foods and beverages and the requisite utensils for preparing and serving your own meals. Each has a microwave/convection oven, coffee maker, toaster, refrigerator and dishwasher. Guests will find a limited selection of groceries at the island outpost market; however, grocery delivery service from Key West is also offered for more extensive orders. If you'd prefer to leave the cooking to someone else, simply walk a few steps to the full-service gourmet restaurant, Latitudes, or arrange for a private chef to prepare a meal in your own kitchen. Room service is also available and a complimentary breakfast basket of muffins and freshly squeezed orange juice is delivered daily, along with the newspaper, to your doorstep.

In addition to a white sandy beach, the island features a freshwater pool, hot tub and two tennis courts. A health club is currently under construction. No cars are permitted on Sunset Key. However, parking is available in the Key West Hilton garage.

Reservations for specific cottage assignments are accepted but not guaranteed; cottages are assigned on a first-come, first-served basis upon arrival. All cottages are nonsmoking, and pets are not allowed. Guests must be older than 25 unless accompanied by an adult. Children younger than 18 stay free with parents or grandparents

Inns, Bed and Breakfasts and Guesthouses

Key West's Conch-style mansions and captains' and cigar-workers' homes date back to the 1800s, and many have been marvelously restored to accommodate a thriving tourist industry. Close to 100 intimate hideaways are tucked along the streets, avenues and lanes of Key West's Old Town, and these charming, romantic inns, bed and breakfasts and guesthouses provide a sense of history, tranquility and intimacy within the active city.

The inns, which are within walking distance of Duval Street, offer spacious rooms that often showcase high ceilings, fine antiques and reproductions and ornate woodwork. Renovations have brought about modern amenities: private baths, air conditioning, telephones and cable television with remote control. Some guest rooms continue to share bathroom facilities.

You'll find few waterfront or water-view guesthouse accommodations. Rather, rooms enjoy tranquil garden views or views of the often active, ever-changing streetfront. French doors often lead to private verandas with picket fences overlooking lush courtyards. It is here that deluxe continental breakfasts, full breakfasts and afternoon cocktails frequently are served amid soothing poolside symphonies or alongside goldfish ponds or hot tubs. Several guesthouses provide passes that allow use of beach, spa and fitness facilities at some of the island's full-service resorts.

Ideal for those seeking a quiet escape accessible to restaurants, bars, theater and watersports, these facilities are run by gracious innkeepers who pay careful regard to detail: Fresh flowers, terry-cloth robes and other amenities often are provided in each room, cottage and suite; continental breakfast and sometimes even cocktails are included in the price of the accommodation.

Key West welcomes diversity, and some guesthouses cater primarily or exclusively to the gay crowd. Others are considered all-welcome or gay-friendly. In a separate section at the end of this chapter, we highlight primarily and exclusively gay retreats, many of which maintain clothing-optional policies. Some straight guesthouses and inns also have begun to incorporate a clothing-optional policy. But unlike gay accommodations — where if you disapprove of the policy you shouldn't stay there — heterosexual guesthouses may require clothing upon complaint.

Rates quoted by inns typically are based on double occupancy, and additional guests pay anywhere from $10 to $50 extra per night. Rooms do have a maximum capacity. Inquire about this and all other details when you call to make reservations. If you are certain you'll need full telephone service in your room, check, too, to determine if your service is designed both for call-ins and call-outs.

Pets tend to be more welcome in Key West guesthouses than in hotels or other accommodations throughout the Florida Keys and Key West, but be sure to ask when making your reservation. Where pets are permitted, a refundable deposit or a fee is usually required.

Children are rarely allowed in Key West's guesthouses. In cases where children are permitted, we inform you.

The city's high season is typically December through April, and room rates are even higher — with minimum stays required — during special events and holidays. If you come to Key West for Fantasy Fest in October or during Christmas week in December, the minimum stay may be set at six to seven nights. To ensure space is indeed available when you plan to travel, call and reserve at least six months to a year in advance.

And last but not least, the accommodations cited below are only a sampling of what is currently available in Key West. At last count, the Key West phone book had listings for close to 100 guesthouses and inns. We have done our best to provide a representative sampling. For a complete list of accommodations, contact the Key West Information Center at (305) 292-5000.

The Artist House
$-$$$$ • 534 Eaton St., Key West
• (305) 296-3977, (800) 582-7882
Legend has it that this 1890 Victorian mansion, formerly the home of Key West painter Eugene Otto, is haunted by the ghost of Otto's deceased wife, whose burial place in the Key West cemetery lacks a tombstone. Some guests claim they have seen Mrs. Otto on a winding staircase in a room on the second floor.

With its gingerbread trim and pineapple gate, the home now boasts a West Indian flair; it is included in the Old Town Walking Tour (see our Attractions chapters).

Accommodations do not have the newer appearance that some other Key West guesthouses do, but all are charming and extremely spacious, with 14-foot-high ceilings, private baths and ceiling fans. Rooms have various antique furnishings and wallpaper patterns and large windows with lace curtains. The parlor suite on the first floor features a four-poster queen-size bed and has a sitting area with Chippendale couch and Oriental rugs over wood floors. The Turret Suite, on the second floor, offers a dressing room and a winding staircase that leads to a cupola, or circular, loft-style room with daybed. Four of the six guest rooms have working fireplaces, and three have claw-foot tubs.

In the small backyard is a brick patio and a swimming pool/hot tub combination.

You will find Eugene Otto paintings on display at the East Martello Museum. At the Key West cemetery (see our Attractions chapter), the former artist's tombstone is surrounded by those of his pet Yorkshire terriers, including one that, according to the inscription, was a "challenge to love."

Pets are not allowed. Children 10 and older are permitted.

Authors of Key West Guesthouse
$-$$$ • 725 White St., Key West
• (305) 294-7381, (800) 898-6909
Visiting writers to Key West often select this private three-building compound as their outpost. Each has his or her favorite room, and each room is named after one of Key West's legendary authors, such as Ernest Hemingway or Tennessee Williams. Look for memorabilia on the author of your choice.

The main two-story, eight-room house is tucked neatly behind a cement wall. Lined with lush tropical foliage, it boasts a two-sided sun deck. Two poolside Conch houses, built around the turn of the century, are available for rent; these one-bedroom homes feature queen-size beds and full kitchens. Both have small private porches.

Rooms within the main house are equally diverse, offering views of either the street, the sun deck or the gardens.

Continental breakfast is served daily in the lounge or by the swimming pool. The inn provides off-street parking, and bicycles are available for rent. Pets are not permitted. Children 13 and older are allowed.

Banana's Foster Bed and Breakfast
$$$-$$$$ • 537 Caroline St., Key West
• (305) 294-9061, (800) 653-4888

Owner Foster Meagher, a talented interior designer who restored the Alexander Graham Bell home in Washington, D.C., considers himself bananas — and he is proud of this fact, hence the unusual name for this restored two-story 1880s Conch-style mansion.

Banana's Foster offers six rooms in an intimate and elegant setting. All feature exposed and restored Dade County pine, queen- or king-size beds, 18th- and 19th-century antiques and private baths. Two are accessed through the main house; the remainder have private entrances. For ultimate luxury, splurge for the two-bedroom Banana suite, with private veranda, stereo system, compact-disc player, VCR and refrigerator. A cottage behind the main house features a room with a king-size bed and a queen-size bed. The room opens to the brick courtyard patio and garden surrounding an oversized hot tub.

The inn serves a continental breakfast each morning, and a wine and relaxation hour before guests venture out to Mallory Square (see our Attractions chapter). Guests may not bring pets.

The Banyan Resort
$$-$$$ • 323 Whitehead St., Key West
• (305) 296-7786, (800) 225-0639

The Banyan Resort is a collection of eight beautifully preserved and refurbished Conch-style homes, six of them listed on the National Register of Historic Places. One of these buildings formerly served as a cigar factory.

Homes boast 38 contemporary studios, suites and duplexes, with full kitchens. Some units have been sold as condominiums; others are available as timeshares and guest accommodations. Studios are least expensive, and rates increase with size: one bedroom, one bath; two bedrooms, one bath; and two bedrooms, two baths. All accommodations have French doors leading to private patios and verandas that overlook award-winning gardens. Included among the gardens are jasmine, frangipani, hibiscus, ixora, rare orchids, palm and fruit trees and two magnificent 200-year-old banyan trees. Bicycle rentals are available on the premises.

Children, with restrictions, are permitted; pets are not allowed. Limited parking is available at an additional charge of $4 per day.

Blue Parrot Inn
$-$$ • 916 Elizabeth St., Key West
• (305) 296-0033, (800) 231-BIRD

Built in 1884 with wood pegs that are more hurricane-friendly than nails, the Blue Parrot Inn offers 10 rooms — seven in the main house and three in a servant's-quarters-turned-cottage. Rooms vary in size, number of beds and decor. The only blue parrot in residence here is a stuffed one; however, all six of the cats you'll see wandering the grounds are very much alive.

A large Irish room with two double beds features Celtic prints and green accessories; the pink flamingo room, with a double bed and a twin-size bed, is flocked with feathers and photographs of the famed Floridian birds. Still others remain true to this guesthouse's name through parrot-print bedspreads. All rooms have mini-refrigerators and phones.

Out back, a heated swimming pool surrounded by extensive decking sets the scene for a leisurely continental breakfast consisting of fresh fruit, bagels, English muffins and home-baked quiche or fruit breads served every morning from 8:30 to 10:30. A tremendous staghorn fern strung along branches of a gumbo limbo tree makes a magnificent garden centerpiece.

The atmosphere at the Blue Parrot is

friendly and intimate. Once an exclusively gay guesthouse, it is now open to all adults and is handicapped accessible. Pets are not permitted here.

Center Court Historic Inn & Cottages
$$-$$$$ • 916 Center St., Key West
• (305) 296-9292, (800) 797-8787

Center Court is a fine example of the historic preservation for which Key West is famous. Nestled on a quiet, inconspicuous lane just a half-block from Duval Street, the main guesthouse, constructed in 1874, is surrounded by a collection of former cigar-maker cottages. Owner/operator Naomi Van Steelandt enrolled in construction courses so she could carry out the restoration, which won two Historic Preservation Awards of Excellence in 1993.

Walls are pastel-colored and feature original local art. Guest rooms are cozy and sleep two to six. Rooms are stocked with toiletries and welcome bags containing beach bags, coffee cups, coolies and other goodies. Each cottage has its own bright and cheerful personality, complete with pickled wood flooring, cordless telephones with answering machines, track lighting and CD stereos.

The inn has indoor and outdoor shower facilities. The main building houses a spacious, airy breakfast room; dining takes place out on the back porch overlooking a freshwater swimming pool, spa and exercise pavilion. Two cottages are set beside a lily pond. A spiral staircase alongside one of these cottages leads to a clothing-optional sun deck.

Children are allowed in the cottages but not the inn. Pets are permitted with a refundable deposit.

Van Steelandt also performs and coordinates weddings and makes honeymoon arrangements; call (888) 969-5683.

Chelsea House
$$-$$$$ • 707 Truman Ave., Key West
• (305) 296-2211, (800) 845-8859

Built in the 1880s for a British ship captain who hauled tobacco from Havana and later became the first general manager of Duval Street's La Concha Hotel, Chelsea House was later converted to a guesthouse by the captain's grieving widow to provide lodging to Key West's military visitors. Later, Chelsea House became an apartment complex. In 1985, massive renovations included the addition of private baths throughout and the conversion of the carriage house into guest accommodations.

The Conch-style mansion serves as the main guesthouse, and additions and extensions have increased the total number of units to 19. Each has 10-foot-high ceilings and individualized decor. Guest rooms in the main house feature hardwood floors and heavy mahogany and oak period-antique furnishings. Ceramic-tile rooms in the carriage house offer wicker furnishings and floral prints in ice-cream colors (orange sherbet is co-owner Jim Durbin's personal favorite).

Unlike The Red Rooster (Chelsea House's more casual sister hotel, described in this chapter), this is Durbin's showpiece, boasting four-poster beds and armoires plus nightly turndowns and fresh pool towels.

A full acre of property, shared with the neighboring Red Rooster, is likely the largest of all of Key West's guesthouse properties. Here, a private garden with massive palms and flowering plants forms an L-shaped alcove visible from the windows, French doors and balconies of some rooms in the main house. Every room at Chelsea House either has a balcony or opens onto the pool area.

A daily continental breakfast is served in an enclosed poolside cafe, and clothing is optional on a secluded elevated sun deck. Also available for topless lounging are the gardens, deck, pool and cabana areas. Off-street parking provides a space for every guest.

With prior approval, pets are accepted.

The Conch House Heritage Inn
$-$$$ • 625 Truman Ave., Key West
• (305) 293-0020, (800) 207-5806

Since the 1800s, this historic two-story estate has been passed on from generation to generation. The owners are Sam Holland Jr. and his mother, Francine Delaney Holland. She is the great-granddaughter of Cuban emigre Carlos Recio, a close friend of Cuban revolutionary Jose Marti.

The inn is listed on the National Register of Historic Places and was restored in 1993 to combine Old World decor with modern amenities. The five bedrooms in the main house feature high ceilings, wood shutters, wraparound porches and picket fences. A poolside cottage offers three guest rooms decorated with Caribbean prints and wicker. Guests may have their continental breakfast in the dining room or on the veranda.

Pets are not permitted at the inn.

Cuban Club Suites and La Casa De Luces
$-$$$$ • 422 Amelia St., Key West
• (305) 296-0465, (305) 296-3993, (800) 432-4849

Both Cuban Club Suites and La Casa De Luces share guest check-in and lobby facilities on Amelia Street, but Cuban Club Suites is actually in a separate building at 1102 and 1108 Duval Street. These two-story luxury suites are condominiums occupying second and third floors above boutique shops that are open to the public.

A large living area, full kitchen, bath and bedroom with a queen-size bed occupy the main level of the two-bedroom suites; an oversize loft area above the main level is furnished either with a queen- or king-size bed and features a second bath and a small private sunning deck. One-bedroom suites have a large living area, full kitchen and half-bath on the first floor; the second-floor loft has a queen-size bed, full bath and small sunning deck. All suites have washer/dryers and are furnished primarily with light wicker furnishings or heavy wood furnishings accented by antique reproductions.

At the less exclusive La Casa De Luces (Spanish translation: house of lights) are eight units ranging from two small rooms sharing a bath to large garden suites with king-size bed, living room, washer/dryer and full kitchen. Most rooms are furnished with lightweight wicker furnishings and tropical prints; all have exterior access via private verandas.

Complimentary continental breakfast is delivered to guest rooms each morning, and within the La Casa De Luces lobby is a small museum illustrating the rich Cuban history of both buildings. Neither facility has a swim-

ming pool, but guests are provided passes to the Marriott's Reach Resort pool, beach and health club (see the Marriott's Reach Resort listing in this chapter).

Off-street parking is available. Children younger than 13 stay free; a refundable cash deposit is required for pets.

Curry Mansion Inn
$$-$$$ • 511 Caroline St., Key West
• (305) 294-5349, (800) 253-3466

Curry Mansion Inn's chief claim to fame is its location on the grounds of the estate that once belonged to the Currys, Florida's first home-grown millionaire family. Situated on Caroline Street, just a few steps off Duval, the 22-room mansion was begun by William Curry in 1855 and completed by his son Milton in 1899. Innkeepers Al and Edith Amsterdam purchased the property in 1975. Curry Mansion is today a museum, housing a selection of turn-of-the-century furnishings and memorabilia from Key West's heyday as the richest city in America (see our Attractions chapter). It is also the centerpiece for a guesthouse that is consistently rated among the best in Key West.

Guests at the Curry Mansion Inn do not actually stay in the mansion; they do, however, have full access to it. Guest accommodations consist instead of 28 rooms adjacent to the mansion, most of which open onto a pool and all of which are surrounded by the lush foliage that characterizes the Curry estate. All of the rooms feature wicker furnishings, antiques and ceiling fans; the beds are draped in handmade quilts. Modern amenities include private baths, wet bars, small refrigerators, air conditioning, cable television and telephones.

A complimentary breakfast buffet is offered poolside each morning; complimentary cocktails are served each evening from 5 until 7. The Inn's heated pool and hot tub are open 24 hours. In addition, guests enjoy beach privileges at the Pier House Resort, within walking distance on the Gulf of Mexico, and at Marriott's Casa Marina on the Atlantic side of the island (see separate listings elsewhere in this chapter).

A particularly appealing feature of this

Photo: Hawk's Cay

Kid-friendly resorts offer many options for entertaining – and educating – your children.

guesthouse is its location — right in the heart of downtown Key West. The restaurants, bars, shops and other Duval Street attractions are just steps away; parking is plentiful. Pets are not permitted.

Cypress House
$-$$$ • 601 Caroline St., Key West
• (305) 294-6969, (800) 525-2488

The 40-foot heated lap pool surrounded by lush tropical gardens on the grounds of this 100-year-old mansion is among the largest at any of Key West's inns. The New England-style three-story home, constructed of cypress, is listed on the National Register of Historic Places and is a noted attraction along the Conch train tourist route (see our Attractions chapter).

Rebuilt in the wake of the fire of 1886 that consumed much of Key West, the facility was originally owned by Richard Moore Kemp, a shipbuilder and naturalist credited for the discovery of the ridley turtle (now known as the Kemp ridley turtle). Twenty years after Kemp built his own home, he added another house to the property for his daughter and son-in-law, a pioneer Key West sponger.

Connected by a wood fire escape, the two homes share a sun deck. Rooms throughout the structures feature 12-foot-high ceilings and wood floors with area rugs. In-room telephones allow for outside calling, and most rooms have queen-size beds and ceiling fans. Six of 16 rooms have private baths, one of which is a whopping 14-foot-square. A handpainted floral ceiling border accents one room, and all are furnished with period antiques.

Porches on the first and second floor are accessible to guests. A breakfast buffet featuring home-baked goods is served poolside, as is a nightly complimentary cocktail hour with beer, wine and snacks.

Formerly an exclusively gay guesthouse, Cypress is now an all-welcome, adults-only facility. Pets are not permitted.

Douglas House
$-$$$ • 419 Amelia St., Key West
• (305) 294-5269, (800) 833-0372

Douglas House is a collection of five Victorian homes, four of which are more than 100 years old. Each house contains two to five spacious units for a combined total of 15.

Standard rooms and one-bedroom suites are furnished with a queen-size bed or two double beds; suites have a full kitchen. All units have private baths and outdoor entrances, and each unit is furnished differently. Some are carpeted with standard wood furnishings; others have hardwood floors and wicker furnishings. Suites have French doors opening to a private deck, patio or balcony. Some suites have loft-style bedrooms.

Within the compound is a swimming pool and a hot tub surrounded by gardens. Continental breakfast is served poolside each morning, and coffee perks throughout the day.

Pets are permitted. Children younger than 12 are not allowed during high season.

Duval Gardens
$$-$$$ • 1012 Duval St., Key West
• (305) 292-3379, (800) 867-1234

One of two buildings at Duval Gardens is a post-Victorian two-story Conch house, built in the early 1920s with 9-foot ceilings. The facility has only four guest rooms and is noted for attentive service. All rooms are nonsmoking and have exterior entrances, private baths and refrigerators. Wicker and rattan furnishings make for relaxed, tropical decor, as do pastel colors and wall hangings with beach scenes.

A standard room with a queen-size bed at Duval Gardens is the least expensive; a slightly larger efficiency with sitting area, kitchenette and dining area is priced a bit higher. Commanding the highest rates are two suites, one with one bedroom and the other with two, and each with a living room, bedroom, full kitchen and bath.

Head for cocktails on a wraparound veranda and embrace a daily breeze. Feast on a full gourmet breakfast, including shortbread, croissants and warm main entrees, such as cinnamon-vanilla French toast topped with bananas and fresh fruit.

Membership at a private beach club offers Duval Gardens guests the opportunity to enjoy a nearby pool, beach and health club, and the guesthouse works closely with local dive shops.

Children are permitted; pets are not. Honeymoon, anniversary and dive packages are available.

Duval House
$$-$$$$ • 815 Duval St., Key West
• (305) 294-1666, (800) 223-8825

This two-story inn may be set on busy Duval Street, but its pigeon plums, banyans, heliconia and hibiscus successfully guard it from intrusion. Lounge poolside amid traveler's palms and light jazz music; linger on a shady hammock or chat with others in a gazebo by the fish pond. The inn's breakfast room maintains a library of books, board games, magazines and newspapers and a weather chart listing temperatures throughout the world.

In the 1880s Duval House was inhabited by cigar workers. Today, the 30 standard and deluxe rooms and apartments are furnished with English antiques, white wicker and wood French doors. All are air conditioned. Locally made frangipani soap is placed in each bathroom.

Most rooms have color television, and some feature elegant poster beds and private porches. All except the two apartments and two front rooms look out onto the gardens.

If you visit Duval House, look for Mush, the resident cat, who receives letters from former guests all over the world.

Eaton Lodge
$$-$$$$ • 511 Eaton St., Key West
• (305) 292-2170, (800) 294-2170

Built in 1886, the treasure that is Eaton Lodge was owned by one of Key West's first physicians, Dr. William Warren. His wife, Genevieve, founded the Key West Garden Club. Notice her intricate designs for the home's diverse courtyard, which features a fountain, fish pond, Spanish lime tree, jacaranda and more.

Present owners Carolyn and Stephen West have painted the inn's shutters to match the lavender jacaranda and have preserved all historic appointments within the home's interior, adding a courtyard hot tub.

Eaton Lodge's main house served as both home and office for Dr. Warren. Its elegant living room features Oriental and Turkish carpets over wood floors, a Venetian glass chandelier and an antique fireplace, and bookshelves pose as inconspicuous doors to divide the living room and kitchen.

All 16 rooms and suites, including those within the William Skelton House next door, vary in size, decor and view. The carriage house at the rear of the home provides two-story, garden-view accommodations that connect to create duplexes. (Our favorite is the equestrian-themed red-and-yellow Saratoga room, with pine furnishings and kitchen cabinets and ceiling fans with fringe pulls.)

With their high ceilings and original moldings, rooms and suites in the main house feature 18th-century furnishings (the Recuperating Room), two antique brass beds (the Operating Room), picket-fence porches and private terraces (the Anniversary and Sunset rooms). The unique Sunset Room has a raised bathroom and a terrace that sides a three-story cistern.

Look for the manager's apartment, which has a tree growing out of its bathroom and through the roof. All rooms feature watercolor and oil paintings by local artists and wood plank or parquet flooring with area carpets.

The three-bedroom, two-bath William Skelton House is typically rented in its entirety, and its pool is shared by all Eaton Lodge guests. Homemade tropical breads and fresh fruits are served on the patio each morning, and an open-bar afternoon break is offered on the brick patio.

There are a number of exotic caged birds on the property, so Kuma, the inn's docile Akita, is the only pet allowed. Smoking is also prohibited at Eaton Lodge.

Eden House
$-$$$ • 1015 Fleming St., Key West
• (305) 296-6868, (800) 533-5397

For years Eden House was known as a no-frills, low-budget hangout for writers, intellectuals and Europeans. Over the past few years, owner Mike Eden has added several enhancements.

When producers of the movie *Criss Cross* scouted Key West locations, they opted for this facility. With the enhancements, the c. 1924 building was too polished for the film's needs. They "roughed it up" a bit cosmetically and sent Goldie Hawn here to portray the movie's main character. Rest assured, Eden House was quickly restored to its vintage art deco grandeur.

Constructed of wood and concrete, the facility categorizes units by luxury rooms and efficiencies (two of them have sleeping lofts); private rooms and efficiencies with bath or shower; semiprivate rooms with shared baths; and European rooms with double or twin-size beds, a sink and a bath and shower in the hall. Most other units feature queen-size beds. Prices descend respectively.

Accommodations are decorated in light, subdued colors and tropical prints and furnished with a mix of wicker and rattan. Many units have French doors leading to porches and decks near the center of the facility, where gardens surround a swimming pool, hot tub and gazebo.

A restaurant is on premises. Children are permitted. Bicycle rentals are available.

Fleming Street Inn
$$-$$$$ • 618 Fleming St., Key West
• (305) 294-5181, (800) 820-5397

This old Conch-style home is deceiving from the exterior. Actual accommodations are to its rear, in six rooms, three cottages and two-story townhouse suites with spiral staircases. All buildings are set around two swimming pools and a brick patio. Those farthest from the main building are largest and more expensive.

The idea behind the decor in all units is, "Less is more." Rooms feature tile floors, white-washed oak, all-white comforters, walk-in showers, French doors, and, with the exception of the bathroom, bare walls. Suites have bleached oak floors, walls and ceilings, all-white kitchens and loft-style bedrooms.

Children are permitted, but pets are not.

The Frances Street Bottle Inn
$-$$ • 535 Frances St., Key West
• (305) 294-8530, (800) 294-8530

Tucked away in a quiet residential neighborhood on the edge of Old Town, this charming inn takes its name from the collection of antique bottles and cobalt blue glassware displayed in every windowpane and along several interior shelves. The trim, white frame structure, once a corner grocery store and boarding house, has a unique place in recent Key West history, too. It was the set for the *Meteor* newspaper office in the short-lived television series *Key West*.

The atmosphere here is quiet and intimate. The Bottle Inn has just seven guest rooms, each with private bath, air-conditioning and color television. White wicker chairs line a gracious porch across the front of the house, and in the lush tropical gardens, a complimentary continental breakfast is served each morning under the poinciana trees. Concierge service is available. Although the grounds are too small to allow for a pool, there is a hot tub.

If you're looking for a guesthouse experience well removed from Duval, yet still within walking distance of most Old Town attractions, you'll find excellent value here.

The Gardens Hotel
$$$$ • 526 Angela St., Key West
• (305) 294-2661, (800) 526-2664

In 1930 the late Key West resident Peggy Mills began collecting various species of orchids from Japan, Bali and other exotic parts of the world. As neighboring homes were placed on the market, Mills would purchase and level them, adding to her garden until it encompassed a full city block.

Before she passed away, the Mills garden became public, gaining the attention of botanists worldwide and national magazines. These gardens have been restored to much of their original splendor by Bill and Corrina Hettinger, owners and operators of The Gardens Hotel, a member of Small Luxury Hotels of the World.

A complex of five guesthouses and a carriage house, the hotel offers 17 units, including two two-bedroom suites set around a tiki bar, swimming pool, hot tub, fountain and a winding path of bougainvillea, orange jasmine, palm, mango, breadfruit trees and more. The architecture is classic, and rooms are furnished with mahogany reproductions from Holland and floral chintz.

InStyle Magazine describes The Gardens Hotel as being like a secluded European inn. Famous guests here have included actors George Clooney and Mickey Rourke and singer k.d. lang.

Floors are hardwood, bathrooms marble with whirlpool tubs and telephones, and walls are decorated with original Key West scenes painted by equestrian Peter Williams. All rooms have garden views, and fountains throughout the grounds enhance the sense of tranquility. Each room has a television, coffee maker, mini-bar and private porch. All except the historic rooms and the master suite have separate entrances and private porches.

Heron House
$$-$$$$ • 512 Simonton St., Key West
• (305) 294-9227, (800) 294-1644

Centered around a 35-foot swimming pool, decorated with a mosaic of a heron, and a Chicago brick patio and sun deck, every one of the 23 rooms at the Heron House features unique woodwork and stained glass created by local artists.

Platform-style oak beds are handcrafted, and all accommodations have French doors leading to private porches or balconies overlooking the English-style country gardens. This historic facility was built prior to the turn of the century. It offers basic, upper-standard and deluxe rooms. All are spacious with incredibly high ceilings and double, queen- or king-size beds. Deluxe rooms and junior suites have

wet bars, futon sitting areas and mini-re-frigerators. Coffee is served in the breeze-way. A private sun deck is clothing-optional.
Heron House accepts children older than 15.

The Historic Saltwater Angler Inn
$-$$$ • 219 Simonton St., Key West
• (305) 294-3248, (800) 223-1629
The Saltwater Angler is more than a fly-fishing/sporting goods store. Built in 1850, the structure owned by fly-fishing guide (and informal consultant) Capt. Jeffrey Cardenas offers second-floor lodging in two spacious suites.
The decor here evokes the rustic out-doors, with wood floors, walls and furnish-ings. Suites share a fully-equipped kitchen, dining area and living room with digital ste-reo. The Bonefish Suite has a queen-size bed, private bath and connecting room with twin-size beds and a desk. The Tar-pon Suite has a queen-size bed, private bath and connecting room with a queen-size bed. The Grand Slam combination of the both provides 1,700 square feet of liv-ing space.
A porch and yard with a hot tub and picnic area are available to all guests. Children and small pets are allowed.

Island City House Hotel
$$-$$$ • 411 William St., Key West
• (305) 294-5702, (800) 634-8230
At Island City House, two 1880s homes and a cypress wood house designed to re-semble a cigar factory encompass an Old World-style enclave lined with brick walkways and lush tropical gardens. Wood decking sur-rounds the hot tub and swimming pool tucked neatly at one end of the compound; the swim-ming pool has a tiled alligator motif at bottom.
Central to Island City House is its charm-ing courtyard patio, where antique iron benches and bistro-style tables are set around a fountain and fish pond. This is the setting for the daily continental breakfast.
Island City House itself is a Conch-style mansion originally built for a wealthy merchant family. Here, guests choose from 12 one- and two-bedroom parlor suites with kitchens and antiques that provide a New England mari-time feel. The Arch House, the only car-riage house in Key West, maintains six stu-dio and two-bedroom suites decorated with casual furnishings of rattan and wicker. At The Cigar House, built on a cistern and the former site of a cigar factory, spacious suites feature plantation-style decor that combines antique furnishings with wicker and rattan. The homes have hardwood floors throughout, and many rooms fea-ture French doors leading to private patios and decks.
Children are permitted; pets are not al-lowed. Bicycle rentals are available on pre-mises.

Island Key Court Guest Residences
$-$$$ • 910 Simonton St., Key West
• (305) 296-1148, (800) 296-1148
Two locations provide for a total of 14 units at Island Key Court, and all but two of these units have kitchens. Here you'll find one of the city's few contemporary, one-story guest homes, of wood construction except for one concrete block addition that has been con-verted from garden apartments.
The artist-owner has painted each room differently: The walls of one room feature a marble finish, while another boasts unique spongework. Still another is covered with artistic renderings of lush greenery. All rooms have private en-trances, private baths, ceiling fans, king-or queen-size beds, a mix of period an-tiques and used furnishings and tele-phones for calling out only. Some French doors lead to private porches and lush meditation gardens featuring palms, bro-meliads and a hot tub.
Two-bedroom suites sleep as many as eight or nine guests, with king- and queen-size beds in the master bedroom, twin beds in the second bedroom and a queen-size sleeper sofa in the living area. Guests seek-ing use of a beach, pool, health club and other facilities are provided passes to the oceanfront Marriott's Reach Resort (see list-ing in this chapter).

Key West Bed & Breakfast
$-$$$ • 415 William St., Key West
• (305) 296-7274

When strong winds blow through the city of Key West, you can feel the three-story Key West Bed & Breakfast move with them, for this 1890 home was built by shipbuilders skilled in crafting structures able to weather any storm. Step inside from the front porch and you likely will be greeted by Dave, the inn's resident golden retriever.

All of the inn's eight guest rooms except for one suite feature a mix of bright colors, elegant Victorian furnishings, exposed Dade County pine and 13-foot ceilings. Most have queen-size beds, and third-floor suites in the dormered attic offer a choice of two magnificent views. The back suite has French doors leading to a private deck and is decorated in more muted tones because it gathers color from the backyard's flowering trees, including a wild orchid tree that produces rich purple flowers. The suite at the front of the house is noted for its 5-foot arched Palladian window, which provides a view of the sunset above the city's rooftops and trees.

Continental breakfast, including fresh baked goods and freshly squeezed orange juice, is served outdoors, where tables and chairs line the backyard wood deck. All rooms are air-conditioned, and most have ceiling fans. The inn has no televisions or telephones except for a community telephone to which all guests are provided access.

Owner Jodi Carlson is an artist who weaves, and her bright yarns provide added color to the inn's community room where magazines, Florida Keys-related books and an extensive compact disc collection and player are available to guests. Two of the inn's four porches are furnished with a swing and double hammock, and the oversize backyard hot tub is also used as a dip pool. Pets are prohibited.

La Mer Hotel
$$$-$$$$ • 506 South St., Key West
• (305) 294-5539, (800) 354-4455
Dewey House
$$$$ • 1319 Duval St., Key West
• (305) 296-5611, (800) 354-4455

La Mer is Key West's only oceanfront bed and breakfast. It has the same owner as its neighbor, the Dewey House. Both are marketed as a single luxury getaway with distinctly different names and ambiance.

La Mer is actually a turn-of-the-century Conch house with 11 rooms decorated with wicker furnishings and light, tropical prints; most rooms have a private balcony or patio. Rooms have king- or queen-size beds. One room has two twin beds; some rooms have sleeper sofas.

If this is not luxurious enough for your taste, the eight-room Dewey House offers decor in rich greens and golds with heavy draperies, fine antiques, whirlpool bathtubs and French doors leading to private balconies and patios.

Rooms at both facilities have high ceilings with ceiling fans, mini-bars and Italian marble bathrooms with built-in hair dryers. Most rooms have king- or queen-size beds, and some have fully equipped kitchenettes with microwaves.

In addition to a deluxe continental breakfast of freshly baked banana breads and coffeecakes, plus croissants, English muffins and fresh fruits, the inn serves tea, crumpets, fresh fruits and cheeses at 4:30 PM daily. *USA Today* is delivered to the door of each guest room, an 8-foot-square hot tub is set among beautifully landscaped gardens, and La Mer and Dewey House guests are allowed access to pool facilities at their owner's Southernmost and South Beach Oceanfront motels. Pets are not permitted.

The Lightbourn Inn
$$-$$$$ • 907 Truman Ave., Key West
• (305) 296-5152

Owners/operators Kelly Summers and Scott Fuhriman have drawn upon sojourns in Europe and Asia in decorating rooms in their classic Conch-style mansion, which is listed on the National Register of Historic Places.

All 10 guest rooms within the Lightbourn Inn feature antiques, Key West wicker and signed celebrity memorabilia. Complimentary breakfast, including hot entrees, is one of the inn's most popular features. Wine is served on the deck during wine hour while an outdoor jukebox plays your favorite tunes, and three levels of private decking overlook the clothing-optional pool area.

Because owners Summers and Fuhriman reside on the property, holidays always include home-away-from-home celebrations at the Lightbourn Inn.

The Marquesa Hotel
$$$-$$$$ • 600 Fleming St., Key West
• (305) 292-1919, (800) 869-4631

This cluster of homes dates back to the 1880s. Each standard room, deluxe room, junior suite, standard suite and terrace suite is furnished with ceiling fans and an eclectic collection of antique English and West Indian reproductions that evoke the ambiance of an exquisite English plantation.

Accommodations are spacious, with oversize marble baths; many rooms feature French doors and private porches overlooking two pools and the garden. At the east end of the garden, brick steps accented by a fountain lead to a newer building of complementary architecture.

Breakfast includes a feast of baked goods fresh from the oven of the highly-praised Cafe Marquesa (see our Restaurants chapter).

The Palms Hotel
$$-$$$ • 820 White St., Key West
• (305) 294-3146, (800) 558-9374

Completely restored in 1995, this Conch-style home with wraparound porches was built in 1889. It features Caribbean influences and is listed on the National Register of Historic Places. In the 1970s, the hotel added an L-shaped structure built in a complementary style.

All 20 units are painted in pastels and furnished with wicker and Caribbean-style decor; rooms in the main house have separate access to the porch. Most have queen- or king-size beds or two double beds. Some floors are carpeted, some are tiled, and several rooms in the main house feature all-wood flooring. Private entrances, private baths and ceiling fans are standard.

For a real Old World-style getaway, ask for the mini-suite with turret, where a king-size bed is surrounded by windows and walls of exposed Dade County pine, and the downstairs living area features hardwood floors.

This suite can be connected to a guest room with queen-size bed to accommodate larger parties.

A deluxe continental breakfast is served each morning at the full-service poolside tiki bar, and the large heated swimming pool is open around the clock.

The Palms maintains a small parking lot; on-street parking is also available. Children are permitted; pets are allowed with advance approval.

The Paradise Inn
$$$$ • 819 Simonton St., Key West
• (305) 293-8007, (800) 888-9648

Style and distinction mark the 15 suites and three cottages of the Paradise Inn, one of Key West's newer facilities. Two of the three cottages are refurbished Conch houses; the rest are recently built two-story buildings of coordinating architecture.

Painted white with Caribbean-blue Bahamian shutters, all units have high ceilings, large marble baths, natural oak flooring and unique window dressings that combine stagecoach and handkerchief valances with wood mini-blinds. French doors lead to outdoor porches in all but one cottage, and the interior decor features distressed pine, botanical prints and pale shades of tan. Rooms have queen- and king-size wrought iron and California sleigh beds.

The inn's diverse gardens, designed by award-winning landscape architect Raymond Jungles of Coral Gables, feature Barbados cherry and avocado trees and bromeliads. Even the swimming pool and hot tub, separated by a lily pond, evoke luxury.

Children are permitted; pets are not.

Pilot House Guesthouse
$$-$$$$ • 414 Simonton St., Key West
• (305) 294-8719, (800) 648-3780

Restored in 1991, this 100-year-old Conch-style home provides rooms and suites that mix antique furnishings with functional pieces and tropical rattan prints.

Once a three-bedroom home, the floor plan has been altered so the first-floor library and dining room now accommodate a guest room and two two-bedroom suites.

Suites on the second floor are furnished with its original family in mind.

Built by the late Julius Otto, son of a prominent Key West surgeon, the 3,000-square-foot mansion served as a winter retreat. Julius' brother Eugene inherited The Artist House (see listing in this chapter) around the corner, and the yards of the two Otto homes almost back each other. Here in the gracious Pilot House, curved archways lead from one room to another, and moldings are massive but not over-powering.

The third-floor picture-perfect penthouse features an octagon-shaped bedroom with skylights, exposed chimney and a mix of tile and carpeting, plus a shower with a skylight. A private sun deck — complete with hot tub — off the penthouse provides a panoramic island view from among the treetops.

Frangipani and royal poinciana trees thrive in the yard, and a gumbo limbo grows through the roof of what is known as this facility's spa building. Set along the brick-patio backyard is a Spanish-style stucco cabana building that offers six suites with queen- and king-size beds, full kitchens and in-room hot tubs. Furnishings in the cabana are contemporary white wicker amidst adobe-colored walls. Mirrors are abundant, and 6-foot-square open showers have sleek European-style shower heads jutting from the ceilings.

Passageways rather than doors create privacy for each area of these suites, and all entrances face the swimming pool.

Most rooms in the main house have balconies but are accessed through a formal entrance, and all rooms have kitchenettes, ceiling fans and private baths. The inn does not provide breakfast, but restaurants are nearby. All guests are encouraged to carry on at their own pace.

The backyard swimming pool, at 15 feet by 30 feet, is larger than most in Key West, and an in-ground spa for 12 is sheltered from the sun by a tin roof with lattice and the aforementioned gumbo limbo tree that grows through the roof.

Clothing here is optional. Pets are prohibited, and no off-street parking is provided.

The Red Rooster Inn
$-$$$ • 709 Truman Ave., Key West
• (305) 296-6558, (800) 845-0825

Built in 1870 by the Delgato family, The Red Rooster is considered Truman Avenue's oldest house. At the time, the street was called Hard Rock Road; it later became Division Street and during the 1950s Truman era received the name Truman Avenue.

In the early 20th century, this private house was converted to apartments to house the U.S. Coast Guard; then it was converted to provide casual, low-end guest accommodations. Left to disrepair, the home was purchased by Jim Durbin and Gary Williams, owners of the exclusive Chelsea House next door (see listing in this chapter), and renamed The Red Rooster. Colorful stories about the home tell of a scandalous past, including illicit use by prostitutes and drug dealers. According to local legend, Mrs. Delgato murdered her husband and buried him beneath a concrete porch along the front of the building.

The 18 carpeted rooms, all with private, renovated bathrooms, exude an eclectic flavor, and all but one of the rooms are accessible via exterior doors. Most have queen-size beds, and some are incredibly spacious, with fireplaces and French doors leading to a front veranda. Others are small but cozy.

This reasonably priced, liberal adult guesthouse shares a yard and outdoor facilities with The Chelsea House, and clothing is optional in designated outdoor areas. A coffee bar at the entrance doubles as space for the desk clerk and evokes a European atmosphere. Continental breakfast is served here daily. Impromptu cocktail hours provide a party-like atmosphere.

Pets are not permitted.

Simonton Court
$-$$$$ • 320 Simonton St., Key West
• (305) 294-6386, (800) 944-2687

Situated on 2 acres of property that once boasted a cigar factory, Simonton Court offers 10 varied structures with equally varied accommodations. The inn's four outdoor swimming pools once served as cisterns. Simonton Court's original building is a Victorianesque mansion with maritime influences including a widow's walk. Built by a judge in the late 1880s and known as "the mansion," it now houses the most luxurious rooms and suites on the property.

Some of Simonton Court's six guest rooms are furnished in period antiques and have green marble bathrooms and large terraces; others offer Caribbean-style decor. One has a spa tub and includes the widow's walk.

A two-story clapboard building with porches, once the actual cigar factory, is now known as the "inn." Within the inn today are nine rustic old Key West-style rooms paneled with Dade County pine and featuring high ceilings and heavily shuttered windows. When closed, the shutters effectively bar the heat. Rooms here range from basic units with king-size beds to a triplex with kitchen, bedroom and living and dining area. All rooms at the inn have hardwood floors and private baths.

On the rustic side also are Simonton Court's two-story cottages. Decorated with antique bamboo furnishings and brightly colored handmade fabrics, interiors are bright and airy. The first floor of each cottage has a kitchenette with microwave (no oven) and a queen- or king-size bed. Attic-style lofts with skylights are furnished with two double beds.

Still another building, known as the Manor House suite, offers a spacious two-bedroom complex with full kitchen and living room and a private outdoor pool. Simonton Court's two-story townhouse is extremely plush, decorated in Grand Floribbean-style antiques and white linens. The first floor has a living room, a bedroom with queen-size bed and private patio and a bath with shower. A similar floor plan upstairs is enhanced by vaulted ceilings, skylights and a spa tub. Both floors have separate entrances via a private balcony or brick patio so that only half the townhouse can be rented if desired. Townhouse guests enjoy their own semiprivate swimming pool.

Simonton Court's tropically landscaped gardens, antique brick pathways, swimming pool and hot tub all come aglow at night, when lighting emphasizes all the right places.

Children younger than 18 and pets are not permitted. Expanded continental breakfast is served poolside daily; inn and townhouse guests who visit during high season are greeted by a complimentary bottle of wine and treated to a nightly turndown.

Southernmost Pointe Guesthouse
$-$$$ • 1327 Duval St., Key West
• (305) 294-0715

Throughout Key West, you will discover all kinds of things dubbed "the southernmost" — a southernmost hockey rink and Southernmost Motel, for instance. The Southernmost Pointe Guesthouse, across from the Southernmost House, is a showy, three-story Conch-style mansion built in 1885 for E.H. Gato Jr., one of Key West's first cigar manufacturer.

The home is notable for its wraparound porches and private balconies, some of which afford partial ocean or garden views. Rooms come in varying sizes, but all have private entrances, private baths and ceiling fans. The Ernest Hemingway suite is a deluxe, two double-bed efficiency designed with a jungle-like theme in honor of the legendary author's ardor for hunting, but most rooms are furnished either with queen-size or double beds and antiques with a tropical flair.

Some rooms have kitchenettes, and the largest of all is the two-bedroom master suite with queen-size bed in the master bedroom, with a pullout sleeper sofa, and a private balcony that offers a partial view of the Southernmost Point (see our Attractions chapter). Suite No. 6 is a duplex that comprises portions of the home's second and third floors, and suite No. 5 features a king-size bed and a private porch with a swing.

All guests are provided a key to the hot tub (large enough for 12 people). And because the inn is only 70 yards from South Beach, it supplies complimentary beach towels and chairs. Lounge chairs also are provided amid the guesthouse's tropical gardens of banana, coconut palm, breadfruit and mango trees.

Continental breakfast includes fresh-baked goods and cold cuts, cheeses and boiled eggs. Children younger than 12 and accompanied by an adult stay free, and guests with pets are charged an additional $5 per night. Rollaway beds are available, and cribs are complimentary. Other thoughtful amenities include wine, mints and fresh flowers placed in each room prior to a guest's arrival.

Speakeasy Inn
$$$-$$$$ • 1117 Duval St., Key West
• (305) 296-2680, (800) 217-4884

The turn-of-the-century Speakeasy offers spacious rooms in its main Duval Street house plus three spacious suites in a back-alley building along Amelia Street.

Built as a residence for the owner's stepdaughter, this second building offers what is referred to as the Gallery Suite, considered to be the best offering in the house. The large, apartment-size unit has a queen-size bed and sleeper sofa and features beamed ceilings, hardwood floors, track lighting and patio doors leading to a private deck and yard. This and other rooms at Speakeasy also are furnished with private, tiled baths, refrigerators, wet-bars and ceiling fans.

First-floor rooms feature queen-size beds and private patios; those on the second floor offer queen- or full-size beds but lack a wet bar. And room No. 2 in the main house features an elegant claw-foot bathtub.

Limited passes to Marriott's Reach Resort pool, spa and fitness facilities are provided on a first-come, first-served basis. Children and small pets are allowed; large pets must be kept in kennel carriers.

Travelers Palm Garden Cottages
$-$$$$ • 815 Catherine St., Key West
• (305) 294-9560

Owners Brigid and Clyde Hensley reside in the main building at Travelers Palm, and guest cottages surround them. Off to the corner of their home are a spacious studio and a one-bedroom apartment with a large kitchen. Cottages house a variety of accommodations, including studios and one- and two-bedroom units. Studios all have futon beds. One-bedroom cottages have large living areas with queen-size sleeper sofas, large kitchens and bedrooms with queen-size beds. In most units, rattan furnishings mix tastefully with light tropical prints and Oriental accents.

Units all maintain private courtyards with grills and picnic tables; lush tropical landscaping provides a sense of seclusion. Known as the pool house, the two-bedroom cottage has a master bedroom with queen-size bed, a second bedroom with two twin-size beds and a living room with sleeper sofa. With stained and beveled glass and a private pool with waterfall, this is undoubtedly the most exquisite of Travelers Palm's appealing accommodations.

Available to all guests is a second swimming pool and a hot tub surrounded by a brick patio; a playground is available to children. Hammocks are set in very private places. Pets are permitted.

The Watson House
$$$-$$$$ • 525 Simonton St., Key West
• (305) 294-6712, (800) 621-9405

Though modified, the original portions of this two-story, three-room Bahamian-influenced Conch house were built in the mid-1800s. A detached kitchen with connecting breezeway has been enclosed and extensions to the home added.

Named for the home's original owners, William and Susan Watson, this guesthouse features 11 units of 1930s decor, three of which are suites and two of which maintain a private living room and dining area with full kitchens. Decorated with lots of lace and white Ralph Lauren wicker furnishings, the Susan Suite evokes a feminine, turn-of-the-century feeling. The William Suite has a four-poster queen-size bed and items reminiscent of a ship captain's bunk. The William and Susan suites feature wainscoting and period hand-silkscreened wallpapers. A third suite, referred to as the Cabana Suite, is light, airy and tropical with a triple set of French doors leading to the pool.

All rooms have ceiling fans and telephones with private numbers. A heated, two-tiered backyard pool creates a centerpiece waterfall effect for lush tropical gardens and a hot tub. Continental breakfast is catered to each room, and limited off-street parking is available. Pets are not permitted.

The Weatherstation Inn
$$-$$$$ • 57 Front St., Key West
• (305) 294-7277, (800) 875-2707

Nestled deep within one of Key West's premier residential communities, The Weatherstation Inn could easily be considered one of this town's best-kept secrets in luxury guesthouse accommodations. Guests here are just two blocks off bustling Duval Street, but they'd never know it. Rarely does any sound intrude.

Opened in 1997, this two-story, 8-room guesthouse sits on the grounds of the Old Navy Yard inside the gated Truman Annex compound and just down the street from Harry Truman's Little White House (see our Attractions chapter). Motorized access is limited to the residents of the Annex, and so within these gates, life is always quiet and serene.

With its glistening hardwood floors and elegant island furnishings, the Inn calls to mind the plantation homes of days gone by in the British and Dutch West Indies. The balconies and decks overlook lush tropical landscaping, and from the second-floor rooms guests can catch an occasional glimpse of the cruise ships arriving in the harbor just beyond. Amenities here include a heated pool, concierge service and complimentary continental breakfast. Pets are not allowed.

Westwinds Guesthouse
$-$$$$ • 914 Eaton St., Key West
• (305) 296-4440, (800) 788-4150

At this complex, a 22-room, two-story New England-style home, two-story Conch houses and poolside cottages, the majority of guests are couples. Room decor is wicker throughout, with queen-size beds in suites, private entrances to the cottages and Conch houses and some furnished private and shared porches.

All rooms provide a feel for the tropics, painted in various shades of pastels, with ceiling fans and carpeted floors. Some rooms in the main house share a bath. Suites include one-bedroom cottage and Conch units with kitchenettes and kitchenless accommodations that sleep several guests.

In back of the compound, brick walkways wind through gardens of hibiscus, bromeliads and other flowers and shrubs, and the kidney-shaped swimming pool with waterfall is sizeable. Continental breakfast is served poolside.

Children younger than 12 are not permitted, nor are pets.

Whispers Bed & Breakfast Inn
$-$$$ • 409 William St., Key West
• (305) 294-5969, (800) 856-7444

This house was one of few spared by a great 1886 fire that consumed most of Key West. All seven guest rooms within this Bahamian-influenced home have their own personalities. They are furnished with four-poster iron beds, canopy beds, spindle sleigh beds, sleeping lofts and claw-foot tubs.

The most masculine decor of all is in the third-floor Captain's Hideaway, which boasts peak ceilings, photos of shipwrecks and nautical memorabilia. The room has one full and one twin-size bed and shares a bathroom with the old-fashioned room known as Grandma's Attic. Kitty Cat's Meow, with its Key West cat motif, is the smallest room in the house so small, in fact, that it couldn't be named the Cat's Meow.

All rooms have ceiling fans, hardwood floors and Oriental rugs. A community phone for guests' use is available in the kitchen.

A unique full gourmet breakfast is served daily along the brick patio in the Whispers garden, and menu items have included grilled cheesecakes with peach papaya and mango sauce and omelets filled with snowpeas, carrots, fresh rosemary, scallions and water chestnuts.

Also in the yard is a hot tub, fish pond and sun deck. Guests are provided passes for beach, spa and fitness facilities at Marriott's Reach Resort (see listing in this chapter). Whispers' owners boast that their guesthouse is within walking distance of Duval Street and within crawling distance back.

Some pets and children are permitted; call for details.

William Anthony House
$$-$$$$ • 613 Caroline St., Key West
• (305) 294-2887, (800) 613-2276

Four luxury suites and two guest rooms are the draw at this charming, renovated historic inn just a half block off Duval Street. Amenities in the suites include sitting and dining areas, private baths, kitchenettes, air conditioning and heating, cable TV and phones. However, it's not the phones that will draw you into the aura of idyllic retreat, but the spa, pond, deck and delightful gardens. One room is handicapped accessible.

The inn offers a complimentary continental breakfast and wine at social hour.

Pets are not allowed. While you're here, be sure to check out nearby Mallory Square for a superlative Key West sunset (see our Attractions chapter).

Gay Guesthouses

Alexander's
$-$$$ • 1118 Fleming St., Key West
• (305) 294-9919, (800) 654-9919

The main three-story building of Alexander's, a Conch-style design, was built around the turn of the century and has since been renovated. Two additional two-story Conch houses combine for a total of 17 guest rooms. This guesthouse attracts gay men and women. Some rooms feature hardwood floors, while others are completely carpeted. Throughout the inn, eclectic local art mixes with poster prints. Many units offer VCRs.

At Alexander's, rooms are relatively basic, equipped with queen-size beds; all rooms have private baths, and two share shower facilities. Deluxe rooms, some with private porches and patios, have king-size beds. For larger accommodations, opt for a more luxurious suite with king-size bed and queen-size sleeper sofa.

A highlight is the cobalt blue, tiled swimming pool surrounded by lush tropical flora. Second- and third-level tanning decks are clothing-optional. Expanded continental breakfast is served by the pool each morning; wine and cheese are offered every evening. Pets are not permitted.

Big Ruby's Guesthouse
$$-$$$$ • 409 Applerouth Ln., Key West
• (305) 296-2323, (800) 477-7829

Formerly the home of a sea captain, the main guesthouse at Big Ruby's, like its two additional on-premise structures, is New England-style clapboard architecture on the outside with contemporary styling on the inside.

Rooms of differing sizes and decor feature clean lines, hardwood floors and Simmons Beautyrest mattresses in a variety of sizes. Refrigerators, ceiling fans, robes and beach towels are standard in all rooms.

Four resident miniature dachshunds roam the premises of this exclusively gay male and female property, and all three buildings share a clothing-optional sunning yard and swimming pool. An outdoor rain-forest shower amid the vines allows for rinsing before and after swimming, and a bike rack provides a secured space for those utilizing a two-wheeler as a primary means of transportation.

Continental breakfast and full cooked-to-order breakfasts are served poolside as are early evening wine and juice. Big Ruby's is set back about 20 feet from the narrow, one-way alley through which it is accessed, and all three buildings are surrounded by orchids and bougainvillea. Balconies on the third floor are set amid the trees, and the grounds are so lush that the second-floor porch does not even allow a view of the street.

Limited off-street parking is provided on a first-come, first-served basis. Pets are not permitted.

Brass Key Guesthouse
$$$-$$$$ • 412 Frances St., Key West
• (305) 296-4719

Built around the turn of the century as a hotel for construction workers employed by the Florida East Coast Railway, the primarily gay male and female Brass Key Guesthouse is listed on the National Register of Historic Places.

All 16 rooms have a modern tropical decor: pastel colors, flora and fauna prints and wall hangings that depict historic Key West. Thoughtful amenities at the Brass Key include hair dryers, terry-cloth robes, VCRs and voice mail. Beds are predominately king-size, and two king-size one-bedroom suites are poolside.

Expanded continental breakfast is served in the great room or dining room, and guests have the option of heading outside to enjoy their meal within a shady nook. A combination of decking and keystone surrounds the pool and hot tub, where clothing is optional; an additional second-floor porch overlooking the street allows for sunning in your swimsuit.

The Brass Key's diverse gardens are updated seasonally and feature a wide variety of orchids. Daily afternoon cocktail parties are held poolside, and the facility offers a videotape library and bioyolo rontals to guests.

No off-street parking is provided. Children

younger than 19 and pets are not allowed. The gay magazine *Out and About* awarded this facility a prestigious five-palm rating.

Coral Tree Inn and Oasis Guesthouse
$-$$ • 822 and 823 Fleming St., Key West • (305) 296-2131, (800) 362-7477

With its Main, Lopez and Margaret Houses, the unusual Oasis offers 20 guest rooms on three fronts that share a yard: The Main house faces Fleming Street; Lopez House faces Lopez Lane, and Margaret House looks toward Margaret Street. Guests at the facility, which caters to gay men, check in at Main on Fleming.

Oasis offers a range of accommodations, including standard rooms with one queen-size bed or two double beds, poolside rooms with queen-size beds and living rooms, and a penthouse on the second, and top, floor of Margaret House. All rooms are completely renovated and have new furnishings, custom drapes and matching bedspreads in tropical or paisley prints. Some rooms have baths with whirlpool tubs; still others share a bath.

The Oasis has two pools and a 24-person outdoor hot tub. The pool and the sun deck surrounding it are clothing-optional

Also owned by Oasis proprietors is Coral Tree Inn across the street. When purchased in 1993 this 11-room facility was merely a shell. With all-new fixtures, Coral Tree is now designed as a European-style gay male guesthouse — smaller, more intimate and upscale. Rooms here feature a queen-size or two double beds. They have porches and balconies facing either the pool or Fleming. Penthouse suites are on the third floor.

Coral Tree Inn has a hot tub and sunning area, and guests here and at Oasis share facilities.

Both establishments are known for hospitality. A bottle of wine welcomes guests upon arrival; continental breakfast is served each morning. Tropical cocktails are offered by the pool each afternoon, and wine and hot hors d'oeuvres are served each evening. Pets are not permitted at either location.

Lime House Inn
$$-$$$ • 219 Elizabeth St., Key West • (305) 296-2978, (800) 374-4242

The all-male Lime House Inn is a collection of two Key West Conch-style mansions with a total of 11 rooms. The main house was built in the 1800s, and the second house is relatively new (1970s) but built to look old.

Eight rooms have private baths and kitchenettes, and all have refrigerators, hair dryers, coffee makers, telephone with voice mail, ceiling fans and wall-to-wall Berber carpeting. In addition, fresh flowers are provided in each room upon check-in, and mints are placed on pillows during the nightly turndown.

Appointed with wicker furnishings, rooms offer twin-, queen- and king-size beds. Key West paintings adorn the walls; porches and verandas connect rooms. A harbor-view suite encompassing the entire third floor of the main house offers two queen-size beds and a private balcony overlooking both the harbor and the ocean beyond it.

A buffet-style breakfast with hot and cold items, including an endless variety of pastries, is served by the heated swimming pool each morning, and a full open bar with hors d'oeuvres is offered Monday through Saturday evenings.

Between July and September, the Lime House holds a summer sale, when rates are reduced and the open bar and hors d'oeuvres are replaced with a wine and cheese hour. A new hot tub for six features the latest bubble and therapy jets, and the sun deck that surrounds both it and the pool is clothing-optional. Beer and soda are sold by the pool throughout the day, the coffee maker is always on, and pool towels are available all day long.

The property has two off-street parking spaces; free parking is also available on either side of the street. Children and pets are prohibited.

Mangrove House
$-$$ • 623 Southard St., Key West • (305) 294-1866, (800) 294-1866

Referred to as an eyebrow house (see Close-up in our Attractions chapter), Mangrove is an intimate bed and breakfast featuring

Snowy egrets show off their breeding plumage during courtship rituals.

only two guest rooms and two apartments. Light wood furnishings and tropical pastels are the standard here, as are queen-size beds, private baths and wall-to-wall carpeting in the first-floor standard rooms.

Two one-bedroom apartments with double beds, full kitchens and dining/living room combinations are on the second floor. Living rooms are tiled; bedrooms, carpeted. If you stay on the first floor, your room opens to a poolside deck; private balconies are accessed off the second floor.

Complimentary continental breakfast, expanded during winter, is served out back by the pool and hot tub. Poolside clothing is optional; soft drinks served throughout the afternoon are "on the house." Mangrove House caters to gay men. Children and pets are not permitted.

Newton Street Station
$-$$ • 1414 Newton St., Key West
• (305) 294-4288, (800) 248-2457

Built in Trumbo Point as the home of the Overseas Railroad station master, this one-story structure was moved a half-mile to this quiet residential neighborhood. Now a male-only, clothing-optional, seven-unit facility with a single entrance, the building has its original Cuban-tile floors.

Each room is furnished with a double bed, wicker furniture, a refrigerator and tropical prints. Most rooms have ceiling fans, and some units share baths. Wall hangings include a mix of photography, watercolors and framed posters from local Key West artists.

The outdoor heated swimming pool is surrounded by a large sun deck, where continental breakfast is served each morning. Guests are allowed free use of on-premise bicycles and an outdoor gas grill, and on-street parking is abundant.

Hostel

Hostelling International Key West
$ • 718 South St., Key West
• (305) 296-5719

If you want to save money on accommodations in Key West, one very inexpensive option is Hostelling International Key West. The facility has 10 air-conditioned dormitory-style rooms with bunk beds and separate baths. The hostel accommodates as many as 92 guests for as little as $17 per night (nonmembers pay $3 more) and is near Old Town and beaches along the Atlantic.

Eleven motel rooms at the Sea Shell Motel — the hostel's affiliate in the same building — each have two double beds, a private bath and a mini-refrigerator. Each room sleeps four, and rates are between $50 and $125 per night, depending upon the season.

A common kitchen is open to all hostel and motel guests for food preparation between the hours of 8 AM and 9 PM, and a common dining area is in the courtyard. Those who prefer to have their meals served pay a mere $2 for breakfast and $2 for dinner. Laundry facilities and lockers are available within this wood structure.

Popular with Europeans, students and adults, the Hostelling International Key West, like other hostels worldwide, provides travelers with low-cost, friendly accommodations and an ideal means of meeting a diverse group of individuals. Bicycle rentals and snorkeling, scuba and sunset excursions (see our Recreation and Diving and Snorkeling chapters) all are offered at rates that are discounted as much as 20 percent.

The hostel is open 24 hours a day. Reservations should be made at least one week in advance. No dorm reservations are accepted in March.

Renting allows you to sample the flavors of our diverse neighborhoods – an especially good idea if you are thinking of buying real estate in the Florida Keys.

Vacation Rentals

Become a thread in the intricate fabric of Florida Keys life. Spend a week, a month, a season or a year on any one of our assorted islands. The Florida Keys offer thousands of rental opportunities to nudge you on your way toward joining leagues of full- and part-time inhabitants who have discovered our restful and rewarding Paradise south of the Miami border.

Renting allows you to sample the flavors of our diverse neighborhoods — an especially good idea if you are thinking of buying real estate in the Florida Keys. Short-term rentals often handle the overflow from our hotels, motels and inns, and many travelers prefer the privacy and home-away-from-home comforts of renting residences for vacations.

The selection includes every available facet of the real estate market. Mobile homes, single-family homes, condominiums and duplexes on dry lots and bayfront, oceanfront and canalfront lots all are available for rent on our islands. If you prefer unabridged seclusion, stay on your own private island (see Rent an Island in this chapter). Although few waterfront properties exist in Key West, you'll still find many intriguing rental options here (see the Key West section of this chapter).

Condominiums, town houses and mobile home communities throughout our islands offer shared amenities such as swimming pools, hot tubs, parking and sometimes dockage, while single-family homes frequently have private pools, hot tubs and lush tropical gardens.

Throughout the Florida Keys, rentals primarily are classified as short-term and long-term. Short-term rental agreements range from a weekend to six months; anything exceeding six months is considered a long-term rental.

When it comes to short-term rentals, there's been a bit of trouble in Paradise. The Monroe County Planning Commission has prohibited short-term rentals of 30 days or less throughout residential areas of unincorporated Monroe County. Key Colony Beach, Florida Keys offshore islands and some unincorporated Monroe County condominiums were not affected by that change. However, in 1998, the Key West City Commission took up the issue of short-term rentals, partly in response to full-time island residents who complained about the increased noise and traffic vacationers bring to their otherwise quiet neighborhoods. In the future, individual homeowners whose properties are not specifically licensed for transient rental may find themselves subject to city-imposed restrictions on short-term occupancy. Those in gated communities, as well as condominium owners, may also face limits on the number of times per year they may rent their properties. The bottom line for vacationers is this: Fewer short-term rental options may soon be available in Key West, and the competition will be fierce for those that are. The best advice we can offer in this ever-changing environment is to work through a rental agent who has a handle on what's available and always book early.

Unlike long-term tenants, short-term tenants are required by the state of Florida to pay an 11.5 percent sales tax. Generally not incorporated into the price quoted for short-term rentals, this tax includes the same tourist bed tax charged by hotels, motels, inns and resorts for maintaining, advertising and promoting our facilities and attractions. Quotes for short-term rentals do, however, include furnishings and utilities, with the exception of long-distance phone calls.

The Role of Real Estate Agents

Most short-term rental properties are handled by real estate agents. The exceptions are condominiums that act as hotels and employ on-site managers (see our Hotels and

Motels chapter) and homeowners who market rentals on their own, which, because of changes in laws as indicated above, are becoming more and more scarce.

Depending upon its size and specialty, an agency that handles rentals may list anywhere between 10 to 200-plus short-term rental options. Most large agencies employ sales associates who specialize in short-term rentals. Except for Key West, where agents handle much of the entire island, Florida Keys agents typically specialize within the region of their office (see the Rental Agencies section in this chapter).

www.insiders.com

See this and many other Insiders' Guide® destinations online — in their entirety.

Visit us today!

Finding a rental property through an agency has its advantages. Rental agencies almost always offer descriptions and photographs of available properties and advice on the best option for your needs and desires. Agents ensure that a home is clean and that its grounds are maintained. If appliances such as air-conditioning units or televisions require repair, most real estate agents are on call 24 hours a day to solve the problem. Agents also frequently handle additional rental needs, such as cribs, rollaway beds, VCRs, office equipment, even boats.

In order to manage short-term rentals for stays of fewer than 30 days, real estate agencies and/or property owners and managers of condominium complexes must be licensed by the state of Florida. Units rented for fewer than 30 days are considered resort dwellings, and agents and/or owners and managers must therefore abide by a Florida statute that applies to hotels and restaurants. Depending upon the category of accommodation (condominium or single-family home, for instance), safety and health standards set by this statute may require fire extinguishers, electric smoke detectors in sleeping areas, mattress covers on all beds and deadbolt locks on doors.

Seasonal Rates

As Old Man Winter rolls around, travelers flock to the Florida Keys seeking respite from cold and snow. Referred to locally as "snowbirds," these travelers drive rates up between the months of December and April, the high season.

Summertime is when diving is typically best (see our chapter on Diving and Snorkeling). It's also the time of year when residents throughout the state of Florida head to the Florida Keys for the relief of the ocean breezes. However, the rest of the mass market moves back home, so rents typically decline during the months of May through August.

September through November is relatively quiet, tourism-wise. With the exception of holidays and special events, rates are reduced during this time to about 20 percent less than the high winter standard. One reason for the price drop is, of course, weather-related. Fall is the prime season for hurricanes in the Florida Keys. However, as long as you keep a watchful eye on the forecasts, you'll find this the best season to enjoy relatively uncrowded streets, shops and attractions and to gain a better sense of what laid-back island life is really like.

Some rental agencies offer two price tiers: Christmas through Labor Day and a fall season during which prices are typically reduced 20 to 25 percent. Rates during holidays and special seasons virtually always exceed the high season.

Minimum Stays

Most short-term tenants rent a home in the Florida Keys for a week to three or four months. The bulk of the short-term rental market consists of two-week vacationers, but our islands are also popular with Northern residents and retirees who retreat here for the winter. Virtually no private homes are available for rent on a daily basis, and only a few condominium complexes, those with on-site managers that act as hotels, offer this option (see our Hotels and Motels chapter).

Throughout the year, the minimum stay is typically three days; during holidays such as Christmas and Easter, and special events including lobster season and Fantasy Fest, minimum stays range from four days to two weeks. These policies are established by individual property owners or condominium complexes. Inquire with your rental agent or property owner/manager.

Options and Restrictions

Rental residences are designated by their owners as "smoking" or "nonsmoking." The number of nonsmoking properties is growing.

Children are generally welcome, but some condominium complexes restrict the number of children allowed in a single unit. One adult-only facility, Silver Shores, a mobile home park in Key Largo catering to senior citizens, exists in the Florida Keys.

Condominiums typically do not allow pets, but some single-family homes and mobile home parks do. An additional security deposit or a fee (sometimes both) is often required. The fee covers the cost of spraying the home for fleas, which ensures accommodations free of pesky insects. Tending to pets outside the rental facility, however, is the owner's responsibility, and fleas can be abundant on hot and humid days.

Reservations and Payment Options

Naturally, the most desirable rental properties tend to book the earliest, and many tenants book the same home for the same weeks year after year. To achieve the greatest selection of rentals, we suggest that you reserve at least six months to a year in advance. During holidays, the demand for short-term rentals can exhaust the supply. If you plan to travel to the Florida Keys during the high season (December through April) and holidays (especially Christmas week), you would be wise to reserve one to two years in advance.

Payment options vary according to how far in advance you book and when you check in. Typically, an initial deposit of 10 to 25 per-cent of the total rental cost, made with a personal check or a credit card, will hold a unit. If you book a rental unit one year in advance, you frequently can opt for an installment plan. The balance typically is paid 30 to 60 days prior to your arrival. Some agents allow you to pay with cash or credit card upon arrival, provided that you check in during office hours, which vary from agency to agency. Ask about these specifics when you call.

When you book a unit, your real estate agent will mail you a lease application and reservation agreement that must be completed and returned with a rental deposit. Reservation agreements will list the address and telephone number of the property so you may notify family and friends accordingly.

Security Deposits

Your rental agreement holds you responsible for any damage to the dwelling and its contents. Security deposits provide the homeowner with added protection and a means of paying any telephone charges not billed to your credit card. As a general rule, count on supplying 50 to 75 percent of one week's rent (slightly more for a monthly rental). Agents collect an average of $500 in deposits per property. Security deposits on large homes with expensive furnishings can be very high, into the thousands of dollars.

If you have opted for an installment plan, you will pay the security deposit with your final payment when you check in. The deposit often is returned in the mail two weeks to one month after your departure, or after the homeowner's telephone bill is received and a damage assessment completed.

Cancellation Policies

Homeowners set monetary penalties for cancellations anywhere between 30 days in advance of reservations, with a nominal can-

INSIDERS' TIP

Recent changes in the laws concerning transient rental properties in the Florida Keys and Key West have significantly reduced the number of single-family homes available for short-term rental. To ensure the widest choice of accommodations, book early.

cellation fee for administrative services, to 60 days in advance with a full refund. Don't assume that an impending hurricane or other emergency beyond your control will warrant a refund of your payment. In such cases, some homeowners may be generous in providing full or partial refunds or offering credit toward accommodations at a future date — but don't bank on it. Generally, you forfeit your deposit when weather emergencies cancel your vacation plans.

Refund policies are negotiated between the tenant, real estate agency and property owner and usually are not included in lease agreements. Many real estate agencies sell trip insurance, whereby a third party will refund the full cost of a vacation rental for which you have paid a portion but not used. These policies typically cost 5 percent of the total dollars at risk.

The Florida Keys

Short-term rentals are available from Key Largo to Key West. As reflected in the general organization of this book, regions typically are classified as Upper, Middle and Lower Keys and Key West. Key Largo, Islamorada and Long Key/Layton constitute the Upper Keys; Duck Key through Marathon encompass the Middle Keys; and Big Pine Key through Big Coppitt Key make up the Lower Keys.

The three distinct segments of the Florida Keys above Key West offer a varied menu of lifestyles and housing preferences. To help you tailor your rental requirements to your vacation or residence needs, we felt a quick tour through several of our communities would prove helpful. Keep in mind that rental prices, like real estate prices, fluctuate within these regions and also vary within subdivisions. (For additional information on subdivisions, refer to our chapter on Real Estate).

Community Overviews

For the most part, **Key Largo** is popular with divers interested in the abundant reefs within John Pennekamp Coral Reef State Park, with families and others who enjoy the activity and attractions of this large island and with individuals who commute a little more than 20 miles to the mainland. The exclusive community here is Ocean Reef.

Still accessible to the mainland is **Islamorada**. Narrow islands here almost always offer a view of the water, and you cross scenic bridges in order to reach them. Even if you do not rent a waterfront home in Islamorada, water views are everywhere, and fishing opportunities are abundant. This area maintains the largest charter fishing fleet in the Florida Keys.

Duck Key and **Marathon**, an hour from Key Largo and an hour from Key West, attract families, anglers and divers who desire convenience and a small-town atmosphere with a variety of recreational opportunities.

Rural **Big Pine Key** in the Lower Keys is home to the diminutive Key deer, and residents sacrifice some freedoms (speed limits, building and fencing restrictions) in order to share the island with these gentle creatures. Big Pine Key likely offers the least expensive rentals; prices ascend as islands stretch closer to Key West (see the Key West section in this chapter).

Kinds of Properties

Condos and Houses

Throughout our islands you'll find condominiums and single-family homes on dry (nonwaterfront), canalfront, oceanfront or bayfront lots. Most desirable — and most expensive — are the open waterfront (bayside or oceanside) single-family homes with pools on private but easily accessed streets. Many single-family homes on open water maintain private beaches.

Photo: Victoria Shearer

Keys gardens often include a quiet spot to relax and reflect.

Because a limited number of waterfront homes is available, short-term tenants often opt for single-family homes on canals or dry (non-waterfront) lots or for waterfront condominiums. Both home and condominium sizes average 1,200 to 1,700 square feet but can be as large as 5,000 square feet.

Duplexes are among the least expensive rental properties; they typically consist of two-bedroom, one-bath units on a single level and share a common wall with a neighboring apartment of similar size.

Mobile Homes

The least-expensive rental option often is a mobile home. Mobile home village communities offer permanent fixed homes for rent; these are especially popular with snowbirds. Two excellent communities to consider are: **Outdoor Resorts**, MM 66 Bayside, Long Key; and **Venture Out**, MM 23 Oceanside, Cudjoe

Key. Amenities include a putting green, tennis courts, a pool and a marina. For information on Venture Out, contact Waterfront Realty, (305) 745-1333. Contact Outdoor Resorts directly at (305) 664-4860.

Rent an Island

Tattoo never had it so good. He had to rely on the plane, the plane. When you rent your own private island in the Florida Keys, all fantasies come true just a five-minute boat ride from our connected island chain. The two lush and secluded offshore islands described below offer solar-powered lodge-style homes with freshwater cisterns, ceiling fans and soothing seaside breezes. Telephones are optional. They'd only jangle the peace and quiet anyway.

Offshore islands are not affected by short-term rental limitations. The rates cited below are subject to change without notice, so be sure to verify the correct figures when you call for reservations.

Seabird Key
(305) 669-0044

From a distance, white ibis seeking refuge in the lush greenery of Seabird Key resemble ornaments on a tropical Christmas tree; just off the dock, cockatiels, parakeets and zebra finches sing out from large aviaries beneath the raised chalet-style home. This gentle flock inspired owners Jim and Deborah Davidson to unofficially rename the 8-acre Russell Key to Seabird Key, which sits a half-mile off Marathon bayside.

The 1,600-square-foot cypress-wood home here is a two-story retreat with three bedrooms, 2½ baths and a tin roof. Open and roomy, the first floor features a kitchen with handmade Mexican tiles and a great room with modern rustic appeal. Louvered windows allow breezes to flow into every corner of the home. The two first-floor bedrooms, furnished with double beds, have private baths; each has access to a small deck. Toward the front is a music nook with a piano and small deck; to the rear is a bedroom with bunk beds.

If you step outside between the two bedrooms, you'll discover an outdoor shower and a ladder leading to a scenic widow's walk atop the home. A gas grill with a picnic table and a chickee is set by the cistern. Papaya, Key lime, grapefruit and pineapple trees and banana plants offer the opportunity to eat off the land; a hammock rests beneath a gumbo limbo tree in the distance. Throughout the island, winding pathways guide visitors through lush native foliage that caretakers lovingly groom, including more than 50 varieties of palms. Wildlife is equally plentiful and interesting, including butterflies from all parts of the world brought in and bred for added color.

A white coral sand beach with lounge chairs is surrounded by waters so clear you can see to the bottom.

Tennis celebrity Martina Navratilova vacationed on Seabird Key after competing in a U.S. Open; Jimmy Buffett's crew became true cheeseburgers in Paradise here.

The rate is $3,295 per week for up to four people plus $225 per person if your party has more than four, with a maximum of eight people. The weekly rate decreases from August through mid-December; tax is not included. A 17-foot skiff, along with snorkeling and fishing gear and a canoe, are included in the rate. Caretakers live 10 minutes away. A lot on Marathon has parking for cars, boats and trailers. For more information, contact Deborah Davidson at the number listed above.

Money Key
(305) 745-3084

OK, so we failed to mention how much such a remarkable undertaking costs. The name says it all: When Money Key owner Tom Lesick purchased the 5½-acre island and constructed its only house, a contemporary 3,500-square-footer known as Emerald Isle, he had "green" on his mind — and the venture cost a bundle.

With time and cash to spend, visitors to Money Key, a mile off Summerland Key oceanside, enjoy a three-story, three-bedroom, 3½-bath home with hardwood floors, wood-beamed ceilings and balconies that stretch around each of the structure's eight sides, giving virtually every room balcony access. Bedrooms are spacious and have private baths. The kitchen is roomy and is separated from the dining area by a tiled counter.

Head out and around the balcony to the living room for an all-encompassing view of each side of the island; or take the spiral staircase from the kitchen to the widow's walk (also known as the crow's nest balcony), and see it all from one unobstructed steeple. A handcarved glass table with a mermaid scene takes in the sunlight from French doors on each side of the dining area. The great room is equally plush, with a wet bar atop a saltwater aquarium. The house has a television, VCR and compact-disc stereo system.

Money Key has a partial sand beach — unusual in that it is a floating platform — with chickee for shade and deck space with barbecue grill and lounge chairs. The island has 700 square feet of sunbathing deck space, a thatch-covered picnic table and grill facilities. Nuzzle into a hammock tied between two of more than 100 palms on the island, or roam the grounds and appreciate the idyllic natural surroundings, where resident peacocks roam through the island's black and red mangroves and sea grapes.

Money Key's rental includes a 16-foot skiff; rubber rafts and water toys are on premises, and a caretaker lives five minutes away. A lot on Summerland offers parking for boats, boat trailers and cars. The weekly price of $3,850 reflects high-season rates and does not include an 11.5 percent tax. Rates are higher during major holiday weeks; from July through September the weekly cost is reduced.

P.S. This property is also for sale. Should you be so inclined, the asking price is a cool $2.2 million.

Rental Agents

The following real estate agencies handle property sales and short- and long-term rentals throughout the Florida Keys (see our Key West section for agents in that city). Most are full-service agencies with a variety of properties, including commercial; many maintain property management divisions designed specifically for managing every aspect of rentals, including their upkeep. A few agencies handle rentals or property sales exclusively.

Many agencies maintain rental offices within specific condominiums and communities such as Truman Annex and the Key West Golf Club community, but they are not the exclusive agents for these properties. For details on condominiums throughout the Florida Keys, refer to our Real Estate chapter.

Look toward our Real Estate chapter also for details about various regions of the Florida Keys and Key West and the subdivisions within them.

Generally real estate professionals in Key Largo and Islamorada handle properties throughout the Upper Keys; agencies in Marathon handle rentals throughout the Middle Keys; Lower Keys agents handle the Lower Keys and some of Key West; and Key West agencies cover all of Key West and some of the Lower Keys. Exceptions are noted. In addition, some real estate agencies maintain offices on more than one island and in more than one region.

For more information on the companies listed here, turn to our Real Estate chapter.

Upper Keys

Loveland Realty, (305) 451-5055, (800) 454-5263; MM 103.2 Bayside, Key Largo.

Freelancer Ltd. Inc., (305) 451-0349; MM 103 Bayside, Key Largo.

Century 21 Keysearch Realty, (305) 451-4321, (800) 210-6246; Tradewinds Shopping Plaza, MM 101.9 Oceanside, Key Largo. Other offices are at 91.9 Bayside, Tavernier, (305) 852-5595, (800) 850-7740 and MM 86 Bayside, Islamorada, (305) 664-4637, (800) 541-5019 (formerly Century 21 Coastways Inc.).

Bayview Properties, (305) 852-8585, (800) 741-0541; MM 100 Bayside, Key Largo.

Coldwell Banker Keys Country Realty Inc., (305) 453-0036; MM 100 Oceanside, Key Largo. In Tavernier, (305) 852-5254, MM 91.9 Bayside, Tavernier. In Islamorada, (305) 664-4470, MM 82.2 Oceanside.

Marr Properties Inc., (305) 451-3879, (800) 585-0584; MM 99.9 Bayside, Key Largo.

The Prudential Keyside Properties, (305) 853-1100, (800) 663-9955; MM 91.5 Oceanside, Tavernier.

American Caribbean Real Estate Inc., (305) 664-5152, (305) 664-4966; MM 82 Bayside, Islamorada. In Marathon, (305) 743-7636; MM 52, Oceanside.

Freewheeler Realty, (305) 852-0609; Bayside, Tavernier. In Islamorada, (305) 664-2075, (305) 664-4444; MM 85.9 Bayside.

Middle Keys

K.E. Brenner Realty Inc., (305) 743-5000; MM 61 Oceanside, 796 Duck Key Dr., Duck

Key. Through its subdivision, Duck Key Rental Headquarters, K.E. Brenner Realty handles Duck Key rentals only

Century 21 Heart of the Keys Inc., (305) 743-3377, (800) 451-4899; MM 54 and 47 Bayside, Marathon.

Century 21 PRO-Realty (Hill/Nardone), (305) 743-8560, (800) 473-9393. The agency's main office is in the Lower Keys (see separate listing).

Keys Island Realty, (305) 289-1744, (800) 874-3798; MM 54 Oceanside, 309 Key Colony Beach Causeway, Key Colony Beach.

Coldwell Banker Schmitt Real Estate Co., (305) 743-5181, (800) 366-5181; MM 52.5 Bayside, Marathon.

The Waterfront Specialist, (305) 743-0644; MM 54 Oceanside, Marathon.

All-Pro Real Estate, (305) 743-8333, (800) 766-3235; MM 50 Bayside, Marathon.

Chaplin Real Estate Better Homes and Gardens, (305) 743-9424, (800) 768-0768; MM 50 Bayside, Marathon.

RE/MAX Keys to the Keys, (305) 745-3815, (800) 597-3815, MM 49.5 Bayside, Marathon. Agents handle properties from Long Key to Big Coppitt.

Barefoot Realty, (305) 743-5006; MM 48 Oceanside, Marathon.

Lower Keys

Latitude 24 Real Estate Inc., (305) 872-2800; MM 31.3 Bayside, Big Pine Key.

Miley Real Estate, (305) 872-9403, (800) 553-2827; MM 31.1 Bayside, Big Pine Key.

Century 21 PRO-Realty, (305) 872-2296, (800) 637-7621; MM 30.5 Bayside, Big Pine Key.

Coldwell Banker Schmitt Real Estate Co., (305) 872-3050, (800) 488-3050; MM 30.5 Oceanside, Big Pine Key.

Raymond Real Estate Inc., (305) 872-9116, (800) 747-4206; MM 30.5 Oceanside, Big Pine Key.

ERA Lower Keys Realty, (305) 872-2258,

(800) 005-7642; MM 30 Oceanside, Big Pine Key.

Greg O'Berry Inc., (305) 872-3052, (800) 741-6263; MM 30 Oceanside, Big Pine Key.

Betty M. Brothers Real Estate Inc., (305) 872-2261, (800) 245-0125; MM 28.5 Oceanside, Little Torch Key.

RE/MAX Island Homes, (305) 745-3700, (800) 277-7756; MM 21.5 Bayside, Cudjoe Key.

Key West

Key West offers rental properties in four distinct communities: Old Town, Mid Town, New Town and the beach. Short-term rentals are most likely to be found in Old Town and the beach, which are heavily concentrated with tourists.

Here, few rentals are waterfront, and even fewer mobile homes are available. Except for condominiums, most Key West rentals are on dry lots. However, those who rent in Key West may choose from a cozy cigar-maker cottage, a Conch house or a stately mansion with turrets, lofts, winding staircases and wraparound porches.

Convenience to Duval Street or the beach typically boosts rents. On-site parking is available at condominiums; with private homes in Key West, parking is often curbside. Resident-only parking restrictions along some Old Town streets can be troublesome for visitors. Be sure to ask about available parking when booking your rental property.

Rental Agents

For more information on these Key West companies, turn to the Real Estate chapter.

Beach Club Brokers Inc., (305) 294-8433, (800) 545-9655; 1304 Simonton Street. Beach Club Brokers also maintains an office at La Brisa Condominiums.

Coldwell Banker Schmitt Real Estate

INSIDERS' TIP

If you rent a condominium unit anywhere in the Florida Keys, remember the water-to-wallet ratio: The closer the accommodation is to the water, the higher the rental price is likely to be.

Co., (305) 296-7727, (800) 598-7727; 2720-A N. Roosevelt Blvd. The company has two additional offices in Marathon.

Greg O'Berry Inc., (305) 294-6637, (800) 654-2781; 701 Caroline Street.

Key West Realty Inc., (305) 294-3064, (800) 652-5131; 526 Southard Street.

Olde Island Realty Inc., (305) 292-7997, (800) 621-9405; 525 Simonton Street.

Prudential Knight Realty, (305) 294-5155, (000) 843-9276, 336 Duval Street.

RE/MAX Paradise, (305) 294-6000; 521 Simonton Street.

Rent Key West Properties Inc., (305) 292-9508, (800) 833-7368; 1107 Truman Avenue. The agency handles rentals exclusively.

Sara Cook Inc., (305) 294-8491; 905 Truman Avenue.

The Real Estate Company of Key West Inc., (305) 296-0111; 701 Simonton Street.

McChesney/Rynearson Preferred Properties, (305) 294-3040, (800) 462-5937; 526 Southard Street.

Truman Annex Real Estate Company Inc., (305) 292-1881, (800) 884-7368; 201 Front Street, Building 45. In addition to Truman Annex this agency also handles rentals for Key West Golf Club properties

Whether you enjoy pitching a tent or traveling with a self-contained motor home, the campgrounds of the Keys offer a reasonably priced alternative to motels and resort accommodations.

Campgrounds

Close your eyes and concentrate on this vision: The turquoise waters shimmer like a '57 T-bird. The sun melts like orange sherbet on a hot summer day. The stars sparkle like a gilded mosaic.

Jimmy Buffett has nothing on you when you are camping in the Florida Keys.

Whether you enjoy pitching a tent or traveling with a self-contained motor home, the campgrounds of the Keys offer a reasonably priced alternative to motels and resort accommodations. However, you will find camping rates in the Florida Keys are generally much higher than in other areas of the United States. All our recommended campgrounds have water access; many are perched at the edge of the ocean or the Gulf of Mexico.

A varying range of amenities distinguishes each from its brethren, but one thing is certain: If you wish to camp in the Keys during January, February or March — those winter months when the folks up North are dusting off their snow boots — you must reserve your site a year in advance. The Keys have a second high season in the summer months, when Floridians locked into triple-digit temperatures head south to our cooling trade winds and warm, placid waters. During sport lobster season, the last consecutive Wednesday and Thursday of July, it is standing-room-only in the Keys.

We have listed our recommended campgrounds and RV parks by descending mile marker, beginning in Key Largo and ending at Stock Island. Key West devotes its land use to mega-hotels and quaint guesthouses, presenting a dearth of premium campgrounds. If you think you might fancy a really unusual camping experience, be sure to see "Camping in the Beyond" in this chapter for information on camping in the Dry Tortugas National Park or Everglades National Park.

You may assume that all our inclusions maintain good paved interior roads, clean restrooms and showers, laundry facilities and 20- and 30-amp electrical service. Most campgrounds accept pets if they are kept on a leash at all times and walked only in designated areas and never on the beach. Exceptions will be noted. Most campgrounds enforce a quiet time from 10 or 11 PM until 7 the next morning.

Listed rates, which are subject to change without notice, are stated per day during high season without the 11.5 percent state tax. (State park campground rates include this tax, however.) High season is considered December 15 through Easter unless we specify otherwise. The summer months are also considered high season by some campgrounds. Weekly and monthly rates are usually available at a reduced cost; be sure to inquire when you make your reservation. Major credit cards are accepted unless noted to the contrary.

Rates vary by the type of site you secure. Tent sites, with or without electricity, are so noted. RV sites with hookups will include electricity and water. Sites with full hookups will have electricity, water and sewer. All water is municipal, piped down to the Keys from Miami. Cable TV and telephone hookups are noted when applicable. Toll-free telephone numbers, when stated, are for reservation purposes only.

The Florida Keys

Upper Keys

John Pennekamp Coral Reef State Park
MM 102.5 Oceanside, Key Largo
• **(305) 451-1202**

Rates: site without electric, $23.69; site with electric, $25.84

Aesthetically, the 47 gravel sites at John

Pennekamp Coral Reef State Park don't begin to compare with their waterfront siblings at the Keys' other two state parks, Bahia Honda and Long Key. But the wide range of fabulous recreational opportunities within Pennekamp and its proximity to the nightlife in Key Largo more than make up for any lack of romantic ambiance (see Parks in our Recreation chapter). A canopy of mature buttonwoods shades most of the sites (back-ins, 24-by-50 feet). One vehicle is allowed per site. The park charges an additional fee for each extra vehicle other than one that is towed by the main camping rig, which allows

www.insiders.com

See this and many other Insiders' Guide® destinations online — in their entirety.

Visit us today!

the main rig to remain fixed at the campsite for the duration of your stay. You may park the extra vehicle within the campsite if it does not encroach upon the buffer zones between your campsite and that of your neighbors.

John Pennekamp Coral Reef State Park, like Bahia Honda State Park and Long Key State Recreational Area, follows a strictly regimented reservation policy (see the Making Reservations for State Park Campsites section in this chapter). If you have a guaranteed reservation at Pennekamp and you will be arriving after 5 PM, you must call before 5 PM on the day of your arrival to obtain a site assignment and the combination to open the park's front gate. The park opens at 8 AM and closes at sundown daily. You may stay a maximum of 14 days. The per-night camping fee includes all taxes and allows four people per campsite. An additional fee of $2 is levied for each additional camper to a maximum of eight. Pets are not allowed in the campground. Intoxicants are forbidden anywhere in the park. Water and electric (30/50 amp) are available at all 47 sites.

Key Largo Kampground and Marina
MM 101.5 Oceanside, Key Largo
• **(305) 451-1431, (800) 526-7688**
Rates: tent site, no hookups, $20; tent site with electric, $22; site with hookups, $40; waterfront site with full hookups, $50

Croton and bougainvillea hedges separate the sites in this village-like campground laden with palm trees. Chickees line the arte-

rial canal that connects the marina to the shallow oceanic bonefish flats beyond. These condo campsites justifiably contribute to the five-star rating awarded the Key Largo Kampground and Marina by the Florida Association of RV Parks. Fifty-one sites front the canal; some even have private boat slips. Of the 171 total sites, 68 gravel sites with full hookups and free cable television are available for overnighters (pull-throughs, 26-by-45 feet; back-ins, 24-by-52 feet). Two beaches look out on Newport Bay, and a heated swimming pool and kiddie pool, shuffleboard, horseshoe pits and volleyball add to the fun. John Pennekamp Coral Reef State Park is only a mile north of the 40-acre campground. A security gate is locked from 11 PM to 7 AM; campers gain admittance to the park with an access card available at the office for a $10 refundable deposit.

Stated rates are based on four people (two adults and two children younger than 6) and one camping unit per site. Each additional person costs $3 per day with a maximum of six per site. Weekly and extended rates must be paid in full upon arrival. You must be off your site by noon of your checkout day, or you'll be charged a late fee. A general store is on premises, but the campground's close proximity to shopping in Key Largo provides many alternatives.

America Outdoors Camper Resorts
MM 97 Bayside, Key Largo
• **(305) 852-8054**
Rates: sites with hookups, $35; sites with full hookups, $40; beachfront sites with full hookups, $50

Each of the 155 sites at America Outdoors is carved out of a tropical hardwood hammock, 2½ untouched acres of which have been set aside adjacent to the park as a nature preserve. The towering, lush vegetation, rarely found in campgrounds of the Keys, creates private, shady campsites. The sparkling waters of Florida Bay complete the picture, offering lazy days and dazzling sunsets.

Photo: Victoria Shearer

Pitch a tent in Paradise for an economical stay in the Florida Keys.

Hookups for air conditioning and electric heat are available at an additional charge at the roomy sites (back-ins, 24-by-40 feet). You can secure pump-out service ($10) once a week. America Outdoors provides a dump station, gasoline, diesel and propane.

A sandy-bottom swim area extends into the bay from a 700-foot beach, and the 170-foot pier meets a 140-foot-wide T where the marina takes center stage. Launch your own craft from the boat ramp and rent a slip ($8 to $10 per day with water and electric). Or simply commandeer a rental canoe, sailboat, paddleboat or windsurfer through the placid waters. Convenience stores on the premises supply marine, fishing, RV and provisional needs. Watch the sunset from the marina snack bar.

Rates are based on two people and one vehicle per site, with no charge for children younger than 6. Each additional person is charged $3 per day.

Fiesta Key Resort
KOA Kampground
MM 70 Bayside, Long Key
• **(305) 664-4922, (800) 562-7730**

Rates: tent site, no hookups, $33.95; tent site, water only, $37.95; tent site with hookups, $40; site with hookups, $54.95; site with full hookups, $59.95; waterfront site with full hookups, $72.95

Surrounded by the warm waters of the Gulf of Mexico, which we call "bayside" here in the Florida Keys, Fiesta Key KOA Campground enjoys a tropical milieu and the famed Keys sunsets. Hot-pink oleander hedges lead to the 35-site tent village, and more than 300 campsites welcome RVs. Most of the sites are shaded with large palms or leafy trees and sport a cement patio (pull-throughs, 16-by-52 feet; back-ins, 24-by-40 feet). Full and shared hookups are available, although no tents are permitted on full hookup sites at any time.

Slide-outs may be used only at a select number of designated sites.

Fiesta Key really does resemble a resort: Diversions are endless. A waterfront pub offers libations and relaxed dining. You will enjoy the Olympic-size, heated, freshwater swimming pool and two hot tubs. The children probably will prefer to camp out in the game room, on the playground or the basketball court. On-premises rentals expand your horizons beyond the campground. Pontoon boats, runabouts and center consoles take you over the calm Gulf waters. Fishing rods stand ready should you care to try your luck with a lure. A full marina provides a boat ramp and slips if you want to bring your own craft. And you can get into shape with a hydro-bike, a single bike or a three-wheeler if you tire of lounging aside the sandy beach area.

A propane station, dumping station, grocery store, public telephones and 24-hour on-site management and security simplify your stay. Twenty motel rooms on the premises offer an alternative to camping, which include basic sleeping rooms and small efficiencies that cost between $110 and $130 per night. You must vacate the property by noon of your checkout day. Late checkout requires prior arrangements.

Rates are quoted for two people; children younger than 6 stay free. Additional people incur an extra fee ($8 for adults; $6 for children ages 6 to 17). A maximum of six people may occupy a single campsite at any time. Monthly rates are available.

Long Key State Recreation Area
MM 67.5 Oceanside, Long Key
• (305) 664-4815

Rates: site without electricity, $23.69; site with electricity, $25.84

Every site is oceanfront when you camp at Long Key State Recreation Area. The sandy sites are buffered by wispy Australian pines and subtropical wild flowers (back-ins, 26-by-68 feet). Half the 60 sites offer water and elec-

tric, and all have picnic tables fronting the shallow saltwater flats. The campground is separated from the rest of the park by a padlocked gate. The paved road into the campground parallels the Overseas Highway on one side and the ocean on the other. Each deep site runs from the park road to the ocean.

Like John Pennekamp Coral Reef State Park and Bahia Honda State Park, Long Key State Recreation Area follows a strictly regimented reservation policy (see the Making Reservations for State Park Campsites section in this chapter). Rates are based on four people, one vehicle per site, and include all taxes. Extra people and vehicles incur additional charges. Only one camper and one small tent or two small tents are allowed per campsite. You are asked to avoid parking vehicles or placing any equipment on small plants and grasses at site margins — use sandy areas devoid of vegetation instead. Always park perpendicular to the ocean and refrain from tying ropes, wires or lanterns from trees and shrubs, as such repeated use will severely damage the vegetation.

The dump station is across from site No. 14. You are asked not to dump any gray water on the ground. The park opens at 8 AM and closes at sunset. Pets are not allowed in the camping areas, beaches or concession areas of the park. For a description of nature trails and offerings of Long Key State Recreation Area, see Parks in our Recreation chapter.

Middle Keys

Knight's Key Park Campground & Marina
MM 47 Oceanside, Marathon
• (305) 743-4343, (800) 348-2267

Rates: overflow area, no amenities, $19.95; tent site, no hookups, $33.95; meadow site with hookups, $39.95; ocean site with hookups, $44.95

This family-oriented campground, started

by three Kyle brothers more than 35 years ago, occupies the land once called Knight's Key Junction at the foot of the Seven Mile Bridge. The tracks of Flagler's Railroad ended here. The train unloaded its cargo, which was stowed on ships heading to Key West or Cuba, and then Keys or Cuban cargo was placed aboard the train, which turned around and chugged back north. The deepwater canal and swimming area, which sports a floating swim raft with diving board in waters 30 feet deep, remain from that bygone era when Knight's Key hummed with ship traffic.

Knight's Key Park imports white sand to create a beach at oceanside. During the winter season, a stone aquarium near the canal is stocked with fish. And some big fish stories are told during the other months as well. From December 15 through March 30, the Kyle Inn, a pub-style restaurant with a Chicago-brick floor, provides meals, libation, bingo, cards and billiards.

Unique to Knight's Key Park, you can dock your boat behind your camper at the harborside marina sites. These sites include hookups and boat dockage. If your boat is up to 25 feet, the rate is $52.95 per day ($54.95 for boats up to 30 feet). Most sites are 30 feet wide at Knight's Key, which can accommodate RVs up to 40 feet long and slide-outs. Knight's Key maintains a pump and dump station but offers no sewer hookups. Electricity of 20-, 30- and 50-amp is available, but don't expect cable TV or telephone hookups.

Rates are based on two occupants. Minibikes and motorcycles are forbidden on park roads. All RVs and tents must be at least 20 feet from the beach. Checkout time is noon.

Lower Keys

Sunshine Key Camping Resort
MM 39 Bayside, Sunshine Key
• (305) 872-2217, (800) 852-0348

Rates: tent site, $29.95; site with hookups, $42; site with full hookups, $45; waterfront site with hookups, $53; waterfront site with full hookups, $56

Sunshine Key Camping Resort occupies an entire key, officially named Ohio Key. This bustling place, with a total of 388 sites, cel-ebrated its 25th anniversary in 1996 with a concert by the Tommy Dorsey Orchestra at the Sunshine Key amphitheater. More like a small Midwestern town than a camping resort in the Keys, 75-acre Sunshine Key, with its winding signposted streets and myriad amenities, is friendly and family-oriented. The oceanside portion of Sunshine Key has not been developed. It remains a tangle of mangroves, buttonwoods and palm trees, shielding a feathered montage of wildlife popular with bird-watchers.

You won't miss any of the action if you are lucky enough to snag one of the coveted Marina Wall waterfront sites, which have full hookups and an endless view of the azure waters of the Gulf of Mexico. But whether you are waterfront or back on Ballyhoo Lane or Seminole Summit, your gravel site will be shaded and equipped with water and electric (pull-throughs, 30-by-65 feet; back-ins, 33-by-45 feet). The campground maintains a mobile sewer service, dump station and LP gas. The park also rents a number of double-wide units and some privately owned fixed trailers.

You will have to rise early to pack in all you can do in a day on Sunshine Key. The 172-slip marina, which even has a fishing pier, will shelter your boat, and the experts at the bait and tackle shop will put you on the fish. Two tennis courts, a heated swimming pool, volleyball, horseshoes and a full schedule of adult activities in the clubhouse keep things hopping. A game room, basketball courts, a playground and watersports occupy the children. This self-contained camping resort provides a well-stocked convenience store and service station, an on-premises marine mechanic, an electrician and a mobile-home mechanic. A full-service restaurant offers light meals.

Rates are based on two adults and their accompanying children younger than 12. Extra people incur a charge of $7 per day to a maximum of six people per site. Satellite cable television is free. Sunshine Key considers its high season November 15 through April 15. Maximum stay is six months plus one day. Sunshine Key maintains a kennel. You will not be charged to keep your pet in the kennel, but you will be your pet's only attendant. You must clean the kennel after your pet uses it.

Bahia Honda State Park
MM 37 Oceanside, Bahia Honda Key
• **(305) 872-2353**

Rates: site without electric, $23.69; site with electric, $25.84

Yellow satinwood, gumbo limbo, silver palms and endangered lily thorns speckle the subtropical landscape at Bahia Honda State Park. Claiming the Florida Keys' most beautiful natural beach (2½ miles long), Bahia Honda offers campers three kinds of sites but no pull-through sites. The roomy sites at Buttonwood can accommodate large motor homes (back-ins, 25-by-35 feet) and offer one central dump station. Sandspur is limited to pop-up tents and small sliding truck campers. Because these sites sit deep in a tropical hardwood hammock, the park is very selective as to which rigs are allowed to camp here. Only one car and one tent per site are permitted. Sandspur sites are closed from Labor Day through Thanksgiving to allow the surrounding vegetation to recover from the onslaught of campers. All these sites have water, and half offer electricity. Bayside campsites, accessed by a road passing under the Bahia Honda Bridge, are restricted to tents or small pop-ups. The bridge provides only a 6-foot, 8-inch clearance. These campsites provide water but no electricity.

Three large cabins, each a heated and air-conditioned two-bedroom duplex with a fully equipped kitchen, a full bathroom and all linens, literally perch on the water near the Bayside campsites. You can throw a baited hook from your front porch, rock a little in the old rocker gracing the deck and catch your dinner without missing the sunset. Each cabin will sleep six, but you'll have to rough it without television or radio. No pets are allowed in the cabins, which must be reserved in person or by telephone up to 11 months in advance. A two-day deposit by credit card, check or cash will secure the cabin reservation if it's received within 10 days of your making the

reservation. The minimum stay is two nights; maximum, 14 nights. The rate per cabin, per night, without tax, in season (December 15 through September 14) is $110. Off-season (September 15 through December 14) is $85.

All campsites at Bahia Honda State Park provide a grill and picnic table. The park has a boat ramp, so you may bring your own craft and try your luck at catching a tarpon under the Bahia Honda Bridge, noted as one of the best tarpon fishing areas in the state (see our Fishing chapter). "You really don't even have to know what you are doing," counsels the assistant park manager. "Put a live mullet on the end of a line and the tarpon will bite." (For a description of nature trails and offerings of Bahia Honda State Park, see the Parks section of our Recreation chapter.)

Like John Pennekamp Coral Reef State Park and Long Key State Recreation Area, Bahia Honda State Park follows a strictly regimented reservation policy (see the Making Reservations for State Park Campsites section in this chapter). Rates are based on four-person occupancy and include all taxes. Extra people occupying a campsite who are not members of the campers' immediate family must pay $2 per person per day. Maximum stay at a Bahia Honda campsite is 14 days. No pets are allowed except for seeing-eye or hearing dogs.

Big Pine Key Fishing Lodge
MM 33 Oceanside, Big Pine Key
• **(305) 872-2351**

Rates: rustic sites, $24; sites with full hookups, $28; dockside sites with full hookups, $31

The Big Pine Key Fishing Lodge, operated by the Gladwell family since 1972, abuts a natural oceanside inlet that was a byproduct of the dredging of Spanish Harbor Channel for Flagler's Railroad. This campground and a number of efficiency motel units act as a yearly reunion site for an extended family of loyal anglers and families, some returning more than

INSIDERS' TIP

If you are a Florida resident 65 or older or 100 percent disabled, you need pay only half the base camping fee at John Pennekamp Coral Reef State Park, Long Key State Recreation Area or Bahia Honda State Park.

20 seasons in a row. The 102 sites range from grass or dirt (back-ins, 22-by-44 feet) to rustic tenting sites without water or electricity. Private boat dockage is available at the 19 sites fronting the canal.

The boat basin, a part of the Big Pine Fishing Lodge since the late 1950s, accommodates your small fishing boat (up to 25 feet long) and provides ample fish-cleaning stations to ready the spoils of the day for the frying pan. All boats, whether on a trailer or in the water, are assessed a 20¢-per-foot daily charge. Bait and tackle are available at the convenience store on premises. The Lodge has an oval swimming pool, sunken in a raised deck overlooking a peppering of statuesque coconut palms, all grown from seed. A pretty, pale-peach and teal-green recreation room welcomes guests with an ongoing schedule of special events. Just past the rustic camping sites, a secluded nature trail, Cactus Hammock Addition, winds through 43½ acres of dense vegetation. An unusual assortment of tropical plants, many seeded by the 1935 hurricane, line this little-known path.

Rates are based on one or two occupants with one vehicle and one camping unit. Extra adults must pay $5 per day, and children ages 7 to 17 staying with their parents stay for $2. Children younger than 6 stay free. Air conditioning or electric heat hookups cost extra. No dogs are allowed in the campground.

Lazy Lakes Camping Resort
MM 20 Oceanside, 3000 Johnson Rd., Sugarloaf Key • (305) 745-1079, (800) 354-5524

Rates: tent site, no hookups, $28; lakeside tent site with hookups, $32; lakeside site with hookups, $36; inland site with full hookups, $39; lakeside site with full hookups, $42

Two manmade saltwater lakes surround the 100 gravel sites at Lazy Lakes. Campers enjoy snorkeling, windsurfing and fishing in the 20-foot-deep lakes, but spear guns and motorboats are not permitted. The resort accommodates RVs up to 40 feet long (pull-throughs, 23-by-50 feet; back-ins, 22-by-50 feet). Lazy Lakes provides all the essentials: a small grocery store, a dump station and a few recreational diversions. A heated pool supplements the lakes for swimming, and

paddleboats and kayaks are offered for rent. Ping-Pong, billiards, basketball, line dancing, water aerobics and bingo will keep you occupied if you choose not to partake of the myriad temptations in Key West, just 20 miles away.

Rates are based on two people per site. Additional people (to a maximum of five per site) incur extra charges. Cable television hookup is available at an additional charge. Fully equipped, air-conditioned, Park Model trailers are available for rent starting at $69 per day. Pets are not permitted in the rental units. Checkout time is 11 AM.

Sugarloaf Key Resort KOA Kampground
MM 20 Oceanside, Summerland Key • (305) 745-3549

Rates: tent site with no hookups, $35.95; tent site with hookups, $49.95; site with hookups, $49.95; waterfront site with hookups, $59.95; site with full hookups, $52.95; waterfront site with full hookups, $62.95

Pelicans perched in mangroves near thatched chickees on white sand create an island ambiance in this comprehensive KOA on Summerland Key. More than 200 gravel, grass or dirt sites (back-ins, 20-by-36 feet) offer a choice of full hookups or tent sites but no pull-throughs. Slide-outs are not permitted. Electricity is a maximum of 30-amp service.

The facility offers what you have come to expect from a KOA Kampground: all the necessities plus the amenities of a resort. A public phone, dump station, convenience market, RV supplies, LP gas and optional cable hookups satisfy the mundane basics. A full marina covers the gamut of boating and fishing needs: motorboat, canoe, rowboat and paddleboat rentals; a fishing bridge; and a dock, boat ramp and slips. A large heated pool, hot tub and two- or three-wheel bicycle rentals allow the landlubbers relaxing diversions. The open-air pavilion of the Crew's Nest pub and restaurant looks out over the panorama of the Atlantic. Volleyball, a game room and a playground amuse the children. Only 20 miles from Key West and near Looe Key National Marine Sanctuary, Sugarloaf Key KOA Kampground is close to all the action.

Rates are based on two occupants; children younger than 6 stay free. Additional adults must pay $8 per day; children ages 6 to 17, $6. A wide variety of social activities, crafts and special events is offered during the winter season.

Bluewater Key RV Resort
MM 14 Oceanside, Sugarloaf Key
• **(305) 745-2494, (800) 237-2266**

Rates: site with full hookups, $55; waterfront site with full hookups, $65

As simple and elegant as a sophisticated ball gown, Bluewater Key RV Resort oozes class. The 80 spacious gravel sites (back-ins, 28-by-62 feet) feature metered utility hookups, including telephone and cable television. Uniquely angled toward the water and buffered with palms and scaevola, each privately owned site has a stone patio with benches and a round cement table. No tents, pop-ups or vans are allowed at Bluewater Key. All units must be self-contained RVs.

A clubhouse hosts table tennis or informal card games, and the freshwater swimming pool attracts sun worshipers from up North.

Oceanside flats and a deepwater canal surround the property, affording primo fishing for anglers. And if you want a little action at the end of your day of quiet solitude, you are but 14 miles from the center of Key West. Need we say more?

Those reserving waterfront or canal sites may secure their small boats to the floating docks or bulkhead. The high season at Bluewater Key RV Resort is considered December 1 to April 1. Although the resort accepts reservations for one day or one week to a month or more depending upon availability, we suggest you book a year in advance if you'd like a waterfront spot. Bluewater Key RV Resort has an on-site manager and is protected from intrusion by a 24-hour, phone-operated security gate.

Boyd's Key West Campground
MM 5 Oceanside, 6401 Maloney Ave.,
Stock Island • **(305) 294-1465**

Rates: tent site, $33; waterfront tent site, $40; site with hookups, $43; waterfront site

Every campsite in the Long Key State Recreational Area
is fronted by this prime tidal bonefish flat.

Photo: Victoria Shearer

with hookups, $50; site with full hookups and cable television, $48; waterfront site with full hookups and cable television, $58

Although its brochures state a Key West address, Boyd's is actually on Stock Island, just outside the Key West city limits. Each of the 125 sites (back-ins, 24-by-44 feet) has a cement patio. All sites are level, and most are shaded. Bordering the ocean, Boyd's offers a boat ramp, a small marina and a heated swimming pool. You can catch the city bus into Key West for unlimited diversions, hang out at Boyd's game room or watch the large-screen television, which is tucked in a tiki hut near the pool.

Rates are based on two occupants and one camping unit per site. Additional people younger than 12 stay free. Additional campers 12 and older must pay an additional $8 per day. Small dogs are permitted in hard-shell campers only.

Camping in the Beyond

If there is a little part of you that longs to forge through uncharted territory and live off the land (or the sea), you can fulfill your fantasies here. Everglades National Park and Dry Tortugas National Park, both daytrip excursions from the Florida Keys, offer unique camping experiences for the adventuresome spirits among you.

Everglades National Park

Canoe or commandeer a small motor craft into the backcountry wilderness of Everglades National Park. This 99-mile route, which is recommended for experienced canoeists only, connects Flamingo and Everglades City. The charted routing through such colorfully named spots as Darwin's Place, Camp Lonesome, Lostman's Five and Graveyard Creek encompasses 47 primitive campsites of three basic types.

Chickees: These elevated, 10-by-12-foot wood platforms with roofs are placed along interior rivers and bays where no dry land exists. A design originally used by the Miccosukee Indians, these open-air structures allow the wind to blow through, keeping the insects away. A narrow walkway leads to a

self-contained toilet. You will need to have a freestanding tent, because stakes and nails are not allowed.

Beach Sites: These are set on the coastal beaches, which have been built up through time from a conglomeration of fragmented shells. Campers are warned that Gulf waters can become extremely rough. Loggerhead sea turtles nest on Highland Beach and Cape Sable in the spring and summer. If you see evidence of their nesting, refrain from lighting a campfire nearby. (Campfires are allowed at beach sites only.)

Primitive Ground Sites: These consist of mounds of earth just a few feet higher than the surrounding mangroves. Willy Willy, Camp Lonesome and Canepatch are old Indian mound sites. Coastal aborigines, who lived here before the Seminole Indians, constructed mounds of shells or soil as dry dwelling sites amidst the mangroves. The ground sites, along interior bays and rivers, have a heavier preponderance of insects than either the beach sites or the chickees. Always be prepared for mosquitoes and tiny biting flies called no-see-ums, especially at sunrise and sunset. Mosquito season corresponds with the rainy season, April through October. We do not recommend you try to camp in the Everglades during these months.

You will need a permit (free of charge) to camp in one of the backcountry sites. Contact the main park number at (305) 242-7700; the Gulf Coast Visitor Center, (941) 695-3311; or the Flamingo Visitor Center, (941) 695-294. Canoes and small powerboats may be rented at Flamingo Marina, (941) 695-3101.

Dry Tortugas National Park

Roughing it takes on gargantuan proportions when you consider camping at Dry Tortugas National Park, but it's worth the effort, for this remote bit of Paradise has been preserved in a virginal state. Ten tent sites, available on a first-come, first-served basis, rest in a sandy area on Garden Key in front of Fort Jefferson, shaded by coconut palms. You must pack in all your supplies, including fresh water; only saltwater toilets, grills and picnic tables are provided. There is no food, fresh water, electricity or medical assistance of any kind on the island.

You must take your chances on securing a campsite because reservations are not taken for the individual sites. (The park service says securing a site usually is not a problem.) Campsites accommodate up to eight people. You can reserve a group site for as many as 15 people, however, by contacting the park service, (800) 368-4753. The staff will send you a permit application and, if the site is available when you submit your completed application, a permit reserving the group site will be issued. You may stay up to 14 days at either individual or group sites, but keep in mind you must bring complete provisioning for the duration of your stay and pack out your trash.

You may have left the civilized world behind you in Key West, but the arena of natural splendor surrounding you in the Dry Tortugas is endless. Tour Fort Jefferson (self-guided), America's largest 19th-century coastal fort. The walls of the fort are 50 feet high and 8 feet thick. A white coral beach, nature-made not manmade, provides a tropical backdrop for doing nothing at all. But you can snorkel just 60 yards off the beach or dive the seemingly bottomless blue waters, which, preserved as a sanctuary, are filled with fearless battalions of finfish and squadrons of crawfish that are oblivious to your presence.

Bird-watching is superb. Sooty and noddy terns by the thousands gather in the Dry Tortugas from the Caribbean, nesting on nearby Bush Key. Single eggs are laid in depressions in the sand. Parent birds take turns shading them from the hot sun. The entire colony leaves when the babies are strong enough.

Getting to the Dry Tortugas presents a bit of a challenge — and expense. The National Park Service provides a list of sanctioned concession services, which means they are insured and bonded and have good safety records. The park service cautions, however,

that the criteria is stringent and the list is constantly monitored. So, although we list them below, be sure to contact the park concessions management, (305) 242-7760 or (305) 242-7761, and double-check their inclusion in the concession recommendations.

Seaplane is the fastest means of transportation to the Dry Tortugas, and it's also the most expensive, about $300 per person. Contact Key West Air Service, (305) 292-5201, (888) 359-3678; Adventure Float Plane Inc., (561) 842-0034; or Seaplanes of Key West Inc., (305) 294-0709.

Transportation by sea varies greatly depending on the size of the craft and the number of people in your party. Yankee Fleet, (305) 294-7009, (800) 634-0939, runs a 100-foot, ferry-style excursion three to four days a week for $94 per person and $70 for children 16 and younger; all camping gear is included. Contact these other individual charters for pricing and availability: Andy Griffiths Jr., (305) 296-2639; John Potter, (305) 294-1860; C.J.G. Enterprises, (305) 296-5139; Key West Water Sports Inc., (305) 294-2192; Tortugas Unlimited, (305) 513-9955; Rob Hammer, Katmandu, (305) 255-5785; Lookout III Charter Boat, (305) 292-5076; Seclusive Charters, (305) 872-3940; and Sunny Days Catamaran, (305) 296-5556.

Making Reservations for State Park Campsites

Some of the most beautiful campsites in the Florida Keys nestle in hardwood hammocks or perch on oceanfront beaches in our three state parks. The per-dollar value of these sites cannot be beat, and demand outsteps supply in all seasons. The state of Florida has developed a highly structured procedure for the fair and equitable allocation of these coveted campsites. We hope this synopsis helps you snag a small patch of Paradise for your Florida Keys holiday.

As of October 1997, all the sites at John

Pennekamp Coral Reef State Park, Long Key State Recreation Area and Bahia Honda State Park are available for advance reservation. You must reserve a campsite no more than 11 months in advance in person or by telephone between the hours of 8 AM and 5 PM (phone numbers are listed below). If you plan to reserve your site via telephone, you may begin calling at 8 AM. Expect the line to be constantly busy. Just keep hitting the redial button until you get through, and be diligent. If you are unlucky on your first try and your vacation plans allow, try calling again the next day, when available sites for 11 months forward will again be allocated for reservation. (Because all campers have the option of staying for 14 days, overlap may affect availability.)

Your reservation is secured with your name and credit card number. A one-day deposit by credit card, cash or check by mail is required. The low daily prices, pristine surroundings and proximity to ocean and bay waters make the camping sites at these three state parks very desirable.

To reserve a campsite call:

•John Pennekamp Coral Reef State Park, (305) 451-1202

•Long Key State Recreation Area, (305) 664-4815

•Bahia Honda State Park, (305) 872-2353

The waters
encompassing the
Florida Keys have been
designated a National
Marine Sanctuary
since 1990.

Boating

The voice of the sea speaks to the soul, no more so than in the Florida Keys. Surrounded by the shimmering aquatic prisms of the Gulf of Mexico and the Atlantic Ocean, the Keys volunteer unlimited vistas for watery exploration. Our depths secret famed fishing grounds (see our Fishing chapter) and unparalleled dive sites (see our Diving and Snorkeling chapter). Cruisers the world over seek out our remote, pristine anchoring-out spots as well as our resort marinas (see our Cruising chapter). And peppering the Keys, from Largo to Key West, a proliferation of watersports facilities afford anyone visiting our shores the opportunity to get out on the water via canoe, sea kayak, water skis, personal watercraft, windsurfers, even paddleboats (see our Recreation chapter).

But the most popular means of wandering our aqueous acres is undoubtedly by boat. The waters encompassing the Florida Keys have been designated a National Marine Sanctuary since 1990, a marine zoning plan that imposes certain restrictions and responsibilities on all mariners so that our resources may be preserved for all time. (See the Florida Keys National Marine Sanctuary Regulation section of this chapter.) In this chapter we will introduce you to our waters, alert you to the rules of our hydrous highways and byways, share some safety and navigational tips and provide you with a primer of available public boat ramps, marine supply stores, boat sales and service businesses as well as motor and sailboat rentals, bareboat charters and other sources to enhance your time on the water.

So follow our lighthouse beacon as we illuminate the joys and some of the hazards of boating in the waters of the Florida Keys. The Key West section gives you details of the boating scene in our southernmost city.

The Florida Keys

Bodies of Water

The waters of the Florida Keys conceal multiple habitats that sustain an impressive array of sea life not encountered anywhere else in the United States. Depths range from scant inches (which often disappear altogether at low tide) in the nearshore waters, the flats and the backcountry of Florida Bay to the fathoms of the offshore waters of the deep-blue Atlantic. And buried at sea 4 to 5 miles from our shores runs the most extensive living coral reef track in North America (see our Paradise Found, Fishing, Diving and Cruising chapters for more information on these waters and the creatures dwelling within).

Flats, Backcountry and Shallow Nearshore Waters

Perhaps the most complex of our waters are the shallows of the nearshore waters, those directly off both our coasts, which vary from a few inches to several feet in depth and sometimes stretch for a mile or more from shore. Called "skinny" waters by local captains, these "flats" of the Atlantic and backcountry waters of the Gulf of Mexico and Florida Bay (that portion of the Gulf bordered by the Upper Keys and Everglades National Park) prove a challenge to navigate. Popular with anglers searching for bonefish, permit, tarpon, redfish, snook and seatrout and inhabited by an array of barracudas, sharks and lobsters, the shallow waters cover meadows of seagrass punctuated with patches of sand, which also function as the nursery waters for many offshore species.

As a boater in the Florida Keys, you should familiarize yourself with the necessary nautical charts before venturing off the dock. Learn to "read" the water (see the Aids to Navigation section in this chapter) because waters are littered with unmarked shoals. Nearshore waters are best traversed in a shallow-draft flats boat or skiff, by dinghy, canoe or sea kayak. Operators of personal water craft should steer clear of the flats to avoid disturbing the aquatic life dwelling below.

www.insiders.com

See this and many other **Insiders' Guide®** destinations online — in their entirety.

Visit us today!

If you do happen to run aground here, turn off your motor immediately; the rotating propeller will kill the seagrass. Usually all you need to do is get out of the boat to lighten the load and push the craft to deeper water. Then trim up your motor and proceed. If this doesn't work, wait until the tide rises a bit and try to push off the flat again.

Intracoastal Waterway

The primary navigable waterway in Florida Bay and the Gulf of Mexico is the Intracoastal Waterway. In the Keys it leads from Biscayne Bay at the mainland, under Jewfish Creek, and then parallels the Keys, accommodating boats with drafts of up to 4 to 6 feet. The Intracoastal runs about 2 to 3 miles off the Gulf side of our islands, between shallow nearshore waters and the scattered mangrove islands that lie varying distances from the coast. The Intracoastal is well-marked to about Big Pine Key where it meets the Big Spanish Channel and heads north into the Gulf of Mexico. (Red day markers should be kept to the starboard, or right, side of the vessel when traveling down the Keys in the Intracoastal Waterway.) From the Spanish Channel to Key West, boaters

must pay close attention to nautical charts to navigate safe passage. Boaters will enter Key West through the well-marked Northwest Channel.

Patch Reefs, Hawk Channel and the Barrier Reef

Between the nearshore waters of the Atlantic and the barrier reef some 4 to 5 miles offshore lies a smattering of patch reefs submerged at depths as shallow as 3 feet, with some even exposed at low tide. Surrounding waters vary in depth, but generally are much deeper than the flats and nearshore waters.

Hawk Channel — a safely navigable superhighway frequented by recreational boaters and cruisers — runs the length of the Florida Keys, bordering the reef at depths between 11 and 16 feet. Square red and triangular green day markers guide boaters through these waters; red markers should be kept to the starboard, or right, side of the vessel when traveling down the Keys in Hawk Channel.

Outside of this marked area, the waters are scattered with dive sites designated with anchor buoys and red-and-white flags, as well as marked and unmarked rocks and shoals. If red-and-white diver-down flags are displayed, boaters should steer clear. These flags indicate that a diver is beneath the water. Lighthouses now mark shallow reef areas which at one time claimed ships that encountered bad weather or navigated carelessly close to the coral mountains. Waters covering the coral reef can run as deep as 20 to 40 feet, but as history attests, depths can vary considerably. Always consult your nautical chart and "read" the water.

The Florida Straits

Outside the reef in the Florida Straits, water depth of the Atlantic increases dramatically to as much as 80 feet, deepening further with distance from shore. Although on some days these waters are relatively calm, all offshore boaters should check wind and weather advisories before venturing out.

Creeks and Channels

The channels, or "cuts," between our islands often have extremely strong currents that make traveling between bridge pilings a bit dicey. Current continuously flows from the Gulf of Mexico into the Atlantic because sea level in the Gulf is slightly higher than that of the ocean. Exercise caution when boating in these waters.

Aids to Navigation

Nautical Charts

Always use nautical charts and a magnetic compass for navigation when boating in the waters of the Florida Keys. Use electronic means of navigation (GPS, Loran) only for confirmation of position. Be sure your vessel is equipped with a VHF marine radio.

The U.S. Coast Guard recommends you follow charts issued by the National Oceanic and Atmospheric Administration (NOAA). To secure nautical charts for the entire Florida Keys, you'll need to purchase a chart kit that includes charts for each section. You can also purchase NOAA charts individually. Readily available in many marine supply stores throughout the Florida Keys (see store listings in this chapter), these charts are accurate based on the date marked on them. Store personnel will be able to help you secure the proper, up-to-date chart for the area you will be exploring. Be sure you know how to read the nautical charts before you set off.

Channel Markers

In most waters, boaters follow the adage: "red, right, return," meaning that the square red channel markers should be kept to the right, or starboard, side of the vessel when heading toward the port of origin. This jingle is confusing at best, for in the Florida Keys it does not appear to apply. Red markers should

be kept to the starboard side of the vessel when heading down the Keys, from Key Largo to Key West, through Hawk Channel on the oceanside or the Intracoastal Waterway in the Gulf. Conversely, when traveling up the Keys, in either Hawk Channel or the Intracoastal Waterway, triangular green markers should be kept to your starboard side; keep red markers on your vessel's port, or left, side.

When traversing creeks and cuts from oceanside to the Gulf, red markers should be kept on your starboard side, and when coming from the Gulf the opposite holds true. In any event, always consult your nautical chart to determine the channel of safe passage and the corresponding positioning of the navigational markers.

Tide Charts

It's important to determine mean low tides within the waters you plan to travel so that you do not run aground. In the Florida Keys tides typically rise and fall about 1 to 2 feet. During spring, fall and a full moon, tides tend to rise to the higher and lower ends of this scale. Boaters should, therefore, rely on a tide conversion chart. Most marinas, bait and tackle shops and other businesses that cater to boaters can provide tide information for specific areas in conjunction with a current tide chart available from the U.S. Coast Guard.

"Reading" the Water

In the Florida Keys, visual navigation often means "reading" the water, that is, recognizing its potential depth by knowing which colors indicate safe passage and which connote danger. As water depth decreases, its underlying sea bottom is indicated by distinctive coloration. Be aware that readings may be difficult in narrow channels and in strong currents where the waters often are murky and restrict visibility. Wear polarized sunglasses to better distinguish one color from another.

The easiest way to remember what each water color signifies is to follow some poetic, but fundamental, guidance:

•**Brown, brown run aground.** Reef formations and shallow seagrass beds close to the surface cause this color.

• **White, white you might.** Sand bars and rubble bottoms may be in waters much more shallow than you think.

• **Green, green nice and clean.** The water is generally safely above reefs or seagrass beds, but larger boats with deeper drafts may hit bottom. If you are renting a boat, find out what the draft is.

• **Blue, blue cruise on through.** Water is deepest, but changing tides may cause coral reefs to surface. Allow time to steer around them.

When You Need Help

Although the U.S. Coast Guard and the Florida Marine Patrol work closely together and will make sure you contact the proper party in any event, they do handle different aspects of our waters in the Florida Keys.

Florida Marine Patrol

The Florida Marine Patrol enforces state marine resources law. They deal with violations such as environmental crime, fish and crawfish bag limits and illegal dumping. They also enforce boating safety laws, responding to reports of unsafe boating and wake violations as well as any perceived illegal activity on the water. You can reach the Florida Marine Patrol on a cellular telephone by dialing *FMP or on a regular telephone line at (800) DIAL FMP, (800) 342-5367. The Marine Patrol vessels also monitor VHF 16.

U.S. Coast Guard

The U.S. Coast Guard maintains three bases in the Florida Keys and Key West. Their mission is to ensure maritime safety and handle life-threatening emergencies at sea, such as vessel collisions, drownings, onboard fires or other accidents at sea. The Coast Guard monitors VHF 16 at all times. The U.S. Coast Guard emergency telephone number is (305) 743-6388. If for some reason you do not have a radio or cellular telephone on board, flag a passing boat and ask someone to radio for assistance.

SeaTow®

Run aground? Out of fuel? Motor problems? Instead of calling the Coast Guard, call SeaTow®, a nationally recognized boater assistance service that maintains facilities the length of the Keys. Convey the details of your problem and what you think you need. Don't just ask for a tow if you have run out of gas or need only a minor repair. Describe your problem; the difference in cost between having gas delivered to your stranded boat and a multi-hour tow back to land could be a lot of money. SeaTow® also will provide free advice, such as projected weather changes or directions in unfamiliar territory.

SeaTow® can be reached on VHF 16 at sea by calling "SeaTow, SeaTow." By telephone the offices are: (305) 451-4910 in Key Largo; (305) 743-7556 in Marathon; (305) 872-2752 in the Lower Keys; and (305) 295-0097 in Key West.

Vessel Regulations and Equipment

Vessels must be equipped with Coast Guard-approved equipment, which varies according to the boat's size, location and use (see the Required Equipment section in this chapter). All vessels must either be documented or registered (see below), and the appropriate paperwork must be carried on board.

Federal, state and local law enforcement officials may hail your boat so they can come aboard and inspect it. Among their reasons for imposing civil penalties: improper use of a marine radio and misuse of calling the distress channel VHF 16; boating under the influence (a blood alcohol level of .10 percent or higher); and negligence, including boating in a swimming area, speeding in the vicinity of other boats or in dangerous waters, bow riding and gunwaling. Boaters without the required Coast Guard-approved equipment on board or with problematic boats that are considered hazardous may be directed back to port.

Vessel Registration

Whether or not you are a resident of the Florida Keys, your vessel must be registered in the state of Florida within 30 days of your arrival if one of our islands is its primary location. Registration renewals require your old registration form and a valid Florida driver's license, if you have one; for registering new boats, bring your manufacturer's statement of origin, dealer's sales tax statement (DR 41) and bill of sale. If you are registering a used boat you have just purchased, you will need a title signed over to you and a bill of sale, one of which must be notarized, and the previous owner's registration if available.

Boats must be registered annually; only cash is accepted as payment. Excluded from registration requirements are rowboats and dinghies with less than 10 hp motors that are used exclusively as dinghies. All other boats may be registered any weekday between 8:30 AM and 4:30 PM at one of the following facilities.

• Plantation Key Government Center, MM 88.7 Bayside, Plantation Key, (305) 852-7150. Head bayside on High Point Road and turn left into the Government Center parking lot. Boat registration is handled in the tax collector's office in the annex building.

• Monroe County Tax Collector's Office, MM 47 Oceanside, Marathon, (305) 743-5585. The office is on the Overseas Highway just past the Monroe County Sheriff's Department.

• Harvey Government Center at Historic Truman School, 1200 Truman Ave., Key West, (305) 294-8403. Follow the Overseas Highway until it becomes Truman Avenue. Proceed south on Truman until it intersects with White Street. The Harvey Government Center is on the corner of Truman and White. Head for the tax collector's office.

Required Equipment

The U.S. Coast Guard requires that vessels using gasoline for any reason be equipped with a ventilation system in proper working condition. With the exception of outboard motors, gasoline engines must also be equipped with a means of backfire flame control. In addition, Coast Guard-approved fire extinguishers are required for boats with inboard engines, closed or under-seat compartments with portable fuel tanks and other characteristics. There are additional requirements for vessels of more than 39 feet and boats used for races, parades and other specific purposes.

Personal flotation devices, night distress signals and navigation lights are other required equipment. Contact the U.S. Coast Guard at (305) 292-8727 for specific requirements for your size and style of boat.

Recommended Equipment

Regardless of your boat's size, location and use, the U.S. Coast Guard recommends that you have the following equipment on board: VHF radio, visual distress signals, anchor and spare anchor, heaving line, fenders, first aid kit, flashlight, mirror, searchlight, sunscreen and sunburn lotion, tool kit, ring buoy, whistle or horn, fuel tanks and spare fuel, chart and compass, boat hook, spare propeller, mooring line, food and water, binoculars, spare batteries, sunglasses, marine hardware, extra clothing, spare parts, paddles and a pump or bailer.

The Florida Keys National Marine Sanctuary Regulations

The Florida Keys fall within the boundaries of the Florida Keys National Marine Sanctuary, created by the federal government in 1990 to protect the resources of our marine ecosystem. And while, for

INSIDERS' TIP

If you see a red-and-white diver-down flag displayed while you are boating, stay at least 100 feet away. Divers or snorkelers are in these waters.

the most part, visitors freely can swim, dive, snorkel, boat, fish or recreate on our waters, there are some regulations, as of July 1997, to guide these activities. For a complete copy of the regulations and marine coordinates of the areas, contact the Sanctuary office, (305) 743-2437.

Sanctuary-Wide Regulations

These mandates focus on habitat protection, striving to reduce threats to water quality and minimize human impact of delicate resources. The following are prohibited in our waters:

• Removing, injuring or possessing coral or live rock.

• Discharging or depositing trash or other pollutants.

• Dredging, drilling, prop dredging, altering or abandoning any structure on the seabed.

• Operating a vessel in such a manner as to strike or injure coral, seagrass or organisms attached to the seabed.

• Anchoring a vessel on living coral in water less than 40 feet deep when you can see the bottom. Anchoring on hardbottom surfaces is allowed.

• Operating a vessel at more than idle speed within 100 yards of residential shorelines, stationary vessels and navigational aids marking reefs.

• Operating a vessel at more than idle speed within 100 feet of a diver-down flag.

• Diving or snorkeling without a dive flag.

• Operating a vessel in such a manner as to endanger life, limb, marine resources or property.

• Releasing exotic species.

• Damaging or removing markers, mooring buoys, scientific equipment, boundary buoys and trap buoys.

• Moving, removing, injuring or possessing historical resources.

• Taking or possessing protected wildlife.

• Using or possessing explosives or electrical charges.

• Collecting marine life species — tropical fish, invertebrates and plants — except as allowed by Florida Marine Life Rule (46-42 F.A.C.).

Marine Zoning Restrictions

The Sanctuary's 1997 marine zoning regulations focus protection on portions of sensitive habitats, while allowing public access in others. Only about 2 percent of the Sanctuary's waters fall into the five zoning categories. All sanctuary-wide regulations apply in the special zones as well as a number of additional rules and restrictions.

Western Sambos Ecological Reserve (ER)

All fishing activities, spearfishing, shell collecting, tropical fish collecting, lobstering and other activities that result in the harvest of marine life by divers and snorkelers are prohibited. Direct physical contact with corals and anchoring on living or dead coral are also prohibited. The area will be marked by round yellow buoys.

Sanctuary Preservation Areas (SPA)

Eighteen small SPA zones protect popular shallow coral reefs. Spearfishing, shell collecting, tropical fish collecting, fishing and other activities that result in the harvest of marine life by divers, snorkelers and anglers are prohibited. Direct physical contact with corals and anchoring on living or dead coral is also prohibited. The 18 SPAs are located in portions of Alligator Reef, Carysfort/South Carysfort Reef,

INSIDERS' TIP

U.S. Coast Guard-approved pyrotechnic visual distress signals include pyrotechnic red flares, pyrotechnic orange smoke and launchers for aerial red meteors or parachute flares. Be sure to check expiration dates.

Cheeca Rocks, Coffins Patch, Conch Reef, Davis Reef, Dry Rocks, Grecian Rocks, Eastern Dry Rocks, Rock Key, Sand Key, French Reef, Hen and Chickens, Looe Key, Molasses Reef, Newfound Harbor Key, Sombrero Key and The Elbow. The areas of restricted access will be marked with round yellow buoys.

Wildlife Management Areas (WMA)

The 27 Wildlife Management Areas are posted with one of the following restrictions: idle speed only/no wake, no motor, a buffer of no access or limited closures. The WMAs include portions of Bay Keys, Boca Grande Key, Woman Key, Cayo Agua Keys, Cotton Key, Snake Creek, Cottrell Key, Little Mullet Key, Big Mullet Key, Crocodile Lake, East Harbor Key, Lower Harbor Keys, Eastern Lake Surprise, Horseshoe Key, Rodriguez Key, Dove Key, Tavernier Key, Marquesas Keys, Mud Keys, Pelican Shoal, Sawyer Keys, Snipe Keys, Tidal Flat South of Marvin Key, Upper Harbor Key, East Content Keys, West Content Keys and Little Crane Key.

Existing Management Areas (EMA)

Sanctuary regulations complement those of existing management areas: Looe Key and Key Largo Management Areas; Great White Heron and Key West National Wildlife Refuges; and all the state parks and aquatic preserves.

Special Use Areas

Four areas are designated "research only" sites and may be accessed only by specifically authorized personnel with valid permits. They are closed to the general public. The areas are in the vicinity of Conch Reef, Tennessee Reef, Looe Key (patch reef) and Eastern Sambos Reef. The areas will be marked by round yellow buoys.

Public Boat Ramps

If you trailer your boat to the Florida Keys, you can launch it at any number of public boat ramps. Here is a list of boat launching sites maintained year round for your use.

Upper Keys

•**Barnes Sound Boat Ramp**, MM 116 Bayside, Key Largo. Streetside parking is limited.
•**Harry Harris County Park**, MM 92.5 Oceanside, Key Largo. A $5 admission fee to the park is required; parking is abundant.
•**Indian Key Fill Boat Ramp**, MM 71 Bayside, Islamorada. Streetside parking is limited.
•**Long Key State Park**, MM 70 Oceanside, Long Key. A $5 admission fee to the park is required; parking is abundant.

Middle Keys

•**Marathon Boat Ramp**, MM 56 Oceanside, Marathon. Streetside parking is limited.
•**Marathon Chamber of Commerce Boat Ramp**, MM 48 Bayside, Marathon. Streetside parking is limited.

Lower Keys

•**Bahia Honda State Recreation Area**, MM 37 Oceanside, Bahia Honda Key. A $5 admission fee to the park is required; parking is abundant.
•**Looe Key National Marine Sanctuary**, MM 33 Bayside, Ramrod Key. Streetside parking is limited.
•**Cudjoe Key Boat Ramp**, MM 26 Oceanside, Cudjoe Key. Streetside parking is limited.
•**Sugarloaf Key West Boat Ramp**, MM 23 Oceanside, Sugarloaf Key. Streetside parking is limited.

Marine Supply Stores

Marine supplies and NOAA charts recommended by the U.S. Coast Guard may be purchased at the following facilities.

Upper Keys

Boater's World Discount Marine Center
MM 105 Bayside, Key Largo
• (305) 451-0025
MM 50 Oceanside, Marathon
• (305) 743-7707
Boater's World carries all marine paints, fenders, fishing and tackle supplies, hardware, electrical, clothing and shoes at discount prices.

Cobra Marine
MM 85.9 Bayside, Plantation Key
• (305) 664-4745
For an outboard engine or a small boat, Cobra stocks a complete selection of necessary parts and electrical supplies, as well as paints and latches. Cobra maintains a complete bait and tackle shop.

Middle Keys

Tugboats
MM 48.5 Oceanside, Marathon
• (305) 743-4585
Tugboats offers a comprehensive selection of marine supplies from electric and plumbing needs to pumps, steering wheels, paint, chairs and rope.

West Marine
MM 103.4 Bayside, Key Largo
• (305) 453-9050
MM 47 Oceanside, Marathon
• (305) 289-1009
West Marine is an expansive store that carries hardware and electric, safety, plumbing and maintenance needs for sail and powerboats.

Lower Keys

Keys Sea Center
MM 29.5 Oceanside, Big Pine Key
• (305) 872-2243
Keys Sea Center offers boat sales, ser-

vices and supplies, including hardware, electric and maintenance needs.

Boat Sales, Repairs, Fuel and Storage

Facilities throughout the Florida Keys carry a wide variety of new and used boats. For boat owners, most of these sales centers provide all the necessary services, including local hauling, repairs, bottom painting and fuel.

Upper Keys

Travis Boating Center
MM 106.2 Bayside, Key Largo
• (305) 451-3398
The world's largest dealer of Pro-Line, Travis Boating Center also carries Donzi brand. The store offers a full-service repair department as well as mobile service. Travis Boating Center does not sell fuel.

Plantation Key Boat Mart
MM 90, Bayside, Tavernier
• (305) 852-5424
Plantation Key Boat Mart sells Mako and Hydrasport brand boats and is a Hurricane dealer. You will also be able to buy Johnson, Yamaha, Mercury and Honda engines here. Inside and outside boat storage is offered for vessels up to a maximum of 28 feet in length. Plantation Key Boat Mart maintains a full-service repair department.

Cobra Marine
MM 85.9 Bayside, Tavernier
• (305) 664-4745
Cobra is the place to turn for Evinrude outboard and OMC Cobra stern-drive engines. This facility also offers a full-service repair department. Rack storage for boats of up to 23 feet in length is available, as well as a number of wet slips. You'll find a selection of used boats here. The facility offers Texaco fuel.

Caribee Boat Sales
MM 81.5 Bayside, Islamorada
• (305) 664-3431

Offshore anglers shop at Caribee for Grady Whites, Pursuits and Contenders 20 to 35 feet in length. For fishing the backcountry, the facility carries 16- to 20-foot Hewes, Pathfinder, and Maverick boats as well as Boston Whalers. Indoor and outdoor storage is available, and certified mechanics are on duty seven days a week. Bottom painting and boat hauling are provided; Caribee carries 89 octane fuel and sells live bait, frozen bait and ice. Mobile service is available.

Max's Marine & Boat Yard
MM 80.5 Bayside, Islamorada
• **(305) 664-8884**

An authorized dealer of Mercury Marine products, Max's carries Action Crafts, Force Outboards, Mariners and MerCruisers. This full-service boatyard and marina accommodates boats of up to 40 tons. Hauling and bottom painting is available, along with indoor and outdoor storage. Max's carries 93 octane fuel.

Dusky South
MM 74.5 Bayside, Islamorada
• **(305) 664-4142**

Offshore and flats anglers will find 17- to 26-foot Duskys here, along with a ship's store and all services including bottom painting. Dusky South carries 89 octane fuel and live bait.

Middle Keys

The Boat House
MM 53.5 Oceanside, Marathon
• **(305) 289-1323**

The Boat House offers full sales and service support for Yamaha and Johnson outboard engines as well as Parker and Century boats. It provides dry storage, inside and out, for vessels to a maximum of 33 feet.

Quality Yacht Service
MM 52 Bayside, 10701 Fifth Ave., Marathon • (305) 743-2898

Quality Yacht Service offers marine fuel and tank cleaning for both diesel and gasoline engines. It provides mobile service.

Inflatable Boats of the Florida Keys
MM 48.5 Oceanside, Marathon
• **(305) 743-7085**

Buy, sell or repair your inflatable boat here, for Inflatable Boats can take care of your needs. The establishment offers Achilles, Caribe, Avon and Alliance Rib as well as Tohatsu outboards and pre-owned boats. As the Keys' only inflatable boat repair center, the shop also stocks parts, supplies and accessories. You'll find life rafts here too.

Keys Boat Works Inc.
MM 48.5 Bayside, 700 39th St., Marathon
• **(305) 743-5583**

Keys Boat Works has been an operational boatyard since 1952 and has been owned and operated by Michael and Sharon Bossert for 16 years. Providing a comprehensive range of services for boats up to 67 feet in length, Keys Boat Works maintains two travel lifts — 15-ton and 50-ton. This full-service yard offers fiberglass work, carpentry and Awlgrip topside painting. The six on-premises tenants contribute to the one-stop shopping for boat service: diesel mechanics, an electronics specialist, a yacht refinisher, sign painter and fiberglasser. Keys Boat Works can store vessels up to 60 feet, either in or out of the water. The facility has a capacity for 180 boats.

Marathon Marina
MM 47.5 Oceanside, Marathon
• **(305) 743-6575**

This full-service boatyard offers the option of transient dockage at one of its 80 slips (dockage up to 85-feet length, 11-foot draft). You'll find fresh water, laundry, showers, bathroom facilities and both 30- and 50-amp power. A ship's store is on premises; Shucker's Restaurant is only a few steps away (see our Restaurants chapter). The yard maintains a 50-ton travel lift and dry storage for up to 130 boats with 24-hour security. The Marathon Marina offers boat cleaning and detailing, preventive mainte-

A small skiff is all you need to explore the nearshore waters of the Florida Keys.

nance, bottom sanding and painting, wood work, plumbing and electrical services, fiberglass and epoxy work and mechanics' services. The first marina on the Boot Key Channel (Marker No. 9), Marathon Marina maintains an easily accessible fuel dock. To reach the marina/boatyard, turn at 11th Street Oceanside.

Turn Key Marine
MM 47.5 Bayside, Marathon
• **(305) 743-2502**

A sales and service dealer for Mariner outboard engines and Glacier Bay catamarans, Turn Key Marine also provides Yamaha parts and service. A 12-ton boat lift facilitates vessel storage, both inside and outside. Bottom painting is also available here.

Lower Keys

Skeeter's Marine
MM 30.5 Bayside, Big Pine Key
• **(305) 872-9040**

Skeeter's sells new boats manufactured by Angler, Stamas, Shamrock, Baha Cruisers, Hewes and Sundance Skiffs. Full engine services are available here as well as mobile marine service to your boat. Skeeter's is a dealer for Mercury, Suzuki, Yamaha, Mercruiser PCM, Indmar and Crusader engines. Hauling, dry storage and bottom painting are also available.

Keys Sea Center
MM 29.5 Oceanside, Big Pine Key
• **(305) 872-2243**

Keys Sea Center carries new ProLines and Sea Pro/Citation and services Johnson, Evinrude, Mercury, OMC and Force engines. Bottom painting and limited boat hauling are available. The facility carries 93 octane fuel and maintains a complete marine store with parts and accessories.

Tropical Marine Center Inc.
MM 19.5 Bayside, Crane Blvd., Sugarloaf Key • (305) 745-3663

Among the now boats available at Tropical Marine are Lowe pontoons and Key Largo boats. The facility also carries a varied selection of used vessels. A Johnson outboard engine dealer, Tropical Marine has a full-service department.

Powerboat Rentals

The following rental facilities offer U.S. Coast Guard-approved, safety-equipped vessels complete with VHF marine radios. They also provide operational briefings and nautical chart reviews.

Purchase the nautical chart you need (see the Aids to Navigation section in this chapter) and bring it with you to the boat rental facility of your choice. Some of these facilities require that you remain within a specific locale at all times; others base this decision on weather conditions.

Upper Keys

Club Nautico
MM 99.7 Oceanside, at the Ramada Ltd., Key Largo • (305) 451-4120

Club Nautico rents two sizes of Four Winds Quests — 20-foot center consoles with V-hulls and 125 hp motors and 22-foot cuddy cabins with 185 hp motors. Both types offer walk-though transoms, depth finders, Bimini tops and VHF radios. The 20-foot boats cost $179 for a full day, $139 for a half-day. The 22-foot crafts cost $209 for a full day and $169 for a half-day. Quoted prices are without tax or gasoline. You also can rent the boats for $40 per hour.

Liquid Leisure
MM 90.5 Oceanside, Tavernier
• (305) 853-0222

Liquid Leisure offers open center-console powerboats, tops, coolers and compasses. Rigged for snorkeling, scuba diving, fishing and swimming, these 17- 18- and 20-foot boats rent for $100 to $180 for the day. Half-day and two-hour rentals also are available. A 15-minute briefing is provided before launching.

Cobra Marine
MM 85.9 Bayside, Islamorada
• (305) 664-4745

Bimini tops and dive platforms are featured on 18- to 22-foot center consoles, 18-foot bowriders and 19- and 20-foot pontoon boats. Full-day rentals range from $130 to $260 and half-days from $93 to $195.

Estes Fishing Camp & Marina
MM 83.9 Bayside, Islamorada
• (305) 664-9059

You'll find 18- to 22-foot skiffs, pontoon boats and center consoles at Estes, all equipped with hand-held VHF radios. Half-day rentals costs between $93 and $195; full days run from $145 to $260.

Robbie's Boat Rentals & Charters
MM 77.5 Bayside, Islamorada
• (305) 664-9814

One of the Florida Keys' more interesting boat rental facilities, Robbie's is behind the Hungry Tarpon Restaurant. Visitors come to Robbie's just to feed the many tarpon that lurk close to shore (see our Kidstuff chapter). Boat rentals, too, are popular, since Robbie's is only a half-mile from historic Indian Key (see our Attractions chapter). Robbie's rents boats from 14 feet to 27 feet in length. The 15-foot McKee and the 19-, 20- and 27-foot boats all have marine radios.

INSIDERS' TIP

All recreational boats with installed toilet facilities are required to have an operable Coast Guard-certified marine sanitation device on board.

The McKee also has a depth sounder. All boats have center consoles and Bimini tops. Rental prices range from $70 to $145 for a half-day to $90 to $195 for a full day, depending upon the size and age of the vessel.

Caloosa Cove Boat Rental
MM 73.8 Oceanside, Islamorada
• (305) 664-4455

Lightweight 16- and 18-foot Riviera powerboats with Bimini tops, compasses, dry storage and swimming ladders cost between $115 and $140 for a full day and $90 to $105 for a half-day.

Middle Keys

Bay View Inn & Marina
MM 63 Bayside, Conch Key
• (305) 289-1525

All 14-, 17-, 19-, 22- and 23-foot powerboats are equipped with compasses, VHF radios, Bimini tops and dive/swim ladders. The larger boats (19-, 22- and 23-feet in length) also have depth finders. Full-day rentals cost between $95 and $195; half-days are from $75 to $125.

Bud Boats Inc.
MM 59 Bayside, Grassy Key
• (305) 743-6316

All 17- through 25-foot powerboat rentals are equipped with depth finders and range in price from $115 to $215 for a full day and $70 to $135 for a half-day. This facility has additional locations at the Buccaneer Resort, MM 48.5, Marathon, and in Big Pine Key at MM 30.

Lower Keys

Dolphin Marina Resort at Little Palm Village
MM 28.5 Oceanside, Little Torch Key
• (305) 872-2685

Dolphin Marina maintains a fleet of 18 powerboats that range in size from 18 to 24 feet. All have T-tops or Bimini tops, and those larger than 18 feet have depth finders. Coolers are almost always standard equipment; if you rent a boat without a built-in cooler, the marina will provide one free of charge. Half-, full- and multiple-day rentals are available; marina staff members review nautical charts and explain where you may and may not go. Prices range from $119 for a half-day up to $299 for a full day. Discounts of 10 percent are offered for rentals of three to six days (20 percent for seven or more days).

Cudjoe Gardens Marina
MM 21 Oceanside, Cudjoe Key
• (305) 745-2357

Seventeen- and 21-foot center consoles are equipped with depth finders, compasses, Bimini tops, rod holders and swim ladders. The cost for the 17-foot boats is $135 for a full day, $100 for a half-day; the 21-foot crafts rent for $175 for a full day, $125 for a half-day. The marina also offers 24-foot pontoon boats for $210 and $150, respectively. Multiple-day rentals are discounted.

Sailing

With an abundance of protected anchorages, harbors and marinas and warm tropical waters, the Florida Keys are often described by sailors as the "American Caribbean." Our offshore barrier reef provides protection from swells. Our bayside is so sheltered that many skippers with low-draft boats (typically catamarans or small, monohull sailboats) can trim up their sails and guide their crafts through the Intracoastal Waterway. Catamarans and monohulls with drafts of 4 or 5 feet fare best along the sometimes shallow Intracoastal; monohulls with 6-foot drafts have difficulty getting out of bayside marinas. These boats may also run aground here. Most oceanside marinas and harbors typically run deep enough to accommodate virtually any type of sailboat.

Within the Florida Keys, local sailing clubs organize their own informal races. Sailing in the Florida Keys can include cruising, limited bareboat charters and a combination of snorkeling, fishing, diving or gunkholing. Many head out simply to enjoy the sail. In order to sail the diverse waters of the Florida Keys, however, boaters must know a rig from a right-of-way.

Sailing Courses

Several facilities throughout our islands offer sailing courses for beginner through advanced levels, along with bareboat certification and brush-up sessions. Prices listed here do not include tax.

International Sailing Center
MM 104.3 Bayside, Rick's Place, Key Largo • (305) 451-3287

From basic sailing instruction through advanced race training, International Sailing Center shares their many years of expertise with Keys sailors and visitors from all over the country. Instruction commences on small monohulls and catamarans. International Sailing Center is affiliated with the American Sailing Association and the U.S Sailing Association. A full-day course for one to two people with boat and instructor costs $250. The 2½-day certification course, which includes instructional material, boat, instructor and certification, costs $595 for one person or $725 for two people.

Banana Bay Sailing School
Banana Bay Resort, MM 49.5 Bayside, Marathon • (305) 289-1433

Banana Bay Sailing School extends a potpourri of options for sailing enthusiasts. Utilizing the azure waters of the Gulf of Mexico, the pros at Banana Bay will take you to sea aboard either 14½-foot day sailers or a 38-foot ketch. The five-day course, which allows you a five-night stay at Banana Bay Resort and five full days of instructional sailing, costs $1,725 for two people or $1,475 for one. A two-day course, which includes two nights at the resort and two days of sailing, is $690 for two people or $590 for one person. The courses are also open to interested sailors who are not staying at Banana Bay, costing $150 for two people or $100 for one for a half-day, $250 for two people or $200 for one person for a full day. These are high-season prices, December through April; discounts are generally offered off season and group rates are available in all seasons.

Both the basic courses (aboard a day sailer) and the bareboat courses (aboard the ketch) include classroom instruction and supervised hands-on sailing and cover a range of topics: fundamentals of sailing, terminology, chart reading, sail theory, sail trim, points of sail, rules of the road, safety, seamanship and knots. Half-day brush-up courses and novice instruction are also available. Expect to pay $150 for two people or $100 for one person for these half-day courses.

Annapolis Sailing School
MM 47 Oceanside, Faro Blanco Marine Resort, Marathon • (305) 743-7740

Basic, cruising and advanced cruising classes are offered at this popular school, with bookings handled through its Annapolis, Maryland, base, (800) 000-0100. Two-hour introductory classroom courses cost $50. Two-, three- and five-day basic courses combine classroom experience with time on the water. They cost $250, $340 and $495, respectively. Cruising classes, which help sailors understand and operate the vessel's engine, water, electrical, fuel and waste systems, are offered as two-, five- or six-day courses and include sails to Key West and surrounding waters. Advanced cruising classes are offered for an eight-day sojourn in the bluewater as well as to the Dry Tortugas.

The Annapolis Sailing School fleet includes two 24-foot keel boats, an O'Day 37 and a Morgan 44. Charters aboard the O'Day or Morgan cost $225 per person for two days; each additional day is $205 per person. Coastal navigation is covered for boater safety. Courses and prices are subject to change without notice.

Bareboat Charters

If you already know how to sail or you prefer to explore our waters on your own, the Florida Keys also offers captained and bareboat charters for anywhere from two hours to several weeks. Prices listed here do not include tax.

Treasure Harbor Marine Inc.
MM 86.5 Oceanside, Plantation Key • (305) 852-2458, (800) 352-2628

Treasure Harbor maintains a fleet of 10 sloops and ketch rigs ranging in size from 19 to 41 feet by Cape Dory, Watkins, Hunter and Morgan. Skilled sailors can charter any one of these boats on their own, and written and verbal "exams" will test your sailing experience.

Professional captains will provide nautical charts, overviews of Florida Keys waters and suggestions of places to visit from John Pennekamp and the Everglades to Key West and the Bahamas. Skippers are available for hire at $125 per day. A two-day minimum is required for all boats greater than 25 feet in length. Day sails on any boat 25 feet or smaller cost between $110 and $175 during peak season, and weekly charters range from $675 to $1,500. Security deposits of between $200 and $1,800 are required. Power trawler yachts, 34 to 47 feet, are also available. Weekly rates range from $1,675 to $3,200. Advance reservations for all vessels are suggested.

Sailing Clubs and Regattas

Avid sailors throughout our islands have formed sailing clubs that sponsor casual regattas. These are not your upscale yacht clubs, but membership does have its privileges: discounted race entry fees and dinners and the opportunity to meet enthusiastic individuals who share your interests.

Upper Keys Sailing Club
MM 100 Bayside, 100 Ocean Bay Dr., Key Largo • (305) 451-9972

Established in 1973, the Upper Keys Sailing Club is based in a club-owned house on the bay and is comprised of Upper Keys residents of all ages. Races on Buttonwood Bay are held on a regular basis. Spectators watch from clubhouse grounds. Two offshore races take place over a two-week period.

As a community service, members provide free two-day sailing seminars four times a year. Seminars combine two hours of classroom instruction with extensive time on the water aboard the club's 19-foot Flying Scots. Boaters with Sunfish and Hobie Cats are welcome. Annual dues are $215 per individual. A onetime initiation fee is an additional $500.

Marathon Sailing Club
(305) 743-3546

The Marathon Sailing Club, a young, infor-

mal group, meets the second Wednesday of each month. Typically the club holds monthly regattas on courses around Marathon. The club's three major regattas each year attract sailors from all over the Keys: Marathon to Key West; a two-day Sombrero Cup race; and the bay-to-ocean race, a course running bayside from Marathon to Channel Five and then back oceanside. A Lady Skipper's trophy puts only women at the helm. Annual membership is $75 per person or $125 per couple. For meeting locations and more information, call Commodore Bob Giffen at the number listed above.

Sailmakers

Sail lofts throughout our islands will repair or replace your tattered sails; some even have on-staff riggers. You can satisfy your hardware and electrical needs as well.

Calvert Sails
MM 81.5 Oceanside, 200 Industrial Dr., Islamorada • (305) 664-8056

You can count on Calvert Sails for fast repairs for any size sailboat. Calvert offers sails for performance boats and cruisers and specializes in multihull boats. Custom hardware supplies and services also are provided. The 20-year-old business, which began as a small, two-man operation of hand-designing and sewing sails, has since evolved into a state-of-the-art business that uses computers in design and manufacture.

Abaco Sails
MM 53 Oceanside, Marathon • (305) 743-0337

As long as your boat has a mast, Abaco can accommodate it. Sails here are made to order. A rigger on premises handles all wiring needs, and the facility carries mast and used boat hardware. Abaco Sails also rents ocean kayaks.

Quantum Florida Keys
MM 48 Oceanside, 238 20th St., Marathon • (305) 209-4388

A worldwide franchise with 33 locations, Quantum Florida Keys offers Grand Prix racing sails and Performance cruising sails, as well as sail repair. The business also performs complete canvas and cushion work and rigging.

Houseboat Rentals

Florida Keys houseboats provide all the comforts of home combined with a camplike experience. Whether you seek a weekend excursion or a gently rocking place to spend your vacation, these rentals may very well float your boat. Be aware that some houseboats must remain within a specific distance from shore. Inquire when you call, and note that prices listed do not include tax.

Smilin' Islands Houseboat Rentals
MM 99.5 Bayside, 4 Woodward Way, Key Largo • (305) 451-1930

Smilin' Islands rents houseboats that range in size from 39 to 52 feet long and accommodate six to 10 passengers. All houseboats are equipped with generator-operated air conditioning, televisions with VCRs, microwaves, toasters and blenders. They also come with gas grills, deck furniture, large coolers, refrigerator/freezers, VHF marine radios and tow dinghies with motors. The vessels, which have one or two bedrooms with sleeper sofas, also are furnished with linens and kitchen supplies.

You have your choice of weekend, midweek and seven-night rental packages. You can cruise the Florida Bay and Intracoastal Waterway 10 miles north or 30 miles south of the dock. Anchor out and use the dinghy to explore the southern boundary of Everglades National Park or Hidden Lake, home to South Florida's prized manatee. Or dinghy to public beaches, watersports facilities, restaurants and more conventional accommodations. Little-known tunnels through mangroves, such as Hemingway's Past and The Bogies, where part of the movie *African Queen* was filmed, also are accessible.

The company provides a thorough orientation of rules and regulations for operating within Florida Keys waters and an information package on how to safely operate the boat so that even first-time boaters can properly maneuver the craft.

Weekend rates during peak winter season are $950 to $1,375; a fourth night (the mid-week rate) costs an additional $100. Seven nights start at $1,700 and extend as high as $2,300. Advance reservations and a deposit are required.

Houseboat Vacations of the Florida Keys
MM 85.9 Bayside, Islamorada • (305) 664-4009

Houseboat Vacations of the Florida Keys offers a 40 foot-long vessel that sleeps six people and a 42-foot-long houseboat that accommodates eight. You must have some boating experience to rent one of these floating homes. Boaters must remain within an 18-mile radius of the main facility. Each houseboat offers a full galley and features a gas grill on deck. There is a three-day minimum; weekly rentals are available. Call for current pricing.

Key West

Key West's port, the deepest in all the Florida Keys, has a main channel depth of about 33 feet; it is even deeper on the Atlantic side. Passenger cruise ships now include this island among their ports of call, and recreational cruisers often head for Key West's bustling harbor to prepare themselves and their boats for a Caribbean journey.

The southernmost city's ports have traditionally been gracious, welcoming tall ships, steamships, ferries, barges, powerboats and seaplanes. Pirates, wreckers, spongers, shippers, naval officers and Cuban émigrés all have found shelter here in the midst of their work, play and quest for worldly wealth and freedom.

Navigation

Despite Key West's deepwater harbor, shallow offshore areas exist, particularly toward the island's northern backcountry area. Nautical charts are some of the best tools to map routes and determine water depth. Novices who wish to ply the waters surrounding Key West would do well to enroll in one of the many free boater safety classes offered throughout the country by the U.S.

Power Squadrons and Coast Guard Auxiliaries.

If you plan to spend time on the water in Key West, the U.S. Coast Guard recommends you use navigational chart No. 11441 for the harbor and its approaches or chart No. 11447 for Key West harbor itself. Regular updates are automatically sent to the hundreds of mariners on the Coast Guard's mailing list, but it is the individual's responsibility to keep up with changes. Throughout this chapter, we provide information on boat rental facilities that have navigational charts and on places where boaters can purchase their own charts. Be sure to always verify that any charts you purchase or use are indeed up to date.

Like the rest of the Florida Keys, Key West is protective of its coral reefs and seagrass beds, and despite the fact that harbors run deep, waters in the backcountry are shallow everywhere. First-time and novice boaters often run aground here and by Fleming Key and Sand Key west of the harbor. Other common problems include running out of gas, mechanical breakdowns and losing one's direction out on the water. The U.S. Coast Guard recommends that before venturing out to sea, boaters know how to operate their boats well, including how to start and stop the craft, operate the bilge and locate all safety devices on the vessel. Coast Guard officials also advise boaters to be aware of their limitations and to remain close to shore in cases when navigational knowledge is minimal. The Coast Guard further urges boaters to know the waters by using a nautical chart and by mapping a route in advance.

Public Boat Ramps

There are only two public boat ramps in the Key West area: on Stock Island at MM 5 and in Key West at the end of A1A on Smathers Beach.

Marine Supply Stores

The following marine supply stores carry all sorts of necessary equipment and up-to-date charts for navigating Key West waters.

Andrews Propeller Service
5000 Third Ave., Stock Island
• (305) 296-8887

Got a problem with your boat's propeller? The friendly folks here can help. They've been in the business of repairing and selling new, used and rebuilt boat propellers for more than 30 years. Machine shop work is done here, too.

Boater's World Discount Marine Center
3022 N. Roosevelt Blvd., Key Plaza, Key West • (305) 295-9232

Boater's World is your one-stop shop for everything marine. This giant marine discount store sells fishing gear, safety equipment, lifejackets, clothing and electronic equipment, along with a complete range of parts for boats and sailboats. The name says it all.

Gulf Atlantic Electric Inc.
5790 Second Ave., Stock Island
• (305) 296-8509

Although mainly aimed at commercial fishermen, this business will happily sell batteries, hydraulic hoses, belts and a lot of other marine products to individuals, too. Repairs on starters and alternators are also available.

Island Propeller Service
5638 Third Ave., Stock Island
• (305) 292-1846

You won't even need to take your boat out of the water to have its propeller fixed here. In addition to selling new and rebuilt equipment, the folks at Island Propeller can remove and replace your boat's propeller in or out of the water.

Key West Electrical Repair and Supply
311 Margaret St., Key West
• (305) 296-8548

Get your batteries and rebuilt starters, alternators and generators here. Key West Electrical Repair and Supply also rebuilds raw water pumps.

Key West Marine Hardware Inc.
818 Caroline St., Key West
• (305) 294-3519

This is the place to go for every cleat, bolt, snap or thingamajig your powerboat or sailboat requires, because Key West Marine Hardware has it all. You'll find the complete set of official NOAA nautical charts to the Keys and Caribbean waters along with cruising, fishing and sailing publications of every description. The stock of fishing tackle is limited, but you really can dress your boat in style with all the add-on amenities offered here. You can also dress yourself. Key West Marine carries a large selection of stylish boating togs.

Peninsular Marine Enterprises
6000 Peninsula Ave., Stock Island
• **(305) 296-8110**

This distributor is stocked with up-to-date NOAA navigational charts exclusively for the waters around Key West and the Lower Keys and as far as Cuba. The charts are not waterproof and cost about $14 each.

Standard Marine Supply Corp.
5713 First Ave., Stock Island
• **(305) 294-2515, (800) 273-8885**

Selling heavy-duty shrimping equipment is the primary purpose of Standard Marine Supply Corp., but you can get chains, ropes, anchors, fishing tackle, various pleasure craft items such as bow lights, stern lights, Bimini tops and odds and ends here as well.

West Marine Products
725 Caroline St., Key West • (305) 295-0999

With 150 stores nationwide and a wide array of supplies, West Marine offers wet and dry storage and NOAA charts, charts that point out fishing and diving spots and wrecks plus guidebooks for cruising the waters of Key West.

Boat Sales

Honda Kawasaki
417 Southard St., Key West
• **(305) 294-5551**

Make yourself the proud owner of a brand new Kawasaki Jet Ski here. Or, if yours needs a little work, the staff here will be happy to help.

Murray Marine
MM 5, Stock Island • Sales
(305) 296-0364, Service (305) 296-9555

Stop here to buy a boat, dock it, fuel it, fix it, store it, buy stuff for it and put it in the water. Offering a full-service marina, stor-

age, fuel, a service department, engine sales, boat sales, a ramp and a convenience store, Murray Marine defies easy categorization. This facility is an authorized dealer for Wellcraft, Bayliner and Action Craft skiffs, as well as being a Johnson and Mercury Outboards dealer.

Willett Marine
6000 Peninsula Ave., Stock Island
• **(305) 293-0110**

Specializing in Yamaha outboard motors since 1983, Willett Marine sells Yamahas ranging from two horsepower to 250. The establishment will service your motor as well as do warranty work.

Yamaha — Florida Keys Cycle
2222 Roosevelt Blvd., Key West
• **(305) 296-8600**

WaveRunner sales and service is the name of the game here, so if you have always dreamed of owning your own personal watercraft, dream no more.

Fuel and Storage

Garrison Bight Marina
711 Eisenhower Dr., Key West
• **(305) 294-3093**

This full-service marina offers both long- and short-term storage. Daily rates are $1.25 a foot. Long-term outside storage (anything longer than two months) runs $6 a foot weekly for dry storage or $8 a foot weekly for storage on the water. Long-term inside storage is available at $6.50 per foot. Unleaded fuel may be purchased here, too; prices fluctuate according to the market.

Peninsular Marine Enterprises
6000 Peninsula Ave., Stock Island
• **(305) 296-8110**

This combination boatyard and storage facility caters primarily to sailboats and large powerboats (30 feet or longer). Long-term storage on land runs $225 per month for boats up to 45 feet. Water storage is not available. There is no fork or ramp.

Sunset Marina
5601 College Rd., Stock Island
• **(305) 296-7101**

Long-term boat storage in the water runs $10 a foot per month; for storage docks, it's $5 a foot per month. Sunset Marina is also a full-service marina, offering sales, service and boating equipment.

Powerboat Rentals

The following boat rental facilities offer vessels equipped with marine radios. Charter-boat captains must be experienced and remain within a specific offshore radius.

Club Nautico Boat Rentals of Key West
Hilton Resort & Marina, 245 Front St., Key West • (305) 294-2225

Nonmembers have the option of renting 20-foot Four Winds bowriders and center consoles or 23-foot Four Winds center console and Stratus walk-arounds with cabins. All boats come with a complete Coast Guard safety package, including items such as flares and first-aid kits that the federal agency recommends for prudent boaters. The 20-foot boats rent for $249 for a half-day and $359 for a full day. The 23-footers cost $399 for a half-day and $599 for a full day.

Club Nautico provides charts and local knowledge of the waters and suggests water-accessible-only sites to visit. Captains must complete a verbal exam and a two-page questionnaire of general information about boating. Shallow waters and mud flats are restricted from boat use, and boats must remain within a 15-mile radius of shore.

Key West Boat Rentals
617 Front St., Key West
• **(305) 294-2628, (800) 537-5068**

You can rent Wahoos and Wellcrafts of 20- to 26-feet, all recreational boats with Bimini tops. Prices range from $220 for a half-day (5 hours) and $295 for a full day on the 20-footer to $275 and $350, respectively, on the 26-footer. A 17-foot Jet boat is also available at

$240 for a half-day or $400 for the full day. Navigational charts are provided and reviewed, along with an overview of local waters and suggestions (based on weather conditions) of directions to take and places to see. A questionnaire and verbal review ensure that boaters are experienced.

Land's End Boat Rentals
201 William St., Key West
• **(305) 294-6447**

Boats of varying lengths and styles are available for rental here. The options include a 23-foot Aquasport for $325 per day ($300 per half-day), a 20-foot Wellcraft for $300 per day ($200 per half-day), a 17-foot Mako for $280 per day ($180 per half-day) or a 14-foot Jet boat for $350 per day ($250 per half day). A 26-foot sailboat is also available at $225 for the full day or $200 for a half-day. Full days run 8 hours, a half-day is 5 hours; some boats may be rented by the week. Sailing lessons are offered here, too.

Sailing

Key West's prevailing winds, almost always out of the southeast, make for ideal sailing.

Key West Sailing Club
Garrison Bight Bridge, Garrison Bight Causeway, Key West • (305) 292-5993

The Key West Sailing Club is a private organization open to anyone for membership. There is a onetime initiation fee, plus annual dues of $30 for a single person and $80 for a family. Membership fees are prorated throughout the year, so those who join later in the year do not incur additional cost. The club itself is located at the base of the Garrison Bight Bridge. A membership entitles members to use club facilities seven days a week between 6 AM and midnight.

The club has 10 Sunfish boats, two Day Sailers, eight windsurfers and three Hobie Cats available to members. The club sponsors monthly offshore races for boats 20 feet and larger; call for more information. During daylight-saving time, small boat (20 feet or less) races are held every Wednesday evening at 6 PM. Group and private instruction is available for both adults and juniors (under 18). Dates and times of courses change seasonally; call for details.

Membership also grants possible dockage in a wet or dry slip; rates are based on boat length. Information on courses, boat races and membership is available on the Club's information line listed above, which does double-duty as the business line.

Southernmost Sailing
Oceanside Marina, 5950 Maloney Ave., Stock Island • (305) 293-1883

Southernmost Sailing maintains a fleet of 10 charter catamarans and monohull sailboats — including Frances, Watkins, Hunter and Beneteau — all of which range in size from 26 to 53 feet and rent for between $625 and $4,300 per week. Qualified sailing captains are permitted to sail virtually anywhere except Cuba, including Shark River, Florida's West Coast, the Marquesas and the Dry Tortugas. A charter-boat captain is provided at an additional $125 per day (rental fee for the 53-foot boat includes the captain's fee).

If boats are not out on a multi-day charter, customers may rent them for $175 to $350 per day, depending on the size of the boat, and charter them with captain for the additional $125 per day. All boats are equipped for cruising and have auxiliary engines that reduce fuel consumption.

If you are interested in learning to sail, or if you would like a refresher course prior to chartering, Southernmost has instructors qualified to teach boaters of all sailing skill levels. Classes are customized to the student's needs and desires, from basic seamanship skills, such as knot-tying and navigation, to higher levels of sailing, such as learning to use a spinnaker. Brush-up skills may take anywhere from one to three days on the water to achieve, whereas those who know virtually nothing about the sport would be best served by a five-day program that includes three hours of formal schooling at the dock and four to five hours of sailing per day. Instructors recommend learning on their J-24, but all nonchartered boats are available. Prices are based on charter costs, and instructor fees are an additional $125 per day.

Reservations for both charter and instruction are recommended three to six months in advance.

Sailmakers

Geslin Sailmakers
631 Greene St., Key West
• (305) 294-5854

Although primarily occupied with repairs on boat sails, awnings and Biminis, this business will also repair "anything you can think of that has to do with boats and needles and thread." You can order a new sail here, and although the sail will be made outside the country (because it's cheaper), the measurements, weight and material requests will be taken here. Service runs $50 an hour. Expect to pay about $4,000 to $5,000 for new sails for your 70-foot boat ($7,000 to $8,000 if you prefer to have the sails made in the United States). Geslin's fax number is (305) 292-9102.

Meloy Sails
6000 Peninsula Ave., Stock Island
• (305) 296-4351

Offering full-service work on sails and marine canvas, Meloy Sails will repair damaged sails or make new ones according to your specifications. Meloy is also a UK sailmakers affiliate.

Southard Sails and Awnings
326 Southard St., Key West
• (305) 294-4492, (800) 298-4492

In addition to custom sails and all types of fabric awnings, hurricane shutters may also be purchased here. Hopefully you'll never need them.

Regarded as America's out-islands by seasoned cruisers, the Florida Keys offer sheltered harbors and easily navigated waters.

Cruising

Put on that string bikini. Throw your necktie in the dumpster. And don't you dare bring your shoes. You are cruising the Florida Keys, and you must obey the dress code.

Regarded as America's out-islands by seasoned cruisers of motor and sailing yachts, the Florida Keys can justifiably boast about the sheltered harbors and easily navigated waters enveloping the serpentine stretch. Our waters are well-marked; our charts, up to date; and the U.S. Coast Guard keeps channels dredged to the proper depth. The Atlantic's Hawk Channel runs along the oceanside of the Keys, protected by the only coral reef in the continental United States. The Intracoastal Waterway — called the Big Ditch in the North's inland waters — cuts through the causeway from the mainland at Jewfish Creek and then parallels the Keys through Florida Bay and the Gulf of Mexico. Keys waters are most accessible to boats with drafts of up to 4½ feet, but you can cruise the Keys with 5½- to 6-foot drafts if you're careful.

If you covet first-class creature comforts, put into one of our comprehensive marinas and enjoy the perks of staying at a luxury resort. Do you relish seclusion? Anchor out on the leeward side of a remote uninhabited key. Or, take the best of both worlds and plan a combination of the two.

To help you plan your Keys cruising adventure, we guide you on a tour of our preeminent marinas and little-known anchoring-out destinations (in descending order from the Upper to Lower Keys). Be sure to read our Cruising Key West and Beyond section, where the junket continues.

The Florida Keys

Marinas

All marinas listed in this chapter take transient boaters, but we suggest you make reservations at least a month in advance during the popular winter season from December through March. Transient rates are quoted per foot, per night. Minimums are noted where applicable. You may assume unless otherwise stated that all our recommended marinas supply hookups for both 30-amp and 50-amp service as well as fresh water. You'll find that provisioning is easy along the 120-mile stretch of the Florida Keys. Most marinas have ship's stores or are within walking distance of a convenience market. The occasional exception is noted.

The marinas keep an active list of expert marine mechanics who are generally on call to handle any repair needs that might develop during your cruise. We highlight fuel dock facilities and availability of laundry, showers and restrooms. We also point out restaurants and the hotspots for partying while ashore.

There are no restrictions against bringing children and pets unless specifically noted. Keep your pet on your vessel or on a leash at all times.

If you are a member of a private yacht club that belongs to the Florida Council of Yacht Clubs, the Marathon Yacht Club will reciprocally welcome you and your transient vessel. Contact the Marathon Yacht Club, (305) 743-6739, about availability of slips.

Dockmasters monitor VHF 16, but they

INSIDERS' TIP

Never anchor on a reef. Your anchor will destroy the living coral. Drop anchor only in sandy areas. A sandy sea bottom appears white. Use mooring buoys wherever offered.

will ask you to switch channels once you've established contact. So that you don't have to scribble instructions on the back of a napkin, we include dockmasters' directions for approaching the marinas, but be sure to read your charts closely. Rates are per foot without tax; minimum charges are stated when applicable.

A word about bridge openings: The Jewfish Creek drawbridge (11-foot clearance when closed) marks the point where the causeway of the 18-mile stretch from Florida City makes landfall on Key Largo. When traveling the Intracoastal Waterway be aware that the bridge opens only on the hour and on the half-hour Thursday through Sunday and on federal holidays. During the week you may seek passage on demand. A 1- to 2-knot current courses through Jewish Creek. Note the direction to allow plenty of time if you have to wait for the bridge to open. Sailors take note: A mast taller than 80 feet will not be able to pass beneath cables near the bridge. Gilbert's Marina, on your starboard side as you pass under the bridge, offers fuel and supplies.

Marina Del Mar
MM 100 Oceanside, 527 Caribbean Dr., Key Largo • (305) 451-4107, (800) 451-3483

Of the 31 slips at Marina Del Mar, all but a select few are usually booked far in advance from January through March, so plan ahead. This charming marina, which lies within the underwater boundaries of John Pennekamp Coral Reef State Park and the Key Largo National Marine Sanctuary, will accommodate vessels with a 14-foot beam, but depth at the mouth of the channel drops drastically at low tide, to about 4½ feet — exercise caution. There is no ship's store, but a short walk to the Overseas Highway will satisfy provisioning requirements. Marina Del Mar does not have its own fuel dock, so fuel your craft at Key Largo Harbor Marina in the channel. Laundry, shower and restroom facilities are provided on the premises. Marina rates do not include water and electricity; a minimum daily charge will be levied. Marina Del Mar Resort

(see our Hotels and Motels chapter) has tennis courts, a swimming pool and a hot tub for your use. Gorge yourself at the hotel's continental breakfast for a nominal charge. And don't miss Coconuts, a popular restaurant and percolating nightspot. Transient rates are $1.65/foot ($58 minimum).

Dockmaster's directions: Via Hawk Channel, from up the Keys, follow Hawk Channel south of Mosquito Banks. Put Marker Red No. 2 on your starboard and take a 350-degree heading to Marina Del Mar Resort Channel (a strip of land will be on your starboard). From Key West, take Hawk Channel past Rodriguez Key to Marker No. 37. From Marker No. 37 to Marker Red No. 2 on your starboard, take 350 degrees from Marker Red No. 2 to channel entrance.

www.insiders.com
See this and many other Insiders' Guide® destinations online — in their entirety.
Visit us today!

Key Largo Harbor Marina
MM 100 Oceanside, 100 Ocean Dr., Key Largo • (305) 451-0045, (800) 843-5397, Ext. 4

Associated with the Key Largo Holiday Inn and the Ramada Limited Port Largo Resort (see our Hotels and Motels chapter), the Key Largo Harbor Marina shares the boat basin with Marina Del Mar. Hail the dockmaster on VHF 16, but he works on VHF 11 and advises you reserve your slip by October if you plan to come during the winter months. Most of the 45 slips have cable television and telephone hookups, and you may use the laundry facilities in the hotel. Modern restrooms and showers grace the premises.

You also have access to the hotels' three swimming pools, hot tub, playground, weight room and tiki bar. And be sure to stop at Bogie's Cafe and visit the *African Queen* of movie fame docked nearby (see our Recreation chapter). On the east end, Key Largo Harbor's full-service boatyard, with a 60-ton travel lift, handles vessels up to 60 feet in length. A fuel dock supplies both diesel fuel and gasoline. Remember that the depth of the channel entrance is 4½ feet at low tide. The tide in the area varies 30 inches. Transient rates are $1.50/foot.

Dockmaster's directions: Via Hawk Chan-

Photo: Wayne Moccia

The Dry Tortugas – end of the line in our string of island pearls.

nel, from up the Keys, go past Mosquito Bank Light, Marker No. 35. Then go southwest to the Marker Red No. 2. From Key West, go past Rodriguez Key and look for the Marker Red No. 2 about 1 mile north of the key. In either case, put the Marker Red No. 2 on your starboard side and take a 345-degree heading; look for a lime-green house, which you should put on your starboard side. This puts you into the jetty. Proceed to the end of the canal and turn to port. Go to the turning basin. Slips will be on your starboard side in front of the Ramada Ltd. Port Largo Resort.

Plantation Yacht Harbor GARY
MM 87 Bayside, Islamorada
• (305) 852-2381, (800) 356-3215

Grab a slip close to the Keys' fabled backcountry at the bayside Plantation Yacht Harbor. Accessed from the Intracoastal Waterway or from the Atlantic via Snake Creek, this 90-slip marina can accommodate ves-

sels up to 60 feet in length, drawing 5 feet. Mobile marine mechanics are on call to service needy vessels, and a fuel dock supplies both diesel fuel and gasoline. Plantation Yacht Harbor does not have a ship's store, but a 1-mile walk up the Overseas Highway will put you at a convenience store. You may use the on-site laundry, showers and restroom facilities and, when you're spiffed up, stop in at the Lagoon Saloon for live sunset entertainment (weekends) or have dinner at the Dockside Restaurant. Tennis courts, a swimming pool, a dive shop and a small beach await your pleasure. Transient rates are $1.25/foot.

Dockmaster's directions: Via the Intracoastal Waterway, halfway between Intracoastal Waterway Markers No. 78 and No. 78A, which are about 2 miles apart, take an approximate heading of 150 degrees. (If you use binoculars, you can spot a miniature red-and-white-striped lighthouse at the entrance to the Plantation Yacht Harbor jetty.) If you come from Hawk Channel via Snake Creek, be careful at the headpins on both oceanside and bayside. There are low spots at low tide. And whatever you do, don't turn toward Plantation Yacht Harbor the minute you exit Snake Creek or you'll be left high and dry. Proceed north approximately 1 mile along the Intracoastal and make your turn between Markers No. 78 and No. 78A.

Holiday Isle Marina
MM 84 Oceanside, Islamorada
• **(305) 664-2321, (800) 327-7070**

Hold on to your Rum Runner cocktail — Holiday Isle is where it's all happening. If you're lucky enough to snag one of the 19 transient slips at Holiday Isle Marina, you can party the night away. But first things first. Reserve your slip a couple of months in advance because this is a popular place. The on-premises Chevron has all the essentials: gasoline, diesel fuel and provisions. Mechanics are on call. Laundry, showers and restrooms are available. Cable television hookup is free, but an additional charge is levied for telephone service.

Once you're settled in, graze the scene: Rip's for ribs and chicken, Horizon Restaurant on the rooftop for a more upscale meal, Wreck Bar for burgers and dogs, Raw Bar for seafood, Beach Bar for barbecue, Bimini Treats for eclectic outdoor noshing and Kokomo's for libation and steel-drum music. Take time to shop at the Bimini Row's arty shops before things heat up in the evening. The Tiki Bar presents an afternoon Polynesian show, and live bands begin pulsating at nightfall and continue until the wee hours (see our Nightlife chapter).

Transient rates are $1.50/foot ($37.50 minimum). Daily transient slips are also available for those who just want to stop for a few hours.

Dockmaster's directions: Via Hawk Channel, at Marker No. 40 take a 270-degree head-

ing west, which takes you to the mouth of Whale Harbor Channel. The channel is well-marked. Between Markers No. 1 and No. 2, the charts might show a 5-foot depth. Be aware that at dead low tide the actual depth drops to more like 4½ feet. Take the channel to the split and then take a starboard tack. This brings you to the mouth of the basin, where you will see the Chevron sign.

Hawk's Cay Marina
MM 61 Oceanside, Duck Key
• **(305) 743-7000, (800) 432-2242**

Probably the best all-around marina in the Keys, Hawk's Cay offers a totally protected boat basin and all the amenities of its fine resort hotel (see our Hotels and Motels chapter). Dock your boat at of one of the 50 marina slips (5-foot draft) of this Boat U.S.-participating marina. Hawk's Cay maintains an extensive list of qualified marine mechanics in the area and has divers on call.

The full-service ship's store sells everything, including groceries, fine wines, boating hardware, fishing tackle, clothing and paperback books. A full-service fuel dock pumps regular and premium gasoline and diesel fuel. Showers and restrooms are in the ship's store, and the marina is equipped with a new pump-out station at the fuel dock. Laundry facilities are coin-operated. Cable television hookup is available at an extra fee. Pamper yourself at the Skin Institute with a facial or a massage before you stop in at one of Hawk's Cay's four restaurants (see our Restaurants chapter) for a change of pace. Or visit the Duck Key Emporium gourmet deli for primo filet mignon to throw on your vessel's barbecue grill — and don't forget a Key lime pie for dessert.

Transient rates are $3/foot ($90 minimum) from December 1 through September 1. Off season rates are less. Members of Boat U.S. or NBOA receive a 25 percent discount.

INSIDERS' TIP

Contact the U.S. Coast Guard in the event of life-threatening emergencies such as an accidents at sea, or to report a drowning or onboard fire. The Coast Guard monitors VHF 16 at all times. The Coast Guard emergency telephone number is (305) 743-6388.

Hawk's Cay now also has 60 new slips for dockage of trailered boats up to 35 feet in length. These slips have no shore power, and you may not stay aboard your boat overnight. Rates are the same as for the other transient slips (except there is no minimum) but, as guests of Hawk's Cay, you will receive a 35 percent discount.

Dockmaster's directions: Via Hawk Channel, from up the Keys, find Marker No. 44. Take an approximate 255-degree heading to the channel entrance. When approaching from Key West, find Marker No. 45. Take an approximate 30-degree heading to the channel entrance. In either case, whatever you do, don't take the channel entrance that has only two markers; you'll run aground. Look for the entrance on the south center of Duck Key that has eight markers. The latitude is 24°45.48; longitude is 80°54.40. The TD numbers are 14049.7/43385.9. You will see a small rock pile off the bow as you enter the channel. Turn to starboard side, keeping the coral breakwater on the starboard side and the homes on your port side. Continue straight down the perimeter channel, remembering this is a no-wake zone. Turn to port to go to the yacht basin or continue straight to the main marina.

Faro Blanco Marina Bayside
MM 48.5 Bayside, Marathon
• (305) 743-9018, (800) 759-3276

The 95 slips at Faro Blanco Bayside surround the distinctive black, red and white navigational lighthouse. This full-service marina covers the gamut: on-site diesel repair, fuel dock, laundry, showers and restrooms, pump-out station and ship's store. The marina accommodates vessels up to 125 feet, 7-foot draft. Dockage entitles you to all the amenities of this expansive resort, which spans both sides of the Overseas Highway (see our Hotels and Motels chapter). Be sure to stop in for Angler's happy hour and play the Australian ring-toss game. Transient rates are $1.50/foot.

Dockmaster's directions: Via the Intracoastal Waterway from up the Keys, find Marker No. 15 at Rachel Bank. Take an approximate heading of 215 degrees. From the Seven Mile Bridge find Marker No. 16 at Bethel Bank. Take an approximate heading of 132 degrees.

Faro Blanco Marina Oceanside
MM 48 Oceanside, Marathon
• (305) 743-9018, (800) 759-3276

Faro Blanco Oceanside, off Boot Key Channel, welcomes transient boaters to its 80 deep-dockage slips. Accommodating a 7-foot draft, the oceanside facility offers the same amenities as its bayside sister across the highway. Fuel, however, must be secured from one of the fuel docks in Boot Key Channel — there is no fuel dock at Faro Blanco Oceanside. Break bread at Crocodile's On The Water, a stone's throw from your craft. Or take the complimentary shuttle to Faro Blanco Bayside for a swim or a leisurely dinner at Kelsey's (see our Restaurants chapter). Transient rates are $1.50/foot.

Dockmaster's directions: Via Hawk Channel, come to the west end of Marathon and enter Boot Key Channel between Marker No. 1 and No. 2. Look for Marker Red No. 12.

Little Palm Island
MM 28.5 Oceanside, Little Torch Key
• (305) 872-2524, (800) 343-8567

Arriving at Little Palm Island by sea, you will be certain you missed your tack and landed in Fiji, for this exquisite jewel is more reminiscent of the South Seas than South Florida. Little Palm Island, the westernmost of the Newfound Harbor Keys, lies 4 nautical miles due north from Looe Key Light. And, while the average bank account strains at the tariffs charged for villa accommodations on the island (see our Hotels and Motels chapter), staying at the marina is a real deal. As marina guests you're invited to use all the recreational facilities: windsurfers, day sailers, fishing gear, canoes, snorkeling gear, beach, lagoonal swimming pool and the sauna.

Little Palm's marina, though small, maintains eight slips for boats up to 60 feet, 6-foot draft. The front dock or T-head can accommodate two deep-draft vessels — one up to 135-foot beam, 18-foot draft, one up to 70 feet. The controlling depth coming into the harbor is 7 feet, but the dockmaster will help you navigate around the tides. The dockmaster monitors VHF channels 9 and 16 at all times. Dock hands are available to assist with lines. Hookup for one 50-amp service is included in dockage fees; additional connections depend upo availability. Boats docked at the T-dock enjoy 100-amp service.

Because you're staying on an out-island, offshore from the contiguous Keys and their more plentiful water supply, you will be allowed only one gallon of water per foot per day, with a baseline of 50 gallons. However, the resort offers you use of a lavish bathhouse with showers and a laundry facility during your stay, so this water conservation is not a hardship. There is no cable or telephone hookup at the dock, but the 60-foot refurbished houseboat with a sizable meeting room equipped with a large-screen television assures you can catch those must-see events by satellite hookup.

Little Palm Island's renowned gourmet restaurant welcomes you for breakfast, lunch and dinner, but you must wear shoes. You may choose to cook aboard your vessel, but be advised that you're prohibited from consuming your own food or beverages in island public areas. Children younger than 12 are not permitted at Little Palm Island nor are villa guests allowed to bring pets. Little Palm does accommodate overnight marina guests arriving with pets, but you must keep them on a leash and walk them only in designated areas. In keeping with the tranquil ambiance of the island, motorized personal watercraft also

are banned. Transient rates are $2.50/foot ($100 minimum).

Dockmaster's directions: Little Palm Island, at the entrance to Newfound Harbor, is called Munson Island on the charts and is marked by Channel Marker Red No. 2. When approaching via Hawk Channel from the north, take care to avoid the coral heads, which run parallel to the Newfound Harbor Keys approximately a half-mile offshore. Loran coordinates are as follows: 13981.6/43530.5. Use GPS latitude 24°37.11; longitude 81°24.42.

Anchoring Out

Fancy yourself more Robinson Crusoe than Aristotle Onassis? Then you'll discover that anchoring out in the pristine waters lacing the Florida Keys approaches nirvana. From the northernmost keys of Biscayne Bay to Loggerhead Key at the end of the line, remote havens remain unspoiled, many reachable only by boat. Ibis, white pelicans and bald eagles winter among select out-islands, and whole condominiums of cormorants take over the scrub of tiny mangrove islets. Gulf waters simmer with snapper, redfish, lobster and stone crabs. The Atlantic Ocean sparkles with the glory of the living coral reef beneath. So

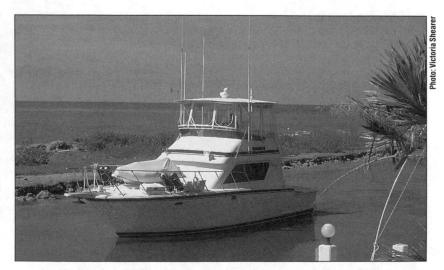

Canals, such as this one in Duck key, allow deep-water access and anchorage for motor yachts and sailboats alike.

pack up and push off for an Insiders' bareboat cruise of the Florida Keys from tip to toe.

Elliott Key

On the eastern side of Biscayne Bay, the island of Elliott Key, which has the ranger station for Biscayne National Park, guards a complex ecosystem from the ocean's battering winds. Anchor on the leeward side of Elliott Key just off the pretty little beach north of Coon Point. The key's proximity to Miami invites a lively weekend crowd of water skiers, but during the week the area is almost desolate. This anchorage, good in northeast to east to southeast winds, is usually accessed by the Intracoastal Waterway. A Columbus Day regatta attracts more than 500 sailboats and powerboats, which pepper the waters around Elliott Key like apples bobbing in a rain barrel.

A strong current rushes through the shallow channel between Sands Key and Elliott Key, and small-boat traffic is heavy on weekends. Although the fishing and diving here are first rate, take care. At the southern tip of Elliott Key, Caesar Creek — named for notorious pirate Black Caesar, who dipped in to stay out of sight in the 1600s — offers dicey passage to Hawk Channel for boats carefully clearing a 4-foot draft at high tide. The more forgiving Angelfish Creek, farther south at the north end of Key Largo, is the favored route from Biscayne Bay to the ocean in this wild and deserted area. Angelfish Creek is the Intracoastal Waterway's last outlet to the ocean until after Snake Creek Drawbridge for large boats or those heading for Hawk Channel.

Pumpkin Key

Safe anchorage surrounds Pumpkin Key, making this island an ideal choice for winds coming from any direction. Be sure to test your anchorage because Pumpkin Key's waters cover a grassy sea bottom. Nearby Angelfish Creek — filled with grouper, snapper and angelfish — almost guarantees dinner. Scoot out the creek to take advantage of the diving at John Pennekamp Coral Reef State Park. Approachable from Hawk Channel or the Intracoastal, this area remains virginal even though it rests in the shadow of Key Largo.

Blackwater Sound

As you anchor in the placid ebony waters of Blackwater Sound, the twinkling lights of Key Largo remind you that civilization is but a dinghy ride away. Have dinner at the Italian Fisherman or sample the local color at the Caribbean Club, Humphrey Bogart's famous bar from moviedom (see our Restaurants and Nightlife chapters). Anchor along the southeast shoreline of Blackwater Sound for a protected anchorage in east to southeast winds. The Cross Key Canal, which connects Blackwater Sound to Largo Sound, passes under a fixed bridge at the Overseas Highway in Key Largo. If your boat clears 14 feet safely, traverse the canal to dive or snorkel in John Pennekamp Coral Reef State Park. Or take your dinghy to the park headquarters on Key Largo Sound, where an interesting museum previews the reef.

Tarpon Basin

Enter Tarpon Basin through Dusenbury Creek or Grouper Creek. Both passages teem with snapper and grouper. Dinghy from this protected anchorage to The Quay restaurant (see our Restaurants chapter), where the famed Bolivar provides rhythmic reggae for the daily sunset celebration ritual.

Largo Sound (John Pennekamp Coral Reef State Park)

John Pennekamp Coral Reef State Park and the adjacent Key Largo National Marine Sanctuary encompass the ocean floor under Hawk Channel from Broad Creek to Molasses Reef. Exit the Intracoastal Waterway at Angelfish Creek and enter Hawk Channel to proceed to Largo Sound. Enter Largo Sound through South Sound Creek. This anchorage, completely sheltered in any weather, is supervised by park staff. Call on VHF 16 to reserve a mandatory mooring buoy in the southwest portion of the sound; anchoring is prohibited. A nominal fee for the moorings entitles boaters full use of park facilities and its pump-out station.

The reefs of John Pennekamp State Park shine brighter than others in the Keys. The bulk of Key Largo's land mass has inhibited development of the erosive channels that cut between the other Keys, preserving shallower waters. More sun filters through the shallow water, causing the coral to flourish. Much of this reef breaks the surface of the water during low tide.

Butternut Key and Bottle Key

Don't worry. Those baby sharks you see in the waters surrounding Butternut Key won't hurt you. The skittish infants leave this nursery area when they reach 2 to 3 feet in length. Prevailing winds will determine anchorage sites near these islands, which offer good holding ground. On the Florida Bay side of Tavernier, Butternut Key and Bottle Key showcase voluminous bird life. Roseate spoonbills breed on Bottle Key, feeding upon the tiny killifishes of the flats. A pond on the island attracts mallard ducks in the winter. And amid this gunk-holers' paradise, the elusive bald eagle rewards the patient observer with a fleeting appearance.

Cotton Key

Approach Cotton Key from the Intracoastal Waterway. This anchorage, protected from north to southeast winds, offers the best nightlife in the Keys north of Key West. Dinghy around the entire island of Upper Matecumbe and the community of Islamorada. Catch the action at Cheeca Lodge, Papa Joe's and the Lorelei (see our Restaurants chapter). Check out the fishing charters at Bud 'n Mary's Marina (see our Fishing chapter). Stop in at the Islamorada Fish Company and take ready-to-eat stone crabs back to your boat for a private sunset celebration (see our Seafood Markets and Specialty Foods chapter). Dinghy through Whale Harbor Channel to the Islamorada Sand Bar, which at low tide becomes an island beach. And, if you'd just like to commune with nature, the forested northeast section of Upper Matecumbe Key hosts a rookery for good bird-watching. Note: There is a no-motor zone on the tidal flat.

Lignumvitae Key

Government-owned Lignumvitae Key stands among the tallest of the Keys, at 17 to 18 feet. A virgin hammock sprinkled with lignum vitae trees re-creates the feeling of the Keys of yesteryear, before mahogany forests were cut and sold to Bahamian shipbuilders. From 1919 to 1953, the Matheson family of chemical company notoriety owned the island, where they built a large home and extensive gardens of rare plantings.

Hug the northwest side of the island for good anchorage in east to southeast winds. Dinghy to Lignumvitae Key for guided tours conducted by the Park Service. You can also dinghy through Indian Key Channel to historic Indian Key (see our Attractions chapter). Nearby Shell Key almost disappears at high tide, so exercise caution. Pods of dolphins romp in Lignumvitae Basin, and sighting lumbering sea turtles is not unusual. But be sure to bait a hook — fishing is prolific.

INSIDERS' TIP

The Florida Marine Patrol enforces state marine resources laws. They deal with violations such as environmental crime, exceeding fish and crawfish bag limits and illegal dumping. The FMP also enforces boating safety laws, responding to reports of unsafe boating and wake violations as well as any perceived illegal activity on the water. You can reach the Florida Marine Patrol on a cellular telephone by dialing *FMP or on a regular telephone line at (800) DIAL FMP, (800) 342-5367. The Marine Patrol vessels occasionally monitor VHF 16, but your best bet is to contact it at one of the other numbers.

Matecumbe Bight

If winds are not good for anchoring near Lignumvitae, Matecumbe Bight provides good holding ground, except in a north wind. Two miles south, Channel Five — east of Long Key — offers a good crossover between Florida Bay and Hawk Channel for large sailboats. Strong currents run in the channel beneath the bridge, which is a fixed span with a 65-foot overhead clearance.

Long Key Bight

Anchor in Long Key Bight, which is accessed via Hawk Channel oceanside or through Channel Five from the Intracoastal Waterway. Bordering Long Key State Park — a 300-acre wilderness area with a good campground, tables and grills — the Bight is protected, yet open. Dinghy through Zane Grey Creek for good gunk-holing. Legendary author Zane Grey angled at Long Key Fishing Club during the days of Flagler's Railroad. Beach-comb for washed-up treasure on the southeast shores of Long Key.

Boot Key Harbor

Boot Key Harbor in Marathon serves as a good, safe port in a bad blow, but, crowded with liveaboards, it is a bit like anchoring out in Times Square. You can dinghy to Shucker's or Crocodile's for dinner (see our Restaurants chapter). Enter this fully protected harbor from Sister's Creek or at the western entrance near the beginning of the Seven Mile Bridge.

NOTE: Moser Channel goes under the hump of the Seven Mile Bridge, creating a 65-foot clearance. The draw-span of the old bridge has been removed, but the rest remains. A portion on the Marathon end now functions as the driveway to Pigeon Key (see our Attractions chapter). A stretch on the Bahia Honda end is maintained for bridge fishing, called the "longest fishing pier in the world." The Moser Channel and the Bahia Honda Channel (with 20-foot clearance) are the last crossover spots in the Keys. You must decide at Marathon if you will travel the Atlantic route or via the Gulf to Key West. If you need fuel, note that the marina at Sunshine Key is the last bayside marina until Key West.

Big Spanish Channel Area

Leave all traces of civilization behind and head out the Big Spanish Channel toward the out-islands. Proceed with care, for this remote sprinkling of tiny keys is part of the Great White Heron National Wildlife Refuge. Before venturing into this backcountry area, secure a Public Use Regulations Map from the Lower Keys Chamber of Commerce, (305) 872-2411. Obey no-entry, no-motor and idle-speed zones. Get your *Florida Bird Guide* out of the cabin and count the species. Then, treat yourself to a swim with the dolphins, who travel in pods throughout these Gulf waters.

Little Spanish Key

The western side of Little Spanish Key provides the best protection from northeast to southeast winds. Explore the surrounding clear waters by dinghy where the endangered green turtles, which weigh between 150 and 450 pounds, have been spotted feeding on seagrass. Catch your limit in snapper and share your bounty with the friendly pelicans.

Content Keys

This beautiful area affords no anchorage because it is designated an idle-speed zone. Row your dinghy or pole through the unspoiled waters for a private eco-tour.

Raccoon Key

If it looks like a monkey and sounds like a monkey, it is a monkey. Like its sister key, Lois, near Little Palm Island, this key is a nursery for Rhesus monkeys ultimately used for laboratory research. Be forewarned: Don't approach too closely. The monkeys are not friendly — and they will jump into your boat.

Sawyer Key

No longer accessible for public use, this beach-lined fantasy island is part of the no-entry zone. The habitat is preserved for nesting birds.

Newfound Harbor

Newfound Harbor, formed by the Newfound Harbor Keys and the southern extension of Big Pine Key, stars as the premier oceanside harbor between Marathon and Key West. Dinghy to exquisite Little Palm Island, the setting for the film *PT-109*, the story of John F. Kennedy's Pacific experience during World War II (see the Marinas listing in this chapter). Newfound Harbor lies within easy reach of Looe Key National Marine Sanctuary, a spur and groove coral reef ecosystem popular with divers and snorkelers.

Key West and Beyond

Welcome to the ultimate cruising destination: Key West. Full of history and histrionics, this vibrant, intoxicating port pumps the adrenaline, pushes the envelope and provides a rowdy good time for all. And when you signal a turn back into the slow lane again, dust off your charts and head out to the wild beyond of the Dry Tortugas, the end of the line.

Marinas

All of our suggested marinas take transient boaters, but the multiplicity of celebrated special events in Key West dictates that you prudently reserve a slip as far in advance as possible. You may assume unless otherwise stated that all our recommended marinas supply hookups for both 30-amp and 50-amp service as well as fresh water. Transient rates are quoted per foot, per night. Minimums are noted where applicable.

Key West offers extensive self-provisioning facilities ranging from supermarkets to gourmet take-out shops (see our Seafood Markets and Specialty Foods chapter). The city also supports a variety of good marine mechanics, which the marina dockmasters will contact on your behalf should the need arise.

Our directions for approaching the marinas will help you find your way, but be sure to hail the dockmaster on VHF 16 and read your charts closely. Rates are figured per-foot without tax; minimum charges are stated when applicable.

A&B Marina
700 Front St., Key West
• (305) 294-2535, (800) 223-8352

A&B Marina is situated in the heart of Old Town, and most of its 50 transient slips will accommodate vessels with up to 7-foot drafts. Cable television hookup is included in dockage fees. A&B does not maintain a fuel dock, but several are available in the harbor.

A&B Marina changed ownership in April 1997. The new owners launched a $3.5 million renovation of the marina, scheduled for completion by the end of 1998. The face-lift will include a convenience store, air-conditioned shower facilities, a laundry room, a 24-hour bar and grill and another full-service restaurant. In the meantime, if you are hungry, A&B Lobster House upstairs has been feeding hungry cruisers for nearly 50 years. Or sit and people-watch from the Dockside Bar, which is labeled by a cryptic sign as the "Dockmaster's Office." Transient rates are $1.75/foot.

Dockmaster's directions: From the Atlantic, come in the main ship channel, which is marked S.E. Channel on the charts, to markers No. 24 and No. 25. From the Gulf, take the N.W. Channel until it intersects with the main ship channel. Take a port turn to markers No. 24 and No. 25. From either direction, turn east between markers No. 24 and No. 25 and proceed about one-eighth mile to Marker Red No. 4. Take a starboard turn around Red No. 4, and you are 400 feet off the dock.

The Galleon Marina
619 Front St., Key West
• (305) 292-1292, (800) 662-7462

Cruisers love the Galleon, probably the most popular of Key West's marinas. The carbonated excitement of Duval Street pulsates only a few blocks away, but the ambiance at the Galleon remains unhurried and genteel. The 91 dockage slips — with good fenders for a scratch-free visit — will accommodate vessels up to 150 feet, 9-foot drafts. One 30-amp or one 50-amp service is included in the daily dockage rate, but you may secure another for an additional fee. Cable and telephone hook-ups result in an extra charge as well. Fuel is available at the Chevron in Key West Bight or the Texaco at Conch Harbor Marina.

The Galleon indulges you with all the amenities and then some: shower and restroom facilities, a laundry, pump-out station, deli, swimming pool, tiki bar, private beach, fitness center, sauna, patio and picnic tables. And if that is not enough, book an afternoon of snorkeling at the on-premises dive shop or plan a fishing expedition with one of the charter boats at the dock. Rent a moped or bicycle and explore Key West, or just kick back and relax on the sun deck.

Pets are welcome in the marina but not on the adjoining resort property. Transient rates are $2.35/foot. A special events rate of $2.75/foot is in effect during holidays, mini lobster season, Fantasy Fest and the like. During September and October, transient rates are reduced to $1.65/foot.

Dockmaster's directions: Follow the main ship channel, NOAA Chart No. 11445, to Marker No. 24, then call the dockmaster on VHF 16. He will guide you to Marker Red No. 4 at the east end of the breakwater and into the entrance to the marina.

Key West Hilton Resort and Marina
245 Front St., Key West • (305) 294-4000

Formerly Truman Annex Marina, this facility is now a part of the new Key West Hilton Resort and Marina offering transients all the perks of the property: pool, hot tub, weight room and Bistro 245 restaurant (see our Hotels and Motels chapter). The south basin of the marina offers 27 floating slips accommodating vessels with 30-foot drafts; the north basin's 600 feet of rigid dock space handles craft with 15-foot drafts or less.

Make reservations up to six months in advance to dock in at the Key West Hilton Resort and Marina. Only one block off famed Duval Street, its location can't be beat and it fills up quickly. Transient rates are $2/foot ($50 minimum). Power is not included in this rate. An additional power fee is levied: $7.50 per night for 30-amp service, $15 a night for 50-amp service. Cable television hookup is included in the dockage fee, and the requisite laundry, shower and restroom requirements are sup-

plied on the premises. Fuel may be obtained a half-mile up the channel at Key West Bight.

Want a wake-up call to go fishing? Need a bag of ice in a flash? Key West Hilton Resort and Marina aims to please with a philosophy of over-the-top personal service. The Key West Hilton Resort and Marina owns the private offshore Sunset Key. Guests of the hotel or marina may daytrip to the island and enjoy its pristine beach, away from the fray of Key West.

Dockmaster's directions: From the south, come up the main cruise-ship channel. At Marker Red No. 14 hail the dockmaster on VHF 16. You will be a half-mile from the marina, which is the first break in the sea wall. From the north, come down the N.W. Channel. At Marker Green No. 17, hail the dockmaster on VHF 16. The marina will be a half-mile dead ahead. On most charts the marina is listed as Pier B. The dockmaster urges you to hail the marina at the specified markers so he can be on hand to assist your dockage.

Key West Yacht Club
Garrison Bight, Key West
• (305) 296-3446

Although Key West Yacht Club is a private club, provisions in its charter with the city of Key West mandate that visiting yachts may make transient dockage. The club allots three of its 66 slips to visiting transients each day. You may make reservations up to 30 days in advance. The marina accommodates vessels with a maximum depth of 6 feet. Be advised: High-tension power lines overhead have a safety clearance of 50 feet. The ship's store offers limited provisions, and there are no on-site laundry facilities, but a supermarket and coin-operated laundry require only a short jaunt on foot. Restrooms and showers are provided. Fuel is available at the Texaco dock. Transient rates are $1.75/foot ($52.50 minimum).

Dockmaster's directions: Enter Garrison Bight. Steer a straight course to Marker Green No. 25, and leave Green No. 25 to port. After passing Green No. 25, turn to port 45 degrees and aim for the blue and white gas station across the street from the sea wall. When you are approximately 40 feet off the sea wall, take another port turn and just point your bow at the lighted Texaco sign, which is the fuel dock.

Oceanside Marina
MM 5, 5950 Peninsula Ave., Stock Island
• (305)294-4676

This top-drawer marina, occupying a finger of Stock Island, offers a Key West alternative for peace and solitude, for it is tucked far away from the fray. Its 106 slips will accommodate vessels up to 150 feet in length with 12-foot maximum drafts. Access to the marina is directly from Hawk Channel. Reservations are suggested 30 days in advance during the winter season. Gas- and diesel-qualified marine mechanics work on the premises. Oceanside provides all the essentials: gas and diesel fuel dock, ship's store and tackle shop, laundry, showers and restrooms and free cable hookups. An additional charge is levied for telephone hookup. Your pet is welcome if kept on a leash. If you don't feel like popping for the taxi ride into Key West for dinner, try the Sailfish Club, which overlooks the boat basin. Transient rates are $1.90/foot ($57 minimum).

Dockmaster's directions: Proceed to latitude 24°32.5 north; longitude 81°43.9 west for the outer marker, which is Marker Red No. 2 at the entrance to Stock Island Channel.

Anchoring Out

The highway may stop in Key West, but the path to adventure continues into the sunset. The Dry Tortugas, the brightest gems in the necklace, mark the real end of the line in the Florida Keys. Once you leave Key West Harbor, you join the ranks of the swashbucklers who have abandoned the safety of civilization to explore the vast unknown.

Be sure you know the range and capabilities of your craft because only self-sufficient cruising vessels can make the 140-nautical-mile trek to the Dry Tortugas and back. There is no fuel, fresh water, provisioning or facilities of any kind once you leave Key West. Unpredictable foul weather could keep you trapped at sea for days, so make sure you are fueled for 200 miles, and stock the larder for extenuating circumstances.

Key West

If you want to anchor out in busy Key West Harbor, look for a spot west of Fleming Key in about 10 to 15 feet of water. You'll find less

current, good holding ground and less fishing vessel traffic than around Wisteria Island. The municipal dinghy dock at the foot of Simonton Street is the only official place to land your dinghy, but you might want to arrange secured short-term dockage for your dinghy from one of the marina dockmasters.

Boca Grande Key

A string of shoals and keys snakes west from Key West, offering unparalleled diving and fishing opportunities. Beyond Man and Woman Keys — popular snorkeling spots — Boca Grande Key offers a good day anchorage on the northwestern side with a beautiful white sand beach. The current is too swift to anchor overnight, but snorkel the small wreck visible just north of the island. Be alert to the constantly shifting shoals around the entrance channel. Note also that this island is a turtle nesting ground — all or parts of it are off limits during specific times of the year, and fines are possible.

Marquesas Keys

About 24 miles from Key West, a broken collar of low-lying, beach-belted islands form the Marquesas Keys. If you pass Mooney Harbor Key on your way into the inner sanctum, watch for coral heads about 1,100 yards offshore. Prevailing winds will determine at which side to anchor, but you should be able to achieve a protected anchorage. Many a ship crashed on the coral heads in this area, leaving interesting wrecks, but check with the Coast Guard before you dive because the U.S. Navy occasionally uses the area west of the Marquesas as a bombing and strafing range. Military practice times are broadcast by the Coast Guard on VHF radio. Don't end up as target practice. Explore the big rookery of frigate birds or take aim with a little spearfishing. Note: A 300-foot no-motor zone is established around the three smallest islands, a 300-foot no-access buffer zone is established around one mangrove island, and an idle speed only/no-wake zone is established in the southwest tidal creek. This pitstop on the way to the Dry Tortugas rates as an end point in itself.

Dry Tortugas

Open water stretches like a hallucination from the Marquesas to our southernmost national park, the Dry Tortugas. Ponce de Leon named these islands the Tortugas — Spanish for turtles — in 1513, presumably because the waters teemed with sea turtles, which he consumed as fresh meat. Lack of fresh water rendered the islands dry.

The first sight of the massive brick fortress of Fort Jefferson, the colorful history of which began in 1846, is breathtaking. The best deep anchorage is usually directly in front of the entrance to the fort on the southeast side of Garden Key, but, depending upon the weather, you may want to check with the ranger first.

Unparalleled diving exists in these unsullied waters. Colors appear more brilliant because the waters are clearer than those bordering the inhabited Keys. The entire area is a no-take zone, so don't be alarmed if you spot a prehistoric-size lobster or jewfish. Be sure to snorkel the well-marked underwater nature trail. From your dinghy, watch for the nesting sooty and noddy terns in their Bush Key sanctuary (landing is forbidden).

Loggerhead Key

Just beyond Garden Key dozes Loggerhead Key, called the prettiest beach in the Keys by those in the know. A good day anchorage with a legion of interesting coral, this is literally the end of the line for the Florida Keys. Nothing but 900 miles of water lies between this point and the Mexican coast. Hope you remembered to fuel up in Key West!

Long after the last bait is cast, tales of captured prizes or the ones that got away evoke visions of the sun, the sea and the smell of the salt air.

Fishing

Angling in the Florida Keys approaches a religion to many. The very essence of the Keys is embodied in gleaming packages of skin and scales, for a day fishing the cerulean waters that lap our islands creates a sensory memory not quickly forgotten. Long after the last bait is cast, tales of captured prizes or the ones that got away evoke visions of the sun, the sea and the smell of the salt air.

Anglers fish here with an intensity rarely seen anywhere else in the United States . . . the world even. Eavesdrop on a conversation anywhere in the Keys and someone will be talking about fishing. As you drive down the Overseas Highway and look out at our acres of shimmering waters, you will feel an overwhelming urge to join in the battle of power and wits, fish against angler, that makes the Keys so special.

The Florida Keys have more than 1,000 species of fish; most are edible, all are interesting. Six of them — bonefish, permit, tarpon, redfish, snook and sailfish — have earned game-fish status, meaning they may not be sold, a reputation justly deserved. To pursue these and other species, you will need a saltwater fishing license (see the Fishing Licenses section in this chapter). You must obey catch and season restrictions and size limits. These regulations change often. Ask for an up-to-date listing when you purchase your fishing license.

The Florida Keys fall within the boundaries of the Florida Keys National Marine Sanctuary, created by the federal government in 1990 to protect the resources of our marine ecosystem. And while, for the most part, visitors freely can swim, dive, snorkel, boat, fish or recreate on our waters, there are some regulations that took effect in July 1997 to guide these activities. Refer to our Boating chapter for information on these regulations before you venture into our waters. For a complete copy of the regulations and marine coordinates of the areas, contact the Sanctuary office, (305) 743-2437.

Catch-and-Release Ethics

Preserve our natural resources. "A fish is too valuable to be caught only once," maintains the U.S. Department of Commerce, the National Oceanic and Atmospheric Administration and the National Marine Fisheries Service. We agree. The spirit behind the catch-and-release policy is to enjoy the hunt and the score, but take a photograph of the fish home with you, not the quarry itself. Taxidermists do not need the actual fish to prepare a mount for you; they only need the approximate measurements. Take home only those food fish you need for table use.

To properly release a fish, keep the fish in the water and handle it very little whenever possible. Dislodge the hook quickly with a hookout tool, backing the hook out the opposite way it went in. If the hook can't be removed quickly, cut the leader close to the mouth. Hold the fish by the bottom jaw or lip — not the gills — with a wet hand or glove so that you don't damage its mucous or scales. Have your photo taken with the fish. Cradle the tired fish, rocking it back and forth in the water until it is able to swim away under its own power. This increases the oxygen flow through its gills, reviving the fish and thereby augmenting its chances for survival against a barracuda or shark.

Where to Fish

To introduce you to our complex watery ecosystem and the species of fish dwelling therein, we have divided fishing destinations into four distinct sections: the flats, the backcountry, the bluewater and the bridges.

The Flats

The continental shelf is nature's gift to the Florida Keys. Stretching from the shoreline like a layer of rippled fudge on a marble slab, it lingers for many shallow miles before plunging to the depths of the bluewater. In the Keys we rather reverently call this area the flats. Waters ranging from mere inches to several feet in depth cover most of the flats, but some areas completely surface during low tide, exposing themselves to the air and intense sunlight. Changing winds, tides, temperatures and barometric pressure ensure that conditions in the flats fluctuate constantly.

www.insiders.com

See this and many other **Insiders' Guide®** destinations online — in their entirety.

Visit us today!

An unenlightened observer might think the flats uninteresting, for most of this watery acreage is covered with dense turtle grass, shell-less sand or muddy muck. But, far from being a wasteland, the flats are the feeding grounds and nursery for a city of marine families whose members inspire dramatic tales of daring and conquest from every person who has ever baited a hook here.

The 4,000 square miles of flats — from Key Biscayne to Key West and beyond — yield a trio of prize game fish, which, when caught in one day, we refer to as the Grand Slam: bonefish, permit and tarpon. And keeping company in the same habitat are the bonus fish — barracuda and shark — that regularly accommodate anglers with exciting runs and fights. Fishing the flats is really a combination of angling and hunting, for you must first see and stalk the fish before you ever cast the waters. The hunt for bonefish, permit and tarpon requires patience and unique angling skills, but most essentially, you must be at the right place at the right time.

We cannot even begin to teach you how to fish for these formidable fighters of the flats in this chapter. You should hire a professional guide, for which there is no substitute — at least while you are a novice. Guides know the local waters well and keep detailed records of where to find fish under every condition, saving you precious hours and money in the pursuit of your mission (see the Guides and Charters section of this chapter). But we will introduce you to the exciting species you will encounter on our flats, relate their personalities, tattle about their habits and point you in the right direction so you can learn all you wish to know to share in the angling experience of a lifetime: fishing the flats in the Florida Keys.

First in the see-stalk-cast sequence so important in fishing the skinny waters of the flats is the visible interpretation of the watery hallucination under the surface. To see the fish of the flats, you must have polarized sunglasses to cut the sun's glare so you can concentrate on looking through your reflection on the top of the water to the shallow bottom. Under the water, fish often look like bluish shadows, or they may appear as indistinct shadings that simply look different than the waters surrounding them.

Most waters of the flats in the Keys are fished from a shallow-draft skiff, or flats boat, although you can wade out from shore in many areas if you prefer. Never motor onto a flat; the fish can hear the engine noise and spook easily. Use an electric trolling motor or, better yet, pole in using a push pole. A push pole is a fiberglass or graphite dowel, 16- to 20-feet long with a V-crotch on one end for traversing the soft bottom of the flats and a straight end on the other for staking out. Using it requires body power and coordination and more than a little practice. A flats boat has a raised poling platform that enables the poler or guide a height advantage to more readily distinguish the fish from its shadowy surroundings in preparation for an accurate cast.

At the turn of the tide, the fish begin to

INSIDERS' TIP

Tune in to local radio stations for fishing forecasts and catches of the day. For more details on these programs, and on Florida Keys fishing publications, refer to our Media chapter.

move into the flats, grazing like sheep in a pasture. Guides know where the fish congregate during an incoming (flood) tide and an outgoing (ebb) tide. While it may prove dangerous for the fish to come up on the flats — they expose themselves to predators — the concentration of food is too enticing for them to resist. The fish prefer feeding during the low, incoming tide; the food is still easy to find, but they won't risk becoming stranded on the flats.

Bonefish: Phantom of the Flats

A sighting of the glistening forked tail of the Gray Ghost — alias of the famed bonefish (*Albula vulpes*) haunting our flats — has been

known to elevate the blood pressure of even the most seasoned Keys angler to celestial heights. This much-respected, skittish silver bullet is considered the worthiest of all opponents, a wily, suspicious street fighter, here one moment, gone the next. The bonefish's superior eyesight, acute hearing, keen sense of smell and boundless speed routinely befuddle anglers, some of whom dedicate their lives to thwarting the fish's Houdini-like escape attempts.

There are three ways to spot a bonefish: tailing, mudding or cruising. When the slender, silvery bonefish feeds, it looks like a washer woman leaning over to get her laundry out of the basket — head down, bottom up. The fork of the tail will break the surface of the water — a tailing fish. The bonefish feeds into the current because its food source is delivered in the drift. As the fish puts its mouth down into the sand and silt, routing around on the bottom of the flats looking for shrimps, crabs and other crustaceans, the water clouds up. This is called "making a mud." As the mudding bonefish continues feeding, the current takes the cloudy water away so he can see his prey once again. Bonefish require water temperatures of 70 degrees and higher for feeding on the flats.

Spotting a cruising fish takes some practice. Look for "nervous water." The bonefish pushes a head wake as it swims, which sometimes shows as an inconsistency on the surface of the water. On other occasions, a mere movement by the fish underwater will cause the surface water to appear altered. Most of the time that the bonefish is cruising, however, it is swimming in deeper water; you will have to spot it. The back and sides of the bonefish are so silvery they act as a mirror. The fish swims right on the bottom of the flats in 8 or more inches of water. The sun shining through the water causes the bottom to reflect off the sides of the fish. So if you think you have seen a ripple of weeds, the image may actually be a bonefish.

The best bait for bonefishing is live shrimp. A guide with an experienced eye will put you "on the fish" by calling out directions like the hands of a clock. The bow of the boat will always be 12 o'clock. You will be instructed by the guide to look in a direction — for instance, 2 o'clock — and at a specified distance to spot the bonefish in preparation for a cast. The cast is the most crucial part of successfully hooking a bonefish. You should be able to cast 30 feet quickly and accurately. A cast that places the bait too close to the fish will spook it and cause the bonefish to dart away at breakneck speed. If the bait is cast too far away, the fish won't find it at all. The bait should land 2 to 3 feet in front of the fish and be allowed to drift to the ocean floor.

Many times the bonefish will smell the bait prior to seeing it because the fish is down-current of the bait and swimming into the current. The bonefish begins to dart back and forth and goes in circles looking for the scented prey. Once the fish locates the source of the scent, it tends to suck in the bait. You, the angler, must make sure there is no slack in the line and that your rod tip is low to the water. Then firmly but gently lift up to set the hook. Hold on tight and raise your rod straight up in the air, holding your arms as high above your head as possible. Once the fish realizes something is wrong — that it's hooked — it will peel way away in an electrifying run, taking out 100 to 150 yards of line in a heartbeat. This whole process — from sighting to hooking — explodes in adrenaline-pumping nanoseconds. Ten to 30 minutes later, after the bonefish makes several pulse-pounding sprints, you can reel in the tired fish to the side of the skiff, where the guide will photograph both victor and spoils. Then quickly release the bonefish so that it may rest up and thrill another angler on yet another day (see the previous section in this chapter on Catch-and-Release Ethics).

Bonefishing is a major playing card of the fishing deck we so lavishly deal here in the Florida Keys. Bonefish usually range in size from 5 to 10 pounds, but the size of this fish deceptively belies its strength. A 5-pound bonefish fights like a 20-pound wannabe. The Keys are the only place in the continental United States where an angler can fish for bonefish. Locals boast that we have the biggest and best-educated bonefish this side of the Gulf Stream. Expect bonefish to grace our flats during April, May, June, September, October and occasionally into November. Cool weather and cold fronts push them into deeper waters from December through March. The hot weather of July and August drives them to cooler, deeper waters as well, although some will stay all year.

Permit: Ultimate Flats Challenge

Though sharing the same waters as the bonefish and stalked in the same manner, the

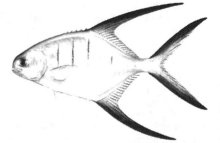

permit (*Trachinotus falcatus*) proves to be a more elusive catch. Spooky, skittish and stubborn, this finicky eater, which can take out line like a long-distance runner, is so difficult to catch that most anglers never

even see one. Three or four times the size of a bonefish — averaging 20 to 30 pounds — the silvery, platter-shaped permit forages in the safety of slightly deeper waters, not risking exposure of its iridescent blue-green back. Its sickle-shaped, black-tipped tail pokes out of the water as it feeds on bottom-dwelling crabs and shrimps, often tipping off its location. The permit's shell-crushing jaws, rubbery and strong, can exert 3,000 pounds of pressure per square inch, enabling it to masticate small clams and crustaceans and dash many an angler's expectations.

The permit will tail or mud like a bonefish. In fact, both fish have been known to have rubbed their snouts so raw from repeatedly routing around in the mud looking for food that they caricature W.C. Fields. But, unlike a bonefish, the permit is often spotted lazily cruising near the surface of the water. Many times its wispy black dorsal fin will break the water, looking like a drifting piece of weed.

The best days to find permit are those glorious, cloudless sunny smiles from Mother Nature, cooled with a slight ocean breeze. Schools of permit will graze the top of the flats and near rocky shorelines in higher tides and poke around in basins and channels during low tides, searching for a meal of small crabs and crustaceans. They often hover above submerged objects such as lobster pots. If you pass over an area littered with sea urchins, be on the lookout for permit searching for gourmet fixings.

Not easily duped, a tailing permit will make you forget all about a bonefish because, if you manage to hook one, you've got a street brawl on your hands that could last an hour or more. When hooked, the permit instinctively heads for deeper water. In the transition zone between the flats and the bluewater, the permit will try to cut the line by weaving through coral heads, sea fans and sponges. The fish will pause in its run to bang its head on the bottom or rub its mouth in the sand to try to dislodge the hook. If you manage to follow the permit through this obstacle course, you may actually catch it a quarter-mile from where you hooked it.

Local Secrets for Tight Lines

• Break off the fanned out portion of a shrimp's tail before baiting your hook. This immediately releases a scent into the water.

• Wet your hands before you handle any fish you catch. When you touch a fish you inadvertently knock off scales and remove the slime layer that protects its skin from microorganisms in the water.

• Bow to the silver king. Whenever a tarpon jumps, lower the rod tip, releasing the pressure from the line when the fish is out of the water. Many hooks have been pulled and lines broken when the angler forgets to release the pressure.

• As soon as a bonefish takes out line, tearing off the flat, put your rod and your arms as high in the air as possible to keep the line out of the water. This keeps the line from breaking on small mangrove shoots or coral ledges of the deeper water.

• When fishing for bonefish, don't use oils, lotions or repellents on your fingers. A keen sense of smell allows the bonefish to discern this odor on your bait. Instead, apply the liquid to the back of one hand and rub it on the back of the other.

• To catch a barracuda: When the barracuda strikes, point the rod tip toward the fish and put a little slack in the line. Let the fish pull against the line, then set the hook with a gentle snap.

• An injured or dying fish will have red, bloodshot eyes. Many game fish will prey on the weak or injured in their midst, so use an artificial lure with red eyes.

• When handling a tarpon, wear wetted gloves. The gloves protect your hands from the tarpon's sharp gill plates and keep the line from cutting your fingers if the powerful fish leaps to escape your grasp. Wet the gloves so as not to injure the fish's scales.

• Don't try to stop a bonefish when it's running. Attempting to reel while the fish is taking out line will only put a severe twist in your line, weakening the strength of the line. When the fish slows down and stops taking out line, begin your retrieve using a pump-and-reel action.

• Look for large stingrays. Red-fish, bonefish and permit will follow

A catch of the silver king, the mighty tarpon, is every angler's dream.

Photo: Bill Beardsley

the stingray as it stirs up the mud on the bottom, hoping for an uncovered morsel or two.

• Noise originating from above the water frightens bonefish. Remember: no loud talking, don't slam the cooler lid, and don't stumble over the anchor.

• Use a quick-release anchor when fishing for tarpon in the current beneath our bridges. Attach your anchor line to a float buoy. Then attach your boat to the float buoy with a snap hook. When you hook a tarpon, start your motor, unsnap the anchor line from the boat and go with the fish. After you have caught and released the fish, return and pick up the float and re-hook your boat to the anchor line. This allows you fast access to the chase and the ability to return to the exact same hotspot.

Tarpon: the Silver King

It is little wonder that the tarpon (*Megalops atlanticus*) is dubbed the silver king, for it wins nine out of every 10 encounters with an angler. The tarpon's lung-like gas bladder allows it to take a gulp of atmospheric air from time to time, enabling the fish to thrive in oxygen-depleted water. This magnificent super hero of the sea, ranging in size from 50 to 200 pounds, will break the surface and "roll" with a silvery splash as it steals an oxygen jolt and

powers on for an intensified fight. The tarpon frequents the deeper flats of 4 to 8 feet or hangs out in the rapidly moving waters of channels or under one of the many bridges in the Keys. Live mullet, pinfish and crabs will entice this hungry but lazy despot, who faces into the current effortlessly waiting for baitfish to be dragged into its mouth. The tarpon's toothless lower jaw protrudes from its head like an overdeveloped underbite, filled with bony plate that crushes its intended dinner.

The successful angler will use heavy tackle and a needle-sharp hook. Hold the rod with the tip at 12 o'clock and wait. When the fish strikes and eats the bait, let the rod tip drop with the pressure, giving minimal resistance. When the rod is parallel to the water and the line is tight, set the hook through the bony structure with a series of short, very strong jabs. Once hooked, the stunned fish runs and leaps repeatedly with reckless abandon, entering the water head first, tail first, sideways, belly-flopped or upside down, an Olympiad confounding its rod-clutching judge. It is important to have a quick release anchor when fishing for tarpon because once the action starts you must be on your way, chasing the

cavorting fish. (See the Close-up: Local Secrets to Tight Lines in this chapter). Be prepared to duke it out, for it is often a standoff as to who tires first, the angler or the tarpon.

Exciting to catch on light tackle is the schooling baby tarpon, which at up to 50 pounds sprints and practices its aerobatic contortions as do its older siblings. Look for baby tarpon in channels and in harbors.

Tarpon season generally begins in April and continues until mid-July. Because the tarpon is primarily a nocturnal feeder, the best fishing is at daybreak and dusk or during the night.

This magnificent creature grows very slowly, not reaching maturity until it is at least 13 years old. Since the tarpon is not an edible fish, some people consider killing it akin to murder.

If you want a simulated "mount" of your catch, take an estimate of the length and girth for the taxidermist, take a photograph with your prize and release the fish quickly and carefully. If you insist on keeping and killing a tarpon, a $50 tarpon tag is required.

Barracuda: the Tiger of the Flats

Look for barracuda (*Sphyraena barracuda*) — which pack a wallop of fight — anywhere the water is about 2 feet deep, especially grassy bottom areas. This toothy, intelligent predator has keen eyesight and moves swiftly. The barracuda's inquisitive nature causes it to make investigatory passes by your boat, where it is oft tempted to sample your baited offerings intended for other species. Pilchards make good bait for catching barracuda. Cut off part of the tail fin of a pilchard before baiting the hook. This injury causes the bait to swim erratically, attracting the insatiable barracuda. When casting to a barracuda, your bait should land at least 10 feet beyond the fish and be retrieved across its line of sight. A cast that lands the bait too close — 5 feet or less — will frighten the 'cuda into deep water. If you are using artificial baits such as a tube lure, be sure to retrieve the bait briskly to pique the barracuda's interest.

The barracuda is eaten by humans in some tropical areas but not in the Keys. The flesh is sometimes toxic, and it is not worth the risk. You are better off quickly releasing the fish so that it might fight another round.

Sharks

Several shark species (order *selachii*) roam our flats looking for a free meal. Sand sharks and nurse sharks are relatively docile, but bonnetheads and blacktip sharks readily will take a shrimp or crab intended for a bonefish or permit, putting up a determined fight. If you happen to catch a shark, wear heavy gloves and cut the leader with pliers. The shark will swim away and will be able to work the hook loose from its mouth. Digestive acids and salt water will corrode the hook in mere days, causing the fish no permanent harm.

The Backcountry

When Mother Nature bestowed the prolific oceanside saltwater flats on the Florida Keys, she didn't stop at our rocky isles. As the Gulf of Mexico meets mainland Florida, a lively ecosystem flourishes in a body of water known as Florida Bay. Hundreds of tiny uninhabited keys dot the watery landscape, referred to locally as the backcountry. Loosely bordered by the Keys — from Largo to Long — and Everglades National Park, backcountry waters offer a diverse habitat of sea grass or mud flats, mangrove islets and sandy basins. The southernmost outpost of the Everglades National Park is at Flamingo, which maintains a marina, boat rentals, houseboats and guide services.

You'll usually be able to find snappers, sheepshead, ladyfish and the occasional shark along the grass-bed shorelines, the open bays and in the small creeks flowing out of the Everglades. And the silver king, the mighty tarpon, frequents backcountry creeks and channels, flats and basins and is rumored to be particularly partial to the Sandy Key Basin in the summer months. But beckoning anglers to these skinny waters is another sporting trio, which when caught in one day are boasted far and wide as the Backcountry Grand Slam: redfish, snook and spotted seatrout.

Redfish, a.k.a. Red Drum

The coppery redfish, or red drum (*Sciaenops oceallatus*), all but disappeared in the 1980s from overfishing, but conservation measures by the State of Florida and the federal government caused a rebirth. This fast-growing fish migrates offshore to spawn when

it reaches about 30 inches (4 years); it is a protected species in federal waters. Regulations open a scant 9-inch window for anglers to keep one captured redfish per day, which must measure between 18 and 27 inches. All redfish measuring less than 18 inches or more than 27 inches must always be released. Because it grows so rapidly, the redfish is exposed to harvest for only one year of its life.

As with fishing for bonefish or permit, you will look for redfish on an incoming tide, when they will be routing for crabs on the shoals and flats. As the water gets higher, the fish work their way up on the flats. You will want to use a shallow-draft boat with a push pole or electric trolling motor and be prepared with polarized sunglasses for enhanced vision in spotting a tailing fish. You'll hear experienced anglers say, "A tailing red is a feeding red." The reddish, squared-off profile of the redfish's tail can be spotted from several hundred feet. When the fish is really hungry, you may see its entire tail exposed, even the shady eyelike spot at the base. Cruising redfish will push a head wake similar to that of a bonefish.

Although a redfish isn't nearly as easily spooked as a bonefish, you should still stay as far away from the fish as possible while still casting a right-on winner. Live shrimps or crabs will entice the fish, which, with poor eyesight, hits most any bait coming its way. The hooked redfish often sticks around and puts up a hard fight. Attracted to its discomfort, other redfish swim to the scene of the accident. You can often catch another redfish if you can get an-

Photo: Cheeca Lodge

Drop a line just about anywhere in the Florida Keys and try your luck.

other baited hook into the water fast enough. The redfish is highly coveted for eating, put on the culinary map by New Orleans' Chef Prudhomme and his famed Cajun blackening process.

The backcountry of the Florida Keys is one of the only places in the world where you can fish for redfish year round, although they prefer cooler waters. It is illegal, however, to buy or sell our native redfish, and they must be kept whole until you reach shore. You are forbidden to gig, spear or snatch the red drum.

Snook

The second member of the Backcountry Grand Slam, the snook (*Centropomus undecimalis*) likes to tuck against the shady mangrove shorelines to feed on baitfish that congregate in the maze of gnarled roots. A falling tide will force the baitfish out of their rooted cages and into deeper holes where the snook can get at them. But the baitfish aren't the only ones getting snookered. This cagey,

sought-after game fish, once hooked, has buffaloed many an angler, vanishing back into the mangroves and snapping its tenuous connection to the rod-wielder like a brittle string.

INSIDERS' TIP

If you're a lobster enthusiast, turn to our Diving and Snorkeling chapter for tips on taking in these tasty crustaceans.

If you win the battle of the bushes or find the snook pushing water in the open or at the mouth of a creek, you still haven't won the war. Once hooked, the snook thrashes about violently, trying to dislodge the barbed intruder. Its hard, abrasive mouth and knife-sharp gill covers can dispense with your line in a flash.

This silvery, long-bodied fish — thickened around the middle like a middle-aged spinster — faces its foes with a depressed snout and a protruding lower jaw. A distinctive lateral black racing stripe extends the length of its body, all the way to its divided dorsal fin. The snook is unable to tolerate waters lower than 60 degrees. And while some anglers feel snook is the best tasting fish in the Keys, Florida law mandates you may not fish for snook from December 15 through January 31, nor in the months of June, July and August. Snook may not be bought or sold, and you must purchase a $2 snook stamp for your saltwater fishing license in order to fish for them.

Spotted Seatrout, a.k.a. Spotted Weakfish

Even though this backcountry prize is called a weakfish, it can be a challenging catch. The weakfish moniker derives from its clan's easily torn mouth membranes. The spotted seatrout (*Cynoscion nebulosus*), actually a member of the fine-flavored drum family, nevertheless resembles a trout, with shimmering iridescent tones of silver, green, blue and bronze.

The seatrout's lower jaw, unlike a true trout's, projects upward, and a pair of good-size canine teeth protrudes from the upper jaw. These predatory, opportunistic feeders enjoy a smorgasbord of offerings but are particularly fond of live shrimp. The seatrout makes a distinctive splash and popping sound as it feeds on a drift of shrimp. These weakfish are easily spotted in the shallow backcountry waters, popular with light tackle enthusiasts who enjoy the stalk-and-cast challenge.

Seatrout prefer temperatures between 60 and 70 degrees. They are highly ranked as a table food because they are so delicately flavored, but the flesh spoils rapidly. Ice it quickly and fillet the fish immediately upon returning to shore.

The Bluewater

The Gulf Stream, or Florida Current, moves through the Florida Straits south of Key West and flows northward, along the entire coast of Florida at about 4 knots. This tropical river, 25 to 40 miles wide, maintains warm-water temperatures, hosting a piscatorial bounty from the prolific Caribbean that constantly restocks the waters of the Keys. The bluewater encompasses deep water from the reef to the edge of the Gulf Stream and is particularly prolific at the humps, which are underwater hills rising from the sea floor. The Islamorada Hump is 13 miles offshore from Islamorada. The West Hump lies 23 miles offshore from Marathon and rises from a depth of 1,100 feet to 480 feet below the surface.

Bluewater fishing is synonymous with offshore fishing here in the Keys. To an angler, it means big game: tuna, billfish, dolphin, cobia, wahoo and kingfish. Also offshore, at the edge of the coral reef and the nearshore patch reefs, you will find a palette of bottom fish, snappers and groupers coveted more for their table value than their fighting prowess, and a grab bag of bonus fish — some good to eat, all fun to catch.

Until you are experienced in our waters, you will need a guide. To troll for big game fish in the bluewater, you should book a private charter, which will put you on the fish and supply everything you need including the professional expertise of the captain and mate, who know when to hold 'em . . . and when to fold 'em. These charters usually accommodate six anglers and though pricey — $500 to $700 per day plus tips — provide the most instruction and individual attention. You can divide the cost with five other anglers, or join with another party and split the tab (see the Guides and Charters section of this chapter).

Alternately, sign on to a party boat, or head

boat, which usually accommodates 50 or more anglers. These boats usually take anglers to the reef for bottom fishing, where you can drop a line and try your luck for snapper, grouper and even kingfish and some of their sidekicks. Mates on deck untangle lines, answer questions and even bait your hook. And although it is a little bit like taking the bus during rush hour instead of a limousine, at $30 to $40 per day — rods, tackle and bait included — a party boat remains the most economical means of fishing offshore.

Billfish: Blue Marlin, White Marlin, Sailfish

Before you head out to the bluewater to hunt for sailfish and marlins, you might want to have a cardiac workup and check your blood pressure because, if your trolled bait takes a hit, it will prove a battle of endurance.

The cobalt-blue marlin (*Makaira nigricans*), largest of the Atlantic marlins, migrates away from the equator in warmer months, enigmatically gracing the Keys waters on its way northward. Females of the species often reach trophy proportions — 1,000 pounds or more — but males rarely exceed 300 pounds. Tuna and bonito provide the mainstay of the blue marlin's diet, but some blue marlins have been found with young swordfish in their stomachs. Anglers trolling ballyhoo or mullet have the chance of latching onto a blue marlin, especially in tuna-infested waters. A fighting blue marlin creates a specter of primitive beauty: A creature the size of a baby elephant plunges to the depths then soars in gravity-defying splendor only to hammer the water once again and shoot off in a torpedolike run.

Less often caught in our waters is the white marlin (*Tetrapturus albidus*), which is much smaller than the blue, averaging 50 to 60 pounds and rarely exceeding 150 pounds. Both marlins use their swordlike bills to stun fast-moving fish, which they then consume. Unlike other members of its family, the dorsal and anal fins of the white marlin are rounded, not sharply pointed. The upper portion of its body is a brilliant green-blue, abruptly changing to silvery white on the sides and underslung with a white belly. White marlin will strike trolled live bait, feathers and lures, hitting hard and running fast with repetitive jumps. The white marlin begins its southward migration as the waters of the North Atlantic cool in the autumn.

A shimmering dorsal fin, fanned much higher than the depth of its streamlined steel-blue body, distinguishes the sailfish (*Istiophorus platyperus*) from its billed brethren. Fronted with a long, slender bill, this graceful creature — averaging 7 feet long and 40 pounds in Florida waters — is meant to be captured and released but stuffed no more. Probably the most popular mount of all time — the flaunted mark of the been-there, done-that crowd — the sailfish, at least in the Florida Keys, is generally allowed to entertain, take a bow and go back to the dressing room until the next show. Taxidermists now stock fiberglass blanks so you need only phone in the prize measurements to receive your representative mount.

The migration of the sailfish coincides with that of the snowbirds, those Northerners who spend the frigid months in the balmy Florida Keys. In late autumn and early winter, the sailfish leave the Caribbean and Gulf waters and head up the Gulf Stream to the Keys. A fast-growing fish — 4 to 5 feet in one year — the sailfish seldom lives more than five years. Feeding on the surface or at mid-depths on small fish and squid, the sailfish also is amenable to trolled appetizers of outrigger-mounted live mullet or ballyhoo that will wiggle, dive and skip behind the boat like rats after the Pied Piper. The sailfish, swimming at up to 50 knots, will give you a run for your money, alternating dramatic runs and explosions from the depths with catapults through the air. The sailfish delights novice and expert alike. The inexperienced angler can glory in the pursuit with heavy tackle while the seasoned veteran can lighten up, creating a new challenge. Both will savor the conquest.

Florida law allows you to keep one billfish per day and mandates size limitations. Sailfish must be at least 57 inches; blue marlin, 86 inches; and white marlin, 62 inches. We recommend, however, that you follow the ethical considerations of catch-and-release, recording your conquest on film instead.

Blackfin Tuna

Highly sought by anglers and blue marlin alike, the blackfin tuna (*Thunnus atlanticus*) is set apart from the other six tunas of North America by its totally black finlets. Rarely exceeding 50 pounds, this member of the mackerel family is not as prized as the giant bluefin of North Atlantic waters, but Keys anglers still relish a substantial battle and the bonus of great eating. Primarily a surface feeder, the blackfin terrorizes baitfish from below, causing them to streak to the surface and skitter out of the water like skipping stones, a move that attracts seabirds. A sighting of diving gulls will tip off the presence of tuna at the feed bag. Blackfin tuna are partial to a chumming of live pilchards but will also attack feathers and lures trolled at high speeds. Tuna fishing on the humps is usually good in the spring months.

Dolphin: Schoolies, Slammers and Bulls

Anyone who has ever seen a rainbow of schooling dolphin (*Coryphaena hippurus*) knows the fish's identity crisis is unfounded. Nothing about this prismatic fish suggests the mammal sharing its name. The dolphin fish resembles a Technicolor cartoon. Its bright green, blue and yellow wedgelike body looks like the fish just crashed into a paint cabinet, and its high, blunt, pugnacious forehead and Mohawk-style dorsal fin evoke a rowdy, in-your-face persona not wholly undeserved. Once out of the water, however, the brilliant hues ebb like a fading photograph, tingeing sweet victory with fleeting regret.

Second only to billfish and tuna, dolphin are prized by bluewater anglers. Frantic fights follow lightning strikes, and the dolphin often throw in some aerobatics besides. This unruly gang fighter rates as a delicacy at the table as

well, celebrated as moist white-fleshed dolphin fillets in the Keys and South Florida, but marketed as mahi-mahi elsewhere. Dolphin fish are surface feeders, attracted to the small fish and other tasty morsels associated with floating debris or patches of drifting sargassum weed. Flying fish, plentiful in the Gulf Stream waters, form a large portion of their preferred diet. A school of dolphin will actually

attack a trolled bait of small whole mullet or ballyhoo, streaking from a distance in a me-first effort like school boys to the lunch gong. It is not unusual for three or four rods to be hit at one time, an all-hands-on-deck effort that approaches a marathon. And, as long as you keep one hooked dolphin in the water alongside the boat, its buddies will hang around and wait their turn for a freshly baited hook.

Dolphin are a rapidly growing fish, living up to five years. The young are called schoolies, generally in the 5- to 15-pound range. Slammers make an angler salivate, for at 25 pounds and up each, an attacking school can get your heart pumping. Doing battle with the heavyweight, the bull dolphin, quite often happens by accident while you are trolling for some other species. But the bull can hold his own in any arena. Dolphin season is generally considered to be from March until August, but the fish tend to stay around all year.

Cobia: the Crab Eater

The cobia (*Rachycentron canadum*), the orphan of the piscatory world, enjoys no close relatives and is in a family by itself. Excellent on the table or on the troll, the adult cobia is a favorite bonus fish, often caught during a day in the bluewater looking for sailfish. Particularly partial to crabs, the cobia also feeds on shrimps, squid and small fish. The young co-

A School for All Seasons

Islamorada, billed as the Sportfishing Capital of the World, is home to the longest-running saltwater fly-fishing school in the world, Sandy Moret's Florida Keys Fly Fishing School. Founded and directed by veteran saltwater fly fisherman Sandy Moret, this weekend "study-class" brings freshwater fly anglers back to school in droves to learn techniques of one of the fastest-growing sports in the world — saltwater fly fishing.

 Close-up

Moret, who also owns and operates Florida Keys Outfitters, is a three-time grand champion of the Gold Cup Tarpon Tournament and four-time grand champion of the Islamorada Invitational Bonefish Fly Tournament. With more than a dozen fly-rod grand slams and four world records to his credit, he has assembled an outstanding team of world-renowned anglers to teach the skills and techniques of saltwater fly fishing to novice and veteran alike. This all-star teaching staff works on a rotating basis.

"A great deal can be accomplished in a weekend," says Moret. "If a student leaves this school knowing what rods, reels and lines to use; how to develop his or her casting; what flies to use; how to tie the proper knots; what to expect from a guide — then we've succeeded."

Typically, class size for the weekend program ranges from 15 to 20 students from all over the world. About a third are women. The student-to-instructor ratio is 5-to-1.

Moret kicks off the first instructive session by reassuringly debunking the myth of the long-distance cast. He says, "A myth has developed through the articles of some outdoor writers, as well as through some movies and videos, that you have to be able to cast long distances in saltwater fly fishing to be successful. For sight fishing on the flats, nothing could be further from the truth. You do need to cast accurately and quickly — but usually only for short distances.

"If the fish is 100 feet away, you can't see him and you can't tell what's going on. You need to be in touch with your surroundings — the wind and currents, the sun and shadows — and you have to see how those elements are affecting the feeding behavior of the fish. Then you have to coax or seduce that fish into biting your fly. And you can only do that in a visual situation, where your target is within sighting distance, usually no more than 30 to 50 feet away."

Chico Fernandez, internationally known outdoor writer, filmmaker and photographer who is considered one of the world's foremost casting instructors, familiarizes students with the anatomy of fly line, including weights and contours — level, double taper, weight-forward, intermediate, sinking, lead cores, shooting taper, etc. — and their uses, care and marking. Freshwater anglers may be daunted by the notion that saltwater fly fishing requires very heavy tackle. "Not so," says Chico. "The best all-around outfit for saltwater fly fishing is an 8-weight."

Flip Pallot, holder of numerous saltwater world records with the fly rod but perhaps best known as the host of the award-winning weekly TV series *Walker's Cay Chronicles*, leads anglers through a discussion of materials, components, actions and care of saltwater fly rods. "The single most important element of tackle in fly fishing is the rod," says Pallot. He recommends that saltwater fly rods measure between 8½ and 9½ feet in length.

Steve Huff, past president of the Florida Keys Fishing Guides Association, has been guiding in the Florida Keys for more than 25 years. He adds an important dimension to

— continued on next page

Photo: Bill Beardsley

Chico Fernandez and Sandy Moret manipulate a "stuffed"
bonefish to explain how to spot a tailing fish.

the course with detailed examination of saltwater fly reels, including such considerations as materials, drives, drag systems, capacity, cost and maintenance.

Anglers gain hands-on training in a knot-tying workshop, during which they master
the art of the nail, blood, Albright, Huffnagle, double surgeon's, improved clinch, Bimini
twist and the Homer Rhode loop. After the knot session, anglers learn about saltwater
flies. Attracting such subtropical species as bonefish, permit, redfish, barracuda and
tarpon, the flies differ in both size and color from their inland cousins. Chico Fernandez
recommends light-colored flies for light bottoms and dark flies for dark bottoms when
fishing the flats, but he also stresses the importance of all three basic elements — size,
color and shape — in fly selection.

The second day of this weekend immersion into the depths of saltwater fly fishing
finds the students learning to cast, but still on dry land. They take to the golf course of
Islamorada's Cheeca Lodge as they practice grip, line control, lift, roll, back and forward
casts and single and double hauls. Instructor Stu Apte — a fly-fishing legend who has
appeared on *The American Sportsman, CBS Sports Spectacular* and *Walker's Cay
Chronicles*, and author of the now-classic book, *Stu Apte's Fishing in the Florida Keys* —
maintains, "There's no substitute for making a good first cast."

A fully rigged flats boat, sitting high on its trailer in the middle of the fairway, provides
the foundation for anglers to learn the setup and shot. Enacted by Pallot on the foredeck
and Huff on the poling platform, the scenario illustrates positioning relative to the wind,
current and shadows, preparation for casting and types of casts used when fishing the
flats. Moret and Fernandez manipulate bonefish mockups to explain and demonstrate
how to spot a fish, when and where to cast to them and how to make a presentation in
such a manner that the fish will encounter the fly in a situation that appears normal, with
nothing arousing suspicion. "The window of opportunity is often fleeting," cautioned
Fernandez, "and you must be ready for it at all times."

The instructors, whose ranks also include veteran Keys guide Rick Ruoff and
champion fly caster Steve Rajeff, share invaluable advice culled from years of

— continued on next page

experience in the saltwater flats of the Florida Keys. "You want to use angles and directions of pressure to tire the fish," Pallot says. "Never keep your rod tip up — that just reduces your mechanical leverage." He instructs anglers to pay particular attention to the angle of pressure: "The tip of your rod can even be held on or below the water's surface to maintain a low angle. The shorter you make the fight, the better your chance of successfully landing the fish."

"Be aggressive," advises Huff. "You'll catch a lot more fish playing them hard than you will by babying them or being timid in your fighting style."

Information on attending Sandy Moret's Florida Keys Fly Fishing School is available by calling Sandy Moret's Florida Keys Outfitters, (305) 664-5423. The school schedule typically offers three options, including introductory and advanced level saltwater fly fishing schools and guided fly-fishing sessions in area waters.

Bill Beardsley, author of this Close-up, is a freelance outdoor writer and fly fisherman for all seasons who divides his time between Duck Key and Sandwich, Massachusetts. Retired from The Wall Street Journal, *Beardsley writes for a number of angling publications, including* Fly Fishing Quarterly. *He is a graduate of The Florida Keys Fly Fishing School.*

---

bia is found often in the flats of nearshore bays and inlets around the mangroves and around buoys, pilings and wrecks.

Wahoo

A fine-eating bonus fish generally caught by fortunate accident while trolling for sailfish or kingfish, the wahoo (*Acanthocybium solandri*) is far from an also-ran. One of the fastest fish in the ocean, the wahoo is a bona fide member of the mackerel family, similar in many ways to the Spanish mackerel. Its long, beak-like snout and slender silver-and-blue-striped body contribute to its prowess as a speed swimmer, for when hooked the wahoo runs swiftly, cutting and weaving like a tailback heading for a touchdown. This loner rarely travels in schools. Wahoo season is in May, but the fish are here year round.

Kingfish: King Mackerel

Here in the Florida Keys, we call the king mackerel — which goes by assorted aliases in other parts of the country — the kingfish. At the turn of the century, kingfish was the most popular catch off the Keys. Sailfish, then unrevered, were considered pests because

they crashed the kingfish bait. The stream-lined kingfish (*Scomberomorus cavalla*) travels in large schools, migrating up and down the coast in search of warm waters. Kingfish commonly frequent the waters of the Keys during the winter months, heading north in the spring.

Kings can be caught by drift fishing, where anglers cut the boat's engines and drift, fishing over the schools. Alternately, you can troll for kingfish with whole mullet or ballyhoo. Some captains prefer to anchor and chum, lacing the slick from time to time with live pilchards. Any method you use, a wire leader is essential when angling for kingfish because the fish displays razor-sharp teeth it is not reticent to use. Kingfish caught in our waters commonly weigh in at about 20 pounds, although the fish have been recorded reaching upwards of 40 pounds. The kingfish is a good sport fish and also makes a fine meal.

Amberjack

When all else fails in the bluewater, you can always find a deep hole and battle an amberjack (*Seriola dumerili*). This powerful bottom-plunging fish, nicknamed AJ, guarantees a good brawl. Bringing in an amberjack is like pulling up a Volkswagen Beetle with light tackle.

The Reef Elite: Grouper, Snapper and the Mackerels

Inhabiting the edge of the barrier reef that extends the length of the Florida Keys and in the smaller patch reefs closer in to shore, several finned species noteworthy for their food value coexist with the brightly painted tropicals

and other coral-dwelling creatures. Like a well-branched family tree, these fish encompass many clans, all entertaining to catch, most delectable to eat. Startled anglers have even brought in permit while fishing the wrecks along the reef line. The brooding presence of the barracuda is always a strong possibility on the reef, because the 'cuda is partial to raw snapper "stew" or grouper tartare when given the opportunity. It thinks nothing of stealing half the hooked fish in one mighty chomp, leaving the angler nothing but a lifeless head.

You will need a boat at least 20 feet long to head out to the reef, some 4 to 5 miles offshore. But with a compass, your NOAA charts, a GPS, tackle, chunked bait and some information locally gathered at the nearest bait and tackle shop, you should be able to find a hot spot on your own. Then all you need to do is fillet the captives, find a recipe and fry up the spoils.

More than 50 species of grouper are found in the Florida waters, but three stand out in waters of the Florida Keys. The black grouper (*Mycteroperca bonaci*) has been known to reach 50 pounds and 3 feet in length. Distin-

guished from other grouper by the black blotches and brassy spots mottling its olive or gray body, the black grouper is nonetheless often confused with the gag grouper. Large adult black groupers are found on the rocky bottom in deep water, although the youth hang out close to shore.

The aforementioned gag grouper (*Mycteroperca microlepis*) reaches a length and proportion similar to that of the black grouper, but its body is a uniform gray color with dark wormlike markings on its sides. The red grouper (*Epinephelus morio*), so named because of its brownish-red pigmentation and scarlet-orange mouth lining, lives on rocky bottoms at medium depths. This makes it an accessible catch for anglers using small boats and light tackle.

All groupers are hermaphrodites, meaning they possess both male and female reproductive organs. The young are females that change into males as they mature. Fond of small fish and squid, groupers can be enticed to hit chunked ballyhoo, mullet and pilchards and shrimp. You will need a stout rod, a heavy leader and a heavy sinker because the grouper will head for the rocks once it comprehends the insult of the hook. The ensuing fight is not for the fainthearted. You will have to horse the fish out of the rocks and corals, where the grouper will make every attempt to cut your line.

The snapper family is a popular bunch in the Florida Keys. The prolific cousins — all pleasurable to eat, delightful to catch and kaleidoscopic to see — confuse Northerners with their dissimilarity. Snappers travel in schools and like to feed at night. Most common on the Keys table is probably the sweet, delicate yellowtail snapper (*Ocyurus chrysurus*), which usually ranges from 12 to 16 inches in length. Big yellowtails, called flags, approach 5 to 6 pounds and 20 inches in length and are prevalent from late summer through October. The yellowtail's back and upper sides shade from

---

INSIDERS' TIP

When you see a boat being propelled by someone pushing it with a pole, please give that boat wide berth. These anglers are stalking game fish in the shallows of the flats. The sound of an engine will frighten all the fish.

olive to bluish with yellow spots. A prominent yellow stripe begins at the yellowtail's mouth and runs mid-laterally to its deeply forked tail, which, as you would expect, is a deep, brilliant yellow. The yellowtail is skittish, line-shy and tends to stay way behind the boat. The fish's small mouth won't accommodate the hooks most commonly used in the pursuit of the other snappers. Successful anglers use light line, no leaders and small hooks buried in the bait (see our Close-up, Recipe for Yellowtail Chum Balls, in this chapter).

The mangrove snapper, or gray snapper (*Lutjanus griseus*), though haunting the coral reef, also can be found inshore in mangrove habitats. Grayish in color with a red tinge along the sides, the mangrove snapper displays two conspicuous canine teeth at the front of the upper jaw. The mangrove is easier to catch than the yellowtail or the mutton snapper. Live shrimp and cut bait added to a small hook will induce these good fighters to strike. Anglers enjoy taking the mangroves on light tackle.

The brightly colored mutton snapper (*Lutanus analis*) shades from olive-green to red, with a bright blue line extending from under its eye to its tail. A black spot below the dorsal fin marks its side like an unwanted birthmark. Mutton snappers are most often caught in blue holes, so called because the water color of these deep coral potholes appears bluer than the surrounding waters. You will also find muttons in channels and creeks and occasionally even on a bonefish flat. The fish range in weight from 5 to 20 pounds. Mutton snappers are rumored to be shy and easily spooked by a bait cast too closely, but they love live pilchards. Usually caught in cloudy, churned up water, the muttons provide a fierce confrontation.

Ergonomically designed for speed, the torpedo-shaped Spanish mackerel (*Scomberomorus maculatus*) distinguishes itself from the king and the cero with a series of irregular buttercup-yellow spots on its stripeless sides that look like the freckles on the Little Rascals. Cherished by light-tackle enthusiasts, the Spanish mackerel averages less than 2 pounds, 20 inches in length. Its razorlike teeth dictate you carefully consider your choice in terminal tackle, for slashing your line rates at the top of the Spanish mackerel's getaway

tactics. Spanish mackerel migrate into Florida Bay in February.

Larger than its Spanish cousin, the cero mackerel (*Scomberomorous regalis*) displays yellow spots above and below a bronze stripe running down its silvery sides from the pectoral fin to the base of its tail. The cero is the local in our visiting mackerel lineup, not straying far from the waters of South Florida and the Keys where it feeds on small fish and squid. The cero makes excellent table fare when consumed fresh, but fillets do not freeze well.

You may encounter the tripletail (*Lobotes surinamensis*) if you fish around wrecks, buoys or sunken debris. Nicknamed the buoy fish, the tripletail has been known to reach 40 pounds and a length of 3 feet. The fish's dorsal and anal fins are so long they resemble two more tails, hence the name tripletail. The tripletail is a mottled palette of black, brown and yellow, looking like an autumn leaf. Young tripletails, which like to stay close to shore in bays and estuaries, are often spotted floating on their sides at the surface, mimicking a leaf on the water. The tripletail will put up a valiant fight, and, though not seen on a restaurant menu, it will make a tasty dinner.

The Bridges

The bridges of the Florida Keys attract fighting game fish and flavorful food fish like magnets draw paper clips. The State of Florida replaced many of the original bridges of the Overseas Highway with wider, heavier spans in the late 1970s and '80s. Monroe County has subsequently fitted many of the old bridges no longer used for automobile traffic for use as fishing piers. These bridges are marked with brown and white signage depicting a fish, line and hook. They offer the general public free fishing access to many of the same species that frequent more far-flung areas of our waters. Parking is provided at the fishing-pier bridges. The Seven Mile Bridge, the Long Key Bridge and the Bahia Honda Bridge have been designated historical monuments.

Fishing is not allowed on all the Keys' 42 bridges. You are permitted to fish only on those structures no longer used by automobile traffic. Many of the old bridge structures have

Photo: Victoria Shearer

Nothing beats the catch of a couple of bull dolphins. Good fight — great eating!

been closed because lack of maintenance has left them unsafe. Be sure to fish only from those bearing the county signage. Some bridges are closed to fishing because a large volume of boat traffic passes beneath them. Fishing lines tangle in the vessels' props. Other fishing bridges screen off a portion of the bridge, allowing a safe passage for the watercraft below and angling access above.

The waters beneath the bridges host a lively population of tarpon, mangrove snappers, snook, baby groupers and yellowtails. See the flats, backcountry and bluewater sections of this chapter for information on these fish. Grunts (*Haemulon plumieri*) also are commonly caught at the bridges. Though little respected in other Keys' waters, this small bluish-gray fish is nevertheless fun to catch and makes a tasty meal. The grunt's name is derived from the sounds escaping the fish's bright orange mouth when it is captured. This grunting sound is actually the grinding of the pharyngeal teeth, which produces an audible noise amplified by the air bladder.

Night fishing is popular from the bridge piers too. An outgoing tide with a moderate flow inspires the fish to continue feeding after dark. Baitfish and crustaceans are funneled through the pilings and out to sea, a temptation too great for many of the finned predators to pass up.

Stop in at one of the local bait and tackle shops to get rigged out for bridge fishing. The local fishing experts working in these shops are encyclopedias of knowledge and will be able to guide you as to times, tides and tackle. Locals recommend you use stout tackle when fishing from one of our bridges. You'll not only have to retrieve your catch battling a heavy current, but also lift it a great distance to the top of the bridge.

Live shrimp, cut bait or live pinfish will attract attention from at least one of the species lurking below. You will need to keep your shrimp alive while fishing from the bridge. Put the shrimp on ice in a 5-gallon bucket with an aerator or in a large Styrofoam cooler with an aerator. You can also lower a chum bag (filled with a block of chum available at all bait shops) into the water. Tie a couple of dive weights to a long rope, lower the chum bag down the surface of a piling on the down-current side of the bridge and tie it off to the railing. Then, fish the slick. The chum will drift with the current, attracting sharks and any finfish in the neighborhood.

You will need sinkers on your line in order for your baited hook to drop to the bottom because a swift current pulses under the bridges. Don't launch your cast away from the bridge. Drop your bait straight down near a piling or down-current at the shore side of the bridge. Rubble from past construction sometimes piled here creates a current break allowing the fish a place to rest, feed or hide in the swirls or eddies. Don't forget to buy a fishing license.

Fishing Licenses

Florida law states you must possess a saltwater fishing license if you attempt to take or possess marine fish for noncommercial purposes. This includes finfish and such invertebrate species as snails, whelks, clams, scallops, shrimps, crabs, lobsters, sea stars, sea urchins and sea cucumbers.

Exempt from this law are individuals younger than 16 and Florida residents 65 and older. You are also exempt if you are a Florida resident and a member of the U.S. Armed Forces not stationed in Florida and home on leave for 30 or fewer days with valid orders in your possession.

Florida residents who are fishing in salt water or for a saltwater species in fresh water, from land or from a structure fixed to land, need not purchase a license. Land is defined as "the area of ground located within the geographic boundaries of the state of Florida that extends to a water depth of 4 feet." This includes any structure permanently fixed to land, such as a pier, bridge, dock or floating dock or jetty. If you use a vessel to reach ground, however, you must have a license. And if you are wading in more than 4 feet of water or have broken the surface of the water wearing a face mask, you also must have one.

You are not required to have a license when you fish with one of our licensed captains on a charter holding a valid vessel saltwater fishing license or if you are fishing from a pier that has been issued a pier saltwater fishing license.

Other more obscure exemptions also apply. Check the summary of fishing regulations issued with your saltwater fishing license.

A Florida saltwater fishing license is available from most bait and tackle shops and from any Monroe County tax collector's office. Residents and nonresidents pay differing amounts for this license. The state defines a resident as anyone who has lived in Florida continuously for at least six months; anyone who has established a domicile in Florida and can provide evidence of such by law; any member of the U.S. Armed Forces who is stationed in Florida, any student enrolled in a college or university in Florida; or an alien who can prove residency status.

Residents pay $10 for a 10-day license, $12 for one year and $60 for five years. Applications for the five-year license may be obtained from the tax collector's office for $1. Nonresidents must pay $5 for a three day license, $15 for seven days and $30 for one year. The tax collector's office charges a processing fee of $1.50. A $2 fee will be levied if you purchase your license at another location. If you wish to take snook or lobster, you must add the appropriate stamp to your Florida saltwater fishing license. Each stamp costs $2.

Florida residents may purchase a lifetime saltwater fishing license. If you are between the ages of 13 and 63, the cost is $300; for those younger than 13, rates are less. Lifetime licenses are available at the county tax collector's office. No snook or crawfish stamps are required. If you are a Florida resident and are certified as totally and permanently disabled, you are entitled to receive, without charge from the county tax collector, a permanent saltwater fishing license.

The penalty for fishing without the required license or stamps is $50 plus the cost of purchasing the proper documentation. A $50 tarpon tag is required if you insist upon keeping and therefore killing a tarpon instead of releasing it (see the Catch-and-Release Ethics section in this chapter).

Tournaments

If you're an angler who would like to compete against your peers instead of just yourself, the Florida Keys offers a plethora of exciting tournaments encompassing most of the finned species enriching our waters. These tournaments, scheduled year round from Key Largo to Key West, award prizes, cash and trophies in a variety of categories ranging from heaviest or longest to most caught and released in a specified time period.

Generally the tournaments fit into one of three categories, although some tournaments have multiple divisions. The billfish tournaments — white marlin, blue marlin and sailfish — are the most prestigious and the most expensive, with entry fees per boat of four anglers of $450 and higher. Billfish tournaments are catch-and-release events. Proof of the catch usually requires a photograph and a sample of the leader, which will be tested for chafing. Scoring follows an intricate point system. A catch of a white marlin, a blue marlin and a sailfish in one day — not your average day, even in the Keys — constitutes a slam.

Dolphin tournaments are more family-type competitions. Generally the fee per angler is about $50. Anglers use their own boats without guides, and if the dolphin exceeds a set poundage, it may be brought in and weighed. Anglers can keep the fish, which are excellent eating.

Flats tournaments — tarpon, bonefish and permit — are always catch-and-release, usually scored by a point system. A catch on a fly rod scores more points than one retrieved on light tackle. The fish must be measured, a photo must be taken, and the process must be witnessed. We recommend you book one year in advance for tarpon tournaments.

Some of our tournaments are restricted to a specific category of angler — women only or juniors only, for instance — or to a particular type of tackle, such as light tackle or fly rods. Others award a mixed bag of catches ranging from game fish to groupers to grunts. Many of the tournaments donate at least a portion of their proceeds to a charitable organization.

In the following section, we introduce you to a sampling of the most important fishing tournaments held annually in the Keys. For a complete listing, call Florida Keys Fishing Tournament Administrator Christina Sharpe at (305) 872-2233.

Cheeca Lodge Presidential Sailfish Tournament
Islamorada • (305) 664-4651

This important tournament, held in mid-January, was named the Presidential back when George Bush was president and fished our Islamorada waters. The name still holds, for it's one of the most popular tournaments of the season. Anglers (four per boat) fish for two full days in search of the most sailfish, which are caught and released. Anglers follow the honor system as to what constitutes a catch. Any disputes are handled with a lie detector test — no kidding! This is the only billfish tournament in the Keys with an outboard division, which affords any angler with a boat the chance to compete, no charter required. Cash prizes and trophies are awarded the winners. Contact person is Julie Olsen.

Ladies Tarpon Tournament
Marathon • (305) 743-6139

The waters under the Seven Mile Bridge and the Bahia Honda bridge are invaded by tarpon-seeking women each year in late April in this ladies-only tarpon tournament. The number of tarpon caught and released in the two-day tournament determines the winners of a cache of rods and reels, trophies and an assortment of jewelry. Points are awarded for catches on 12-pound test and 30-pound test. The 1999 tournament marks the event's 23rd year. Dave Navarro is the contact person.

Texaco Key West Classic
Key West • (305) 294-4042

Big money can be won in this late-April tournament, which holds a pot of $50,000

spread over a variety of categories. The major targets are blue or white marlin, sailfish, tarpon and permit, all catch-and-release except for fun-fish. All boats registered in other divisions can participate in the fun-fish categories, which award a total of $7,500, of which $1,500 is given for the heaviest dolphin, tuna and wahoo weighing in at more than 20 pounds. Proceeds benefit the National Mental Health Association, which has received almost $750,000 since the tournament's inception 10 years ago. Contact Michael Whalton for more information.

Key West & Lower Keys Fishing Tournament
(305) 745-3332, (800) 970-9056

This unusual tournament must have been designed for the angler who just can't fish enough. It lasts eight months, from April to early December, and encompasses a potpourri of divisions and species. Charters and individuals both register for the tournament and participate in a two-day kickoff tournament-within-a-tournament, which in itself awards $6,000 in prizes. Anglers weigh their food-fish catches or record their releases at participating marinas and are awarded citations for their efforts. The end-off-of-the-kick-off is the Team Challenge, where a minimum of two anglers, maximum of four anglers amass points as a team. The event, which is the last of the tournament, awards Key West vacation packages and cash prizes. At the grand finale of the tournament, the tabulated results are announced, and all prizes are presented. Contact person is Capt. Linda Luizza.

Coconuts Dolphin Tournament
Key Largo • (305) 451-4107

The largest dolphin tournament in the Florida Keys, Coconuts Dolphin Tournament at Marina Del Mar in mid-May regularly hosts more than 700 anglers. This three-day tournament, with cash prizes of $25,000, runs from 8 AM to 3 PM each day. You can book a charter to fish the tournament or use your own boat.

INSIDERS' TIP

Never discard your fish line in the water. It can injure marine life, sea turtles or seabirds.

Recipe for Yellowtail Chum Balls

Take one bag of good quality chum (packed from a commercial fish market in clear plastic, not a box). Allow chum to defrost overnight. Drain liquid. In a large container, mix chum with an equal portion of fine-grained mason's sand. Add flour, oatmeal and glass minnows. Mix together well and form into solidly packed 2-inch balls (much like you would a snowball). Add more flour to the mixture if the balls do not hold together. Bait a hook (size 4 to size 1) with 1-inch, cut-up pieces of ballyhoo or mackerel. Bury the hook and bait inside the chum ball. Your hook should be tied directly to the line — no leader, no swivels, no double lines and no sinkers. The weight of the chum ball will carry your bait to the bottom.

Open the bail on your reel or set your reel to free-spool and drop your baited hook in the water. As it goes down to the bottom, bits of the chum ball will break off. When it hits the bottom, the chum ball will break up completely, freeing your baited hook. The cloud of swirling chum will attract the yellowtails. Keep your line in free-spool until the yellowtail grabs the bait and peels off line. Close the bail and set the hook. The rest is history.

Photo: Wayne Moccia

Yellowtail snapper - fun to catch, great to eat.

The director says there has been no proven advantage to having a charter. Scoring is determined by weight of the fish. Since this is a food-fish tournament, anglers may bring in all dolphin of more than 10 pounds. Chester Marr is the contact person.

Don Hawley Invitational Tarpon Tournament
Islamorada • (903) 454-6178

The oldest tarpon-on-fly tournament in the Keys and the first all-release tournament, the Don Hawley event is a five-day fishing extravaganza of all-fly, all-tarpon and all-release. Anglers are awarded 1,000 points for a catch-and-release on 12-pound tippet, 750 points on 16-pound. Winners amassing the most points secure original Keys art by such notables as Al Barnes, Bill Elliott and Kendall Van Sant. Proceeds of the tournament benefit the nonprofit Don Hawley Foundation, which supports the study of tarpon fishery and preservation in the Florida Keys and provides assistance to guides and their families in time of need. The tournament is held in early June. Eddie Miller is the person to call for information.

Women's World Invitational Fly Championships — Tarpon Series
Islamorada • (305) 664-9279

This ladies-only, three-day tarpon catch-and-release tournament is limited to 30 anglers, one per boat. The tarpon must be taken on fly only and measure at least 4 feet. Touching the leader is a catch in this release tournament. Regulation measuring sticks and the honor system determine size of the catch. Winners are awarded original artwork of the Keys, crystal trophies and an assortment of rods and reels. Sponsored by Yamaha Outboards, Scientific Anglers and Maverick Boats, this nonprofit tournament, held in mid-June, awards a scholarship to a local high school student who will pursue studies in environmental or marine science, thereby giving back the gift of knowledge to the Keys. There is usually a waiting list for this tournament, so contact Amy Knowles as soon as possible.

Mercury Outboards' S.L.A.M. Tournament
Key West • (305) 664-2002

First in the Celebrity Tournament Series each year is the S.L.A.M. (Southernmost Light-tackle Anglers Masters) event in early September directed by Gary Ellis for the benefit of cystic fibrosis research (see the Baybone and Redbone tournament events). Participants in this two-day fishing event angle to score a grand slam: the catch and release of a bonefish, permit and tarpon in two days. Points are awarded for each release in categories of fly, spin/plug and general bait. Each release is photographed against a measuring device.

Like the other two tournaments in this series, the S.L.A.M. awards original art and sculpture to its winners. Anglers can fish as a two-person team or one angler can opt to fish with a celebrity such as Gen. Norman Schwarzkopf, Chris Evert or Wade Boggs. Celebrity host is Curt Gowdy. The contact person is Gary Ellis.

Little Palm Island Grand Slam
Little Torch Key • (305) 664-2002

This small and select two-day tournament in mid-September, with a kickoff and awards banquet at the elite Little Palm Island, is a catch-and-release event in search of the elusive grand slam: tarpon, bonefish and permit in two days. Winners of the 30-boat event (two anglers per boat) receive original paintings, limited-edition prints and pieces of sculpture. Proceeds of this tournament, like the Celebrity Tournament Series, benefit research by the Cystic Fibrosis Foundation. Contact Gary Ellis for more details.

Women's World Invitational Fly Championships — Bonefish Series
Islamorada • (305) 664-9279

Sponsored by Yamaha Outboards and Maverick Boats, this women-only late-September event cashes in on the growing popularity of saltwater fly fishing. Participants will be fishing for bonefish on fly only. Proof of the catch in this release tournament will be determined by camera and regulation measuring sticks. Prizes include original art pieces, fine crystal and tackle. The director will book you a guide if desired. Contact Amy Knowles for more information.

Mariner Outboards' Baybone
Ocean Reef Club, North Key Largo • (305) 664-2002

Event No. 2 in the Celebrity Tournament Series, the prestigious catch-and-release Baybone tournament in early October, run by Gary Ellis, benefits cystic fibrosis research. Ellis is particularly interested in this worthy cause because his daughter, Nicole, has cystic fibrosis. The Celebrity Tournament Series, which includes the Redbone and the Mercury Outboards' S.L.A.M., donates 100 percent of its proceeds to the Cystic Fibrosis Foundation for research. The stalked catch for the Baybone is bonefish and permit, which are photographed against a measuring device and released. Points are awarded for catches on fly, spin/plug or general bait; nothing heavier than 12-pound test may be used in all divisions. An intricate point system determines the winners, who receive original paintings and sculptures as

INSIDERS' TIP

Dispose of your garbage back at the boat dock. Be careful that trash does not blow out of the boat. Do not leave anything behind that cannot be immediately consumed by the ecosystem.

prizes. Anglers can fish as a two-person team or one angler can be paired with a celebrity such as John Havlicek, Mark Sosin or Mike Stanley.

Mercury Outboards' Redbone
Islamorada • (305) 664-2002

Third in the Celebrity Tournament Series, the prestigious Redbone (first held in 1988) attracts anglers in competitive search for bonefish and redfish in early November. Also benefiting cystic fibrosis research, the Redbone follows the rules and regulations of the other two tournaments in the series. Many anglers try to fish all three tournaments. The grand champion of the series wins a gold Rolex Yachtmaster watch. Again, Gary Ellis is the one to call for more on this tourney.

George Bush/Cheeca Lodge Bonefish Tournament
Islamorada • (305) 664-4651

Perhaps the most prestigious of all tournaments in the Florida Keys is the George Bush/Cheeca Lodge Bonefish Tournament, held in autumn. The former president himself competes in this event. (He has not won.) Preceded by a kickoff meeting, 1½ days of intense fishing are followed by an awards banquet at Cheeca Lodge. Forty-five boats participate, two anglers per boat. Other than those included in the most-catches category, bonefish must weigh at least 8 pounds to qualify. All must be released. Trophies are awarded to winners. Proceeds benefit a variety of Keys environmental groups. Contact Julie Olsen for more information.

The Florida Keys
Guides and Charters

Nearly 1,000 charter captains and guides — be it flats, bluewater or backcountry — do business in the Florida Keys. Our guides are the most knowledgeable in the world — licensed captains who maintain safe, government-regulated watercraft. Hiring a guide allows the first-time visitor or the novice angler an opportunity to learn how to fish the waters of the Florida Keys and catch its bounty without having to spend too much time learning about the fish's habits. And guides will be your best teachers, for they usually have a lifetime of experience. Once you fish our waters, however, you will be the "hooked" species, for this unforgettable angling experience is addictive.

Book a guide as soon as you know when you are coming to the Keys because the guides here book up quickly, especially during certain times of the year. If you hope to fish our waters with a guide during tarpon season, especially the months of May and June, plan a year ahead. Holidays such as Christmas and New Year's book up quickly also. Traditionally, the months of August through November are a bit slower. You may be able to wing it during those months, but we wouldn't advise it. Even if you don't take a charter trip, stop at a fishing marina about 4 PM and check out the catch of the day.

Bluewater or offshore fishing charters can accommodate six anglers. The captain guides the vessel to his or her favorite hotspots, which are anywhere from 6 to 26 miles offshore and are usually closely guarded secrets. Often he will stop on his bluewater trek so the mate can throw a cast net for live bait. The mate will rig the baits, ready the outriggers and cast the baited hooks for you. Big game fish are usually stalked by trolling, as are dolphin. You need do nothing but relax, soak in the sea air and wait for the call, "Fish on!" Then the action is up to you.

Bluewater charter boats range in size from 35 to 50 feet. Each generally has an enclosed cabin and a head (toilet) on board. Everything you need for a day's fishing is provided except your refreshments, lunch and any personal items you may need. Expect a half-day charter to cost $350 to $450. A full day will run anywhere from $500 to $700, depending upon the size of the boat. It is customary to tip the mate 10 to 15 percent cash if you have had a good day.

Guides for flats fishing or backcountry angling usually take a maximum of two anglers per boat. A few with larger skiffs will take an additional person for an extra $50 to $100. The guide will pole the skiff or flats boat through the skinny water, attentively looking for fish from atop the poling platform. This sight fishing dictates both guide and anglers stand alert, all senses engaged. The angler, whether fly fishing or spin casting, casts to the desired location directed by the guide.

Flats boats measure 16 or 18 feet and are not outfitted with any shading devices, nor do they have a head. Be aware you may have to use rather primitive facilities; many of the guides will dip into shore for a pit stop, but others will not, so inquire before you leave the dock. All fly or spin rods, reels, tackle and bait are provided. Some guides even tie their own flies, providing special furry or feathery creations proven to entice the fish. A half-day flats or backcountry guide will charge between $225 and $250. A full day will cost $325 to $350. It is customary to tip the guide 10 percent to 15 percent in cash if you were happy with the excursion.

When booking a charter, inquire about penalties for canceling your reservations. No-shows frequently will be charged the full price.

Always bring sunscreen, polarized sunglasses, a hat with a long bill lined with dark fabric to cut the glare and motion-sickness pills (even if you've never needed them before). Anglers are responsible for providing their own lunches and refreshments. Keys tradition is to bring lunch for the captain and mate on a bluewater charter or for the guide on a flats trip.

Many guides are known only on a word-of-mouth basis, but we have compiled a source list of fishing marinas and outfitters you may call to secure an offshore charter or flats or backcountry guide. The chambers of commerce in Key Largo, Islamorada, Marathon and the Lower Keys also act as referral sources (see subsequent listings).

Some guides are willing to captain your private vessel at a much-reduced charter rate. If this interests you, inquire when you call one of these central booking or referral sources. Often hotels maintain a source list of guides or charter captains they will recommend. Inquire when you reserve your accommodations.

Central Booking Agents

Establishments acting as central booking services will determine your needs and book your flats/backcountry guide or bluewater/offshore charter directly. They accept credit cards. Deposit information and cancellation policies are listed below.

Upper Keys

Holiday Isle Marina, MM 84 Oceanside, Islamorada, (305) 664-2321. A $100 deposit is required.

Whale Harbor Dock & Marina, MM 83.5 Oceanside, Islamorada, (305) 664-4511. Whale Harbor requires a $100 deposit.

Sandy Moret's Florida Keys Outfitters, MM 82 Bayside, Islamorada, (305) 664-5423. A 25 percent deposit is required; balance is to be paid 30 days before the booked date. A booking may be rescheduled or canceled one month ahead of time with no penalty.

Islamorada Tackle, MM 81.6 Bayside, Islamorada, (305) 664-4578. A 50 percent deposit may be required. Walk-ins are welcome; guides can almost always be secured, even in high season.

World Wide Sportsman Inc., MM 81.5 Bayside, Islamorada, (305) 664-4615, (800) 327-2880. World Wide Sportsman acts as a full-service travel agency, booking a large stable of local guides by reputation. It also can arrange your hotel and rental car.

Bud n' Mary's Fishing Marina, MM 79.8 Oceanside, Islamorada, (305) 664-2461, (800) 742-7945. Required deposits include $200 for an offshore charter and $100 for a flats/backcountry guide.

Papa Joe's Marina, MM 79.7 Bayside, Islamorada, (305) 664-5005. A credit card number will be taken by telephone as a deposit. There is no penalty if the booking is canceled prior to 72 hours of the excursion. If you cancel within 72 hours, a 50 percent penalty will be charged to your credit card. No-shows will incur full charges.

Middle Keys

Hawk's Cay Marina, MM 61 Oceanside, Duck Key, (305) 743-9000. A credit card number will be taken by telephone as a deposit. There is no penalty if the booking is canceled up to 48 hours before the scheduled departure. After that, half the charter fee will be charged.

Photo: Victoria Shearer

Monroe County has converted spans of the Keys' old highway bridges as fishing bridges. Look for the hook, line and fish signs along the Overseas Highway.

Key Colony Beach Marina, MM 54 Oceanside, Key Colony Beach Causeway, (305) 289-1310. A $100 deposit is required.

Captain Hook's Marina, MM 53 Oceanside, Marathon, (305) 743-2444. A $100 deposit is required.

World Class Angler, MM 50 Bayside, Marathon, (305) 743-6139. Charters will require a deposit of half the fee.

Faro Blanco Outfitters, MM 48.5 Bayside, Marathon, (305) 743-9018. A 50 percent deposit is required.

Lower Keys

Strike Zone Charters, MM 29.5 Bayside, Big Pine Key, (305) 872-9863, (800) 654-9560. A $100 deposit is required. There is a 48-hour cancellation policy.

Sea Boots Outfitters, MM 30 Bayside, Big Pine Key, (305) 745-1530, (800) 238-1746. A $150 deposit is required on a credit card with a faxed signature.

Sugarloaf Marina, MM 17 Bayside, Sugarloaf Key, (305) 745-3135.

Referral Agents

Businesses functioning as referral sources maintain an active list of reputable flats/backcountry guides and bluewater/offshore captains and will provide you with names and telephone numbers. You must call the captain directly and work out the details of your charter. You should inquire if the captain takes credit cards; some do not. Our recommendations are listed in descending mile-marker order beginning with Key Largo.

Garden Cove Marina, MM 106.5 Oceanside, Key Largo, (305) 451-4694.

Yellow Baithouse, MM 101.7 Oceanside, Key Largo, (305) 451-0921.

Bluewater World, MM 100.5 Bayside, Key Largo, (305) 451-2511.

Key Largo Harbour at the Holiday Inn, MM 100 Oceanside, Key Largo, (305) 451-0045.

Marina Del Mar Resort and Marina, MM 100 Oceanside, Key Largo, (305) 451-4107, (800) 451-3483.

Zappie's Bar & Tackle, MM 99.5 Bayside, Key Largo, (305) 451-0531.

Kona Kai Resort, MM 98 Bayside, Key Largo, (305) 852-7200.

Smugglers' Cove Marina, MM 85.5 Bayside, Islamorada, (305) 664-5564.

H.T. Chittum & Co., MM 82.7 Bayside, Islamorada, (305) 664-4421.

Lorelei Yacht Basin, MM 82.5 Bayside, Islamorada, (305) 664-4338.

Bonefish Bob's, MM 81 Bayside, Islamorada, (305) 664-9420.

Jigs Bait and Tackle, MM 30.5 Bayside, Big Pine Key, (305) 872-1040.

Chambers of Commerce

Key Largo Chamber of Commerce & Florida Keys Visitors Center
MM 106 Bayside, Key Largo
• **(305) 451-1414, (800) 822-1088**

This chamber will provide names of guides who either belong to the Key Largo Chamber of Commerce or those from other areas of the Keys who pay a fee to the Florida Keys Visitors Center for representation.

Islamorada Chamber of Commerce
MM 82.5 Bayside, Islamorada
• **(305) 664-4503, (800) 322-5397**

This chamber maintains an active list of guides in the Islamorada area.

Greater Marathon Chamber of Commerce
MM 53.5 Bayside, Marathon
• **(305) 743-5417, (800) 262-7284**

Upon request, this chamber will send you a list of guides belonging to the Marathon Guides Association. The list specifies the guide's name, address, telephone number, type of fishing (i.e., bluewater or flats), fishing specialties (spin or fly) and size and make of boat. If you don't have time to wait for this list by mail, the chamber will provide several selections over the telephone.

Lower Keys Chamber of Commerce
MM 31 Oceanside, Big Pine Key
• **(305) 872-2411, (800) 872-3722**

The Lower Keys chamber goes beyond its membership list to refer you to a wide range of guides and captains in the area.

Party Boats

Party boats, sometimes called head boats, offer a relatively inexpensive way to fish the waters of the Keys. These U.S. Coast Guard-inspected and certified vessels generally can hold 50 persons or more, but most average no more than 25 to 30 anglers. Party boats take anglers out to the reef where they anchor or drift and bottom fish for more than 40 species of fish. Spring and summer find a plethora of groupers, snappers, dolphin fish and yellowtails, while kingfish and cobia are more apt to make an appearance in the winter months. Porgies, grunts and some species of snappers and groupers show up all year. Occasionally even a sailfish or a big shark has been caught from a party boat here.

The party boat offers rod and reel rental at $3 to $5 per trip. This includes your terminal tackle — hook, line and sinker — and all bait. If you bring your own fishing gear, bait is included in the excursion fee. You do not need a fishing license on a party boat. While most party boat information mentions your license is included in the excursion fee, this actually is only a temporary license. Two or more mates work the boat, helping you bait your hook, confiding fishing tips and untangling the inevitable crossed lines.

Most of the party boats have seats around the periphery of the lower deck and a shaded sun deck up top. You are advised to wear shorts rather than swimsuits and durable sneakers or deck shoes, not thongs or sandals. Remember, there will be a lot of anglers with many flying hooks on the boat. Put some sturdy cloth between your skin and that accidental snag. Most captains recommend bringing a long-sleeved lightweight shirt for protection against the sun and a jacket to ward off cool breezes. Bring sunglasses, sunscreen, a hat and motion sickness pills (many people who never suffered from seasickness before find drifting in the swells causes them *mal de mer*). Also bring a fishing rag or towel to wipe your hands on during the day.

After you land a fish, a mate will help you take it off the hook and will check the species to make sure it is not one of those protected by law, such as Nassau grouper. The mate then will measure the fish to ensure it meets the required size limit, tag it with your name and place it on ice. At the end of the fishing trip, you may reclaim your catch. The mate will clean your fish, usually for tips. Party boats with a set cleaning-fee policy will be noted in the descriptions. Mates work for tips aboard party boats, the standard tip being 10 to 15 percent if you had a good day and if the mate was helpful.

The following party boats may be booked for day or evening charters. It is always a good idea to arrive at the docks 30 minutes before departure to stow your gear on the boat and secure a good position on deck. All boats have restrooms on board. Most have an enclosed cabin and offer a limited snack bar, beer and soda. Exceptions will be noted.

In all cases you are allowed to bring your own cooler filled with lunch and refreshments. All party boats recommended in this section take credit cards unless otherwise stated. Children's rates refer to youngsters 12 and younger unless otherwise stated.

Atlantic Star
Holiday Inn Marina, MM 100 Oceanside, Key Largo • (305) 451-5894

The crew aboard the *Atlantic Star* are not just deck hands, they all are experienced anglers, anxious to share their intimate knowledge of the Keys' waters. The anglers aboard this excursion have even hooked into a shark from time to time.

Excursions go out daily from 9:30 AM to 4:30 PM at a cost of $47 for adults and $25 for children 16 and younger. Evening outings are Wednesday through Sunday from 7:30 PM to 12:30 AM; the cost is $30 for adults and $20 for children 16 and younger.

Sailor's Choice
Holiday Inn Marina, MM 100 Oceanside, Key Largo • (305) 451-1802

The *Sailor's Choice*, a 60-foot, aluminum, custom-built craft with an air-conditioned lounge, offers plenty of shade and seating for anglers on its daily fishing excursions. Though not forbidden on the evening excursion, children enjoy the daytime trips more, says the captain. During the day, they can easily see the big fish in the water and seabirds, porpoises and sea turtles. The evening fishing trip goes farther offshore and is devoted more intensely to fishing.

The two daily excursions are from 9 AM to 1 PM and 1:30 to 5:30 PM at a cost of $28 for adults and $17 for children. Evening outings are from 7:30 PM to 12:30 AM and cost $33 for adults.

Captain Michael
Holiday Isle Resort, MM 84.5 Oceanside, Islamorada • (305) 664-8070

If you just can't get enough fishing, the *Captain Michael* offers a money-saving option: Fish the morning excursion and go out again in the afternoon for only an additional $15. Rates for children younger than 5 who will only be "assisting" mom and dad are further reduced. The 65-foot *Captain Michael*, with spacious decks and an air-conditioned cabin, is available for private charters, sunset cruises and wedding receptions.

Daily trips are from 9:30 AM to 1:30 PM and 1:45 to 5:45 PM; the cost is $25 for adults and $20 for children. The evening excursion is from 7:30 PM to 12:30 AM, the prices are $30 for adults, $22 for children.

Miss Tradewinds
Whale Harbor Marina, MM 83.5 Oceanside, Islamorada • (305) 664-8341

The captains of *Miss Tradewinds*, each with more than 15 years of fishing the Keys' waters, can put their experience to work for you. Docked at Whale Harbor Marina for 26 years, the vessel makes a quick 30-minute trip to the reef so you can maximize a full three hours of fishing time.

Two daily excursions are available, at 9:30 AM to 1:30 PM and 1:45 to 5:30 PM. The cost is $26.50 for adults and $20 for children. The evening trip takes place from 7 PM to midnight for $31.95 for adults, $22 for children.

Gulf Lady
Bud n' Mary's Fishing Marina, MM 79.8 Oceanside, Islamorada • (305) 664-2628, (800) 742-7945

Mates are stationed at the bow and at the stern of the *Gulf Lady*, and the captain also works the boat, so you'll get plenty of assistance on this fishing trip. If you bring your own tackle, the captain recommends you have both 12-pound and 20-pound test. This 65-foot vessel also is available for private fishing charters and wedding receptions.

Daily trips are from 9:30 AM to 4:30 PM at a cost of $45 for adults, $40 for children. The evening outing is from 7:30 PM to 12:30 AM; cost is $35 for adults, $30 for children.

Marathon Lady and Marathon Lady III
Marathon Lady Dock at the Vaca Cut Bridge, MM 53 Oceanside, Marathon
• **(305) 743-5580**

Children fish for significantly reduced rates aboard the *Marathon Lady*. Inquire when you make your reservations. If you rent a rod and reel for the excursion, your tackle is included, but if you prefer to bring your own gear, terminal tackle is available for only $1. The mates will clean your catch for 25¢ a fish. A cooler with lunch and refreshments is allowed on all-day winter excursions. However, on summer evening excursions, which replace the all-day winter ventures, the captain prefers you bring your refreshments in a plastic bag; the crew will put them on ice for you.

June through August, daily trips are conducted from 8:30 AM to 12:30 PM and 1:30 to 5:30 PM. The cost is $25 for adults. September through May, daily excursions are from 9:30 AM to 4:30 PM at a cost of $42 for adults. Evening excursions are conducted June through August only, from 6:30 PM to midnight, for $35.

Outfitters

Upper Keys

Bluewater World
MM 100.5 Bayside, Key Largo
• **(305) 451-2511**

Specializing in offshore and light tackle, Bluewater offers Star and Key Largo custom rods and Penn, Daiwa and Shimano reels. The shop carries an assortment of flies and fly-tying materials and sells G. Loomis fly rods. Bluewater acts as a Penn service center, so it provides rod and reel repair. Look for AFTCO, Columbia, Sebago, Sportif and Hook & Tackle clothing. You can also purchase rigged and unrigged bait here.

Zappie's Bar & Tackle
MM 99.5 Bayside, Key Largo
• **(305) 451-0531**

You'll find more than just a wide selection of custom rods at Zappie's, now a "happening" in the Upper Keys offering live music and live bait. Insatiable anglers can quench their thirst, enjoy live blues, jazz and rock entertainers and choose from light to super-heavy custom tackle, which is built on the premises (see our Nightlife chapter). Shimano and Penn reels are available, but custom is really the name of the game here. The shop rigs its own baits and specializes in custom rigging of offshore bait.

H.T. Chittum & Co.
MM 82.7 Bayside, Islamorada
• **(305) 664-4421**

It took a local fly fisherman, Hal Chittum, to open H.T. Chittum & Co., the popular outfitter in Islamorada (see our Shopping chapter). Specializing in light and fly tackle, Chittum's offers products from Winston, Penn, Shimano, Daiwa, Diamondback and Redington. Fly reels from Tibor, Abel, Lamson, Scientific Anglers and Bauer are always in good supply.

The store stocks a complete selection of fly-tying materials and more than 25,000 saltwater flies. On-premises flytiers will quickly make custom flies of any hot pattern you request. And free advice on fishing techniques and expert tackle rigging are yours for the asking. Sportif and Woolrich are among the fishing togs on offer to complete the picture.

Sandy Moret's Florida Keys Outfitters
MM 82 Bayside, Islamorada
• **(305) 664-5423**

The focus here is on fly fishing, and the personnel rank as some of the most experienced in the sport (see our Close-up, A School for All Seasons, in this chapter). You'll find Sage, G. Loomis and Scott fly rods and Islander, Tibor, Abel, Sage and Scientific Angler fly reels, plus a wide selection of flies and fly-tying materials (owner Sandy Moret suggests trying the Bead Chain Eye Merkin for bonefish). In addition to Columbia, Sage, ExOfficio,

Patagonia and Orvis clothing, Florida Keys Outfitters sells Reef Rider and Teva sandals as well as Sebago and Columbia boat shoes. An angling art gallery features originals and prints by Millard Wells, Al Barnes, Don Ray, Tim Borsky, C.D. Clark and Kendall Van Sant.

World Wide Sportsman Inc.
MM 81.5 Bayside, Islamorada
• (305) 664-4615, (800) 327-2880

World Wide Sportsman's new 29,000-square-foot super store opened bayside in Islamorada in late 1997, celebrating 30 years in the Florida Keys. Owned by Johnny Morris of Bass Pro Shops, World Wide continues its longstanding tradition of booking complete fishing tours through its six-person travel agency (see previous listing under Guides and Charters). The new facility features a full-service marina of 40 to 50 slips, accommodating boats up to 42 feet in length. Many of the area guides launch from these facilities. The marina offers a fuel dock (both gas and diesel) as well as frozen, live and fresh bait. Seacraft and SilverKing boats are sold here. World Wide is stocked to the rafters with a wide assortment of fishing tackle, including Billy Pate, Tibor, Penn, Sage and Orvis. You'll find fly-tying materials and an assortment of flies — even the Cockroach for tarpon. A rod and reel repair center is on premises. ExOfficio, Woolrich, Bimini Bay, Sportif and Columbia fishing clothes for both men and women are offered. This fishing emporium is every angler's dream store.

Bonefish Bob's
MM 81 Bayside, Islamorada
• (305) 664-9420

This unique outfitter carries all kinds of tackle but specializes in fly-fishing gear and collectibles. Bob stocks Thomas & Thomas and Winston rods and Penn, Abel, Sea Master and Lamson reels. One of the 6,000 flies he has in stock is a Clouser Minnow, a chartreuse and white fly that entices bonefish, snook, trout, permit and even tarpon. You can find a nifty fly-tying table and all supplies here too. Bob sells more than 400 used rods and maintains a collection of antique fishing memorabilia, including everything from old books to bam-

boo poles. Expert advice is free for the asking, and the owner gives free fly-casting lessons on the lawn out back.

Middle Keys

World Class Angler
MM 50 Bayside, Marathon
• (305) 743-6139

World Class Angler sells Penn, Shimano, Daiwa and Shakespeare reels and Star and Ricky's rods. Ricky's rods are custom-made in Miami, ready in a couple of days to your specifications. The store stocks an assortment of flies — look for the Tarpon Bunny — and Redington and Penn fly rods. World Class specializes in the tarpon worm lure. The worm hatches at night for two nights in a row, and then in two weeks another worm hatch takes place. No one can predict exactly when the hatchlings will happen, usually in June, but the tarpon go wild over the worms. So, we are told, do the anglers.

Faro Blanco Outfitters
MM 48.5 Bayside, Marathon
• (305) 743-9018

In the base of the Faro Blanco lighthouse, off-road in the Faro Blanco Marine Resort, this full-service outfitter carries G. Loomis and Star rods, Shimano and Penn reels and Abel, G. Loomis, Tibor and Scientific Anglers fly gear. A local fly-tier works on the premises; bonefish like his Crazy Charlie. You'll find Columbia, Sea Harbor, AFTCO and Canyon Gear clothing.

Lower Keys

Jigs Bait and Tackle
MM 30.5 Bayside, Big Pine Key
• (305) 872-1040

Jigs features Ace, Island and Hair Ball lures, handmade in the Keys. The store carries Ricky's rods, custom-made in Miami, and Fenwick and Sea Star. Jigs also carries Penn, Fin-Nor and Shimano reels and rents kayaks and rods. You'll have a choice of fresh (dead but not frozen), live or frozen bait. Jigs also stocks guns, ammo and accessories.

Ahh! The joys of cleaning the catch at the end of day.

Sea Boots Outfitters
MM 30 Bayside, Big Pine Key
• **(305) 872-9005,**
(800) 238-1746

This friendly, family-owned and operated outfitter is a Pro Fly Shop with a complete assortment of flies, including the famous Lefty Deceiver for tarpon, designed by famous angler Lefty Kreh. You'll find G. Loomis and Star spin or fly rods, Penn reels and Islander fly reels as well as a selection of Columbia, Kahala and Rum Reggae fishing togs and Sebago deck shoes. Sea Boots sells the Sportsman Collection of Florida Keys fishing videos, so you don't have to wait for that Saturday morning television show.

Key West

Because all the Keys share the same ecosystem and the same waters, fishing off Key West mirrors fishing experienced in the rest of the Keys, with several added bonuses. With the Atlantic to the south and the Gulf of Mexico to the north, there is no end to angling excitement, both in the flats and in the bluewater. In the accessible waters of the Gulf alone, more than 30 wrecks, such as the *Luchenbach* and the *Gunvor*, harbor legions of fish within their graveyard decks and holds. Hundreds of square miles of flats emanate out from Key West, all the way to the Marquesas, 28 miles west, where there is a particular abundance of permit.

Commercial shrimping is big business in Key West bluewaters, and the bonito and tuna like to follow these boats, scavenging the smorgasbord the shrimpers leave behind. You can follow too and stalk the stalkers. The most famous bluewater angler in Key West's collective consciousness remains Ernest Hemingway, who augmented his famous writing with a passion for fishing these waters. Photographs of Hemingway with his prized monster-size tarpon and sailfish cause many a covetous angler to turn green with envy.

Perhaps even more than the rest of the Keys, you'll need a guide to find the fish in the waters surrounding Key West. A busy harbor for centuries, Key West's marinas and bights are a bustling maze to the uninitiated. In this section, we describe some of the best fishing guides and charter boats doing business in Key West, with referral sources to help you locate them.

Guides and Charters

See the Guides and Charters listings in our Florida Keys section for information on prices, gear, licenses and other aspects of arranging a day on the water.

In addition to a limited number of fishing marinas and outfitters booking or referring guides or charters, Key West's fishing excursions are put together by charter agencies operated out of booths peppering Mallory Square, Duval and other major streets of Key West.

You can also book party boats at these booths. However, more than 25 charter boats dock at the City Marina at Garrison Bight, which is accessed on Palm Avenue just off N. Roosevelt Boulevard. This marina is locally referred to as Charter Boat Row. From 7 to 7:30 AM and 3:30 to 5 PM, the captains are available at their vessels to take direct bookings. You can meet them and their crews, see the offshore vessels and save money to boot. Booking a charter directly with the captain instead of a charter agency will save you a whopping 20 percent. The captains assure us a visit to Charter Boat Row, even in high season, will net you a score, for there will always be a boat available for charter.

This is the place to come to see the catch as well. The boats come in between 3:30 and 4 PM and hang their catch for all to see. You can watch the mates clean the fish and greedy pelicans feast on the remains.

We have compiled a list of fishing marinas, outfitters and charter agencies to call to secure an offshore charter or flats guide in Key West. Some guides are willing to captain your private vessel at a much-reduced charter rate. If this is of interest to you, inquire when you call one of these central booking or referral sources.

Central Booking Agents

Central booking services will determine your needs and book your flats/backcountry guide or bluewater/offshore charter directly. Credit cards are accepted. Deposit information and cancellation policies are listed below.

Oceanside Marina, 5950 Peninsula Avenue, Stock Island, (305) 294-4676. Credit card and deposit policies vary by captain. Inquire when booking.

The Saltwater Angler, 219 Simonton Street, (305) 294-3248, (800) 223-1629. Saltwater Angler will put 15 percent of the total fee on your credit card as a deposit. The balance must be paid to the guide in the form of cash or check.

Referral Agents

Referral agencies maintain an active list of reputable sources and will provide you with names and telephone numbers of guides. You must call the captain directly and work out the details of your charter. You should inquire if the captain takes credit cards; some do not. If you book directly with a captain at Charter Boat Row, be sure to inquire as to method of payment.

A & B Marina, 700 Front Street, (305) 294-2535.

Key West Chamber of Commerce, Mallory Square, (305) 294-2587, (800) 648-6269. The staff will mail you a list of guides or captains who are chamber members.

Murray Marine, Stock Island, MM 5, (305) 296-9555.

Party Boats

Key West party boats take anglers out to the reef, where they anchor or drift and bottom fish for more than 40 species of fish. See our discussion of party boats in The Florida Keys section for details about party-boat fishing. Be sure to note that rod rental is an extra charge, costing between $3 and $5.

All three Key West party boats are docked at Charter Boat Row on Palm Avenue off N. Roosevelt. You can call the numbers listed to make reservations, book a space at one of the booths on Duval Street and in the Mallory Square area, or simply come down to the docks and make arrangements directly with the captain. All three vessels operate at far

less than maximum capacity during most seasons, so finding a spot should not present a problem.

Can't Miss
Charter Boat Row, City Marina, Garrison Bight, Key West • (305) 296-3751

The excursion fee with the *Can't Miss* includes your rod, reel, terminal tackle and bait. Senior citizens and members of the military services receive a $3 discount on the all-inclusive fishing excursion fee. The onboard snack bar serves a selection of sandwiches and other refreshments. Mates will clean your fish, but negotiate the fee before they begin. The *Can't Miss* is available for sunset charters and private trips to the Dry Tortugas.

Daily excursions are from noon to 5 PM and cost $30 for adults, $20 for children. Evening outings, June through August only, are at 6:30 PM to 1 AM and cost $30 for adults.

Capt. John's Greyhound V
Charter Boat Row, City Marina, Garrison Bight, Key West • (305) 296-5139

The *Greyhound V* gears up for the busy holiday season by offering two daily four-hour trips, at 8:30 AM and 1 PM, from December 26 to December 31. The party boat does not operate in the month of September. The mates charge 25¢ to clean a small fish and $1 for a fish 20 inches and longer.

Daily trips are from 11 AM to 4 PM and cost $25 for adults and $18 for children. Passengers who would like to ride along and use the sun deck instead of fishing may do so for $12.

Gulf Stream III
Charter Boat Row, City Marina, Garrison Bight, Key West • (305) 296-8494

The *Gulf Stream III* provides a full-service lunch counter offering sandwiches, beer and soda. Ever prepared, the crew will provide free motion-sickness pills if the need arises. The mates will clean your catch for 30¢ apiece.

Daily excursions September through June are from 9:30 AM to 4:30 PM and cost $30 for adults, $20 for children. Evening outings are conducted in July and August only, from 6:30 PM to 1 AM. The price is $30 for adults and $20 for children. Sunbathers may come along on this party boat for half-price.

Outfitters

The Saltwater Angler
219 Simonton St., Key West
• (305) 294-3248, (800) 223-1629

Owned by Jeffrey Cardenas, the 1989 Fly Fishing Guide of the Year, The Saltwater Angler specializes in fly tackle. Look for Sage, G. Loomis, Billy Pate, Orvis, Scott and Thomas & Thomas rods; and Orvis, Lamson, Sage, Tibor, Loop, Fin-Nor, Sea Master and Abel reels. The store also stocks a full assortment of flies and fly-tying materials. You'll find the tarpon's favorite, Black Death, here. You can also select from a complete line of top-brand fishing apparel by Royal Robbins, ExOfficio, Orvis, Patagonia and Columbia. Books and artwork with an angling theme round out their offerings. Look in the racks for Cardenas' *Marquesa*, a natural history of the Marquesas Keys and a description of the author's houseboat sojourn in those waters.

Probably the most popular and hassle-free way to dive or snorkel in the Florida Keys is to go out with a dive charter.

Diving and Snorkeling

The greatest treasure of the Florida Keys, the most extensive living coral reef system in North America, lies 4 to 5 miles offshore beneath the sea, hidden but not yet lost (see our Paradise Found chapter).

Ranking as the third-largest reef system and one of the most popular dive destinations in the world, the Florida Keys' reef runs 192 miles from Virginia Key in Biscayne Bay all the way to the Dry Tortugas in the Gulf of Mexico. A fragile symbiotic city of sea creatures crowds our reef — fishes, sponges, jellyfish, anemones, worms, snails, crabs, lobsters, rays, turtles and, of course, both soft and stony corals — sometimes mixing it up with sunken bounty of a different kind: shipwrecks of yesteryear.

Although our coral reef appears sturdy and, indeed, has proved intractable to the many unfortunate wooden-hulled vessels it has so callously pierced throughout the centuries, this barrier of teeth is actually made up of colonies of tiny living animals. These coral polyps secrete calcium carbonate, developing so slowly it can take years for some species to grow just one inch. The careless toss of an anchor can destroy decades of coral growth in just seconds. Even the gentle touch of a finger can kill the delicate organisms instantly. When polyps are damaged or killed, the entire colony becomes exposed to the spread of algae or disease, and the reef is at risk.

To protect and preserve our marine ecosystem, Congress established the Florida Keys National Marine Sanctuary in 1990, signed into law by President George Bush. Extending on both sides of the Florida Keys, the 2,800-square-nautical-mile sanctuary is the second-largest marine sanctuary in the United States (see our Paradise Found chapter). The sanctuary encompasses two of the very best diving areas in the reef chain of the Keys: the Key Largo National Marine Sanctuary, established in 1975, which in turn envelops John Pennekamp Coral Reef State Park; and the Looe Key National Marine Sanctuary, formed in 1981. The proliferation of marine life, corals and finfish is incomparable anywhere on this continent.

Several years ago, the State of Florida adjusted its offshore boundaries from 7 miles to 3 miles. This means many of the underwater dive and snorkel sites that used to be referred to as John Pennekamp Coral Reef State Park are now actually part of the Key Largo National Marine Sanctuary. Many dive operators and much promotional literature still refer to diving and snorkeling in Pennekamp Park. The actual boundaries of the park are much smaller than they used to be. To clear up the confusion remember: Key Largo National Marine Sanctuary encompasses the waters of John Pennekamp Coral Reef State Park, but Pennekamp is not synonymous with the sanctuary.

In this chapter we provide you with a rundown of great reef and wreck dives and snorkel adventures from Key Largo to the Dry Tortugas. Our reefs are not within swimming distance of the shore, so you will need to make your way by boat. If you plan to venture out on your own craft or in a rental boat, be sure to stop at a dive center or marine supply store and purchase a nautical map that notates the exact coordinates for dive and snorkel sites (see our listings in this chapter). Motor to the reef only if you know the waters, are an experienced boat handler and can read the nautical charts well. You are financially liable for damage to the reef, so always anchor only at mooring buoys when provided or on sandy areas of the sea bottom. Florida law dictates you fly the diver-down flag, which is red with a diagonal white stripe, to warn other boaters that divers are underwater within 100 feet of your craft.

Probably the most popular and hassle-free way to dive or snorkel in the Florida Keys is to go out with a dive charter. Most reputable dive centers in the Keys belong to the Keys Association of Dive Operators, which sets standards of safety and professionalism. Crews are trained in CPR, first aid and handling dive emergencies. Emergency oxygen supplies are kept on board. The dive captains, who must be licensed by the U.S. Coast Guard, judge weather conditions and water visibility each day and select the best sites suited to your experience level. Often their coveted knowledge of little-visited patch reefs and wrecks affords you an experience you could not duplicate on your own. We offer you a guide to dive centers, noting the comprehensive services ranging from instruction and underwater excursions to equipment rentals and sales.

In the Florida Keys, divers usually are not accompanied in the water by the crew or dive master. Divers spread out across a shallow reef, two by two, swimming in a buddy system. The dive master stays on board and watches everyone from the boat. You must prove your experience level by showing current dive certification and your dive log before you may go out on a dive charter. If you have not have made a comparable dive within the past six months, you must hire an instructor to accompany you in the water. Be sure you are comfortable with the sea conditions and that they are consistent with your level of exper-

tise. If this is your first dive, alert the crew so they can help you.

Whether you dive on your own or go out to the reef with a charter, you should be aware of the strong current of the outgoing tidal flow and in the Gulf Stream. It is easy to overlook the current in the fascination of your dive until, low on both energy and air, you must swim against it to get back to the boat. Begin your dive by swimming into the current. To determine the direction of the current, watch the flow of your bubbles or lie back into a float position and see which way the current carries you.

Be careful around bridges. The tremendous energy of the tides passing through the pilings of our bridges creates coral outcroppings that would not normally be so close to shore. Divers and snorkelers without boat transportation to the patch reefs or the Gulf waters like to take advantage of this underwater terrain to look for lobsters. Be forewarned: It is very dangerous to dive or snorkel under and around our bridges. The currents are swift and the tidal pull is strong. Boat traffic is often heavy. If you do decide to dive or snorkel here be sure to carry a diver-down flag with you on a float, and follow the buddy system. The best and safest time to tackle these turbulent waters is just before slack tide, during slack tide and immediately following slack tide. The time of this cycle varies with wind, the height of the tide and the phase of the moon.

With the privilege of diving and snorkeling in our waters comes responsibility. We sprinkle Insiders' Tips throughout this chapter because we know you also would like to preserve our fin-tastic coral reefs for all time.

For the most part, visitors freely can swim, dive, snorkel, boat, fish or recreate on our waters, but there are some Florida Keys National Marine Sanctuary regulations that took effect in July 1997 to guide these activities. Refer to

www.insiders.com

See this and many other **Insiders' Guide®** destinations online — in their entirety.

Visit us today!

Photo: Victoria Shearer

Sand Key, one of Key West's favorite dive and snorkel
sites, is marked by Sand Key Lighthouse.

our Boating chapter for information on these
regulations before you venture into our waters. For a complete copy of the regulations
and marine coordinates of the areas, contact
the Sanctuary office, (305) 743-2437.

Whether you'd like to spend a few hours,
days, weeks or a lifetime exploring our coral
reefs and wrecks, you'll find in this chapter all
you need to know to "get wet," as divers like
to say, in the Florida Keys.

In Emergencies

Divers in the Florida Keys are in good
hands in the face of a recompression emergency. The Florida Keys Hyperbaric Center,
(305) 743-9891, in Marathon operates 24 hours
a day, 365 days a year. Mariner's Hospital in
the Upper Keys (see our Healthcare chapter)
has a small hyperbaric chamber, but there are
no hyperbaric facilities in Key West.

Dive shop personnel, instructors, dive masters and boat captains have joined with members of the local EMS, U.S. Coast Guard, Marine Patrol, NOAA, Monroe County Sheriff's
office and the Florida State Highway Patrol to
develop a coordinated evacuation program to
get injured divers off the water and to the hyperbaric chamber quickly. In case of a decompression injury, call 911 and got the vic-
tim to the nearest emergency room as rapidly
as possible.

The Keys to the Reef

Most diving and snorkeling takes place on
the barrier reefs of the Florida Keys. These
linear or semicircular reefs, larger than the inner patch reefs, have claimed a graveyard of
sailing vessels, many laden with gold and silver and other precious cargo. Salvaged by
wreckers for centuries, the remains of these

wrecks entice experienced divers, some of whom still hope to discover a treasure-trove. Lighthouses were erected on the shallower, more treacherous sections of the barrier reef during the 19th century as an aid to navigation. They now also mark popular dive and snorkel destinations.

The coral reef system of the Florida Keys is distinctively known as a spur-and-groove system. Long ridges of coral, called spurs, are divided by sand channels, or grooves, that merge with the adjoining reef flat, a coral rubble ridge on the inshore edge of the reef. The ridges of elkhorn coral thrive in heavy surf, often growing several inches a year. The spurs extend 100 yards or more, with shallower extremities sometimes awash at low tide while the seaward ends stand submerged in 30 to 40 feet of water. Small caves and tunnels wind through to the interior of the reef, home to myriad species of marine plants and animals. The white grooves separating the spurs are covered with coarse limestone sand, a composite of coral and mollusk shell fragments and plates from green calcareous algae. The wave action passing between the spurs of coral creates furrows in the sand floor of the grooves.

Generally, the shallower the reef, the brighter the colors of the corals, for strong sunlight is a prerequisite for reef growth. Legions of fish sway back and forth keeping time with the rhythm of the waves. While deep dives yield fascinating discoveries for those with advanced skills — such as long-lost torpedoed ships — sport divers will not be disappointed with the plethora of sea life within 60 feet of the surface. Night dives reveal the swing shift of the aquatic community. While the parrotfish may find a cave, secrete a mucous balloon around itself and sleep the night through, sparkling corals blossom once the sun sets, and other species come out of hiding to forage for food.

Supplementing our coral barrier and the broken bodies of reef-wrecked ships, artificial reefs have been sunk to create underwater habitats for sea creatures large and small. The Florida Keys Artificial Reef Association, a non-profit corporation of Keys residents, banded together in 1980 to capitalize on putting to use the many large pieces of concrete that became available during the removal of some of the old Keys bridges. More than 35,000 tons of rubble were deep-sixed throughout the Keys' waters between 1981 and 1987, creating acres of artificial reefs. In recent years, steel-hull vessels up to 350-feet long have been scuttled in stable sandy-bottom areas, amassing new communities of fish and invertebrates and easing the stress and strain on the coral reef by creating new fishing and diving sites.

Always use a mooring buoy if one is available. The large blue-and-white plastic floats are drilled directly into the sea bottom and installed with heavy chains or concrete bases. They are available on a first-come, first-serve basis, but, if you are a small craft, it is courteous to tie off with other similar boats, allowing larger vessels use of the mooring buoys. Approach the buoy from downwind against the current. Secure your boat to the pickup lines using a length of your own rope. Snap shackles provide quick and easy pickup and release. Large boats are advised to give out extra line to ensure a horizontal pull on the buoy. If no mooring buoys have been provided, anchor only in a sandy area downwind of a patch reef, so that your boat's anchor and chain do not drag or grate on nearby corals.

Safety Tips for Divers

• Always display the red-and-white diver-down flag while you are scuba diving or snorkeling. Approaching boats must stay 100 yards from this flag or vessel and slow down to idle speed. Be sure to stay within 100 yards of your diver-down flag when you are diving or snorkeling.

• Be careful of fire or false corals of the genus *Millepora*. These tan or golden-brown platelike vertical growths topped with white

Each July, Looe Key National Marine Sanctuary hosts an underwater music festival for divers and snorkelers. See our Annual Events chapter.

Diving for Lobster

Umm, umm good. Lobster.

Now, you Easterners may conjure up scarlet visions of the mighty Maines, but when we say lobster here in the Florida Keys, a totally different creature comes to mind. Equally delectable and much in demand, the Florida lobster, or spiny lobster, is actually a crustacean whose relatives include crabs, shrimp and crawfish. Unlike its downeaster cousin, the Florida lobster is clawless. Ten spiderlike legs support its spiny head and hard-shell body, and radar-like antennae make up for bugged eyes and weak eyesight. But its best defense, and most coveted by hungry humans, remains its powerful tail muscle, which propels the lobster backward at breakneck speed.

Close-up

Diving for lobster is a popular sport in Florida Keys' waters. Like any other hunt, you will need to understand your intended prey, for self-preservation will be their only consideration. Nocturnal feeders, spiny lobsters hide underwater in crevices, between rocks, in caves, under artificial reefs, near dock pilings or in dead coral outcroppings during the day. They are not easy to spot. They occasionally peek out from their protective holes, but most often only a single antenna will be visible. The good news is that a whole gang may be hiding out together.

So how do you catch these potentially tasty morsels locals call "bugs"? We have found a few basic tools — and tricks — help swing the scales in our favor. You will need a pair of heavy-duty dive gloves, for the two large horns on the lobster's head and the sharp spines of his whipping tail can draw blood. To store your captive prizes, get an easy-to-open mesh game bag that has a fastener that you can hook to your weight belt. Be sure this bag does not drag over the reef, which would damage coral and other marine life. A probe, or "tickle stick," which is a long metal or fiberglass rod with a short, 90-degree bend on one end, allows you to wisely restrain from poking your arm into a crevice or hole in order to coax out a lobster. That hole could just as easily house a moray eel as a lobster. (This toothsome green eel has been known to clamp its enormous mouth firmly and painfully into many an unsuspecting diver's arm.) And, finally, a lobster net is a must if you hope to capture the tickled lobster.

Florida law mandates lobster hunters carry a device to measure the carapace of each lobster. (The carapace is that portion of the lobster shell beginning between the eyes and extending to the hard-end segment just before the tail). The carapace should measure at least 3 inches, otherwise the lobster — deemed a "short" — must be returned to the sea. The measuring device is most often made of plastic or metal and can be attached to a string and secured to your game bag. Measure the lobster before you put it in your bag; do not bring it to the boat to be measured.

To recreationally harvest lobsters in the Florida Keys, you must possess a valid Florida saltwater fishing license with a current crawfish stamp (see our Fishing chapter).

Look for lobsters in the patch reefs on the oceanside. Patch reefs can usually be found by using the NOAA navigational charts. Look for relatively shallow areas (15 to 20 feet) surrounded by deeper water (25 to 30 feet). If your boat is equipped with a chart recorder, use this device to detect bottom contours and the presence of fish. Look for irregular bottom areas, which will usually mean coral outcroppings and sponges. When you find the suspected patch reefs, check them out with a quick dive to the bottom before anchoring your boat. You will need to scuba dive for lobsters in the patch reefs.

Alternately look for lobster "holes" in the shallow gulfside waters and, wearing mask,

— continued on next page

fins and snorkel, free-dive for the crustaceans — a one-breath challenge for sure. These areas will appear as patches of brightness in the turtle grass floor as you skim across the water in your skiff. Sandy sea bottom looks bright also, so you must slow to idle speed and look for a hunk of coral. It helps to throw a buoy marker at this spot (connect a dive weight to a Styrofoam buoy with a length of line), because these coral outcroppings are few and far between. Send a dive scout over the side to bird dog the outcropping for antennae, and with a little luck, the hunt will begin.

You have displayed your diver-down flag. You're equipped. You're psyched. You're underwater. Now what? Stay cool and calm; move slowly. These crusty crustaceans are a wily group. When frightened, the lobster will contract its powerful tail and propel itself like a bullet backward to the far recesses of its shelter or deep into the seagrass. Tickle your way to victory. Slowly slide your tickle stick behind the lobster and tap his tail. Bothered from behind, the lobster is persuaded to slowly leave his shelter to investigate. Once the lobster is out of the hole, place the net behind (yes, behind!) the lobster with the rim firmly resting on the sandy bottom if possible. Tap the lobster's head with the tickle stick. This time, irritated, the lobster will propel backward into your net. Quickly slam your net down on the sea floor so the lobster cannot escape. Then secure the net closed with your other hand. The lobster may thrash and become tangled in the net.

Holding the netted lobster firmly with one hand, measure the carapace. Carefully remove the lobster from the net. If the lobster is a short, release it to be captured another day. If it is legal size, place it securely in your game bag, tail first. One thrust of the vigorous tail could negate all your efforts. Also, be careful not to release any other "bugs" you have already bagged. If you see a dark spot or reddish-orange nodules under the tail, this lobster is an egg-bearing female. By Florida law you must release her.

Place your captured lobsters in the saltwater-filled bait well of your boat or store them on ice in a cooler with a lid. Do not wring the tails from the lobsters until you get back to shore. It is against Florida law to separate the tail from the body while on Florida waters. Once on dry land you may pull the tails. There is negligible meat in the body of the Florida spiny lobster, so it may be discarded unless you want to boil it to make

— continued on next page

Photo: Wayne Moccia

If the lobster is of legal size, place it in your game bag, tail first.

lobster stock. After wringing the tail, break an antenna from the severed body of the crawfish. Insert the antenna, larger end first, into the underside base of the tail and then pull it out. The spiny thorns of the antenna will snag the intestinal tract, which will be removed with the antenna. If you wish to freeze the lobster tails, place several in a small plastic zipper bag, fill the bag with fresh water and place the bags in the freezer for up to six months.

We think the best way to cook Florida lobster tail is on the grill. First, with a sharp knife or kitchen scissors, butterfly the tail by cutting through the outer shell and meat. Spread the tail open and sprinkle with melted butter, salt, pepper and onion powder or garlic powder if desired. Place the tail on a double-thick piece of aluminum foil and fold the foil envelope-style, sealing tightly. Grill over hot coals for 15 to 20 minutes or until the shell is bright red and the meat is no longer translucent. Serve grilled lobster tail with clarified butter or a slice of Key lime.

Sport Lobster Season

Sport lobster season takes on festival proportions in the Florida Keys, but the competition is keen. Previewing the official opening of lobster season, the last consecutive Wednesday and Thursday in July are a designated sport season in the state and federal waters for the nonprofessional spiny lobster hunter. Every motel, hotel and campground in the Florida Keys is filled beyond capacity. Divers are allotted six lobsters per person per day; sunrise to sunset is considered a day. Diving at night is not permitted. John Pennekamp Coral Reef State Park is closed to lobstering during the sport season.

Regular Lobster Season

Regular season, which is when commercial lobstermen begin putting out their traps, commences in early August and ends in late March. Rules differ slightly in state and federal waters. The bag limit in state waters is six lobsters per person per day, or 24 per boat, whichever is greater. State waters surround the Florida Keys out to 3 miles oceanside and 9 miles on the Gulf. You may dive for lobster at night in state waters during regular lobster season.

Areas of John Pennekamp Coral Reef State Park restricted from lobstering include Turtle Rocks, Basin Hills North, Mosquito Bank North, Three Sisters North, Higdon's Reef, Basin Hills East, Mosquito Bank Southeast, Three Sisters South, Cannon Patch and Basin Hills South. Lobstering is prohibited year round in Everglades National Park, Biscayne Bay/Card Sound Spiny Lobster Sanctuary and Dry Tortugas National Park. Those waters beyond the state limits are deemed federal waters; see a NOAA chart for the official boundary lines. The bag limit in federal waters is six lobsters per person per day, or six per person per trip when the trip is longer than one day. The per-boat quota does not apply in federal waters. You may not combine the federal bag limit with the state bag limit.

Be sure to check The Florida Keys National Marine Sanctuary section of our Boating chapter for new 1997 restrictions before diving for lobsters.

Words to the Wise

- Always display your diver-down flag when you are diving or snorkeling for lobster.
- Be careful not to damage coral while you are harvesting lobster.
- Anchor in the sand or use a mooring buoy.
- Use an official NOAA navigational chart when navigating our waters.
- Do not molest, damage or take lobster from traps. It is a felony offense in Florida.
- You may not use spears, hooks or wire snares to capture or dismember lobsters.

are very smooth and lack the well-defined cups of true stony corals. If you brush against the toxic fire corals, you will feel an intense, though short-lived, sting, which usually causes a painful welt. Wear a thin-skin jumpsuit when you dive, even in the summer months, for protection.

• Float a line with a buoy behind your boat when diving in waters where there is a strong current. If you surface from your dive behind your boat, grab the line so the current does not carry you farther away. You can pull yourself into the boat, saving air and energy.

• Always dive with a buddy and keep track of each other time. Always have an octopus (extra mouthpiece connected to your air tank) as part of your dive gear. If your buddy's air runs out, you will have to share your air until you both can get to the surface.

• Snorkelers, be sure to wear a float vest so you don't have to stand on the coral to make any necessary adjustments to your gear. Divers, wear only the minimum weight you need to maintain neutral buoyancy so you do not have contact with the ocean floor. Areas that appear lifeless may, in fact, be supporting new growth.

The Florida Keys

Diving and Snorkeling Sites

We highlight 20 of the better-known and most enchanting dive and snorkel sites, listed in descending order from the top of the Keys in the Key Largo National Marine Sanctuary to the Looe Key National Marine Sanctuary in the Lower Keys. See our Key West and Beyond section for information on dive sites and dive centers from Key West to the Dry Tortugas.

Carysfort Reef

At the extreme end of Key Largo National Marine Sanctuary, Carysfort Reef appeals to both novice and intermediate divers. British vessel H.M.S. *Carysfort* ran aground here in 1770. The reef, now marked by the 100-foot

steel Carysfort Lighthouse, undulates between 35 and 70 feet. Lush staghorn corals, which look like bumpy deer antlers, and masses of plate coral, which overlap each other like roofing tiles, cascade down the 30-foot drop to the sandy bottom. Schools of algae-grazing blue tang and pin-striped grunts circulate among the coral heads of a secondary reef. The H.M.S. *Winchester*, a British man-of-war built in 1693, hit the reef in 1695 after most of her crew died of the plague while en route from Jamaica to England. The wreck, discovered in 1938, was cleaned out by salvagers in the 1950s. It rests southeast of Carysfort Light in 28 feet of water.

The Elbow

Aptly named, The Elbow looks like a flexed arm as it makes a dogleg turn to the right. Prismatic damselfish and angelfish, so tame they will swim up and look you in the eye, belie this graveyard of sunken cargo ships, the bones of which litter the ocean floor. The 191-foot *Tonawanda*, built in 1863 in Philadelphia, ended her short career as a tug and transport vessel in 1866 when she stranded on the reef. The c. 1877 passenger/cargo steamer *City of Washington*, cut down and sold as a barge, piled up on the Elbow Reef in 1917 as it was towed by the *Edgar F. Luchenbach*. Dynamited so it would not impede navigation, the barge's scattered remains rest near the *Tonawanda* in about 20 feet of water covered with purple sea fans and mustard-hued fire coral trees. The unidentified Civil War Wreck, now nothing more than wooden beams held together by iron pins, sits in 25 feet of water. A search of the area may yield a sighting of an old Spanish cannon, probably thrown overboard to lighten the load when one of the ships ran aground. The Elbow, marked by a 36-foot light tower, provides good diving for the novice. Depths at this spur-and-groove reef range between 12 and 35 feet and currents vary.

Christ of the Deep Statue

Perhaps one of the most famous underwater photographs of all time is of the *Christ of the Deep Statue*, which stands silhouetted against the sapphire-blue ocean waters bordering Key Largo Dry Rocks. This 9 foot figure of Christ, arms upraised and looking toward the heavens, was donated to the Underwater Society of America by Egidi Cressi, an Italian industrialist and diving equipment manufacturer. Designed by Italian sculptor Guido Galletti and cast in Italy, the statue is a bronze duplicate of the Christ of the Abysses, which stands underwater off Genoa. Surrounded by a flotilla of nonchalant skates and rays, the statue's left hand appears to be pointing to the massive brain corals peppering the adjoining ocean floor. With depths ranging from shallow to 25 feet, snorkeling is outstanding. Schools of electric-blue neon gobies congregate in cleaning stations, waiting to service other fish who wish to be rid of skin parasites. A slow offer of an outstretched arm may net you a goby-cleaned hand.

Grecian Rocks

This crescent-shaped patch reef, which ranges in depth from shallow to 25 feet, ranks as a favorite among snorkelers and novice divers. Colonies of branched elkhorn corals, resembling the racks of bull moose or elk, provide a dramatic backdrop for the curious cruising barracudas, which often unnerve divers by following them about the reef but rarely cause a problem. Colossal star corals dot the area, which is populated by a rainbow palette of Spanish hogfish and a scattering of protected queen conch. An old Spanish cannon reportedly is concealed in one of the more luminous of the star coral, placed there some time ago by rangers of John Pennekamp Coral Reef State Park. Look for a small patch reef near Grecian Rocks where old cannons and fused cannonballs litter the landscape.

Benwood Wreck

The English-built freighter *Benwood*, en route from Tampa to Halifax and Liverpool in 1942 with a cargo of phosphate rock, attempted to elude German U-boats early in World War II by running without lights. Unfortunately, the American freighter *Robert C. Tuttle* also took a darkened route. In their ultimate collision, the American ship ripped the *Benwood's* starboard side open like a can

opener. As she limped along a fire broke out on deck and attracted a German U-boat, which finished her off with two torpedo hits. A memorable first wreck for novice divers, the bow of the ship remains in about 50 feet of water, while the stern rests in but 25 feet. She lies in line with the offshore reef about 1.5 miles north of French Reef.

French Reef

Even novice divers can negotiate the caves at French Reef. Swim through the 3- to 4-foot limestone ledge openings or just peer in for a glance at the vermilion-painted blackbar soldierfish, who often swim upside down, mistakenly orienting themselves to the cave ceilings. Limestone ledges, adorned with tub sponges, extend from the shallows to depths in excess of 35 feet. Follow the mooring buoys for the best route. A mountainous star coral marks Christmas Tree Cave where, if you swim through the two-entrance passage, trapped air bubbles incandescently flicker in the cave's low light. Hourglass Cave sports a shapely column of limestone that divides the space in half, and White Sand Bottom Cave, a large swim-through cavern, shelters a potpourri of groupers, dog snappers, moray eels and copper-colored glassy sweepers.

White Bank Dry Rocks

A garden of soft corals welcomes snorkelers and novice divers to these patch-reef twins. With calm waters and depths ranging from shallow to 25 feet, White Bank Dry Rocks extends north and south along Hawk Channel at the southern end of Key Largo National Marine Sanctuary. You will feel as if you are swimming in a giant aquarium, for the lacy sea fans, feathery sea plumes and branching sea whips create surreal staging for the fluttering schools of sophisticated black and yellow French angelfish. Bring an underwater camera.

Molasses Reef

Shallow coral ridges of this well-developed spur-and-groove reef radiate from the 45-foot light tower that marks Molasses Reef. Mooring buoys bob in deeper water, about 35 feet.

Just off the eastern edge of the tower lies a single windlass, all that remains of the so-called Winch Wreck, or Windlass Wreck. Look for Christmas tree worms among the masses of star coral. The conical whorls, resembling maroon and orange pine trees, are actually worms that reside in living coral. If you slowly move a finger toward these faux flowers, they will sense your presence within a half-inch and disappear like Houdini into their coral-encased tube homes.

U.S.C.G. Bibb and U.S.C.G. Duane

Advanced divers will relish the exploration of the two U.S. Coast Guard cutters sunk as artificial reefs 100 yards apart near Molasses Reef. Both these vessels, c. mid-1930s, saw action in World War II and the Vietnam War. Both did search and rescue in their later peacetime years and were decommissioned in 1985. A consortium of dive shops and the Monroe County Tourist Development Council bought the cutters, which were subsequently stripped of armament, hatches and masts, then cleaned. In 1987 the Army Corps of Engineers sank the 327-foot vessels on consecutive days. The *Bibb* rests on her side in 130 feet of water with her upper portions accessible at 90 feet. The upright *Duane* sits in more than 100 feet of water, but you can see the wheelhouse at 80 feet and the crow's nest in 60 feet of water.

Pickles Reef

Pickles Reef got its name from the coral-encrusted barrels strewn about the ocean floor near the remnants of a cargo ship, called the Pickles Wreck, that carried them to their demise. The kegs are said to resemble pickle barrels, hence the name of the reef, but more likely were filled with building mortar bound for burgeoning construction in Key West. Look

for the distinctively marked flamingo tongue snails, which attach themselves to swaying purple sea fans, grazing for algae. Flamboyantly extended around the outside of the flamingo tongue's glossy cream-colored shell is a bright orange mantle with black-ringed leopard-like spots. Don't be tempted to collect these unusual creatures, for the colorful mantle is withdrawn upon death. With depths between 10 and 25 feet and a moderate current, Pickles Reef is a good dive for novice to intermediate skill levels.

Conch Reef

Dive charters usually anchor in about 60 feet of water at Conch Reef, but the area actually offers something for everyone. With depths ranging from shallow to 100 feet and currents varying from moderate to strong, beginners as well as intermediate and advanced divers will be entranced here. The shallow section, festive with swirling schools of small tropicals, extends for a mile along the outer reef line. Conch Wall steeply drops from 60 to 100 feet, where sea rods, whips, fans and plumes of the gorgonian family's deepwater branch congregate with an agglomeration of vaselike convoluted barrel sponges. The coral of Conch Reef was nearly decimated by heavy harvesting in bygone eras; dead stumps of pillar corals can still be seen.

Hens and Chickens

A brood of large star-coral heads surrounds a 35-foot U.S. Navy light tower within 7 feet of the water's surface on this inshore patch reef, bringing to mind a mother hen and her chicks. Less than 3 miles from shore, this easily accessed 20-foot-deep reef remains popular with novice divers. Plumes, fans and candelabra soft corals intermingle with skeletons of the coral graveyard (almost 80 percent of the reef died in 1970 after an unusually cold winter).

INSIDERS' TIP

Remember, queen conch is a protected species in the Florida Keys. All conch you see offered on restaurant menus or in seafood markets is imported. Please respect our Queen of the Conch Republic.

Jailhouse-striped sheepsheads mingle with shy notch-tailed grunts and the more curious stout-bodied groupers, but don't be tempted; spearfishing is not allowed here. Remains of the Brick Barge, a modern casualty, and an old steel barge torpedoed during World War II lie among the coral heads.

Eagle

In 1985 an electrical fire disabled the 287-foot *Aaron K*, a freighter that carried scrap paper between Miami and South America. Declared a total loss, she was sold to the Monroe County Tourist Council and a group of local dive shops and then scuttled for use as an artificial reef. The vessel was renamed the *Eagle* after the Eagle Tire Company, which provided much of the funding for the project. A must-do for advanced divers, the Eagle landed on her starboard side in 120-foot waters, though her upper portions lurk within 65 feet of the surface. Densely packed polarized schools of silversides flow and drift within her interior. The tiny fork-tailed fish will detour around divers swimming through the school.

Alligator Reef

Launched in 1820 in Boston, the U.S.S. *Alligator* hunted pirates in Florida as part of the West Indies Squadron. A 136 foot light tower now marks her namesake, Alligator Reef, which claimed the copper- and bronze-fitted warship in 1825. The Navy stripped the ship's valuables and blew her up. The *Alligator* rests offshore from the 8- to 40-foot-deep reef, now a bordello of brilliant tropicals, corals and shells.

Coffins Patch

Gargantuan grooved brain corals join staghorns and toxic fire corals at Coffins Patch, a 1.5-mile reef popular with Middle Keys divers. A drift of yellow-finned French grunts and festive angelfish join an escort of mutton snappers, each distinctively branded with a black spot below the rear dorsal fin, as they guard the remains of the Spanish galleon *Ignacio*, which spewed a cargo of coins across the ocean floor in 1733.

Thunderbolt

In 1986 the artificial reef committee bought the *Thunderbolt*, a 188-foot cable-laying workboat, from a Miami River boatyard. The vessel was cleaned and her hatches removed. She then was towed south of Coffins Patch, where she was sunk as an artificial reef. Sitting majestically upright in 115 feet of water, the *Thunderbolt's* bronze propellers, cable-laying spool and wheelhouse are still recognizable. A stainless steel cable leads from the wreck to a permanent underwater buoy. Current is strong at this wreck. Clip a line to the eye on the buoy and walk down the line. This dive is suitable for those with advanced certification.

Delta Shoals

This shallow 10- to 20-foot shoal claimed many an unsuspecting ship through the centuries. Perhaps the most colorful history is that of an old vessel that ran aground in the 1850s. The ship yielded no treasure, but recovery of unique relics and elephant tusks led to the name Ivory Wreck. Among the wreckage were leg irons and brass bowls, leading historians to believe this was a slave ship from Africa.

Sombrero Key

A 142-foot lighthouse tower marks this living marine museum. Coral chasms, ridges and portals support a proliferation of fuzzy, feathery or hairy gorgonians as well as a salad bowl of leafy lettuce coral. A battalion of toothy barracudas swim reconnaissance, but don't be alarmed. You are too big to be considered tasty.

The Horseshoe

You spot a U-shaped jetty bayside as you crest the Bahia Honda Bridge, MM 35, while heading down the Keys. What is that thing? A couple of cars are parked on the outer two arms, and you notice a brightly colored bobbing life vest in the waters. This unmarked bit of mangrove-shrouded county land is locally called The Horseshoe, or Cuban Quarry. When fill was dug during the building of the Bahia

Photo: Wayne Moccia

Schools of colorful fish cruise the coral reef, delighting snorkelers and divers alike.

Honda Bridge years ago, a jetty-lined lagoon was formed that is now a natural aquarium popular with those in the know. A shallow sandbar at the open end keeps barracudas and sharks at bay (no pun intended) protecting a menagerie of marine life.

The shallow waters and preponderance of colorful fish make this spot an easily accessible, unpopulated "exploratorium" for snorkeling and fishing. A large pile of broken-up lobster traps, once set on fire by partying spring-breakers, litters one end of the jetty. Several local artisans regularly create patio floors from the big stone slabs used to weight the traps. To find The Horseshoe: Turn right at the first opportunity after crossing Bahia Honda Bridge when heading down the Keys. Follow the dirt road past the stack of leftover bridge pilings to the water's edge. No camping or overnight stays by RVs are allowed.

Looe Key National Marine Sanctuary

In 1744 Capt. Ashby Utting ran the 124-foot British frigate H.M.S. *Looe* hard aground on the 5-square-mile Y-shaped reef now bearing her name. Remains of the ship are interred between two fingers of living coral about 200 yards from the marker in 25 feet of water. The ballast and the anchor remain camouflaged with centuries of vigorous coral growth. Preserved as a national marine sanctuary since 1981, the 5- to 35-foot-deep waters surrounding Looe Key protect the diverse marine communities from fishing, lobstering or artifact collecting, all forbidden.

The sanctuary, like Key Largo National Marine Sanctuary in the Upper Keys, offers interesting dives for novice, intermediate and advanced divers alike. The spur-and-groove formations of Looe Key National Marine Sanctuary are the best developed in the Keys, and you can observe a complete coral reef ecosystem within the sanctuary's boundaries (see the Paradise Found chapter).

Take a laminated reef-creature guide sheet (readily available in dive shops) on your dive to identify the senses-boggling array of sea life at Looe Key: the yellowhead jawfish, which excavates a hole in the sand with his mouth and retreats, tail-first, at the first sign of danger; the wary cottonwick, which sports a bold black stripe from snout to tail; the prehistoric-looking red lizardfish, which rests camouflaged on rocks and coral; and the occasional blue-spotted peacock flounder, which can change color, chameleon-like, to match surroundings. Commercial dive charters provide excursions to Looe Key from Big Pine Key, Little Torch Key and Ramrod Key.

Dive Centers

As you drive down the Overseas Highway from Key Largo to Key West, you will notice banner-size red-and-white diver-down flags heralding one dive shop after another. More than 100 such establishments are listed in the phone book alone. To help you navigate this mine field of choices, we supply you with the best ammunition: information.

Many of the dive operations offer the same basic services and will take you to similar, if not the same, spots. But each also differs in many ways. Snorkelers and divers often are taken to the reef in the same excursion, for the varied depths of our spur-and-groove reefs can be experienced with multiple levels of expertise. Snorkel-only trips also are an option. The size of dive excursions varies greatly, ranging from 20 individuals or more to a small-boat group called a six-pack.

Dive rates are based on a two-tank, two-site daylight dive. Excursion only, without tanks or weights, ranges from $35 to $50. Excursion plus tanks and weights ranges from $50 to $65. Finally, excursion plus a full-gear package — generally including two tanks, buoyancy compensator, weight belt, regulator, octopus breathing device, gauges and occasionally mask, fins and snorkel — ranges from $65 to $80. A wet suit (only needed in the winter months) will cost between $10 and $15 extra. Always ask exactly what is included if you need a full-gear package. Snorkel-only rates, quoted for the excursion alone, run between $35 and $45. Children usually are offered a reduced fare. If equipment is routinely included, it will be so noted. You can rent mask, fins and snorkel for $5 to $15.

Virtually all of our listed dive centers offer optional dive packages, either for multiple days of diving or for hotel/dive combinations. If you plan to dive on several days of your holiday, you will save money with a package, but you will be limited to diving with one exclusive dive center. All our recommended dive centers make a one-tank night-dive excursion on demand unless otherwise specified.

You may assume, unless stated to the contrary, all featured dive centers rent full equipment and maintain a retail dive shop where you can purchase equipment, accessories and underwater camera housings if needed. You may also count on the fact that all recommended dive centers offer a one-day "let's give it a try" resort course (it averages $150) and a basic open-water certification ($350 to $400), as well as a wide selection of PADI, NAUI and other advanced classes.

You will be required to show your certification card and logbook, and you must wear a buoyancy compensator and a submersible pressure gauge. Snorkels are required equipment for all divers. To dive deeper than 60 feet, considered a deep dive, you must hold advanced certification or a logbook entry showing dives to equivalent depths within the last six months. If you cannot meet these specifications, you will be required to be accompanied by an instructor or guide, which requires an additional fee that can vary between $30 and $40. You must wear an octopus (an emergency breathing device to share air with your

INSIDERS' TIP

Please do not try to feed the fish from your hand. This changes the natural behavior and diet of the fish.

Spearfishing

One of the oldest methods for securing food from the sea was with a spear. Originally, this weapon was used at the water's surface while the hunter stood near or on the shore. Today spearfishing is practiced underwater by divers equipped with scuba gear and spear guns, equalizing the suboceanic playing field.

The 3-foot to 6-foot stainless steel shaft of the spear gun is operated with a system of rubber slings. At the end of the arrow is a sharp barb.

You must first commence the hunt. Swim very quietly and peer over every rock and ridge of the outer edges of the reef until you find the fish. Reef fish are territorial, seldom found far from their habitual hiding place. (Mutton snapper and black grouper are considered prizes.) Move slowly and carefully as you stalk the fish until it is in range. Lead the fish like you would if you were hunting with a rifle and try to hit its head. Be sure not to spearfish near any other divers.

Once you spear a fish, it thrashes about and causes justified commotion. Blood will be released into the surrounding waters and may attract sharks cruising the area. Be alert to their presence. While they will be after the injured fish, not you, the sharks may not readily make the distinction.

Be sure to check The Florida Keys National Marine Sanctuary section of our Boating chapter for restrictions before spearfishing in our waters.

The fish in our waters know the rules. Do you? You may not spearfish:

• Within 100 yards of a public bathing beach, a commercial or public fishing pier or any part of a bridge from which public fishing is allowed.

• Within 100 feet of any part of an above-surface jetty, unless the final 500 yards of the jetty extend more than 1,500 yards from shore.

• In state waters (from shore to 3 miles out) from Long Key Bridge north to the Dade County line.

— continued on next page

Photo:Frankie Wilson

The mutton snapper ranks as a favorite prey among spearfishing enthusiasts.

• In Key Largo National Marine Sanctuary, Looe Key National Marine Sanctuary, Everglades National Park and Dry Tortugas National Park.

• Without a valid Florida saltwater fishing license.

• For redfish (red drum) or these protected species: jewfish, sawfish, saw shark, basking shark, whale shark, spotted eagle ray or sturgeon.

• For ornamental reef fish such as puffers, parrotfish, angelfish, dorsal fish, trunkfish, squirrel fish or porcupinefish.

dive buddy) or carry spare air for a deep dive, and you must be equipped with a depth gauge or a timing device. You do not need advanced certification to participate in a night dive, but you must own or rent a dive light and carry a cylume stick as a backup lighting system.

All dive centers request you check in at least 30 minutes prior to the excursion's departure. Allow even more time if you are renting a full-gear package. We list the dive centers in descending order from Key Largo through the Lower Keys. See our Diving and Snorkeling Key West and Beyond section of this chapter for the underwater finale.

Upper Keys

Captain Slate's Atlantis Dive Center
MM 106.5 Oceanside, 51 Garden Cove Dr., Key Largo • (305) 451-3020, (800) 331-3483

Watch Captain Slate feed bait fish to a barracuda, mouth to mouth. See him cuddle with a moray eel. The Friday morning dive trips are showtimes at Captain Slate's Atlantis Dive Center, when the captain himself performs these fearless feats underwater at the *City of Washington* and *Mike's Wreck*. Divers from all skill levels enjoy outings with the Atlantis Dive Center. A minimum of only two divers is necessary for a charter to head for the reef or for one of the nearby wrecks. Snorkelers accompany divers to two locations, or they can make a snorkel-only excursion to one destination aboard a glass-bottom boat at 9:30 AM, 12:30 PM and 3:30 PM. Snorkeling rates here include mask, fins, snorkel and safety vest. Dive

departure times at Captain Slate's are 8:30 AM and 1 PM.

A special feature of Captain Slate's is the custom underwater wedding package. Divers are married in front of the Christ of the Deep Statue at Key Largo Dry Rocks. Vows are made via underwater slates as guest-divers watch the ceremony from the ocean floor and guest-snorkelers view the proceedings from overhead. Guest-landlubbers are accommodated in the glass-bottom boat, where the perspective varies yet again. Videos and still-photography of the blessed event are also available.

Sharky's Dive Center
MM 106 Bayside, Key Largo
• (305) 453-3711, (800) 935-3483

Sharky's high-speed catamaran transcends the waters covering dive sites from Carysfort Reef at the north end of Key Largo National Marine Sanctuary to the *Eagle* in Islamorada. If desired, Sharky's will design a custom, three-tank dive trip for you, consisting of one deep dive and two shallower ones. Dive departures are at 8:30 AM and 1 PM.

Snorkelers head out to the shallower reefs of the sanctuary at 9:30 AM, 12:30 and 3:30 PM daily. Uniquely available during these trips is the option of a guided snuba tour, which is a combination of scuba and snorkeling, to 20 feet below the surface. Instead of using your snorkel, you are attached to the surface with a long air hose, from which you breath much as you would if you were scuba diving. An instructor gives you a short training session on board the boat before you go down under. All you need is snorkel gear and your bathing

INSIDERS' TIP

There are old divers and bold divers, but few old, bold divers.

suit. Those wishing to simply go along for the ride may do so for $15.

Harry Keitz's American Diving Headquarters Inc.
MM 105.5, Bayside, Key Largo
• **(305) 451-0037, (800) 634-8464**

Hop aboard and explore virtually all the dive sites of Key Largo National Marine Sanctuary with this, the oldest dive operation in the Keys, which has helped folks get wet since 1962. Harry Keitz and company extends a watertight guarantee that you'll have a good time. He guarantees you'll be happy with the boats, crew and dive sites, or he'll refund your money. Dive departures are at 8:30 AM and 1:15 PM.

Snorkelers may accompany divers on the two-destination daytime trips, or they may book a snorkel-only trip at 9 AM, noon or 3 PM. Night dives are scheduled if the demand is great enough. American Diving Headquarters customizes instruction so you can take your open-water certification over two consecutive weekends if you want.

Kelly's on the Bay and Aqua-Nuts Dive Center
MM 104.2, Bayside, Key Largo
• **(305) 451-1622, (800) 226-0415**

At Kelly's on the Bay, you can literally step off the boat and fall into bed, because this dive operation is a complete waterfront resort. Aqua-Nuts will take divers to all the popular reefs in Key Largo National Marine Sanctuary and John Pennekamp Coral Reef State Park, including *Christ of the Deep Statue*, the wreck of the *Benwood*, Molasses Reef, The Elbow, the *Bibb* and the *Duane* and even to Conch Reef. Aqua-Nuts regularly schedules one-tank night dives. And unlike most dive shops, you can rent its gear without booking onto one of its charters — a real plus if you are venturing out on your own. Dive departures are at 8:30 AM and 1 PM. Snorkelers are accommodated on the same trips as divers. Night dives regularly are offered on Tuesdays, Fridays and Saturdays and other times on demand.

Amy Slate's Amoray Dive Resort
MM 104 Bayside, Key Largo
• **(305) 451-3595, (800) 426-6729**

Hop out of bed and onto the deck when you scuba on an excursion with Amy Slate's. The Amoray Dive Resort's villa lodging options, complete with hot tub and pool, will cater to your every diving whim (see our Accommodations chapter). Amoray's catamaran will whisk you to the reefs of the Key Largo National Marine Sanctuary for a two-tank dive. Departures are at 8:30 AM and 1 PM. Snorkelers may accompany divers to the reef. Night dives are regularly scheduled on Thursdays and Saturdays.

Silent World Dive Center Inc.
MM 103.2, Bayside, Key Largo
• **(305) 451-3252, (800) 966-3483**

Silent World regularly visits The Elbow, Key Largo Dry Rocks, the *Benwood*, French Reef, Carysfort Reef and other popular sites within Key Largo National Marine Sanctuary. Departures are at 9 AM and 1 PM. Snorkelers may accompany divers, and family members who just want to ride along may do so for $18.50.

Pennekamp State Park Boat Rentals & Dive Center
MM 102.5 Oceanside, Key Largo
• **(305) 451-6322**

Pennekamp State Park Boat Rentals & Dive Center prides itself on being the "only authorized dive center" in John Pennekamp Coral Reef State Park, although all the Key Largo dive centers advertise themselves as diving Pennekamp State Park. The only dive center actually situated inside Pennekamp's grounds, this company's scuba shuttles regularly visit such novice sport dives as Molasses Reef, French Reef and Christmas Tree Cove, the wreck of the *Benwood* and the *Christ of the Deep Statue*. All dives are less than 60 feet, and certification requirements are stringent. If you have not dived in the past two years, you must hire a guide. If you have not dived in three years, you will have to take a review course. Dive departures are at 9:30 AM and 1:30 PM. Pennekamp does not offer night dives.

Pennekamp offers occasional telephone specials, so it pays to call and inquire. Discount coupons are available at the Key Largo Chamber of Commerce, MM 106. Snorkelers are not routinely taken with divers at this operation (see Coral Reef Park Company below), but members of your party who don't dive may go on the dive shuttles and snorkel above you. You may rent one of Pennekamp State Park's 19- to 28-foot boats if you would like to try a dive excursion of your own. Personnel will provide detailed maps of underwater sites within the park and show you exactly where to go. When choosing the size of your craft, be certain to consider that three full air tanks take up the equivalent space of one person. A 19-foot boat would be considered a four-person vessel; 22-foot, eight-person; 24-foot, 10-person; and 28-foot, 12-person. Figure in the weight of your tanks so you stay afloat.

Coral Reef Park Company
MM 102.5 Oceanside, John Pennekamp Coral Reef State Park, Key Largo
• **(305) 451-1621**

Snorkel-only excursions in John Pennekamp Coral Reef State Park leave the docks three times daily. The shallow-reef sites vary, depending upon where the least current, least wave action and best visibility conditions exist. The snorkel trip lasts 2½ hours, with 1½ hours of actual snorkeling time at Molasses Reef, White Bank Dry Rocks, Grecian Rocks, Key Largo Dry Rocks or Cannon Patch. Departures are 9 AM, noon and 3 PM.

Another option is a four-hour sail and snorkel aboard a 38-foot catamaran, which leaves daily at 9 AM and 1:30 PM. If you feel like staying close to shore, you can rent mask, fins and snorkel for $10 and paddle around in the water off Cannon Beach, where, yes, there really are a couple of sunken cannons and ancient anchors.

Ocean Divers
MM 100 Oceanside, 522 Caribbean Dr., Key Largo • (305) 451-1113, (800) 451-1113

Each day of diving with Ocean Divers brings a different adventure, for the company tries to maintain a rotating schedule of set dive sites if conditions allow. Visiting the popular sites within the Key Largo National Marine Sanctuary, Ocean Divers slips into Eagle Ray Alley and Fire Coral Cave at Molasses Reef, Christmas Tree and Hourglass Caves at French Reef and between the stands of the

rare day-feeding pillar coral. Advanced divers have a chance to visit the *Bibb* and the *Duane*. Regular departures are at 8:30 AM and 1 PM. Snorkelers ride and snorkel with divers. Night dives regularly are offered on Tuesdays, Thursdays and Saturdays and other times on demand.

Ocean Divers is adjacent to Marina Del Mar Resort. It maintains two dive shops (the second is at MM 102.5, just south of the entrance to Pennekamp Park.

Tavernier Dive Center
MM 90.7 Oceanside, Tavernier
• **(305) 852-4007, (800) 787-9797**

Tavernier Dive Center will take you as far north as French Reef and all the way south to the wreck of the *Eagle* or to Alligator Reef. While the center caters to all skill levels, if you want a three-tank dive or an all-day charter, this outfit will accommodate you. A two-tank dive with Nitrox tanks and weights is $65. Regular departures are 9 AM Monday through Friday and 8 AM on Saturdays and Sundays; the afternoon excursion leaves at 1 PM. Snorkelers may accompany divers to reef destinations.

Florida Keys Dive Center
MM 90.5 Oceanside, Tavernier
• **(305) 852-4599, (800) 433-8946**

The Florida Keys Dive Center offers divers combo wreck/reef dives. A dive to the 100-foot-deep *Duane* is followed by shallower dives at Molasses or Pickles Reef; an excursion to the *Eagle* is followed by a trip to Crocker or Davis Reef. Departures are 8:30 AM and 1 PM.

Florida Keys Dive Center will video your adventure or arrange for Nikonos or video rentals if you want a do-it-yourself setup. The center will book accommodations for you at the Ocean Point Suites, offering a discount diving package if you so desire.

Lady Cyana Divers
MM 85.9 Bayside, Islamorada
• **(305) 664-8717, (800) 221-8717**

Cyana first dove beneath the Aegean Sea in the fifth century B.C. to cut the anchor lines of the invading Persian fleet. Today you are in good hands, too, when you join a dive excursion with Lady Cyana. The friendly staff knows the dive sites within the 6-mile stretch of reef off Islamorada so well you can get wet for 10 days and never be taken to the same location twice. Lady Cyana will offer you either a two-reef dive or a wreck and a reef, visiting Pickles, Davis and Alligator reefs as well as the *Eagle* and the *Duane*.

To dive a wreck with Lady Cyana Divers, you must have made a 70-foot unsupervised wreck dive or an equivalent saltwater dive within the past year, or you will be required to hire a guide. Departures are 8:30 AM and 1 PM. Snorkelers may go out on the dive boat, although when the excursion is to a wreck and a reef, snorkelers will only be able to get wet during the second dive because the water will be too deep at the wreck to see anything.

Middle Keys

Abyss Dive Center
MM 61 Oceanside, Hawk's Cay Marina, Duck Key • (305) 289-4433, (800) 432-2242

Personal attention to each diver's every need and some friendly confidence building when necessary distinguish Mike and Elizabeth Giglio's Abyss Dive Center on Duck Key from the plethora of dive centers lining the Overseas Highway. Compact and efficient, Abyss takes only six divers to the boiler stacks of Duck Key Wreck, Porkfish Reef, the Wreck of the *Conrad* and other little-known spots, where, at 25 to 30 feet, it focuses on longer bottom time rather than extremes of depth. If you have advanced certification or have logged a dive to 90 feet in the past six months, you can dive the *Thunderbolt*, the Middle Keys' famed wreck. Missing this criteria, you can hire an instructor to accompany you. Depar-

tures are at 8:30 AM and 12:30 PM. Abyss will take snorkelers if the sea conditions and visibility allow.

Abyss Pro Dive Center
MM 54 Oceanside, Holiday Inn Marina, Marathon • (305) 743-2126, (800) 457-0134

The Abyss Pro Dive Center in Marathon subscribes to the less-is-more theory of diving, which guarantees lots of personal attention. The company takes a maximum of six divers to 48 sites spread over the reefs at Sombrero Key, Coffins Patch, Yellow Rock and Delta Shoals. Abyss will take you to the *Thunderbolt* if your certs are current or your dive experience warrants, or you can hire an instructor and explore the wreck with a guide. Departures are at 8:30 AM and 12:30 PM. Snorkelers may accompany divers on a space-available basis.

The Diving Site
MM 53.5 Oceanside, Marathon • (305) 289-1021, (800) 634-3935

If you would like to dive the *Thunderbolt* with The Diving Site, you will need to show advanced certification or three logged dives of 100 feet or greater. If that is not in the cards, don't despair. You can hire an experienced instructor to guide you through the fascinating wreck. The Diving Site finds plenty of good dives for novices and intermediate divers alike, including Yellow Rocks, Coffins Patch, Delta Shoals and Sombrero Reef. Departures are at 8 AM and 12:30 PM (1 PM during Daylight Savings Time). Snorkelers may accompany divers on the afternoon excursion.

The Diving Site offers a reduced price for the PADI resort course if two persons take it together ($125 each instead of $149).

INSIDERS' TIP

Shipworms, or teredo worms, are sea animals that have decimated the wood-timbered sunken ships off the Florida Keys. Shipworms (actually bivalves) resemble tiny clams when they are young and swim about freely. They attach to wood and bore downward and inward with their two clamlike shells, tunneling as much as three-quarters of an inch per day. Shipworms have been known to honeycomb timbers within six months.

Christ of the Deep Statue, deep in the waters of Key Largo
Dry Rocks, is a must-see on every diver's list.

Photo: Florida Keys Tourist Development Council

Fantasea Divers
MM 49.5 Bayside, Marathon
• **(305) 743-5422, (800) 223-4563**

From Sombrero Reef through Duck Key, Fantasea Divers fulfills your underwater fin-filled illusions. Coffins Patch and the Barge Wreck delight sport divers, and those with advanced certifications or a recent 90-foot dive relish the *Thunderbolt* wreck. Departures are at 8 AM and 1 PM. Fantasea Divers, formerly named Tilden's Pro Dive Shop, will take snorkelers along with divers if the site is compatible.

Hall's Diving Center and NAUI Career Institute
MM 48.5 Bayside, Marathon
• **(305) 743-5929, (800) 331-4255**

If you are an advanced certified diver or have an 80-foot dive under your weight belt, head out to the *Thunderbolt* with Hall's. This deep wreck is sitting in 120 feet of water, with her upper deck levels in slightly shallower depths. Divers of other skill levels will enjoy diving the Middle Keys' 25- to 90-foot reef specialties, from Looe Key to Coffins Patch and especially around Sombrero Reef. Departures are at 9:30 AM and 1:30 PM.

In addition to standard equipment, a deluxe full-gear package, featuring top-of-the-line

Nitrox clean gear, is also available. Snorkelers are welcome with divers at shallow reef locations. Or you can rent mask, fins and snorkel and explore the Gulf waters or the Atlantic off Sombrero Beach with a buddy.

Hall's rents and provides certification in the use of a re-breather, the newest wave in scuba diving. Four re-breathers are available. Hall's Diving Center, in Marathon for more than 20 years, offers multiple-day dive/lodging packages in conjunction with Faro Blanco Marine Resort.

Lower Keys

Underseas Inc.
MM 30.5 Oceanside, Big Pine Key
• **(305) 872-2700, (800) 446-5663**

In the Lower Keys, when you've said Looe Key National Marine Sanctuary, you've said it all. And when you need a dive center, Underseas, in business for 27 years, will take you there. With depths to satisfy all levels from snorkelers and novice divers to those with advanced skills, Looe Key is endlessly fascinating. Departures are at 9 AM and 1 PM. Underseas offers dive/lodging packages with Parmer's Place or the Big Pine Motel.

Strike Zone Charters
MM 29.5 Bayside, Big Pine Key
• **(305) 872-9863, (800) 654-9560**

Docked out back and ready to transport you to the reef for a spectacular two-tank dive are Strike Zone Charter's 40-foot catamaran, *Emerald See*, and the 45-foot *Holiday Princess*. Or maybe you'd like to visit the reef at night and witness the underwater marine life that emerges after dark. Either way, you can get wet with Strike Zone Charters when staff escort you to the Looe Key National Marine Sanctuary. Departures are at 9:30 AM and 1:30 PM.

If you'd rather see the reef from atop the water, Strike Zone will take snorkelers to the reef as well. Those who just want to come along and view the reef life through the boat's glass-bottom may do so for $25.

Looe Key Reef Resort & Dive Center
MM 27.5 Oceanside, Ramrod Key
• **(305) 872-2215, (800) 942-5397**

The friendly crew at Looe Key Reef Resort whisks you off to the Looe Key National Marine Sanctuary, where you will visit two sites with at least an hour bottom time available at each location. Snorkelers may accompany divers. Departures are at 9 AM and 1:30 PM.

Looe Key Reef Resort and Dive Center offers dive/lodging packages at its adjoining motel. The dive boat leaves from its mooring directly behind the motel so schlepping your gear is not a burden here.

Key West and Beyond

Toss out your preconceptions, because Key West is not the final destination on our reef and wreck tour of the watery underworld. Our coral reef system heads west into the sunset as it swings by Cayo Hueso into the untamed and isolated but charted waters leading to the Marquesas and the Dry Tortugas. The half-day dive excursions based in Key West do not venture as far as these outer, uninhabited Keys. You will have to charter private overnight dive excursions or travel the distance in your own motor or sailing yacht if you wish to explore these waters (see our Cruising chapter).

The reefs in the Key West area have swallowed many a ship, for this port has bustled with trade and military maneuvers for centuries. We highlight 18 of the most interesting dive and snorkel sites from Key West to the Dry Tortugas National Park. The order does not line up quite as neatly as those marching down the barrier reef from Key Largo to Looe Key. Purchase a NOAA nautical chart, which notates the exact coordinates for dive and snorkel sites, at a dive center or marine supply store before you try to find these locations in your own vessel.

Be sure to read the first part of this chapter for discussions of our barrier reef and for diver safety tips, because the information applies to the Key West portion and beyond as well.

Diving and Snorkeling Sites

Eastern Sambo

An underwater ridge at 60 feet dropping off sharply to the sand line at 87 feet goes by the name of Eastern Drop-off in this immensely popular reef area southeast of Key West. Reddish-brown honeycomb plate corals encrust the sloping reef face while boulder corals pepper the base at the outer margin of the reef. The Hook, a long spur-and-groove canyon, extends south from the Eastern Sambo reef marker. Look for cruising tarpon during the summer months. West of Eastern Sambo is a site commonly referred to as No. 28 Marker, where sea turtles and nurse sharks make their rounds of the elkhorn coral.

Middle Sambo

Coral heads and soft corals cover the sand beneath the 30- to 40-foot depths of Middle Sambo. You won't be alone as you observe the prolific lobsters haunting this area, especially in the summer months. Look for squadrons of tarpon and snook.

Western Sambo

Mooring buoys mark this popular reef area with a variety of dives to 40 feet. Fields of branch coral stretch into the blue infinity while mountains of sheet, boulder, star and pillar corals cover the dramatic drop from 28 to 40 feet. Small yellow stingrays, which are actually covered with dark spots and can pale and darken protectively when the environment dictates, lie on the bottom with their stout venomous tails buried in the sand. In the protected mid-reef area of the Cut, goggle-eyed blennies mill about with a colony of yellowhead jawfish, retreating tail-first into their sand holes when frightened.

A half-mile south of Western Sambo, the remains of the *Aquanaut*, a 50-foot wooden tugboat owned by Chet Alexander, was scuttled in 75 feet of water as an artificial reef. Scattered about amid drifts of mahogany snappers and nocturnal glasseyes, the wreck is alive with spiderlike yellow arrow crabs.

Cayman Salvager

The 187-foot-long, steel-hulled buoy tender *Cayman Salvager*, built in 1936, originally sank at the Key West docks in the 1970s. Refloated and innards removed, she went back down under in 1985 for use as an artificial reef, coming to rest on her side. Hurricane-force waves later righted her and she now sits in 90 feet of water on a sandy bottom. Look for the fabled 200-pound jewfish and 6-foot moray eel residing in her open hold.

Joe's Tug

Sitting upright in 60 feet of water, *Joe's Tug*, a 75-foot steel-hulled tugboat, was scuttled as an artificial reef in 1989. She rests inshore from the *Cayman Salvager* on a bed of coral. This is one of the most popular wreck dives in the Key West circuit. Look for Elvis, the resident jewfish who hangs out at the tug with yet another large moray eel.

Eastern Dry Rocks

Shells, conchs and the ballast stones, cannonballs and rigging of disintegrating wrecks litter the rubble zone, coral fingers and sand canyons of Eastern Dry Rocks. With depths between 5 and 35 feet and only light current, this dive is suited to novices.

Rock Key

Twenty-foot cracks barely as wide as a single diver distinguish Rock Key from nearby cousins at Eastern Dry Rocks. A 19th-century ship carrying building tiles from Barcelona went aground on Rock Key, scattering her bounty about the ocean floor. Tiles carrying the Barcelona imprint are reportedly still occasionally recovered.

Sand Key

Originally called Cays Arena by early Spanish settlers, Sand Key, 6 miles south of Key West, is partially awash at low tide. Topped by a distinctive 110-foot red iron lighthouse, Sand Key's shape, comprised of shells and ground coral, changes with each hurricane and tropical storm. Sand Key shines as a good all-weather dive and, with depths ranging to 65 feet, appeals to all skill levels. The shallows of the leeward side provide good snorkeling, with elkhorn corals and artifacts from the old brick lighthouse that was destroyed in 1846. In spring and summer, the Gulf Stream movement over the shallows provides great visibility and vibrant colors. You can easily reach Sand Key on your own in a 17- to 18-foot boat on a calm day.

Ten-Fathom Bar

Advanced divers peruse a gallery of deep dives on the western end of the outer reef system, which is nearly 4 miles long. The southern edge, Fennel Ridge, begins at about 60 feet deep, giving the site its name, then plunges to the sand line undulating between 90 and 120 feet. Encrusted telegraph cables at 45 to 55 feet, apparently snaking a line to Havana, cut across the eastern end of the Ten-Fathom Bar, competing with man-size sponges and dramatic black coral. Near the cable, Eye of the Needle sports a plateau of coral spurs. Deep, undercut ledges shelter the spotted, white-bellied porcupinefish. Divers can swim under a ledge and up through a broad "eye" to the top of the plateau. Depths max out at 120 feet, but you'll see much more between 40 and 80 feet. Be prepared for a sea squadron of fin-driven tropicals to shadow your every move.

Western Dry Rocks

Experts will love the unusual marine life at Western Dry Rocks. Novices and snorkelers will, too, because this site ranges in depth from 5 to 120 feet. Lots of coral fingers with defined gullies and coral formations laced with cracks and caves showcase species normally found more in the Bahamas than in the Keys. The deep-dwelling candy basslets hide themselves away at 90 feet, while their more gregarious cousins, the orangeback bass, hang out in the open. The dusky longsnout butterflyfish prefer dark recesses, though they will sometimes curiously peer out to see what's happening. Sharks have been witnessed regularly enough to prompt advice against spearfishing.

Alexander's Wreck

Commercial salvor Chet Alexander bought a 328-foot destroyer escort from the U.S. Navy at the bargain price of $2,000 and sank her (still sporting her deck guns) in about 40 feet of water west of Cottrell Key as an artificial reef in 1972. Though the current fluctuates from moderate to strong, the relatively shallow depths allow conscientious novices a chance to swim among the prison-bar-striped spadefish, whose bodies resemble the spade figures in a deck of playing cards; zebra-striped sheepshead, so curious if you remain stationary they may come over to investigate; or the flashy metallic gold- and silver-striped porkfish, apparently the victim of a cruel creator, for two bold black diagonal bands slash across its glittery head.

Cottrell Key

A snorkeler's paradise at 3 to 15 feet, gulfside Cottrell Key saves the day for divers when the weather is foul on the Atlantic. The grassy banks of the adjoining lakes protect the reef in east-southeast to southwest winds. Ledges and solution holes run for several miles amid intermittent coral heads and swaying gorgonians. The pits, crevices and coral caves hold great treasures: encrusting orange sponges, which look like spilled cake batter; lustrously mottled cowries camouflaged by their extended mantles; the Florida horse conchs, which will venture out of their long conical spire if you wait patiently; and the spindle-shaped freckled tulip snails.

The Shipwrecks of Smith Shoal

Between June and August 1942, four large ships met their demise near Smith Shoals, apparent unwary victims of American military mines. U.S.S. *Sturtevent*, a 314-foot-long four-stack destroyer, was only two hours out of port escorting a convoy when two consecutive explosions ripped her apart. She rests in 65 feet of water. The 3,000-ton American freighter *Edward Luchenbach*, en route from Jamaica to New Orleans with a cargo of tin, zinc and tungsten, joined the *Sturtevent* after hitting the same mine field. The *Bosiljka* also made a navigational misstep, succumbing to an American mine as she carried her pharmaceutical cargo from New Orleans to Key West. Groupers, jewfish, snappers and cobias populate the sunken 277-foot Norwegian ship *Gunvor*, taken by a mine on her way to Trinidad from Mobile, Alabama. The wreckage is scattered in 60 feet of water.

Marquesas Keys

This group of 10 mangrove islands surrounded by shallow waters has alternately been called the remains of a prehistoric meteor crater and an atoll. The ring of keys was named for the Marquis de Cadierata, commander of the 1622 Spanish fleet that included the wrecks *Atocha* and *Santa Margarita*. The wrecks were partially salvaged until 1630 by the Spanish, who enticed slave divers to search the remains, promising freedom to the first diver to recover a bar of silver from the site. The ships were rediscovered in 1985 by Mel Fisher, the famous 20th-century salvor who found a mother lode of treasure in the holds.

The islands evidence little human influence, for they remain uninhabited. Clusters of coral heads shrouded in grouper and snapper mark the southern edge of the islands. Twenty-five miles from Key West, the Marquesas appeal to divers cruising in their motor yachts or on an overnight charter or to hale and hearty daytrippers. West of the Marquesas several wrecks dot the suboceanic landscape. Exercise caution before diving, however, because the U.S. Navy uses them as bombing and strafing targets from time to time. Before you strap on your tanks, check your radio for a Coast Guard bulletin regarding this area.

Northwind

The *Northwind*, a large metal tugboat belonging to Mel Fisher's Treasure Salvors Inc., tragically sank in 1975 while working on the *Atocha* project. Said to have a malfunctioning fuel valve and a leaky bulkhead, the *Northwind* capsized while at anchor, taking Fisher's son and daughter-in-law to a watery grave. The vessel lies on her side in 40 feet of water 3.5 miles southwest of the Marquesas.

Cosgrove Shoal

A 50-foot skeletal lighthouse marks the northern edge of the Gulf Stream, 6 miles south of the western Marquesas. This rocky bank runs for miles, a prehistoric dead reef where caves and ledges support gardens and forests and social clubs of marine fin and flora. A contingent of giant barracudas patrols the shallows, and black coral grows up from the depths, which extend beyond recreational diving capacities. Be sure to take the strong outgoing tide into consideration before you dive here.

Marquesas Rock

Moderate to strong currents and depths to 120 feet dictate that this dive is only suited to advanced skill levels. A can-buoy marks the rocky plateau of Marquesas Rock, the cracks and crevices of which reveal a potpourri of sea life. A school of jacks, apparently attracted by your bubbles, may make a swing past. Saucer-eyed reddish squirrelfish, with elongated rear dorsal fins resembling squirrel tails, mind their own business in the shaded bottom crevices. Occasional sightings of sailfish, sperm whales and white sharks have been reported. Keep in mind that when diving Marquesas Rock you are 30 miles from the nearest assistance.

Dry Tortugas

The end of the line in the Florida Keys, the Dry Tortugas lie some 80 miles beyond Key West. Small boats are discouraged from making the trip, because strong tidal currents flowing against prevailing winds between Rebecca Shoals and the reef of the Tortugas can be treacherous. There is no fuel, fresh water or provisioning facilities nor any emergency assistance. Nonetheless, if your vessel is self-sufficient, if you are with a charter out of Key West, or you have traveled to the Dry Tortugas by seaplane or ferry to camp on Garden Key, you are in for the treat of a lifetime.

The eight-island chain is guarded as our southernmost national park. All living creatures below are protected from collection or capture, so a virtual mega-aquarium exists beneath the sea. The constant Gulf Stream current cleanses the waters, allowing visibility of 80 to 100 feet over the 100-square-mile living coral reef. Just off the beach on the west side of Loggerhead Key slumbers a snorkelers' paradise. About a mile offshore lies the remains of a 300-foot steel-hulled French wreck. Divers report that a monster-size jewfish estimated to be 150 years old resides under the wreck. Other wrecks are littered about the ocean floor, claimed by the reef over centuries past.

Dive Centers

We have listed the Key West dive centers for you in the same fashion and by the same criteria as their siblings up the Keys. Dive rates are again based on a two-tank, two-site daylight dive. Excursion-only charges range from $35 to $50. Excursion plus tanks and weights varies between $50 and $65. Finally, excursion plus a full-gear package ranges from $65 to $80. Snorkelers can expect to pay between $35 and $45 for their excursion. Snorkeling equipment is $10 to $15 extra. If this gear is included, it will be so noted. See our earlier section on dive centers for more information on what other features the dive centers have to offer. Descriptions of Stock Island and Key West dive centers are arranged in alphabetical order below.

Captain Billy's Key West Diver Inc.
MM 4.5 Oceanside, Stock Island
• **(305) 294-7177, (800) 873-4837**

This is the place to be if you want to dive the deep, 200-foot wrecks such as the U.S.S. *Wilkes Barre*. Captain Billy's teaches a full range of technical and decompression diving skills, including Trimix (helium, oxygen and nitrogen). Mornings see Captain Billy and crew guiding a wreck and a reef dive, visiting such popular sites as *Joe's Tug*, the *Cayman Salvager* and the *All Alone*. This excursion is $3 more than the regular reef-dive prices in all categories. In the afternoon the 30-foot dive boats head for two reefs, often the Sambos, No. 1 Marker or Cable Ledge. Captain Billy's will customize the trips to suit divers' wishes, never taking more than 12 divers on a boat. Departures are at 9 AM and 1:30 PM. Snorkelers may accompany divers to the reefs.

Captain's Corner Dive Center
Zero Duval St., Key West
• **(305) 296-8865**

Get wet with a wreck and a reef dive with Captain's Corner Dive Center, whose boat leaves from Conch Harbor on Caroline Street opposite PT's each day at 10 AM and 2 PM. Captain's Corner takes you to Western Dry Rocks, Lost Reef toward the Marquesas and the Sambos, as well as *Joe's Tug*, the *Cayman Salvager* and the airplane wreck, *All Alone*. Regular departures are at 9:30 AM and 1:30 PM. Snorkelers are welcome on the dive charters.

On Tuesdays, Thursdays and Saturdays, you can dive the twilight wreck and reef dive. First you dive a wreck, then watch the sunset from the deck of the boat. After dark, experience the after-hours sea life during a reef dive.

Captain's Corner always has instructors in the water with you, so you can sign on even if you are a novice diver. Snorkelers and riders who would like to accompany diving members of their party for the twilight dive may come at no charge.

Captain's Corner's staff of 10 dive instructors is multilingual.

Dive Key West Inc.
3128 N. Roosevelt Blvd., Key West
• **(305) 296-3823, (800) 426-0707**

Dive Key West offers "reef du jour," customizing the schedule based on diver demand and weather conditions. It concentrates on the 30-foot reef lines where the light is better and the colors are more brilliant, allowing you more bottom time. The inner reefs have large stands of coral and a high concentration of tropical fish, while at the outer reefs you will see less coral, more huge sea fans, sponges and larger finfish. For your two-dive combo you can choose between a wreck and a reef or two reefs. Dive Key West visits the wrecks of the *Cayman Salvager*, *Joe's Tug* and the *Alexander*, which, at 90 feet, 60 feet and 30 feet, respectively, offer a skill level for everyone. Regular departures are at 9 AM and 2 PM.

If you do not have the skill level for the wreck dive of your choice, you may hire an instructor to accompany you. Snorkelers will be custom-fitted with gear at no extra charge, and free instruction is available. Night dives, scheduled on demand, are always accompanied by an instructor. Departure times for the night dive vary by daylight-saving time.

Dive Key West's boats are docked at Oceanside Marina.

Lost Reef Adventures
261 Margaret St., Land's End Marina, Key West • **(305) 296-9737, (800) 952-2749**

Lost Reef Adventures customizes its dive trips one day before departure based upon the skill levels and dive site desires of interested divers. The wreck/reef (leaves at 8:30 AM) and reef/reef combinations visit the celebrated *Joe's Tug*, *Cayman Salvager* and *Alexander* wreck sites and reefs from Western Sambo to the Western Dry Rocks. Regular departures are at 9 AM and 1:30 PM. Lost

Reef offers night pilgrimages seasonally. First you can pay homage to the sun as it sinks into the water; then you will take the plunge for a one-tank twilight dive. Snorkelers may accompany divers; equipment is included in the fee.

SeaBreeze Charters of Key West
2319 N. Roosevelt Blvd., Key West
• **(305) 292-7745, (800) 370-7745**

Join SeaBreeze Charters of Key West for either or two daily dive charters. The two-tank, two-reef dives reach a maximum depth of 45 feet. Times of the excursions vary, synchronized with the setting sun. During standard time, departures are 11 AM and 3 PM. During daylight-savings time, the dive charters leave at 10 AM and 2 PM. The sunset one-tank dive, from 6 to 8 PM, visits one location. You will be treated to champagne after your sunset dive in addition to the usual refreshments of juice, snacks, beer and wine that SeaBreeze stocks on board for your post-dive enjoyment.

Snorkelers may accompany divers; equipment is included in the fee. SeaBreeze does not venture out for night dives nor does it have a dive shop. You also can book a dive package with accommodations at the adjoining Banana Bay Resort if you like.

Southpoint Divers
714 Duval St., Key West
• **(305) 292-9778, (800) 891-3483**

Southpoint Divers' two state-of-the-art Pro custom jet boats whisk you away from the dock at the Hyatt Key West in record time so you don't miss a moment of bottom time. The jet-drive systems of these boats feature no propellers and a shallow draft (like a Jet Ski), enabling them to travel in knee-deep water at top speeds of 20 to 30 knots. Morning excursions feature a deep wreck and a shallower outer reef, appealing to divers with advanced skills. The afternoon session visits shallower areas of between 25 and 40 feet,

where students and novices will delight in unmarked reefs that experience limited exposure to dive traffic. Departures are at 9 AM and 2 PM. Southpoint does not take snorkelers on its outings, preferring instead to take fewer divers to the exclusive reef sites of Trinity Cove, Kedge Ledge and the Ball and Chain. However, family members of divers are allowed to come along and snorkel on occasion. Night dives regularly are offered on Wednesdays and Fridays.

Subtropic Dive Center
1605 N. Roosevelt Blvd., Key West
• **(305) 296-9914, (800) 853-3483**

Wednesday, Friday and Sunday finds Subtropic's dive boat anchored at *Joe's Tug* for the wreck portion of its daily morning wreck/reef dive. Monday mornings the boat visits the *Alexander*. Tuesday, Thursday and Saturday it takes divers to the *Cayman Salvager*. These wreck dives require divers to hold advanced certification or equivalent experience. Subtropic also offers trips to two reefs every morning for those who are not as experienced. The afternoon reef/reef trips and the reef-dive portion of the wreck/reef excursions visit the Sambos, Rock Key, Sand Key and the Dry Rocks. Regular departures are at 9 AM and 2 PM. Snorkelers may accompany divers. The snorkeling fee includes equipment, and those snorkelers enjoying the morning trip will also enjoy a rate discount. Night dives regularly are offered on Wednesdays and Saturdays.

Situated at the far end of Garrison Bight Marina, Subtropic Dive Center also has a large selection of spear guns and offers special spearfishing courses and charters on Saturday afternoons for $99, which includes tanks, weights and spear gun. There is a four-person minimum for the spearfishing excursion to be scheduled, and visibility must be 20 feet or better. Subtropic Dive Center is a full-service repair facility for all gear.

Hit the beaches and parks, or go sky diving, parasailing, gunk-holing and bicycling. Indoors or out, the Keys have all the action.

Recreation

What's happening?

If you want to scuba dive, fish, sail or motor in our abundant waters, see the related chapters in this book. For a plethora of other stimulating diversions, read on. We show you where the action is — from sky diving, parasailing and watersports to sunset cruises, gunk-holing eco-tours and bicycling. You'll find out about our beaches and public parks in this chapter. And, if the weather isn't fine — which is rare — or you would just like to stay indoors, look here for billiards, bowling and bingo.

We give you an idea of the price range for each of your recreational choices in the preface to each category. Look for fee information for those one-of-a-kind activities within the write-up. Recreation facilities in the Keys are organized by category from Key Largo to Stock Island. Be sure to consult the Key West section of this chapter for the fun-filled selections at MM 0.

The Florida Keys
Air Tours and Sky Diving
Lower Keys

Fantasy Dan's Airplane Rides
MM 17 Bayside, Lower Sugarloaf Airport, Sugarloaf Key • (305) 745-2217

Fantasy Dan takes passengers in his Cessna 182 on 10- to 45-minute flights 500 feet over the Florida Keys. Excursions, which cover areas from the Seven Mile Bridge to Key West, operate from 9 AM to sunset. Air tours range in price from $20 to $50 per person; children's rates are less. Call in advance

or stop by the airport. To reach Lower Sugarloaf Airport, turn toward the bay at the paved road bordering the west end of Sugarloaf Lodge.

Skydive Key West
MM 17 Bayside, Lower Sugarloaf Airport, Sugarloaf Key • (305) 745-4386

Try tandem skydiving from 10,000 feet over the Lower Keys and Key West with Skydive Key West. First-timers are welcome. Allow one hour per person for this venture, including training and the jump. Soft landings are provided on Lower Sugarloaf Key. Skydive expeditions aboard a Cessna 182 depart Sugarloaf Airport between 10 AM and sunset seven days a week. Skydivers are advised not to scuba dive for 24 hours before their jump. Videos and photographs are available for purchase as souvenirs. Jumps are by reservation only. Book several days in advance during the winter season. Expect to spend between $200 to $300 for this adventure.

Beaches and Public Parks

"Life's A Beach," the T-shirts say, but first-time visitors to the Keys who expect to find soft, white, endless sand along the ocean are bound to be disappointed. The coral reef protects the Keys from the pounding surf that grinds other shorelines into sand, and so most of ours must be carted in by the truckload. Nevertheless, if stretching out in the sand tops your recreational must-do list, Man and Nature have teamed up here to bring you a stretch or two. Some of our parks and beaches, as designated, charge admission fees, and most have specific hours of accessibility.

Keys beaches do not maintain lifeguard stations. Swim at your own risk and never venture out alone or after dark.

Upper Keys

John Pennekamp Coral Reef State Park
MM 102.5 Oceanside, Key Largo
• **(305) 451-1202**

Well-known to divers and snorkelers as the first underwater state park in the United States, John Pennekamp also serves a wide palette of diversions within its land-based boundaries. You can explore most of the fascinating habitats of the Florida Keys here (see our Paradise Found chapter). Enjoy campfire programs, guided walks and canoe trips. The park offers a nature trail, beaches, picnic areas, campsites (see our Campgrounds chapter), restrooms, showers and watersports concessions (see listings in this chapter) where you can rent any equipment you might desire, from scuba gear to sailboats.

Admission to the park is $4 per vehicle, plus 50¢ for each passenger older than 5. Car and driver only may enter for just $2.50. The park is open 8 AM to sunset.

www.insiders.com

See this and many other **Insiders' Guide®** destinations online — in their entirety.

Visit us today!

Friendship Park
MM 101 Oceanside, Key Largo

This relatively recent addition to our list of parks sports a playground, a Little League field, swings and a basketball court. It's perfect for those lazy afternoons with children in tow, and it's especially inviting for picnics. The park is open from 8 AM until dusk or when a Little League game is scheduled. Admission is free.

Harry Harris Park
MM 92.5 Oceanside, Tavernier
• **(305) 852-7161**

Bring the kids along to Harry Harris, where a small beach fronts a tidal pool protected by a stone jetty. You'll find a playground, ball field, volleyball net and picnic grounds. An in-line skating park was added in 1997. Restrooms are available. To reach the park, follow signs leading toward the coast along the oceanside by MM 92.5 (Burton Drive). Stay on Burton Drive about 2 miles and follow the signs to the left. Admission is free except for

nonresidents (persons residing outside Monroe County) on Saturdays, Sundays and federal holidays, when it is $5 per person. The park is open from 8 AM to sunset.

Plantation Yacht Harbor Resort & Marina
MM 87 Bayside, Islamorada
• **(305) 852-2381**

Tucked in a tiny alcove beside the massive grounds of this resort and marina is a quiet bayside beach with a tiki bar, a grill and a watersports concession. Open to the general public, the resort offers opportunities for you to sun and swim, rent a Hobie Cat or a paddleboat and enjoy live entertainment on weekends. Lounge chairs are available for rent, and restrooms are on the premises.

Holiday Isle Resort & Marina
MM 84 Oceanside, Islamorada
• **(305) 664-2321**

Holiday Isle Resort offers two beaches with watersports concessions, volleyball and limitless grazing and quaffing at numerous lively tiki bars and waterfront grills. Lounge chairs are available for rent. Body watching and mingling top the list of pastimes at this singles favorite. Restrooms are dubbed "Kokomo Toilets." This beach extravaganza is open to the general public.

Beach Behind the Library
MM 81.5 Bayside, Islamorada

This stretch of beach has no more official name than the general location, but it does offer a playground, restrooms and showers. There is no admission charge.

Indian Key Beach
MM 78 Oceanside, Islamorada

Although there isn't much of a beach here, a swimming area and boat access are available. Admission is free.

Anne's Beach
MM 73.5 Oceanside, Islamorada

At low tide, tiny Anne's Beach holds enough sand to accommodate several blankets, but it

Photo: Victoria Shearer

Feast your eyes on the sunset while sailing aboard a cocktail/sunset cruise.

attracts sun worshipers by the dozens. Swimming waters are shallow. Parking is limited. To find Anne's Beach, slow down along the Overseas Highway southwest of Caloosa Cove Resort and look toward the ocean for a small parking lot. Blink and you'll miss it. There is no charge.

Long Key State Recreation Area
MM 67.5 Oceanside, Long Key
• **(305) 664-4815**
A long, narrow sand spit comprises the "beach" at this state park, which is fronted by a shallow-water flat. Waters are calm and easily accessible, and bird-watching and fishing conditions are ideal. The picnic area is equipped with charcoal grills. Long Key State Recreation Area offers superb oceanfront campsites (see our Campgrounds chapter), restrooms and shower facilities. Rent a canoe or walk the nature trail. Admission is $3.25 per vehicle plus 50¢ per person. Long Key State Recreation Area is open from 8 AM to sunset.

Middle Keys

Sombrero Beach
MM 50 Oceanside, Sombrero Beach Rd., Marathon
This spacious, popular public beach offers a picnic area, playground and sweeping views of the Atlantic. Swimming waters run deep off Sombrero Beach. Restrooms are available. Marathon Chamber of Commerce, along with volunteer organizations, work to keep this gem of a beach in pristine condition. There is no admission charge, and parking is plentiful.

Lower Keys

Little Duck Key Beach
MM 39 Oceanside
Offering restrooms and picnic shelters, this beach makes for an ideal lunch spot. The small

beach provides a swimming area but no life-guards. Open from 8 AM until dusk, the beach is free to the public.

Bahia Honda State Park
MM 37 Oceanside, Bahia Honda
• **(305) 872-2353**

Across the Seven Mile Bridge from Marathon, Bahia Honda State Park sparkles like a diamond. Boasting the best natural beach in all of the Florida Keys (it has been cited as such by several travel magazines), Bahia Honda State Park is a popular destination in any season. Narrow roads wind through the mangrove thickets, many of which have been fitted as campsites (see our Campgrounds chapter). Tarpon fishing beneath the Bahia Honda Bridge attracts seasoned anglers and novices alike, and the park has its own marina with boat ramps and overnight dockage. At the dive shop in the concession building, you can rent snorkeling equipment or book a trip to Looe Key National Marine Sanctuary. Groceries, marine supplies and souvenirs are sold here, too.

Bahia Honda offers picnic facilities, restrooms, guided nature walks and charter boat excursions. Admission is $4 per vehicle, plus 50¢ per passenger; car and driver only may enter for just $2.50. The park is open 8 AM to sunset.

Bicycling

You'll be able to get a "wheel" deal when you rent a bike and cycle the Keys. Rentals are offered by the day (9 AM to 5 PM), 24 hours, multiple days, week or month. The one-speed cycles, which we call beach cruisers, average about $6 for eight hours or $8 for a 24-hour rental. Weekly rentals are around $35. Most of these establishments sell parts and new bicycles, do repairs and rent helmets and other gear. Remember, Florida state law requires helmets for bicyclers younger than 16.

Upper Keys

Among the best places to bike the Upper Keys are Harry Harris Park, where bicycle lanes are provided, and on the bicycle paths in the median and along the oceanside of the Overseas Highway in Key Largo. Down the Keys, you may safely cycle through Islamorada's Old Highway, which borders the Overseas Highway on the oceanside. A bike path on the bayside now finishes a tour through Upper Matecumbe Key and on through Lower Matecumbe Keys, thereby making it possible to safely cycle from about MM 90 to approximately MM 72.

Tavernier Bicycle and Hobbies
MM 92 Bayside, Tavernier
• **(305) 852-2859**

Tavernier Bicycle and Hobbies rents cruisers (one-speed bicycles) for men, women and children by the day, week or month. Per-day prices decrease with multiple-day rentals.

Middle Keys

There are few bicycle paths in the Middle Keys. In Marathon, you'll need to cycle on the old Seven Mile Bridge to Pigeon Key (a good 2-mile-plus jaunt), use the Key Colony Beach bicycle lane (turn onto the Key Colony Causeway at MM 53.5 to get to Key Colony) or pedal along the relatively traffic-free streets of the Sombrero residential area (turn onto Sombrero Beach Road, MM 50, by the Kmart).

Key Colony Beach Marina
MM 53.5 Oceanside, 589 Sixth St.,
Key Colony Beach • (305) 289-1310

Bicycles are available for daily, weekly and monthly rentals. You'll find the marina on the Key Colony Beach Causeway on the left side.

INSIDERS' TIP

If you plan to make frequent visits with friends and family to John Pennekamp, Bahia Honda, Fort Zachary Taylor or any of the 47 state parks in Florida, consider purchasing an annual pass. The pass, which costs $69.50, allows unlimited park access for up to eight people per vehicle for one year from the date of purchase. You need not be a Florida resident to buy one.

Equipment Locker Sport & Bicycle
MM 53 Bayside, Marathon
• (305) 289-1670
MM 101.4 Oceanside, Key Largo
• (305) 453-0140

Equipment Locker rents beach cruisers by the 24-hour period or by the week. The store also offers 21-speed mountain bikes for $15 per day ($75 per week). Here, too, you can rent in-line skates with complete gear for $25 a day, knee boards, water skis or towable tubes, each for $15 per day.

Lower Keys

The Lower Keys span 30 miles, but you will have the best luck finding rental bikes toward the end of the Lower Keys, on Stock Island especially. From Stock Island, it's an easy ride across Cow Key Channel and into Key West. See our Key West section for information on Stock Island bike rentals.

Billiards, Bingo and Bowling

Yes, we do occasionally have inclement weather here in the Keys, but we never let rainy days and Mondays get us down. In addition to the three indoor leisure pastimes described in this section, the Florida Keys has a busy bridge league schedule. For dates, times and locations of weekly games with the American Contract Bridge League, see our Retirement chapter.

Upper Keys

St. Justin Martyr Catholic Church Bingo
MM 105.5 Bayside, Key Largo
• (305) 853-3442

Doors open Tuesday night at 6 PM; early birds begin at 7 PM, and regular bingo is at 7:30 PM.

Key Largo Lion's Club Bingo
MM 99 Oceanside, 232 Homestead Ave., Key Largo • (305) 451-1271

Public bingo is held Thursdays at 7 PM and Sundays at 11:30 AM.

Elks Lodge BPOE 1872 Bingo
MM 92.5 Bayside, Tavernier
• (305) 852-5615

Friday nights at the Elks Lodge feature 7 PM bingo.

Jammers Grill Room & Party Pub
MM 86.7 Oceanside, Plantation Key
• (305) 852-8786

In addition to four pool tables, Jammers offers assorted video games, electronic basketball, football, air hockey, dart boards and pinball machines. Televisions are typically tuned in to sports; a jukebox plays your favorite hits, and you can nosh the day or night away with offerings from the grill room (see our Restaurants chapter).

Coral Bowl
MM 83.5 Bayside, Islamorada
• (305) 664-9357

Even non-pin fans may enjoy the facilities at Coral Bowl, where six coin-operated and rental billiard tables ($5.50 per table per hour) are available, along with video and pinball machines. Half-court basketball in the gymnasium-style lounge is open to those older than 20. The facility — the only public bowling alley in the Keys! — has 12 bowling lanes. Rates per game for bowling before 6 PM are $2.20, adults; $1.70 for children younger than 12. In the winter season, evening prices are 50¢ higher. Coral Bowl's lounge, designed like a high school gym, offers weekend entertainment. Bowling leagues play on Thursday nights.

Middle Keys

Loyal Order of Moose Lodge 1058 Bingo
MM 54 Bayside, Marathon
• (305) 743-6062

Monday night bingo begins at 7 PM; Thursday matinee games start at 1 PM.

Disabled American Veterans Bingo
MM 52 Bayside, Marathon
• (305) 743-4705

You'll find another Monday night game here. Bingo is at 7 PM.

Elks Club Bingo
MM 51.5 Oceanside, Marathon
• (305) 743-2652

The Elks Club holds bingo on Sundays from 2 PM to 5 PM.

Gary's Pub & Billiards
MM 49 Oceanside, Marathon
• (305) 743-0622

Visitors and residents alike revel in Gary's, the upscale billiard parlor with a long, mahogany bar that is a welcome addition to the Marathon recreational scene. Brass-trimmed overhead lights dimly illuminate the nine coin-operated pool tables. A jukebox, dart boards and video and pinball machines in the back entertain those not playing pool. Some 25 television sets dot the interior. Billiard tournaments are held Sunday afternoons (see our Nightlife chapter).

American Legion Post 154 Bingo
MM 48.5 Oceanside, Marathon
• (305) 743-4783

Bingo is held each Wednesday at 7 PM and Saturday at 2 PM.

San Pablo Catholic Church Bingo
MM 53.5 Oceanside, 670 122nd St., Marathon • (305) 743-3955

Tuesday night is bingo night at San Pablo. Games are played from 7 to 10 PM. Proceeds go toward college scholarships for local students.

Lower Keys

Boondocks
MM 27.5 Bayside, Ramrod Key
• (305) 872-0022

You'll find one billiard table at this popular Lower Keys watering hole and restaurant (see our Restaurants and Nightlife chapters).

Loyal Order of Moose Lodge 1585 Bingo
MM 28.5 Oceanside, 21 Wilder Rd., Big Pine Key • (305) 872-4063

The only year-round bingo in the Lower Keys, these Monday night games begin at 6 PM.

Boat Excursions, Sunset Cruises and Gambling Junkets

Our crowning glory rests in our encompassing waters. Explore the backcountry and the waters of the Everglades National Park on group gunk-holing eco-tour expeditions (see our Paradise Found chapter) or take a glass-bottom boat trip to the reef to view the fascinating creatures residing there. Relax aboard a sunset cocktail cruise or fire up for a casino cruise.

Snorkeling-only trips average $25 per person. See our Diving and Snorkeling chapter for charters that take both divers and snorkelers to the reef. Glass-bottom boat rides cost between $15 and $20. Plan on paying about $20 per hour for a guided gunk-holing eco-tour jaunt, for these are generally small, intimate excursions. Sunset and sailing cruises range from $25 to $35 per adult, depending on the size of the vessel and length of the cruise. In most cases, children's rates are less.

Upper Keys

Everglades Cruises and Sightseeing Adventure Tours
MM 103.5 Bayside, Key Largo
• (305) 451-0639

Capt. Jerry McCauley has converted his 22-foot centerboard sailboat into an old-fashioned powerboat with a surrey top. On it, he provides one- and two-hour personalized tours of areas so secluded within the waters of Everglades National Park they are not listed on charts. Depending upon wind, tide and weather conditions, McCauley opts for any one of 100 routes. The boat carries two to six passengers; tours are provided by appointment only.

San Jose
MM 102.5 Oceanside, John Pennekamp Coral Reef State Park, Key Largo
• (305) 451-1621

Pennekamp's 65-foot glass-bottom catamaran, the *San Jose*, carries as many as 98 people on tours of the reef. Tours are offered three times daily.

Sea Dancer
John Pennekamp Coral Reef State Park, MM 102.5 Oceanside, Key Largo
• **(305) 451-1621**

If you would like to sail the wondrous waters of John Pennekamp Coral Reef State Park, this new 38-foot catamaran departs the park marina twice daily.

Everglades Safari Tours
MM 102 Bayside, The Quay Restaurant, Key Largo • (305) 451-4540, (800) 959-0742

Venture 17 miles into the waters of the Everglades National Park, in and around mangrove and bird rookery islands (see our Paradise Found chapter). Tours depart three times daily, and one- and three-hour versions are offered. A 1 ½-hour champagne sunset cruise for six passengers departs aboard an 18-foot pontoon boat at the whim of the setting sun.

African Queen
MM 100 Oceanside, Holiday Inn Docks, Key Largo • (305) 451-4655

The legendary *African Queen* — featured in the Humphrey Bogart, Katharine Hepburn movie of the same name – can be boarded in Key Largo for daily 1-hour cruises and sunset or charter excursions during the autumn and winter months. In summer, the boat goes on tour.

Morning Star Sailing Charters
MM 100 Oceanside, Marina Del Mar Resort & Marina, 527 Caribbean Blvd., Key Largo • (305) 451-7057

This 50-foot sailboat is available for private, personalized charters of up to six people (minimum of two) to the best reefs of the Key Largo National Marine Sanctuary. Half-day snorkeling, diving or sailing excursions cost $55 per person; a full day is $110 per person. A full-day charter until dark with an onboard barbecue runs $450 per couple.

Quicksilver Catamaran
MM 100 Oceanside, Holiday Inn Docks, Key Largo • (305) 451-0105

Snorkel and sunset sails through John Pennekamp Coral Reef State Park are offered daily aboard the 50-foot catamaran, *Quicksil-*

ver. Discounts and family rates are available on snorkel/sunset sail combinations. Private and group charters also can be arranged.

Key Largo Princess Glass Bottom Boat
MM 100 Oceanside, Holiday Inn Docks, Key Largo • (305) 451-4655

This princess carries passengers on royal narrated two-hour tours that drift above the reef. A full bar is on board, and guests can buy hot dogs and snacks. *Key Largo Princess* tours are offered three times daily. Family rates and private charters are available. The boat is wheelchair accessible.

Sun Cruz Casino and Key Largo Resorts
MM 100 Oceanside, SunSpreer Resort, Key Largo • (305) 451-0000

Sports betting, blackjack, slot machines, dice, roulette and video poker are among the many diversions on board *Sun Cruz Casino*. A full bar and à la carte sandwich menu satisfy hungers of another kind; a welcome aboard cocktail and hors d'oeuvres are served to all free of charge. Guests at Key Largo's Holiday Inn, Ramada or Marriott sail for free, as often as they desire. The general public may board the 100-plus foot vessel's afternoon gambling sails for $7; evening excursions are $10. The actual casino is moored each day 3 miles offshore in federal waters. Water taxis take guests to and from the casino vessel every two hours.

Caribbean Watersports
MM 97 Bayside, Westin Key Largo Resort, Key Largo • (305) 852-4707 Cheeca Lodge, MM 82 Oceanside, Islamorada • (305) 664-9598

Glide through the Everglades with Caribbean Watersports' two-hour guided Hobie Sailing Safaris and explore uninhabited mangrove islands all along Florida Bay. Environmental gunk-holing tours (see our Paradise Found chapter) at both locations provide the same guided ride in a 17-foot rigid inflatable boat that has a fiberglass hull and stabilizing inflatable side pontoons. All enviro-tours depart about every two hours beginning at 9:15 AM daily. Tours are limited to six people; you must call ahead to reserve a spot.

Freya Sailing Cruises
**MM 85 Bayside, Lorelei Restaurant
and Marina, Islamorada • (305) 664-2692**

The two-masted 63-foot schooner *Freya* makes sunset trips through the bay daily from December through April. Passengers bring their own coolers, food and beverages. The *Freya* accommodates a maximum of 35 passengers. Advance reservations are suggested.

Bud n' Mary's Glass-bottom Boat
**MM 79.5 Oceanside, Islamorada
• (305) 664-2211**

Sightseers and snorkelers aboard this glass-bottom boat stop at two locations along the reef. Depending upon weather conditions, the three-hour trip departs daily at 1:30 PM. If you plan to go, call at 10:30 AM to confirm that the trip is scheduled.

Florida Keys Paddler
**MM 77.5 Bayside, Islamorada
• (305) 664-4424**

Explore the different worlds of the Keys via kayak. Take a guided tour to the backcountry, see the botanical preserve at Lignumvitae Key, investigate the history of Indian Key, explore the wreck of the *San Pedro* or take a leisurely sunset paddle. Whew! Florida Keys Paddler offers rentals,

custom trips and instruction. They'll even deliver a kayak to you.

Middle Keys

Hawk's Cay Resort and Marina
**MM 61 Oceanside, Duck Key
• (305) 743-7000**

Sail aboard the 40-foot custom sailing catamaran *Horizon* at up to 20 knots or sign on for a more leisurely sunset cruise. Board the *Osprey*, a glass-bottom boat, on one of the twice-daily narrated trips to the reef. Or travel into the backcountry with a naturalist for a real Keys-style gunk-holing eco-tour of the out-islands near Duck Key. All these excursions may be booked at Hawk's Cay.

Many other water-related activities are available at Hawk's Cay, including charter fishing, from small backcountry trips to reef trips in full-cabin offshore boats. For those not interested in fishing, many other amusements are available, including WaveRunner and small-boat rentals, pontoon party barge rentals, parasailing and for the diver, a full-service dive shop.

Caribbean Queen Cruise Ship
**MM 47.5, 11 St. Oceanside, Marathon
• (305) 289-0400**

Take this 2½ hour sunset cruise every night

Photo: Cheeca Lodge

Parasailing allows you to soar over the waters of the blue Atlantic.

for a week and you will see something different every time. Admission is $15, boarding begins at 5 PM and departure is at 6 PM. Thursday nights offer a country theme, Friday night is Caribbean Fun Cruise Night and Saturdays and Sundays are Island Party Nights. A weekend Suntan Cruise boards at 12:30 PM on Saturday and Sundays and is only $10. A full bar is available. The boat is located next to Shucker's Raw Bar and Grill.

Spirit Catamaran Charters
MM 47.5 Oceanside, Porky's Bayside Restaurant, Marathon • (305) 289-0614

A 40-foot catamaran named *Spirit* takes passengers snorkeling to popular Middle Keys reefs twice a day, makes family charter cruises to Pigeon Key, offers marine biology tours with classrooms of children and sets off for a daily sunset cruise at the end of the day. Call in advance to make reservations.

Hoot Mon Charters
Banana Bay Resort MM 49.5 Bayside Marathon • (305) 289-1433

A conjunctive business with Banana Bay Sailing School (see our Boating chapter), Hoot Mon Charters offers an array of adventures on the water. For $25 per person, you can enjoy a snorkel trip aboard the *Hoot Mon*, a large sailboat, gear included. In the evening, the *Hoot Mon* sets off for a sunset cruise; price is $25 and includes champagne. Hoot Mon Charters also rents an assortment of do-it-yourself watercraft — kayaks, windsurfers and day sailers.

Lower Keys

Strike Zone Charters
Island Excursion
MM 29.5 Bayside, Big Pine Key
• (305) 872-9863, (800) 654-9560

This five-hour backcountry out-island excursion, which includes a fish cookout on a secluded island, will entice your entire family (see our Kidstuff chapter for more details). Tour cost is $45 per adult; children ages 6 to 9, half-price; and children younger than 6, free. A senior citizen discount is offered. (See our Diving and Snorkeling chapter for Strike Zone's underwater offerings.)

Golf and Tennis

Putters and players drive the Keys links, and racketeers of all ages play to love on our courts. Read on and be on the ball.

Upper Keys

Gator Golf
MM 93 Bayside, Tavernier
• (305) 852-3499

Offering the only miniature golf in the Upper Keys, Gator Golf is a sure favorite with the kids. With alligators and waterfalls on the premises, it's easy to see why. A full game of 18 holes is $4.50 for adults and $3.50 for children 12 and younger. Gator Golf is open weekdays from 4 PM to 10 PM, Saturdays and Sundays from 1 PM to 10 PM.

Islamorada Tennis Club
MM 76.8 Bayside, Islamorada
• (305) 664-5340

This facility maintains four clay and two hard courts, five of which are lighted for extended play into the evening hours. Two pros offer private lessons, clinics, round robins and tournaments. Open to the general public, Islamorada Tennis Club will arrange games at all levels. A pro shop and boutique are on premises. Same-day racket stringing is available. Court fees are $10 per person per hour (singles); $12 per person per match (doubles).

Middle Keys

Duck Key Tennis Garden
MM 61 Oceanside, Hawk's Cay Resort, Duck Key • (305) 743-7000, Ext. 3551

Hawk's Cay expanded its tennis program in 1997 and offers a wide range of organized tennis to both hotel guests and the general public. Regular events include a ladies' clinic, men's round robin, mixed doubles round robin, stroke of the day, one-hour free clinic and assorted drill sessions. Special event tournaments are planned around such holidays as Thanksgiving, Valentine's Day and St. Patrick's Day. Courts can be rented by the hour: $5 per person per hour for clay; $3 per person per hour for hard surface. Clay courts are lighted. Ball machine rental and private lessons are also available by reservation.

Key Colony Beach Golf and Tennis
MM 53.5 Oceanside, Eighth St., Key Colony Beach • (305) 289-1533

You can rent clubs ($2) and pull carts ($1) when you play Key Colony Beach's nine-hole par 3 public course. Greens fees are $7 for the first nine holes and $7 for each subsequent nine. Tee times are not required. The course is open 7:30 AM to sunset. Key Colony Beach Golf Course is the only public course in the Keys outside Key West.

Tennis players can enjoy the two lighted hard courts, which are open from 8 AM to 9 PM. Courts cost $4 for singles; $6, doubles.

To find the golf course, turn toward the oceanside onto Key Colony Beach Causeway at the traffic light at MM 53.5.

Wonderlin Tennis
Sombrero Resort Lighthouse and Marina, MM 50 Oceanside, Sombrero Blvd., Marathon • (305) 743-2250, Ext. 526

Marathon's favorite pro, Tim Wonderlin, together with Sombrero Resort, offers a tennis package that is difficult to beat. A $5-per-day guest fee entitles you to unlimited tennis and pool privileges at the resort; you can also purchase a seasonal membership. The four hard courts are lighted so play commences at 7 AM and can continue until 10 PM. During the high season (November 15 through April 15), Wonderlin offers morning two-hour special clinics and organized round-robin play: women's day, men's day or mixed doubles. These events are an additional $5. Private lessons may be scheduled.

Sombrero Country Club
MM 50 Oceanside, Sombrero Blvd., Marathon • (305) 743-2551

Members of Golf Association country clubs in the United States may obtain reciprocal golfing privileges at the private Sombrero Country Club by following a specific procedure; call for details. Monthly memberships are also available for nonmembers who do not own property in Monroe County.

Watersports

Pick your pleasure and make a splash — parasailing, water-skiing and kayaking. You'll find personal watercraft and paddleboat rentals in this section. For a rundown of scuba diving/snorkeling trips to the reef, see our Diving and Snorkeling chapter. Parasailing ranges in cost from $35 to $45, depending on length of the ride and height achieved. Kayaks range from as much as $10 per hour to only $35 per day. Personal watercraft single seaters cost anywhere from $30 to $45 per half-hour, $60 to $65 per hour. Two-seaters are about $45 per half-hour, $80 per hour. Count on spending about $15 to rent a paddleboat.

Upper Keys

Feet First Water-Ski Center
MM 105 Bayside, 38 S. Blackwater Ln., Key Largo • (305) 451-7194

Feet First offers lessons for beginners on two skis through advanced barefoot water-skiing. You can learn knee boarding, trick skiing and wake boarding. Half-hour, hour, half- and full-day lessons and excursions take place in Lake Surprise toward the north end of Key Largo. The water here is always smooth. Instruction/excursions range from $70 to $125. Call in advance for reservations and directions.

Florida Bay Outfitters
MM 104 Bayside, Key Largo • (305) 451-3018

Owner Frank Woll offers a wide selection of kayaks, canoes and camping supplies and provides basic lessons for using paddle floats, spray skirts and bilge pumps. The company offers guided and self-guided tours through the fascinating waters of the Everglades National Park. Guided tours include virtually all areas of the Florida Keys: through North Sound Creek, Lignumvitae Key and Indian Key, Great White Heron Refuge, John Pennekamp Coral Reef State Park and Everglades National Parks. Tours vary and range in length from half-day to overnighters. They are priced between $39 and $629. Full-moon tours also are offered on specific dates. From July through August, the facility is closed each Tuesday and Wednesday and some holidays.

It's a Dive Watersports
MM 103.8 Bayside, Marriott Key Largo Bay Beach Resort, Key Largo
• **(305) 453-9881**

It's a Dive offers personal watercraft and kayak rentals. Parasailing, water-skiing and scuba instruction are available, and snorkeling trips aboard a glass-bottom boat depart twice daily.

Coral Reef Park Company
MM 102.5 Oceanside, John Pennekamp Coral Reef State Park, Key Largo
• **(305) 451-1621**

Coral Reef Park Company rents snorkeling equipment at Pennekamp Park for unguided exploration of the nearshore Pennekamp waters off Cannon Beach, or you can sign on with one of the snorkeling tours to the reef (see our Diving and Snorkeling chapter for details). Rent canoes, kayaks or Spyaks here and paddle the mangrove water trails. Small boats also are available for hire.

Caribbean Watersports
Westin Key Largo Resort, MM 97 Bayside, Key Largo • (305) 852-4707 Cheeca Lodge, MM 82 Oceanside, Islamorada • (305) 664-9598

Caribbean Watersports maintains watersports concessions, otherwise known as beach huts, at two Upper Keys resorts. Both carry 13- to 21-foot Hobie Cats and sailboats and provide a refresher course or an overview of how to sail before you head out on the water. You'll find parasailing (try the tandem flight with a friend) every hour; snorkeling trips twice daily; snuba dive excursions (instead of wearing a tank, you are tethered to a topside oxygen tank with a 27-foot hose), for which

you must take a one-hour lesson; kayaks; windsurfers and five-passenger Jamaican bobsleds (long, inflated pontoon-style kayaks pulled by powerboats). You'll find personal watercraft at the Westin facility and water-skiing at the Cheeca, which also has a full dive center. For all these watersports, call ahead for reservations.

Kawabunga Jet Ski Rental
MM 92.5 Bayside, Key Largo
• **(305) 852-1423**

Owner Scott Ammon maintains a fleet of six 650-Yamaha WaveRunner IIIs and 750-Kawasaki Super Sports. Ammon works out of his home and provides half-hour instruction including safety tips and parameters of where and where not to go. His half-day minimum and full-day rentals include pickup and delivery between Key Largo and Lower Matecumbe Key. (He'll head farther down the Keys for an additional fee.) Discounts apply to multiple watercraft rentals or rentals for consecutive days. Call for reservations.

Roman Watersports
MM 84.8 Oceanside, Coconut Cove Resort, Islamorada
• **(305) 664-2882**

Personal watercraft rentals are available in three categories: half-hour, hour and 1½-hour outings. Water-skiing, flats fishing and customized boat charter excursions also are available.

Splash Watersport Rentals
MM 84.5 Oceanside, Pelican Cove, Islamorada • (305) 664-8892

On the beach at Pelican Cove, Splash rents personal watercraft and 16-foot skiffs for visits to the Sand Bar (a popular snorkeling and swimming site) and back. A reef boat takes snorkelers on excursions, and 16-mile guided personal watercraft tours depart before sunset and head through the backcountry.

Island Sports of Islamorada
MM 84 Oceanside, Holiday Isle Resort, Islamorada • (305) 664-9494

This facility is the only full-service windsurfing rental and retail establishment south of Miami. Professional instruction for catamaran sailing is offered. Various guided tours are also available, including historical tours of nearby Indian Key, guided kayak tours and nature tours.

Holiday Isle Watersports
MM 84 Oceanside, Holiday Isle Resort, Islamorada • (305) 664-5390

Raft, kayak and windsurfer rentals are at the southwest end of Holiday Isle's beach. Personal watercraft are available by the half-hour or hour, and parasailing trips lead adventurers 300, 600 and 1,000 feet in the air. Takeoffs and landings are smooth and dry from specially designed winch boats. WaveRunner eco-tours are also offered.

Pier 68
MM 68 Bayside, Long Key
• (305) 664-9393

You can't possibly miss the bright yellow and red building next to Lime Tree Bay Resort. Here, personal watercraft, Hobie Cats and day-sailers are available for half- and full-day rentals. If a powerboat is more your style, get that here too. A gift shop is also on the premises.

Middle Keys

Hawk's Cay Resort and Marina
MM 61 Oceanside, Duck Key
• (305) 743-7000

The watersports facility at Hawk's Cay offers parasailing, pontoon or center-console boat rentals, personal watercraft and kayak rentals.

Rick's Watercraft Rentals Inc.
MM 49.5 Bayside, Banana Bay Resort, Marathon • (305) 743-2450

Rent a WaveRunner or Jet Ski from Rick's for a half-hour or hour. Try the two-seater Yamaha IIIs. Rent your own 22-foot boat for a day for $160, but be sure to gas it up before you bring it back.

Skimmers Kayaking
MM 50 Bayside, 371 69th St., Marathon
• (305) 743-0771

Skimmers carries the Aquaterra line of sit-atop kayaks, and a variety of singles and some doubles are available for full-day guided nature tours. Your guide will arrange transportation from your accommodations. All-day guided tours ($49 per person) allow you to explore some of 10 locations, covering 4 to 6 miles, at a leisurely pace. Your guide will lead you through canals and into mangroves and take you for lunch on an uninhabited island where you can snorkel off its shores. Beverages and a light lunch are provided. Call in advance for reservations.

Wet Willy's Watersports
MM 48.5 Bayside, Buccaneer Resort Hotel, Marathon • (305) 743-9822

Yamaha Wave Ventures and Wave Raiders are available at Wet Willy's for half-hour and hourly rentals. Kayaks are rented by the day or week, and the Buccaneer beach and pool are available to all customers. New to Willy's is a guided two-hour, 26-mile sunset Wave Venture or Raider tour around the islands, harbors and mangroves. Tours must be arranged in advance, and reservations are recommended for holiday watercraft rentals. A large selection of windsurfing boards is available.

Seven Mile Marina
MM 47.5 Bayside, Marathon
• (305) 289-9849

Chris Fisher runs the watersport shop at Seven Mile Marina, where personal watercraft are available for rent by the half-hour, hour, half-day or full day. Riders must remain within his sight.

Lower Keys

Reflections Kayak Nature Tours
MM 28.5 Bayside, Parmer's Place, Little Torch Key • (305) 872-2896

Kayak tours through the Lower Keys backcountry waters of the Great White Heron Refuge make for superb gunk-holing (see our Paradise Found chapter). Guided eco-tours on sit-atop kayaks are an option. If you prefer to head out on your own, you'll be given operational and chart instructions and suggestions of where to explore. Paddle on over to the Sandbar Restaurant (see our Restaurants chapter) for lunch, a mere 10 minutes away. Kayak reservations are required. Conch cruiser bike rentals and windsurfers are both available as well.

Let's Go To The Movies

Cinema buffs can screen the latest flicks here. Tickets are about $6.

Tavernier Towne Twin Cinema
MM 91.5 Bayside, Tavernier Towne Shopping Center, Tavernier
• (305) 852-2023
This twin cinema offers Hollywood's latest creations twice nightly. Monday through Thursday individuals 65 and older benefit from discounted rates. Take advantage of the matinee on Wednesdays and Saturdays.

Marathon Community Cinema
MM 50 Oceanside, Marathon
• (305) 743-0288
This is no average movie theater. Owned and operated by the Marathon Community Theater, the cinema is small and intimate, although the screen is large. Seating is informally arranged in comfy barrel chairs around cocktail-style tables. A single movie is shown twice nightly. Matinees are offered on Saturdays and Sundays. The theater is tucked behind Marathon Liquors & Deli.

Physical Fitness

Upper Keys

Body Balance Fitness Center
Tradewinds Plaza Shopping Center, MM 101.4 Oceanside, Key Largo
• (305) 451-5761
At Body Balance you'll find Nautilus equipment, free weights and cardiovascular equipment such as NordicTrack, LifeStep and LifeCycle. Aerobics and karate are offered

here, and a pro shop carries weight-training accessories. Personal trainers are available, and the center offers a wellness program that works in conjunction with local physicians. Body composition testing provides body-fat analysis. Vitamins and vitamin supplements are sold on premises.

Middle Keys

Marathon Health & Fitness
Town Square Mall, MM 53 Bayside, Marathon • (305) 743-7618
Patrons work out in this full-service gym with Nautilus-type machines, free weights and cardiovascular equipment, including treadmills, step machines and stationary bikes. Aerobics, weight management, body-fat testing and certified personal trainers are other features here.

Lower Keys

The Body Joint
MM 30 Oceanside, 27 Quail Roost Trail, Big Pine Key • (305) 872-1142
It's a simple name for an all-encompassing place. The facility has cardiovascular equipment, stationary bicycles, treadmills, a rowing machine, a NordicTrack cross-country skier, Precor Elliptical Trainer and a full line of weights. Personal trainers offer body-fat testing and weight management. Aerobics sessions are also offered.

Key West

Air Tours

Seaplanes of Key West
Key West International Airport, 3471 S. Roosevelt Blvd. • (305) 294-0709, (800) 950-2359
There is simply no faster, easier, more incredible way to reach Dry Tortugas National Park — 70 miles due west over open water from Key West — than via seaplane. With Seaplanes of Key West, everyone on board gets a

window seat for the 45-minute flight to Fort Jefferson. In addition to navigating the skies, your pilot will point out the sights as you glide just 500 feet above the emerald waters of the Gulf of Mexico. Along the way, you're likely to spot sea turtles, rays, dolphins and a shipwreck or two.

Seaplanes of Key West offers half-day (morning or afternoon) and full-day trips to Fort Jefferson. The half-day trip encompasses 4 hours (45 minutes' flying time each way, plus 2½ hours on the island). Half-day round-trip fares are $159 for adults and $109 for children ages 6 through 12; kids 5 and younger fly for $80 each. The full-day trip takes 8 hours, 6½ of which are spent on the island. Full-day round-trip fares are $275 for adults, $195 for children ages 6 through 12 and $140 for children 5 and younger. Soft drinks and snorkeling equipment are included with the fare, but if you want lunch, you'll have to pack your own.

A drop-off/pickup service is provided for campers at a cost of $299 for adults, $205 for children 6 through 12 and $149 for children 5 and younger. Campers must carry everything, including water, into and out of the park; the extra charge covers the cost of transporting their gear.

A maximum of nine passengers can be accommodated per trip, and reservations are required. Allow plenty of lead time, especially in season, to secure your place.

Beaches and Public Parks

Higgs Beach and Rest Beach
Atlantic Blvd., Key West

These twin beaches are so close together they are often mistaken for each other. Higgs Beach offers a playground, picnic tables and nearby tennis courts. It is between White and Reynolds Streets on Atlantic Boulevard. An old wood pier makes for excellent sunbathing. The beach is open sunrise to 11 PM. There is no admission charge.

Rest Beach is smaller than Higgs Beach and is dwarfed by the massive White Street

Pier. This pier is a favorite with hopeful fishermen and dog walkers, and is sometimes called the "Unfinished Road to Cuba." Rest Beach has the same hours as Higgs Beach. Right across the street is an extensive playground called Astro City — a favorite with the kids.

Smathers Beach
S. Roosevelt Blvd., Key West

Across from Key West International Airport, Smathers is a long strip of sand that bustles with food vendors, watersports concessions and beautiful bods in itsy-bitsy, teeny-weeny suits. Beach admission is free, but bring plenty of quarters for the streetside parking meters (you'll need one per hour). The beach is open sunrise to 11 PM.

Fort Zachary Taylor
Truman Annex at the end of Southard St., Key West

Look to the left of the brick fort for a pleasant, although rocky, beach with picnic tables and barbecue grills. The locals call this place "Fort Zack"; this is where they come in droves to sunbathe and snorkel. The water is clear and deep, and you're likely to see many colorful fish congregating around the limestone-boulder breakwater islands constructed just offshore. When it gets too hot on the beach, head for the shade — there's plenty of it available under the lofty pine trees in the picnic area. The beach area is open 8 AM to sunset (see our Attractions Key West chapter for admission charges).

South Beach
Duval St., Key West

Rivaling the popularity of Smathers is South Beach, where an adjacent seafood grill and raw bar add to the appeal. South Beach is open sunrise to 11 PM. It's at the end of Duval Street near the Southernmost Point.

Dog Beach
Waddell and the ocean, Key West

Tucked in right next to Louie's Backyard Restaurant is a tiny little beach. It is a favorite with locals mainly for one reason — dogs are allowed.

Bayview Park
**Truman Ave. and Jose Marti Dr.,
Key West**

You will definitely notice Bayview Park if you are driving into Key West on North Roosevelt Boulevard, which becomes Truman Avenue. On your left as the road narrows and you head into Old Town, Bayview Park is one of the largest green spots still left in Key West. Several picnic tables are strewn throughout the park and come highly recommended for a shady afternoon lunch.

Bicycling

Rental bikes in Key West are generally referred to as beach cruisers, which are one-speed bicycles for leisurely pedaling and getting around. Rentals average about $6 to $7 for eight hours or $8 to $10 for a 24-hour rental. Weekly rentals are between $35 and $45. Tandem bicycles, offered at some of the facilities, are around $15 per day.

Adventure Scooter
& Bicycle Rentals
**Key Plaza Shopping Center, 2900 N.
Roosevelt Blvd., Key West**
• **(305) 293-9933**

Adventure has 10 locations in Key West and offers beach cruisers with locks and adjustable padded seats.

The Bicycle Center
523 Truman Ave., Key West
• **(305) 294-4556**

Single-speed bicycles with coaster brakes, locks and baskets are available at The Bicycle Center.

The Bike Shop
1110 Truman Ave., Key West
• **(305) 294-1073**

The Bike Shop offers one-speed cruisers with baskets and locks.

Conch Bike Express
(305) 294-4318

Strictly a delivery service, Conch Bike rents one-speed cruisers with baskets, locks and lights. Pickup, delivery and road service from 9 AM to 5 PM daily are free. Bike rental is $10 for the first day and $5 for each additional day.

Island Bicycles
929 Truman Ave., Key West
• **(305) 292-9707**

Island Bicycles offers a full selection of bicycles for sale and rent, including one-speed cruisers and adult trikes. Repairs and accessories are also available here.

Moped Hospital
601 Truman Ave., Key West
• **(305) 296-3344**

Single-speed bicycles with coaster brakes, baskets and locks are rented hourly, daily and weekly at the Moped Hospital.

Paradise Rentals Inc.
**Holiday Inn LaConcha,
430 Duval St., Key West • (305) 293-1112
105 Whitehead St., Key West**
• **(305) 292-6441**

Weekly rentals on beach cruisers are offered at both locations.

SUN-N-FUN Rentals
1316 Duval St., Key West
• **(305) 296-1543**
1019 White St., Key West
• **(305) 295-0696**

In addition to single-speed bicycles, SUN-N-FUN rents multispeed bikes from single-speed beach cruisers to 18- to 21-speed mountain bikes; tandem bikes (for two) also are available. Bicycles may be rented by the hour but require a two-hour minimum.

TJ's Fudge Cycle
**MM 5 Oceanside, 5704 Maloney Ave.,
Stock Island • (305) 294-7090**

TJ's relatively new cruisers may be rented for a half-day period in addition to the standard rate designations.

Billiards and the Cinema

Regal Cinema 6
**Searstown Shopping Center, 3338
Roosevelt Blvd., Key West**
• **(305) 294-0000**

Six movies run concurrently at the Florida Keys' only multiplex cinema. Tickets are $6.50 for adults and $4.50 for children and senior citizens. All tickets for shows before 6 PM are $4.50.

Cinema Shores
Atlantic Shores Resort, 510 South St., Key West • (305) 296-2491

Enjoy a movie under the stars poolside every Thursday night, weather permitting, beginning at 9 PM. The movie changes weekly; call for details. Recent offerings have included adult-oriented short subjects, foreign films and popular feature flicks you may have missed on the big screen. All tickets are $4, which includes popcorn. Cocktails are available for purchase. In case of rain, the film is postponed until Friday night.

Down Under Sports Bar
1970 N. Roosevelt Blvd., Key West • (305) 294-1970

This sports bar features two billiard tables, darts, pinball machines, video games and a half-dozen televisions that offer satellite programming. Billiards at Down Under is free.

Stick and Stein Sports Rock Cafe
Key Plaza Shopping Center, 2922 N. Roosevelt Blvd., Key West • (305) 296-3352

At Stick and Stein, 13 billiard tables are set around four bars with sports playing on 23 large- and small-screen televisions. Billiards is free before 4 PM and after 11 PM (see our Nightlife chapter).

Boat Excursions and Sunset Cruises

Snorkel-sail cruises run about $35 to $45 per person (see our Diving and Snorkeling chapter for charters that take both divers and snorkelers to the reef). Sunset cruises cost $25 to $30 depending on the libation selection and the size of the boat. Guided kayak gunk-holing tours range from $35 to $45. Glass-bottom boat rides cost about $15 to $20. Plan on paying about $20 per hour for a gunk-holing eco-tour jaunt, for these are generally small, intimate excursions. In most cases, children's rates are less.

A Key West Reef Trip
MM 5.5 Oceanside, Safe Harbor Marina, 6810 Front St., Stock Island • (305) 292-1345

Board a classic, wood sailing schooner for dive and snorkel trips to Sambo Reef or for leisurely day, sunset and evening sails. Sailing lessons and music cruises are also available on the 65-foot schooner *Reef Chief*, a classic Chesapeake Bay-style schooner. A Dead-in-the-Water Party, usually held on Friday nights, features nonstop Grateful Dead music, and a Blues Cruise each Sunday evening highlights a mix of musical sounds.

Adventure Charters
MM 5.5 Oceanside, Safe Harbor Marina, 6810 Front St., Stock Island • (305) 296-0362

Captain Tom of Adventure Charters provides half-day snorkel cruises, half-day backcountry nature excursions and half-day backcountry trips with kayaks aboard a 40-foot trimaran and 42-foot power catamaran. If kayaking is your thing, you can head through tidal streams and along mangrove islands unreachable by larger boats. To find Adventure Charters, turn at MacDonald Avenue near Chico's Cantina.

Appledore Charter Windjammer
201 William St., Key West • (305) 296-9992

Daily snorkel trips aboard this 85-foot oak-framed pine schooner head for the reef. The excursion includes a full lunch, a fruit platter, snacks and beverages, plus beer and wine for after-snorkeling libation. Gear is provided, and passengers need only bring towels and sunscreen. A nightly sail-only excursion out of the Northwest Channel offers all-you-can-drink

---

INSIDERS' TIP

Frequent and even application of your sunscreen is every bit as important as its SPF. Do not venture into the hot, intense Florida sunshine without sunscreen protection, and if you get wet, be sure to reapply it.

Snorkeling adds a new perspective to water fun for Keys kids.

beer and wine (champagne during sunset) and crudites.

During the high season, the *Appledore* fills up quickly; call with a credit card to confirm reservations in advance. The *Appledore*, which has circumnavigated the world, summers in Maine and is in Key West October through May.

Conch Charters Inc.
Holiday Inn La Concha, 430 Duval St., Key West • (305) 295-9030

Snorkel trips to the reef aboard the 42-foot catamaran *Queen Conch* last four hours and include lunch, gear and beverages. Sunset cruises also are offered.

Danger Charters
Hilton Resort & Marina, 231 Front St., Key West • (305) 744-8476 days, (305) 296-3272 evenings

Don't let the moniker fool you: *Danger* is the name of the boat, a Chesapeake Bay Skip

Jack sailboat, not any situation you will encounter on this adventurous charter. Up to six people board *Danger,* and right away owner and captain Wayne Fox assigns one of his new crew as first mate. The fun begins as the new mate learns the intricacies of tending to a huge sailboat and tacking into the wind. The boat soon travels to the backcountry, where the crew disembarks into three double kayaks and journeys through the mangrove islands. Then the sailboat moves to another location where snorkeling gear is donned. Finally, after much adventure, the boat sails back home. This half-day charter trip costs $55 per person, but there are others to choose from: full-day trips, sunset cruises and specialized bird-watching trips. Call for details.

Fury Catamarans
201 Front St., Key West • (305) 294-8899

Climb aboard one of *Fury's* 65-foot catamarans for a sail by day or night. *Fury* offers two three-hour trips to the reef daily for snorkeling — one in the morning, one in the afternoon — plus a two-hour champagne sunset sail each evening. You can buy separate tickets for either day snorkeling or sunset sailing or purchase a combination snorkeling/sunset sail ticket. Beer, wine, sodas and snorkeling gear are included in the price of your ticket. *Fury* also offers parasailing as well as a land/sea excursion package that includes a trip to the reef and a tour of Key West aboard either the Conch Tour Train or Old Town Trolley.

Discovery Glass Bottom Boat
Land's End Marina, 251 Margaret St., Key West • (305) 293-0099
This 78-foot, 124-passenger triple-decker vessel makes three trips daily to Eastern Dry Rocks. A 45-minute excursion through the harbor and out to the reef includes a narration of Key West history. Once the vessel arrives at the reef, passengers head downstairs beneath the water line where windows provide the main viewing and glass-bottom wells at the stern add to the visual feast. All trips, with the exception of *Discovery's* sunset cruise, are two hours long. At sunset, the captain cruises by Mallory Square on his two-hour and 20-minute itinerary so that passengers can view the unusual live entertainment from the oceanside (see our Attractions chapter).

Easy Day Charters
Garrison Bight Marina/Harbor Lights Restaurant, Key West • (305) 294-3095
Capt. Tom Halford takes private parties of up to six people on special interest cruises such as snorkeling or light-tackle fishing. Nature-, dolphin- and bird-watching tours head through the Lower Keys backcountry in the Great White Heron National Wildlife Refuge. Halford's 24-foot Wellcraft is equipped with a cabin, head, freshwater shower and canopy. Half-day ($300) and full-day ($450) trips are available; all equipment and a cooler with ice and beverages are included.

Eco-Charters Murray Marina
Stock Island • (305) 294-4213
Gunk-hole within the Great White Heron Natural Wildlife Refuge aboard the 30-foot river cruiser *Mangrove Mistress*, a 1930s-style wood

craft. Snorkel gear is onboard, including equipment for children. Capt. Lynda Schuh's Eco-Charters offers two half-day trips daily, each of which costs a total of $250, a price that can be shared by six people. You'll enjoy serene sunsets through the mangroves during late-day cruises at a cost of $35 per person or $175 for a charter.

Mosquito Coast Island Outfitters
1107 Duval St., Key West
• (305) 294-7178
Full-day kayak trips depart Key West by van for Geiger Key or Sugarloaf Key where guided backcountry tours include a narration of the trees, birds, fish, coral, sponges, seagrass and sea creatures (see our Paradise Found chapter). Single and double kayaks are available; half the trip is devoted to snorkeling. Gear, snacks and bottled water are provided. Children are welcome, but must be at least 9 years old to participate in the tours.

Phallosea Southern Comfort Sailing Charters
201 William St., Key West
• (305) 296-8985
The 47-foot Gulfstar motorized sailing vessel takes gay men and women on daily five-hour clothing-optional snorkel trips to reefs such as Eastern Dry Rocks and Cottrell Key. Snorkel gear and instruction plus lunch, beer, soda, snacks and sunscreen all are provided. Passengers need only bring a towel. Snorkel trips cost $70 per person. Two-hour sunset cruises include beer, soda and snacks and cost $35 per person. Summer prices are usually lower than the high season.

Liberty Fleet of Tall Ships
Hilton Resort and Marina, 201 Front St., Key West • (305) 292-0332
The 49-passenger *Liberty* summers in Boston and winters in Key West. While here, she sails the harbor twice daily, during which passengers can participate in hands-on sailing or sit back and let the captain do the work. Sunset and occasional full-moon sails also are offered. Sailors of all levels will appreciate sailing on the new 125-foot, 115-passenger *Liberty Clipper* in the waters of the Florida Keys and the Dry Tortugas. On Thursday nights,

passengers can dine on Hard Rock Café's Caribbean-style barbecue aboard the *Liberty Clipper,* and on Sundays brunch is served on board from 11:30 AM until 2 PM.

Sebago Catamarans
200 William St., Key West
• (305) 294-5687

Head out to the reef for a snorkeling/sailing adventure aboard Sebago's 60-foot catamaran or cruise Key West harbor at sunset. Complimentary drinks are served on both excursions.

Stars & Stripes Catamaran Tours
Land's End Marina, Margaret St.,
Key West • (305) 294-7877

The 53-foot catamaran *Gold Coast* is equipped to carry as many as 44 passengers but typically takes smaller groups. Don Kincaid, one of the vessel's owners, is a former underwater photographer who has established full-day nature and history tours to Western Dry Rocks, Stripe Point and Woman Key. Sandwiches, salads and beverages are included in the $69.95 per-person price for the all-day cruise. For an extra $10, add the sunset cruise with beer, wine, champagne and champagne punch. The sunset cruise alone costs $25 per person.

Kincaid also maintains a 22-foot powerboat, *Magic Hour,* that makes daytrips to the uninhabited Marquesas ($400) and half-day nature tours ($225). The boat has a maximum capacity of six.

Starship Yacht Charters
Conch Harbor Marina, Key West
• (305) 294-4346

Choose from any number of fun activities with Starship Yacht Charters. Owner Julie Airtrip will personally insure that you have a blast on her private 40-foot sailing catamaran *Starship* when you go snorkeling, sport fishing, spearfishing, scuba diving or lobstering. And be sure to avail yourself of the only boat

water slide in the world. Free snack food and cold drinks are offered, as is a photo of you snorkeling underwater. Charters are limited to six to eight passengers, so you can count on privacy.

Half-day trips are $50, and sunset trips with beer and champagne included cost $35. A new boat, a 45-foot Sea Ray, has recently been added to the operation and offers gourmet dinner cruises around Key West ($250 per couple), daytrips to the Dry Tortugas with breakfast and lunch included ($200 per person) and reef trips ($100 per person).

The Schooner Wolf
201 William St., Key West
• (305) 296-9653

This 74-foot steel-hull schooner offers nightly two-hour sunset sails, which include beer, wine, champagne and nonalcoholic beverages and feature a guitarist who strums sea chants and Jimmy Buffett music. The price for children is always half the adult price. Other offerings include an 11 AM two-hour, casually narrated cruise through the harbor ($20) and a romantic starlight sail that includes live music, $1 alcoholic drinks and 50¢ sodas. Advance reservations for all sails are recommended. Locals and visitors alike clamor to get aboard the monthly full-moon sails.

Sunny Days Catamaran
201 William St., Key West
• (305) 296-5556

Sunny Days bills itself as the "high-speed catamaran service" to Dry Tortugas National Park. Passengers aboard *Sunny Days* arrive at Fort Jefferson in approximately 2½ hours instead of the three or more needed to make the passage aboard some other vessels. As a result of the time saved, passengers aboard *Sunny Days* get a little something extra, a snorkeling side trip to one of three locations: the *Windjammer* wreck, Little Africa or Loggerhead Key. The destination of choice varies from one

INSIDERS' TIP

If you plan to explore the backcountry or go on a guided eco-tour, first read our Paradise Found chapter for a gunk-holing primer of the fascinating creatures you will discover.

day to the next depending on water conditions and visibility.

Sunny Days leaves from its berth at the foot of Elizabeth Street at 8 AM and returns at 5:30 PM daily. The daytrip fare for adults is $85 ($50 for children). A continental breakfast and lunch are included in the fare, along with snorkeling gear and instruction. Campers pay a slightly higher fee to accommodate their gear.

Western Union
202 William St., Key West
• **(305) 292-1766**

A sail aboard the 130-foot schooner *Western Union* is truly a voyage back in time. Built and berthed in Key West, the *Western Union* was launched off Simonton Beach in 1939 as a working schooner. Until 1974, she sailed the Caribbean and South Atlantic, logging more than 30,000 miles and maintaining thousands of feet of communications cables for the Western Union Company. In 1997, she returned to Key West to begin her second career as a passenger vessel.

From her slip at the Schooner Wharf at the foot of William Street, the *Western Union* offers two-hour afternoon sails and sunset and starlight cruises; she is also available for private charters and other seafaring adventures. The sunset sails include music and complimentary beer, wine and champagne.

Yankee Fleet Ferry to Fort Jefferson and Dry Tortugas National Park
Land's End Marina, Key West
• **(305) 294-7009, (800) 634-0939**

Visit Dry Tortugas National Park, 70 miles west of Key West, for a spectacular ride back in history. The seven islands were named Las Tortugas (The Turtles) by Ponce de Leon in 1513. The word "Dry" was later incorporated into the title to let seafarers know that there is no fresh water available on the islands. You'll be able to take a self-guided tour of the massive and historical Fort Jefferson on Garden Key. The protected waters surrounding the Tortugas sparkle with all the sea creatures of the coral reef and a good many shipwreck remains. With natural sand beaches and calm seas, snorkeling and swimming are a must. There is no food, fresh water, electricity or medical assistance at Fort Jefferson.

The air-conditioned tour boat, *Yankee Freedom*, departs at 8 AM and returns at 7 PM daily. The daytrip fare is $85 for adults; $76 for senior citizens, military and students with identification; and $50 for children 16 and younger. Fare includes round-trip transportation on the 100-foot vessel; snorkeling gear; a 45-minute guided tour of Fort Jefferson; continental breakfast of bagels, doughnuts, cold cereal and juice; and lunch consisting of cold salads and a make-your-own sandwich bar. Coffee, iced tea and water are complimentary; you can buy sodas, beer, wine and mixed drinks on board. Passengers are not permitted to carry alcohol to the Dry Tortugas.

Only campers staying the night on Garden Key may bring large coolers (see our Campgrounds chapter). Campers pay slightly higher fees for passage aboard *Yankee Freedom* to accommodate their gear: adults, $94; children 16 and younger, $70.

Golf and Tennis

Island City Tennis
1310 Truman Ave., Key West
• **(305) 294-1346**

Using the tennis courts at Bayview Park, Island City Tennis offers private and group lessons. It also offers racket rentals, repairs and stringing. The pro shop features Wilson tennis gear. The courts are open to all on a first-come, first-served basis; reservations are neither required nor accepted. There are no court fees for play, but lessons will incur a charge. Courts are lighted until 10 PM.

INSIDERS' TIP

Look to our Diving and Snorkeling chapter for information on dive sites and dive/snorkel excursions to the reef. Rather go fishin'? See our Fishing chapter.

Key West Golf Club
MM 5 Bayside, Stock Island
• **(305) 294-5232**

The only public 18-hole course in the Keys, this par 70 offers a clubhouse, pro shop and lessons. Designed by Rees Jones, the course has been renumbered, and a new clubhouse has been completed. Greens fees are $60 from June 1 to October 31 and $80 from November 1 to May 31, not including tax.

Key West Tennis
811 Seminole Ave., Key West
• **(305) 296-3029**

Affiliated with the Marriott's Casa Marina Hotel and adjacent to it, Key West Tennis utilizes the hotel's three hard-surface courts. Newly installed tournament lights make nighttime play possible. A pro offers lessons by appointment, a ball machine is available for rent, and a complete pro shop carries Head and Tail clothing lines and Head, Dunlop and Wilson rackets. Stringing is done in-house. Guests of Marriott's Reach or Casa Marina hotels play for $8 per hour. The public pays $15 per hour.

Watersports

Key West watersports concessions make sure you have enough toys to play with during your visit. These playthings do not come cheaply, however. Figure on $35 to $45 for parasailing, $35 and higher for kayaking depending on whether or not you have a guide, $35 to $85 for a one- or two-seater personal watercraft depending on size and length of rental and $15 to rent a paddleboat.

Beachside Watersports Inc.
**Holiday Inn Beachside, 3841 N.
Roosevelt Blvd., Key West**
• **(305) 294-5934**

Motorized Sun Kats, paddleboats and personal watercraft are available for rent here. Beachside also offers guided personal watercraft island tours, four-hour snorkeling trips aboard the *Holiday Cat*, two-hour sunset cruises and booking services for kayak tours, parasail trips, gambling boats, offshore fishing and seaplane trips to the Dry Tortugas.

Island Watersports
**245 Front St., Hilton Resort and Marina,
Key West** • **(305) 296-1754**

Jet Skis and jet boats are available for rental by the half-hour ($45) or hour ($80). This business also boasts the largest riding area in Key West. If you like, wet suits and Oakley goggles are also offered. A 1½-hour guided tour around the island runs $95 and is a great way to see the island.

Key West Boat Rentals
617 Front St., Key West • **(305) 294-2628**

Personal watercraft are rented by the half-hour and hour here. Backcountry personal watercraft tours are available for different lengths and prices: five hours for $240, 2½ hours for $120, and 1¼ hours for $85. Parasail for 10 to 12 minutes over Key West Harbor. A package of sports includes a half-hour personal watercraft rental, a parasail excursion, a snorkeling trip to the reef, a sunset cruise, a day's scooter rental and lunch, all for $125.

Key West Water Sports Inc.
**714 Seminole St., Marriott's Casa Marina
Resort, Key West** • **(305) 294-2192**

A wide variety of watersports gear is ready and waiting for you here. Feel like a lazy afternoon just drifting? Try a Sun Cat floating lounge chair. Or maybe a Sea Peeper — a two-person glass bottom boat — is more your style. Try either of these for $20 per half-hour. Key West Water Sports is also home to high-performance short boards — quality windsurfing equipment. And if you've never tried the sport before, climb aboard the Cat Surfer. The folks here guarantee that anyone can learn to windsurf aboard this baby. For the rest of you, Hobie Cats, WaveRunners, baby-seat bikes, double-seater scooters, water skiing and parasailing are also available.

Land's End Boat Rentals
**End of Margaret St., Land's End Marina,
Key West** • **(305) 294-6447**

Rent all sorts of boats from this place, including sailboats, powerboats and jet boats. Rentals are available by the hour, half-day, full day and week. Take advantage of the guided island tours or just take some sailing lessons.

Parawest Watersports Inc.
700 Front St. • (305) 292-5199

This enterprise prides itself on offering more free falls and dips than any other excursionist in Key West. Regular rides of 8 to 10 minutes include heights of 300 feet with one free fall and one dip; longer, higher rides of 10 to 12 minutes reach 600 feet and include several free falls and dips. Most parasailing is done behind Christmas Tree Island and Sunset Key. Single and double personal watercrafts also are available for rent. Individuals who rent personal watercraft must remain within a limited riding area.

Sunset Watersports
Smathers Beach, Key West
• (305) 296-2554
3031 N. Roosevelt Blvd., Howard
Johnson's, Key West • (305) 296-2554

This outfit offers something for everyone. Parasailing, Hobie Cats, kayaks and windsurfing are all provided on Smathers Beach. A Jet Ski rental operates out of the Howard Johnson's. For an all-inclusive daytrip, take the "Do It All": From the Key West Seaport, a 44-foot catamaran takes you out about 3 miles to a shallow wreck. From there, take turns doing it all with WaveRunners, water-skiing and just about anything else they can think of, for $89 per person.

Tropical Sailboats
Higgs Beach, Key West
• (305) 296-0423
Smathers Beach, Key West
• (305) 296-4185

Two locations provide an extensive list of watersports rentals. Choose from Hobie Cats, windsurfers, kayaks, rafts and snorkeling equipment. Both locations offer free instruction, and both are authorized Hobie Cat dealers. Rentals are available by the hour or half-day.

Physical Fitness

Club Body Tech
1075 Duval St., Key West
• (305) 292-9683

Some of the most high-tech equipment in the fitness industry, including the David 900 Series machines, is available at Club Body Tech. This circuit-type equipment allows individuals to strap themselves in for easy exercise, and they can move from machine to machine. Cardiovascular equipment and free weights also are available. The center offers classes in aerobics, step, abdominals and back and leg. Personal training and massage services are available.

Coffee Mill Cultural Center
916 Pohalski St., Key West
• (305) 296-9982

This local center promotes good health. It's the home of the Key West Dance Theatre and also offers many workout opportunities. Get ready for some yoga meditation in the morning, or opt for aerobics, dance or martial arts. Classes are held daily and visitors are welcome. Attend a single class or sign up for a month's worth.

Pro Fitness Center
1111 12th St., Key West • (305) 294-1865

Also known as Body Zone South, this facility offers Nautilus and cardiovascular equipment and free weights. Floor instructors are on hand for all equipment use, and personal training, nutritional counseling and fitness evaluations are offered. Juices, vitamin supplements and workout wear are sold on premises.

Shape U
2740 N. Roosevelt Blvd., Overseas
Market, Key West • (305) 292-6323,
(305) 292-6328

Key West's largest, this gym offers something for everyone. A full range of exercise equipment is available, including treadmills,

INSIDERS' TIP

What is a turtle moon? This full-moon phenomenon coincides with the journey of the female loggerhead turtle from the sea to the shore, when she buries her eggs in the warm sand.

bikes, a stair climber and plenty of free weights. Exercise programs come in all shapes and sizes, from those for children to seniors and from low impact to hard core. A juice bar and play care for children are both convenient services.

Yoga College of Key West
812 Southard St., Key West
• (305) 292-1854
This is the real thing and is not for wimps — yoga with an attitude. Renowned yoga experts often give seminars here, expounding upon what they call "Rambo Yoga." Classes are held daily; call for details.

Just Plain Fun

Climb Key West, Inc.
245 Front St., Hilton Resort and Marina, Key West • (305) 292-5462
The highest point on the island of Key West is Solares Hill, which rises a scant 16 feet above sea level at the intersection of Elizabeth Street and Windsor Lane. But just because Key West sits on some of the flat-test terrain on earth doesn't mean you can't find a hill to climb here. There's one, in fact, just waiting to be scaled each night alongside the water at the Hilton Resort and Marina. It's artificial, of course, but this 24-foot, portable wall provides all the challenge any mountain climbing wannabes would need. What's more, anyone — or so say the folks who run it — can climb this wall in 18 seconds to five minutes depending on the route and skill of the climber. Kids as young as 3 have scaled it; so has a 74-year-old man. And at least 95 percent of those who've tried to climb the wall have made it to the top their first time out.

A single climb costs $12 ($9 for children younger than 12), which includes shoes, harness, instruction and a spotter. The wall beside the Hilton is available for climbing on weekdays from 6 PM to 9 PM and on Saturdays and Sundays from noon to 9 PM. Climb Key West will also set up a wall for group gatherings, special events and fund-raisers. And if you're interested in getting into the wall climbing business yourself, the folks here can sell you the equipment and show you how.

Don't wait for a rainy day (you might not have one) to explore our historic sites, out islands, museums, nature preserves and marine research centers.

Attractions

Our land mass is but a drizzle of frosting across our seas, but this yummy confection of coral yields some tantalizing attractions. Don't wait for a rainy day (you might not have one) to explore our historic sites, out islands, museums, nature preserves and marine research centers.

We've organized the attractions described in this chapter by mile marker in descending order down the Keys, beginning in Key Largo. In our Key West section, we offer several categories of attractions scattered throughout our southernmost city. Many are free or charge a nominal amount for admission. You'll find the majority of our most popular land-based diversions bordering the Overseas Highway, for our string of islands is not very wide.

And don't miss this chapter's final section, "And Beyond...," where we reveal the hidden treasures of our three nearby national parks — Biscayne, Everglades and the Dry Tortugas.

So put on your sandals, grab your hat and look for those car keys. Dally with us on an Insiders' tour of the distractions in Paradise.

The Florida Keys
Upper Keys

Maritime Museum of the Florida Keys
MM 102 Bayside, Key Largo
• (305) 451-6444

This tiny museum packs a lot of history into a little bit of space, for the displays chronicle the voyages of the Spanish plate fleets of the 18th century and showcase recovered relics such as leg and arm irons from the slaver *Henrietta Marie*, which went down about 1700. A video of pioneer treasure salvor Art McKee takes you back to the diving days of the 1950s when, tethered to the surface with an air hose, he searched for remains of the *San Pedro*, which ran aground with the Spanish fleet of galleons in 1733. Take home a piece of treasure from the adjoining gift shop.

The Maritime Museum is open from 10 AM to 5 PM every day except Thursday. Admission is $5 for adults, $3 for children ages 6 through 12 and free for children younger than 6.

Dolphins Plus Inc.
MM 100 Oceanside, Ocean Bay Dr., Key Largo • (305) 451-1993

This marine mammal research and education facility offers you the opportunity to learn the fascinating habits and lifestyles of the bottle-nosed dolphin and enter its world for a compatible swim. Offered twice daily (9 AM and 1:30 PM), a 2½-hour environmental education program teaches you all about dolphins, including their social pod structure, communication methods and anatomy. You'll learn how to conduct yourself in the water for your 30-minute swim with the dolphins. Participants who do not wish to swim are also welcome. Individuals 10 and older may swim with dolphins, but those younger than 18 must be accompanied by a participating adult. Cost of the full environmental education program, including the dolphin swim, is $85.

Dolphins Plus also offers a 2-hour, structured, in-water orientation program where you can be in the water involved directly with the dolphins. After an educational briefing, you will experience a structured water session encompassing platform behaviors and in-water behaviors. Interaction varies in each session, depending on the dolphin and the instructor. Two sessions for the structured orientation program are offered daily: at 8:45 AM and noon. Participants must be age 7 or older. Anyone younger than age 18 must be accompanied by a participating parent or guardian. Pregnant women may not participate in the structured program. Cost of this program is $100 per participant.

Nonswimmer admission for both programs is $8 for ages 8 to adult and $5 for ages 7 to 17; children younger than 7 are admitted at no charge. Participants in all programs must call for reservations. Directions to Dolphins Plus are complicated. Call the center for detailed instructions.

Florida Keys Wild Bird Center
MM 93.6 Bayside, Tavernier
• (305) 852-4486

Dedicated to the rescue, rehabilitation and release of ill, injured and orphaned wild birds, the Florida Keys Wild Bird Center will fascinate visitors of all ages. Artificial environmental hazards such as entanglement with anglers' lines or fishhooks also can render the birds injured and helpless. This rapid-care aviary treats the wounds, supervises the convalescence and releases the birds back into the wild. Meanwhile, you may walk along a boardwalk path through the birds' natural habitats, which have been discreetly caged with wire enclosures.

The Wild Bird Center is open seven days a week from 8:30 AM to 6:30 PM. The center is funded by public donations; there is no admission charge. Look for the two great white heron statuettes marking the roadside driveway to the center.

Windley Key Fossil Reef State Geologic Site
MM 85 Bayside, Windley Key

Quarried long ago by workers building Flagler's railroad extension, the fossilized coral reef that forms the bedrock of the Keys (see our Paradise Found chapter) is exposed here for all to see. You'll be able to examine fossilized imprints of ancient shells and marine organisms still embedded in the coral quarry walls.

www.insiders.com
See this and many other Insiders' Guide® destinations online — in their entirety.
Visit us today!

The state site is open from 9 AM to 1 PM on the third Saturday of every month, when guided tours are given. At all other times, visitors may check out a key to the locked geologic site from the ranger station at Long Key State Recreation Area, MM 67.5 Oceanside, (305) 664-4815, and visit the quarry for a self-guided tour. The key must be returned by 5 PM. There is no charge for admission.

Theater of the Sea
MM 84.5 Oceanside, Islamorada
• (305) 664-2431

With continuous dolphin shows offered daily from 9:30 AM to 4 PM, Theater of the Sea is the Florida Keys' answer to SeaWorld. The natural-looking lagoons, created by excavations for Flagler's railroad and filled with saltwater, host the popular marine mammals. Other marine exhibits showcase our locals: game fish, tropicals, sea turtles and more.

Admission costs $15.25 for adults and $8.75 for children ages 3 to 12. Children younger than 3 get in free. The Trainer for a Day program, open to those 10 and older, allows you to assist the animals' trainers and includes general show admission and a ride in the bottomless boat ($75). The Dolphin Adventure Package includes park admission plus a 30-minute swim with the dolphins and a half-hour orientation ($95). Or, after orientation you can snorkel with a stingray for 30 minutes, when you can feed and touch the marine creatures for $40. Restrictions apply for participants younger than 13.

Pioneer Cemetery
MM 82 Oceanside, Cheeca Lodge, Islamorada

Their gravestones defiled in the hurricane

of 1935, the founding fathers and mothers of Islamorada — the Parkers, Pinders and Russells — still rest in the Pioneer Cemetery, now a part of the extensive grounds of Cheeca Lodge. The cemetery was once bordered by a schoolhouse and the Methodist church, both destroyed in the hurricane (see our Paradise Found chapter). The angel statue marking the grave of Etta Dolores Pinder was found on the highway, miraculously intact except for a broken arm and wing. In 1989 Cheeca Lodge and University of Miami historian Josephine Johnson researched the cemetery, leading to the designation of the Pioneer Cemetery as a historic site by the Historical Association of Southern Florida. A plaque at the cemetery gate commemorates the event. You'll find the tiny Pioneer Cemetery surrounded by a white picket fence near the beach on the Cheeca Lodge grounds. The cemetery is open for free viewing by the general public.

Hurricane Monument
MM 81.6 Oceanside, Islamorada

Honoring the hundreds of residents and railroad workers in Islamorada who lost their lives in the Labor Day hurricane of 1935, this monument depicts the fury of nature's elements with a bas-relief of high seas and wind-battered palm trees. Carved out of local coral limestone, the Hurricane Monument may be

viewed just off the Overseas Highway near Grove Park Cafe.

Indian Key State Historical Site
MM 77.5 Oceanside, Indian Key
- **(305) 664-4815**

A colorful history paints Indian Key, a 10-acre oceanside island about .75 mile offshore from Lower Matecumbe Key. Now uninhabited, this tiny key has yielded archeological evidence of prehistoric Native American cultures. Visited by Spaniards and pirates alike, the island was purchased in 1831 by Jacob Housman, who established a thriving settlement. Indian Key became the Dade County seat in 1836. Physician Henry Perrine sat out the Second Seminole War here, which proved a misguided decision, for Indians attacked the island in 1840, and he lost his life after all. Fires destroyed all the structures except for the foundations. Although some people returned after the assault, by the early 1900s the key supported only burgeoning vegetation.

Each year the history of Indian Key is recreated during the Indian Key Festival (see our Annual Events chapter). Indian Key is accessible only by boat. Limited private dockage is available, but the site has no restrooms or picnic facilities. The historic site is open daily from 8 AM to sundown.

Robbie's Marina, MM 77.5 Bayside, (305) 664-9814, offers the only regularly scheduled tour transportation to the island. Tours depart Thursday through Monday to Indian Key and Lignumvitae Key (see the following write-up). No tours are given on Indian Key on Tuesdays and Wednesdays, but the island is open to those with their own transportation. The boat shuttle to Indian Key departs Robbie's docks at 8:30 AM and 12:30 PM. The launch will carry you to Lignumvitae Key at 9:30 AM or 1:30 PM. Cost for either excursion is $15 for adults, $10 for children. If you'd like to visit both islands — one in the morning, one in the afternoon — the cost is $25. Reservations are preferred. And while you are awaiting the boat, buy a cup of bait and feed the tarpon that come around the docks regularly.

Lignumvitae State Botanical Site
MM 77.5 Bayside, Lignumvitae Key
• (305) 664-4815

Named after the lignum vitae tree, Lignumvitae Key — our highest island at 17 feet above sea level — supports one of the best examples of a virgin hardwood hammock in the Florida Keys (see the Hardwood Hammock section in our Paradise Found chapter). Also on the island is the 1919 home of the Matheson family, of chemical company notoriety, who owned the island for many decades. The stilt-style home sports two storm hatches — bedroom and porch — so doors would not be blown off their hinges in a bad blow. The screened porch enabled the Mathesons to leave via the hatch, keeping the mosquitoes at bay.

One-hour ranger-guided walks at 10 AM and 2 PM allow visitors to tour the house and the hardwood hammock. Cost is $1 per person (children to age 6 tour for free). You may not enter the hammock unless accompanied by a ranger. Park officials suggest you come equipped with mosquito repellent and sturdy shoes. Like Indian Key, Lignumvitae Key may be accessed only by boat, and limited private dockage for small crafts is available (see previous write-up for information on Robbie's Marina, which offers transportation to the key).

Lignumvitae Key is closed Tuesdays and Wednesdays.

Middle Keys

The Dolphin Connection
MM 61 Oceanside, Duck Key, Hawk's Cay Resort • (305) 743-7000, Ext. 3030

Dolphin Discovery at Dolphin Connection provides an interactive, in-water encounter with the most famous of our Florida Keys marine creatures, bottle-nosed dolphins. The Connection's dolphins are young males, just teenagers, named Chinook, Ranier and Sebastian. They came to Hawk's Cay as "Navy surplus," no longer needed for official government programs. You will not actually "swim" with the dolphins here, but rather get to know them up-close and personal. You'll be able to touch, feed, pet and play with them from the security of a submerged platform (great for nonswimmers or those people with physical limitations).

After a 15-minute classroom orientation reviewing dolphin and people etiquette, you will sit in the water on a shallow platform where the trainer will familiarize you with the dolphin's anatomy. Trainers enlighten participants not only about the dolphins and their marine environment, but also on the greater Florida Keys' ecosystem. From the submerged platform you will move to the deep area, standing in water 4 feet deep. Here you will play games with the dolphins, who will jump, splash and fetch and thoroughly entrance you.

The Dolphin Discovery program is open to participants who are 4 feet, 6 inches or taller. The encounters are held at 10 and 11:30 AM and 1 and 4 PM. There is a maximum of six people per program, with the intimate ratio of three people to one trainer and one dolphin. Cost is $70 for Hawk's Cay Resort guests, $80 for the general public.

Kids have a ball as participants in the unique Dolphin Detectives program. From the dry docks, the children, who must be at least

---

INSIDERS' TIP

Many Florida Keys attractions offer a group discount for parties of six or more.

Interaction with bottle-nosed dolphins — up-close and personal —
is available at several locations in the Florida Keys.

age 5, learn how to be a dolphin trainer. The kids learn the trainer's hand signals and get to try them out on the playful dolphins during a supervised training session. The participants are taught how to feed to the dolphins — touching, weighing and preparing those fish the mammals like so much. Adults who do not wish to get wet in the Discovery program can participate in Dolphin Detectives, as can pregnant women, who are not allowed to join in the in-water Dolphin Discovery.

Dolphin Detectives kicks off every day at 2:30 PM. Cost is $25 for resort guests; $30 for the general public. Advance reservations are required for all programs. Bookings are accepted up to three months in advance.

The Dolphin Connection conducts ongoing genetic and neutral buoyancy research with the dolphins as well as other studies. The Connection staff devotes a good portion of their time to public education, hosting Monroe County school children to entertaining, informative sessions highlighting the dolphin's natural environment. They also maintain a college internship program and a one-day-a-week volunteer program.

Dolphin Research Center
MM 59 Bayside, Grassy Key
• (305) 289-1121

Look for the giant statue of a dolphin and her calf that heralds the Grassy Key home of the Dolphin Research Center. Once the lodging for Flipper, the famed television star of yesterday, the Dolphin Research Center today offers a variety of fascinating encounters with these smart marine mammals.

One-hour narrated walking tours introduce you to the dolphins in their natural environments where you'll witness their training sessions. Walking tours are offered five times a day (10 and 11 AM and 12:30, 2 and 3:30

PM), every day and require no reservations. Admission for adults is $12.50; senior citizens, $10; and kids ages 4 to 12, $7.50. Children younger than 4 are admitted free.

The half-day Dolphin Encounter enables you to learn how people interact with the dolphins. You'll attend a workshop, take the walking tour and then spend 20 minutes in the water with two dolphins and up to five other people. The ratio of people to dolphins is never more than 3-to-1. Children ages 5 to 12 must be accompanied in the water by a paying adult. Life jackets will be supplied to participants of all ages who desire them. This program is very popular, and access is limited. You must call for reservations the first or 15th day of the month preceding the month you'd like to swim (i.e., call October 1 if you'd like to reserve a dolphin swim from November 1 to November 14; call October 15 if you'd like a reservation from November 15 to the end of the month). Cost is $90 per person regardless of age.

DolphInsight offers a nonswimming half-day alternative to interact with the dolphins. On Wednesday or Saturday at 9 AM you will meet with a trainer who will teach you hand signals to allow you to communicate with the dolphins. You'll get the chance to try out your new skills from the floating docks of the dolphin lagoon, where you can "talk" to the dolphins. You'll also listen, by means of a hydrophone, to the dolphins communicating with each other under water. Reservations are required for this unique experience. Cost is $75.

You also can earn college credit at the week-long DolphinLab, a series of dolphin behavior seminars and hands-on encounters. You'll live on-premises in the center's dormitory and enjoy side trips to Key West and snorkeling at Looe Key National Marine Sanctuary. Cost is $1,100.

Two baby dolphins were born in 1997. Pax, a male whose name means peace, was born at sunrise on Easter morning; Pandora, a female was born on November 22. Breeze, a female dolphin who resided for 18 years at the Cedar Point Marine Mammal Park in Ohio, moved to the Dolphin Research Center in 1998 after the Ohio park closed.

Tropical Crane Point Hammock
MM 50.5 Bayside, Marathon
• **(305) 743-9100**

The small, interesting Museum of Natural History and the adjoining Florida Keys Children's Museum (see our Kidstuff chapter) sit on the skirt of the Tropical Crane Point Hammock, which covers a bit of history in itself. The museum houses a potpourri of Keys icons. Exhibits, which were refurbished in July 1997 by Wilderness Graphics, include creatures of the reef, authentically re-created in tropical splendor and accompanied by an audio of the sounds of the deep; the inhabitants of the Pinelands habitat — slash pines, red mangroves, silver buttonwood, Key deer and miniature raccoons; ancient shipwreck memorabilia; shells of giant sea turtles; tree snails of the tropics; even a stuffed osprey, great white heron, egret, frigate bird and the like.

Between the two museum structures, a fish-filled lagoon attracts fin fanciers of all ages. You'll see a Caribbean-style sailing canoe, paddled here in 1989 by three Guatemalan refugees, and an authentic Cuban freedom raft. Guided tours of the museum are offered weekdays from October through April at 10 AM and 1:30 PM.

After you tour the exhibits, traipse down the nature trails that loop through Tropical Crane Point Hammock, which is named for the Cranes, the family that owned the property until the early 1970s. Although hurricanes Donna and Betsy wreaked havoc in the hammock, flooding the sinkholes with saltwater and damaging much of the vegetation, the efforts of the Cranes to protect the area from development has preserved the forested land as a good example of our rare hardwood hammock habitat (see our Paradise Found chapter). New trails were created in 1997.

The museum provides a self-guided tour pamphlet that also lists some of the unusual tropical hardwoods you'll see along the nature trails. The Adderley House walk, about a half-mile long, leads to the restored Bahamian-style house built around 1905 by George Adderley, a black Bahamian settler of the Middle Keys. The concrete-like walls of the one-room structure are constructed from ground shells.

The attractions are open Monday through Saturday from 9 AM to 5 PM and Sundays from noon to 5 PM. One admission charge gives access to both walks and both museums: Cost for adults is $7.50; ages 65 and older, $6; and students, $4. Children age 12 and younger get in free.

Pigeon Key National Historic Site
Old Seven Mile Bridge, Bayside,
Pigeon Key • (305) 289-0025

Though undoubtedly Pigeon Key was known to Native Americans and Bahamian fishermen in the early days of the Keys, it was Henry Flagler's East Coast Railroad Extension that put the tiny key on the historical map. And it is the volunteer-staffed Pigeon Key Foundation that keeps it there. The island, which is connected to the mainland by a bridge originally built for the railroad, served as a construction and maintenance site for the railroad from 1908 to 1935. The hurricane of 1935 flooded Pigeon Key and caused so much damage to the railroad the company decided not to rebuild (see our Historical Evolution chapter). When the Seven Mile Bridge was built over the railroad spans in the late 1930s, Pigeon Key became headquarters for the Bridge and Toll District.

Over the ensuing decades the key was used as a fishing camp, a U.S. Navy site, a park and a marine biology center for the University of Miami. In 1982 the new Seven Mile Bridge was constructed, bypassing Pigeon Key from auto traffic. The Pigeon Key Foundation, a nonprofit local organization with the stated mission "to preserve the history and environment of the Florida Keys" was established in 1993, securing a long-term lease to the island from Monroe County.

Pigeon Key is a living testament to the Florida Keys of 1912 to 1940. The foundation has restored seven of the 5.3-acre island village's buildings dating from the early 1900s. Automobiles are not allowed on the Old Seven Mile Bridge. A trolley shuttle leaves the Pigeon Key Visitors Center (campily occupying an old green railway car, still resting on Flagler's tracks at MM 47 Oceanside, Knight's Key) every day on the hour from 10 AM to 4 PM. You may return on any shuttle you wish; the last one leaves the island at 5 PM.

Visitor's fees, which include shuttle service, are $7.50 per person ($5 for children 12 and younger). You can get out to Pigeon Key under your own steam, if you'd rather — the 2 miles of renovated bridge make for a good workout via walking, jogging, in-line skating or biking. Stop by the visitors center to purchase tickets before your jaunt. Or, you may rent bicycles at the Pigeon Key Visitors Center (open daily 10 AM to 4 PM in season, closed Mondays in the summer) for your trek through history. Pigeon Key hosts a number of festivals and special events each year (see our Annual Events chapter).

Lower Keys

National Key Deer Refuge and Watson Nature Trail
MM 30.5 Bayside, Key Deer Blvd.,
Big Pine Key • (305) 872-2239

The National Key Deer Refuge protects the pineland habitat frequented by the Key deer, a small species not much larger than a German shepherd that is found nowhere else in the world (see our Paradise Found chapter). Some areas of the refuge, which encompasses a large portion of Big Pine Key, are off limits to visitors and are so marked. Boundaries of the refuge open for daytime public access on designated trails are marked by a National Wildlife Refuge sign depicting a flying bird.

You can find the nearly mile-long Watson Nature Trail 1.5 miles north of the intersection of Key Deer and Watson boulevards. The trail winds throughout the pineland habitat of the refuge (see our Paradise Found chapter).

The Key deer are protected by law — even feeding them is a misdemeanor offense. Road

Key West Architecture

The mix of Key West architecture, like the cultural melting pot of the 19th century, is duplicated nowhere else in the world. Many of the nearly 3,000 frame structures in historic Old Town were built by self-taught craftsmen who worked from their own designs. These ship carpenters and captains drew upon their knowledge of wooden vessels to construct their new homes. They were primarily influenced by the structural techniques of their homeland, the Bahamas. Several houses were actually dismantled in the Bahamas and transported to Key West where they were reassembled.

The climate of Key West and the Bahamas is similar, so every attempt was made to capture breezes and keep the houses cool. Houses had to be built to withstand the hot sun, heavy rains and hurricanes. Builders used hand-hewn wood instead of plaster because plaster cracks and decays in high wind and humidity. Dade County pine, when available, was imported from the Upper Keys and Pensacola. It was preferred because the heavy resin content made it dense and impenetrable to termites. But much of the time wood from wrecked ships or the cargo salvaged from them was used. Nails were scarce because they were handmade and expensive, so wooden pins held the timbers together.

Most of the houses were built on wooden posts or coral rock piers for protection from high tides and storm waters. Roofs were designed to shed heavy water, with gutters and downspouts carrying the runoff to cisterns, where it was collected for later use. The roofs featured scuppers, or scuttles, which are openings that allow the hot air from the upper stories or attics to escape. Window and door openings were protected from the sun by louvered wood blinds. Wide covered verandas protected windows and doors from rain. And the houses were trimmed with intricately carved wood molding that has come to be known as gingerbread.

The 19th-century Key West homes preserved today through ongoing restoration efforts are unique architectural mutations we call Conch houses, after the original Bahamian settlers who first designed them. These styles are often referred to as Classic Revival, Victorian or Queen Anne.

The so-called eyebrow house is easy to spot because the sloping front roofline all but covers the upper story windows like bushy eyebrows over glassy orbs.

The two-story Conch temple has distinctive columns supporting roof overhangs on both levels.

The simple shotgun houses are so called because the interior rooms are lined up one behind the other with a hallway extending the length of the house from front to back. Hence, a bullet shot from the front door would hit no wall at all before it reached the back of the house. Most shotgun houses were built in the 1800s by cigar factories to house their workers.

You'll find other elaborate frame structures laden with capitals and pediments, porches and bay windows, gingerbread and other decorations borrowed from styles throughout the ages, as distinctively individual as their owners and defying easy classification.

For a good, thorough look at the architecture of Key West, get a copy of *The Houses of Key West* by Alex Caemmerer (available at Key West bookstores). Caemmerer describes the architectural styles in detail, inside and out, and gives addresses of

— continued on next page

classic examples of these private homes so all you need to do is put on your walking shoes and stroll back in time down the streets of Key West's historic district.

The road to restoration and preservation of Key West's charming architecture is paved with official actions at several levels of government. In 1965 the city of Key West established the Old Island Restoration Commission; its mission was to preserve the historic buildings in Old Town. The U.S. Congress passed the National Historic Preservation Act in 1966, creating a National Register of historic buildings, sites and districts. The Florida legislature created the Historic Key West Preservation Board of Trustees in 1972 to specifically deal with Key West. In 1986 the Historic Architectural Review Commission (HARC) assumed responsibility for the ongoing restoration and preservation of Key West's historic areas and does so to this day.

kill remains a primary hazard to the Key deer. Speed limits on U.S. Highway 1 through Big Pine Key are reduced to 45 mph during the day and 35 mph at night and are strictly enforced. The best time to look for Key deer is early in the morning or at dusk.

You can sometimes spot Key deer beside U.S. 1, but you are more likely to see them along the back roads and especially on No Name Key, where there are fewer human inhabitants. To reach No Name Key, turn right at the intersection of Key Deer and Watson boulevards. The road will take you through a residential neighborhood and over a cement bridge to No Name Key, ending abruptly at a pile of boulders. In between the bridge and the boulders, drive slowly and keep your eyes peeled.

The Blue Hole
MM 30.5 Bayside, Key Deer Blvd., Big Pine Key • (305) 872-2239

You may wonder why all those cars are parked on the side of Key Deer Boulevard, for from the roadside the area looks like an uninhabited stand of slash pines. Park your vehicle and join the crowd. A few steps into the thatched palm understory you'll see a large,

water-filled barrow pit, known as The Blue Hole. Inhabiting this incongruous water hole are a couple of resident alligators who have replaced the now legendary "Grandpa," a big 'gator that was deported to the Gulf Coast on a charge of bad behavior. If you're lucky, you may catch a glimpse of one of these illusive reptiles. An assortment of ducks and wading birds gingerly stays out of the alligators' path. The Blue Hole is 1.25 miles north of the intersection of Key Deer and Watson boulevards.

Perky Bat Tower
MM 17 Bayside, Sugarloaf Key

Richter Perky may have had bats in his belfry in 1929 when he decided to build this Sugarloaf Key tower, but such are dreams that lay the foundations for legends. Perky believed that the uniquely designed, louvered pine tower, when laced with the proper bait, would attract a Keys population of mosquito-loving bats, thus solving his insect-infestation problem. Alas, the nocturnal flyers bypassed his offering, and Perky had to go back to the drawing board. The structure has withstood the tests of time and the elements, however. Perhaps he should have called it a hurricane shelter.

To find Perky Bat Tower, turn right (bayside) at the Sugarloaf Airport sign just beyond Sugarloaf Lodge when heading down the Keys. When the road forks, bear to the right. No admission is charged.

Key West

Key West's historic Old Town district is perfect for a leisurely stroll to take in the history and eccentricity of this tiny island. Or how about an aquarium, a cemetery, a garden? Or maybe a tour of haunted houses or an old wrecker's house filled with antiques? We've checked out all the high points for you, including a few "only in Key West" attractions guaranteed to keep you entertained.

Key West attractions have been divided into three categories: Historic Homes and Museums, One of a Kind, and Guided and Self-Guided Tours. Within each category, attractions are listed in alphabetical order. The prices cited below are the advertised admission fees; they may or may not include sales tax.

Historic Homes and Museums

Audubon House & Tropical Gardens
205 Whitehead St., Key West
• (305) 294-2116

It was 12 years before the house was built, but in 1832 John James Audubon did spend time on the grounds of John Geiger's huge garden. Legend has it that Audubon sketched the white-crowned pigeon and the geiger tree he found in the garden here. During his stay in the Keys, Audubon produced 18 sketches of native wildlife. Original lithographs of these drawings are on display at the Audubon

House. The house and environs, however, are more reminiscent of the family of Capt. John Geiger, a wrecker who built the house and lived here with his family. Set your own tour pace with a free pair of headphones and a tape that brings the house alive.

Audubon House is open daily from 9:30 AM to 5 PM, but last entry is at 4:45 PM. Admission for adults is $7.50; senior citizens, $6.50, students, $5; children ages 6 through 12, $3.50; and children younger than 6, free.

Curry Mansion
511 Caroline St., Key West
• (305) 294-5349

This imposing home evokes images of an opulent, old Key West, although the three-story Conch house now serves as the focal point for a bed and breakfast inn and a museum. Built in 1905 by Milton Curry, Florida's first homegrown millionaire, the inn's public rooms display a selection of antiques and memorabilia. Poke around in the attic, and you'll find an 1899 billiards table among the old dresses and luggage. From the attic you can climb the widow's walk for a panoramic view of Key West Harbor. Self-guided tours are available daily from 10 AM to 5 PM. Admission is $5 for adults and $1 for children 12 and younger.

Duval Street Wrecker's Museum — The Oldest House
322 Duval St., Key West • (305) 294-9502

Withstanding every storm since 1835, the former Watlington House has rightly earned its Key West nickname as the oldest house in the city. Capt. Watlington bought the house in 1839, and it was family-occupied for the next 130 years. Donated to the State of Florida in 1974, it is now the Wrecker's Museum, housing nautical photos and memorabilia from the Key West wrecking era, including an authentic wrecking (some prefer to call it salvaging) license. Highlights are a shipwreck display, which shows the location of many a wreck on

---

INSIDERS' TIP

What about alligators? With the exception of the 'gators relocated to the Blue Hole in Big Pine Key, you won't find these critters in the Keys since they are freshwater dwellers. To find an alligator in the wild, you'll have to visit Everglades National Park.

local reefs; an antique dollhouse that even has a miniature Key West mural; and the detached cookhouse kitchen, separated to safeguard against fires.

The Wrecker's Museum is open from 10 AM to 4 PM daily. The tours are self-guided, but a docent is always available on-premises to answer questions. Admission is $4 for adults and teens; children 12 and younger are admitted for 50¢.

East Martello Museum
3501 S. Roosevelt Blvd., Key West
• (305) 296-3913

This enchanting, artifact-filled former fort will bring you up to speed on Key West history. Built during the Civil War, the brick fortress was never completely finished because the circular Martello design became antiquated before it was ever armed. Operated today as a museum and gallery by the Key West Art and Historical Society, the 8-foot-thick walls support pictures, artifacts and historical documents. Featured in the small gallery are the charming wood carvings of Key West's Mario Sanchez and the funky welded sculptures fabricated by the late Stanley Papio of Key Largo from bedsprings, toilet fixtures and other so-called "junk." You can climb the citadel to the lookout tower for an unobstructed view of the Atlantic coast.

East Martello Museum is open daily from 9:30 AM to 5 PM, but the last admission is at 4 PM. Cost is $6 for adults and teens and $2 for children ages 7 to 12; kids younger than 7 get in free. Adults may purchase a combination ticket that allows admission to both this museum and the Key West Lighthouse Museum (see its description later in this chapter) for $10.

Harry Truman's Little White House Museum
111 Front St., Key West • (305) 294-9911

Ordered by his doctor to retreat to a stress-free climate and recover from a lingering cold, President Harry S Truman came to Key West for the first time in 1946. Like so many others, he was instantly smitten with the island and spent 11 working vacations in the commandant's quarters, dubbed the Little White House. Built in 1890, the house was renovated for its famed visitor in 1948. Opened to the general public as a museum dedicated to Give 'Em Hell Harry in 1991, the home has once again been restored to its 1948 splendor. You'll be able to view Truman's Winter White House as it looked when he spent his 175 working vacation days here. The family quarters, poker porch, dining room and living room (complete with Truman's piano) are open to the public.

The guided tour takes you into the rooms and lives of Harry and Bess. The Exhibition Room displays a permanent collection of photographs of Presidents Eisenhower and Kennedy. Eisenhower spent two weeks here recuperating from his second heart attack, and Kennedy held a summit meeting here before the Bay of Pigs action. Jimmy Carter visited in 1996. A 10-minute video recounts the history of the home, and a collection of presidential memorabilia is on display in the museum gift shop.

Guided tours are conducted daily between 9 AM and 5 PM. Admission is $7.50 for adults and teens and $3.75 for children ages 6 through 12. Children younger than 6 are admitted free.

Hemingway House and Museum
907 Whitehead St., Key West
• (305) 294-1575

Once the home of Key West's most famous writer, Ernest Hemingway, the Hemingway House and Museum ranks at the top of the must-do list and is Key West's most popular attraction. Built by wrecker Asa Tift in 1851, the home took on historic significance when Ernest and Pauline Hemingway moved in. Pauline spearheaded extensive remodeling, redecorating and refurnishing and fitted her backyard with the island's first swimming pool. Hemingway wrote several of his most celebrated works, including *For Whom the Bell Tolls*, *Death in the Afternoon*, *The Green Hills of Africa* and *To Have and Have Not*, from his poolhouse office out back. The Hemingways lived in this Key West home from 1931 to 1939.

Guided tours lasting approximately 45 minutes are offered every 10 minutes from 9 AM to 5 PM daily; the last tour begins at 4:30 PM. Admission is $6.50 for adults and teens and $4 for children ages 6 through 12; children

Photo: Wayne Moccia

The lighthouse at Loggerhead Key, at the tip of the Dry Tortugas, is the last outpost for 900 miles.

younger than 6 enter free. Be sure to look for the equally infamous six-toed cats.

Heritage House Museum and Robert Frost Cottage
410 Caroline St., Key West
• (305) 296-3573

The memorabilia in the Heritage House Museum pays tribute to Jessie Porter, a cultured, well-traveled woman at the center of Key West society in the mid-1900s. Visitors to the house included Tallulah Bankhead, Thornton Wilder, Gloria Swanson, Tennessee Williams, Pauline Hemingway and, of course, regular visitor Robert Frost, who stayed in the small cottage in the rear garden when he wintered in Key West, which he did off and on from 1945 through 1960. Visitors are invited to make themselves at home in the comfortable original surroundings and even play the antique piano.

Tours of Heritage House are offered Monday through Saturday from 10 AM to 5 PM and on Sunday from 1 PM to 4 PM. The last tour begins a half-hour before closing. Heritage House is generally closed the first two weeks of September, and in summer hours may be shortened; in either case, it is best to phone ahead. Admission is $6 for adults ($5 for senior citizens) and $3 for students. Children younger than 12 get in free.

Key West Lighthouse Museum
938 Whitehead St., Key West
• **(305) 294-0012**

This 1847 structure, inland on a Key West street just across from the Hemingway House, affords visitors a bird's-eye view of Key West from atop its 90-foot light tower. It was positioned here to avoid the fate of its predecessor on Whitehead Point, which toppled in a hurricane the previous year. The keeper's quarters houses maritime memorabilia and a gift shop.

The lighthouse museum is open daily for self-guided tours from 9:30 AM to 5 PM; last admission is at 4:30 PM. Admission for adults and teens is $6; children ages 7 to 12, $2; and children younger than 7, free.

Mel Fisher Maritime Heritage Society and Museum
200 Greene St., Key West
• **(305) 294-2633**

For 16 years, "today's the day" was the hope of treasure salvor Mel Fisher, who finally struck pay dirt on July 20, 1985. Finding the *Nuestra Señora de Atocha*, which Fisher has estimated to be worth $400 million, ensured his legacy as treasure hunter extraordinaire. Heavy gold chains, jeweled crosses and bars of silver and gold are among the artifacts on display at the permanent first-floor exhibit. Hefting a gold bar worth more than $18,000 is a highlight. The second-floor exhibit changes frequently — call for details. A museum shop offers a variety of pirate and nautical gifts.

The museum is open daily from 9:30 AM to 5 PM. The last video shows at 4:30 PM. Admission charge for adults and teens is $6.50; children ages 6 to 12, $2; and children younger than age 6, free. AARP, AAA and student discounts are available.

San Carlos Institute
516 Duval St., Key West • (305) 294-3887

Founded in 1871 by Cuban exiles, the San Carlos Institute was established to preserve the language and traditions of the Cuban people. Dubbed "La Casa Cuba" by legendary poet and patriot Jose Marti, the Institute helped unite the exiled Cuban community. The present building was completed in 1924 and operated as an integrated school until the mid-1970s, when deteriorating conditions necessitated its closing. With the perseverance of the Hispanic Affairs Commission, a state agency headed by Rafael Penalver, restoration of the San Carlos was completed and the Institute reopened on January 3, 1992, 100 years to the day after Jose Marti's first visit. Today the San Carlos Institute is a museum, library, school, art gallery, theater and conference center. The Institute is open 11 AM to 5 PM daily except Mondays, and admission is free.

West Martello Tower
Joe Allen Garden Center
Atlantic Blvd. and White St., Key West
• **(305) 294-3210**

Built in 1862, the West Martello Tower, like the other forts on the island, was never involved in an actual war. It was, however, used for target practice by the U.S. Navy, which accounts for its somewhat shabby condition. Today the tower is also the Joe Allen Garden Center, and the Key West Garden Club operates here. Use the self-guided tour to spot local flora, including a Key lime tree, or just find an inviting spot to relax.

West Martello is open Tuesdays through Saturdays in season from 9:30 AM until 3:15 PM. The schedule may be different in the summer months; call for more information. Admission is free, but note that shirt and shoes are required.

One of A Kind

A Key Encounter
Clinton Square Market, 291 Front St., Key West • (305) 292-2070

When your feet get weary and you need a break, head up to the second floor of Clinton Square Market for a 25-minute, triple-screen movie showcasing the natural habitats of the Florida Keys and the flora, fauna and marine creatures dwelling therein. The narrated feature, which is set to music, will set the stage for your exploration of our islands (see our Kidstuff chapter).

A Key Encounter is open daily except Saturday from 11 AM to 5 PM with showings every 30 minutes. Admission is $3 for adults and teens and $1 for children ages 4 to 12.

Fort Zachary Taylor State Historic Site
Truman Annex at Southard St., Key West
• **(305) 292-6713**

Although not fully completed until 1866, this Key West military bastion served the Union well during the Civil War, when it guarded against Confederate blockade runners. So impressive were its defenses, the fort was never attacked. It saw continuous usage by the military until the federal government deeded the structure to the State of Florida for use as a historic site. The Florida Park Service opened Fort Zachary Taylor to the public in 1985.

Today, however, much of the fort is again closed to public exploration, this time because the structure has succumbed to the ravages of time. The park service secured a $1.25 million grant, used to restore the north curtain, which is where the guns were mounted. As portions of the fort are structurally repaired, they will be reopened. At present, only the parade ground, the south curtain observation deck and the north curtain can be toured. The museum is also closed for repairs and will remain so indefinitely. Exhibits have been transferred to East Martello Museum (see previous listing) until the restoration is complete.

The surrounding park offers a beach for fishing, swimming or snorkeling, as well as picnic areas equipped with tables and grills, outside showers, snackbar and restroom facilities. It also offers one of the best, unobstructed views of the sunset.

Admission charges are uniquely computed: It's $1.50 if you are walking or riding a bicycle or scooter, $2.50 if you drive in alone. Cars with passengers are charged $5. The car and driver are included in this fee; an additional 50¢ is charged for each passenger. Fort Zachary Taylor is open daily from 8 AM to sunset. Hang on to your ticket stub; you may leave the park and return at any time through-

out the same day by simply showing your ticket to the booth attendant. Hint: Lots of people leave the beach in the afternoon, then return here to watch the sunset away from the craziness going on down at Mallory Square (see description later in this chapter).

Key West Aquarium
1 Whitehead St. at Mallory Sq., Key West
• **(305) 296-2051**

Key West's oldest tourist attraction (built in 1934) and still one of the most fascinating our southernmost city has to offer, the Key West Aquarium affords you a diver's-eye view of the marine creatures of our encompassing waters. Stroll at your leisure alongside the backlit tanks recreating our coral reefs, but don't miss the guided tours (11 AM and 1, 3 and 4:30 PM daily) when you'll witness the feeding of the species. You'll marvel at the feeding frenzy of the sharks and sawtooths; the nurse sharks and stingrays flipping and splashing for their rations; and the tarpon, barracudas, game fish and sea turtles recognizing the hands that feed them in the outdoor Atlantic Shores Exhibit, created to look like a mangrove lagoon.

A highlight for kids is the "touch tank" just inside the front door. Here, they can reach in and grab hold of horseshoe crabs, hermit crabs, conch, sea cucumbers and many other creatures that populate the waters surrounding Key West. Be sure to bring your camera — you'll want to capture the expression on your child's face when the horseshoe crab in his or her hand suddenly flexes its legs.

The aquarium is open daily from 10 AM to 6 PM. Admission for adults and teens is $8; children ages 4 to 12, $4; children age 4 and younger, free. Discounts are available. Adults holding a trolley, train or cruise ship coupon may enter for $7. Do hang on to your tickets. Should you forget to pack your camera, you can use those tiny slips of paper to re-enter the following day at no additional charge.

Key West City Cemetery
Bordered by Angela, Frances and Olivia Sts., and Windsor Ln., Key West

Built in 1847 after the horrific hurricane the year before washed out the sand sanctuary at the island's southernmost point, Key West City

Cemetery, right in the center of town, adds a human element to the history of Key West. The marble monuments of the wealthy were shipped to the island; local markers were generally produced from brick or coral-based cement. Carved with symbols and prosaic sayings, such as "I told you I was sick" and "Devoted fan of Julio Iglesias," the gravestones are a living legacy for those lying beneath. Some of the tombs are "bunked," or stacked, because digging in the coral rock proved difficult and seawater percolates just under the surface.

The Historic Florida Keys Foundation makes it easy to explore the Key West City Cemetery. The organization's self-guided tour pamphlet lists graves of 42 of Key West's most prominent or notorious deceased citizens, with brief personality profiles and a translation of the meaning of the carved symbols on the gravestones. Pick up a free *Historic Key West City Cemetery Self-guided Tour* pamphlet in the Florida Room at the Monroe County Public Library, 700 Fleming Street, or at the Key West Chamber of Commerce, Mallory Square.

If you'd like a guided tour of the cemetery, join the Historic 1847 Cemetery Stroll conducted by historic preservationist Sharon Wells (see the "Guided and Self-Guided Tours" section of this chapter). The cemetery stroll is $13 per person. Tour times vary, and reservations are required. Call (305) 294-8380 for information.

Key West Botanical Gardens
Botanical Garden Way and College Rd., Stock Island

Follow College Road, then turn right just past Bayshore Manor, to find this little-known slice of serenity tucked between the Aqueduct Authority plant and the Key West Golf Course. Maintained by volunteers from the Key West Botanical Garden Society and funded by donations, this 11-acre garden contains one of only two undeveloped native hardwood hammocks remaining in Key West. Despite its proximity to U.S. Highway 1 and a busy public golf course, the garden is surprisingly peaceful — home to numerous birds, butterflies and other native creatures. On any given day, you're apt to see a turtle sunning itself on a log or an egret searching for food right next to the bridge

that spans Desbiens Pond. Pick up a map near the front gate, but don't be surprised if you find it hard to follow. Many of the labels on the plants and trees have disappeared over time; society volunteers are working to replace them. In the meantime, this is still a pleasant place to wile away a quiet hour and marvel at what Key West once looked like before we humans arrived.

The gardens are open daily during daylight hours. There is no admission fee, but donations are welcomed.

Key West Historic Memorial Sculpture Garden
Mallory Square, Key West
• (305) 294-4142

Located on Key West's original shoreline just behind Mallory Square, this tiny fenced-in "garden" pays homage to 36 men and women whose lives and deeds have had tremendous impact on the southernmost city. Here you will find the stories and likenesses of such former influential citizens as wreckers Asa Tift and Capt. John Geiger, railroad magnate Henry Flagler and Sister Louise Gabriel whose Grotto to Our Lady of Lourdes is said to have protected Key West from hurricanes for more than 75 years. All of the bronze busts, as well as the imposing wreckers sculpture that is the centerpiece of the Garden, are the works of sculptor James Mastin of Coral Gables, Florida.

As you wander through the garden, be sure to look down, too — the walkways are paved with commemorative bricks purchased by individuals and families in remembrance of their friends and relatives. Monies derived from the sale of these bricks (each costs $60) help support construction and maintenance of the Garden. The Sculpture Garden is open daily during daylight hours; there is no admission charge.

Key West Shipwreck Historeum
1 Whitehead St., Mallory Square, Key West • (305) 292-8990

Relive the days of wreckers, lumpers and divers at the Shipwreck Historeum — part museum, part theater — where actors, video footage and interactive presentations re-create vestiges of Key West's once-lucrative wrecking industry. During the 1800s about 100 ships passed by the port of Key West daily, many running aground on the reef. Asa Tift, one of the 19th-century wreckers and the original owner of what would one day become the Hemingway House, tells his story of salvaging the goods of the SS *Isaac Allerton*, which was downed by a hurricane (see our Kidstuff chapter).

Shows are daily every 30 minutes from 9:15 AM to 4:45 PM. Admission for adults and teens is $8; children ages 4 to 12, $4; children younger than 4, free.

Mallory Square Sunset Celebration
1 Whitehead St., Key West
• **(305) 296-4557**

A do-not-miss event during any visit to Key West is the famous (perhaps infamous) sunset celebration. Buskers and street players, vaudevillians and carny wannabes strut their stuff every day as the sun sinks into the horizon over Sunset Key off Mallory Square. Beverage and nosh vendors hawk refreshments while the entertainers compete for your attention. From fire eaters to furniture jugglers, tight-rope walkers to sword swallowers, you'll rarely see the same routine two nights in a row.

This daily Key West tradition is free to all, but pack your pocket with small bills because the performers play for tips. The fun starts approximately one hour before sunset at Mallory. Entertainers can also be found nightly along the pier at the Hilton Resort and Marina next door to Mallory Square.

Mile Marker 0
Corner of Whitehead and Fleming Sts., Key West

Key West is truly the last resort and here's the proof: The official green-and-white Mile Marker 0 signifying the end of U.S. Highway 1 is posted at this corner. Have someone snap a picture of you in front of the sign that reads "End — U.S. 1." It will make a wonderful reminder of that very moment you finally arrived at the end of your road.

Nancy Forrester's Secret Garden

1 Free School Ln., Key West
• **(305) 294-0015**

The garden isn't a secret anymore, because Nancy Forrester's arboreal and botanical prowess has become legendary. A knowledgeable expert on specimen palms and tropical plants, Forrester has created a garden rain forest that offers a welcome respite from the flesh-pressing masses churning up and down Duval Street. Examine the panoply of exotic vegetation or bring a picnic lunch and just sit a spell. Outdoor tables and chairs are peppered about the garden.

The garden is open for self-guided tours daily from 10 AM to 5 PM during the winter season. During summer, call for hours of operation. Admission for adults is $6; children ages 6 to 14, $2; children younger than 6, free. In-depth, personalized horticultural tours are also offered with advanced reservations. Call for information and fees. The Secret Garden is at the end of Free School Lane, behind the wooden gate. Free School Lane is off the 500 block of Simonton Street between Fleming and Southard streets.

Ripley's Believe It or Not! Odditorium
527 Duval St., Key West • (305) 293-9694

Robert L. Ripley was no accidental tourist. This adventurer knew exactly what he was doing when he traveled the world amassing unusual artifacts, real and imagined, now displayed in "odditoriums" around the world. So, believe it or not, Ripley's Key West even displays a few Keys-style "artifacts" you won't find in the other odditoriums. Be brave as you encounter a monster-size hammerhead shark.

Ripley's is open daily from 9 AM to 11 PM. Admission charge for adults and teens is $9.95; children ages 4 to 12, $6.95; children younger than 4, free.

The Southernmost Point
Corner of Whitehead and South Sts., Key West

Look for the traffic jam at the Atlantic end of Whitehead Street and you'll see the giant red, white, green and yellow marker buoy that

INSIDERS' TIP

Stop in at any of our fishing marinas (see our Fishing chapter) around 4 PM and take a look at the catch of the day.

designates the southernmost point of the continental United States. And standing in front of it, in the street, blocking traffic trying to turn left onto South Street, preen a never-ending stream of Key West visitors, trying to capture the moment they stood closer to Cuba than anyone else in the country. Call it touristy if you like, but the crowds love it.

Wildlife Rescue of the Florida Keys
**Atlantic Blvd. and White St., Key West
(305) 294-1441**

On the grounds of McCoy Indigenous Park, a large, quiet park full of rare and native species of flora, lies Wildlife Rescue of the Florida Keys. Since 1993, Wildlife Rescue has released more than 2,000 healed animals back into the wild. At any given time, approximately 100 animals, ranging from sea birds to raccoons to chickens, are recovering here. Wildlife Rescue will rescue animals anywhere from the Seven Mile Bridge to the Dry Tortugas.

The center is open Monday through Friday from 7 AM to 4 PM and Saturdays from 10 AM to 2 PM. Admission is free, but donations are appreciated, and volunteers are always needed.

Guided and Self-Guided Tours

Conch Tour Train
**301 Front St. at Mallory Square,
Key West
Key West Welcome Center, 3840 N.
Roosevelt Blvd., Key West
• (305) 294-5161**

Some folks might think a narrated motor tour spells tourist with a capital T, but the quirky little Conch Tour Train is a great way to garner an overview of Key West in the shaded comfort of a canopied tram. You'll pass by most of the attractions we've written up in this chapter, sometimes twice, because in tiny Key West the train weaves a circuitous route that often changes from one hour to the next depending on road construction and special events that necessitate street closures. Regardless of the path, you're sure to enjoy the ride as your guide recounts fact and legend, tall tales and sad stories about life in Key West.

Tours start at Mallory Square from 9 AM to 4:30 PM and at the Welcome Center from 9:30 AM to 3:30 PM. Tickets for adults and teens

Sunken treasures and pirate tales entertain in the Maritime Museum in Key Largo.

are $15; children ages 4 to 12, $7; children younger than 4, free. The tour lasts 90 minutes, with one 10-minute rest break at the Conch Tour Train ticket station, 501 Front Street. Train passengers can also get off at Land's End Village at the foot of Margaret Street to explore the Historic Seaport area on foot, then reboard another train to complete the tour.

Ghost Tours of Key West
(305) 293-8009

Key West's No. 1 haunted attraction, Ghost Tours offers a chance to get an in-depth introduction to the most famous ghosts of our island. Highlights include a haunted doll and the city's original hanging tree. Narrated by a spooky, caped, lantern-bearing guide, the tour wends its way through Key West after dark and lasts around an hour and 20 minutes.

Tours leave nightly just after sunset from the lobby of the La Concha Hotel, 430 Duval Street. Ticket prices are $15 for adults, $12 for students and $10 for children 12 and younger. Reservations are required.

Key West Literary Seminar Writer's Walk
Various sites • (888) 293-9291

Put on your tennies for a one-hour, 1-mile guided walking tour through literary Key West. Your guide will share with you the secret to why Key West has attracted so many writers throughout the decades. You'll see the exteriors of the houses these writers called home for a time, and your guide will point out distinctive architectural features of the buildings. (You will not be touring the interiors of any homes.) The tour offers insights into the lives and times of such writers as Ernest Hemingway, Tennessee Williams, John Hersey, Shel Silverstein, James Leo Herlihy and Elizabeth Bishop.

From December through May, small, intimate tours are offered twice weekly. On Saturdays the group leaves at 10:30 AM from the Heritage House Museum, 410 Caroline Street. On Sundays the tour embarks at 10:30 AM from the Hemingway House, 907 Whitehead Street. Call the toll-free number to book a tour at other times. Tours must have a minimum of five people. Tickets are $10 per person and

may be purchased at the Heritage House or the Key West Island Bookstore, 513 Fleming Street. Writer's Walk is sponsored by the Key West Literary Seminar, a nonprofit corporation whose mission is "to promote and preserve the island's literary heritage."

Key West Nature Bike Tour
(305) 294-1882

Join local character Lloyd Mager on his two-hour tour of Key West's lesser-known spots. Highlights of this easy-to-ride tour include tasting many local species of flora, including mangoes, tamarind fruit, Key limes and whatever else may be in season. You'll see a sand palm so large it is hard to fathom. Call for a schedule and reservations. The tour departs from the Moped Hospital, 601 Truman Avenue. Mager will arrange for rental bikes at $15 per person.

Old Town Trolley Tours
Key West Welcome Ctr., 3840 N. Roosevelt Ave. • (305) 296-6688
Old Town Trolley Car Barn, 1910 N. Roosevelt Blvd. • (305) 296-6688

Join the Old Town Trolley Tour for an informative, convenient entry into Key West. The trolley stops at most major hotels, handy if you're staying in the southernmost city. Daytrippers will appreciate the free parking at the Key West Welcome Center or the Trolley Car Barn where you can pick up the tour. The trolleys depart every 30 minutes, and, best of all, you can get off at any of the stops and reboard the same day whenever you like. All along the way the tour guide will treat you to a Key West history lesson, full of anecdotes and legends.

Old Town Trolley Tours run daily from 8:55 AM to 4:30 PM. Ticket cost per day for adults and teens is $16; children ages 4 through 12 pay $7.

Pelican Path
Old Island Restoration Foundation • (305) 294-9501

Visitors who like to wander on their own should be sure to first pick up a copy of the *Pelican Path* brochure at the Chamber of Commerce on Mallory Square. This handy compact walking guide and map offers a short history of Key West as well as a suggested route that will take you past 50 of our most prominent historic structures. Most of the buildings described in this brochure are today private homes and guesthouses. Those that are open for touring are highlighted in yellow. Don't be surprised, however, if you can't spot those yellow and blue Pelican signs described in the brochure as path markers; many of them have disappeared over the years. Even so, the Pelican Path remains relatively easy to follow and is a great way to get acquainted with island history.

The Pub Tour
(305) 294-9255

Key West is a small island with a big thirst. So big, it seems, that when one local balladeer compared the number of watering holes to the island's square footage, he came up with this interesting bit of trivia: There's a bar every 67 feet in Key West. With numbers like these, it was only a matter of time before some vehicle would be created to bring tourists and taverns together in an organized fashion. That vehicle is The Pub Tour. Brought to you by the same folks who bring you Ghost Tours of Key West (see the previous description), this two-hour guided pub crawl takes you to five of Key West's most infamous saloons. Included in the $25 price are five drinks — your choice of a domestic draft, a nonalcoholic beverage or a house specialty at the bars featured on the tour — and a souvenir mug for sipping them.

Tours start every afternoon at 2:30 in the Green Parrot Bar, 601 Whitehead Street. Reservations are required. Sorry, no kids allowed. You must be 21 years old to participate.

Sharon Wells' Walking and Biking Guide
(305) 294-8380

This organizational wonder created by historic preservationist Sharon Wells leads you through 10 free, self-guided tours. The maps highlight the architectural and historic treasures of Key West. From November through May, Wells also offers personally guided tours called Island City Strolls. These include a 90-minute architectural stroll which winds through the historic neighborhoods of Old Town, a 90-minute cemetery stroll and two bike tours —

the 90-minute "Island Trek" through Key West's historic neighborhoods and the 2-hour "Literary Landmarks Trail" which leads past the homes of famous Key West writers. Upon request, Sharon can also put together a personalized tour for individuals or groups. Space is limited on all guided tours and reservations are required. Call for prices and tour times.

If you prefer to explore on your own, you'll find copies of Sharon Wells' *Walking and Biking Guide* at more than 200 locations in and around Key West, including the Key West Public Library, 700 Fleming Street; and the Key West Chamber of Commerce, Mallory Square. Up the Keys you'll find the guide at the chambers of commerce in Big Pine Key, MM 30.5 Oceanside; Marathon, MM 53.5 Bayside; Islamorada, MM 82.5 Bayside; and Key Largo, MM 106 Bayside.

And Beyond . . .

Biscayne National Park
National Park Service • (305) 242-7700, (800) 368-4753
Main Visitor Center, Convoy Point

Only 4 percent of Biscayne National Park's 181,500 acres are above water, consisting of about 45 tiny keys and a mangrove shoreline. The crystalline depths shelter the northern portion of the Florida Keys' barrier reef and all the marine life lurking in the submerged coral nooks and crannies. Biscayne's complex ecosystem, like that of the Florida Keys, extends from the mangrove-lined shoreline to the Gulf Stream. The northernmost of the Florida Keys protects the waters of Biscayne Bay from the pounding surf of the Atlantic.

The best time to visit Biscayne National Park is from mid-December to mid-April. Unless you have your own boat, you will have to explore the park's waters by concessionaire-run cruises. You'll find glass-bottom boats that will take you on a reef cruise or for a snorkeling or diving excursion. More than 200 species of fish, as well as spiny lobsters, crabs, shrimp, sponges, sea turtles and other marine life, will be visible as you pass from the nursery grounds of the turtle grass at 4 to 10 feet to the deeper waters of the reef. Some of the excursions visit Adams Key, Elliott Key and

Photo: Victoria Shearer

Buy a bucket of bait at Robbie's Marina and feed the
remarkable tarpon that hang around the docks.

Boca Chita Key where picnic facilities, restrooms and nature trails have been established for visitors.

Visitors may also enjoy swimming, water skiing, fishing and bird-watching. Canoes are available for rent. Biscayne National Park is open year-round. There are no entrance fees, but concessionaire boat trips levy a charge. From Homestead, take SW 328th Street to the park entrance.

Everglades National Park
**National Park Service • (305) 242-7700,
(800) 368-4753
Main Visitor Center, Fla. Hwy. 9336**

The largest remaining subtropical wilderness in North America and one of the world's richest biological preserves, Everglades National Park encompasses the eight ecosystems of the Everglades within its 1.5 million acres. Endlessly fascinating, the Everglades is so much more than the ubiquitous alligator that quickly comes to mind. From the acres of sawgrass prairie to the pinelands, the hardwood hammocks and the mangrove-lined inland waterways, the Everglades supports a fascinating array of organisms at all levels of the food chain.

Ranger-led activities emanate from the various visitor centers of Everglades National Park, which is located at the southern tip of the 100-mile-long stretch of the Everglades: Main Visitor Center, at the park's main entrance; Royal Palm, off the main park road a few miles inside the main entrance; Flamingo, on the main park road at Florida Bay; Shark Valley, at the north end of the park on U.S. Highway 41; Gulf Coast Ranger Station, at Everglades City on Fla. Highway 29 at the northwest entrance.

You'll find naturalist-led hikes and talks, guided canoe trips and evening programs under the stars. Also available are tram tours and scenic, narrated boat tours into the backcountry waterways of Whitewater Bay or the Gulf waters of Florida Bay. Available for rent are motorboats, canoes, kayaks, bicycles, even houseboats. Fishing is good in the waters of Everglades National Park, and birdwatching is unparalleled, for the 'glades is home to the multispecied heron, egret and ibis families as well as wood storks, ospreys, bald eagles, snail kites and more. The Anhinga Trail at the Royal Palm Visitors Center teems with wading birds and alligators in January and February. Bring your camera.

The best time to visit Everglades National Park is the dry season, mid-December through mid-April, when mosquitoes are minimal. Many park activities are curtailed during the rainy season. Entrance fee is $10 per car, per week. From Florida City take Fla. Highway 9336 and follow signage to the Main Visitor Center.

Dry Tortugas National Park
National Park Service • (305) 242-7700, (800) 368-4753

Visit Dry Tortugas National Park, the end of the line in the Florida Keys, for a spectacular ride back in history. Accessible only by boat or seaplane (see our Cruising, Camping and Recreation chapters for transportation options), the Dry Tortugas, 70 miles west of Key West, harbor a rich history and an even more prolific underworld.

The seven islands were named by Ponce de Leon in 1513, presumedly for the multitude of sea turtles (tortugas) and the lack of fresh water (dry) on these keys. You'll be able to take a self-guided tour of Fort Jefferson on Garden Key, America's largest 19th-century coastal fort, which was started in 1846 but never completed. The walls are 50 feet high and 8 feet thick. For years, the fort operated as a military prison. Fort Jefferson's most famous inmate was Dr. Samuel Mudd, who was convicted of conspiracy after he set the broken leg of President Lincoln's assassin, John Wilkes Booth.

The protected waters surrounding the Tortugas sparkle with all the sea creatures of the coral reef as well as a good many shipwreck remains. With natural sand beaches and calm seas, snorkeling and swimming are a must. All the waters of the Dry Tortugas National Park are designated a no-take zone, so you may see fish and lobsters of gargantuan proportions.

There is no food, fresh water, electricity or medical assistance at Fort Jefferson. Salt water toilets, grills and picnic tables are provided. No lodging exists out here in the beyond, but you may camp on Garden Key if you pack in and pack out all water and supplies (see our Camping chapter). Campers pay slightly more than daytrippers for passage to Fort Jefferson, mostly to cover the cost of transporting the gear they must carry in and out.

The Florida Keys and
Key West serve up an
alphabet soup of things
kids can do and see,
from touch tanks to
trolley cars.

Kidstuff

Get ready, get set, go!

It's time to explore the alphabet soup of things to do in the Florida Keys and Key West, especially for kids. But we have to warn you. Your parents will want to come along.

We deviate from our usual geographic arrangement in this chapter, but all our attractions include addresses and phone numbers for convenience in finding them. Look to related chapters for a comprehensive listing of hours of operation and admission costs.

Tell Mom and Dad if they want to find out more details of our ABCs (and 1, 2, 3s in Key West), they can look in our Recreation and Attractions chapters, where they'll find lots more fun things to do.

The Florida Keys
Fun From A to Z

A is for . . .

affectionate sea lions that may try to kiss you at **Theater of the Sea**, MM 84.5 Oceanside, Islamorada, (305) 664-2431 — so be prepared. You can pet the sharks in the touch tank and touch the dolphins in another tank. In the main lagoon, created by excavations for Henry Flagler's railroad (see our Historical Evolution chapter), the dolphins put on quite a show. Watch them walk on their tails and jump high in the air. You'll see tropical fish and game fish, stingrays and sea turtles. There is even a boat ride through the lagoon. (For more on Theater of the Sea, see our Attractions chapter.)

B is for . . .

baiting a hook. Go fishing on one of our group party boats (see our Fishing chapter for complete information). You may catch the prismatic dolphin fish, which has a blunt forehead that makes it look a little like Bart Simpson. Or reel in some yellowtail snappers; they really have yellow tails. Almost certainly you'll catch grunts. They make a funny grunting sound when you take them out of the water. Keep a lookout for the playful mammal dolphins and sea turtles.

C is for . . .

crayon rubbings over an imprint of a moray eel, a queen angelfish, a loggerhead turtle or a lemon shark. These treasures are yours to create at the **Florida Keys Children's Museum** at Tropical Crane Point Hammock, MM 50.5 Oceanside, Marathon, (305) 743-9100. This hands-on museum has a hop-aboard pirate ship with dress-up pirate clothes, a real Cuban freedom raft, a fish pond (where you can feed the barracudas and the sharks), a touch tank full of hermit and horseshoe crabs, a huge seashell exhibit and even a thatched chickee sandbox built by the Miccosukee Indians. And don't miss Buoy, the broad-wing hawk, or the four resident iguanas — Mr. Iggy, Gossamer, SweetPea and Jade. (For more, see our Attractions chapter.)

D Is for . . .

"Don't touch!" If you touch the sap of the poisonwood tree when you walk through the nature trails at the **Tropical Crane Point Hammock**, MM 50.5 Oceanside, Marathon, (305) 743-9100, it will make you itch like poison ivy does. This tropical Keys forest is full of interesting sinkholes, red mangroves, thatch palms and lots of cool lizards, land crabs and birds. One fee covers admission to the hammock and the Florida Keys Children's Museum. And you'll enjoy the adjoining Museum of Natural History too. (See our Attractions chapter.)

E is for . . .

examining a treasure castle. Ours is filled with silver, gold and copper coins and artifacts retrieved from ancient shipwrecks on our coral reefs. The **Maritime Museum of the Florida Keys**, MM 102 Bayside, Key Largo, (305) 451-6444, shelters some of the buried bounty found underwater by Art McKee, the pioneer of treasure diving. Watch a black-and-white video of his early salvage attempts of the 1733 *San Pedro*. He wears 200 pounds of weights — some even on his feet — and a hard-helmeted diving hat that is connected to an air compressor on the surface for oxygen. (See our Attractions chapter for more on the museum.)

www.insiders.com

See this and many other **Insiders' Guide®** destinations online — in their entirety.

Visit us today!

F is for . . .

feeding the tarpon from the end of the dock at **Robbie's Marina**, MM 77.5 Bayside, Islamorada, (305) 664-9814. You can purchase a cup of bait fish, the tarpon's favorite snack, at the marina. These giant "silver kings" will swim in a frenzy before your very eyes, jockeying to be first in line when you throw the fish in the water.

G is for . . .

grabbing some rays at the beach. Play in the sand or look for crabs and crustaceans at **Sombrero Beach** in Marathon, MM 50 Oceanside, Sombrero Beach Road, which even has picnic tables so you can make a day of it. There is no admission fee. **Bahia Honda State Park**, MM 37 Oceanside, has two beaches. A small one near the concession stand at the south end of the park is calm, sheltered and roped off for safety. The other, the Sandspur, is much longer. You can wade in the soft sand through waters that vary from several inches to 3 feet deep looking for sea

creatures and washed up treasure. (See our Recreation chapter for more on beach options.)

H is for . . .

hopping aboard the *Emerald See* for a 5½-hour ecological tour of the Lower Keys backcountry with **Strike Zone Charters**, MM 29.5 Bayside, Big Pine Key, (305) 872-9863, (800) 654-9560. You'll learn the history of the Key deer and the tiny out-islands, the hurricanes, the wreckers and the Indians. You'll see bald eagle nesting sites, great white herons, egrets and dolphins feeding in the wild. You can snorkel and fish a little too. And to top it all off, you'll enjoy a fish cookout picnic on a private island. (See our Recreation chapter for more information.)

I is for . . .

investigating the **Blue Hole** — but don't feed the alligators. This freshwater sinkhole at MM 30.5 Bayside, Key Deer Boulevard, Big Pine Key, is home to a couple of curious 'gators, and they'll swim almost up to the viewing platform. Keep your puppy on a leash because its barking will ring the alligator's dinner bell. You'll see turtles in the Blue Hole, and Key deer come 'round at dusk. There is no admission charge.

J is for . . .

jumping into your jammies and listening to bedtime stories read for you at **Marathon Public Library**, MM 48.8 Oceanside, Marathon, (305) 743-5156, on Wednesday from 7 to 8 PM. Mom and Dad can come along, and don't forget your blankie. Or, if you are ages 3 to 6 or even older, come to the Saturday story hour from 10:30 to 11:30 AM. Summertime brings an assortment of activities at the library

INSIDERS' TIP

Take the kids fishing on one of Key West's party boats. See our Fishing chapter.

Life's a beach when you are young and carefree in the Florida Keys.

on Thursdays from 10 to 11 AM. The program is appropriate for ages 6 to 13 and runs from mid-June to early August. All these programs are free of charge.

K is for . . .

kicking your finned feet as you practice snorkeling in the shallow waters of the protective U-shaped jetty called **The Horseshoe**, MM 35 Bayside, just over the Bahia Honda Bridge as you head down the Keys (see our Diving and Snorkeling chapter). You'll see a natural aquarium of colorful tropical fish with no danger from sharks or barracudas 'cause they can't get in. It's free.

L is for . . .

looking a great white heron in the eye at the **Florida Keys Wild Bird Center**, MM 93.6 Bayside, Tavernier, (305) 852-4486. Although

some of the birds you'll see are permanent residents at the shelter because they can't exist in the wild anymore, others are recovering from injuries — like the hawk with the broken wing and the roseate spoonbill with an amputated leg — and will leave the center once healed. All the birds live in natural habitats that have been enclosed by huge wire cages. You can even go into the pelican cage yourself. (See our Attractions chapter for more on the center.)

M is for . . .

meeting friendly dolphins up close and personal at the **Dolphin Research Center**, MM 59 Bayside, Grassy Key, (305) 289-1121. The dolphins' behavior trainers will put them through learning exercises in the saltwater lagoon. Or spend a half day at **DolphInsight**, where you can listen to live underwater conversations through a hydrophone and learn the verbal and hand signals the trainers use to communicate with the dolphins. You can swim with dolphins in the **Dolphin Encounter** if you are between 5 and 12 years old. (See our Attractions chapter for more information.)

N is for . . .

navigating your way through two marked mangrove trails or the Largo Sound of **John Pennekamp Coral Reef State Park**, MM 102.5 Oceanside, Key Largo, (305) 451-1621, in a sea cycle. You can rent one here for $10 an hour. Your legs will be doing all the work in this two-passenger, pedal-driven pontoon craft. Look for the white herons and egrets feeding among the mangroves, and keep your eyes peeled for a sighting of a manatee. (For more information, see our Recreation chapter.)

O is for . . .

observing the catch of the day when you visit one of our fishing marina docks between 3:30 and 4 PM (see our Fishing chapter). That's when the charter boats come back in from offshore, and if their luck held, so will yours. You'll see giant dolphin, tuna, snapper, wahoo, grouper and cobia. But you probably won't see sailfish and marlin because, since they aren't good to eat, we prefer to release them back into the ocean so they may continue to live. This is free fun.

P is for . . .

paddling your very own kayak through the mangrove creeks and the backcountry of Florida Bay. If you are at least 10 years old, Mom and Dad can rent a Sit-on-Top or an enclosed cockpit kayak called a Keowee for you from the folks at **Florida Bay Outfitters**, MM 104 Bayside, Key Largo, (305) 451-3018.

The staff will provide you with a life jacket, paddle, paddle floater and chart. You and your family can go off on your own or take a three-hour family tour. You can even rent camping gear here and spend the night on one of the little out-islands in Florida Bay. (See our Recreation chapter.)

Q is for . . .

qualifying as a super sleuth when you participate in the Dolphin Connection's Dolphin Detectives Program. If you are at least 5 years old, you can learn how to be a dolphin trainer. You'll get your hands all fishy preparing the dolphin's food. And you might get splashed as you supervise a dolphin training session from the dry docks. You'll find **Dolphin Connection at Hawk's Cay Resort**, MM 61 Oceanside, (305) 743-7000, Extension 3030. (See our Attractions chapter.)

R is for . . .

riding out Watson Boulevard in Big Pine Key and crossing the bridge to **No Name Key**. If you come just as the sun is setting, you'll probably see our miniature Key deer — they're only 3 feet tall — wandering along the roadside. To get to No Name Key, go to MM 31 Bayside. Turn right on Key Deer Boulevard, then right on Watson and over the bridge. This is a free ride.

S is for . . .

swimming in the tidal pool at Key Largo's **Harry Harris Park**, MM 92.5 Oceanside, (305) 852-7161, if you get tired of swinging or playing on the slide. This state park has a small beach collared by a stone jetty so the waters are always calm. When the tide goes out, you can look for sea creatures. (For more information, see our Recreation chapter.)

T is for . . .

taking in a movie at the **Marathon Community Cinema**, at the side of Marathon Liquors and Deli, MM 50 Oceanside, Marathon, (305) 743-0288, or at the **Tavernier Towne Twin Cinema** in the Tavernier Mall, MM 91 Bayside, Tavernier, (305) 852-2023.

U is for . . .

unlocking the mysteries of a hardwood hammock on a nature walk with a naturalist on **Lignumvitae Key**. You'll have to take a boat trip from Robbie's Marina, MM 77.5 Bayside, Islamorada, (305) 664-9814, for Lignumvitae is out in Florida Bay. This is the way all the Keys looked long ago. You'll see the red bark of the gumbo limbo tree, called the "tourist tree" because the bark peels like a sunburned vacationer. You'll also encounter leafy trees with unusual names like mastic, strangler fig and pigeon plum. The lignum vitae tree (its name means "wood of life") grows very slowly. (See our Attractions chapter for more information.)

V is for . . .

viewing the fascinating world under the sea through the glass bottom of the *Osprey*, a nifty undersea viewing boat. You can see everything a snorkeler sees without ever getting wet. And the boat's captain will narrate some fascinating tales as he takes you out to the coral reef. You'll find the *Osprey* at MM 61 Oceanside, Hawk's Cay Marina, Duck Key; call (305) 743-7000.

W is for . . .

watching pottery being made by hand at **Bluewater Potters** in Treasure Village, MM 86.7 Oceanside, Islamorada, (305) 853-0616. Treasure Village is a castle-like arts and crafts village with a gigantic lobster statue out front. Or pull Mom and Dad into **Rudy's Kids Club**, (305) 853-1265, for an alligator T-shirt or one of their unusual environmental toys. You can climb a short stairway to the top of the castle building, where you can get a bird's-eye view of the Overseas Highway while your parents have a cup of coffee in the cafe.

X is for . . .

x-ing out the bad guys when you rent the latest equipment from **Blockbuster Video**, MM 100 Oceanside, Key Largo, (305) 451-1313, and MM 50 Bayside, Marathon, (305) 743-3034. Blockbuster has Super Nintendo, Sega Genesis, Sony Playstation, Sega Saturn and Nintendo 64. You can also rent all the game machines.

Y is for . . .

"Yow!" That's what you'll say when you see a shark really close up. Stop at **Captain Hook's Marina**, MM 53.1 Oceanside, Marathon, (305) 743-2444, and look at their 48,000-gallon outdoor aquarium. Every day at 4 PM you can watch the sharks — and lots of other big fish too — receive their evening meal. Keep your fingers out of the tank so you don't become dessert. It's free fun.

Z is for . . .

zipping across the old Seven Mile Bridge to **Pigeon Key** in the old-time trolley car. Or you can walk, jog or ride a bicycle to this 5-acre island, rich in history. Pigeon Key was the construction camp for workers building Henry Flagler's Railroad. Now the preserved early-19th-century buildings are listed on the National Register, and you can see them and take an island tour with a volunteer. Catch the trolley shuttle or rent bicycles at the Visitors Center, MM 47 Oceanside, Knight's Key, (305) 743-5999, or walk the old bridge to Pigeon Key. (See our Attractions chapter for more information.)

Kid-Friendly Resorts

Several of our premier resorts in the Florida Keys offer special organized programs for children, ensuring that you, Mom and Dad, have some time to pursue your own interests or just unwind and relax with a good book by the swimming pool. You will find more information about these hotels in our Accommodations chapter.

Photo: Steven C. Cook

Sun, fun and sand mark the interactive play at Camp Cheeca.

Westin Kids Club
Westin Beach Resort Key Largo, MM 97
Bayside, Key Largo • (305) 852-5553

Kids are special at the Westin Kids Club. If you are staying at the Westin or are a local resident with a membership to use the hotel grounds, your children can really take advantage of some interesting activities.

The children have sessions in the swimming pool and take walks along a nature trail and to the pier in search of bird and animal life. They snorkel at the beach or build sand castles. Lunch is served at Splashes, on premises. Crazie Crafts rate high on the agenda of favorite pastimes at the Westin Kids Club. Beading and coconut crafts, hat making and spin art, sand art and hand painting, toy boat modeling and puppet creation, all keep little fingers busy.

An all-day session at the Westin Kids Club runs from 10 AM to 4:30 PM. The cost, which includes lunch, is $25 per child. A half-day session, from 10 AM to 1 PM or 1:30 to 4:30 PM, is $15. Children between the ages of 5 and 12 are eligible. All participating children receive a Kids Club T-shirt.

Friday and Saturday nights Westin Kids Club offers kids special themed activities and frees up Mom and Dad to enjoy a romantic dinner alone. Friday nights kids enjoy a special pizza pool party complete with waterfall basketball, volleyball, water balloons and splash contests. On Saturday nights, the Kids Club hosts themed Super Splash parties where Crazie Crafts and such events as Tropical Travels, Clown Capers and Pirate Parades are featured. The evening activities run from 6 to 9 PM, include dinner and a Kids Club T-shirt, and cost $15 per child.

The Westin Beach Resort Key Largo also offers some optional activities for children: kayak lessons, a tennis workshop, and acting and drama workshops. Babysitting service is available through the hotel for $10 per hour (up to two children). All sitters are bonded and well screened.

Camp Cheeca
Cheeca Lodge, MM 82 Oceanside, Islamorada • (305) 664-4651

Camp Cheeca maintains an environmental focus through its never-ending selection of children's activities. From windsurfing to sewing, nutrition to cooking, exercise to massage and facials, the kids learn while they have fun. In the summer, Everglades Alert teaches them about the endangered ecosystems of the Everglades National Park and about Florida's trees and plants. The winter season brings Earth Alert, when the children learn how to protect species all over the world.

The kids make recycled art: pencil holders formed from Styrofoam meat trays and paper towel or toilet paper cardboard rolls are finished off with glue and sand for a stucco effect. Or the participants may braid plastic grocery bags into a rug. Nature art sessions result in weavings of palm fronds, painted coconuts or sand sculptures. And the Cheeca Challenge, team problem-solving initiatives, prove that everyone is important, even the little people, as the children work together to achieve a common goal.

The mysteries of the coral reef unfold in a classroom-like setting. Then the children learn to snorkel in the swimming pool and finally are taken out to the reef itself or under the oceanfront pier, where they experience the undersea wonders first hand. The children even cast a few lines, displaying the environmentally sound practice of catch-and-release fishing.

Camp Cheeca operates daily except Monday during holiday periods throughout the high season (the last three weeks of December, the first two weeks of January and the end of February through April). From June to Labor Day the camp is open from Monday through Sunday (Sunday is a half-day). During the rest of the year Camp Cheeca is open on weekends. Children ages 6 to 12 are invited to participate if they are guests of the hotel or if their families are members of the Cheeca Club (a membership fee is required to use hotel facilities). A full-day session, 9 AM to 4 PM, costs $26. Half-days (9 AM to noon or 1 to 4 PM) are $15. Cheeca Club members pay a lower rate. A half-day morning session will replace the all-day session if fewer than four children sign up.

Some nights are special at Cheeca Lodge. Kids Social Nights, on Thursdays and Saturdays, provide movies, games and arts and crafts from 7 to 9 PM and cost $6 per child. These evening activities are open to the children of anyone dining at Cheeca Lodge, but, since dinner is not included in the Kids Social Nights, parents should feed their children prior to dropping them off. Children ages 3 (must be completely potty-trained) through teen years are welcome to attend. All quoted prices are based on the 1997 rates and may be subject to change.

INSIDERS' TIP

Don't let your kids miss the sunset celebration at Key West's Mallory Square pier. As the sun sinks into the water, performers on land eat fire, juggle coconuts, play music and entertain everyone. And it's free.

Island Adventure Club

**Hawk's Cay Resort and Marina, MM 61
Oceanside, Duck Key • (305) 743-7000
Ext. 3175**

Island Adventure Club is a themed day camp offering ever-changing daily activities that are sure to attract the interest of kids of all ages. From Save the Planet Day, Sand Castle Day, Happy Easter Day, Marine Life Day to Back to the '60s Day and more, kids enjoy structured activities that teach about the Florida Keys' environment while they entertain. Arts and Crafts projects always incorporate a Keysy twist — fish, sand, shells, dolphins — so the children go home with a souvenir of the Keys. Swim activities include noodle races, treasure dives and tiki boat activities in Hawk's Cay's calm lagoon.

The Island Adventure Club offers themed interactive evening sessions on Wednesdays, Fridays and Saturdays as well. Dinner is included. Wednesday night is Florida Keys Island Night, where the children create a fish art project, play lagoon games and watch the movie Flipper. Friday night is Pirate Adventure Night, where the kids build their own pizza, go on a treasure hunt and watch *Muppets Treasure Island*. And its all-aboard to Safari Excursion Night on Saturday evening, when the art activity is making an animal pin out of Sculpsy clay and watching *George of the Jungle* or *Jungle to Jungle*.

The Island Adventure Club is staffed by degreed professionals year around as well as 12 interns, college juniors who participate for 16-week sessions. These exuberant young adults bring a special zest to the programs offered to the children. Kate Price is the club's director.

Children ages 3 to 11 are welcome at the Island Adventure Club. Children ages 3 and 4 may attend the morning session only. A full-day session lasts from 9 AM to 4 PM and costs $25 (includes lunch). A half-day, which runs from 9 AM to noon or 1 to 4 PM, is $15 (no lunch). Evening sessions last from 7 to 10 PM and cost $19 (includes dinner). The Island Adventure Club runs daily during the summer and during other high peak times, such as Christmas and Easter week, Presidents' weekend and other holidays.

Key West

Calling all kids. Come and join the countdown of the Top 5 things to do in Key West. We know you won't want to miss a single one.

No. 5

Step back in time as you explore the Civil War era fort at **East Martello Museum and Gallery**, 3501 S. Roosevelt Boulevard, (305) 296-3913. The brick walls are 8 feet thick, and you can climb the winding steps right to the top of the tall citadel. You'll find some piratical loot here too. Look for treasure chests, hiding rocks and manacles. And the outdoor gallery sports some pretty neat junk-art sculptures. (For more on the museum, see our Attractions chapter.)

No. 4

You'll love this movie adventure that envelops you on three screens. You might think you are under the sea as *A Key Encounter* explores the underwater mysteries of our coral reef — the corals, the fish and the fascinating plant life. This 25-minute video adventure also takes you to Big Pine Key and introduces you to our tiny Key deer, Blue Hole's alligators and other animals of the Florida Keys. It's open Sunday through Friday from 11 AM to 5 PM, with showings every 30 minutes. The theater is at Clinton Square Market, 291 Front Street, (305) 292-2070. (See our Attractions chapter.)

INSIDERS' TIP

Club Bounce is a kids' center in Key West open to elementary schoolers on Wednesdays from 6:30 to 8:30 PM and to middle school students on Fridays from 8 to 11 PM. Call Jimmy or Joanne Cooper, (305) 294-0965, for more information.

No. 3

At the **Mel Fisher Maritime Heritage Society Museum**, 200 Greene Street, (305) 294-2633, you'll see all kinds of gold and silver treasure recovered from the ancient ship *Atocha*, which sank off the Marquesas in 1622. Every 30 minutes a documentary movie shows how Mel Fisher searched for the fortune, a task that took nearly 20 years. Examine gold coins, bars of silver, gold chains and giant emeralds. You can even make a crayon-rubbing of a silver bar or some Spanish coins. Upstairs, the museum features interactive children's exhibits that change every six months. Children receive a special coloring guide at the front desk and upon successful identification of objects in the museum they are awarded a small prize. (For more information on the museum see our Attractions chapter.)

No. 2

Deep in a dark cistern, a foot below sea level, you'll meet a 175-year-old wrecker named Asa Tift at the **Key West Shipwreck Historeum**, 1 Whitehead Street at Mallory Square, (305) 292-8990. Surrounded by thick ropes, jugs, rigging and cannonballs, he'll tell all about the wreck of the *Isaac Allerton*, the richest Key West shipwreck of all. This funny little man (really an actor) asks if you'd like to hire on as a lumper or a wrecker or, if you can hold your breath a long time, as a diver to help salvage the cargo off the wreck. You'll see a video about old Key West, then Mr. Tift will personally invite you to the upper deck of the "ship," where you can see all kinds of interesting things he has salvaged. Each exhibit has headphones you can put on to hear recorded messages chock-full of information. Don't miss the laser mannequin, Capt. Philip Philpot — you'll swear he's real. Climb up to the top of the lookout tower and do as Asa Tift tells you: Shout "Wreck ashore!" (See our Attractions chapter for more information.)

No. 1

This is it. The place where you'll meet all the fish and sea creatures we tell you about in our Diving and Fishing chapters: The **Key West Aquarium**, 1 Whitehead Street at Mallory Square, (305) 296-2051. Be sure not to miss the guided tours — 11 AM and 1, 3 and 4:30 PM — because you'll be able to watch the feeding sessions of the stingrays, sharks, sawfish and barracudas. A splash from the eager stingray may even get your shirt wet. You'll get the chance to pet the tail of a nurse shark. The tour guide will show you the touch tank, where you can handle the hermit crabs, horse conchs, horseshoe crabs, sea cucumbers, pencil urchins and common starfish. The guide will pick up a queen conch and let its slimy brown body slither out of its pretty pink shell. Walk around the aquarium, and look at all the saltwater species of brightly colored tropical fish, blooming corals and sea fans. Look for the giant green moray eel. Go outside to the Atlantic Shores exhibit, re-created to give you the experience of a Florida Keys mangrove habitat. You'll see huge tarpon, snook, jacks and sea turtles swimming in the crystal-clear water. If you don't get a chance to snorkel or dive in the ocean waters of our coral reef, this is the next best thing. The aquarium is open daily from 10 AM to 6 PM. (See our Attractions chapter.)

Kid-Friendly Resorts

Coral Reef Kids Club
Sheraton Key West, 2001 South Roosevelt Blvd. • (305) 292-9800, (800) 452-3224

Kids have it all in their very special club room of the Coral Reef Kids Club at the Sheraton Key West. Finished by local artists, all surfaces of the room re-create our coral reef. The floor is painted to resemble the ocean floor. The ceiling depicts the surface of the ocean waters, complete with a snorkeler looking down into the room and the bottom of a boat, suspended — with hook, line and sinker — from above. Adorning the walls are realistically detailed creatures of the reef, such as colorful coral and tropical fish, stingrays and barracudas. A television set perches atop a harbor piling.

Children ages 4 to 12 enjoy a changing rota of highly interactive activities, all with an

Children discover a friendly Keys bottle-nosed dolphin at the Dolphin Research Center.

educational twist. They learn about the creatures of the reef and other Keys wildlife. Face-painting, storytelling and hair braiding prove popular diversions. But most popular are the pool activities held each day. A state-of-the-art outdoor playground opened in May 1997, featuring slides, crawl-through tubes and hanging bridges.

The Coral Reef Kids Club, which opened in January 1997, is open on Wednesday, Saturday and Sunday from 10:30 AM to 4 PM, for full day or half-day sessions, and Tuesday and Friday evenings from 6 to 10:30 PM. Full-day sessions include lunch and cost $25. Half-day sessions (no lunch) are $15. The evening sessions feature a PG-rated movie, dinner and unlimited soft drinks and popcorn throughout the movie. Evening sessions are $25. If more than one child from the same family attends the all-day or evening session, cost for the additional children is $20 each.

Marriott's Casa Marina Resort
1500 Reynolds St. • (305) 296-3535

Free for guests at Marriott's Casa Marina Resort is a potpourri of organized children's activities from 10:30 AM to 1:15 PM. Listed and posted on the bulletin board by the pool deck each day, these activities are open to children ages 6 to 12. Three 45-minute sessions explore arts and crafts (clay painting, jewelry making, weaving), active games (Frisbee throws, dodge ball, croquet, horseshoes) and passive games (board games, Pictionary, checkers, bingo). The children particularly like coconut bowling and shell hunts on the beach. No swimming activities are planned within the program. Parents are asked to remain on the premises of Casa Marina Resort while their children are participating in the activities. Babysitting is also available anytime through the concierge for $10 per hour. Each additional child in the family adds $1 to the rate, so that the rate for two children is $11 per hour, rate for 3 children is $12 per hour and so forth.

Immerse yourself in Florida Keys arts and culture at our historic observances, music festivals or arts and crafts fairs.

Annual Events

No one knows how to throw a party better than residents of the Florida Keys. Come dress with us in period attire as we relive eras of our past. Or join locals — and folks from all over the world — in a challenging road race on a bridge spanning miles of open sea.

We also have boat parades, bikini contests, battle reenactments and our own unplugged underwater concert. Or try your angling skills in one of our many fishing tournaments (see our Fishing chapter for an expanded listing). Immerse yourself in Florida Keys arts and culture at our historic observances, music festivals or arts and crafts fairs.

And my, how we love to eat. From Key Largo to the Lower Keys, food festivals abound. These events provide an inexpensive means of sampling incredibly fresh seafood and menu items from leading local restaurants.

The following selection of festivals and events is a sampling of what we offer annually in the Florida Keys; a separate calendar of events for Key West follows the Florida Keys section. Additional events occur sporadically from year to year. Months, dates and locations sometimes change, and admission prices vary; events may even be cancelled on the spur of the moment. We suggest you call festival organizers in advance to confirm all details. You can pick up the annual *Attractions & Events* brochure at any of our chambers of commerce: Key Largo, MM 106 Bayside, (305) 451-1414, (800) 822-1088; Islamorada, MM 82.5 Bayside, (305) 664-4503, (800) 322-5397; Marathon, MM 53.5 Bayside (305) 743-5417; (800) 262-7284; Lower Keys, MM 31 Oceanside, (305) 872-2411, (800) 872-3722; Key West, Old Mallory Square, (305) 294-2587, (800) 527-8539.

January

Organized Fishermen of Florida (OFF) Seafood Festival
Plantation Yacht Harbor, MM 87, Plantation Key • (305) 664-5596

Your boats — commercial fishing, that is — have just come in. And what fine catches they have made. Our commercial fishing industry's largest fund-raiser often features a raw bar, split lobster and dolphin all heaped generously onto your plate at extremely reasonable prices. The OFF booth provides educational literature about commercial fishing in the Florida Keys plus handy recipes for preparing seafood dishes at home. Live entertainment is on hand, and arts and crafts vendors peddle stained glass, beads, copper sculpture and pottery. Kids will like the carnival rides, including a Ferris wheel and mini-roller coaster. This event is held the third weekend in January. Admission is $2 for adults and free for children younger than 13. The fee does not include food, rides and other incidental purchases.

Cheeca Lodge Presidential Sailfish Tournament
MM 82, Oceanside, Islamorada • (305) 664-4651

One of the most popular sailfish tournaments of the season, the Presidential received its name back when George Bush was president and came to fish our Islamorada waters. Cash prizes and trophies are awarded in this catch-and-release tournament. See our Fishing chapter for details.

Florida Keys Renaissance Faire
MM 50 Oceanside, Sombrero Beach Park, Marathon • (305) 743-5447, (800) 262-7284

How gallantly we begin the year, stepping into the medieval era as professional performers portray members of the royal court. You'll enjoy jousting, a living chess match and an ever-changing montage of Renaissance entertainment. Medieval rides and games are on-site for the enjoyment of young and old alike. Enticing aromas fill the air, and master craftspeople hawk their wares in the Market Lanes. Music from the Shire's Minstrels resounds throughout the faire grounds. The event is held annually on the Martin Luther King Jr. holiday weekend. Tickets at the gate cost $7 for adults, $6 for senior citizens and $5 for students (ages 7 to 17); children 6 and younger enter for free when accompanied by an adult.

February

Treasure Village Outdoor Art Show
MM 86.7, Oceanside, Plantation Key • (305) 852-0511

The grounds outside the late treasure salvor Art McKee's legendary castle and treasure museum (now an arts and crafts mall) teem with activity throughout the third weekend in February and then again in March and the second weekend in April. Artists and crafters from throughout the country display watercolors and acrylics, wood works, handpainted clothing and more. Admission is free.

Holiday Isle Hawaiian Luau
MM 84, Oceanside, Islamorada • (305) 664-2321

Aloha! You'll be greeted at this annual American Red Cross fund-raiser with an artificial lei, a beachside pig roast, grilled kabobs,

live tropical music and Hawaiian dancers. Limited tickets are sold for a reverse raffle, whereby the last tickets drawn win cash prizes. Admission is free. Food and beverages are sold individually. The luau is typically held the last weekend in February.

Florida Keys Art Fest
Key Colony Beach City Hall, 600 W. Ocean Dr., Key Colony Beach • (305) 743-5151

In addition to the works of artists throughout the country, local high school students display their talents at this intimate showing. Bronze, stone and metal sculptures, oil paintings, watercolors and other fine arts and crafts are among the items featured. Judging is held for the work of high school students only. Food, beverages and live entertainment are offered throughout the weekend, and a raffle drawing affords you the chance to win some of the work on display. Florida Keys Art Fest is typically held during the third weekend in February. Admission is free.

Pigeon Key Art Festival
Pigeon Key • (305) 289-0025

More than 50 artists from throughout the country gather on the shores of Pigeon Key the first weekend in February to display a variety of works. This is a juried show, meaning artists' works have been screened for quality prior to being included. At weekend's close, judges bestow awards for the best artwork in categories such as watercolor, oil and acrylic painting, jewelry, photography, sculpture, glass, pottery and graphics. Live entertainment features the music of steel-drum bands, jazz groups, classical ensembles and country-and-western performers. Local restaurants sell food, and raffle drawings include original artwork donated by each participating artist.

Getting to this festival by your choice of water taxi, trolley or Pigeon Key "choo-choo" is half the fun, and transportation is included in the admission price ($7.50 for adults, $2 for students and free for children 12 and younger). All proceeds are donated to the Pigeon Key

Foundation for restoration of the island (see our Attractions chapter). Artists pay $100 entry fees, and half the show's work has a Florida theme.

Pigeon Key Jazz Festival
Pigeon Key • (305) 289-0025

Jazz at its finest comes to the Florida Keys the second weekend in February, and you won't want to miss it. Come hear Maynard Ferguson and other legendary jazz greats as they get together for a jam session under the stars at the Pigeon Key National Historic Site. Tickets are $30 per person, which includes tram transportation to the island from the Pigeon Key Visitors Center at MM 47 Oceanside, where you can park your automobile. Food, beer and wine are available at an additional charge.

March

Taste of the Keys Bird Bash
Key Largo • (305) 453-9643

Some of the best Upper Keys restaurants offer everything from soup to sushi at this, the largest fund-raiser for the Florida Keys Wild Bird Center, a rehabilitative facility for sick and injured birds (see our Attractions chapter). Prizes go to the best dishes in a variety of categories, including soup, salad and entree. Live entertainment typically features a one-man band. Silent and live auctions offer the opportunity to purchase a variety of items at reasonable prices.

Exact dates and locations vary, but the event is typically held on a Sunday in March. The admission price of $20 includes all food; beverages are sold separately.

Rain Barrel Arts Festival
MM 86.7 Bayside, Plantation Key
• (305) 852-3084

This juried art show is so popular that thousands of artisans from throughout the country apply, but only 100 are selected as exhibitors. Held the third weekend in March at the Rain Barrel Village of Artists & Craftspeople, the event features mixed media with a cross-section of artwork, including stained glass, leather works, watercolors, oil paintings and more. First-, second- and third-place cash prizes are awarded to the best in each of six categories: paintings, crafts, jewelry, sculpture, photography and graphics. Live entertainment offers a cultural mix, including instrumental Native American, reggae and jazz. Food and beverages are sold separately, and admission is free.

Holiday Isle Bikini and Body Building Contests
MM 84, Oceanside, Islamorada
• (305) 664-2321

This marks just the beginning of Holiday Isle's body-baring events. Throughout spring break and Memorial Day, Labor Day and July 4th weekends, women romp in their skimpiest swimsuits for one of the largest cash prizes of its kind: $1,000. This same purse is split equally among the male and female winners of bodybuilding contests. Spectators receive complimentary souvenirs and T-shirts. Admission is free.

Save A Turtle Picnic
Marathon • (305) 664-8252

Designed to raise funds to find a cure for fibropapilloma tumors that plague green sea turtles, this annual barbecue is held at a public beach or on park grounds. Founded in 1985 and co-sponsored by the Florida Park Service and the Game and Freshwater Fish Commission, Save A Turtle researches turtle nesting and conducts protective beach patrols. When you adopt a baby turtle through this organization, you'll receive a certificate of adoption with a photo of your hatchling. The picnic costs $6 for adults and $3 for children ages 6 through 12; it's free for children 5 and younger. This fee includes food, live entertainment and the company of a local turtle. Dates and locations change annually.

The Original Marathon Seafood Festival
Marathon • (305) 743-5417

We've been on Keys Time long enough to realize it isn't necessarily the early bird that always catches the worm. If you missed the Organized Fishermen of Florida (OFF) Seafood Festival in January, here is your opportunity to reap its rewards while supporting the

Florida Keys commercial fishing and tourism industries. Sponsored by the Marathon Chamber of Commerce and OFF, The Original Marathon Seafood Festival features thousands of pounds of fish, including cobia ceviche, golden crabs, conch fritters, Florida lobster and a raw bar. Landlubbers can munch on hot dogs, hamburgers and ethnic dishes.

Educational literature on the commercial fishing industry is distributed, and the Mid Keys Marine Association hosts a festival flea market with new and discontinued marine items at below-retail prices. Rides, games, vendors and raffles mean fun for the entire family, and live entertainment is provided.

Held the last weekend in March, the OFF Seafood Festival location changes annually. Admission is $2 for adults; children younger than 12 get in free. Food and rides are priced additionally.

April

Bay Jam
Plantation Yacht Harbor, MM 87 Bayside, Plantation Key • (305) 451-1414

Continuous concerts by the sea are the highlight of this daylong event featuring local and out-of-county musicians. You can lounge on the beach or on the extensive grounds at Plantation Yacht Harbor and enjoy a variety of performances including reggae, calypso, blues and jazz. Better yet, anchor offshore and sway to the sounds while aboard your boat. Typically held the second Sunday in April, Bay Jam offers food, beverages and games at an additional cost. Admission is free.

Chamber of Commerce Taste of Islamorada
Islamorada • (305) 664-4503

Islamorada's most popular restaurants all come together for this annual Chamber of Commerce fund-raiser. Booths at the event allow visitors to sample a variety of unlimited cuisines from 15 to 20 fine dining establishments, all at one minimal cover charge. If you have never dined at Islamorada's local restaurants, this is a wonderfully inexpensive opportunity to try out several. Live entertainment and raffle prizes make this a popular family event.

Locations change annually. Admission is $20; beverages are sold separately.

Don Hawley Invitational Tarpon Tournament
(903) 454-6178

This Don Hawley event is the Keys' oldest tarpon-on-fly tournament and the original all-release event. Proceeds benefit the nonprofit Don Hawley Foundation, which supports the study of tarpon fishery and preservation in the Florida Keys. See our Fishing chapter for details. Eddie Miller is the contact.

Earth Day at Cheeca Lodge
MM 82 Oceanside, Islamorada
• (305) 664-4651

Every year, Cheeca Lodge puts on quite a spectacle in honor of Mother Earth. The big draw here is the land-based aerial display, where revelers put together the words "Earth Day" in huge letters made out of sand. Other events include fishing tournaments, cooking demonstrations, costume contests, live entertainment and barbecues. Open to the public, Cheeca Lodge's Earth Day celebration raises funds for environmental causes. Admission is free.

Seven Mile Bridge Run
Marathon • (305) 743-8513

Men and women from all over the world flock to this seven miles of roadway spanning the open water between Marathon and Bahia Honda. In the wee morning hours, these spirited individuals participate in the most scenic competition of its kind: a run across one of the world's longest bridges. Organized by the Marathon Runners Club, sponsored by a number of Florida Keys businesses and designed to raise money for local schools and youth groups, the run is said to be the only one in the world held completely over and surrounded by water. Post-race prizes are awarded in various categories, and runners gather for what is likely the world's largest early morning celebratory bash. Held usually on the second Saturday in April and beginning on the Marathon end of the Seven Mile Bridge, the run requires a $25 entry fee. Spaces are limited, so if you plan to run, reserve your spot early.

Note: The run closes the Seven Mile Bridge

Fantasy Fest

Kookier than Carnival and merrier than Mardi Gras, Fantasy Fest is Key West's own decadent decibel of dreamy delight.

Fantasy Fest was originally conceived as a way to boost tourism in an otherwise soft season. It succeeded — and how! Today, more than two decades after its conception, this event annually doubles the island's population for one week in October, culminating with the arrival of some 50,000 revelers on Duval Street for the Saturday night parade.

 Close-up

Fantasy Fest is a nine-day adult Halloween celebration that commences on a Friday night with the Royal Coronation Ball, where the King and Queen of Fantasy Fest are crowned. The competition is open to all, and campaigning for the titles begins as early as late August. The winners are the ones who "buy" the most votes (translation: They raise the most money for AIDS Help Inc.). The closer it gets to Fantasy Fest, the fiercer the competition becomes and the more creative the candidates must become at finding sponsors and venues for their fund-raising efforts.

Contributions are accepted right up to the last minute when the final tally takes place at the Coronation Ball. The man and woman — or man and man-in-drag — are dubbed "royalty" only after emerging from a field of entrants whose votes have been bought and sold and bought and sold all over again. The King and Queen receive regal robes, crowns and scepters and preside over all official Fantasy Fest events. While it's considered quite a coup to be named King or Queen, the real winners in all of this are the people served by AIDS Help Inc.

The competition doesn't end with the race for King and Queen. It continues over the weekend as captains seek the winner's cup in the Fantasy Yacht Race's Victory at Sea. On Masked Monday, fines are imposed on anyone (including any unsuspecting tourist) who does not comply with the loony law of the land: You must be masked to meander Duval Street, or the Mask Rangers will make an example of you.

Each year, Fantasy Fest features a new theme, which is emblazoned on posters and T-shirts promoting the events, all of which are for sale, of course. In keeping with Key West's penchant for parties, a poster-signing celebration is held on Masked Monday. The following night, you can enjoy a preview of some courageous/outrageous costumes at the Masked Madness and Headdress Ball. Then on Wednesday, be sure to enter your pet (and yourself) in the Pet Masquerade and Parade. No species is excluded.

The complete list of Fantasy Fest events portends a good time by all: Celebrities Look-Alike Contest, Beach Party, Pretenders in Paradise costume

— continued on next page

Photo: Stuart Newman Associates

At Fantasy Fest, designers vie for the most beguiling masquerade creations.

competition, Toga Party, Fantasy Fest Street Fair, Tea Dance in the Street and the Masquerade March from the Key West Cemetery to Mallory Square. But all of these are only a mere tease to the culminating event yet to come.

On the Saturday preceding Halloween (or on Halloween night, if it happens to fall on a Saturday), Duval Street becomes one huge costume party. Floats, bands and masked marchers flaunt their flash — and often flesh — in the Twilight Fantasy Parade that begins at the Gulf of Mexico and ends at the Atlantic Ocean. The parade is supposed to last 2½ hours, but it often takes longer. As the floats make their way down Duval, the partying spectators spill into the street and often halt their progress.

Fantasy Fest has become a Key West tradition that rivals even Mardi Gras. It's bewitching. It's bedazzling. Best of all, significant bits of it benefit charity organizations, including the nonprofit Florida Keys-wide AIDS Help Inc. and the Florida Keys Children's Shelter.

---

on a Saturday morning for approximately 2 hours. If you need to be somewhere at a certain time that day and your route requires a trip across the bridge, make sure you're on the desired side before 7:30 AM.

May

Holiday Isle Bartenders in Paradise Party
MM 84 Oceanside, Islamorada
• (305) 664-2321

This weeklong event marking the end of the tourist season draws bartenders from throughout the Keys to participate in games of bartending skill, water basketball, volleyball and tug-o-war. There's also a bikini contest, beachside barbecue and live entertainment daily. Typically held the second week in May, this party is open to the public. There is no admission fee; food and beverages are sold individually.

July

Fourth of July Parade
Overseas Highway, Key Largo
• (305) 852-3216

From Mardi Gras to Native American, this old-fashioned community-oriented parade goes the distance from MM 98 to MM 105. The Overseas Highway is closed during the hourlong parade, which begins at 10 AM, except when the holiday falls on a Sunday, in

which case the parade begins at 1 PM. All are welcome to participate. Award plaques are presented to the best floats in seven categories, including most beautiful, best use of theme and best use of natural materials. A barbecue at the Elks Lodge traditionally follows. The parade is free. Admission price to the barbecue varies.

Fourth of July Fireworks
Bayside, Key Largo • (305) 451-4502

View this half-hour fireworks display from land or, if you are a boater, by sea. Funded by local merchants, the show typically begins at 9 PM. The best coastal viewing spots are the Caribbean Club, Señor Frijoles, Sundowners and Marriott Key Largo Bay Beach Resort. Some of these facilities host barbecues with live entertainment. Admission is free, but you must be a patron to enjoy the view from a private business. Food and drinks are sold separately.

Star Spangled Event
Sombrero Beach, MM 50 Oceanside, Marathon • (305) 743-5417

On July 4, follow a parade to the beach, where fireworks decorate the sky, and enjoy all-American hot dogs, hamburgers and fish sandwiches. Live entertainment is provided, games are available for the kids, and an afternoon volleyball tournament welcomes last-minute sign-ups. Many people see the fireworks display from the decks of their boats, anchoring offshore for the extravaganza. The traffic jam at sea rivals the one on land. No admission or entry fee is required. Food and games are priced individually.

Holiday Isle Independence Day BBQ & Fireworks
MM 84 Oceanside, Islamorada
• **(305) 664-2321**

One of Holiday Isle's largest gatherings, this weekendlong celebration features live music, Bikini contests and volleyball games. An evening fireworks display lasts nearly 30 minutes. Admission is free (food and beverages priced separately).

Underwater Music Fest & Chamber Food Festival
MM 31 Oceanside, Big Pine Key
• **(305) 872-2411**

Whether you dive, snorkel or merely swim, here is an unplugged series of "concerts" that beats music videos fins-down. Six hours of prerecorded commercial-free music -- from Beethoven to the Beatles — can be enjoyed in synchronicity with tropical fish swimming across the reefs of the Looe Key National Marine Sanctuary. Dance the day away underwater and look out for surprises such as mermaids and the Keys' very own Snorkeling Elvises.

Typically, the music fest runs from midmorning to midafternoon and is broadcast live on radio. Landlubbers and those who have danced up an appetite can enjoy this same music plus a variety of foods, arts and crafts and family games at the Lower Keys Chamber of Commerce, MM 31 Oceanside. Admission to both the concert and the food festival, hold the second Saturday in July, is free. See our Diving chapter for a list of dive and snorkel charters that will take you to the reef.

August

Historic Seacraft Race & Festival
Big Pine Key • (305) 872-2411

Designed to accentuate the maritime history of the Florida Keys, this gathering combines rowing, kayak and canoe races with new and historic watercrafts, arts and crafts vendors, ship carvings, macrame, displays, jewelry sales and a variety of ethnic cuisine. The

Historic Seacraft Race is held at different places and times each year. Admission is free, but race entry requires a fee.

September

Florida Keys Poker Run
Miami through Key West
• **(305) 294-3032**

With so many magnificent bridges, the Florida Keys is extremely popular with motorcycle riders. For this event, more than 10,000 motorcyclists ride from Miami to Key West, stopping at various points within our islands to pick up playing cards. At the end of the ride, the player with the best poker hand wins, and all enjoy live bands, field events and runs-within-a-run on Duval Street. Bikers can also get their machines blessed before returning home. Entry is free; each poker hand costs $5.

Nikona Shootout
Key Largo • (305) 451-2228

Hundreds of divers head for Key Largo for a weekendlong photo competition. Sponsored by Nikon and coordinated by Waterhouse Photo Tours, the competition offers divers the opportunity to capture images of the diverse marine life, coral reefs and the abundant wrecks in Key Largo waters. About $25,000 in prizes, including dive trips, camera and dive equipment and more, go to the photos judged best in such categories as standard and wide-angle lens. Host hotels offer parties and photography seminars. This event is typically scheduled two weeks after Labor Day and runs from Thursday through Sunday. Registration is free.

October

Mariner Outboards' Baybone Tournament
(305) 664-2002

Event No. 2 in the Celebrity Tournament Series (see our Key West's September section for the first event), this is a catch-and-release tournament in pursuit of bonefish and permit. Proceeds benefit the Cystic Fibrosis

Foundation. See our Fishing chapter for details. The Key Largo contact is Gary Ellis.

Holiday Isle Volleyball Tournament
MM 84 Oceanside, Islamorada
• (305) 664-2321

Sponsored by Miller Brewing Company, the tournament attracts professionals and amateurs to vie for round-robin or two-man team volleyball championships on the beach. In the past, the two-day tournament has attracted athletes from all over the world, including a Cuban Olympian. Admission is free.

Indian Key Festival
Islamorada • (305) 664-4704

One of the Upper Keys' most anticipated events, the Indian Key Festival consists of weekendlong guided tours, interpretive displays and living-history re-enactments, such as the 1840 attack on this island during The Seminole Wars. Indian Key is accessible only by boat, and transportation is provided from the Indian Key Fill at MM 78.5. Income from food and T-shirt sales at this festival helps fund the nonprofit group Friends of the Islamorada State Parks in its efforts to preserve and protect natural resources while at the same time making them available to the public. Admission is free, and the event is usually scheduled for the second weekend in October.

Holiday Isle Halloween Costume Party
MM 84 Oceanside, Islamorada
• (305) 664-2321

Unlike Key West's Fantasy Fest parade, which is always staged on the last Saturday in October, not necessarily the 31st, Holiday Isle's Costume Party is actually held on Halloween night. Dress as outlandish as you like, and you may win any number of cash prizes in the center-stage costume contest. Also enjoy live music and drink specials at Holiday Isle's infamous tiki bar. Admis-

sion is free. Food and beverages are available at an additional cost. The event is for adults.

November

Island Jubilee
Harry Harris Park, MM 92.5 Oceanside, Tavernier • (305) 451-1414

This two-day festival has been voted best of the Upper Keys. Held in conjunction with the Miss Island Jubilee Pageant, the Island Jubilee Talent Quest and the Island Jubilee Cook-Off, the festival features arts and crafts and food booths, games for kids and local entertainment performed by professional bands and talent quest winners. The cook-off culminates in prizes for the best recipes in the categories of professional, amateur and haute cuisine entrees, appetizers and desserts. Even if you do not enter the contest, you can take part in a post-judging public tasting. Admission costs $3 (free for children younger than 12). Food, beverages, rides and games are additional.

George Bush/Cheeca Lodge Bonefish Tournament
MM 82 Oceanside, Islamorada
• (305) 664-4651

Former President George Bush himself participates in this, the most prestigious of all our tournaments. All bonefish must be released. Winners are awarded trophies. See our Fishing chapter for details.

Mercury Outboards' Redbone Tournament
Islamorada • (305) 664-2002

Third in the Celebrity Tournament Series is the Redbone, the competitive search for bonefish and redfish. Proceeds in this tournament also benefit the Cystic Fibrosis Foundation. See our Fishing chapter for details. Contact Gary Ellis at the number listed above.

Sky Dive Marathon
Marathon Airport, MM 52 Bayside, Marathon • (305) 743-5417

Between 800 and 1,000 skydivers from throughout the United States participate in this two-day event which is typically held the second weekend of November on the grounds of the Marathon Airport. Weekend activities include skydiving demonstrations and an air show. There is no admission fee. Food and beverages are available for purchase.

December

Christmas Boat Parade
Bayside, Key Largo • (305) 451-4502

Deck the boats with boughs of holly. . . . Come watch a festive parade of between 30 and 50 lighted boats glow its way through Blackwater Sound. Prizes are awarded in various categories. At recent events we've spotted Santa Claus catching a sailfish and Frosty the Snowman water-skiing. As with the Fourth of July Fireworks, the best coastal viewing locations are the Caribbean Club, Señor Frijoles, Sundowners and Marriott Key Largo Bay Beach Resort. Some of these facilities host barbecues with live entertainment. Admission is free, but you must be a patron at any of these facilities to enjoy the view.

Holiday Isle New Year's Fireworks Celebration
MM 84 Oceanside, Islamorada • (305) 664-2321

Whatever your party preference, you can find a way to ring in the New Year at Holiday Isle. The resort offers a casual outdoor celebration with party hats, party goods and drink specials and a formal dinner in its elegant Horizon restaurant. Join in the countdown to midnight wherever you are, and see a spectacular fireworks display over the Atlantic. Admission is free.

Key Colony Beach Boat Parade
MM 53.5 Oceanside, Key Colony Beach • (305) 289-1212

A more intimate, equally spectacular version of the Key Largo boat parade, this one is held along the landmark canals of Key Colony Beach. Admission is free.

Key West

Honk a conch! It's party time at the end of the line.

Outwitting, outstanding and outlandish, festivals and events in Key West reflect the dreams and schemes of the very varied individuals who have discovered their place within this potent post. Writers, rebels and restorers are among them. Ride with us on this roller coaster of revel and rally — and then join us when the real frills and thrills begin.

January

Annual House and Garden Tours
Various Key West sites • (305) 294-9501

Olde Island Restoration, a nonprofit organization that encourages preservation of Key West's many historic structures, sponsors this popular tour to show off some of the city's finest private properties. At intermittent times during January, February and March, foundation members guide visitors on tours of a select group of five or six privately owned historic homes. Tours explore shotgun-style cottages, Conch-style mansions and everything in between (see our Architecture Close-up in the Attractions chapter).

Guides discuss the builders responsible for these c. 1800s homes. Some residences were built by stranded sailors and wreckers who added gingerbread detail and hurricane-proof components to what otherwise would be pleasing but rather conventional abodes.

Participants meet at Olde Island Restoration offices along Mallory Square and then embark on a Conch Trolley tour. Home tours typically are held in the evening. Scheduled dates vary from year to year.

Key West Yachting Race Week
Waters off Key West • (305) 294-2587

Sailors from throughout the world flock to Key West the second week in January for this event, the biggest annual regatta in America. More than 250 sailboats compete for no money, just glory and prestige. America's Cup teams use this event for training and to scope out the competition. Everyone who's anyone in sailing is sure to be here. The event lasts five days, with races beginning each day at around 10 AM.

Island Food & Music Festival
Bayview Park, Key West
• **(305) 294-9575**

The premier charity fund-raiser of the Key West Sunrise Rotary Club of the Conch Republic offers a carnival-like atmosphere of food, fun and games for the entire family. A Ferris wheel, merry-go-round and other rides are available for children, and more than 13 local bands perform throughout the weekend. Mallory Square's infamous sunset performers (see our Attractions chapter) also grab a piece of the action.

Come hungry! Fish sandwiches, fritters and funnel cakes make satisfying entrees, topped off by Key lime pie, candy apples and fudge.

Bayview Park is at the intersection of four main roads: N. Roosevelt Boulevard and Truman Avenue and Jose Marti and Eisenhower Drives. Held either the last weekend in January or the first weekend in February, the festival requires admission and parking fees. More than 20 charities, including local high schools, youth clubs and the Salvation Army, benefit from the event.

Key West Craft Show
Whitehead and Caroline Sts., Key West
• **(305) 294-1241**

Key West ends the month of January with a weekendlong exhibit of original crafts. Among the one-of-a-kind items offered for sale are handmade jewelry, leather goods, wood carvings, kitchen accessories and beach and lounge chairs. Exhibitors come from throughout the United States. The craft show takes place in the street — on Whitehead Street between Eaton and Greene and along Caroline Street in Truman Annex. The Island Food & Music Festival (see listing in this section) is sometimes held this same weekend. Admission is free.

Key West Literary Seminar
San Carlos Institute, 516 Duval St., Key West • (888) 293-9291

In 1981 Key West author David Kaufelt and a group of his colleagues capitalized on Key West's literary reputation by bringing writers from throughout the world together to discuss their works. Since then, the Key West Literary Seminar has blossomed into a highly respected, annual theme event featuring such prominent panelists that the seminar sells out months in advance.

Not all attendees are writers. Some are professors; others are plumbers. They travel the world over for this event because they share a common interest or hobby: writing and reading. Past themes have included "American Writers in the Natural World," which addressed all forms of nature writing and featured Annie Dillard, Jim Harrison and Peter Matthiessen. A journalism seminar brought together the likes of David Halberstam, Anna Quindlen and Louis Harris. Other topics covered by the Key West Literary Seminar include literature in film and travel, new directions in American theater and children's literature.

Panelists deliberate among themselves the evolution of each form of writing and the issues that affect it; they then open their discussion to a public Q-and-A session.

Key West's San Carlos Institute, 516 Duval Street, typically serves as the home base for these sessions. Writing workshops, tours of legendary local authors' homes and cocktail parties also are offered to seminar participants. Included in the core seminar price, these parties offer the opportunity to mingle with panel guests. Workshops and tours cost an additional fee. The four-day event is typically held during the second week of January. Call for information on registration and workshop fees, but reserve early. These events are typically sold out nine to 10 months in advance.

February

Old Island Days Art Festival
Whitehead St., Key West
• **(305) 294-0431**

If you appreciate art, your heart is bound to beat faster at the sight of several blocks of exhibits by talented local artists. Inspired by this southernmost city, they take this opportunity to showcase their vivid creations. Virtually all artistic mediums are represented in this pre-juried weekendlong show, including oil, wa-

Photo: Andy Newman

You never know what you'll get into at the Florida Keys Renaissance Faire in Marathon.

tercolor and acrylic paintings; graphics; wood, metal and stone sculptures; glasswork; and photography. Judges provide merit awards within each category. Old Island Days Art Festival exhibits line Whitehead Street from Greene Street to Caroline and into Truman Annex during the last weekend in February.

March

Key West Garden Club Flower Show
West Martello Tower, Atlantic Blvd. and White St., Key West • (305) 294-3210

Established in 1949 by former Key West politician Joe Allen, the Garden Club organizes monthly educational seminars for the public. Plant-swapping sessions also are popular. The group holds a pre-juried show every other year (the next is scheduled for 1999). Held at the Joe Allen West Martello Tower,

home of the Key West Garden Club, the show features some 800 entries of floral arrangements, potted plants, palms and rare tropical flowers and hybrids. Judges from garden clubs throughout the state of Florida award ribbons and prizes in several categories. The Flower Show is typically held during the spring, not necessarily always in March. Admission to the flower show is $5 for adults and $2 for children younger than 12.

April

Conch Republic Independence Celebration
Various Key West sites • (305) 296-8803

Key West has always been marked by an independent spirit, and this 10-day festival exalts it. It officially commemorates the city's attempt to secede from the United States on April 23, 1982, after the U.S. Border Patrol established roadblocks at the end of the mainland to screen for drugs and illegal aliens. Independent Key Westers rebelled, creating their own flag and attempting to secede from the United States.

The secession fizzled, of course, but locals here find the brief attempt at independence a reason to party nevertheless. Around this same time every year, officials of the fictitious Conch Republic — secretary general, prime ministers, navy, air force and all — host a picnic, fashion show and buffet and a pirate's ball. Events also include "Conch cruiser" car shows and what has been dubbed "the world's longest parade" — spectators lining the route simply join in the fun as the floats pass by.

A final word on emancipation in the southernmost city: Duck! During the Great Battle of the Conch Republic, all forms of food whiz through the air and ultimately find their marks on participants and spectators. The battle engages the Conchs and the U.S. Coast Guard in a "water fight" held "at sea" just off Mallory Square. Conch Republic Celebration events are held all over the island and on the water.

Conch Shell Blowing Contest
Sunset Pier, Ocean Key House, 0 Duval St., Key West • (305) 294-9501

Feel free to toot your own horn. The Conch Shell Blowing Contest offers adults and children the opportunity to sound off. Prizes are awarded to the loudest, the funniest and the most-entertaining conch shell blowers in several divisions. This one-day springtime event takes place on the waterfront and on various dates each year. Participation is free.

A Taste of Key West
Various Key West sites • (305) 294-2587

"So many restaurants, so little time," is the lament we often hear from visitors to Key West. Our tiny island boasts well over 100 eateries, and on an average visit, you simply can't try them all. But if you're lucky enough to be here in April, you may have the chance to sample the best of the best on one night, at one location.

A Taste of Key West, which benefits AIDS Help Inc., brings together chefs and their favorite dishes from many of Key West's finest restaurants. There is no admission charge, but you must buy tickets to eat. Each ticket costs $1, and the individual restaurants set the number of tickets you will need to sample their wares. For three tickets, you can nosh on a salad or a dessert; entrees typically cost four or five tickets. In addition to cash, be sure to bring your appetite; the portions are always generous.

The location for this annual event keeps changing as it grows, but it is always held outdoors and typically on a Tuesday night in mid-April.

Texaco Key West Classic
Various Key West sites • (305) 294-4042

This tournament holds a total pot of $50,000 spread over a variety of categories — blue or white marlin, sailfish, tarpon and permit. Proceeds benefit the National Mental Health Association. See our Fishing chapter for details.

May

Annual Key West Minimal Regatta
Schooner Wharf Bar, 202 William St., Key West • (305) 292-9520

Putting together a boat with as few supplies as possible is the goal at the Minimal Regatta, which is held every year at the Schooner Wharf Bar. Contestants must create a floatable object (a "boat") from such materials as glue, nails and a couple of boards. The boat that floats the farthest wins the prize. Food and drinks are available at the bar. Come early and register even earlier for this memorable event. The Regatta is free to watch, but entry costs $10.

June

Swim Around Key West
Waters off Key West • (305) 745-1331

Call early for information on this great event, which started more than 20 years ago. The swim was originally scheduled to take place on the Fourth of July, but as the organizers seek the best tides and currents, the actual date may vary. The swim usually lasts six hours or more, so plan well if you want to participate. Swim Around participation is free, but you need to register in advance. Entrants must, obviously, be competent swimmers, but there are no other restrictions.

July

July 4th VNA/Hospice Picnic
Marriott's Casa Marina Resort, 1500 Reynolds St., Key West • (305) 294-8812

The whole town turns out for this old-fashioned beachside picnic to benefit the Visiting Nurses Association/Hospice of the Florida Keys. There are plenty of hot dogs, hamburgers, watermelon and fun for all, plus special activities for the kids, continuous live entertainment and a raffle. The picnic begins around 5 PM, but because the beach at the Casa is one of the best places to view the fireworks, you'll probably want to come early and stick around until well after dark. Tickets for the picnic are $15 for adults and $8 for kids 11 and younger.

July 4th Fireworks
White Street Pier, White St. and Atlantic Blvd., Key West • (305) 294-2587

The Key West Rotary Club sponsors this pyrotechnic extravaganza every July 4 beginning at 9 PM and lasting approximately 30 minutes. Best viewing spots are Higgs Beach and Marriott's Casa Marina. There is no admission charge; the fireworks are funded strictly by donations.

Reef Awareness Week
Reef Relief, 201 William St., Key West • (305) 294-3100

Reef Relief is one of the best known and largest of the organizations with the sole purpose of protecting North America's only living coral reef. And when these folks throw a party, they invite everyone. This weeklong event offers all sorts of information to those who want to learn about the coral reef. Visit the art auction and poetry readings, or become a member of this worthy organization during the kickoff week. For more information, call Reef Relief, or visit the organization's retail store at the

address above. Admission is usually free, but some events may carry an entry fee.

Hemingway Days Festival
Hemingway House and Museum, 907 Whitehead St., Key West
• (305) 294-2918

Celebrate the legendary author's birthday with residents of the old man's former hometown by the sea. Tours of the Hemingway House and Museum are offered, along with a street fair, literary seminars and workshops and a Hemingway look-alike contest at what was one of his favorite haunts: Sloppy Joe's (see our Nightlife chapter). This weeklong event centers on the author's July 21 birthday. Fees for some events are required. Call for more information.

September

Mercury Outboards' S.L.A.M. Tournament
(305) 664-2002

First of the annual Celebrity Tournament Series is the Southernmost Light-Tackle Anglers Masters (S.L.A.M). Anglers try to score a Grand Slam by catching and releasing a bonefish, permit and tarpon in one day. Proceeds benefit the Cystic Fibrosis Foundation. See our Fishing chapter for details or contact Gary Ellis at the number listed above.

WomenFest Key West
Various Key West sites • (305) 296-4238

They are women, hear them roar. Each week after Labor Day, thousands of women from all over the country gather in Key West for a bit of female bonding. They include women from diverse races, religions, professions and sexual preferences; motto is "Free to Be You with Me in Key West." Sponsored by American Airlines, the seven-day celebration includes women-only watersports, cocktail comedies and concerts. Organizers host wine-tasting dinners, parties and picnics, and women ship off together on sunset sails.

Most events are free, including the "Sisters for Brothers" blood drive to compensate for the gay male population not being permitted to donate blood. Discounted party passes are available for groups of events that come at a cost, such as the Old Town Trolley Tour that highlights infamous Key West women.

Gay male and female guesthouses and mainstream hotels provide accommodations, and some of the island's "all-boys" houses (see our Accommodations chapter) become all-women instead.

October

Fantasy Fest
Various Key West sites • (305) 296-1817

This is Key West's biggest party — a citywide celebration similar to Mardi Gras in New Orleans (see our Close-up in this chapter).

Goombay Festival
Petronia St., Key West • (305) 293-8898

A Caribbean tradition comes to Key West, where new practices also have originated. Designed to showcase the cultural customs of the city's Bahamian community through food, music and crafts, this grassroots affair has grown to include African, Filipino and Latin traditions, too. Food booths dish up typical festival fare such as gyros, sausage and peppers, and Thai, but tucked among them are the treasures of this event: Jamaican-jerk chicken and pork and Bahamian cracked conch, conch salad, fried fish and pigeon peas and rice, all highly seasoned.

Dance in the streets to African and steel drummers or calypso bands. Stop by the simulated Nassau straw market to see straw hats and fruit baskets in-the-weaving.

Goombay is organized by the Key West Neighborhood Improvement Association, a nonprofit organization that raises funds to help the city's economically disadvantaged. The festival stretches from the corner of Petronia at Duval down to Emma Street and now encompasses many of the streets that comprise a good share of the neighborhood known as Bahama Village.

Held the first weekend of Fantasy Fest (see our Close-Up in this chapter), Goombay sets the stage for an even wider segment of society to flaunt their heritage. There is no admission charge.

Key West Theatre Festival
Various Key West sites • (305) 292-3725

Emerging playwrights rarely are offered the chance to see their work produced, but the Key West Theatre Festival provides one such opportunity. Throughout the year, members of the nonprofit organization Theater Key West receive hundreds of scripts. For this 10-day festival, they and more than 100 community members pool their talents to produce about five of them. The festival features script readings, seminars on writing and acting and public presentations in theaters throughout the islands (see our Arts and Culture chapter).

Events are priced individually and take place at a variety of locations. The Key West Theatre Festival is typically held during the first two weeks of October.

November

Offshore Power Boat Race Week
Waters off Key West • (305) 296-8963

Just as Key West begins to recover from Fantasy Fest, the big boats roar into town to compete in a week's worth of offshore races that culminate in the naming of the world's champ. These are no little, put-put motorboats; they are high-performance ocean racers costing more than $1 million each and boasting speeds of 125 to 150 miles per hour. Close to 50,000 fans line the waterfront to view the competition which generally takes place the second week of November. There's no charge to watch, and the best viewing spots are along Mallory Square and at the harborside hotels — the Pier House, Ocean Key House, Hyatt and Hilton. Even if you're not a particular fan of powerboats, these are something to see.

INSIDERS' TIP

Local radio stations broadcast live from many annual Florida Keys events. If you can't make the parade or fest, tune in. See our Media chapter for station listings.

December

Christmas by the Sea
Various Key West sites • (305) 294-2587

Lighted boat parades are common throughout our islands, and Key West is no exception. In addition to the magical entourage of skiffs, schooners and cruisers, viewers may enjoy the pre-parade sunset activities at Mallory Square. The boat parade begins at Schooner Wharf Bar at the foot of William Street, but it can best be viewed from Mallory Square and the pier beside the Hilton Resort and Marina. The boat parade is typically held on the second Saturday in December. Participation is free, but call Schooner Wharf, (305) 292-9520, to reserve your spot.

Christmas by the Sea also includes a traditional land parade, complete with floats, marching bands and Santa Claus in full regalia riding atop a fire truck. Unlike most parades in Key West which begin and end on Duval Street, the route for this one follows Truman Avenue (U.S. 1) instead. The Christmas street parade is sponsored by the city of Key West and is usually scheduled for the first Saturday night in December.

Other Christmas events in Key West include the annual Christmas concert at St. Paul's Episcopal Church, 401 Duval Street, on the Sunday night immediately preceding Christmas and the lighting of the nation's southernmost Christmas tree on the first Saturday afternoon in December. The tree, and accompanying carolers, are carried by Conch Train from the Christmas tree lot at the old Harris School, 812 Southard Street, to the Southernmost Point at the foot of Whitehead.

Christmas House Tour
Heritage House Museum, 410 Caroline St., Key West • (305) 296-3573

Explore the historic Heritage House Museum at a leisurely pace during this one-day free open house. Sip some punch and munch on cookies along the way as the Key West High School chorale carols from a distance. Heritage House Museum's original cottage dates back to 1834; years of renovations and additions were completed in 1995. Rare antiques and unusual seafaring artifacts adorn the inside. Don't miss the lush colorful garden and the Robert Frost Cottage, which hosted the famous poet between 1944 and 1960. The event is typically held during mid-December.

New Year's Eve on Lower Duval
Duval St., Key West • (305) 294-2587

Times Square has nothing on us when it comes to knowing how to ring in a new year. We close off the street and, in typical Key West style, party outdoors 'til the bars close down at 4 AM. So come New Year's Eve, grab your hat and horn and head for Duval to watch the Conch shell drop from the top of Sloppy Joe's Bar at the stroke of midnight. Just don't wear your best silks and satins for this celebration because it will be raining champagne for sure!

Whatever muse may be at work in the sun-struck Keys, the result is a proliferation of art galleries, fine crafts boutiques, theaters and literary seminars.

Arts and Culture

Creative juices flow freely in the Florida Keys. Is it the sunshine? Or maybe the profusion of riotous colors everywhere you look? Perhaps our pervasive nothing-is-impossible, sky's-the-limit attitude is a contributing factor. Or maybe the reason is when you're in the Keys, you take the time to smell the bougainvillea.

Visit our proliferation of art galleries and fine crafts boutiques while you are here. See a play; take in a concert under the stars. Or, if your timing is right, catch an arts festival, literary seminar or theater gala for a creative night out. See our section on Key West, a city that quickens our inventive pulse. And be sure to check our Annual Events chapter for descriptions of special arts festivals and events.

The Florida Keys Arts Organizations

The Monroe Council of the Arts Corp. is considered the official arts organization in the Florida Keys, and many regional organizations offer members in the Upper, Middle and Lower Keys the opportunity to network and showcase their talents.

Monroe Council of the Arts Corp.
(305) 294-4406

This 14-year-old organization was established as the Monroe County Arts Council by the State of Florida to act as the "chamber of commerce" of arts throughout the Keys. In 1997 the organization became a 501-3C nonprofit organization, which receives supportive funding from the county. Members evaluate and develop arts and cultural institutions throughout the Keys.

Among its current initiatives are instituting a comprehensive registry of Florida Keys artists, assisting in the development of an Upper Keys cultural center and helping children and students develop skills as artists and employees of the arts and culture industry. The Arts Council writes state grants and is supported by Monroe County and private donations. It maintains several hundred members throughout the Florida Keys, along with 15 county commission-appointed board members. A referral and support service, the Arts Council provides thousands of artists throughout the Keys with a means of political clout.

South Florida Center for the Arts
(305) 453-4224

After Hurricane Andrew tore through South Miami and Dade County in 1992, the South Dade Center for the Arts moved to Key Largo and established itself as the South Florida Center for the Arts (SFCA). A private, nonprofit organization, SFCA offers art and music instruction for children and adults, including programs in voice, piano, drama and the fine arts. SFCA also provides a community concert series and art lectures, and some years offers jazz and chamber music programs as well as concerts for children.

Local fund-raisers support a scholarship program, Arts for Youth, which encourages young audiences to participate in the arts. Members also provide workshops and arts programs in local schools. Between its arts and concert association members, this organization has approximately 350 members, many of whom reside in the Upper Keys.

Purple Isle Art Guild
(305) 852-7464

Purple Isle Art Guild encourages art in the Upper Keys and welcomes artists at all levels of experience, from beginning amateurs to professionals. The guild holds an annual multimedia exhibit that includes mixed-media presentations, photography, sculpture and watercolor, oil and acrylic paintings. Participation in the show is open to members only, who are each allowed to submit three pieces of their work. Purple Isle Art Guild meets once a month. The meeting, open to the public, features a speaker and a demonstration.

Each year the guild offers a three- to four-day workshop taught by a well-known artist, such as watercolorist Janet Walsh. A paint-out group called the Brown Baggers meets every Wednesday and paints together, usually outdoors, sharing ideas and expertise. Membership in the Purple Isle Art Guild includes a monthly newsletter and discount excursions to Miami museums and art shows such as the Coconut Grove Art Festival.

Florida Keys Art Guild
(305) 743-5151

Anyone interested in the arts is invited to attend the monthly meetings of the Florida Keys Art Guild, where speakers and technique demonstrations bring the world of the arts to life. Members of the guild are artists in a variety of media as well as the creators of fine crafts. The group holds five shows between December and March at venues in Marathon. For more information, contact Rene Anderson at the number above.

Lower Keys Artists Network
MM 30.5 Bayside, Big Pine Shopping Center, 122 Key Deer Blvd., Big Pine Key • (305) 872-1828

Formed in 1994, the Lower Keys Artists Network has about 50 members, and anyone in the Lower Keys interested in art is welcome to join. Meetings are held from December to May at Artists in Paradise, a co-op gallery the network's fund-raisers have helped purchase (see the listing in this chapter). Through corporate sponsorships, the group raises funds for art scholarships. Members assist in judging student art competitions and work with the public library to provide arts and crafts programs for children. Lower Keys Artists Network also provides demonstrations and seminars on all forms of art, including watercolor, wood sculpture, food sculpture, stained glass

and etching. Contact Barbara Hettinger at the above number for more information.

Performing Arts

Give our regards to Broadway . . . Throughout the year theater-lovers in the Florida Keys enjoy quality professional presentations without traveling to the Big Apple.

Key Players
(305) 852-8586

Established in 1979, the Key Players community group was the dream of former Key Largo School principal Ed Caputo, who was interested in the arts and influential in getting a group of friends together to produce plays. The first production of Caputo and friends was *Curse You, Jack Dalton*, an old-fashioned melodrama. Soon after, the group formed the nonprofit corporation, Key Players. Membership has since grown from 30 to nearly 100, and the group puts on three productions annually, in the fall, winter and spring. The group also produces and directs area school-age children in a Key Players Kids production each year.

Toward summer's end, Key Players holds an open house, a free play or musical review to express appreciation to the community for its support throughout the year. Shows are held in local school auditoriums. All community members are welcome to audition for productions and to join the Key Players. Members often wear a variety of hats, including set and costume design and publicity. A seven-member board of directors handles financing.

Marathon Community Theatre
MM 50 Oceanside, Marathon • (305) 743-0994

Providing topnotch live theatrical entertainment to locals and visitors for 25 years, the Marathon Community Theatre purchased a playhouse and adjoining movie theater (see our Recreation chapter) in 1996. The 100-member group annually stages three productions, such as *Hello, Dolly!* and *Play it Again Sam*,

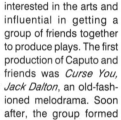

that each run for a month. Productions utilize full sets and full costuming; actors hail from all over the Keys, from Key Largo to Key West. The group also hosts other productions, from chamber symphony orchestras to professional company road shows.

Marathon Community Theatre works with the community schools to encourage children's theater productions. The playhouse building, which sports a recently renovated lobby and bathrooms, is used for fund-raisers and other community events between theater productions.

The Middle Keys Concert Association, Inc.
(305) 289-1078, (305) 289-1419

Every year since 1969 the Middle Keys Concert Association has brought live concert artists to the Florida Keys for the cultural enrichment of our residents and visitors. Five or six concerts are held annually at Marathon venues, quite often San Pablo Catholic Church (MM 53.5 Oceanside). A well-balanced season of offerings includes classical and semi-classical music encompassing voice, strings, brass and organ.

You may purchase a subscription to all concerts for $50 or buy tickets at the door for $15 (some productions may cost more). Children are admitted for free. You can pick up a current brochure at the Marathon Chamber of Commerce, MM 53.5 Bayside, (305) 743-5417 or (800) 262-7284. You may also write to the association at P.O. Box 522636, Marathon Shores, FL 33052, or call Lukina Sheldon or Robert Weil at the numbers listed above.

Art Galleries

Unique galleries dot the Florida Keys, often tucked amid commercial shops in a strip mall or gracing a freestanding building off the beaten track. Join us for a gallery hop down the Keys. And be sure to continue your rambling in the Key West section of this chapter.

The Gallery at Kona Kai
MM 97.8 Bayside, Key Largo
• (305) 852-7200

Opened in January 1997 to rave reviews, The Gallery at Kona Kai secrets away a small yet exquisite changing exhibit of fine art treasures. The galley features the works of such prominent South Florida artists as Clyde Butcher, known for his hauntingly surreal black-and-white photography of the Everglades and Big Cypress National Preserve; Gregory Sohran, a watercolorist who chronicles quintessential scenes of the Keys in a spectrum of pastel hues; and John David Hawver, who captures the ebb and flow of Keys' waters in a symbiosis of line and color.

An integral element of the charming Kona Kai Resort (see our Hotels and Motels chapter), the gallery's exhibits expanded into other resort buildings in 1998. Owners Joe Harris and Ronnie Farina now display a revolving selection of works in the resort's 11 individual rooms and suites.

The Rain Barrel Gallery
MM 86.7 Bayside, at The Rain Barrel, Islamorada • (305) 852-3084

The main gallery of The Rain Barrel is owned and operated by Carol Cutshall, The Rain Barrel's founder and proprietor for more than 20 years. At the entrance to the "village," this gallery features an array of media — painting, sculpture, woodwork and decorative glass — all in one location. More than 100 artists from all over the United States are represented here. You'll find an eclectic assortment of art and craft creations, including whimsical ceramics and an expansive wind chime collection. Two resident artists, Nathan P. Hall and Dan Lawler, maintain studio galleries within The Rain Barrel complex.

INSIDERS' TIP

If you own property and pay taxes in Monroe County — even if you live here for only a portion of the year — you can obtain a library card for free. If you're visiting the Keys temporarily and would like to borrow books, you can purchase a card for $15.

AmeriCaribbean Stained Glass
MM 86.7 Bayside, at The Rain Barrel, Islamorada • (305) 853-0280

Carol and John Chilson used to run their stained-glass studio out of their home, but now their wonderful secret is revealed to all who enter the Rain Barrel. Lining the walls of AmeriCaribbean are stained-glass pieces in a variety of sizes, shapes and designs, including the Chilsons' popular parrots and tropical fish as well as a magnificent image of the pirate Blackbeard. Stop by and watch Carol sketch these figures, transfer them to architectural paper, cut them and solder ground glass. Much of the Chilsons' work is commissioned by homeowners seeking to add a touch of beauty to front doors, windows, even ceilings. They also make dramatic wall hangings that mirror tropical scenes of the Florida Keys.

Joan Purcell's Sunshine Art Gallery
MM 86.7 Bayside, at The Rain Barrel, Islamorada • (305) 852-3960

Etcher/lithographer Joan Purcell uses slabs of ancient coral as her canvas for oil paintings of fanciful tropical marine life. Two coats of resin make the coral creations shimmer like the sea. She has held exhibitions in galleries throughout the United States and in London, Paris and the Caribbean.

Spectrum Studio
MM 86.7 Bayside, at The Rain Barrel, Islamorada • (305) 852-4516, (800) 488-7780

Artist Michael Robinson creates delicate blown-glass sculptures through the ancient process called lampworking. All pieces are created off hand, meaning no molds are used. You'll find exquisite images of dolphins, fish and exotic wildlife as well as fragile floral blossoms and even a plump strawberry.

Jefferson Clay Creations
MM 86.7 Bayside, at The Rain Barrel, Islamorada • (305) 852-6911

Nancy Jefferson, resident potter at The Rain Barrel, handcrafts creative vases and dinnerware in the shape of our Keys tropical fish. She also works in the medium of raku, a Japanese technique of quick firing and rapid cooling that creates a unique, crackled glaze on the pottery pieces. Her crystalline-glazed vases are also striking. You'll see the blazing inferno of Jefferson's kiln on the premises.

Rain Barrel Sculpture Gallery
MM 86.7 Bayside, at The Rain Barrel, Islamorada • (305) 852-8935

The commanding sculptures of Kendall Van Sant, Leon Kula and Fernando Rodriguez dominate the floor space of this fascinating gallery. And the creations stand in good company. From the fired copper of Kevin Jenkins to the winged driftwood sculptures of Felix Velez, talent oozes from every corner of the expansive room.

Bluewater Potters
MM 86.7 Oceanside, at Treasure Village, Islamorada • (305) 853-0616

High-fire stoneware and functional pottery set the theme for Bluewater Potters, where most of the work is accomplished on the premises by husband-and-wife owners Corky and Kim Wagner. The couple creates collaborative pieces: He manages the throwing, and she does the hand-building. The Wagner's inventory includes everything from spoon rests to full dinnerware and architectural pieces. Some work is brought in by outside artists. Among the pieces offered are wine goblets and baking dishes. All glazes are oven, microwave and dishwasher safe. Custom dinnerware is a specialty of the Wagners.

Art Lovers Gallery
MM 86.7 Oceanside, at Treasure Village, Islamorada • (305) 852-1120

More than 50 artists and sculptors from the Keys, South Florida and other parts of the United States are represented at Art Lovers Gallery. The creations span all media. Most of the originals and signed lithographs, such as those by locally known artists Sandy Kay, Jeannine Bean and Kathleen Denis, depict tropical subjects. Art Lovers also sells a wide selection of artists' supplies.

Island Glass Art
MM 86.7 Oceanside, at Treasure Village, Islamorada • (305) 852-0710

Intricate sandblasting and airbrushing creates an exquisite selection of glass table tops, mirrors, plaques and other one-of-a-kind items

Photo: Victoria Shearer

Creative juices flow here like no place on earth.

in Bill White's Island Glass Art Wineglasses, mugs and cocktail glasses sport the creatures of our reef. Custom orders are the norm here, where imaginative designs predominant.

Redbone Art Gallery
MM 82 Oceanside, 200 Industrial Dr., Islamorada • (305) 664-2002

The Ellis family of Islamorada began this non-profit organization as a means of raising funds for research for cystic fibrosis, a disease that afflicts their young daughter. Each year the Ellises hold a trilogy of backcountry fishing tournaments in order to raise these funds (see the Tournaments section of our Fishing chapter), and their art gallery defrays the cost of office expenses.

The gallery sports a variety of saltwater and marine art and sculptures from local artists and others noted for their works related to sport fishing, such as Don Ray, Diane Peebles, James Harris and C.D. Clarke. Redbone Art Gallery exclusively showcases the original watercolors of Chet Reneson in South Florida.

The Gallery at Morada Bay
MM 81.6 Bayside, Islamorada • (305) 664-3650

Upscale crafts bedazzle the browser here at this enticing gallery, which opened in 1997 on the lushly landscaped grounds of the restaurant Morada Bay. Offered here is a selection of the metal hollowware plates and candle-

INSIDERS' TIP

Anyone can borrow paperbacks from the Monroe County Library, no card required. Take out as many as you like and keep them as long as you like. Access is strictly on the honor system.

sticks of Thomas Markusen, whose work graces the White House. You'll also find handcrafted paper shades by Galbraith & Paul and Correia glass, as well as blown creations from Rogers Glassworks and brightly colored paperweights and perfume bottles by Schmidt/Rhea Glass Studio. Especially striking are the *pate de verre* vases by Daniel Gaumer. Don't miss D.M.Z. Coyle's funky ceramic sculptures of "over the top" ladies. Could they be caricatures of the Keys?

Wyland Gallery
MM 80.9 Oceanside, Islamorada
• **(305) 517-2625, (888) 323-9797**

What more fitting location for Wyland's new gallery than Islamorada, "Sportfishing Capital of the World." Situated in the Galleria, this dramatically striking gallery showcases Wyland's fine art and collectibles, testament to his commitment to saving our oceans and creatures dwelling within. Also displayed are works by Jim Warren, James Coleman, Walfrido, John Pitre, William DeShazo, Michael Maiden, Tracy Taylor, Dan Mackin and Janet Stewart as well as Oggetti glass from Murano, Italy. You can see one of Wyland's famous whaling wall murals adorning the Kmart building in Marathon.

Kennedy Studios
MM 48 Oceanside, Marathon
• **(305) 743-2040**

Kennedy Studios frames the Keys, thanks to the steady, creative hand of owner Diane Busch. Custom framing of any and all objets d'art is the specialty of this studio, which resembles the chain — established by Robert Kennedy, a watercolorist, and his wife, Michele, an oil painter — in name only. Works by both Kennedys are included in the collection here, including limited edition prints of Pigeon Key, the Seven-Mile Grill and the Faro Blanco lighthouse. Also displayed are original works by such local artists as Lynn Voit, Joan Howe, Jeanne Dobie, Marilyn Bernardo, Christi Mathews and wildlife artist Dan "Spider" Warren.

In addition to custom framing, Kennedy Studios provides creative matting for needle arts and shadow boxes. The studio also does museum and conservation framing. Folks come back year after year just to hear Busch's Quaker parrot, Scout, imitate her infectious laughter from the back room.

Key West

Key West is the cultural center of the Florida Keys. This scintillating port has long attracted free spirits and adventurers — wreckers, sailors, spongers, shrimpers and pirates — who played an enormous role in Key West's settlement and development. But an enigmatic quality inherent in the essence of Key West also draws fertile minds and searching souls to its inner sanctum like moths to a flame. Creative juices flow here like no other place on earth. Sunshine, starshine or moonshine, Key West supplies the props.

From Ernest Hemingway to earnestly trying, Key West has hosted for a time the famous, the infamous and the obscure. Join us for an Insiders' look at the arts in Key West, some traditional, others not so. Enjoy our music, theater and dance while you are here and tour our myriad galleries. Walk the streets of Key West's Old Town and make the acquaintance of our architectural treasures, which, if they could talk, would tell a few tales of their own.

Performing Arts

Red Barn Theater
319 Duval St. (rear), Key West
• **(305) 296-9911**

Quaint and charming, the restored carriage house that houses the Red Barn Theater has stood in the shadows of one of Key West's oldest houses, now the Key West Women's Club, for more than 50 years. Up from its humble beginnings as an animal stable, the

---

INSIDERS' TIP

The theaters in Key West are small, and tickets sell out quickly, but do check with the box office. A few single seats may be available at the last minute.

building hosted the Key West Community Players for a time and also was the venue for puppet shows and piano concerts. Lovingly restored in 1980, the 88-seat structure shines with professional regional theater at its finest. And because of its size and layout, there isn't a bad seat in the house.

The Red Barn Theater does five or six shows each year, including original comedies, musicals and dramas by published writers. Its season runs from late November through June. Past productions have included *Always Patsy Cline*, *Sylvia*, *The Food Chain*, *Ruthless the Musical* and *The Bathroom Plays* by Key West's own Shel Silverstein. Full sets, costumes and orchestrated scores are featured.

Ticket prices range from $16 to $25. Tickets to musicals cost a bit more than other productions and usually sell out first. Visitors should purchase their tickets as early as possible for all productions, although individual seats are often available at curtain time.

Tennessee Williams Fine Arts Center
5901 W. College Rd., Stock Island
• **(305) 296-1520**

The Tennessee Williams Fine Arts Center opened in January 1980 on the campus of Florida Keys Community College with the world premiere of Tennessee Williams' unpublished play, *Will Mr. Merriwether Return From Memphis?* Named after one of Key West's most illustrious writers, this 478-seat air-conditioned theater features a thrust stage extending 8 feet in front of the curtain line, a fly system and a state-of-the-art lighting and sound system.

The Tennessee Williams Fine Arts Center produces a full season of dance, theater, chamber music and shows by nationally known performing artists. In-house productions involve amateur actors from the community and feature students working toward associate of science degrees in acting and theater production. Professional touring companies bring a wave of nationally and internationally recognized artists to the Florida Keys. The St. Petersburg Ballet of Russia has appeared here, as did the Irish Rovers and singer Cleo Laine with Johnny Dankworth. Chamber music concerts are sprinkled throughout the copious performance calendar of the Tennessee Williams Fine Arts Center, which runs from late November through April.

Most of the productions are held in the evening, but some events offer matinees on weekends as well. Ticket prices range from $15 to $32, depending upon the event. The Florida Keys Community College Chorus, which is coed, performs here three times each year, including early December and mid- to late March. (The chorus also offers a concert under the stars at Fort Zachary Taylor Historic Site in April.) Tickets for the concerts cost about $7.

Waterfront Playhouse
Mallory Square, Key West
• **(305) 294-5015**

Community theater at its finest shines from an unlikely thespian arena on the waterfront. Once the site of Porter's warehouse, the physical structure served as an icehouse in the 1880s, storing blocks of ice cut from New England ponds and brought to Key West as ships' ballast. The Waterfront Playhouse restored the old warehouse into the present theater, infusing the crumbly stone walls with enduring creativity and talent.

The Waterfront Playhouse, dedicated to expanding knowledge of dramatic works to the general public, presents a variety of musicals, comedies, dramas and mysteries each season. Past productions include *Six Degrees of Separation* and Terrence McNally's *Lips Together, Teeth Apart*. The community thespians also offer a children's theater workshop in the summer and other participatory theater experiences to Key West school children throughout the year.

Tickets for productions at the 180-seat theater are generally easy to obtain and cost about $15. The performance season is from November through April.

Participatory Theater

Theatre des Seances
Porter Mansion, 429 Caroline St., Key West • **(305) 292-2040**

You say you don't believe in ghosts? This re-creation of a turn-of-the-century seance might just change your mind. The adventure begins at 8 PM each night in the sitting room of the old Porter Mansion, one of Key West's oldest houses, at the corner of Duval and Caroline streets. First, you'll learn about some of this city's more bizarre tales of house hauntings and grave robbers, then you'll take a few psychic tests to be sure you and your companions on this journey are prepared to meet the spirits.

Once your host determines that all in your group are receptive, you'll be ushered into the seance parlor, where you'll take your seat around a large antique dining room table for the main event. Once the candles are extinguished, the real fun begins. Every presentation is unique, and success depends on the energy and focus of the group. Past groups are said to have experienced some strange, not easily explained phenomena. It's a little scary, but a lot of fun — a real Key West experience for the not so faint of heart.

Tickets are $29 per person, and reservations are required. Book early; seances are limited to 13 participants per night.

Art Galleries

Galleries abound along Duval Street, and you'll also find small lofts and garrets secreted off the beaten track down narrow lanes. Come along for a gallery crawl through the high spots of the Key West art scene.

Alexandre Art Gallery
718 Duval St., Key West • (305) 296-7722

If your tastes lean toward seascapes and watercolors depicting Old Town Key West, skip this gallery. But if you want something on your walls that will have your friends talking, this is the place to find it. The owner of this gallery is French, and the works he chooses to display are most definitely avant-garde. Bright colors and bold techniques abound here.

Becky Thatcher Designs
425B Eaton St., Key West
• **(305) 296-0886**

If one-of-a-kind jewelry creations from un-usual gemstones such as tourmaline, boulder opal, fancy sapphire, tanzanite, sugalite and chrysocolla pique your interest, visit Becky Thatcher Designs. Set in gold or silver, the gemstones join with shells and ancient beads from around the world, creating what Becky calls "picture" necklaces and earrings that capture the essence of spirit and individuality.

Bordello Gallery
729 Thomas St., Key West
• **(305) 292-1323**

Situated within the confines of the celebrated Blue Heaven Restaurant (see our Restaurants chapter), this gallery offers a taste of Key West at its funkiest. You'll find a selection of scrimshaw, natural jewelry, handpainted clothing and even a few decorated bicycles.

Call of Africa's Native Visions Gallery
821 Duval St., Key West • (305) 295-9364

Big names, big talents, big prices. This classy gallery, which operates Native Visions in Hawaii and California, showcases remarkable works celebrating the wildlife resources of South Africa and the world: the Zimbabwe realism of Craig Bone; the impressionist pastels of Kim Donaldson's travels in Botswana and the Namibian desert; the hammer-and-chisel sculptures of James Tandi; South African wildlife captured by the oil-on-board techniques of Brian Scott-Dawkins; and the sculptural furniture designs of Dale J. Evers. David Miller's extraordinary palette of acrylics on Lexan depicts scenes of the coral reef a little closer to home. This shop is a must-see.

Caribbean Gallery
1000 Duval St., Key West
• **(305) 292-0060**

Don't miss this nifty gallery. The vibrant colors of Shari Hatchett Bohlmann's romantic Key West oils shown here also reside in the

INSIDERS' TIP

The Marathon Airport has an interesting display of artwork. Even if you aren't flying, stop by for the cultural experience.

permanent White House collection. Todd J. Warner's whimsical metal sculptures surface all over the world, including at Caribbean. And America's number one pop artist, Romero Britto, of Absolut Vodka and Pepsi International advertising fame, lives six months of the year in Key West. President Bush and Frank Sinatra own his work, and so does Caribbean Gallery.

Celeste
531 Whitehead St., Key West
• **(305) 295-9918**

The sign posted outside this tiny shop says it all: "Inner Peace thru Impulse Shopping." There's nothing inside that you need, but plenty that you'll probably want. The goods here include everything from pottery bowls to picture frames. In addition to accent pieces for your home, you'll find an array of handcrafted jewelry. And be sure to look for the whimsical windchimes, crafted from old butter knives, forks and spoons.

Florida Keys Community College
5901 W. College Rd., Stock Island
• **(305) 296-9081**

Florida Keys Community College stages four art shows a year in the Library Gallery. Invitational shows are held in October and February, and the Florida Artist series is showcased in January and February. Student work is exhibited during the month of April.

The Gallery on Greene
606 Greene St., Key West
• **(305) 294-1669**

Think you can't afford fine art? Think again. This gallery prides itself on displaying original art priced for every pocketbook — from $10 to $25,000! Among the offerings here are works by part-time Key West resident Jeff MacNelly (he draws the cartoon strip "Shoe"), critically-acclaimed abstract-expressionist Kim Northrup, and Henry La Cagnina, the last survivor of 12 artists brought to Key West in the 1930s by the WPA.

This gallery also supports working artists: There is always at least one artist-in-residence, bent over his or her work, in a corner of the gallery.

Gamefish Gallery and Outfitters
608 Greene St., Key West
• **(305) 294-7111**

This gallery offers primarily prints and artwork of big game fish and wildlife. A souvenir from here is perfect for the fishing aficionado or the sports enthusiast. Choose from large framed original oil paintings, small prints or sports-themed gear, including hats, shirts, belts and shoes. Shipping is available.

Gingerbread Square Gallery
1207 Duval St., Key West
• **(305) 296-8900**

Billed as Key West's oldest private art gallery, Gingerbread Square Gallery on upper Duval features sculptures, art glass, one-person shows and ongoing presentations of the highly acclaimed works of Key West's favorite artists. Sal Salinero's oils depict the treasures of the rain forest. John Kiraly's fanciful paintings capture the spirit of locales real and imagined, and George Carey's photo-realistic acrylics depict Key West, then and now.

Glass Reunions
825 Duval St., Key West • (305) 294-1720

Glass is the business here, and you can get it in almost any form or color imaginable. Lamps, vases and mirror wall hangings all showcase the talents of the various artists. For the traditionalist, a wide selection of stained-glass art is available.

Guild Hall Gallery
614 Duval St., Key West • (305) 296-6076

Up to 20 local artists display their work here, presenting a vast array of mixed media. Most of the pieces focus on island life, with a definite Bahamian and Caribbean influence thrown in. Head upstairs for more unusual and bigger, works of art.

Haitian Art Company
600 Frances St., Key West
• **(305) 296-8932**

Bold, wild colors and primitive designs mark the artistic offerings of Haiti, displayed in the multiple rooms of Haitian Art Company. The intricate paisley-style designs often weave an image of a serpent or wild animal

Photo: James DiLoreto

Marathon Airport, also known as an "artport," showcases
tropical accents and local art within its terminal.

within the overall picture. The work of Haiti is a study of form and color not readily encountered in this country. All pieces are originals. This gallery is tucked in a residential neighborhood at the corner of Frances and Southard streets, way off Duval, but it's definitely worth the walk.

Heliographics Gallery Story
814 Fleming St., Key West
• **(305) 294-7901**

The emphasis here is on wearable, useable art, all of which is produced locally. Handscreened throw pillows, pottery, glassware, humidors and T-shirts are among the items available. Much of what you see is one-of-a-kind, and many of the works on display are simply that — display. They must be special ordered. Shipping is available.

Island Arts
1128 Duval St., Key West
• **(305) 292-9909**

This co-op of local artists fashions itself after a Caribbean bazaar, and many of the items herein illuminate just how fertile the imagination can be. Welded sculptures created out of scrap iron, metal junk, old screws and tools turn up as a rooster, ostrich, duck or dinosaur. Paper Smash is sculpted recycled paper made into snakes, pelicans, fish and manatees. You'll find a potpourri of handpainted tiles, stained-glass pieces and ceramics, all with an island theme.

Jack Baron Folk Art Gallery
1075 Duval St., #18 in Duval Square, Key West • (305) 294-3629

One of Key West's long-term favorite artists has been plying his trade for more than

20 years and is still going strong. Baron's pieces evoke a rustic childhood, with brightly painted dressers, shelves and carved animals. His paintings are festive and colorful, portraying people and animals in a whimsical, merry fashion.

Joy Gallery
1124 Duval St., Key West
• (305) 296-3039

A little sign that hangs amid the surreal paintings of out-of-body experiences by Lucie Bilodeau in the Joy Gallery reads: "Warning — The purchase of fine art is not necessarily a logical decision." Bilodeau's brooding pieces are joined by copper etchings by Francine Desbiens and Key West watercolors and prints by various artists.

Kennedy Gallery
1130 Duval St., Key West
• (305) 294-5997

This gallery of Kennedy originals deserves mention, for it should not be confused with the bevy of Kennedy Studios franchises that sell prints across the nation as well as down Duval Street a few blocks. This gallery, like its siblings in Provincetown, Boston and Nassau, features only originals by Michele Richard Kennedy, Robert Kennedy and other celebrated artists from around the world.

Key West Art Center
301 Front St., Key West • (305) 294-1241

You can duck out of the teeming crowds of tourists at Mallory Square for a serene perusal of the pastels, watercolors and oils of local Key West artists at this spacious two-story gallery. Catch your breath and see Key West from the locals' perspective.

Kokopelli Contemporary Gallery
824 Duval St., Key West • (305) 292-4144

If you'd rather hang your favorite art around your neck than on your walls, be sure to visit this gallery, where handcrafted jewelry is the focus. You'll find everything from sterling silver and amethyst earrings to rings crafted from 14k gold and black opals. Most of the offerings are one-of-a-kind, and the artists hail from throughout the U.S.

Pandemonium
825 Duval St., Key West • (305) 294-0351

Music from the 1950s will help you toe-tap through Pandemonium, a funky, eclectic shop featuring imaginative crafts and objets d'art created from recycled items. Pick out a travel-log journal covered with an old automobile license plate — from the state of your choice. Or perhaps you'd like a tin man sculpted from an old typewriter or a horse made from used rubber tires. You'll find an airplane whose prop is fashioned from beer cans, a leather belt adorned with beer-bottle caps and even a chenille dress, every bit as soft as grandma's bedspread — from which it was probably made.

Pelican Poop Shop
314 Simonton St., Key West
• (305) 292-9955

This eclectic collection of artwork includes originals from all over the Caribbean. If you're in the market for a life-size stone Mayan deer dancer or a Haitian oil drum sculpture, this is the place to come. You'll browse to the tropical sounds of Harry Belafonte's "Matilda," and, if you buy $10 in merchandise or pay a $2 fee, you can tour the private Casa Antigua gardens out back, linked forever to Ernest Hemingway by a quirky twist of fate. According to tour literature, he wrote *A Farewell to Arms* while staying here on a visit in 1928.

Plantation Potters
521 Fleming St., Key West
• (305) 294-3143

Plantation Potters handles quality crafts in traditional and contemporary styles in many media, including ceramics, wood, metals and glass. Local artists create functional pieces, such as bowls and mugs, along with non-functional artwork, such as ceramic wall hangings.

INSIDERS' TIP

The Rain Barrel Village of Artists and Craftsmen on Plantation Key allows shoppers the opportunity to watch artists at work.

Whitehead Street Pottery
1011 Whitehead St., Key West
• (305) 294-5067

Occupying a renovated 100-year-old Cuban bodega, or wine shop/grocery store, potters Charles Pearson and Timothy Roeder specialize in raku-fired pieces. Using a Japanese firing method to lend the works primitive characteristics, sculptured handbuilt slab constructions are glazed with metallic oxides, fired individually to 1,900 degrees, removed from the kiln and then buried in seaweed. Watch the potters at work.

Wild Side Gallery
Clinton Square Market, 291 Front St.,
Key West • (305) 296-7800

From carved wood walking sticks to ceramics, jewelry and watercolors, all objets d'art in this interesting and affordable gallery depict some element of nature. Artists and craftspeople represented here are from all over the United States.

Wings of Imagination, The Butterfly Gallery
1108-C Duval St., Key West
• (305) 296-2988
Clinton Square Market, 291 Front St.,
Key West • (305) 296-2922

Art really does imitate life in the case of these two galleries. Raised in butterfly farms and imported from South America, Africa and Southeast Asia, the butterflies live out their 10-day life cycle and are then shipped to the Key West production studio, where they are arranged in geometric compositions and preserved in acrylic cases. Don't miss this fruition of Sam Trophia's childhood dream, capturing the everlasting beauty of the "flowers of the sky."

Woodenhead Gallery
907 Caroline St., Key West
• (305) 294-3935

No truer words could be used to describe this unimposing gallery than those on the sign out front, which reads "Definitely not Duval." There's no glitz, no glamour, no watercolors of gingerbread houses here, just nonconformist works reflecting real-life Key West by real-live starving artists, most of whom hold day jobs just to make ends meet. The emphasis here is on art for art's sake, and special exhibits, like last year's Valentines Day Erotic Art Show, are sometimes controversial.

Wyland Galleries
102 Duval St., Key West • (305) 294-5240
719 Duval St., Key West • (305) 292-9711

The first East Coast display venues of Wyland, the world's leading marine life artist, these two Key West galleries display a wide range of the environmental artist's work. His world-renowned life-size whaling wall murals — one of which adorns the Kmart building in Marathon and another the Waterfront Market building at the Key West Bight — reflect Wyland's unshakable commitment to saving the earth's oceans and thereby its marine creatures. Also displayed are several paintings from the "above and below" series, for which Wyland collaborated with other talented artists to create a scene looking beneath and above the sea concurrently.

Zbyszek Art Gallery
519 Fleming St., Key West
• (305) 295-9085

Billed as the "home of the piano dog," this gallery features the works of Zbyszek and Tippi Koziol. Here you'll find paintings, toys, wood

---

INSIDERS' TIP

Almost all art galleries in the Florida Keys offer shipping, so you never have to carry it with you.

sculptures, painted furniture and wearable art in vibrant colors and whimsical designs. Not for every taste, but definitely fun to own and worth a look.

Participatory Art

Gone To Pot
Corner of Front and Simonton Sts.,
Key West • (305) 295-7373
Paint-A-Pot
208 Telegraph Ln., Key West
• (305) 292-3322

Ever had a hankering to create a work of art yourself? Key West offers two opportunities for you to become a potter of sorts. Here's how it works: You pick a ceramic piece from the shelf — such as a mug, salt and pepper shakers, a bowl, a platter, a teapot, etc. —

paint it in your own distinctive style, then leave it overnight to be fired in the kiln. You pick up your finished piece the next day, and voila! You have your own personalized souvenir of Key West. If your schedule doesn't permit you to return for your finished pot, don't despair. Shipping is available.

Both shops listed here have similar selections of items to paint and colors from which to choose. The biggest difference between the two is pricing. At Paint-A-Pot, the posted prices include the ceramic item, paints, firing and studio time (no matter how long it takes you to create your work of art). At Gone To Pot, you will pay a per-hour fee for studio time, in addition to the price of the item. Both offer group rates and special prices for kids. In either case, painting a pot is a great way to spend a rainy afternoon or to wile away an hour or so when your feet just can't carry you to one more T-shirt shop.

We don't require much
in the way of clothing
here in the Keys'
tropicality, just a suit
(small and stringy),
shoes (light and
strappy) and a hat
(woven and floppy).

Shopping

"Born to shop."

"Shop 'til you drop."

"He who dies with the most toys wins."

We've heard them all in the Florida Keys, and then some. Stretched along our 100 miles of Overseas Highway is every diversion imaginable for the serious (and not so serious) shopper. Scuba aficionados find nirvana here, reveling in state-of-the-gear offerings from our plethora of dive shops (see our Diving and Snorkeling chapter). Anglers, who may readily concede that you might be able to be too thin or too rich, staunchly maintain that you can never have too many fishing rods or an excess of tackle (see our Fishing chapter). And boaters, who all know that a vessel is really a floating hole into which you pour money, find a virtual smorgasbord of shopping options guaranteed to fertilize their needs exponentially (see our Boating chapter).

But what about the rest of us, free spirits who like to see the ocean through the rim of a glass, preferably while lying prone by the swimming pool in the shade of a coconut palm? We have pent up shopping desires too. We know we don't require much in the way of clothing here in the Keys' tropicality, just a suit (small and stringy), shoes (light and strappy) and a hat (woven and floppy).

So here it is: the ultimate road map to the shops. We describe our favorite shops, in geographic order from Key Largo to Key West. Our Key West section picks up the buyers' gauntlet. Be sure to scope out our Arts and Culture chapter for descriptions of galleries selling creative works, many by local artists. And turn to our Seafood Markets and Specialty Foods chapter to find piscatory treasures and other palate pleasers.

The Florida Keys

Upper Keys

Cuda Wear
**MM 103.5 Bayside, Pink Plaza,
Key Largo • (305) 453-0210**

Cuda Wear carries well-known brands of clothing, shoes, belts and accessories with nautical or tropical themes. In addition to Kahala and Hook & Tackle lines for men, the store sells stain-resistant apparel for hiking and fishing. Among the footwear brands offered here are Rockport, Sperry and Sandals by Scott. Women will find bathing suits and Hawaiian and Indonesian print blouses, dresses and sarongs. Cuda Wear's nautical children's clothing is equally popular. The store also offers shoe and leather repair and a mail-order catalog.

Caribbean Cigar Shop & Factory
**MM 103.5 Bayside, Pink Plaza,
Key Largo • (305) 453-4014**

Cigar aficionados can watch the stogies being hand-rolled at Caribbean Cigar Shop & Factory. The in-house line here includes Santiaga Cubano, Havana Classico and Calle

---

INSIDERS' TIP

All the treasures of the Keys are not in the watery deep. Some of the best "salvaging" goes on at our flea markets. Here are three of our favorites, which are open Saturdays and Sundays: Key Largo Storage/Flea Market, MM 103.5 Bayside, Key Largo; Grassy Key Flea Market, MM 60 Oceanside, Grassy Key; Big Pine Flea Market, MM 30 Oceanside, Big Pine Key.

Ocho. Imports include Partagas, Macanundo and Punch. This full-service store also carries a wide variety of humidors, lighters, cutters and accessories and imported cigarettes.

Tropical Details
MM 103 Bayside, Key Largo
• **(305) 453-9100**

Upmarket furniture accents and interior accessories, all with a classical island plantation feeling, dominate Tropical Details. And the exquisite appointments, those details that make your private tropical abode a true paradise, are fascinating and unique. Many come from the Far East and Indonesia, such as baskets of ficus-leaf-covered Styrofoam balls and polished coconut-shell salad servers. This is an enchanting place to browse, even if you don't have a tropical home. You'll find silk bromeliads, orchids and birds of paradise if your thumb is less than green. Or avail yourself of Tropical Details' orchid leasing service — blooming orchids are delivered to your home and maintained twice weekly.

Steve & Co.
MM 101.4 Oceanside, Tradewinds Shopping Center, Key Largo
• **(305) 451-5646**

Offering a wide selection of men's casualwear, Steve & Co. is the place to go if you need to dress up, Keys style. Look for racks and racks of tropical print shirts, de rigueur here for a night on the town. You'll also find top brands of shorts and knit shirts, including Kahala, Sportif, Weekenders, Reggae and Hook & Tackle.

The Book Nook
MM 99.6 Oceanside, Waldorf Plaza, Key Largo • **(305) 451-1468**

If reading rates a spot in your Florida Keys vacation, The Book Nook packs a multitude of bestsellers, popular paperbacks, children's books and specialty publications into a compact space. The shop, with friendly and helpful personnel, also carries national and international daily newspapers.

Elsie's Kingdom
MM 99.5 Oceanside, Port Largo Plaza, Key Largo • **(305) 451-3772**

If crafting is your passion, head to Elsie's, where bountiful supplies of beads, bangles, ribbons, baskets and fabric painting necessities are just the beginning. You'll be able to fuel your imagination here for sure.

www.insiders.com

See this and many other **Insiders' Guide®** destinations online — in their entirety.

Visit us today!

Rogers Furniture
**MM 99.5 Oceanside,
Key Largo** • **(305) 451-1429**
**MM 30.5 Oceanside,
Big Pine Key** • **(305) 872-9611**

You'll find good quality wicker and rattan furniture, including Henry Link, Lane and Lloyd Flanders brands, at either of Rogers' two locations in the Keys. In Key Largo, you must access Rogers from the northbound lane. Don't miss the unusual (and expensive) custom metal sculptures in front of Rogers' Big Pine store. Inquire within for information about the artist and prices of the sculptures.

Flamingo Books, Inc.
MM 99.5 Oceanside, Port Largo Plaza, Key Largo • **(305) 451-5303**

You'll find lots and lots of used paperback books at Flamingo Books and an unusual deal to boot. For each used paperback you bring into the shop, Flamingo will give you one-fourth its cover price and one purchase credit. Used books sell to the general public for one-half the cover price. You may use one purchase credit for each used book you buy, thereby paying only a quarter of the cover price. What a deal! Flamingo stocks

INSIDERS' TIP

If you need to buy a gift for a newborn infant, visit Fishermen's Hospital Gift Shop, MM 48.8 Oceanside.

new bestsellers and will place custom orders for you as well.

Arteffects
MM 98.5 Bayside, Key Largo
• (305) 852-5933

Almost like an outdoor mini-museum, Arteffects warrants a "look-see." Heralded by an 8-foot mummy, gigantic stone statues line the Overseas Highway. You'll see a changing rota of fascinating creatures: pig, cowpoke, bull, giraffe, camel, dolphin, mermaid, cranes, cherubs, elephants, even Poseidon, a pharaoh and a selection of Buddahs. Arteffects features handcarved stone lanterns and old filigreed wood trims that can be recycled as an unusual architectural accent. Look for tribal art and jewelry too. Merchandise is from Southeast Asia, Africa and Central and South America. Arteffects closes from mid-June through mid-December when the operation moves to Bar Harbor, Maine.

Anthony's Women's Apparel
MM 98.5, in the median, Key Largo
• (305) 852-4515
MM 50.5 Bayside, Gulfside Village,
Marathon • (305) 743-5855

At Anthony's you can expect to find a constantly changing array of reasonably priced casual attire in petite, junior and misses sizes by such manufacturers as Liz Sport and Ocean Pacific. The shops offer a wide variety of swimsuits and cover-ups as well as a decent selection of lingerie and nightwear. Anthony's sales and bargain basement are not to be missed.

Banana Hill Healing Arts Center
MM 98.3, in the median, Key Largo
• (305) 852-6161

Spiritual, New Age and natural remedies and cosmetics are carried at Banana Hill, hidden within the median and accessible from the northbound lane of the Overseas Highway. Instrumental CDs and cassette tapes sold and played here are rejuvenating, as are the incense, oils and crystals.

Kids' Closet
MM 95 Oceanside, Key Largo
• (305) 852-4710

Kids' Closet is a treasure chest of better-than-new clothing for infants to teens. The mixture of new and consignment items, including some toys and accessories, takes it easy on your wallet too! Kids' Closet has a wide range of baby equipment available for weekly rentals, perfect for when your grandkids come for a visit or when you enjoy one of the Keys' hotels or rental properties. Available are cribs, porta-cribs, playpens, highchairs, sassy chairs, boosters, car seats, strollers, double strollers, umbrella strollers, baby walkers, toddler beds

— even adult roll-away beds. The delivery charge is $25 each way.

Island Feet
MM 94 Oceanside, Tavernier
• **(305) 852-5691, (800) 442-3338**

Accessed from the northbound lane of the Overseas Highway, this dome-shaped building shelters Island Feet. Providing foot relief in the form of sandals, boat shoes and sneakers, Island Feet carries such brands as Reef, Teva, Birkenstock, Sperry and New Balance as well as a good selection of sport sandals and flip-flops.

Island Custom Embroidery
MM 92.2 Bayside, Tavernier
• **(305) 852-6317**

Within this pink-and-white gingerbread cottage a selection of shirts, shorts, kids' togs, towels and terry-cloth robes awaits your request for custom embroidery. Choose from a wide selection of stock designs and lettering that will be custom-stitched for you.

Grant Gallery & Antiques
MM 92, in the median, Tavernier
• **(305) 853-0562**

You'll find a potpourri of collectibles, oil paintings and furnishings secreted away in the upstairs rooms of Grant's place, so browsing often yields unexpected treasures. The first floor is packed with an interesting assortment of ladies' fashions and accessories.

Florida Keys Handbag Factory
MM 91.5 Oceanside, Tavernier
• **(305) 852-8690, (800) 462-7112**

Handpainted tropical designs grace Florida Keys handbags, which have been constructed in the Keys from heavy-duty marine vinyl for more than 20 years. From shrimp boats, palm trees and pelicans to hibiscus, macaws and creatures of the coral reef, imagination is the only limitation to the design you can custom order. And these unique purses wipe clean with the whisk of a cloth and are virtually indestructible. You'll also find an interesting selection of ladies' tropical fashions here.

Kelly's Shoes
MM 91.2 Bayside, Tavernier
• **(305) 852-0082**

Although you'll find a small selection of ladies' long and short tropical dresses in this shop in Tavernier Towne, Kelly's is primarily a shoe store. You'll be able to outfit your weary feet with a wide selection of brands, including Fila, Sebago, Nine West, Easy Spirit, Sperry and Nike.

Bensons Camera
MM 90.2 Bayside, Tavernier
• **(305) 852-0106**

You can't miss Bensons' screaming yellow building, bayside in Tavernier. Expect to find all the major brands of cameras, equipment and supplies at Bensons, including Nikon, Cannon, Pentax, Olympus, Minolta and Leica. Bensons also sells Sony camcorders, televisions and VCRs, as well as binoculars and both video and still underwater photo equipment. The only lab in the Florida Keys that processes APS film, Bensons also will develop your 35 mm or 120 film in one hour. You can purchase either amateur or professional Kodak or Fuji film here.

Cover to Cover Books
MM 90.1 Oceanside, Tavernier
• **(305) 852-1415**

You can lose yourself for hours in this nifty book-shop-cum-coffee-bar. Situated in a pale gray building surrounded by lush landscaping on the old road just off the Overseas Highway, Cover to Cover sparkles with the warmth and friendliness of its owners, Joy McIntosh and Linda Johnson. Expanded in May 1996, Cover to Cover stocks more than 35,000 titles. You'll find a good Florida collection, and the selection of children's books and educational games is outstanding. Sprinkled throughout the shop are gift items, specialty wrapping papers and even some interesting jewelry. Stop and sip a spell at the coffee bar — cappuccino, espresso, caffe latte and caffe mocha are all on offer here, even iced if the Keys heat is too much for you. And you can buy gourmet coffee beans and Paradise Spice Tea here as well.

Gerry Droney Tropical Gardens
MM 88.7 Bayside, Tavernier
• **(305) 852-4715**

A riot of orchids, bromeliads, anthuriums, gingers and other exotic tropical plants greets you as you wander through Gerry Droney's Tropical Gardens. This is tropical browsing at its finest. You'll find pots galore of every shape, size and color, as well as a full line of insecticides, fertilizers and soil additives. Even if you eventually have to hop a plane for home, stop in here to see how Paradise blooms.

The Rain Barrel Village of Artists and Craftspeople
MM 86 7 Bayside, Islamorada
• **(305) 852-3084**

A lush, tropical hideaway greets you in this artisan village as artists and crafters work in retail shops that are peppered beneath the gumbo limbos and amid the bougainvillea. At King's Treasure, (305) 852-9797, you'll find shipwreck coin jewelry as well as a fascinating selection of silver charms. Jeweler Dwayne King works on the premises. Be sure to check out our Arts and Culture chapter for a rundown of the other fine art and crafts galleries within the Rain Barrel: Rain Barrel Gallery, AmeriCaribbean Stained Glass, Joan Purcell Gallery, Spectrum Studio, Jefferson Clay Creations, Rain Barrel Sculpture Gallery and the studio/galleries of Nathan P. Hall and Dan Lawler.

Treasure Village
MM 86.7 Oceanside, Islamorada
• **(305) 852-0511**

From the road, Treasure Village does evoke memories of a pirate's castle, but inside the portals, a charming boardwalk fronts a potpourri of interesting shops. In the center of the square, tropical plantings shade picnic tables and lounge chairs, and island steel-drum music lilts from every corner. Island Body and Sol is a great-smelling little shop where you'll find all manner of lotions, salves, oils, balms and aromatherapy to pamper your body. Bahama Bob's Flotsam & Jetsam fea-

tures handmade creations of wood and leather, such as cutting boards, toys, utensils, sculptures, even wooden combs and switch plates decorated with frogs, geckos and turtles.

At P.J. Max Caribbean Clothing, all the clothing, for ladies and tots, is custom-made on premises. That includes a selection of island-style swimsuits. Rudy's Kids Club is the place for kidstuff, all with an environmental theme. Clothes, books, toys, games, puzzles and even pint-size furniture all focus on some wonder of our natural world. At Treasure Harbor Trading Co., a treasure trove of men's and women's clothing and T-shirts mingles with an eclectic array of costume jewelry, books and Keys memorabilia. Entry to this store is just beyond Big Betsy, known as the world's largest lobster. You'll be able to spot Big Betsy from the highway.

At Ziggy's Candles you'll find unusual handcarved and custom-made candles. Especially popular are the one-of-a-kind lighthouses. Made in the Keys, the lighthouses remain long after the candles burn down. Caribbean Furnishings displays one-of-a-kind tropically colored furniture made from Ponderosa pine as well as brightly hued dishes and creative sculptures.

Don't miss the listing for Made To Order in our Seafood Markets and Specialty Foods chapter or Bluewater Potters, Island Glass Art and Art Lovers Gallery in our Arts and Culture chapter.

Anna Banana
MM 86.7 Oceanside, Islamorada
• **(305) 853-1200**

Anna Banana offers draped Moroccan cottons and elegantly long casual linen dresses amid their tropical ladies' fashions. Plus sizes are available here. Look for funky costume jewelry to finish off your ensemble.

Blue Marlin Jewelry
MM 86.7 Oceanside, Islamorada
• **(305) 852-9880**

Discover gold in this interesting jewelry shop. Blue Marlin sports a great selection of gold charms depicting most of the species of our ecosystem. Especially striking are the black coral fish. Many pieces are also offered in sterling silver.

Expressions Sun N' Swimwear
MM 86.7 Oceanside, Islamorada
• **(305) 852-1155**

Ladies, tropicalize your wardrobe at Expressions, which offers Jams' wonderful Caribbean prints in a variety of comfortable styles. You'll find swimsuits and floppy hats as well as cover-ups — everything you need for a sojourn, Keys style. Men can dress down as well, finding Kahala, Madison Trader, Baja Blue and Mobility casualwear here.

Somewhere in Time
Spanish Treasure
MM 82.8 Oceanside, Islamorada
• **(305) 664-9699**

Step into Somewhere in Time, and you'll find a tiny shop chock-full of shipwreck treasure — coins, jewelry, bits of pottery, bottles, cannons, guns and other collectibles. It's been set up like a museum by jeweler-owner Dick Holt, but most of the treasure is for sale.

H.T. Chittum & Co.
MM 82.7 Bayside, Islamorada
• **(305) 664-4421**

A step inside this low-lighted, paneled sports emporium evokes a big-game feeling from yesteryear. An old carriage suspends from the wood slat ceiling. Massive mounted tarpon, blue marlin, swordfish and jewfish adorn the walls. Anglers can sate all tackle cravings here (see Outfitters in our Fishing chapter), and they'll find a good selection of Costa del Mar sunglasses and a wide offering of knives as well. Top brands of both men and women's casual clothing are featured, such as Timberland, Royal Robbins, Tarponwear, Tommy Bahama, Lilly Pulitzer, Ruff Hewn, Woolrich, Sigrid Olsen and Signatur. Holland Bros. leather goods are on offer.

Katie's Collection
MM 82.6 Oceanside, Islamorada
• **(305) 664-8306**

Housed in a cute little white shop with blue trim, Katie's displays sundresses, shorts, swimsuits and other tropical island fashions. A separate room houses a display gallery of Guy Harvey fine art prints. Rumor has it Katie's sales are not to be missed.

Garden of Eden
MM 82.3 Oceanside, Islamorada
• **(305) 664-5558**

Noticed those cute manatee mailboxes along the Overseas Highway? Well this is the place to find them. You can also get a giant grouper to gulp your mail if you like. Garden of Eden is filled with silk flowers and arrangements, including orchids, bromeliads, crotons and many other faux tropicals. Look for the handcarved bottle stoppers; the caricatures are a riot, sure to remind you of someone back home.

The Mayan Way
MM 82.2 Oceanside, Islamorada
• **(305) 664-9670**

The Mayan Way brings together an unusual collection of handcrafted items from Central and South America. Of particular interest is the assortment of fruit carved from mahogany and polished to a deep, realistic color. Don't miss the Argentinean facial sculptures, handcrafted from scraps of leather, which are reminiscent of tribal men and women.

Lion's Lair
MM 82.1 Oceanside, Islamorada
• **(305) 664-9922**

Artist/owner Kimberly White airbrushes custom designs on T-shirts, jeans, jackets and an assortment of kids' gear. You'll find realistic looking wild animals and Keys birds. And here's a Grandma Alert: Don't miss the cute baby sneakers decorated with lace, bows, rhinestones and glitter.

Caribbean Village Shops
MM 82 Oceanside, Islamorada
• **(305) 664-4732**

Steel drum music accompanies you on a stroll through a potpourri of shops billed as "Caribbean Village, a feel of Old Islamorada." You'll follow brick walkways under a canopy of tropical foliage with hanging baskets of bromeliads. You'll meet the resident scarlet macaw, Fred, as well as his "mates," an assortment of parrots, cockatoos and lovebirds. The Caribbean Village Gift Shop, a ubiquitous, something-for-everyone tourist shop, stocks quality gifts items that exude a Caribbean feel-

Photo: Victoria Shearer

Funky shopping oases, such as this one in Marathon,
are sprinkled along the Overseas Highway.

ing, along with an outdoor display of kitschy
shells, fountains, bromeliads, garden statues
and Caribbean furnishings.

Justine's Jewelry
MM 82 Oceanside, Islamorada
• **(305) 664-5120, (800) 211-5120**

Easy to miss sandwiched between Tropical Optical Boutique and Island Silver and
Spice, Justine's small shop holds a mother
lode of silver treasure inside. The porch is laden
with Old West memorabilia, foreshadowing the
gems within. You'll find a good selection of
creative sterling silver jewelry, many inlaid with
turquoise and other semiprecious stones. The
one-of-a-kind pieces are strikingly unusual.

Island Silver & Spice
MM 82 Oceanside, Islamorada
• **(305) 664-2715**

Billed as the Keys' department store, Island

Silver & Spice offers a quality sampling of many
things. A small men's department tucks away
in the rear of the store, allowing the much larger
ladies' section to predominate. Fine jewelry is
offered as well as a limited selection of shoes,
children's clothing, books and games. The
peach-and-green building also houses an eclectic assortment of gourmet kitchen items, including a selection of gourmet coffee beans that
fills the air with a vanilla-mocha scent. Bath and
household accessories are upstairs, along with
a bargain corner.

The Sandal Factory
MM 82 Oceanside, Islamorada
• **(305) 453-9644**

This sandal outlet allows you to fit yourself. Pick from a copious selection of strappy
ladies' sandals as well as Reef and Birkenstock
brands. Men and children can be accommodated here too. You won't find every style in

every size, but there are hundreds of designs from which to choose.

Angelika
MM 81.9 Oceanside, Islamorada
• **(305) 664-9008**

Upmarket ladies' fashions with an old-fashioned twist and whimsical designs mark the merchandise at Angelika's. You'll find natural fabrics in these casual fashions, which include Blue Fish, Flax Linen, Surrealist, Nothing Matters and BCBG brands. Don't miss Angelika's great hats.

Sunny Exposures
MM 81.9 Bayside, Islamorada
• **(305) 664-8445, (800) 725-0801**

See suits, suits and more suits here — for surf and sun, not the office, for sure. Ladies' swimsuits of every style and description for every imaginable body type join ranks with cover-ups, lotions and sunglasses. Sunny Exposures even carries some kids' suits.

World Wide Sportsman Inc.
MM 81.5 Bayside, Islamorada
• **(305) 664-4615, (800) 327-2880**

World Wide Sportsman's stately new store — a former in-and-out storage building renovated in an old-fashioned faux exposed-brick motif and surrounded by native trees and shrubs — showcases the exact replica of Hemingway's 42-foot ship, the *Pilar*. Visitors can climb aboard and examine Hemingway's chair and even his typewriter. Rumor has it that he wrote at least one novel while fishing on the *Pilar*. A 6,000-gallon saltwater aquarium presents the creatures of our reef, including baby tarpon, bonefish and redfish. A small art gallery upstairs features works of local artists.

Memorabilia aside, World Wide is stocked to the rafters with a wide assortment of fishing tackle (see the Outfitters section in our Fishing chapter), and a full line of men's and women's technical clothing is offered: ExOfficio, Woolrich, Bimini Bay, Sportif and Columbia. You'll also find Reef Rider belts and wallets and extensive gift and jewelry sections.

If your stamina runs out before your money does, sit a spell in one of the rocking chairs lining the back porch and watch the action on the Gulf of Mexico. Or pop up to the Zane Grey Bar, sink into a leather chair, look at the vintage fishing photos of Grey and his cronies, and sip a tall, cool one. World Wide Sportsman is one place you won't want to miss.

Coral Reef Gifts
MM 80.4 Oceanside, Islamorada
• **(305) 664-2622**

Lots of fun stuff is to be had in this long, narrow coral pink building punctuated with teal blue trim. You'll see coconut pelicans, flamingos and parrots, wooden postcards, one-of-a-kind gift items and unusual baskets. Cat lovers will fancy the kitty memorabilia. From plaques to cards, cats adorn many things, including the signs: "Cat Crossing" and "Attack Cat." A small selection of gourmet food items includes the wildly popular Paradise Tea that is served at Morada Bay (see our Restaurants chapter). At one end of Coral Reef Gifts is the JCPenney Catalog Merchant Store, (305) 664-4417.

Middle Keys

All That Glitters
MM 61 Oceanside, Duck Key
• **(305) 743-0058**

All That Glitters is a jewelry store specializing in custom-made items. Don't miss the black Tahitian pearls — the largest collection in Florida — which come from the black-lipped oysters of Tahiti. You'll see a large collection of treasure-coin jewelry as well. All That Glitters buys coins directly from the divers who explore the ancient wrecks that litter our reefs. This is the place to take any jewelry that needs fixing (even many of the area jewelers send items here to be repaired).

Pier 61 — A Tropical Bazaar
MM 61 Oceanside, Duck Key
• **(305) 743-1934**

Like a tropical garden, the affordably priced colorful island togs at Pier 61 will entrance you. Flowing, flattering and fun, short or long, swimsuits and shorts — everything you need for an island vacation is here. You'll be hard-pressed to leave empty handed.

The Enchanted Elephant
MM 54 Bayside, Quay Village, Marathon
• (305) 289-0646, (800) 689-0646

Celebrating all things animal — but especially the five-toed, long-tusked Elephantidae family — The Enchanted Elephant is full of just plain fun stuff. One whole room, called the Elephant Adoption Center, is devoted to elephantine icons and statuettes (better take one home today!). And a corner of another room is decked out as a shrine: The World's Smallest Museum for the World's Largest Animal showcases the owner's antique elephant collection. You can pick up a regulation "manatee crossing" sign, or maybe your street needs one to caution for tigers. The four animal-filled rooms will enchant you.

Bayshore Clothing and Small World
MM 54 Bayside, Quay Village, Marathon
• (305) 743-8430

Actually three adjoining rooms of the same shop, Bayshore caters to men's and women's garment needs, while the little people's shop beckons parents and especially grandparents with a cute selection of swimsuits, Big Bird terry-cloth cover-ups and warm-weather togs. You'll even find a pint-size grass skirt, halter-top and floral lei. Pick up a soft, fuzzy hand puppet. You'll be a hero with your wee one when you get home. You can order personalized baby blankets also.

Martha's Caribbean Cupboard and Dangerous John Hubert's Hot Sauces & Cigars
MM 54 Bayside, Quay Village, Marathon
• (305) 743-9299

Living proof that when you're hot, you're hot, John Hubert now has his own brand of hot sauce, barbecue sauce and jellies to complement the wide range of cigars and outrageously named hot sauces in this captivating store. This place is a hoot (see our Seafood Markets and Specialty Foods chapter).

Key Bana Resort Apparel
MM 53.5 Oceanside, Marathon
• (305) 289-1161

We know you ladies will find a new swimsuit or tropical cotton item here that you will like. We always do. And Key Bana has a roomful of shorts and shirts for men too. It gives them something to do as you browse. Key Bana also has a good selection of shoes.

Joanne's Discount Depot
MM 53.5 Bayside, Marathon
• (305) 289-1166

Joanne's is not part of the national fabric chain bearing the same name. Nevertheless, fabrics are Joanne's specialty — room upon room of gorgeous, riotously colored bolts that will inspire you to run for your sewing machine. You'll even find swimsuit fabric. Joanne's stocks every thread, ribbon, button or notion you could imagine, including wedding paraphernalia. You can supply your craft and knitting needs here, and quilters will love the unusual tropical cotton prints. Joanne's maintains a workroom for custom reupholstering, slip covers and window treatments.

Equipment Locker Sport & Bicycle
MM 53 Bayside, Marathon
• (305) 289-1670

Peppermint-striped tennis balls are just a fraction of the sporting gear offered here, where you can find a good selection of Trek bicycles and related biking gear, exercise equipment and the gamut of necessities for every sport from hoops to in-line skating. Top-brand athletic shoes line the walls.

Book Key & Gallery
MM 53 Bayside, Marathon
• (305) 743-5256

Just past Ornamental Tile and directly next to Dr. Alexander's dental office, this cozy, inviting book nook hides behind an iron gate in five cubbyhole-size rooms. The shop is virtually wallpapered with books, half new, half used. The used books, walls and walls of which are paperbacks, are sold for half the retail price. Special-interest books line one whole room, which the locals call "the interesting room."

Out n Out Gifts
MM 52.5 Bayside, Marathon
• (305) 289-9911

This nifty shop is chockablock with interesting "stuff" — all very reasonably priced. Picture frames, wind chimes, mobiles and memorabilia compete with household accessories and decorative items, all-in-all creating a bazaarlike hodgepodge of curiosities. Be sure to allow enough time to poke around for a while.

Keyker's-N-Co.
MM 52 Bayside, Marathon
• (305) 743-0107

Fifty-seven local artisans display their talents at Keyker's, the artists' co-operative tucked into a nook between a hardware store and a dive shop just beyond the Marathon Walgreen's. Four clothing designers create custom island clothing for women and children. And don't miss the cute Keyker's, from which the store got its name: They are skid-resistant slippers made out of bathing suit material, perfect for infants in walkers or pint-sized novice swimmers in the pool. You'll find framed watercolors and photography of familiar Keys locations as well as a wide selection of crafts, even coconut bunnies. This is a must-stop place for a Keysy browse.

Island Junction
MM 51.5 Oceanside, Marathon
• (305) 743-2580,
(800) 255-4803

Island Junction sells a complete selection of the famed Key West Aloe products as well as handpainted clothing and interesting costume jewelry. This is the place to find Pool Pal infant and toddler swimwear — those nifty swimsuits for the little ones that have floats built into the lining.

Wicker Web
MM 51.5 Oceanside, Marathon
• (305) 743-3696

Across from the Marathon Airport runway in the Southwind Building, you'll discover the Wicker Web, three showrooms chock-full of tchotchkes for every room in your house. You'll find a wide selection of baskets, wall hangings, wicker items, lamps, plasticware and bath accessories.

P & J Antiques
MM 51.2 Oceanside, Marathon
• (305) 743-0136

P & J Antiques displays collectible glassware and antique items in a cozy little warren, perfect for those who like to rummage through the spoils of antiquity. We even spotted an ancient sled nestled among the memorabilia.

General Rental & Party Center
MM 51 Oceanside, Marathon
• (305) 743-2158

It's party time! Or at least it should be, because the Party Center's fantastic selection of party paraphernalia keeps growing and growing. You'll find a smorgasbord of paper and plastic supplies as well as a great selection of linens, grills, tables, chairs, china, glassware, flatware, serving dishes, food warmers, tents and helium balloons.

Driftwood Designs
MM 50 Bayside, Gulfside Village, Marathon • (305) 743-7591

Driftwood's claim of being "The Definitive Gift Store" is well-deserved. Browsing the eclectic selection of bronze and fine-art sculptures, jewelry, wearable art and pottery is like exploring a museum, but more fun, because you can actually purchase the curiosities. From a Civil War chess set to brass herons, enameled tropical fish, Caribbean inspired tableware and more, the smorgasbord of merchandise here is upmarket and fascinating. This is the place to find the fabulous "Lunch at the Ritz" earrings, pins, bracelets and chokers. A small grouping of children's puzzles, books, games and stuffed Gund bears and ostriches will prove popular with your kids.

The Port Hole
MM 50 Bayside, Gulfside Village, Marathon • (305) 743-3552

Don't miss The Port Hole, an upmarket ladies' clothing boutique guaranteed to pry open your pocketbook. Jean and her crew keep even more temptations in the back room, so be sure to clue them in to your tastes, and they'll dress you in style. This is one of the few shops around where the clerks pamper you with service while you're in the dressing room, exchanging sizes and styles, replacing the clothes on the hangers and suggesting smart accessories.

Beachcomber Jewelers
MM 50 Bayside, Gulfside Village, Marathon • (305) 743-2245

Beachcomber's showcases more than just fine jewelry. You'll find Key West dinnerware, Lenox and Mikasa china and a selection of crystal goblets. Beachcomber Jewelers also stocks the popular mother-and-child necklaces, all the rage with the '90s new moms.

Food for Thought
MM 50 Bayside, Gulfside Village, Marathon • (305) 743-3297

Food for Thought is really two shops in one: half books and magazines, half health foods (see our Seafood Markets and Specialty Foods chapter). You can fuel your mind and your body at the same time. Custom orders are the norm here.

Marathon Men's Shop
MM 50 Bayside, Gulfside Village, Marathon • (305) 743-5657

Perhaps the oldest men's clothing establishment in Marathon, this men's shop features such brands as Hook & Tackle and Sperry Topsiders. This is the place in the Middle Keys to rent a tuxedo for your next formal affair.

Sandpiper
MM 50.5 Oceanside, Marathon • (305) 743-3205

You might want to pop in to the Sandpiper, a clothing-cum-gift store mainly specializing in women's sportswear, including Liz Claiborne. The men are not slighted, however, for they can find Nautico and Hook & Tackle brands as well as Sperry Topsider boat shoes.

The Brown Pelican
MM 50.5 Oceanside, Marathon • (305) 743-3849

The Brown Pelican, a cozy shop crammed full of tropical cottons, Florida Keys handbags and Key West Aloe products, perches just next to Kmart.

Lazy Lizard
MM 49.8 Bayside, Marathon • (305) 743-5001

Full of cool cottons, fun aprons, Keysy jewelry, stationery, cards and glassware, Lazy Lizard is a shop for all occasions. You'll find everything from stuffed hand puppets to mirrors bordered with palm trees. This is the place to find a campy touch of the Keys for your memory box.

Patio & Home Decorating Shop
Furniture Gallery at Gulfside Village, MM 50.5 Bayside, Gulfside Village, Marathon • (305) 289-2038
Furniture Art Gallery, MM 49.6 Oceanside, Marathon • (305) 743-2740
Casual Furniture Gallery, MM 48.6 Bayside, Marathon • (305) 743-2776

The Furniture Gallery at Gulfside Village is the first of three stores that make up the sprawling Patio & Home Decorating Shop. The Gallery crams a warehouse full of bargains in its spacious, good-deal shop. Better check it out; you may find an item you can't live without. Sometimes we stroll through the enormous Furniture Art Gallery just to see what wild new things they've added to the collection. Besides offering the most complete selection of quality furniture you'll find in the Keys, the Furniture Art Gallery peppers the showroom with accessories that range from the sublime to the outrageous. You have to see it to believe it. You'll find a wide range of Oriental antiques and artifacts here as well. The Casual Furniture Gallery is the third of the trio of furniture stores. This large showroom stocks all the name brands in outdoor and casual furniture and has a way-out selection of only-in-the-Keys accessories.

Paradise Ltd.
MM 49.6 Oceanside, Marathon • (305) 289-9090

These are not your average tourist trivialities, although most everything has a decidedly Keys feeling and theme. Tropically inspired quality accessories, tableware and correspondence materials join ranks with one of the best Florida Keys book selections around.

Marathon Discount Book Center
MM 48.2 Oceanside, Marathon • (305) 289-2066

The newest addition to the Middle Keys book shop scene, Marathon Discount Book Center offers all books at 10 to 90 percent off retail prices. Selling primarily publisher's overstock, the store also offers best sellers and local interest books. The staff also will place special orders.

Golden Nugget
MM 48 Bayside, Faro Blanco Resort, Marathon • (305) 743-3059

Tucked on the grounds of the Faro Blanco Marine Resort in a floating houseboat at harbor's edge, it is easy to miss the Golden Nugget jewelry store if you haven't talked to an Insider. Check out these upmarket treasures, however, because Golden Nugget stocks a mother lode. The sand-glass enamel reef necklaces represent a lost art. The colorful tropical fish "swim" against an 18-karat gold "coral reef." You'll also find gold omegas and a wide selection of gold slides — shells, swordfish, lobsters and other nautically themed pieces, some set with gemstones.

Pigeon Key Foundation Gift Shop
MM 47 Oceanside, Pigeon Key Visitors Center, Marathon • (305) 743-5999
MM 52 Bayside, Marathon Airport, Marathon • (305) 289-0506

Look for the old green railway car, still sitting on the tracks of Flagler's railroad at MM 47 Oceanside. Hidden unassumingly inside resides the Pigeon Key Visitors Center Gift Shop, a potpourri of Keys memorabilia and gift items you won't want to miss. The gift shop, like everything on Pigeon Key, is run by a contingent of loyal volunteers, and all proceeds go to the Pigeon Key Foundation. You can even buy a piece of Flagler's dream, for Pigeon Key will sell you a bit of the track. You can rent bicycles here for a spirited ride down the old Seven Mile Bridge to Pigeon Key. A giant sign heralding Knight's Key marks the spot you should turn to find the gift shop. Many of the same items and more are available at the airport terminal shop as well so you can pick up those last-minute gifts before heading home.

Lower Keys

Big Pine Shopping Center
MM 30.5 Bayside, Key Deer Blvd., Big Pine Key

Turn right at the light in Big Pine to find this shopping center. Locals shop at the Winn-Dixie, the only supermarket for miles around, but the plaza has interesting shops as well. Inside Whalton's Pet Shop, Ralph, the 18-year-

old celebrity hyacinth macaw, holds court. Beware: If you are not a fan of birds on the loose, do not enter this shop, because Ralph and his friends — a multicolored sun conure and a white umbrella cockatoo like the one in the old television show Baretta — are not caged. Whalton's places kittens from the Lower Keys Friends of Animals group, charging customers $30 for the privilege of providing the cats with a new home. The money pays for spaying or neutering and for the kittens' first shots.

Down the way a bit, Edie's Hallmark Shop markets a potpourri of cards and collectibles, puzzles and pocket novels, cookbooks and even a sweet shop of chocolates. You'll finally find those Revo or Hobie polarized sunglasses you've been searching for at The Sunglass Shop. Check out a video at Now Showing Video or shop for a swimsuit, shorts or T-shirt at Beall's Outlet; the prices are quite reasonable.

Big Pine Village
MM 29.5 Bayside, Big Pine Key

First, stop at the angel shop, A Glimpse of Heaven. Angels of every description adorn this tiny haven, inspired by the untimely death of the owner's daughter. The owner started collecting angels as therapy during her grieving process, finally amassing so many her friends suggested she open a shop. Spirits soar in this unique collection of jewelry, books, cards, wall hangings and handcrafted items. Walk along the boardwalk and visit Granny's Attic. You'll swear you just arrived in New England. Chock-full of country crafts and antiques — Sandy Clark makes the crafts, Harry Clark fashions the handmade wood furniture — this testimony to the nostalgia of yesteryear will hasten memories for some. Remember that china-faced doll in her lace christening dress? What about that Remington manual typewriter? Or the silver tea service like the one your grandmother used? You'll likely find them here.

The Blue Moon Trader and The Crystal Loft
MM 29.7 Oceanside, Big Pine Key • (305) 872-9390

The Blue Moon Trader is a New Age boutique where mysteries lurk inside a quirky, multistory frame house along the Overseas Highway. A half-moon collars the psychic's window, and frolicking dolphins and rock crystals adorn the clapboards, which are shaded from mauve to blue to pale peach. Inside you will be transcended by all things mystical, magical and metaphysical: books, incense, clothing and more. Even the kids have a special room with books of affirmations and meditations. Upstairs in the Crystal Loft you can immerse yourself in crystals, gems and minerals, even medicine pouches and dream catchers.

Little Palm Island Gift Shop
MM 28.5 Oceanside, Little Torch Key
• (305) 872-2524

Stop at this mainland substation of the Little Palm Island Gift Shop, which tripled in size in 1998 and now rivals its sister shop on the island. You'll find interesting Mexican glassware and handpainted plates in addition to upscale clothing and straw hats. If you go out to Little Palm Island itself, for lunch or dinner or to stay the night, don't miss the island shop. The tropical ambiance will tempt you to discard your shorts and don an island caftan.

Sherman's Nautical Emporium
MM 24.5 Oceanside, Summerland Key
• (305) 745-1748

The merchandise here includes everything from frozen bait to women's designer dresses. But souvenirs are your best bet, and you'll score big if you're looking for note cards, greeting cards, kidstuff, T-shirts, shower curtains, picture frames or just basic Keys stuff.

Woodcarvings, Etc.
MM 24 Oceanside, Summerland Key
• (305) 745-2726

The terrain becomes wilder and appears more remote on this part of the Overseas Highway. Christina Dube swims the ocean waters every morning in search of cypress posts and boards that she recycles into sculptures with a chisel and mallet in her home on Summerland Key. Displayed in several rooms, these creations evoke Ms. Dube's subtle sense of humor. Look for the unusual collection of Santa Clauses. The Key West Santa stands with a gummy, rummy grin, holding a bottle of wine behind his back. Some Santas even have pelicans peeking out of their sacks. A display of snapshots shows Ms. Dube's specialty — caricature portraits. You can have your features chiseled for posterity in any style you like. The back room holds a selection of antiques. Kayak rentals are available, and you can take them out right on the premises. Expect to spend about $10 an hour or $30 for 4 hours.

Belle's Trading Post
MM 14 Oceanside, 2 Bluewater Dr., Sugarloaf Key • (305) 745-1842

The address reads Sugarloaf Key, but this tiny shop is actually tucked in a roadside shanty near Bluewater Key Resort on one of the Saddlebunch Keys and is not visible from the road. Turn in at the Bluewater sign and bear right. A rabbit warren of collectibles and antiques awaits the scavenger-at-heart.

Key West

For shoppers, Key West lives up to its reputation as Paradise. Colorful, funky, one-of-a-kind shops abound on our fair island, and choosing from among the plethora of goods may seem daunting to some, a challenge to others. Here we have taken the best of Key West — a little of this, a little of that — and presented it in a simple format. Duval Street is home to some of the classiest merchandise for sale anywhere, and we take you on a tour of it, pointing out the highlights along the way.

We also include a section called simply Old Town. This category encompasses stores not on the main stretch of Duval Street. Often, you will find these Old Town shops epitomize the eccentricities and color of Old Key West. Tucked in and about small quiet streets and the heavenly scents of local flora are many stores that are sometimes tough to find but not to be missed. To simplify, we consider the line of demarcation between Old Town and New Town to be White Street.

We've also included a section devoted to shopping in New Town, the more conventionally developed part of Key West. New Town shops are mostly organized into several large plazas, where one-stop shopping makes souvenir fetching easy and, usually, more inexpensive than on pricey Duval Street. Finally, we've attached a separate section on bookstores. This tiny island boasts no less than seven of them. And no wonder. Eight Pulitzer Prize winners have come from our island, and close to 60 working writers live here all or part of the year. Whether they draw inspiration from our sunshine and warm breezes or from the quirky cast of characters who populate our streets, it seems that Key West has become not only a haven for those who write prose and poetry but for those who read it as well.

So get ready, get set, go shopping. But be sure to make your first purchase a pair of comfortable shoes. You'll need them to make the most of your shopping spree in Key West.

Best of Duval

If you like to think of shopping as a game, then Key West will seem like a giant Monopoly board of clever boutiques and colorful shops. A lucky roll of the dice lands you on some of our favorite spots along the city's most popular promenade, Duval Street. We move through our virtual tour of Duval Street from Upper Duval (Oceanside) to Lower Duval (Gulfside).

We have selected a sampling from among the premier shops on this 1.1-mile stretch of road. However, some of you will want to take home a T-shirt or two, and you will surely pass by many shirt shops, which we have excluded here. Many such places on Duval carry virtually the same stock. But be aware, and do not let yourself be overcharged for such additions as special designs. All T-shirt shops are required to post a list of prices inside the store. Be sure to confirm the total price before consenting to the purchase. If you feel you have been overcharged by any store, call Key West Code Enforcement at (305) 292-8191.

Now, on to world-famous Duval Street.

Key West Havana Cigar Company
1117 Duval St., Key West
• **(305) 296-2680**

Make your selection from among the many brands of quality, handcrafted cigars and accessories in this small shop that doubles as the front entry of the Speakeasy Inn. A prompt mail-order service is offered, so you can send cigars to the folks back home.

City Zoo
1108 Duval St., Key West
• **(305) 292-1711**

Get your animal memorabilia here. Faux animals of all shapes and sizes bound unbridled in this fetching little store. If an adorable little stuffed frog doesn't tickle your fancy, then perhaps a tropical fish mobile will. You'll find plenty for the children on your shopping list.

Décor of Key West
1075 Duval St., Duval Square, Key West
• **(305) 296-4146**

Don't let the name confuse you. This shop is filled not with furnishings but with women's apparel and accessories. If an upcoming occasion calls for something slightly more formal than a T-shirt and shorts, this may be your place. An array of stylish dresses, skirts and trouser/shirt ensembles awaits your inspection.

Fletcher on Duval Island Furniture
1024 Duval St., Key West
• **(305) 294-2032**

Decorate your home with the fine-crafted furniture offered by Fletcher. The specialty here is coral keystone, wrought into strange and wonderful forms. Coffee tables with end stands of this intricate rock hold a glass top in place. Choose also from among artistic pedestals, fireplace mantels and much more. Be prepared to spend a considerable amount — art like this doesn't come cheaply.

Curtis & Sons
913 Duval St., Key West • **(305) 296-2082**

Take home a piece of the Florida Keys in the form of an accessory for your living room, dining room, den or office. In this tiny shop nestled beside the Wicker Guesthouse, you'll find a unique array of lamps, mirrors, tropical throw pillows, pottery, picture frames, glassware, ceramics and more. Among the fanciful clothing displayed you might even find the perfect lightweight, loose-fitting dress for tonight's cocktails by the sea.

Tikal Trading Company

912 Duval St., Key West • (305) 293-0033
129 Duval St., Key West • (305) 296-4463

Two locations hold a vast store of women's apparel. Flowery dresses perfect for the warm climate of the islands invite passersby into the site. The same prints and styles are available in several sizes so mothers and daughters can be outfitted alike.

Cuba! Cuba!

814 Duval St., Key West • (305) 295-9442

Get a little "Libre!" in your life with this quaint little shop that espouses a passion for all things Cuban. Art is very much a part of the selection, evidenced by nostalgic wood carvings depicting a typical Cuban kitchen. Other passions evinced are those of cooking and music: Cookbooks and authentic jams and marmalades line the shelves, and guitars and maracas are just begging to be played. A selection of cigars is also on display.

Towels of Key West

806 Duval St., Key West • (305) 292-1120

Towels in all shapes, sizes and budgets fill this simple store. Get the best-selling colorful print terry robe, or immerse yourself in a big warm oversized colorful towel.

H.T. Chittum & Co.

725 Duval St., Key West • (305) 292-9002

Lovers of the outdoors find H.T. Chittum & Co. among the most charming of sports apparel stores. Don't let the two-story log cabin or the seaplane hanging from the ceiling distract you from finding some of the finest clothing labels in the country. The buyers for this store travel the country to bring in the best from Tommy Bahama, Sigrid Olsen, Lilly Pulitzer, Timberland, Lacoste, Sportif, Reyn Spooner, and Holland Bros. leather goods. You will find the same quality island gear here as at the H.T. Chittum & Co. store in Islamorada (see other listing in this chapter).

Last Flight Out

706 Duval St., Key West • (305) 294-8008

The story is that many visitors in the '70s fell so in love with the island that they waited as long as possible and took the last flight out. In fact, some are still waiting. Dreamers and doers are invited to wander around in this charming store, dedicated mostly to flight. If you love the islands as much as we do, be sure and take the Last Flight Out. Especially appealing are the T-shirts and posters bearing the phrase "Contrary to popular opinion, life is not a dress rehearsal."

Open Minded

703 Duval St., Key West • (305) 295-9595

Tiffany lamps of all shapes and vivid colors perch daintily in the front display window of this unusual store. Part New Age and part boutique, Open Minded caters to those who wish to decorate their lives and homes in an otherworldly manner. Colorful wall hangings, chimes and women's apparel co-mingle with incense, Tarot cards and colorful serenity.

Worldwide Flags

626 Duval St., Key West • (305) 292-9301

Sometimes the name says it all. Flags it is, and if you are French, Dutch or even Lithuanian, you'll find a flag to rouse your patriotism. Vast quantities of official flags from many countries and all 50 states are offered here, but don't forget a Conch Republic flag or a Key West rainbow flag. Or just take home a colorful windsock.

ACA Joe

617 Duval St., Key West • (305) 294-1570

Need some cargo shorts? A pair of deck shoes? A lightweight jacket for your sunset cruise? ACA Joe has a wide assortment of cool, comfortable cotton clothing for men and women as well as shoes that are perfect for boating and beachcombing. You'll find a nice selection of tropical print camp shirts here, too — tasteful enough to even wear back home.

Hot Hats

613 Duval St., Key West • (305) 294-1333

If you're heading out into the midday sun, you'd best wear a hat. And you're sure to find a flattering one at this shop devoted entirely to headgear. Everything from canvas caps to straw boaters can be found here. There's even a rack full of multicolored baseball caps with propellers for catching those island breezes in a whimsical way.

Latitude 24
612 Duval St., Key West • (305) 294-4255

Latitude 24 sounds out to surfers seeking swimwear separates, Teva sandals, Rollerblades and more. Sports enthusiasts can deck themselves out for a game of beach volleyball and be properly dressed for a dip in the pool.

Birkenstock
610 Duval St., Key West • (305) 294-8318

Essentials for island life, Birkenstock has a large full-service store right in the middle of it all. Although Birkenstocks don't come cheaply, the shoes are exceptionally durable and comfortable. Count on paying anywhere from $45 up for a pair of these.

Wizard's Attic
**506 Southard St., Key West
• (305) 294-6180**

For all your alchemy and arcane needs, the Wizard's Attic, just a few steps off Duval, is the shopping center for today's New Age aficionado. Herbs, oils, New Age literature, aromatherapy products, candles and crystals beckon the novice; a genuine black cauldron

is for the expert. Workshop seminars and lectures are held monthly; call for details.

Environmental Circus
518 Duval St., Key West • (305) 294-6055

A Deadhead's delight lies within this cozy store, filled to the brim with tie-dyed T-shirts, essential oils, lava lamps, dyed wall hangings and smoking accessories.

Sunlion Jewelry
513 Duval St., Key West • (305) 296-8457

You'll know you've struck treasure when you see the gold and gemstone bracelets, necklaces, earrings and rings designed on-premises by Fantasy Fest's official jeweler. Conch pearls and treasure coins also are among the elegant trinkets here.

Margaritaville Store
500 Duval St., Key West • (305) 296-3070

Everything here is tuned to one thing — the works of Key West's favorite son, Jimmy Buffett. All his albums are available here, along with tons of shirts, books, photos, and other Parrothead paraphernalia. Spend some time perusing the walls — they're

Photo: Victoria Shearer

Flea markets attract bargain hunters of all kinds — locals and visitors alike.

packed with photos and memorabilia related to events in the life of the man from Margaritaville. This place is a must-stop for Buffett fans old and new.

Fast Buck Freddie's
500 Duval St., Key West • (305) 294-2007

If there weren't literally hundreds of stores to explore in Key West and you never reached the bottom of your pockets, Fast Buck Freddie's, at the southeast corner of Duval and Fleming, would be your one-stop shop. FBF's carries men's and women's clothing in metropolitan and tropical styles. Just around the bend from the mega-store's clothing section are imported items from around the world, such as clocks, candle holders, picture frames and some of the most unusual home furnishings you'll see anywhere. Look to Freddie's kitchenware department for an extensive selection of cookbooks, gourmet kitchen accessories, herbs, flavored oils and Godiva chocolates sure to have you walking on air for the rest of your excursion. And be sure to check out the unusual toys, novelty items and greeting cards in the back of the store. But beware — some may be R-rated.

Shades of Key West
335 Duval St., Key West • (305) 294-0519
306 Front St., Key West • (305) 294-0329

Protect your eyes from the intense tropical sunlight with a wide selection of brand-name sunglasses, including Oakley, Ray-Ban, Vuarnet, Armani, Arnet and Hobie. These are not your cheap, dime-store sunglasses; everything's top-quality.

Earthbound Mining Co.
419 Duval St., Key West • (305) 292-8604

Semiprecious stones and minerals fill this shop, in more forms than you thought possible. Big pieces of lovely purple amethyst and golden citrine are offered in their natural form, but you could also opt for a marble chess set, wood-carved animals, beautiful sliced opaque rock chimes, bead jewelry or agate bookends.

Gecko's
419 Duval St., Key West • (305) 295-0046

Not just your ordinary animal-theme store, Gecko's is the perfect place to shop for children. Right inside the door is a selection of glow-in-the-dark room schemes, along with the requisite black lights for emphasis. Choose from Outer Space, Ocean Life, Rainforest and Glow Frogs. Past that, take a chance and sponsor a wild dolphin or wolf, or take home an animal figurine. A large selection of stuffed animals brings out the child in everyone.

Leslie Miller, Ltd.
419 Duval St., Key West • (305) 293-0790

This fine jewelry store offers some exotic original creations. Jewelry incorporating black pearls is a specialty, but jewelry is not the only offering — some of the pieces definitely qualify as art.

Michael's Pirate World
400 Duval St., Key West • (305) 294-2488
431 Front St., Key West • (305) 293-9700
123 Duval St., Key West • (305) 293-9926

If treasure coins are your thing, then no visit to Key West would be complete without setting foot inside this store dedicated to treasure coins and coin jewelry. The most popular coins are from the *Atocha* (see the entry on Mel Fisher's Maritime Heritage Museum in our Attractions chapter), but coins from all ages and places, including ancient Greece and Rome, are available.

Becky Thatcher Designs
425 Eaton St., Key West • (305) 296-0886

Just a few steps off Duval Street on Eaton lies this quaint store, named after the designer. Jewelry is the specialty, and the designs incorporate any number of unusual precious and semiprecious stones. The opals are especially exquisite (see our Arts and Culture chapter).

Hair Wraps —
A Bead and Braid Shop
310 Duval St., Key West • (305) 293-1133

If you want to make a real statement or you just want to get your hair done in a new

Remember when heading down the Keys on the Overseas Highway, bayside is on your right, oceanside is on your left.

way, head over to Hair Wraps in the courtyard of the Garden Cafe. Tons of beads are available, and they have just about any color or detail you'd like.

Key West Candle Company, Inc.
310 Duval St., Key West • (305) 296-8447

Candles galore abound in this small store, tucked in the back of the courtyard of the Garden Cafe. All candles are made on the premises, and, if you are lucky, you just might happen upon the candlemaker at work.

Neptune Designs
301 Duval St., Key West • (305) 294-8131

Most of the jewelry filling this shop is of an oceanic nature and is wrought in gold or silver. Leaping silver dolphin necklaces frolic with golden, gliding sea turtles on a black background. Noah's Ark figurines are on display — tiny ships decked with all manner of wildlife.

Biker's Image
121 Duval St., Key West • (305) 292-1328

Get your Harley tuned up and race over to Biker's Image, where you can splurge on your fantasies with leather, Harley T-shirts, helmets, smoking accessories and just about anything that complements the biker lifestyle.

The Partridge Christmas Shop
120 Duval St., Key West • (305) 294-6001

This little wedge of a store is packed at Christmastime with gift buyers looking for that perfect Key West memento. Ornaments of snorkeling Santas, Christmas dolphins and anything of an island nature are favorites.

Old Town

Throughout Key West's intricate roadways, a wealth of interesting shops emerges. You can walk to all of them, of course, but you might want to consider getting around by bicycle or moped instead. There's a lot of territory to cover.

Bird in Hand
203 Simonton St., Key West
• (305) 296-6324

Newly relocated from Mallory Square, this shop is one of Key West's oldest and most respected establishments. Here you'll find local handmade jewelry (both fine and costume), collectibles (including Lladro and Hummel pieces) and a wide selection of local and imported gifts.

Cavanagh's
520 Front St., Key West • (305) 296-3342

An exotic array of clothing, furniture and collectibles awaits you here. Among some of Cavanagh's highlights are ornate offerings from the Orient.

The China Clipper
333 Simonton St., Key West
• (305) 294-2136

For more inspiration for your interiors, head to The China Clipper, where prices are clipped on quality Oriental furnishings and artwork.

Clinton Square Market
291 Front St., Key West • (305) 296-6825

Enclosed within Clinton Square are a number of shops worth stopping in to see. Island Jewelry combines local design with native elements such as sea turtles, dolphins and manatees. All are carved or emblazoned in 14- and 18-karat gold and sterling silver. It's You or, at least, the handpainted clothing and hats at the store of the same name may very well be you. Footweary travelers will find solace in the wide array of sandals and shoes available at Happy Feet. Club West, Sublime and Paradise of Key West offer tropical clothing and souvenirs. Wings of Imagination is a shop devoted to butterflies. And for feline fanciers, there's The Blue Cat, fully stocked with all manner of cat-related merchandise.

Fabric World
613 Simonton St., Key West
• (305) 294-1773

Founded in 1970, Key West's only shop devoted solely to fabrics is like a box of crayons — plain on the outside, a riot of color within. The owners have handpicked all of the fabrics, including the tropical fish prints for which this shop is justly famous and the more than 200 bolts of upholstery materials. Patterns, sewing notions and decorator trims are also available. This is a must-shop for anyone who sews.

From the Ruins
219 Whitehead St., Key West
• **(305) 293-0897**
No one — and we mean no one — should pass up the opportunity to experience From the Ruins, where one-of-a-kind handmade garments and accessories make for a mellifluous museum. Wear your heart on your sleeve with a handbag crafted in the form of your favorite dog breed or pick up an intricate hand-blown glass vase. Be sure to bring a full wallet — these one-of-a-kind artifacts have one-of-a-kind prices. Look for the cozy cottage with a white picket fence and welcoming front porch.

Half Buck Freddie's
726 Caroline St., Key West
• **(305) 294-6799**
Slightly dated, overstocked or slow-moving merchandise from Fast Buck Freddie's (see listing above) never dies. It simply ends up across Duval and down a few blocks at Half Buck Freddie's on Caroline. Everything here, from clothing to calendars to kitchen gadgets, was once on sale at Freddie's. Now it's moved out and marked down 50 percent from its original price. The stock changes regularly, and the hours are limited. Shop for bargains here Thursdays through Sundays only.

Heatwave Swimwear
403 Greene St., Key West
• **(305) 296-0292**
One of South Florida's best bikini shops, Heatwave carries a variety of styles and sizes with a Caribbean flair.

Island Needlework
527 Fleming St., Key West
• **(305) 296-6091**
For wearable crafts, Island Needlework carries original handmade accessories, including belts, as well as needlepoint canvases and the yarns to complete them. Carpets sold here make any floor a bit fancier.

Key West Aloe
524 Front St., Key West • (305) 294-5592
Step into the Key West Aloe on Front Street for a showroom of the only perfumes, skin-care products and cosmetics to boast a "made in Key West" label. Then be sure to

visit the factory outlet store at 540 Greene Street for discounts on these items and to take a free tour of the laboratory where the products are made.

Key West Hand Print Fabrics and Fashions
201 Simonton St., Key West
• **(305) 294-9535**
At Key West Hand Print Fabrics and Fashions, you can watch silkscreen craftspeople create original men's and women's fashions on 60-yard-long tables. Original copyrighted Key West prints adorn men's shirts and various ladies' fashions, all ready to wear for your next outing. The prints are also sold by the yard; be sure to ask for a label to sew inside your own personal creations.

Key West Kite Company
409 Greene St., Key West
• **(305) 296-2535**
The Key West Kite Company is just waiting to make windy days wondrous with flags, banners and flying tours. The first kite store to set up shop in all of Florida, Key West Kites offers everything from handmade to high-performance sport kites.

Kino Sandals
107 Fitzpatrick St., Key West
• **(305) 294-5044**
Whatever you do in Key West, do not miss Kino Sandals. Tucked in the corner of Kino Plaza across from the Key West Cigar Factory, this factory offers handmade leather footwear for less than $10. Now that's something to wiggle your toes about.

Local Color
276 Margaret St., Lands End Village
• **(305) 292-3635**
This is where locals and tourists alike come to purchase the colorful, comfortable clothing that fits the Key West lifestyle. In addition to casual apparel for men and women, you'll find hats, handbags and costume jewelry to complete your island look.

Low Key Tye Dye South
528 Front St., Key West • (305) 294-5114
This is where quality tie-dyed clothing

makes a sensational '60s statement; with some help from these folks, so can you,

Noah's Ark
416 Fleming St., Key West
• **(305) 294-2757**

Noah's Ark is an animal-theme gift shop in a Conch house more than 100 years old. This fetching store showcases room after room of collectibles, stuffed animals, clothing and housewares that cover hundreds of species.

Perkins & Son Chandlery
901 Fleming St., Key West
• **(305) 294-7635**

Perkins can supply everything you need to set out to sea or add a nautical theme to your home: brasswork, ships' clocks, models, charts and books, plus jackets, shorts, hats and foul-weather gear. Allow plenty of time just to browse; this shop is stuffed from floor to ceiling. Many of the antiques are for display purposes only and not for sale. However, if you see something you like, ask. Some sales are negotiable.

Rainy Day Records
515 Fleming St., Key West
• **(305) 292-4793**

Vinyl records and used CDs are the focus here. You can buy, sell or trade your favorites for reasonable prices. You really can't go wrong because all used products are pre-checked and guaranteed. New CDs (they're the sealed ones) are also available for around $6 to $8. New shipments arrive here regularly so if you don't see something you like on your first visit, check back again in a few days.

Records and Rogues
1018 Truman Ave., Key West
• **(305) 296-4115**

Offering CDs from $2 to $10, Records and Rogues is Key West's largest discount music store. Take your old CDs and trade them for credit, or just find that old record your collection has been lacking.

The Restaurant Store
313 Margaret St., Key West
• **(305) 294-7994**

The Restaurant Store is chock-full of kitchen and cooking gear to feed five or 50. You'll discover state-of-the-art utensils, pots and pans and accessories for culinary aficionados and chefs alike.

Sign of Sandford
328 Simonton St., Key West
• **(305) 296-7493**

This store specializes in wholesale fabrics but also offers a selection of wearable art created by designer Sandford Birdsey for retail sale.

SwashBucklers
309 Petronia St., Key West
• **(305) 295-6357**

Shiver me timbers — it's a store devoted entirely to pirates. Among the booty you'll find pirate paintings, videos, books, flags, hats and vintage clothing. For kids (or adults who just want to act like kids), there are treasure chests of hooks and swords, eye patches and parrots starting as low as 99¢.

Timmy Tuxedo's
812 Fleming St., Key West
• **(305) 294-8897**

Believe it or not, we islanders occasionally have to go formal. But that doesn't necessarily mean black tie. At this, the only formal wear outlet in Key West, the ties and cummerbunds are just as likely to be tropical prints. Tuxedos, dinner jackets and all the accompaniments are available for rent or sale here in a wide array of sizes and styles.

INSIDERS' TIP

To preserve the vibrant colors of your brand-new, hand-screened Florida Keys T-shirt, soak the garment for approximately 10 minutes in a cold saltwater solution before tossing it into the machine for the first time.

T-Shirt Factory Outlet
316 Simonton St., Key West
• (305) 292-2060

No trip to Key West would be complete without the purchase of at least one T-shirt to commemorate the event. Key West is loaded with T-shirt shops, but most of them carry exactly the same styles. So, you can purchase your shirt on Duval and risk looking like everyone else or you can come here and find a shirt that's truly unique. These tees are screen-printed right on the spot using vivid colors and designs supplied by local artists. You'll find a wide variety of sizes and styles here, including tank tops and crop tees for kids and adults. The average price is around $12.

Victoria Lesser Design Statement
1102 Truman Ave., Key West
• (305) 292-0101

Get some stylish clothes made to order or buy them straight off the rack. Designer Victoria Lesser is affectionately called "Pajama Mama" by Bill Cosby, because she designed all the pajamas he wore on his popular television show. She has designed clothes for many others, including Barbara Mandrell, The Bee Gees, Sophia Loren, Aerosmith and Goldie Hawn.

Whitfield Jack
200 Elizabeth St., Key West
• (305) 294-7092

Were it not for the cases of jewelry lining the walls of Whitfield Jack, you likely wouldn't realize you are inside a store at all. Set inside a simulated tropical garden, Whitfield Jack jewelers carries original 14-carat designs.

Bookstores

Ever since Hemingway penned some of his most famous works here, Key West has enjoyed a reputation as a writer's colony. We have played host to the likes of Tennessee Williams, John Hersey, Thomas McGuane and Robert Frost, to name but a few. But this town of writers is also a town of readers, and we have more than our fair share of bookstores to prove that point. You'll find the works of the aforementioned Key West authors and many others at the following stores.

Bargain Books and Newsstand
1028 Truman Ave., Key West
• (305) 294-7446

South Florida's largest retailer of pre-read books is right here on our tiny island. Wander through room after slightly dusty room of fiction, sci-fi, romance and literature. A couple of cats may find your lap a cozy spot to take a nap as you peruse a favorite title from one of the comfortable chairs strewn throughout. If you love books and you love a bargain, you won't be disappointed. But be prepared to spend some time here. Half the fun of finding your bargain book is in the search for it.

Blue Heron Books
1018 Truman Ave., Key West
• (305) 296-3508

A two-in-one deal is what you'll get here, as this bookstore does double-duty as a coffee shop. Cafe con leche in hand, browse the aisles for your favorite Key West author, new release, classic title, foreign book or gay literature.

Flaming Maggie's Books, Art & Coffee
800 N. Fleming St., Key West
• (305) 294-3931

A large selection of works by local writers is available here, as well as one of the island's best selections of gay and lesbian literature. The store, which used to be Caroline Street Books, is housed in the former site of Maskerville. Fresh-ground coffee is available while you browse.

Key West Island Bookstore
513 Fleming St., Key West
• (305) 294-2904

This shop sells everything from the classics to the bestsellers, along with topical nonfiction and the works of Florida Keys and Key West writers. The bookstore often has booksigning events that generate lots of local excitement and a party atmosphere.

L. Valladares and Son
1200 Duval St., Key West
• (305) 296-5032

Billing itself as "Key West's Oldest Newsstand," L. Valladares offers a wide selection of regional and national newspapers and magazines. An array of works by Key West authors is on display.

Upstart Crow Books
218 Whitehead St., Key West
• **(305) 293-0709**

Home of the Key West Poetry Guild, Upstart Crow Books boasts a large selection of Key West subject books and Key West authors. For your correspondence needs, this bookstore has a myriad of greeting cards, note cards and stationery. And for your psychological needs, a display of New Age books is offered. Coffee and other drinks are on hand to assist with leisurely perusal.

Waldenbooks
2212 N. Roosevelt Blvd., Key West
• **(305) 294-5419**

Not surprisingly, this is Key West's largest bookstore and, perhaps, its most visible. It's a stand-alone shop on U.S. 1 with plenty of free parking. On the inside, the store looks much like every other Waldenbooks you've ever been in with a notable exception: Right up front, there's a huge display of titles by Key West authors as well as an impressive array of books on a variety of Florida-related subjects. In addition to several guides to Key West and Florida Keys' attractions, you'll find island cookbooks, maps, history tomes and nature guides to help you identify our native flora and fauna. You'll also find especially helpful clerks here as well as frequent book signings/sales, the proceeds of which are often earmarked for local charities.

Best of New Town

The New Town area is often overlooked by shoppers anxious to partake of the tiny, funky stores lining the streets of Old Town. But this is where the locals shop because the stores in New Town tend to cover all the bases, and prices are often much cheaper than those in Old Town. Since New Town is more spread out than the rest of Key West, the stores are often clumped together in plazas — most of which are within blocks of each other.

Shopping Plazas

Searstown
3200 block of N. Roosevelt Blvd., Key West

This conglomerate of stores lends itself to one-stop shopping. Sears is undoubtedly familiar to most people, and is the namesake and anchor of the plaza.

Nearby is Quality Home Furnishings, where you can get a great variety of top name brands and fashion designs on household furniture and supplies at affordable prices.

Carey's Home Fashions is a favorite with those redecorating their tropical pads. Searstown Jewelers can satisfy any jewelry or repair need. Both Champs and The Letterman Sporting Goods will keep you pumped up. Restock for Fido at Searstown Pet Store. And be sure to stop at The Imagination Station. It's Key West's largest toy store and a great local favorite for kids and their parents. You'll find the best in creative toys, puzzles and games for all ages inside.

Payless has one of two shoe outlets in Key West here. For all the fixings for a cheeseburger in Paradise, and other grocery needs, head to Publix. Key West's only big movie theater, Regal Cinema, is located here, too (see our Recreation chapter). To send souvenirs to the folks back home, avail yourself of the services of The Mail Spot, or if you need some pens and paper to write that letter, check out Incubator Business Supply. Last but not least, if you've decided to chuck it all and move to Paradise, sell your Rolex at the Key West Pawn Shop.

Key Plaza
2900 block of N. Roosevelt Blvd., Key West

Kmart dominates this large plaza situated just down the street from Searstown. To get a

---

INSIDERS' TIP

Make time to browse the gift shops at our museums and attractions, too. You might just find the perfect Keys book, trinket or T-shirt for that special someone on your shopping list.

really good look at Paradise, have your eyes checked at Eckerd Optical. Upton's is your one-stop shop for apparel for the whole family. The Cat House is the place to be for pet lovers, and Key West has plenty of those. Boaters World has all the essentials for a day on the water and Keep on Truckin' offers necessities for campers and survivalists. For electronics aficionados, there's Radio Shack. Other stores in the plaza include Party Time, Key West Florist, The Pampered Pet, Spec's Music and Blockbuster.

Overseas Market
2700 block of N. Roosevelt Blvd., Key West

Perhaps the largest of New Town's many plazas, the Overseas Market offers a plethora of places to shop. Grocery shopping is taken care of here at Winn-Dixie. JCPenney is located here, as is Pier One Imports. Jewelers are very much in evidence, with Beachcomber Jewelers, Robert Garcia Jewelry and Zales. The home furnishings you don't get at Pier One can be picked up at the Bed and Chair Depot and you can find floor coverings at Classic Carpet. To outfit your feet, head to the Foot Locker and Payless, then stop in for a haircut at Supercuts — no appointment needed. Take care of the dog at Keys Pet

Market, grab a supply of vitamins at GNC, and send some cards back home at the U.S Post Office substation. Get music at Sam Goody, perfume at Turtle Walk Perfumery and basics at Eckerd Drugs. Whew! That's a lot of shopping.

Kennedy Plaza
Northside Dr. and Kennedy Dr., Key West

This plaza is relatively new. High points include 7 Days Deli and Video Store, where you can pick up a mean Cuban mix and a movie to boot. Joppa Furniture is here to help you decorate in Paradise. Pick up your favorite rare baseball card at Southernmost Sports Cards. Lynn's Alley is like a little side-street plaza right next to Kennedy Plaza. Offerings include Kari's Dance Factory, First Impressions Hair and Nail Salon and MacArthur Music.

Luani Plaza
Northside Dr. and Flagler Ave., Key West

This out-of-the-way strip mall offers some good places to shop. Budde's Arts and Crafts has everything you need for home crafts, and Budde's Hobbies is the place for model car and train enthusiasts. Off Duval provides casual apparel for men and women at "off Duval" prices. Images by Alison is a favorite for those who want portraits in Paradise.

Real Estate

Finding your place in the sun could mean owning a piece of Paradise.

Our crime rate is low, our tropical climate warm year round and our surrounding waters simply spectacular. All of this comes at a cost, however, and prospective homebuyers soon learn that our delicate ecosystem was never intended for unlimited habitation.

In 1975, the Florida Keys was designated an area of critical concern because of the conflict between resource protection and population growth. Evacuating the islands safely in the face of an oncoming hurricane was a real concern, calling for official action. What resulted was a two-pronged effort that includes a land-use plan and enforced zoning ordinances in Monroe County, which encompasses the Keys. A finite number of building permits is allocated per year, and approval can take months. Except in the incorporated areas of Layton, Key Colony Beach, Islamorada and Key West, land owners often endure lengthy waits to obtain building permits. Monroe County issues a specific number of building permits quarterly based on a point system that takes into consideration the land's environmental sensitivity, the proposed structure's architectural desirability and other factors.

The less complicated and, indeed, less frustrating approach to owning property in the Florida Keys is to purchase an existing home. These include mobile homes, single-family homes and condominiums. The Keys have few cookie-cutter-type subdivisions, where one home looks pretty much like the others in a single area. In many neighborhoods all three housing styles mingle, with mobile homes clustered in areas zoned specifically for them.

Real estate prices in the Florida Keys depend largely upon access to the water. Direct oceanfront or bayfront property garners the highest prices, followed by property on a canal with an ocean or bay view and by property on a canal with access to the ocean or bay. Other developments, such as Ocean Reef, Duck Key and Sunset Key, have special features that make homes desirable, such as gated security, golf courses, swimming pools, strict building covenants and other community amenities.

Some relief in the cost of owning a Keys home is available for certain owners in the form of a homestead exemption. In Florida, this exemption allows $25,000 of the assessed value of a house purchased as a primary residence to be exempt from property tax. Real estate taxes in Monroe County are based on a millage rate which changes annually with the county budget.

Between Key Largo and Long Key alone, there are nearly 500 subdivisions and condominium complexes. It would be impossible for us to review each one, so we provide you with a general overview of each area. At the end of the chapter, we include listings of real estate professionals who can assist you in finding your bit of Paradise. But first, to familiarize you with the residential choices and the range of prices you're likely to face as you begin your search for Keys property, here are the basics about mobile homes, single-family homes and condominiums.

Types of Property

Mobile Homes on Lots

First the good news: A mobile home is the least expensive real estate you can buy in the Florida Keys, with the exception of some vacant, difficult-to-build-on sites. The bad news? Most vulnerable to hurricane damage, mobile homes are the first properties ordered for evacuation during severe-storm watches in the Florida Keys. Zoning ordinances restrict mobile homes to specific communities. Fortunately, the Keys have several mobile home subdivisions and communities, many of them on desirable waterfront land.

Often the least expensive mobile homes are those that have existed in residential subdivisions since before zoning ordinances were established. These mobile homes, which have individual septic tanks, lack the recreational and service-oriented amenities typically offered in mobile-home communities here. Prices range from $40,000 to more than $100,000, depending largely on location and whether the lot is purchased or rented.

Buyers who purchase property in a mobile home community pay more but frequently enjoy a clubhouse atmosphere complete with a swimming pool, shuffleboard court, boat ramp, dockage, on-site manager, sewage treatment and a convenience store. Depending on how the community's lots are deeded, prices range from about $70,000 to more than $150,000. The price of any mobile home increases with a concrete or wood-frame addition — an elevated Florida room, built-up gravel roof, poured concrete slab and other features. (Check Monroe County's building ordinances before adding on to a mobile home yourself; new add-ons may be restricted.)

Condominiums

Condominiums are scattered throughout the Upper and Middle Keys, and many homebuyers find them a low-maintenance way to keep up a part-time residence. For full-time residents, condos offer commonly owned amenities rarely available with a single-family home, such as swimming pools, fitness facilities, saunas, hot tubs, boat dockage and covered parking. Condos also are likely to have more affordable water views than single-family homes.

During our peak tourist season (generally December through April), condominiums often are teeming with activity, affording residents the opportunity to meet renters from across the country. When the low season rolls around and occupancy typically drops to 30 percent or less at any given time, full-time residents have the facilities nearly all to themselves. If you plan to become a full-time Florida Keys resident in a condominium, be sure to check on whether the complex you have your eye on maintains an active rental program. You may not enjoy living alongside transient residents. Some of our condominiums employ on-site managers and desk clerks and act as hotels, which keeps them busy year 'round (see our Accommodations chapter).

What you'll pay for a condo depends on the size of the unit, its location and its view. You also need to factor monthly maintenance fees into the overall cost; these increase with unit sizes and cover caretaking of the common area, a reserve account for future major maintenance and insurance for damage by flood, wind, storm, peril and salt air.

Older condominiums (those built in the 1970s) offer efficiencies and one- and two-bedroom units that are not as luxurious as those in newer complexes. These units are typically small, with some efficiencies a tiny 500 square feet or less and two-bedroom units consisting of 900 to 1,200 square feet. The smaller residences typically cost between $50,000 and $100,000 and carry maintenance fees of $150 to more than $250 per month. If the unit is waterfront or has a water view, the price range increases to between $75,000 and

$150,000, with a monthly maintenance fee of $200 to $300 and up.

In condominiums built within the past decade, you will rarely find units smaller than two-bedrooms and 1,200 square feet. Most of these buildings are on or near the water, affording waterfront views and boat dockage, each of which holds almost equal value. More contemporary-style condominiums command even higher prices than those of our older established facilities, reaching well into the $150,000 to $200,000 range and higher.

Single-Family Homes

Dry-lot homes — those not fronting a water view or canal — are more often purchased by full-time residents and typically sell for anywhere between $75,000 and $250,000, with water access a major factor in determining where within this range a home fits. Canalfront homes generally sell for between $150,000 and $500,000. These days it's difficult to find a home on the open water for less than $400,000. Local real estate agents report that the number of homes selling for more than $1 million is now higher than ever. Many of our million-dollar estates are opulent and grand, featuring everything from Spanish Colonial arches and verandas to contemporary curves with generous expanses of glass.

Since 1975, the county has required that most homes be constructed of concrete block, set on stilts and have hurricane shutters, but pre-restriction days yielded some interesting variations: an Islamorada home with a bomb shelter and a backyard cemetery, a Cudjoe Key house constructed with ties from Henry Flagler's railroad and several historic homes moved from island to island so they wouldn't face a bulldozer. Today a "grandfather" clause applies to many of these homes, including homes with piers, allowing nonconforming uses to exist. However, if 50 percent or more of the dollar value of a nonconforming use structure is destroyed and requires rebuilding, new zoning laws and building restrictions apply.

Much of a buyer's decision to purchase a home in the Florida Keys depends upon the structure's ability to withstand a hurricane. Concrete block-style (CBS) stilt-level homes are more solid than those made of wood and are considered to be elevated enough to avoid potential flooding. CBS ground-level homes typically cost less than stilt homes of comparable sizes, and ground-level homes allow easier access.

A large percentage of Lower Keys homes are factory-built wood-frame modulars. Because they are constructed under controlled circumstances and designed to withstand 135-mile-per-hour winds, some homeowners believe they're stronger than wood-frame homes built on-site. CBS homes typically command higher prices than all wood-frame structures.

If you are considering buying a home in the Florida Keys, landscaping also may influence your decision. Some buyers prefer intricate vegetation, which requires irrigation, while others want low-maintenance pearock and xeriscaping (landscaping using indigenous plantings that require no irrigation). Because many real estate purchases here are made by boaters, homes that sit closer to a bridge — providing access to both the ocean and the bay — sell more quickly.

Area Overviews

Upper Keys

Key Largo

Because Key Largo is within 20 miles of the mainland, property here often is in great demand by weekday commuters and South Floridians purchasing weekend retreats. In real estate terms, Key Largo generally includes the exclusive Ocean Reef subdivision at the extreme northeast and encompasses all land southwest to Tavernier at the points where Key Largo and Plantation Key are nearest. Ocean Reef maintains a slightly higher cost than most of Monroe County.

In an effort to subdivide Key Largo in the 1930s, canals were dug throughout the island. A trailer set up along the Overseas Highway acted as a sales office for developers who sold platted subdivision plots for $100 down and the remainder, a few hundred more, to be paid in small installments.

In a few instances, these developers never

sold a lot, and some subdivisions have since been purchased by the county. Land near Card Sound Road is a prime example of platted subdivisions that never fully developed. Homes in this sparsely populated area begin at about $100,000, which is considerably lower than prices for homes throughout most of the Florida Keys. A large portion of vacant land in this area is government-owned.

After Hurricane Andrew displaced many South Dade County residents in 1992, scores moved south to Key Largo, driving up the island's real estate values. Prices have since leveled off, but Port Largo remains Key Largo's most sought-after subdivision in terms of dollar value, lot size and prestige. The cost of a home here ranges from about $120,000 to more than $500,000. Lot sizes throughout the island tend to be small, and even some million-dollar estates barely have enough space for parking.

There are always exceptions to the rule, but older communities, such as Winston Waterways, Largo Sound Village and Stillright Point, tend to blend contemporary homes with older homes. Dry-lot homes in these communities may list for as low as $80,000, and you can occasionally find good buys on "fixer-uppers."

Mobile-home communities and subdivisions are more prevalent in Key Largo than in the rest of the Keys. Cross Keys Waterway, at about MM 103, is one of this area's largest mobile home subdivisions; Hammer Point — where most homes are on canals and may cost upward of $300,000 — is undoubtedly the most prestigious. Ocean Shores is a gated mobile-home community, and adults-only Silver Shores is one of few mobile-home parks designed exclusively for retirees.

Ocean Reef

A luxury subdivision in North Key Largo, Ocean Reef is a private, all-inclusive gated community of large single-family homes, condominiums and town houses. Properties here attract buyers seeking privacy, exclusivity and the opportunity to fish, dive, snorkel, swim, shop and dine out without ever leaving the complex. This community has three golf courses, a marina and other amenities open only to residents. Prices begin at $200,000 for condominiums and $400,000 for single-family homes. Residents pay a fee for additional services.

Tavernier

Toward the southern end of Key Largo is Tavernier, one of the Florida Keys' oldest settlements. If you are intrigued by the history of our islands, this is a fascinating location. Some Tavernier homes date back to the early farming settlements at the turn of the century. Plantation Key (its northern end also maintains a Tavernier postal designation) has a wide range of real estate opportunities, with single-family subdivisions primarily bayside. Tavernaero, along Tavernier Creek, is a gated community with a 2,000-foot grass landing strip and stilt homes designed to accommodate private planes underneath. These homes usually sell for $300,000 and up.

The Snake Creek Drawbridge makes Plantation Key an ideal homesite for owners of large yachts and sailboats. Venetian Shores, with homes on wide canalfront lots as large as 100 feet by 100 feet, is the most upscale subdivision. Other desirable bayside communities here include Kahiki Harbor, Plantation Key Colony, Indian Harbor, Indian Waterways and Plantation Beach. Because of the large, individually owned tracts of land on which private estates are nestled, much of the oceanfront on Plantation Key is referred to as "Millionaire's Row."

Islamorada

Islamorada, which was incorporated in 1998, stretches from Plantation Key to Lower Matecumbe. Lot sizes in Islamorada typically are larger than those in other areas of the Florida Keys, a factor intended to attract builders of large, impressive homes.

Upper Matecumbe Key is the heart of Islamorada, commercially developed but with homes tucked along the waterfront in quiet residential areas. Several gated single-family communities, including Pen Key Club, Coral Cove and Bay Hammock, offer such shared facilities as boat basins and swimming pools.

Lower Matecumbe Key is Islamorada's predominantly residential island, with a bike path, tennis club and private beach. Subdivi-

sions here, such as Port Antigua, Safety Harbor, Toll Gate Shores and Lower Matecumbe Beach, maintain distinct personalities and offer waterfront homes starting at about $200,000. Sapodilla Drive at MM 74 is considered one of this area's prestigious addresses, with home prices typically starting at about $500,000.

Layton

The late Del Layton, a Miami grocery store owner, developed Layton into a subdivision in the 1950s. Later, he incorporated it as a city. Except for two oceanfront homes, all single-family residences in Layton are on oceanside canals, with the nearby Channel 5 Bridge allowing access to the bay. Fifteen miles from Marathon and Islamorada, Layton is largely a community of retirees, with a population of approximately 250.

The city has a couple of good restaurants, a hotel, a gift and watersports shop and the Department of Environmental Protection's State Marine Laboratory, where studies on Florida Keys marine life are conducted. Old and new homes found throughout Layton typically sit on 75-foot-by-100-foot lots, and homes constructed more recently start at about $195,000.

Layton employs its own mayor and city council, and the costs for these services are tacked onto property tax bills.

Middle Keys

Greater Marathon and the Middle Keys generally comprise all areas southwest of the Long Key Bridge to the Seven Mile Bridge.

Duck Key

Duck Key is composed of five islands connected by white Venetian-style bridges. A series of flow-through canals encircle each island, ensuring that nearly half the homes or lots offer canalfront dockage or open water views. The uniquely situated islands allow direct access to both the ocean and the Gulf of Mexico. Homes on dry lots (those not on canals or open water) are offered between $150,000 and $250,000; canalfront homes average between $350,000 and $500,000. Oceanfront homes, which are also bordered by the deep-water canal system, are priced in excess of $500,000.

The Duck Key Property Owners Association, an active group, maintains rights of way and public area plantings, has established distinctive signage and sponsors myriad social events throughout the year. Residents pay a small out-of-pocket tax to employ a private security firm to supplement county services. Hawk's Cay Resort and its sister vacation community, The Village at Hawk's Cay, are on the first island, Indies Island, which is zoned differently than the rest. The other four islands —

Center, Plantation, Harbour and Yacht Club — are designated for single-family residential housing only. All homes must be of CBS construction.

Grassy Key

Grassy Key, a sleepy, rural island with a few oceanfront bungalow courts and several restaurants, is distanced from Marathon by preservation lands. Single-family homes here cost in the low $100,000s on a dry lot or in excess of $1 million along the Gulf of Mexico and the Atlantic. With no canals on Grassy Key, there is no pricing middle ground.

Key Colony Beach

Incorporated in 1957 by developer Phil Sadowski, Key Colony Beach encompasses 285 acres. The city has 1,216 residential units, including 460 condominiums and 207 single-family homes.

Key Colony Beach is one of the most developed areas of the Florida Keys, employing its own police and enforcing its own signage and zoning ordinances. Accessed by a causeway, Key Colony Beach has a few small shops and restaurants.

Oceanfront condos and half-duplexes begin at about $150,000, with condo prices stretching well over $500,000. A new Coury subdivision has single-family homes that begin at $500,000.

Marathon

Marathon was heavily developed in the 1950s, when dredging was relatively commonplace. This area probably has more canals and waterways, and thus more canalfront properties, than any other region of Monroe County. (It also has a few unpaved roads that do not alter home values as they do vacant lots.)

Marathon's Coco Plum subdivision features beachfront condominiums ranging from $75,000 to $400,000-plus and includes Bonefish Towers, a 75-unit, 14-story building that is the Florida Keys tallest. Coco Plum's single-family homes all are on large lots on canals. These three-bedroom, two-bath homes begin at about $225,000.

Extending from the Vaca Cut Bridge to the Seven Mile Bridge is the city of Marathon, which has several subdivisions. Considered

prime are the Sombrero and gated Stirrup Key communities, with high-quality homes on lots averaging 1,500 square feet commanding prices upward of $225,000. A half-duplex here will cost about $150,000 or more, and condominiums range from $90,000 for a canalfront efficiency to $400,000 for a three-bedroom, two-bath with an oceanfront location.

Slightly farther down on the price scale but certainly still desirable are the Paraiso Estates, Flamingo Island, Sombrero Isle and Walorris subdivisions, where non-waterfront homes begin at about $150,000 and canalfronts at $275,000. In subdivisions such as Little Venice, which is popular with first-time buyers, homes and half-duplexes on 50-foot-by-55-foot canal lots range from $75,000 to $125,000. Marathon's Old Town area offers a number of mobile-home subdivisions, where prices range from about $50,000 to $120,000.

Lower Keys

Big Pine Key

This rural, semi-isolated island has acres of open space and limited development potential. Home to the National Key Deer Refuge, this island is popular with many Key West and Marathon workday commuters. This area probably offers the best value for the money in affordable housing. Though large oceanfront homes on extremely private Long Beach Road begin at about $350,000, it is possible to find a small, non-waterfront home in the Eden Pines and Port Pine Heights subdivisions in the $100,000 range.

Big Pine Key features a number of canals, and canalfront homes are listed at about $150,000. The exception is prime Pine Channel Estates, where canalfront homes begin at about $175,000. Many natives began their Big Pine Key residency in the largely dry Sands subdivision, where mobile homes and travel trailers are listed for about $50,000, and those on canalfront lots are as steep as $175,000. Homes and transient RV lots also are located here.

Little Torch and Ramrod Keys

On Little Torch Key, homes in the Jolly Roger Estates oceanside subdivision begin at

$179,000 and can climb as steep as $400,000 on the Atlantic side. This subdivision's bayside is also becoming more pricey, with homes offered from $130,000 to $220,000-plus.

The major development on nearby Ramrod Key is Breezeswept Beach Estates, where all homes are priced between $150,000 and $500,000. On the gulfside, houses on dry lots and plugged and open canals range from about $90,000 to $150,000.

Summerland, Cudjoe and Sugarloaf Keys

Heading closer to Key West and into the more exclusive subdivisions of Summerland, Cudjoe and Sugarloaf Keys, you'll find luxurious properties. Summerland features a number of waterfront homes, along with a small airstrip that allows residents to park their private airplanes directly beneath their homes.

Even mobile homes on these islands are more costly. Average mobile-home prices within Venture Out, a large, gated-mobile home community on Cudjoe Key, are about $90,000. In the Cudjoe Gardens subdivision, single-family homes are surrounded by lush landscaping and native trees and are priced upwards of $250,000. You may find a home for as little as $135,000 in Cutthroat Harbor Estates, Cudjoe's largest development, but prices also extend beyond $200,000.

On Sugarloaf Key, you can buy large $200,000-plus properties on the inland bay at the ends of cul de sacs, but on the Gulf, homes can be had for anywhere from $75,000 to $200,000.

Baypoint, Shark Key, Big Coppitt and Key Haven

Shark Key is a gated community developed with strict architectural guidelines. Large open-water lots on Shark Key are beautifully landscaped, and houses set on them typically are valued at $500,000 and more. Key Haven is a premier location, with homes selling from

$300,000 to much more than $1 million. Saddlebunch, Baypoint, Big Coppitt and Key Haven offer community lifestyles from $200,000 upward. These areas are in demand for their convenient location only minutes from Key West.

Real Estate Companies

Though all of Keys agents share a multiple listing service (MLS) with properties available throughout Monroe County, each agency tends to specialize in its own territory. We describe some of the largest agencies in the sections that follow. This is not meant to be a comprehensive listing of all real estate companies by any means. For a complete list, consult the Yellow Pages for the appropriate communities or pick up copies of the many real estate guides available free of charge at supermarkets and other locations throughout Monroe County.

Upper Keys

The Prudential Keyside Properties
31 Ocean Reef Dr., Ste. A 101, North Key Largo • (305) 367-2336, (800) 692-7653
MM 91.5 Oceanside, Tavernier
• (305) 853-1100, (800) 663-9955

The Prudential Keyside Properties is the only real estate company in the Florida Keys that covers the area from the top of the Keys to Key West. All three offices of the company, which is owned by William H. Dickinson, are members of MLS. The North Key Largo office focuses exclusively on properties in the private Ocean Reef community. The Tavernier office covers both residential and commercial properties from Key Largo to Marathon. Prudential Knight Realty in Key West covers real estate from Key West to Marathon (see our Key West section of this chapter for a separate listing).

INSIDERS' TIP

For details about our recycling program and obtaining a recycling bin, call (305) 296-8297. Aluminum and metal cans, glass bottles and jars, plastic containers and newspapers are recyclable.

Loveland Realty
MM 103.2 Bayside, Key Largo
• (305) 451-5055, (800) 454-5263

Diane Loveland, a broker and former president of the Women's Council of Realtors, has been in the real estate business for close to 20 years; she established Loveland Realty in 1993. Loveland is a member of the Florida Keys Board of Realtors.

Freelancer Ltd. Inc.
MM 103 Bayside, Suite 53, Key Largo
• (305) 451-0349

In 1995 real estate broker Eric Beatty, a member of the Florida Keys Board of Realtors, inherited the business that his now-retired father purchased in 1980. The original Freelancer Ltd. agency was established in 1947 by a man named Joseph Lance.

Century 21 Keysearch Realty
MM 101.9 Oceanside, Key Largo
• (305) 451-4321, (800) 210-6246
MM 91.9 Bayside, Tavernier
• (305) 852-5595, (800) 850-7740
MM 86 Bayside, Islamorada
• (305) 664-4637, (800) 541-5019

Established in 1992 by real estate broker George Nyman, Century 21 Keysearch is a member of the Florida Keys Board of Realtors. The company has three offices in the Upper Keys. The Islamorada office was formerly Century 21 Coastways.

Bayview Properties
MM 96.5 Bayside, Key Largo
• (305) 852-8585, (800) 741-0541

What began as Ganim Realty in the 1980s was purchased in 1995 by broker Tom McDermott, who changed the name to Bayview Properties. The agency is a member of the Florida Keys Board of Realtors; Bayview maintains an on-site office in the Buttonwood Bay Condominium complex at MM 96.5 Bayside.

Coldwell Banker Keys Country Realty Inc.
MM 100 Oceanside, Key Largo
• (305) 453-0036
MM 91.9 Bayside, Tavernier
• (305) 852-5254
MM 82.2 Oceanside, Islamorada
• (305) 664-4470

This agency was purchased in 1984 by broker Ralph Berard and wife/agency manager Jeane. They renamed the business Keys Country and, in 1990, became an affiliate of Coldwell Banker. The agency is a member of the Florida Keys Board of Realtors.

Marr Properties Inc.
MM 99.9 Bayside, Key Largo
• Sales, (305) 451-4078, (800) 277-3728
• Rentals, (305) 451-3879,
(800) 585-0584

Marr Properties dates back to 1965, when it was established by Stuart Marr. Today the agency is owned by Joy C. Martin and Marr's son Trent; she is the active broker, he maintains a nearby property appraisal office. The agency is a member of the Florida Keys Board of Realtors.

American Caribbean Real Estate Inc.
MM 81.8 Bayside, Islamorada
• (305) 664-4966, (305) 664-5152
MM 52 Oceanside, Marathon
• (305) 743-7636, (800) 940-7636

American Caribbean has been owned since 1993 by James Terra. Managed by broker Howard Corr, the agency is a member of the Florida Keys Board of Realtors.

Freewheeler Realty
MM 98 Bayside, Tavernier
• (305) 852-0609
MM 85.9 Bayside, Islamorada
• (305) 664-2075, (305) 664-4444

Alexa Wheeler established this agency in 1989 as the first rental-only agency in the Up-

INSIDERS' TIP

If you purchase a part-time residence in the Florida Keys, you can contract a reliable agency to look after your property while you're away. Ask your real estate agent for a referral.

Photo: Victoria Shearer

Gracious plantation-style homes are tucked amid a riot of tropical foliage.

per Keys. She has since expanded into property management and sales. Both locations handle property sales and rentals. Freewheeler is a member of the Florida Keys Board of Realtors and the Monroe County Vacation Rental Managers Association. Freewheeler is a primary agent for rentals at The Palms of Islamorada and Summer Sea condominiums.

Middle Keys

K.E. Brenner Realty Inc.
MM 61 Oceanside, 796 Duck Key Dr.,
Duck Key • (305) 743-5000

Established in 1977 by Elaine Brenner, this agency has, since 1989, been owned and operated by her daughter, broker Kristen E. Brenner. Through its subdivision, Duck Key Rental Headquarters, K.E. Brenner Realty handles Duck Key rentals. The agency is a member of Marathon and Lower Keys Asso-

ciation of Realtors and the Monroe County Vacation Rental Managers Association.

Century 21 Heart of the Keys Inc.
MM 54 and 47 Bayside, Marathon
• (305) 743-3377, (800) 451-4899

Broker Max Bayard purchased this local franchise in 1988. In the fall of 1995 he opened a second office at MM 47. Both agencies are members of the Marathon and Lower Keys Association of Realtors.

Marathon Key Real Estate Inc.
MM 54 Bayside, Marathon
• (305) 743-9088

Brokers for more than a decade, Sue Demaras and Connie Tucker became co-owners of Marathon Key Real Estate in October of 1995. This all-broker office at the very entrance to the greater Marathon area offers comprehensive real estate services. The company is the exclusive selling broker for Sombrero Resort condominiums (see our Accommodations chapter). Marathon Key Real Estate sells waterfront properties and even has private islands to offer. The company is a member of MLS and both the national and local Association of Realtors and sells commercial properties as well as a wide range of single-family dwellings and condominiums.

Century 21 PRO-Realty
(305) 743-9393, (800) 473-9393

Morgan Hill and Paula Nardone handle Marathon residential and Layton through Summerland Key commercial real estate sales for Century 21 PRO-Realty. The agency's main office is in the Lower Keys (see separate listing). Hill and Nardone are members of the Marathon and Lower Keys Association of Realtors. Their partnership was established in 1991.

Keys Island Realty
MM 53.5 Oceanside, 309 Key Colony Beach Causeway, Key Colony Beach
• **(305) 289-9696, (800) 253-8677**

When broker James Senhoff purchased Sara Island Realty in 1995, the firm had been in business for about 30 years. He changed the agency name to Keys Island Realty; this agency is a member of the Marathon and Lower Keys Association of Realtors.

Coldwell Banker Schmitt Real Estate
MM 52.5 Bayside, Marathon
• **(305) 743-5181, (800) 366-5181**
MM 30.5 Oceanside, Big Pine Key
• **(305) 872-3050, (800) 488-3050**

In 1955 Alan Schmitt established Schmitt Real Estate in Marathon. Alan is still active as a property appraiser; his son Brian is the agency broker. In 1980 Alan opened an office on Big Pine Key; in 1996 he and Brian opened an office in Key West.

The Waterfront Specialist
MM 54, Oceanside, Marathon
• **(305) 743-0644, (800) 342-6398**

A Realtor for more than 25 years and a

Marathon resident since 1953, broker Diane Chaplin is on the board of directors for the Marathon and Lower Keys Association of Realtors.

All-Pro Real Estate
MM 50 Bayside, Marathon
• **(305) 743-8333, (800) 766-3235**

All-Pro Real Estate was established in 1990, and broker Suzanne Goodlow has owned it since 1995. She is a member of the Marathon and Lower Keys Association of Realtors, the National Association of Realtors and the Florida Association of Realtors.

Chaplin Real Estate
Better Homes and Gardens
MM 50 Bayside, Marathon
• **(305) 743-9424, (800) 768-0768**

Established in 1972 by F. James "Jim" Chaplin, this is a family-run agency. In 1986 his wife, Bettye, joined the team. The Chaplins grew up in the Middle Keys; working with them are a cousin and a high school friend. In 1988 Chaplin Real Estate became affiliated with Better Homes and Gardens. The agency is a member of Marathon and the Lower Keys Association of Realtors.

RE/MAX Keys to the Keys
MM 49.5 Bayside, Marathon
• **(305) 745-3815, (800) 597-3815**

Broker Karen Farley-Wilkinson opened this agency in 1986; in 1991 it became a RE/MAX affiliate. The agency is a member of the Marathon and Lower Keys Association of Realtors and the Monroe County Vacation Rental Managers Association. Agent Richard Kerwick handles properties from Long Key to Big Coppitt.

Barefoot Realty
MM 48 Oceanside, Marathon
• **(305) 743-5006**

Established in 1991 by broker Dee Millis, Barefoot Realty is a member of the Marathon and Lower Keys Association of Realtors and the Vacation Rental Managers Association. Millis has worked in the real estate business since 1988.

INSIDERS' TIP

Homes featuring capitals, pediments, porches, bay windows, gingerbread trim and tin roofs are most often found in Key West.

Lower Keys

Latitude 24 Real Estate Inc.
MM 31.3 Bayside, Big Pine Key
• (305) 872-2800

Broker Chuck Vowels, who grew up in the Middle Keys, established Latitude 24 in 1988. Seven years later, he merged with Key Deer Realty and created Latitude 24 Real Estate Inc. Latitude 24 is a member of the Marathon, Lower Keys and Key West Association of Realtors as well as the Florida Keys Board of Realtors. Vowels is the association's former president and was named Realtor of the Year in 1994 and 1996.

Miley Real Estate
MM 31.1 Bayside, Big Pine Key
• (305) 872-9403, (800) 553-2827

This agency has existed since about 1981; Donna Slevers and her husband, Garry, both brokers, purchased it 10 years later. The couple has more than 10 years of experience in the real estate business. Their agency is a member of the Marathon and Lower Keys Association of Realtors and the Monroe County Vacation Rental Managers Association.

Century 21 PRO-Realty
MM 30.5 Bayside, Big Pine Key
• (305) 872-2296, (800) 637-7621
MM 22 Oceanside, Cudjoe Key
• (305) 745-3340
MM 17 Bayside, Sugarloaf Key
• (305) 745-1856, (800) 745-8610

Owned and operated by broker Concetta McSorley, this Century 21 office became PRO-Realty when she purchased it in 1989. The agency is a member of Marathon and the Lower Keys Association of Realtors and the Monroe County Vacation Rental Managers Association. Additional agents are assigned to handle the Middle Keys.

Raymond Real Estate Inc.
MM 30.5 Oceanside, Big Pine Key
• (305) 872-9116, (800) 747-4206

Brokers Alma and John Raymond established Raymond Real Estate in 1981. They have been in the real estate business since 1978; their agency is a member of the Marathon and Lower Keys Association of Realtors.

ERA Lower Keys Realty
MM 30 Oceanside, Big Pine Key
• (305) 872-2258, (800) 859-7642

Broker Len Van Stry purchased ERA Lower Keys Realty in 1993. He has been in the real estate business since 1989 and was formerly on the board of directors for the Marathon and Lower Keys Association of Realtors. Scott Beskin, who joined the firm in July 1996, has more than 20 years of real estate experience.

Greg O'Berry Inc.
MM 30 Oceanside, Big Pine Key
• (305) 872-3052, (800) 741-6263

Greg O'Berry established this agency in 1976, two years after he opened his Key West agency. In 1989 broker Gene Moody, founder and first president of the Monroe County Vacation Rental Managers Association, purchased both offices. The agency is a member of the Key West Association of Realtors, the Real Estate Brokerage Council, Florida Vacation Rental Managers Association and the national Vacation Managers Association.

Betty M. Brothers Real Estate Inc.
MM 28.5 Oceanside, Little Torch Key
• (305) 872-2261, (800) 245-0125

Betty Brothers has been in the Florida Keys since 1946; in 1963 she established this real estate agency. Her agency primarily handles property sales and appraisals; it is a member of the Marathon and Lower Keys Association of Realtors.

RE/MAX Island Homes
MM 21.5 Bayside, Cudjoe Key
• (305) 745-3700, (800) 277-7756

Established in 1989, this agency is owned and operated by Dyne Vaughn and Denise Marvel. RE/MAX Island Homes is a member of the Marathon and Lower Keys Association of Realtors and Monroe County Vacation Rental Managers Inc.

Key West

Despite the fact that Key West is heavily developed, with old and new homes on generally small lots throughout the city, real estate agents report that the demand for homes far outstrips the island's supply. Also, while waterfront property is a prime attraction for homebuyers throughout the rest of the Florida Keys, it is rarely found in Key West.

Nevertheless, real estate in the southernmost city is expensive. According to the Multiple Listing Service, the average price for a single-family home in Key West is $253,400. Buyers seem so enchanted by Key West's rich architectural heritage, which falls under the watchful eye of the Historical Architecture Review Commission (HARC), that they're willing to pay top money to reside in this predominantly year-round community.

The island of Key West is an incorporated city governed by local elected representatives as well as by Monroe County. Consequently, the property tax structure here includes both city and county government expenses. Like the rest of Monroe County, Key West also must adhere to the county's rate-of-growth ordinance, which was designed to reduce population density and control growth and development.

Of the 5,700 building permits available countywide, Key West is allowed to issue 1,093. The city divided these into specific numbers of permits to be allocated each year over a period of 11 years, or until the year 2002. The good news for builders is that Key West issues its permits more quickly than other Florida Keys communities. The bad news is all the permits are gone.

Key West has its own land-use plan with zoning ordinances, permitted units, density requirements and building height and setback minimums. Within the historic district of Old Town, another layer of controls and reviews exists. The five-member Historical Architecture Review Commission, mentioned earlier, reviews applications for improvements and new construction. Established in 1986, HARC works to ensure the integrity of the historic district.

Key West offers a selection of styles in single-family homes, town houses and condominiums. The island has few mobile home parks, and the only mobile home communities here are small and hidden away. There are also several on Stock Island.

Town houses, typically adjoining structures with a common wall, allow homeowners to own the ground beneath them. The center of the common wall is the dividing line, and party wall agreements determine who maintains responsibility in cases of repair or destruction. In Key West, town houses typically range in price from $225,000 to $300,000, and townhouse owners pay the appropriated taxes plus maintenance fees that range from as little as $60 to $80 per month to as much as $500 per month. Maintenance fees depend upon the age of the building, its number of units, the size of its property, the amenities and rules and restrictions. Owners of town houses are, for the most part, full-time Key West residents.

If you wish to purchase beachfront housing, owning a condominium is without a doubt the way to go. Along the south side of Key West are several relatively new, multistory beachfront condominiums with elevators, enclosed parking, pools, tennis courts and hot tubs. Units range in size from one bedroom, one bath to three or four bedrooms and two or three baths. Only a few units have waterfront or partial water views, however, and prices range from $135,000 to $600,000 depending upon the size of the unit and its view.

Even Key West by the Sea, the island's sole "old" beachfront condominium complex, is only slightly lower in price. This particular complex offers many of the above amenities, but parking is outdoors. La Brisa II is a newer, more expensive, condominium complex, and The Beach Club offers only waterfront units. Other condominium complexes include 1800 Atlantic and Casa Casalles.

Typically, condominiums are owned by part-time residents and investors, handled by on-site managers and by real estate agents for the purpose of short- and long-term rentals. The population in any one complex varies according to the time of year. Thanksgiving through March is typically the peak resident season when occupancy is full, while May begins the low season of less than 50-percent occupancy. Recent revisions in the law restrict the number of times per year that condominium owners may rent their units.

The majority of single-family homes in Key West are in areas known as Old Town, Mid Town and New Town, and real estate agents further break two of these regions into "old" and "new" Old Town and "old" and "new" New Town. Boundaries are roughly established, with some overflow, and within all Key West areas you'll discover a diverse array of properties dating between the early 1800s to the late 1900s.

Convenience to the water or to touristy Duval Street is not usually a factor in the cost of Key West property. Rather, prices generally depend on the size and condition of the house, its lot and its location. The island itself is only 2 miles long by 4 miles wide, so beaches and harbors are never far away. Some homebuyers seek property as far from the busy roadways and attractions as possible.

Within Old Town, lot sizes typically are 30 feet by 60 feet. Because the living space in Key West's large Conch-style homes can be as spacious as 5,000 square feet, some homes have virtually no yards at all. In residential Mid Town and New Town, homes average 1,500 square feet, with lot sizes roughly 50 feet by 100 feet.

Community Profiles

Old Town

Settled in the early to late 1800s and the turn of the century, Old Town is characterized by large wood-frame houses of distinctive architectural styles (see Architecture in our Attractions chapter). Typically built by shipbuilders and carpenters for New England sea captains, many of these homes feature Bahamian and New England influences and high ceilings. Peaceful, shady William Street, with its classic homes on larger-than-usual lots, is among the most prestigious and pricey areas.

Conch-style homes along Eaton Street are generally large, but this is not the rule. Lots along this busy street also are smaller, and the real estate therefore is less valuable. Both house and lot sizes diminish toward the outskirts of Old Town, where large estates coexist with shotgun cottages, which are described in the Architecture section of our Attractions chapter. Neighbors are almost always just an arm's length away.

From Truman Avenue south is the area once known as Little Havana because it was primarily inhabited by Cuban cigar workers. The majority of one-story homes here are re-

ferred to as shotgun houses, designed with all rooms off the left or right sides.

Due to renovations and extensions, cottage sizes range from 800 square feet of floor space with two bedrooms and one bath to 1,500 square feet with three bedrooms and three baths. Some have been gathered into cottage compounds. Many homes have been cosmetically restored to their original splendor and in some cases are experiencing a second renewal for structural improvements.

The historic district includes numerous houses owned by part-time residents. Owners are permitted to renovate their homes only after the proposed changes are reviewed by the HARC. Paint colors are limited to those approved by this watchdog commission, and floor plans may be altered only if the resulting changes do not detract from the historic appearance of the neighborhood.

Gone are the days in Old Town when you could plunk down a relatively small amount of money — $150,000 for a Conch temple or $50,000 for a cigar-maker's cottage — and renovate your "bargain" into a beauty. The renovation process has been going on since the mid-1970s, so such finds are all but extinct. Today even the smallest, most run-down shotgun house is priced upward of $150,000; Conch-style estates, with as many as six bedrooms and five baths, sell for $2 million plus.

In addition to its obvious aesthetic qualities, Old Town is desirable because it is within walking distance of just about everything Key West has to offer, including shops, restaurants, nightlife and galleries. Among the community's residents are a large number of artists and writers. Children's author/poet Shel Silverstein has a house in Old Town, and former U.S. Poet Laureate Richard Wilbur resides in a cottage compound where Pulitzer Prize-winner John Hersey also lived for many years before his death in 1993.

Toward the southern end of Whitehead Street and west of Duval on Petronia Street, about a block from the Ernest Hemingway Home and Museum, lies Bahama Village. This community now is undergoing gentrification as homebuyers purchase and renovate existing properties here.

One of Key West's newest developments in Old Town is Truman Annex, where private homes, town houses and condominiums all boast features of Key West's distinctive architecture. This self-contained development once was an extension of the island's Bahama Village section and later a portion of the Key West naval base.

Truman Annex was constructed and renovated according to a unified plan reminiscent of Old Town but with more green space and winding streets. Because of the charm that this gated development exhibits, even the hubbub created by large cruise ships entering the nearby harbor does not affect its pricey real estate values. Condominiums in the Harbour Place complex of Truman Annex are almost directly on the water and are priced accordingly — at around $300,000. Units in the more affordable Shipyard complex typically sell for between $175,000 and $200,000. Homes are in the multimillion-dollar price range. Vacant lots cost between $80,000 and $100,000.

Suburbia meets the city at the upscale but affordable Key West Golf Club community, which, though miles away on Stock Island, looks a lot like Truman Annex, in part because it was created by the same developer. Here, single-family homes, town houses and condominiums display elements of Conch-style architecture. Each residence overlooks the Florida Keys' only 18-hole public golf course, along with its surrounding lakes and ponds. If you are not in the market to buy at this time, a variety of long-term rental options is available. All residents have free access to tennis courts, nature walks, several swimming pools and, of course, golf.

Mid Town and New Town

Stretching from White Street all the way east to Kennedy Boulevard, Mid Town boasts a mix of wood-frame and concrete-block ground-level homes built in the late 1950s and 1960s. New Town, developed a bit later, spreads out along North Roosevelt Boulevard, near stores such as Kmart and JCPenney.

Ground-level homes of CBS construction in these residential communities primarily offer 1,500 square feet of living space and feature three bedrooms and two baths. Garages and carports are a scarcity throughout Old Town but are fairly common in Mid Town and New Town. Prices here range from $150,000 to more than $1 million for larger homes (about 2,000 square feet) typically on large lots and canals.

Both areas are popular with families because of their proximity to the city's elementary schools.

Coming soon to the Mid Town area is Roosevelt Annex, a gated community of 25 single-family homes and town houses fronting the Gulf of Mexico on the former county fairgrounds along N. Roosevelt Boulevard. Billed as the last developable site in Key West with open water views, Roosevelt Annex is currently under construction by the developer of Truman Annex and the Key West Golf Club. Prices start at around $350,000.

Sunset Key

If you would truly like to live on a secluded island — but not too far from civilization — consider a home on Sunset Key. Formerly known as Tank Island (the Navy once stored its fuel in huge tanks here), Sunset Key is just a stone's throw across the harbor from Mallory Square. About half of the island is devoted to guest cottages and a beachfront restaurant/bar operated by the Hilton Marina and Resort (see our Accommodations chapter); the rest is reserved for single-family homes. Prices start at $400,000. In addition to fabulous open-water sunset views, homeowners on Sunset Key enjoy such amenities as a health club, pool, tennis courts and putting green. Their cars, however, must remain behind at the Hilton parking garage on Key West; only golf carts and bicycles are permitted on Sunset Key. Regular ferry service is available from the Hilton Marina. To arrange an island visit, call the Sunset Key sales office at (305) 296-7700.

INSIDERS' TIP

CBS is a term frequently used in real estate advertisements throughout the Florida Keys. It refers to our most commonly designed home: concrete block construction with a stucco finish.

Real Estate Companies

Beach Club Brokers Inc.
1304 Simonton St., Key West
• (305) 294-8433, (800) 545-9655

Owner Dawn Thornburgh, principal broker of Beach Club Brokers, established this agency, a member of the Key West Association of Realtors in 1984. A former president of the association, Thornburgh has more than 13 years of experience in the industry. Beach Club Brokers also maintains an office at La Brisa Condominiums.

Coldwell Banker Schmitt Real Estate Co.
2720-A N. Roosevelt Blvd., Key West
• (305) 296-7727, (800) 598-7727

The Schmitt family has a long history in the Florida Keys real estate business (see Middle Keys/Marathon listing). In 1996 father and son Alan and Brian Schmitt opened an office in Key West. They maintain two additional offices in Marathon.

Prudential Knight Realty
336 Duval St., Key West
• (305) 294-5155, (800) 843-9276

A part of the trio of The Prudential Keyside Properties offices owned by William H. Dickinson, Prudential Knight Realty concentrates sales efforts on properties from Key West to Marathon. This is the only one of the three Prudential offices that handles rental listings.

Century 21 All Keys Inc.
1720 N. Roosevelt Blvd., Key West
• (305) 294-4200, (800) 373-4200

Century 21 All Keys Inc. has been owned and operated by Michael Larson since 1980. A member of MLS and the Key West Association of Realtors, the company services Key West and the Lower Keys, specializing in commercial properties and property management as well as residential listings.

Sara Cook Inc.
905 Truman Ave., Key West
• (305) 294-8491, (305) 294-3340

Established by broker Sara Cook in 1980, this agency is a member of the Key West Association of Realtors, the Monroe County Va-

cation Rental Managers Association and the Florida Vacation Managers Association.

Greg O'Berry Inc.
701 Caroline St., Key West
• (305) 294-6637, (800) 654-2781

In 1989 broker Gene Moody, founder and first president of the Monroe County Vacation Rental Managers Association, purchased this agency from Greg O'Berry, who had established it in 1974. The agency is a member of the Key West Association of Realtors, the Real Estate Brokerage Council, Florida Vacation Rental Managers Association and Vacation Managers Association, a national enterprise.

Key West Realty Inc.
1109 Duval St., Key West
• (305) 294-3064, (800) 652-5131

In 1988 broker Tim Henshaw began working as a property manager at the full-service Key West Realty Inc. After the owner of the agency passed away in 1990, Henshaw purchased it. Key West Realty is a member of the Key West Association of Realtors.

Olde Island Realty Inc.
525 Simonton St., Key West
• (305) 292-7997, (800) 621-9405

Olde Island Realty was established by broker Edward Czaplicki in 1986. The agency is a member of the Key West Association of Realtors, Monroe County Vacation Rental Managers Inc., Florida Vacation Managers Association and National Trust for Historic Preservation.

RE/MAX Paradise
521 Simonton St., Key West
• (305) 294-6000

Broker Ed Clark established RE/MAX Paradise in 1989. The agency is a member of the Key West Association of Realtors.

The Real Estate Company of Key West Inc.
701 Simonton St., Key West
• (305) 296-0011

Specializing in upscale residential properties, this agency was founded in 1986 and became the exclusive affiliate in Key West and the Lower Keys for Sotheby's International Realty in 1991. James A. Blum is the owner and princi-

The two-story Conch temple stlye of Key West architecture distinctively
features columns supporting roof overhangs on both levels.

pal broker. In addition to five brokers, the staff here includes a full-time property manager who oversees luxury vacation rentals ranging from cottages to multi-bedroom estates.

McChesney/Rynearson Preferred Properties
526 Southard St., Key West
• (305) 294-3040, (800) 462-5937

Brokers Laurie McChesney and Kirk Rynearson are founders and partners in this agency, which offers residential and commercial property sales as well as vacation rentals, investment properties and long-term property management.

Truman Annex Real Estate Company Inc.
201 Front St., Blg. 21, Ste. 101, Key West
• (305) 2960-7078, (800) 884-7368

Don't let the name fool you. Truman Annex Real Estate Company has been listing and selling property all over Key West — not just in Truman Annex — for more than 10 years. The primary focus here is, however, on the sale, financing and construction of Truman Annex properties as well as those in the Key West Golf Club community. A separate division handles rentals at Truman Annex and the Key West Golf Club (see our Vacation Rentals chapter).

Each year, about the time Jack Frost starts whistling up North, the influx of snowbirds to our sun-kissed islands begins, and the collective pulse of our communities quickens.

Retirement

If we are to believe Noah Webster, retirement means "withdrawing from active life." Not so in the Florida Keys. Our retirees are anything but retiring. Nowhere will you find a more active, vibrant group of seniors. Each year, about the time Jack Frost starts whistling up North, the influx of snowbirds to our sun-kissed islands begins, and the collective pulse of our communities quickens.

Unlike other retirement areas in Florida, our seniors usually don't keep to themselves in pre-planned communities. You'll find them living in residential neighborhoods and condominiums, RV parks and mobile-home villages. Our seniors contribute an added dimension to our communities. They form a much-needed core of volunteers for many of our public services, such as the county libraries, the local hospitals and the area schools.

The American Association of Retired Persons accepts individuals 50 and older into membership, which means the first wave of baby-boomers are reaching "senior" status. Some are already taking the Florida Keys by storm. These prime-of-lifers have taken a career course detour, leaving that corporate 9-to-5 (or, more likely, 9-to-9) grind to venture off the track into uncharted territory.

Regardless of age, the retirees in the Florida Keys remain youthful. Our warm tropical climate is kind to old bones (young ones too!). The pace of our lifestyle moves to a different drummer . . . more of a reggae beat. Some people even feel we live longer down here . . . and they're in their 90s. Our energetic retirees enjoy fishing and scuba diving, golf and tennis, boating and bridge. They are active in myriad special-interest organizations the length and breadth of the Keys. Many pursue artistic hobbies long put on the back burner while the rest of their lives simmered. Some go back to school, developing new skills and honing others.

At the heart of the retirement community in the Florida Keys are the senior citizen centers, which serve as cohesive units of companionship and support to retirees of all ages and circumstances. The centers were constructed and are maintained as a joint venture between Monroe County and the local chapters of AARP. The county nutrition sites are in the centers (see Nutrition Services later in this chapter). Membership in AARP is not a prerequisite for most activities of the senior citizen centers, but anyone age 50 or older may pick up an application to AARP at any of the centers. Membership is $3 per year.

We begin with a summary of senior activities in the Upper, Middle and Lower Keys; a Key West section follows.

The Florida Keys
Senior Citizen Centers

Upper Keys AARP Senior Citizens Center
MM 88.7 Bayside, Plantation Key
• **(305) 852-7132**

This active group of seniors in the Upper Keys has a series of fund-raisers, such as its annual rummage sale, to raise money for 12 to 15 community organizations, including the fire department, the ambulance corps and the local Red Cross chapter. Members also help with the Santa Claus party at the Theater of the Sea each Christmas, serving refreshments. Besides its monthly meetings, this Upper Keys group enjoys bingo on Tuesday evenings; members donate the money raised to Hospice. During the winter season, when the ranks swell by some 60 to 75 percent, Spanish classes are offered at the center.

Many of the retirees in the Upper Keys are active in conservation and preservation organizations, fraternal organizations, the Monroe County Fine Arts Council and the Key Players (see our Arts and Culture chapter), and human service groups such as Hospice and the Domestic Abuse Shelter.

The center is next to the Sheriff's Sub-station.

Middle Keys AARP Senior Citizens Center
MM 48.8 Bayside, 535 33rd St., Marathon • (305) 743-4008

This lively bunch in the Middle Keys maintains a whirlwind of activities, especially during the winter season. There is a regular exercise group as well as weekly bingo on Tuesday afternoons, bridge and crafts. The seniors trip the light fantastic with special events, such as the Valentine Sweetheart Dance and the St. Patrick's Day party. They charter buses and go on special excursions to the Monkey Jungle or Everglades National Park, to Homestead or Miami, even an overnight to Busch Gardens in Tampa. The trips usually cost a nominal fee and include entrance fees and dinner.

The center offers Arrive Alive instruction for seniors four times per year. Arrive Alive is a book-work driving course that when passed nets the senior citizen a discount on auto insurance. The crafting groups hold boutiques in October, November and December, where they display and sell their creations. The seniors have a series of yard sales throughout the year to make money to maintain the center. Volunteers also go to the elementary schools several times a week and, like grandparents, assist children in reading or math, or just talk to the child and give a hug when needed.

The Marathon Senior Citizens Center has a big lending library. It also has free income tax preparation when that dreaded time rolls

www.insiders.com
See this and many other **Insiders' Guide®** destinations online — in their entirety.
Visit us today!

around. Free flu shots and blood-pressure checks are available on a regular basis.

The center is near the Marathon Yacht Club.

Lower Keys AARP Senior Citizens Center
MM 31 Bayside, 380 Key Deer Blvd., Big Pine Key • (305) 872-3990

Not to be outdone by the other Keys centers, the seniors in the Lower Keys boogie in a bevy of activities like their compatriots up the Keys. The winter season finds them line-dancing and exercising, taking French lessons and attending classes in hatha-yoga. Every month the center shows a classic movie, and Sunday evening is bingo night. The group has an active barbershop quartet and a serious chess club. Two times each month seniors can get free blood-pressure checks.

The Lower Keys Senior Citizens Center, which is right behind the Big Pine Key firehouse, is open every day for card playing and puzzle-making. The seniors sponsor Arrive Alive driving classes much like the group in the Middle Keys. Every Friday night during the winter season the center holds a dance, playing recorded Big Band music.

College Courses

You are never to old to learn. In fact, seniors in the Keys know learning keeps you young, and they think going to school is fun.

The Florida Keys Community College offers a selection of courses of interest to seniors. Classes cost $42.45 per credit hour (for Florida residents) with a onetime $15 application fee. Those students from out of state must pay a higher fee. There is no tuition break for senior citizens. The fall class session runs from August through December; the spring term is January to beginning of May. The summer is divided into two segments: May through the first half of June; second half of June through early August. (See our Key West section in this chapter for courses at the main campus of FKCC.) Class offerings change often, so call the college branch of your choice for the most recent schedule.

Upper Keys Campus
MM 89.9 Oceanside, Coral Shores High School, Tavernier • (305) 852-2737

Seniors and retirees particularly enjoy the computer classes offered at this branch of Florida Keys Community College. They also sign up for conversational Spanish, watercolor painting, beginning drawing, creative writing and American and English literature. A class in financial planning is available through FKCC Continuing Education, (305) 296-9081, Extension 305.

Middle Keys Campus
MM 50 Oceanside, 900 Sombrero Beach Rd., Marathon • (305) 743-2133

The Middle Keys branch of FKCC offers general-interest classes in foreign language and computer science as well as some more unusual fare. There are nature walks and tours of the Everglades, conservation classes and photography instruction. You can even take a game-fishing class, where you'll find out how to throw a cast net for bait and learn the habitats of both the baitfish and the game fish. A custom rod-making class and instruction in fly fishing is available through FKCC Continuing Education, (305) 296-9081, Extension 305.

Public Libraries

The four Monroe County libraries outside Key West are popular reading-room destinations with seniors in the Keys. They all maintain ever-growing large-print collections and a wide selection of current magazines. In addition, most of the libraries have a burgeoning number of videotapes and books-on-tape that may be checked out. Card catalogs in each of the libraries list all the materials in the system. Your local li-

brary will be able to get information from other branches for you upon request.

The libraries also host special events, such as lectures and film screenings, throughout the year. The library system has a strong volunteer program as well.

The county library system includes the Key Largo Public Library, (305) 451-2396, MM 101.4 Oceanside, Tradewinds Shopping Center, Key Largo; Islamorada Public Library, (305) 664-4645, MM 81.5 Bayside, Islamorada; Marathon Public Library, (305) 743-5156, MM 48.5 Oceanside, next to Fishermen's Hospital, Marathon; and Big Pine Public Library, (305) 289-6303, MM 31 Bayside, 213 Key Deer Boulevard, Big Pine Key.

Special-Interest Activities

It is not uncommon here in the Florida Keys to hear a senior citizen complain, "Since I've retired, I've never been so busy in my life!" Seniors get involved in civic clubs and fraternal organizations such as the Elks, Eagles, Moose and Shriners. They work with human-service organizations such as Big Brothers & Sisters, Florida Keys Children's Shelter, Domestic Abuse Shelter and the AIDS Prevention Center. Retirees donate valuable time to the Monroe Fine Arts Council, the American Cancer Society and Guardian Ad Litem. And they participate in activities helping the Florida Keys themselves such as Reef Relief, Florida Keys Wild Bird Rehabilitation Center, Friends of the Everglades and the Nature Conservancy's Bay Watch (see our Paradise Found chapter).

Contact the chamber of commerce in your area for a complete listing of the special-interest organizations of the Florida Keys. Area chambers include those in Key Largo, (305) 451-1414, (800) 822-1088; Islamorada, (305) 664-4503, (800) 322-5397; Marathon, (305) 743-5417, (800) 262-7284; and Lower Keys, (305) 872-2411, (800) 872-3722. (See our Key West section for the telephone number of the Key West Chamber of Commerce.)

Garden Clubs

Some of the most popular organizations in the Florida Keys are its garden clubs, perhaps because we have so many days of glorious sunshine or because our subtropical climate fosters the growth of such exotic flowering foliage and palms. But our planting medium is unyielding coral rock that must be pickaxed into a hole into which we put imported (from the mainland) dirt. To complicate matters further, a bulging cupboard of insects hangs around all year long, feasting on the fruits of our labors. There is a lot to learn about gardening in the Keys.

Membership in garden clubs in the Florida Keys is open to all interested parties. The groups generally have annual dues of $20 or less.

Upper Keys Garden Club
MM 94 Bayside, Key Largo
• **(305) 852-8629**

Built about 1960, the Frances Tracy Garden Center (next to the Red Cross Building) hosts the 110 members of the Upper Keys Garden Club on the third Tuesday of every month. The group often hears a lecturer speak on some phase of subtropical horticulture. In the fall they hold a Plant Ramble sale as a fund-raiser. The group sponsors a garden walk through six lovely private gardens of the Upper Keys each January. In March or April, depending upon when Easter falls, the Garden Club has an accredited flower show, which is judged by professional judges in the categories of artistic (flower arranging) and horticulture (plants).

The Upper Keys Garden Club is affiliated with the Florida Federation of State Garden Clubs and the National Council of State Garden Clubs. The club passes a donation basket at each meeting in support of the Florida Keys Wild Bird Rehabilitation Center (see our Attractions chapter). They also support the community's landscaping needs by donating plants and labor in landscaping the Coast Guard Station, Coral Shores High School and Plantation Key Elementary School.

The Upper Keys Garden Club helps a fledgling group of junior gardeners at Key Largo Elementary School with money and shared talents. Junior gardeners, under the instruction of the school's horticulture teacher, participate in the Garden Club's annual flower show.

Marathon Garden Club
MM 50 Bayside, Marathon
• **(305) 743-4971**

The Marathon Garden Club was organized in March 1955, when the Keys were in desperate need of beautification. Beginning as a small grass-roots group that held meetings in each other's homes, the ranks have burgeoned to almost 200. Much of the lovely landscaping gracing public areas of Marathon is the work of the Marathon Garden Club. You'll notice their creative handiwork at the American Legion, the chamber of commerce building, the firehouse, Fishermen's Hospital, the public library, the Key Colony Causeway and plantings of trees along the Overseas Highway and at Marathon High School.

Since the 1970s the group has sponsored successful house tours, plant and craft fairs and flower shows. The club furnished the live plants in the new Marathon Airport facility (see our Getting Here, Getting Around chapter) and cares for them on a regular basis.

In 1990 the Marathon Garden Club started a conservation program called Save the Queen Conch. A state environmental grant of $8,700 was given to the club to help enforce fines and educate the public by erecting signs on water and land, warning about taking the endangered conch. They were awarded the Governor's Environmental Education Award in 1992. The same year, the club purchased the William B. Bradley building and adjoining nursery property for use as the Marathon Garden Club Center. A recent addition augments the original structure with a new 40-foot by 60-foot meeting room.

In 1997 the Marathon Garden Club presented its first annual Christmas Around The World display: 17 Christmas trees, each decorated in the traditional ornaments of a different country. In addition to opening the event to the general public, the club hosted more than 900 Monroe County school children to this exhibit. Garden club members also take their collective expertise into the Monroe County schools, where they teach the children about plants and trees as well as flower arranging.

The Marathon Garden Club meets the third Friday of each month from October through May. The public is invited. The gift shop, which

Our subtropical climate fosters the growth of exotic
flowers and palms, like this red leaf palm.

offers a changing rota of unusual specialty gift items, is open year round from Tuesday through Saturday, 10 AM to 2 PM.

American
Contract Bridge League

Duplicate bridge passes muster as the game of choice among those addicts of the sport. "If there's a game in town, we'll find it," says one duplicate player. There are seven regular weekly games of duplicate bridge in the Florida Keys, and bridge players come from as far as Key West to participate. The play is recognized by the National American Contract Bridge League, and you can earn Life Master's points. The games are open to all. If you don't have a partner, don't worry, the director will pair you with a partner for the day's game. Play costs about $3.

It is best to call the director before the day of play to make sure the schedule has not been changed. The groups are listed here by location.

•**Barnett Bank**, MM 100 Oceanside, Key Largo. Play is year round on Mondays at 1 PM. Director is Lucy McGraw, (305) 451-2302.

•**Barnett Bank**, MM 100 Oceanside, Key Largo. Play is year round on Tuesday evenings at 7:30 PM and Fridays at 1 PM. Director is Carol Duffy, (305) 852-5369.

•**San Pablo Catholic Church**, MM 53.5 Oceanside, 550 122nd Street, Marathon. Play is year round on Thursdays at 12:30 PM and Fridays at 10:30 AM. Director is Sally Whitman, (305) 743-7154.

•**Kirk of the Keys**, MM 51 Oceanside, Marathon. Play is October to June 1 on Wednesdays at 12:30 PM. Director is Richard Foley, (305) 743-3296.

•**Sombrero Country Club**, MM 50

Oceanside, Sombrero Boulevard, Marathon. Play is October to June 1 on Mondays at 12:30 PM. Richard Foley, (305) 743-3296, is director.

Golf and Tennis

Two of the most religiously played sports among seniors are golf and tennis. See our Recreation chapter for information on facilities in the Florida Keys.

Quilter's Club

Next to avid gardeners, bridge fanatics, loyal golfers and tireless tennis players, quilters rank as a group prepared to go the distance. We've never known a quilter who could pass up a fabric store or a quilt shop, and it is a hobby that has burgeoned across the nation.

Totally hooked on quilting in the Florida Keys are the members of the Quilter's Club, who come from all over the Keys, and even South Florida, to attend meetings at the Key Largo Library the first and third Saturdays of the month at 10 AM. The group does not jury any bodies of work, but they have a popular show-and-tell of projects in process. Each month members also hold a themed fabric exchange of 6-inch squares and a "block of the month" drawing.

Every other year the Quilter's Club has a quilt show on National Quilting Day in March, complete with national advertising. They draw a worldwide audience, we're told. Contact the Key Largo Public Library, (305) 451-2396, for more information.

Senior Services

Monroe County Social Services

The Florida Keys offers senior citizens a wide range of services through the Monroe County Social Services Agency, whose main administrative offices are in Key West. We have listed the branch office locations in the Upper and Middle Keys below and the contact numbers of each department in the individual de-

scriptions. Note that services in the Middle Keys also include Big Pine Key, which ordinarily is included with the Lower Keys throughout the book. The rest of the Lower Keys are handled from the offices in Key West.

Alternately, you can call the Elder Help Line, (800) 273-2044, and describe your problem or need, and they will refer you to the proper agency. Monroe County Social Services office locations include: in the Upper Keys, Plantation Key Government Center Annex, MM 88.8 Bayside, Tavernier; in the Middle Keys, Marathon Government Annex, MM 50.5 Oceanside, 490 63rd Street, Suite 190, Marathon; and, in the Lower Keys, Public Service Building, Wing III, 5100 College Road, Key West.

Welfare Department
Upper Keys • (305) 852-7125
Middle Keys • (305) 289-6016
Lower Keys, Key West • (305) 292-4408

The Florida Keys have the highest cost of living in the state of Florida, but no adjustment is made in eligibility requirements for aid for senior citizens, who are usually managing on a fixed income. This county agency works with seniors on a case-by-case basis as an interim assistance agency, helping solve unexpected crises that put them at temporary financial risk. They also aid seniors in matters of lost checks, robbery and fraud; provide equipment loans of wheelchairs and walkers; and help out with short-term medical needs such as prescriptions, eyeglasses and hearing aids. This help is designed to restore the individuals to self-sufficient status or to refer them to the appropriate state or federal agencies for more long-term support. Documentation of need is required to qualify for assistance.

Senior Community Service Employment Program
Upper and Middle Keys
• **(305) 852-1469, Ext. 6328**
Lower Keys and Key West
• **(305) 292-4593**

The Senior Community Service Employment Program is a national program funded by Title V of the Older Americans Act. It provides temporary work experience and training for persons 55 and older who meet financial and eligibility guidelines. Most seniors living on Social Security payments alone will qualify. The training occurs at governmental and non-profit community service agencies. Jobs include library aides, nutrition site aides, senior citizen center receptionists or aides in the Social Security office, job service office or Red Cross office. The employment prepares candidates for jobs in the private sector.

The program director has determined that seniors ages 55 to 62 fit into the work force well. Monroe County (the Florida Keys) is allocated 35 slots for these light-duty projects. Workers are covered under the Worker's Compensation Law. The agency is mandated to place 30 percent of the participants in jobs off the program. This 32-year-old government program has been deemed the most successful job training program in any age group, because these seniors want to work.

In-Home Services
Upper Keys • (305) 852-7154
Middle Keys • (305) 289-6324
Lower Keys, Key West • (305) 292-4583

In-Home Services networks information and referrals between the private and public sector for family members, friends and other agencies seeking services on behalf of impaired elderly persons. Participants must be at least age 60. The program is designed so the elderly may maintain quality of life while remaining in their homes.

The information and referral telephone line, (800) 273-2044, is staffed by case managers from 8 AM to 5 PM, Monday through Friday. They will specifically target the needed assistance and refer the caller to the resources available. Case management provides a social worker to support and help those requiring assistance.

Chore services for impaired elderly who can no longer accomplish the tasks for themselves are available. These include yard work, heavy-duty cleaning services and small minor household repairs. Homemaking support with light housekeeping, meal preparation and planning, shopping, laundry tasks and other essential errands assist clients in need. Personal care, in-home respite aides will help with bathing, dressing and other personal needs, providing relief for caregivers. A fee schedule assessment based on the person's income will determine what or if they will have to pay for these services.

Nutrition Services
Upper Keys • (305) 852-7133
Middle Keys • (305) 743-3346
Lower Keys • (305) 872-3617
Key West • (305) 294-7646,
(305) 294-0708

Funded by the Older Americans Act of 1960 and the Alliance for Aging for Dade and Monroe Counties, and aided with a 10 percent cash match by the Monroe County Board of Commissioners, seniors 60 and older may take advantage of many county nutrition programs. Homebound persons can receive a daily hot meal from Meals on Wheels. Other congregate sites throughout the Keys offer a noontime, complete balanced meal for only $1.50. The midday repast is supplemented with lecturers and instruction on nutrition, hygiene, healthcare concerns and hurricane preparedness, and the group also participates in card games and organized activities.

One help to seniors is the ongoing registration for special telephones that BellSouth supplies the hearing-impaired elderly of the Florida Keys. The sound of these telephones is enhanced, and the numbers are extra large. All seniors are eligible for one of these free telephones. Call one of the congregate centers (see earlier listings) and request an application form for a telephone for the hearing-impaired. Telephones will be delivered to the homebound. All customers of BellSouth pay 10¢ to 15¢ per month, probably without even

---

INSIDERS' TIP

Senior citizens and those who are disabled can register with Monroe County Social Services for emergency or disaster evacuation assistance: Upper Keys, (305) 852-7125; Middle Keys, (305) 289-6016; and Lower Keys, (305) 292-4591.

knowing it, to provide this service to the elderly.

The midday congregate meals for the Upper, Middle and Lower Keys are held at the respective AARP Senior Citizens Centers. The congregate centers and Nutrition Services contacts in Key West are Douglas Community Center, 800 Emma Street, (305) 294-0708, and the AARP Senior Citizens Center, Old Truman School Cafeteria, 1016 Georgia Street, (305) 294-7646.

Transportation Program
Upper Keys • (305) 852-7148
Middle Keys • (305) 289-6052
Lower Keys, Key West • (305) 292-4424

Monroe County maintains eight mini-buses throughout the Keys, providing transportation for individuals 60 and older or those physically challenged or transportation-disadvantaged (those who don't or can't have a driver's license for some reason). Travelers must be able to get to the bus unassisted, but the vehicle has a wheelchair lift to aid entry. The bus picks up and drops off at your door between 8:15 AM and 5 PM (last pickup is 4:30 PM). Seniors must call for bus service 24 hours in advance, no later than 3 PM. The route is figured every day, based on the pickup times and locations requested. Riders must allow plenty of time to get to their appointments and can expect actual pickup to be 30 minutes before or after requested pickup time.

Each of the eight buses has a set territory: The Lower Keys circuit is considered Key West to Big Pine Key. The Middle Keys territory is between Sugarloaf Key and Marathon. The two Upper Keys routes travel between Marathon and MM72 and between MM 72 and MM 112 at the county line on the 18-mile stretch. Fees are figured on a sliding scale based on mileage. The scale begins with zero to 14.9 miles (50¢, one way), capping out at $4 for more than 75 miles. Transportation vouchers

are available in booklets of 20 coupons in 50¢ denominations ($10).

Adult Day Care

Marathon Adult Day Center Inc.
MM 52.5 Oceanside, Marathon
• (305) 743-0996

Fully licensed by the State of Florida and fully insured, Marathon Adult Day Center opened it doors in autumn 1996 as a social day-care program for the aged population. David and Debra Kelly, both registered nurses, strive to provide entertaining, adventurous experiences for the elderly in a protective, homelike environment. These social, health and therapeutic activities include full nursing health assessments, blood pressure and weight monitoring, cognitive memory games, ambulation programs, gardening and a full lunch daily.

Participants in the adult day care, who must be older than 55, should call ahead to make arrangements. They may attend on a full-time, part-time or vacation enrollment basis. Full-time is considered 24 to 40 hours per week; part-time, at least 10 hours but less than 24 hours per week. Fee structures vary depending on length of program chosen. Call the center for more information on other health services offered. Marathon Adult Day Center accepts Medicaid.

Key West

The seniors of Key West have a wealth of special interest activities and organizations at their fingertips. Unlike the rest of the Keys, the active retirees of Key West have regularly scheduled public bus transportation available, allowing them easier access to desired destinations.

Some activities, such as the duplicate bridge games of the American Contract Bridge League in the Middle and Upper Keys and the Quilter's Club of Key Largo (see previous sections) entice Key Westers to trek up the Keys. The young-at-heart Key West retirees play golf and tennis (see our Recreation chapter) and spend time fishing, diving and boating too (see related chapters).

Senior Center

AARP Senior Citizens Center
1216 Georgia St., Key West
• **(305) 292-3565**

The seniors in Key West often go their own way, we are told, so not as many organized activities emanate from this center as from others in the rest of the Keys. The seniors are active in the Key West Garden Club and the Art and Historical Society, the Maritime History Society and the Key West Yacht Club (see our Cruising chapter), the Power Squadron and fraternal organizations such as Moose and Elk. More than 50 seniors regularly come to the center for the county-supplied hot meal each day (see "Nutrition Services" in this chapter), staying to play bingo or cards afterward. Bridge is popular at the center too. There are more than 200 card-carrying members of AARP in Key West.

College Courses

Florida Keys Community College
5901 W. College Rd., Stock Island
• **(305) 296-9081 Ext. 495 or 496**

The main campus of the Florida Keys Community College offers many more classes of interest to seniors than the other branches up the Keys. The fee structure remains the same, however. Each credit hour costs $42.45 (Florida residents), with a onetime $15 application fee (no tuition discounts for senior-citizen status). Out-of-state students must pay a higher credit-hour fee.

Art classes in ceramics, stained glass, jewelry making, lettering and calligraphy, drawing, wheel throwing, print making, photography, graphic arts, painting and sculp-

ture will intrigue the artistically inclined. New courses in computerized photography and graphic arts are also offered. Many foreign languages are available, and the selection of literature courses includes one on Florida Keys writers and literature. Seniors can try their hands at creative writing and dabble in the natural sciences with marine data collection, marine archaeology and the culture and environment of the Florida Everglades. Vocational courses include marine propulsion technology (good for those with boats to repair) and electronic engineering technology (to fix VCRs, etc.).

FKCC has a brand new swimming pool and offers classes in water aerobics and fitness swimming. Seniors can take classes as non-degree-seeking students or work toward an Associate of Arts or Associate of Science degree.

FKCC Continuing Education
5901 W. College Rd., Stock Island
• **(305) 296-9081, Ext. 305**

Offered under the umbrella of Florida Keys Community College are constantly changing mini-classes through the Division of Continuing Education. Seniors particularly enroll in expansive computer classes, such as Windows 95, Creating a Web Page, Getting on the Internet, Office '97, Computer for the Timid and others. Courses are offered in business skills, grant-writing skills and financial strategies for women. Unusual offerings include basic bookbinding, box making, portfolio making, cake decorating, making and repairing custom rods, saltwater fly fishing, meteorology for the non-meteorologist (a must for every boat owner who'd like to learn to navigate by the stars) and even a motivational seminar titled "Developing the Power Within." Continuing Education also offers a class in Security Officer Training and a fun decorating course titled "What Do You Say To A Bare Wall?" Caregiver and guardianship classes are available for those who are interested.

Continuing Education is a nonprofit entity. Classes typically cost between $10 and $110. Any group of 10 people with a common interest can contact the FKCC Continuing Education office to have a course custom created.

Public Library

Monroe County Public Library
700 Fleming St., Key West
• **(305) 292-3595**

The Monroe County Public Library maintains a large-print collection just as the other libraries up the Keys do. In addition, a well-stocked Florida History Room provides a fascinating look back through the centuries in Key West and all of the Keys. Volumes of old photographs are housed here. The Friends of the Library sponsors a lecture series dealing with topics from finances to fiction, taxes to investments. This is the place to go if you have to sort something out with a government agency. The library will help you get information on regional government offices, such as telephone numbers for the Internal Revenue Service or the Social Security Administration. It can also provide you with information on government-sponsored healthcare.

Special-interest Activities

Key West Garden Club
West Martello Towers, Atlantic Blvd.,
Key West • (305) 294-3210

The Key West Garden Club, a spirited group of 200, maintains the gardens of West Martello Towers, an old Civil War fort at Higgs Beach on Atlantic Boulevard. The Garden Club meets once a month for a short business meeting followed by a presentation by a guest speaker, often a visiting horticulturist. These events are open to the general public. Twice a year the group holds a plant sale at its West Martello Towers headquarters. You can walk away with beautiful plants at bargain prices and a wealth of free gardening tips and information to boot. Every March the Key West Garden Club sponsors a garden tour during which the general public can visit five private gardens in Key West.

Photo: Victoria Shearer

Our seniors are anything but retiring.

Senior Services

The main offices for countywide programs administered by Monroe County Social Services in Key West are in the Public Service Building, Wing III, 5100 College Road, Stock Island. Contact numbers for Key West include the Welfare Department, (305) 292-4408; Senior Community Service Employment Program, (305) 292-4593; In-Home Services, (305) 292-4583; Nutrition Services, (305) 294-7646, (305) 294-0708; and Transportation Program, (305) 292-4424. See the descriptions of these programs in the Florida Keys section of this chapter.

Alternately, you can call the Elder Help Line, (800) 273-2044, and describe your problem or need, and they will refer you to the proper agency.

Assisted-Living Facility

Bayshore Manor
MM 4, 5200 College Rd., Stock Island
• (305) 294-4966

Bayshore Manor is the oldest assisted-living facility in Monroe County and the only such facility in the State of Florida owned and operated by county government. It is staffed on a 24-hour basis by State Certified Nursing Assistants and is licensed to provide full residential care for up to 16 clients.

In addition to full-time residents, Bayshore Manor also operates the only respite/daytime program in Monroe County for elderly residents who either require constant nonmedical attention at home because of mental, emotional or physical limitations or simply because their families are concerned about them remaining at home alone during the day. This program provides daily group activities such as field trips, arts and crafts, music, games and simple calisthenics plus a daily hot lunch. This service is available seven days a week.

Additionally, bed space permitting, short-term admissions for up to 30 days are available for caregivers who require longer periods of time away from the person in their care. Residents live in private rooms each equipped with a color television. The facility is centrally air-conditioned, and meals are served in a communal dining room. In addition to assistance with activities of daily living, Bayshore Manor provides a full laundry service.

The monthly fee for residential service is based upon the client's ability to pay, and the admission procedure is a joint process involving both the Bayshore Manor director and the Monroe County Social Services Department's social workers. Daytime respite services are available at $24 per day, which includes a hot lunch.

The Florida Keys and Key West are served by physicians in nearly every specialty, as well as by osteopaths, chiropractors, podiatrists, dentists and optometrists.

Healthcare

In case you need healthcare while you're here, this chapter offers a synopsis of options, listed by category in descending mile-marker order from Key Largo to Key West.

We have included information on healthcare options ranging from full-service hospitals and specialty care-providers for patients in need of cancer or dialysis treatments to physical therapy clinics and mental health services. And don't miss the information on veterinary-care options. We care about Spot and Fluffy, too!

Please be reminded, however, that this is not intended to be a comprehensive listing of all possible health services. The Florida Keys and Key West are served by physicians in nearly every specialty, as well as by osteopaths, chiropractors, podiatrists, dentists and optometrists. So if, while visiting our islands, you should develop a sudden toothache from downing one too many frozen coladas or drop a contact lens somewhere in the sand, don't despair. One of our many healthcare providers will be available to help you, even on short notice. Ask your hotel concierge for a referral to the appropriate specialist or consult the phone book's Yellow Pages.

And should your situation call for medical expertise that is not available in the Florida Keys, rest assured that you will still be able to receive state-of-the-art treatment in a timely manner. The University of Miami's renowned Jackson Memorial Medical Center as well as other mainland hospitals and trauma facilities are just a helicopter ride away.

Emergency Numbers

While we sincerely hope you won't ever need to use the following telephone numbers, it is good to keep this information in a convenient place.

Police, fire or rescue emergencies — 911.

Florida Poison Information Center — (800) 282-3171

U.S. Coast Guard Marine and Air Emergency — (305) 295-9700, (305) 295-9735

Florida Marine Patrol — (305) 289-2320; after 5 PM, (800) DIAL-FMP; (800) 342-5367

Crisis Intervention and Help Lines

Abuse Registry — (800) 96-ABUSE; (800) 962-2873

AIDS Help Inc. — (305) 296-6196

Aids Hotline for Counseling and Information — (800) 590-2437

Alcoholics Anonymous — Key Largo, (305) 852-6186; Islamorada, (305) 664-8683; Marathon, (305) 743-3262; Lower Keys and Key West, (305) 296-8654

Codependents Anonymous — (800) 672-2632

Consumer Helpline — (800) 435-7352

Crisis Intervention 24-hour Helpline — (305) 296-4357, (800) 273-4558

Elder Helpline — (800) 273-2044

Hospice of the Florida Keys — Upper Keys, (305) 852-7887; Middle Keys, (305) 743-9048; Lower Keys, (305) 294-8812

Insurance Consumer Hotline — (800) 342-2762

Missing Children Information Clearing House — (888) FL-MISSING; (888) 356-5774

Narcotics Abuse 24-hour Helpline — (800) 234-0420

Narcotics Anonymous — Islamorada, (305) 664-2270; Key West, (305) 296-7999

Overeaters Anonymous— (305) 293-0070

Teenline (24-hour crisis intervention) — (305) 292-8440; (800) 273-4558

Acute-Care Centers

Upper Keys

Keys Rapid Care Center
MM 101.4 Oceanside, Tradewinds Shopping Center, Key Largo
• **(305) 453-0666**

Immediate care for cuts, insect bites, allergies, minor emergencies and illnesses is available for children and adults at this readily accessible clinic located at the Tradewinds Shopping Center between Publix and Kmart. Medical specialties here include family practice, pediatrics, gynecology and dermatology. The center is open Monday through Saturday. Appointments are appreciated but not necessary; walk-ins and tourists are welcome. A second clinic, offering in-house laboratory services and X-rays, is located across from Mariner's Hospital at MM 91.4 in Tavernier.

Vivra Renal Care of Upper Florida Keys
MM 92.2 Bayside, Tavernier
• **(305) 852-0255**

Opened to patients in June 1997, this dialysis center provides those in need of dialysis an opportunity to receive treatment close to home instead of traveling to Homestead on the mainland, about 40 to 50 miles away. Vivra Renal Care is based out of California and is a for-profit corporation. Vivra regularly assists about a dozen patients.

Mariners Hospital
MM 88.5 Bayside, 50 High Point Rd., Tavernier • **(305) 852-4418**

Mariners Hospital, established as a nine-bed physicians' clinic in 1959, today is a state-of-the-art hospital facility completed at the end of 1998. Among the services provided here are 24-hour emergency care, surgery (including outpatient), respiratory therapy, pulmonary rehabilitation, cardiac rehabilitation and radiology (including MRI, CT scans and mammography). Mariners maintains a sleep diagnostic center, laboratory and pharmacy and has a hyperbaric, or decompression, chamber (see our Diving and Snorkeling chapter). Mariners has a helicopter pad for transfer of severe cases to mainland hospitals.

The hospital is an affiliate of Baptist Health Systems of South Florida, a nonprofit organization. Mariners Hospital also operates a state-of-the-art physical therapy center in a separate location at MM 100.3 Bayside, Key Largo, (305) 451-4398.

Middle Keys

Fishermen's Hospital
MM 48.7 Oceanside, Marathon • **(305) 743-5533**

The medical staff at this 58-bed facility offers cardiology, cardiac rehabilitation, family practice, general surgery, gynecology, oncology, internal medicine, neurology, pathology, radiology, rheumatology and plastic/reconstructive surgery. A CT scanner, known as a helical scanner, provides three-dimensional images with extraordinary clarity. Emergency service and same-day surgery also are available.

In 1996 the hospital expanded by 4,400 square feet. A helicopter pad allows for emergency chopper services, and a hyperbaric emergency response team is on call for divers. Fishermen's Overnight Guest program provides testing and pre-surgery (the night prior to surgery) room and board. Also licensed to provide home healthcare, Fishermen's accepts most forms of insurance. Other offerings include a certified diabetes educator and nutritional support services. Fishermen's Hospital also offers physical therapy services at two separate locations: at MM 54, across from the Quay on Marathon Key, and at the Big Pine Key Medical Complex in the Winn Dixie Shopping Plaza on Big Pine Key. For information on either of these physical therapy centers, phone (305) 289-9950. This hospital is a for-profit organization.

Florida Keys Hyperbaric Center
MM 54 Oceanside, Marathon
• (305) 743-9891

Florida Keys Hyperbaric Center uses high concentrations of oxygen to treat decompression sickness, often called "the bends," and medical emergencies such as carbon monoxide poisoning, smoke inhalation, cyanide poisoning and crush injuries. See our Diving and Snorkeling chapter for more information.

Lower Keys
and Key West

Associates in Orthopaedics and Sports Medicine
MM 100.3, Key Largo • (305) 451-0361
13357 Overseas Highway, Marathon
• (305) 743-2182
3138 Northside Dr., Key West
• (305) 293-9231

At these three full-service orthopaedic and sports medicine facilities, physicians perform both surgical and nonsurgical intervention on orthopedic problems. Other services available include arthroscopic surgery, joint replacement and hand and spine surgery. X-ray facilities are on the premises, and minor surgical procedures are performed in the office. The centers are open during regular business hours.

RMS IntegraCare Outpatient Center
MM 100 Bayside, Key Largo
• (305) 453-0409
MM 52 Oceanside, Marathon
• (305) 743-1881
33 Ships Way, Big Pine Key
• (305) 872-2720
3156 Northside Dr., Key West
• (305) 292-1805

IntegraCare maintains a network of therapists who specialize in physical, speech and occupational therapy. Audiologists offer hearing tests and provide hearing aids. Some locations also offer orthopedist, family physician and internist referrals.

Lower Florida Keys Health System
5900 College Rd., Stock Island
• (305) 294-5531

This accredited primary-care hospital is the only hospital in the Florida Keys to offer maternity services. Lower Florida Keys Health System maintains 169 beds, a 24-hour emergency room, clinical lab and a heliport. Added services include pediatrics, inpatient and outpatient psychotherapy, physical therapy, radiation therapy, chemotherapy and cardiovascular and ambulatory care. The hospital offers substance-abuse assistance and comprehensive wellness programs.

Keys Cancer Center
5900 College Rd., Stock Island
• (305) 296-0021

External and internal radiation therapy for all types of cancer, including breast, skin, prostate, lung and AIDS-related malignancies, is provided at the Keys Cancer Center by Dr. Mark Perman, a board-certified radiation oncologist. Patients are generally referred by other physicians, but walk-ins are always welcome. The center also offers state-of-the-art seed implants for prostate cancer.

The Keys Cancer Center is open Monday through Friday from 8 AM to 4:40 PM. The staff actively works to educate and promote cancer awareness within the community, sponsoring screenings and working closely with cancer support groups.

INSIDERS' TIP

Heat stroke is no laughing matter. To avoid dehydration in the hot Florida sun, always tuck a bottle of drinking water into your beach bag.

Big Pine Professional Plaza
MM 29.7 Bayside, Big Pine Key
• (305) 872-0040

This clinic is an extension of Lower Florida Keys Health System and allows those who live outside Key West to schedule an appointment with their doctor at a location closer to home. The clinic is open Monday through Friday and offers all the services of the Lower Florida Keys Health System (see previous listing). Appointments must be made through the individual doctors' offices.

www.insiders.com

See this and many other **Insiders' Guide®** destinations online — in their entirety.

Visit us today!

Integrated Medical Services of the Florida Keys and Mount Sinai Florida Keys
3428 N. Roosevelt Blvd., Key West
• (305) 294-2500

Services offered at this new center include cardiology, general surgery, hematology/oncology, internal medicine, neurology, obstetrics and gynecology, orthopedic surgery, pediatrics and ear, nose and throat. The group practice of 16 local doctors also has diagnostic facilities for general radiology, nuclear medicine, CT scans, MRI and lab testing. IMS also operates clinics with more limited services on Big Pine Key, (305) 872-3192, and Marathon, (305) 289-3420.

V.A. Outpatient Clinic
1350 Douglas Cir., Key West
• (305) 293-4810

Available to all military veterans are outpatient services such as office visits with a physician or psychological counseling. The clinic employs two doctors, one nurse and a social worker.

Vivra Renal Care
3114 Flagler Ave., Key West
• (305) 294-8453

This center offers dialysis for kidney patients who would otherwise have to travel to the Upper Keys or Homestead. Approximately 25 to 30 patients receive dialysis at the center, which is open during regular business hours and on Saturdays as well.

Home-Health Services

Tenet Home Care of the Florida Keys
MM 92 Bayside, Tavernier
• (305) 852-4051
MM 53 Oceanside, Marathon
• (305) 743-6408
1200 Kennedy Dr., Key West
• (305) 294-2591

This network of health professionals offers individualized home-care services: registered nurse care, physical therapy, IV therapy, home-health product supply, occupational therapy, speech therapy and medical social worker consultation. Companion care also is available. Tenet Home Care maintains offices throughout the Florida Keys and serves children, adults and senior citizens. Care for the terminally ill is typically provided by Hospice (see subsequent listing). Medicare and Medicaid are accepted.

Hospice of the Florida Keys/ Visiting Nurse Association
MM 92 Oceanside, Tavernier
• (305) 852-7887
MM 50.5 Oceanside, Marathon
• (305) 743-9048
1319 William St., Key West
• (305) 294-8812

Hospice provides care for terminally ill patients with six months or less to live. Services are provided in private homes and nursing homes throughout the Keys by a staff of registered nurses, patient-care managers and social workers. Certified nursing assistants tend to personal needs such as bathing, grooming and bedding, and all home-care patients must be referred to the agency by a physician. Comfort Care, which is private-duty nursing care, is now available. Hospice's purpose is to ensure patients' comfort so that the last days of their lives are quality ones.

Within this same nonprofit organization, the Visiting Nurse Association provides more aggressive home care for patients still undergoing various treatments or who require blood tests or care for wounds. This service also is provided upon a physician's request. Both Hospice and VNA are on call 24 hours a day, seven days a week. Medicare and Medicaid are accepted.

Nursing Homes

Upper Keys

**Plantation Key
Convalescent Center**
**MM 88.8 Bayside, 40 High Point Rd.,
Tavernier • (305) 852-3021**

Comprehensive Care is a 120-bed facility specializing in long- and short-term convalescent care and physical and occupational therapy. This center, Marathon Manor and Key West Convalescent Center (see subsequent listings) are under the same ownership.

Middle Keys

Marathon Manor
MM 50 Bayside, 320 Sombrero Beach Rd., Marathon • (305) 743-4466

A long-term skilled-care facility, Marathon Manor also responds to a variety of medical needs including IV therapy, short-term rehabilitation and physical and occupational therapy. The facility maintains 120 beds and a day-care center for community children.

Lower Keys and Key West

Key West Convalescent Center
**5860 College Rd., Stock Island
• (305) 296-2459**

The 120-bed Key West Convalescent Center provides skilled and acute care as well as physical, speech and occupational therapy. Psychologists are on staff.

Mental-Health Services

Upper Keys

The Counseling Center
**MM 99.5 Oceanside, Key Largo
• (305) 453-9443**

The Counseling Center is staffed by two clinical social workers and a psychiatrist who provide individual, family, group and premarital therapy. Other areas of emphasis are stress reduction, alternative lifestyle counseling for gays and lesbians and hypnosis for weight control and smoking cessation.

Coastal Counseling Services
**MM 87.4 Oceanside, Islamorada
• (305) 852-6023**

At Coastal Counseling Services, licensed mental health counselor and licensed massage therapist Rosanne B. Walsh offers individual and couple's counseling. She specializes in the treatment of depression and anxiety, life transitions and adjustment disorders for children and adults.

Middle Keys

The Guidance Clinic of the Middle Keys
**MM 49 Oceanside, 3000 41st St.,
Marathon • (305) 743-9491**

This mental health facility offers inpatient and outpatient services for substance abuse and mental illness. Other programs include day treatment, job coaching, case management, medication management, a detox unit, a crisis stabilization unit and a residential program. The staff consists of a psychiatrist and several qualified and licensed care providers.

Lower Keys and Key West

Care Center For Mental Health
1205 Fourth St., Key West
• **(305) 292-6843**

This traditional outpatient community mental health center offers psychiatric diagnosis, treatment, evaluation and testing; psychological services; substance-abuse treatment services; 24-hour emergency services for those in imminent danger; crisis services during business hours on a walk-in basis; and acupuncture service.

Alternative Healthcare

Many of the people who reside full-time in the Florida Keys are laid-back types who were drawn to our islands by a desire to pursue a less-than-conventional lifestyle. In many cases, their approach to healthcare is as nontraditional as their approach to life. Fortunately, a burgeoning alternative healthcare industry is now available to meet their needs.

The Florida Keys, and Key West in particular, boast a wealth of options in the alternative healthcare category. These include everything from yoga classes and massage therapy on the beach to acupuncture, homeopathic medicine, organic foods and herbal remedies. A logical place to start in Key West is at **Island Wellness**, 530 Simonton Street. In addition to a juice bar and shelves fully stocked with a variety of vitamins and homeopathic remedies, Island Wellness also offers substance abuse counseling, facials, manicures, pedicures and massage therapy.

For a complete list of other alternative healthcare options/practitioners throughout the Florida Keys, consult the local Yellow Pages under the following categories: Acupuncture; Health Clubs; Health and Diet Food Products; and Massage Therapists.

Veterinary Services

Your four-legged friends and "family" sometimes need healthcare, too. These pet clinics cater to their needs from the top of the Keys to Key West.

Upper Keys

Animal Care Clinic
MM 100.6 Bayside, Key Largo
• **(305) 453-0044**

Animal Care Clinic is run by Dr. Fred Peacock. Boarding and grooming are a small part of the operation at Animal Care. Peacock maintains oxygen-intensive critical-care units and offers surgery, lab testing, X-rays, EKG and ultrasound dentistry. For emergencies, he is on call 24 hours a day, seven days a week. When you visit, notice the caged cats and kittens in the Animal Care Clinic window: Dr. Peacock takes them in and offers them for adoption as a means of reducing the large number of euthanized strays in the Keys.

Upper Keys Veterinary Clinic
MM 87 Oceanside, Islamorada
• **(305) 852-3665**

Dr. Robert Foley, who is among the best-known animal hospital veterinarians in the Keys, operates this clinic. He and four other veterinarians provide comprehensive services for all types of animals, including dogs, cats, birds, reptiles, ferrets and exotics. Twenty-four hour emergency care is offered seven days a week. Boarding is provided for clients.

Middle Keys

Marathon Veterinary Clinic
MM 52.5 Oceanside, Marathon
• **(305) 743-7099**

Marathon Veterinary Clinic is run by Drs. Jim Greene, Dave Gallagher and Geraldine Diethelm. The facility itself is small, but the

INSIDERS' TIP

Reapply sunscreen often. In the Florida Keys, the sun burns hotter than it does up north.

vets here offer full services, including 24-hour emergency care.

Keys Animal Hospital
MM 52.5, Bayside, Marathon
• (305) 743-3647, (305) 743-2287

Drs. Robert Defield and Ralph Sellman operate this full-service hospital. Twenty-four hour emergency care and boarding are available.

Lower Keys

Cruz Animal Hospital
MM 27 Bayside, Ramrod Key
• (305) 872-2559

Dr. Rene A. Cruz offers a variety of medical services to virtually all pets. He also provides 24-hour emergency service.

The Vetmobile
(305) 872-7997

This mobile service based in Big Pine Key is available for veterinary house calls. Dr. Edie Clark is the vet.

Doc Syn's Veterinary Care
MM 22.7 Bayside, Cudjoe Key
• (305) 744-0074

At Doc Syn's, the motto is "we treat your pets as if they were our own." Dr. Cynthia Sandhusen offers complete medical and surgical care for dogs, cats, birds, ferrets and reptiles.

Key West

Lower Keys Animal Hospital
3122 Flagler Ave., Key West
• (305) 294-6335

This facility treats small exotics but mostly sees cats and dogs. The staff offers regular annual checkups, surgery, dentistry, X-rays, vaccinations and treatment of other internal medical problems of pets.

All Animal Clinic and Hospital
5505 Fifth Ave., Stock Island
• (305) 294-5255

Drs. Diane Chesebro, Joan Wheeler and Lisa Bramson operate this facility. They offer medicine, surgery, dentistry, an in-house laboratory and X-rays. This clinic provides emergency care and offers house calls by appointment.

Animal Hospital of Olde Key West and Stock Island
6150 Second St., Stock Island
• (305) 296-5227

Veterinary services are provided in a modern, full-service facility that offers a yearly healthcare plan. A complete boarding facility is also on the premises.

Cross Animal Clinic
928 Truman Ave., Key West
• (305) 294-9551

Rex Cross, DVM, offers full-service care including vaccinations, worm testing, cat boarding and drop-off service. Evening and weekend hours are available.

Thanks to a visiting institute and college degree programs at the Boca Chica Naval Air Station in the Lower Keys, students can earn bachelor's, master's and doctoral degrees without ever leaving our islands.

Education and Child Care

The Florida Keys and Key West are served by public and private schools, preschools and a community college. Thanks to a visiting institute and college degree programs at the Boca Chica Naval Air Station in the Lower Keys, students can earn bachelor's, master's and doctoral degrees without ever leaving our islands. In addition, several institutions of higher education in Miami are within commuting distance.

Following the information on education options is a comprehensive look at the child-care scene in the Florida Keys and Key West. We explore traditional child-care services along with other handy (sometimes vacation-saving) options such as drop-in care, babysitting, sick-child and respite care, family child-care homes and public after-school programs.

Education

The Florida Keys

Public Schools

The Monroe County School District oversees schools from Key Largo to Key West, including three high schools. Some elementary and middle schools within our county occupy the same building; other middle and high schools share facilities.

Upper Keys students attend Coral Shores High School in Tavernier or Key Largo Elementary and Middle School or Plantation Elementary and Middle School in Tavernier. The site for a new Upper Keys high school has been chosen, but construction has not begun.

Students in the Middle Keys are taught at Stanley Switlik Elementary School and Marathon Middle and High School.

Lower Keys elementary-age students are taught at Big Pine Neighborhood School or Sugarloaf Elementary/Middle School. High school students may choose between Key West High School and Marathon High School.

Key West elementary schools are Glynn Archer on White Street, Gerald Adams on W. College Road, Poinciana on 14th Street and Sigsbee on Felton Road. Grades 6 through 8 are at Horace O'Bryant Middle School on Leon Street, and grades 9 through 12 are at Key West High School on Flagler Avenue.

The school system, which operates on a school year that runs from late August through early June, offers computer technology and other innovative programs, including a television production lab and theatrical program at Key Largo School and a mentoring program and a welcome package for new students at Coral Shores High School in Tavernier. Dropout prevention programs and college credit courses taught in high school are other special programs.

Our public schools are governed by an elected board headed by an elected superintendent who oversees five district representatives. Board members serve four-year terms. School funding comes from Monroe County property taxes.

Private Schools

Private schools typically offer smaller student-teacher ratios and a variety of learning curricula. Tuition in the Florida Keys is usually about $2,000 to $3,000 per child per year. The cost to send additional siblings to the same private school is typically discounted. Following are private schools operating in the Florida Keys and Key West.

Montessori Island School
MM 92.3, Oceanside, Tavernier
• (305) 852-3438

Montessori schools across the country work on the principle of self-pacing for children. This Montessori school, established in 1996, works on the same idea of purposeful action. The school provides education for preschool through elementary children with Montessori-certified teachers. Year-round programs are available.

www.insiders.com
See this and many other **Insiders' Guide®** destinations online — in their entirety.
Visit us today!

Island Christian School
MM 83.4 Bayside, Islamorada
• (305) 664-4933

Established in 1974 by a group of parents from Island Community Church, Island Christian began with 54 students. As grade levels were added and the school became accredited, enrollment increased to 300. Island Christian today teaches pre-kindergarten through high school level students in a traditional college preparatory curriculum that incorporates the Abeka and Bob Jones Christian teachings. The average class size is 18. The school offers a full interscholastic sports program to junior and senior high school students. Each elementary-level class has computers, and junior and senior high levels have computer labs. Some creative senior scheduling is allotted to allow hands-on experience as teacher aides.

Marathon Lutheran School
MM 53.3 Bayside, 325 122nd St.,
Marathon • (305) 289-0700

A service of Martin Luther Chapel and Lutheran Church Missouri Synod, a national Lutheran organization, Marathon Lutheran School offers education from kindergarten through 6th grade. Using the School of Tomorrow PACE program, Marathon Lutheran's two teachers offer its 14 students the opportu-

nity to learn at their own speeds with several class levels combined. Established in 1987, the school requires students to attend weekly chapel service and take religion classes. Music and karate instruction also are offered here, and students work on computers at least once a day. The school year at Marathon Lutheran is the same as that of public schools.

Vineyard Christian School
MM 30 Bayside, 100 County Rd., Big
Pine Key • (305) 872-3404

Within Vineyard Christian Church, this 9-year-old school serves kindergarten pupils beginning at age 3 (age 5 is typical for other schools) and has classes through 6th grade, with a total enrollment of approximately 90 students. Grade levels are combined for classroom instruction. Students are taught using the traditional Christian-based Abeka curriculum, which incorporates Bible study into the basic reading, writing and arithmetic textbook education. All students receive computer training, and additional computer instruction and gymnastics are offered as extracurricular activities. Weekly chapel attendance is required. The school is behind the Coca-Cola Building.

Higher Education

The Union Institute
Venture Centre, 16853 N.E. Second Ave.,
Ste. 102, North Miami Beach
• (305) 653-7141, (800) 486-3116

Since 1994, The Union Institute has acted as a remote adult-education facility that offers bachelor's and doctoral degrees to Florida Keys residents via self-directed independent study. Fully accredited by the Commission on Institutions of Higher Education of the North Central Association of Colleges and Schools and licensed by the State Board of Independent Colleges and Universities, The Union Institute was founded in 1963. Current enrollment is about 1,400; classwork is accomplished via computer. Courses of study include criminal justice, hotel management, social work, psychology, public administration, maritime archaeology, multicultural studies, coastal resource management and more. Financial aid is available.

Additional Educational Opportunities

Residents and visitors to the Florida Keys may participate in a number of hands-on educational opportunities listed below.

National Undersea Research Center
515 Caribbean Dr., Key Largo
• (305) 451-0233

Run by the University of North Carolina and funded by the National Oceanic and Atmospheric Administration, the National Undersea Research Center operates the Aquarius Undersea Laboratory, the nation's only underwater research habitat. It conducts day-boat operations for scientists who are conducting studies on water quality and the marine life environment. The center's primary participants are scientists who have presented a research proposal that has completed a peer review process, but graduates from all over the world may attend with the sponsorship of a professor. Their research proposals must be presented to an established scientist and operated under his or her name.

The National Undersea Research Center is open year round. It has been featured on ABC's *20/20* and has hosted The Jason Project, an interactive education program for students throughout the world.

MarineLab Marine Resources Development Foundation
51 Shoreland Dr., Key Largo
• (305) 451-1139

Offering students an in-depth introduction to the ecology of the Keys, the nonprofit Marine Resources Development Foundation provides customized programs for students. Learn about sea life in the Emerald Lagoon or explore the MarineLab Undersea Laboratory. Customized programs can include scuba certification, coral reef ecology, mangrove ecol-

ogy or a trip to the Everglades. Teacher workshops are also offered.

Outward Bound Florida Sea Program
MM 32 Oceanside, Big Pine Key
• (305) 872-4102, (800) 643-4462

Based in Rockland, Maine, the nonprofit Outward Bound educational organization offers wilderness courses for middle school students through adults. Other adventures are tailored to women, families and educators. Probably the most publicized of all Outward Bound excursions are those within the organization's Career/Life Renewal program, whereby adults at various crossroads in their lives are rewarded by teamwork and the ability to meet physical challenges.

The organization was founded in 1941 with the belief that action and thought should not be separated from educational experiences. Its 44 schools throughout the world offer days of sailing, mountain climbing, kayaking, dogsledding and other outdoor activities coupled with community service work. The goal is to help students develop self-esteem, self-reliance and concern for others and the world around them. Outward Bound's Lower Keys program includes sailing, snorkeling, swimming and natural history instruction. Classes are held here from November through May.

For course information and a complete catalog of Outward Bound programs in South Florida and elsewhere, call the toll-free number listed above.

Seacamp Association
MM 30 Oceanside, Newfound Harbor Rd. and 1300 Big Pine Ave., Big Pine Key
• (305) 872-2205, (305) 872-2331

This scuba and marine science camp for children ages 12 through 17 has been in Big Pine Key for more than 30 years. Children from all over the world sign up for Seacamp's 18-day program to experience scuba diving, sailing, snorkeling and windsurfing. Marine science classes teach about such subjects as exploring the seas, animal behavior and Keys critters. Scuba certification is available.

The camp operates from June through August and offers a day camp in summer for resident children ages 10 through 14. In addition, Seacamp is affiliated with the Newfound Harbor Marine Institute, which hosts three-day winter field trips for teachers and students from 4th grade through high school.

Key West

Public Schools

Key West has four elementary schools, a middle school and a high school. See the discussion of Monroe County's public school system in The Florida Keys section of this chapter for additional information.

Private Schools

Grace Lutheran School
2713 Flagler Ave., Key West
• **(305) 296-8262**
Established in 1952 and designed for pre-kindergarten 3-year-olds through 2nd graders, Grace Lutheran offers computers and teaches Spanish in all but pre-kindergarten level classes. During "God Time," students learn about Christian ideals and how to live them. The school maintains an active parent-teacher group.

Mary Immaculate Star of the Sea
700 Truman Ave., Key West
• **(305) 294-1031**
Mary Immaculate follows a pre-kindergarten through 8th grade curriculum outlined by the Archdiocese of Miami, including religious instruction. The school's mission is to provide opportunities for all Lower Keys families to experience a Catholic education. Within a Christ-centered environment, the instructors foster spiritual, academic and social development. Class sizes average 15 to 25 students.

Montessori Children's School of Key West
1221 Varela St., Key West
• **(305) 294-5302**
Montessori is designed to support a child's need for purposeful action. Here teachers guide students without unnecessary interference — all furnishings are child-size, and photos are hung at a child's viewing level. Allowed freedom within certain guidelines, Montessori children work at their own pace on their own projects. Classes are mixed in age (ages 3 through 5 and grades 1 through 3 study together). The idea is to foster learning by example and learning to share. A director and assistant director are assigned to each class of about 28 students. Summer day-care programs also are offered.

Higher Education

Florida Keys Community College
5901 College Rd., Key West
• **(305) 296-9081**
When Florida Keys Community College began operation in fall 1965, it became the first institution of higher education in the Florida Keys. FKCC was established through funding provided to Monroe County by the Florida state legislature after parents and teachers had expressed concerns over the lack of a college in the Keys. Today the school boasts an enrollment of 5,000 and offers Associates of Science and Arts degree programs in such fields as business administration, electronics engineering, nursing and marine biology. Credits earned at FKCC may be transferred to other institutions of higher learning for application toward a bachelor's degree.

FKCC's performing and visual arts programs are enhanced by the college's Tennessee Williams Fine Arts Center. Its marine biol-

INSIDERS' TIP

The University of Miami, Florida International University and Barry University, all well-known institutions of higher education, are within driving distance of the Upper Keys. All of these universities offer student housing. For commuters, Miami-Dade Community College is also nearby.

The great blue heron fishes for its next meal.

ogy and dive programs are especially popular. Certificate programs are offered at FKCC in business data processing, marine propulsion technology, small business management and more. Vocational training is also available for law enforcement and correctional officers. In 1995, FKCC opened the Mario F. Mitchell Aquatic Safety Center for dive technology and a new oceanfront pool.

Through FKCC's dual enrollment/dual credit program, students in the Monroe County School District can begin earning college credit in high school. Distance learning is provided through telecourses that air on TCI cable Channel 5.

In addition to its main campus on Stock Island, Florida Keys Community College also offers a limited number of classes at two other Keys locations: The Middle Keys Center at 900 Sombrero Beach Road, MM 50, Marathon, (305) 743-2133; and the Upper Keys Center at MM 90, Tavernier, (305) 852-8007.

Troy State University
Florida Region
718 Hornet St., Boca Chica Naval Air Station • (305) 293-2987

Established by the Alabama legislature in 1887 as Troy State Normal School, this university began as a normal, or teachers', college. Troy State grew steadily, earning university status in 1967. The institution serves civilian citizens throughout the United States and military personnel here and abroad. With its main campus and three sites in Alabama, 10 sites in Florida and 40 more around the world, Troy State has graduated more than 75,000 men and women.

In the Florida Keys and Key West, the university offers graduate degree programs in counseling and psychology and in management. Many of these programs consist of weekend-intensive courses or evening classes and may be completed within one year.

Saint Leo College —
Key West Center
718-A Hornet St., Boca Chica Naval Air Station • (305) 293-2847

Saint Leo College offers the only regionally accredited bachelor's degree program in the Florida Keys. Located in Key West since 1975, Saint Leo is a private college offering Associate of Arts and Bachelor of Arts degrees. Annual enrollment exceeds 1,200 students who are pursuing degrees in business administration, criminology, human services and/or human resource administration. Situated at the Naval Air Station, Saint Leo College is open to all civilian and military personnel and their families in the Florida Keys. Classes are designed for the working adult.

Additional
Educational Opportunities

San Carlos Institute
516 Duval St., Key West • (305) 294-3887

In keeping with its century-old mission of promoting Cuban culture and democratic ideals, the historic San Carlos Institute offers Spanish language classes for adults in two terms: winter and summer. Taught by native speakers, these eight-week sessions are available at three levels: beginner, intermediate I and intermediate II. The course fee is $50, which includes all materials.

Child Care

Gone are the days of Ward and June, Ozzie and Harriet and Lucy and Ricky, those televised icons of the '50s nuclear family. In their TV Land, Pop went to the office while Mom stayed home with the children. Nowadays, when fathers go off to work, most mothers are right behind them on their way to jobs; grandparents work too. Child care has become a necessity, and the Florida Keys' scenario differs little from this national norm.

The problem of finding good, competent child care is compounded here by a shortage of available providers at any cost. According to the National Association for the Education of Young Children, child care is the fourth-largest item in the family budget after food, housing and taxes. Infant care (birth to age 1) and weekend and evening care are in particularly short supply in Monroe County, which encompasses the Keys.

Day-to-day child care in the county generally falls into two categories: center-based care and family child-care homes. Results of a study of child-care costs in Monroe County, compiled by Wesley House Resource & Referral Network in May 1996, show that full-time child care in a preschool/child-care center averages between $75 and $84 per week. The average weekly fee in a family child-care home is slightly less, $75 to $78. That means parents in the Florida Keys can expect to pay almost $20,000 for full-time child care during the first five years of a child's life.

In this section, we describe qualities you should seek in child-care providers and provide information on resources, types of child-care programs and contacts for centers that serve the Florida Keys and Key West.

Resources

Wesley House Community Coordinated Child Care Agency
1011 Virginia St., Key West
• (305) 296-8964, (305) 296-5231

With offices in Key West and serving all of the Florida Keys, Wesley House assists families in making the best of a difficult situation. The Wesley House Resource & Referral Network is perhaps the most important resource in the Keys for parents looking for appropriate, quality child care. (Wesley House is a national division agency of the United Methodist Church and a United Way of Monroe County agency.) WHR&R acts as a link between families and the child-care services they seek. It can recommend affordable child care for children up to 5

years old and after-school and summer care for children up to 12 years old.

Other assistance comes in the forms of subsidized child care and scholarships and help in obtaining legal aid, medical aid, food stamps and other services. The network conducts classes for parents in money management, parenting skills, nutrition and handling everyday pressures. It provides personal help for families with at-risk children, assisting them in filling out paperwork to meet eligibility requirements. Wesley House also offers transportation to and from child-care centers for children in at-risk situations.

Types of Programs

This section describes the center- and home-based child-care options available to parents in Monroe County.

Child-Care/ Preschool Centers

The minimum state licensing requirements dictate that a child-care center must hold a valid license from the Health and Rehabilitative Services department of the State of Florida. The license must be posted in a conspicuous place within the center.

The center must adhere to the number of children for which it is licensed, and it must maintain the minimum staff-to-child ratio for each age level: Younger than 1, one teacher for every 4 children; age 1, 1-to-6; age 2, 1-to-11; age 3, 1-to-15; age 4, 1-to-20; and age 5, 1-to-25. We stress that this is the minimum ratio.

INSIDERS' TIP

During the days of school segregation in the 1950s, black children in the Middle Keys had to travel to a Key West boarding school to receive an education. Few could afford the expense. Grace Jones, a Keys educational pioneer, pressured the county and state government for a school for black children in Marathon. Now the Grace Jones Community Center, housed in the converted school building, is a child-care center for all races. The center is at MM 49.3 Bayside, 230 41st Street, Marathon. Call (305) 743-6064 for information.

It may not be sufficient to give your child the level of care you desire.

Licensing standards mandate health and safety requirements and staff training requirements. These include: child abuse and neglect training, a 20-hour child-care training course, a 10-hour specialized training module and eight hours of in-service training annually. In addition, there must be one CPR- and first aid-certified person on site during business hours. Some centers are prepared to accept infants; others are not.

Some child-care centers are exempt from HRS licensing. They are accredited and monitored by religious agencies, the school board or the military. Care provider-to-child ratio, quality of care and training standards vary and may be lesser or greater than that of licensed centers.

None of the child-care centers is open weekends or evenings in the Keys.

Contact Wesley House for a list of HRS-licensed and license-exempt child care/preschool centers in the Florida Keys and Key West.

Family Child-Care Homes

Family child care is considered by the State of Florida to encompass home-based child care with five or fewer preschool age children from more than one family unrelated to the caregiver. Any preschool children living in the home must be included in the maximum number of children allowed. The adult who provides the child care is usually referred to as a family child-care home operator.

Some counties in Florida require that family child-care homes be licensed. Monroe Country, which includes the Florida Keys, requires only registration with the Department of Health and Rehabilitative Services. Every adult in the household must be screened. Registration requires no on-site inspection of the home for minimum health,

safety and sanitation standards, however. Nor is there a requirement that the family child-care operator have CPR or first-aid training.

Military programs are exempt from this registration (see military-certified programs in this chapter). They have their own accreditation procedures and are available only to family members of military personnel.

Wesley House actively recruits for and offers a three-hour course covering basic health and safety issues to persons who wish to operate registered family child-care homes.

Public After-School Programs

Most of the public schools in the Florida Keys and Key West run their own after-hours programs for school-age children from 2:15 to 5:30 PM and also on school holidays and summer weekdays. Most schools do charge for this service.

Key Largo After School
Key Largo Elementary School, 104801 Overseas Hwy., Key Largo
• **(305) 453-1250**

The school offers after-school care and activities for elementary children until 5:30 PM.

Plantation Key After School
Plantation Key School, 100 Lake Rd., Tavernier • (305) 853-3278

Students are entertained until 5:30 PM Monday through Friday.

Marathon Swit City After School
Stanley Switlik Elementary, MM 48.8 Bayside, Marathon • (305) 289-2490

This program provides games and activities until 5:15 PM Monday through Friday for preschool through 6th-grade children attending Stanley Switlik Elementary School.

Big Pine Annex After School
Big Pine Key Neighborhood School, Palomino Horse Tr., Big Pine
• **(305) 872-1266**

Kindergarten through 2nd grade students have fun until 5:30 PM Monday through Friday with outdoor games and card games.

Sugarloaf Afterschool
Sugarloaf School, 255 Crane Rd., Summerland Key • (305) 745-3282

Middle school students in 6th through 8th grade may stay an hour after school and participate in the activity of their choosing, academic or otherwise.

Poinciana After School
Poinciana Elementary, 1212 14th St., Key West • (305) 293-1630

This program operates until 5:30 PM Monday through Friday.

Sigsbee After School
Sigsbee Elementary, Sigsbee Naval Base, Key West • (305) 294-1861

Students at Sigsbee in kindergarten through 5th grade can stay until 5:30 PM for various games and activities. The program is limited to children of military families.

Gerald Adams After School
Gerald Adams Elementary, 5855 College Rd., Key West • (305) 293-1609

The Gerald Adams program entertains students until 5:30 PM Monday through Friday.

Sick and Respite Care

Preschool/child-care centers cannot care for your sick child. Wesley House (see listing above) refers families needing sick care to in-home nursing specialists. You should expect to pay about $10 per hour.

Drop-Ins

Some centers, if they are not filled, will offer drop-in care. The list is in constant flux so call Wesley House (see previous listing) for the latest information.

Babysitting

Personal knowledge of the person you choose to care for your child in your absence is the best of all possible worlds, but it isn't always a reality. If you are a visitor to the Florida Keys or Key West or a newly relocated resident, you may have to take a leap of faith and entrust your child to someone you do not know. Therefore, you should check references. For referrals, contact Wesley House (see previous listing) or ask the concierge at your hotel.

You can also contact local chambers of commerce, which often keep lists of local residents who babysit: Key Largo, (305) 451-1414, (800) 822-1088; Islamorada, (305) 664-4503, (800) 322-5397; Marathon, (305) 743-5417, (800) 262-7284; Lower Keys, (305) 872-2411, (800) 872-3722; and Key West, (305) 294-2587, (800) 527-8539. Be sure to ask by what criteria these referrals have been checked for suitability.

Military- Certified Programs

Military-certified family child-care homes on the military bases in Key West can accept up to six preschool children of military families but are restricted to two children under the age of 2. A home inspection is required. Training, which is provided by the military, is required in CPR, first aid and family day care. The Military Family Home Care program loans and delivers start-up supplies, including cribs, gates, toys and fire extinguishers to all family child-care homes while they are in operation. For a list of all military family child-care homes in Key West, call (305) 293-4441.

The military's child-care center, **The Child Development Center at Trumbo Point**, (305) 293-4376, is available to members of the U.S. military only.

Five community
newspapers are
circulated between Key
Largo and the Lower
Keys and two dailies
between the Florida
Keys and Key West.

Media

Even after Henry Flagler's extension of the Florida East Coast Railway provided Florida Keys residents access to the mainland, communications on our islands were limited. In order to receive local news and news outside the South Florida area, residents relied on radio broadcasts from Miami, sporadic postal service and what was probably their most effective and timely means of dispatch: word-of-mouth.

Today, five community newspapers are circulated between Key Largo and the Lower Keys and two dailies between the Florida Keys and Key West. Key West is home to five weekly papers as well. TV reception includes more than 50 local, network and cable television channels. Online publications, such as *CyberConch Zine*, also are becoming more popular, and most community newspapers receive subscription requests and letters to the editor via e-mail.

With the exceptions of *The Miami Herald*, a daily that devotes one page of coverage to the Florida Keys, and the daily *Key West Citizen*, the Florida Keys are served by community newspapers, published once or twice a week and on alternate days. We also have alternative publications — some that often take strong stances on issues and oppose what their writers perceive as mainstream, politically correct newspapers.

The coverage offered by radio stations is restricted by wattage, and broadcasts for any one radio station typically reach segments, but not the entire length, of the Keys and parts of south Dade County. Except for a few strains of Howard Stern heard some mornings as far as Marathon on Miami's WBGG, 105.9 FM, Florida Keys radio listeners will find local AM and FM programming to be a mix of Latin,

country or contemporary music, reggae, jazz and Jimmy Buffett specials, fishing forecasts, special live broadcasts and local and syndicated national news.

Unless you have a satellite dish or your antenna is high enough to pull network programs off the translator, you will probably want to sign up for basic cable through either TCI Cablevision of Florida or Keys Microcable (see the Television section of this chapter). Although network programs may be seen without cable access, reception is "iffy." TCI's Channel 5 is the local television channel in the Florida Keys except in Ocean Reef, which has its own cable system.

Newspapers

Newspapers are often sold in curbside vending racks. Grocery stores, pharmacies, convenience stores and bookstores offer local publications, and a handful of shops carry national and international newspapers. Because the Florida Keys are considered a remote distribution site, some national newspapers, such as *The New York Times*, are sold at a higher newsstand price. A rule of thumb: Get to the newsstand early. The farther you travel from the mainland, the more quickly the out-of-town papers sell out.

Dailies

The Miami Herald
1 Herald Plaza, Miami • (800) 437-2535
619 Eaton St., Key West • (800) 278-3083
The largest-circulation daily newspaper in the Southeastern United States, this Pulitzer

---

Prize-winner has for decades maintained Key West correspondents and now has a bureau in the southernmost city. *The Miami Herald* features crisp writing and tends to favor features over hard news except when issues are pressing. Keys circulation is 12,500 on weekdays, 20,000 on Sundays.

Herald humor columnist and Pulitzer Prize winner Dave Barry is popular in the Keys as he is most everywhere else. His column is syndicated nationally.

The newspaper costs 50¢ every day except Sunday, when it sells for $1 to $1.25, depending on where you purchase it. Newspapers in vending racks are priced to absorb the sales tax; elsewhere, the tax is added to the cover price. Home delivery is available.

www.insiders.com

See this and many other **Insiders' Guide®** destinations online — in their entirety.

Visit us today!

The Key West Citizen
3420 Northside Dr., Key West
• (305) 294-6641

Newspaper publication in Key West dates as far back as some of the island's earliest settlers. The island's first newspaper, the 1829 *Register*, made a brief run, followed by several short-lived publications appearing and disappearing through 1845. Other early publications included an English/Spanish daily and *The Democrat*, founded in part by Key West's first millionaire, William Curry of Curry Mansion fame (see our Attractions chapter). In 1904 the small, weekly newspaper known as *The Citizen* appeared. It was later consolidated with the 1899 Inter-Ocean to form *The Key West Citizen*.

Thomson Newspapers, a Canadian chain, owns *The Key West Citizen*, along with *The Islamorada Free Press*, *The Keys Advertiser* and *Florida Keys News Service*. *The Citizen* shares editorial coverage and classified advertisements with its sister publications and features a significant amount of syndicated material and lifestyles coverage. *Citizen* circulation is approximately 12,000.

The Citizen's editorial focus is primarily on features. "Paradise," a tabloid appearing in Thursday's edition, is a comprehensive compendium of what's currently happening in the theaters and at the clubs and galleries around town; it's handy to have for weekend planning. Free copies of "Paradise" are available at hotels, guesthouses, restaurants and other businesses throughout Key West. *The Citizen's* most popular department, however, is the Crime Report, which appears daily on page 2. Locals always turn here first, partly for entertainment and partly to make sure their own names are not there after a night of revelry on Duval Street. The kind of incidents that make the daily Crime Report are the kind that get mentioned by Letterman and Leno — the scooter driver assaulted by a flying burrito, the snake held hostage for an engagement ring, the man who lived with a corpse, etc. Yes, truth is stranger than fiction. The Crime Report has become so popular that in 1997, *The Citizen* issued its first annual "Best of the Crime Report" booklet, which sold separately for $1 and soon became a collector's item.

The Citizen is published every day except Saturday. It sells for 50¢ on weekdays and $1 on Sundays. Home delivery is available.

Weeklies and Biweeklies

The Florida Keys Keynoter
MM 48.6 Oceanside, Marathon
• (305) 743-5551, (305) 451-4960,
(305) 745-1313

The award-winning *Florida Keys Keynoter* is owned by Knight-Ridder Publishing and is considered *The Miami Herald's* sister newspaper. *The Keynoter* is Monroe County's second-oldest publication, and with a circulation exceeding 15,000 during season, its largest as well.

With offices in Marathon and Key Largo, a stringer in Key West and a local television news program (see the Television portion of this chapter), *The Keynoter* offers some of the most comprehensive coverage of the Florida Keys. Of particular interest are the "South of Reality" feature, showcasing only-in-the-Keys experiences; the weekly "Top 10 List," merging lo-

Catching the Big one is easy with a subscription to
FISHING
THE FLORIDA KEYS
Florida Keys Captains share secrets and techniques on how to catch the Big Ones.
• BackCountry
• Flats • DeepSea
Only $12.00 a year (six issues) out of county
Brought to you by the
KEYNOTER
(305) 743-5551 • Fax (305) 743-9586
3015 Overseas Hwy., Marathon, FL. 33050
Visa • MasterCard • American Express
35

cal wit and satire à la David Letterman; and the letters to the editor. Classified advertising covers all of the Florida Keys, with most ads stemming from Marathon.

This tabloid-style newspaper featuring a four-color cover sells for 25¢ and is published each Wednesday and Saturday. Subscriptions are sold at a discounted rate, and home delivery is available.

The Islamorada Free Press
MM 81.5 Oceanside, Islamorada
• (305) 664-2266, (800) 926-8412

This paper was established in 1987 by Key Largo resident Dave Whitney, a 30-year veteran reporter and editor who felt that Islamorada needed a community newspaper. *The Free Press* eventually grew to include news and sports coverage throughout the Florida Keys as well as an Ocean Reef edition.

Whitney sold the publication in June 1995 to Thomson Newspapers, a Canadian company that also owns *The Key West Citizen*, *The Keys Advertiser*, *Florida Keys News Service* and other publications nationwide. Whitney became executive director of the Pigeon Key Foundation (see our Attractions chapter for further information).

The Free Press primarily covers south Dade County through Marathon, but its recent merger with other Thomson papers here brought more extensive Florida Keys news coverage and an all-encompassing classifieds section. It is published each Wednesday and is available free in grocery and convenience stores and in curbside racks from Homestead to Duck Key. Subscriptions are available.

The Reporter
MM 91.6 Oceanside, Tavernier
• (305) 852-3216

When the Rufer family began publishing *The Reporter* in the early 1900s, the newspaper, which was printed via mimeograph, was based in Key Largo. As the publication grew, its owners bought what was at the time a top-of-the-line printing press — a monumental

event in Keys publishing, since few newspapers were actually printed in this stretch of Monroe County. (Even today, newspapers are sent down the Keys to Key West or up to Dade County for printing.) *The Reporter* is now published by Knight-Ridder, which also publishes *The Miami Herald*.

This tabloid, circulation 8,000, packages community news from south Dade County to Marathon in a traditional, black-and-white format. Its society column, written by Nancy Thompson, is one of the few offered in Florida Keys newspapers, and its weekly calendar is thorough. Classified ads generally cover the Key Largo and Upper Matecumbe areas.

Published each Thursday, *The Reporter* sells for 25¢ and is available in stores throughout the Upper Keys. Subscriptions also are available; residents of the Keys pay a slightly reduced rate.

The Keys Advertiser
MM 52 Oceanside, Marathon
• (305) 743-8766

Owned by Thomson Newspapers, this free tabloid dubs itself an extension of *The Key West Citizen*. The paper covers the Middle and Lower Keys, and its news content is almost exclusively community-oriented. Circulation is 8,000. The classified section shares Key Largo through Key West advertisements with *The Citizen* and *The Islamorada Free Press*. *The Keys Advertiser* is published on Wednesdays.

The Lower Keys Barometer
MM 30.3 Oceanside, Big Pine Key
• (305) 872-0106

Former radio disc jockey, advertising copywriter and salesperson Keith Monti moved to the Florida Keys in the early 1990s and became a real estate agent. In 1995 he and his wife, Diane, started this newspaper to provide strictly Lower Keys coverage. Their *Lower Keys Barometer*, published Thursdays, combines columns and news in an op-ed format.

Monti, a self-proclaimed citizens' rights advocate, reflects his philosophy in his tab-

INSIDERS' TIP

FM stations may be more popular with listeners, but AM stations beam farther-reaching signals.

loid. The free newspaper also offers local news items and features individuals and businesses as a way to "help neighbors become better acquainted." The Lower Keys Barometer also has a small classifieds section. It is distributed to restaurants, hotels, shops, convenience stores, supermarkets and pharmacies between Grassy Key and Key West.

Key West

El Faro
1908 Flagler Ave. • (305) 296-3719

El Faro editor and publisher Jose Cabaleiro was working in the accounting department of a company in Cuba that printed Spanish versions of *Reader's Digest*, *Time* and *Life* magazines when the Castro regime confiscated the business. Cabaleiro fled to Venezuela. In 1962 he moved to the United States, and in 1971, he established *El Faro* newspaper.

Published on the 15th and 30th of each month, this free Spanish/English newspaper covers social and political issues affecting residents of Monroe and Dade counties. Approximately 10,000 copies of each edition of *El Faro* are printed and distributed throughout Monroe County.

Solares Hill
330-B Julia St. • (305) 294-3602

Founded in 1971, the free weekly *Solares Hill* provides "the straight truth plainly stated," as its longtime slogan declares. The focus here is primarily on politics and business, along with a smattering of restaurant, theater and book reviews. The insightful tell-it-like-it-is editorials garner much interest in the community.

The newspaper, distributed free of charge from Key West to Big Pine Key, covers the Lower Keys and Key West exclusively. About 10,000 copies of *Solares Hill* are circulated on Thursday mornings. Subscriptions are available.

Key West The Newspaper
711 Eisenhower Dr. • (305) 292-2108

Since its debut in January 1994, *Key West The Newspaper* has found its niche in the realm of politics and entertainment. While the paper boasts a hearty entertainment section full of live music listings, reviews and local color, it is perhaps best known for its investigative reporting. Publisher/editor-in-chief Dennis Reeves Cooper and takes the news seriously, and it shows. During season, 13,000 copies (11,000 in summer) of this free weekly are distributed every Friday morning in Key West and Stock Island, and subscriptions are available.

The Island News
1315 Whitehead St. • (305) 296-1566

Established in 1996, Key West's newest paper has a specific mission: Be the locals' hometown weekly paper. The focus is a broad one, covering aspects such as lifestyles, health, education, sports and community news. Publisher Winston Burrell, former publisher of *The Key West Citizen*, has nearly 20 years of journalism experience. So do most of the staff writers, some of whom were also previously associated with *The Citizen*. The *Island News* distributes 12,000 free copies across Key West every Friday. Subscriptions are available.

Celebrate Key West
1315 Whitehead St. • (305) 296-1566

Celebrate Key West is the sister paper to *The Island News* and caters to the gay and lesbian population of Key West. Offering various community features along with gay-perspective editorials and stances on issues, *Celebrate Key West* provides a new forum in Key West publishing. This free paper prints 12,000 copies that are distributed throughout Key West each Friday. Subscriptions are available.

Magazines

Fishing the Florida Keys
MM 48.6 Oceanside, Marathon
• (305) 743-5551

Originally issued six times a year by *The Florida Keys Keynoter* as a stand-alone publication, *Fishing the Florida Keys* is now incorporated into *The Keynoter* on a quarterly basis. This newsprint magazine devoted to fishing combines the expertise of columnists, writers and sources who are experienced Florida Keys anglers and charter boat captains.

Editorial content focuses on a wide variety

of angling topics. Past articles have included tips on the movement patterns of dolphin (fin-fish, not Flipper) and on preparing rods and rigs for blue marlin. Copies can be found at locations throughout the Florida Keys and Key West where *The Keynoter* is sold. Annual subscriptions to *FFK* only are available for $8.

Alternative Publication

Bone Island Sun
812 Southard St., Key West
• (305) 296-3492

For more than five years, the *Bone Island Sun* has entertained visitors and locals alike with its satirical brand of humor. This broadsheet newsprint paper focuses its wit primarily on local issues. One recent article, for example, reviewed "Key West at Seaworld." Published "sporadically but usually quarterly," the *Bone Island Sun* is available free throughout Key West. The Bone Island Press, parent company of the *Sun*, also publishes a free guide to Key West (copies are available at the offices inside the old Harris School on Southard Street) as well as fiction and nonfiction by local authors.

Radio

Radio reception in the Florida Keys is heavily influenced by factors such as weather and distance from the transmitter. We have therefore grouped stations according to the areas where your chances for clear reception are the best. Clear skies and sunshine will optimize good reception; luckily, we have plenty of both most of the time.

Upper Keys

WKLG Star 102.1 FM (Key Largo): Hits from the '70s through the '90s, traffic and weather reports, syndicated news.

WFKZ SUN 103.1 FM (Tavernier): Pop/con-temporary music with a mix of oldies, live local news, daily live fishing reports, weather and tide information.

WCTH Catch FM 100 (Islamorada): Contemporary music with fishing reports, community calendar, news and sports.

Middle Keys

WAVK Wave 105.5 FM (Marathon): Adult contemporary music from the '60s to today, local talk shows, news, daily fishing and dive reports.

WGMX 94.3 FM (Marathon): Adult contemporary music from the '70s to today.

WFFG 1300 AM (Marathon): All-talk sports (Miami Dolphins, Miami Heat, NASCAR) and news 24 hours a day.

Lower Keys

WWUS (U.S. 1 Radio) 104.7 FM (Big Pine Key): Oldies music, reggae and Jimmy Buffett, daily fishing reports, on-air flea market, morning magazine (interviews) and live local news.

WPIK PIK'n 102.5 FM (Summerland Key): Modern country.

Key West

WAIL 99.5 FM: Classic rock.

WCNK Conch 98.7 FM: Smooth jazz.

WEOW 92.5 FM: Contemporary hits.

WIIS Island 107 FM: Adult-alternative music, local news, weather, fishing reports, tide and wind information.

WKRY Key 93.5 FM: Soft adult contemporary music, weather and tide information, daily stock reports, health tips, cultural and community calendars. Special programs feature classical, jazz and Latin music.

WKWF/AM 1600: All sports radio.

WSKP 107.9 FM: Spanish language/music.

Television

Florida Keys residents must pay for cable television service in order to receive clear und consistent reception of network channels. Our primary provider, **TCI Cablevision of Florida Inc.**, (800) 477-8881 — (305) 743-5776 in Marathon, (305) 852-2288 in Islamorada and (305) 296-6572 in Key West — offers local-origination programming and national advertorials on Channel 5 in all regions of Monroe County except Ocean Reef. TCI, the largest cable television provider in the United States, serves about 30,000 subscribers nationwide, including 12,000 in Key West.

TCI's public-service programming includes live coverage of city commission meetings and political debates, as well as real estate listings and even a dating service. News related talk shows include *Keynoter Live at Five*, with *Keynoter* publisher Tom Schumaker. Some local shows offer live call-in sessions; all are scheduled weeknights between 6 and 9 PM.

An alternative provider to TCI Cablevision in Key West and up to mile marker 15 is **Keys Microcable**, (305) 296-8112, (800) 279-9288.

Until 1881 the ministerial needs of the sparsely populated Florida Keys (except for Key West) were filled locally by lay preachers.

Worship

The Florida Keys owes much of its religious history to the Conchs, the group of seafaring settlers who emigrated from the Bahamas.

Some of the Conchs were the descendants of members of the Eleutherian Society, who left England in 1649 and 1650 to seek religious freedom. Others were descendants of loyalists who fled the Carolinas and Georgia during the American Revolution to settle in the Bahamas, which was then still controlled by England. They settled primarily in Key West, bringing with them devout religious beliefs, mostly Methodist.

Until 1881 the ministerial needs of the sparsely populated Florida Keys (except for Key West) were filled locally by lay preachers. Settlements were scattered and rustic, their inhabitants farming the unyielding coral rock with attempts at growing pineapples, tomatoes, limes and melons. Many worked the sea as fishermen, harvesting a bounty more prolific. Two Key West ministers began making rounds of the Keys communities by boat, holding services for the next six years anywhere they could find a welcoming group of worshipers.

The main Upper Keys settlements in the late 1800s were Tavernier at the southern end of Key Largo; Planter, a mile north of Tavernier; Rock Harbor (present-day Key Largo); Newport, between Rock Harbor and Tarpon Basin; and Basin Hills, at the northern end of Key Largo. The first actual building outside Key West dedicated solely for worship services was built at Newport in 1885. Then a church was built in 1886 in Tavernier, named Barnett's Chapel in honor of its pastor. By 1887, a minister from the Florida Methodist Conference traveled a month-long circuit of the Upper Keys, visiting Basin Hills, Newport, Tavernier and Matecumbe. Plantation Key Methodists built their own church in 1899, and other congregations began assembling in private homes.

After the turn of the century, with the advent of Flagler's East Coast Railway Extension, the population of the Keys above Key West began to grow, and this growth spawned churches of diverse denominations. After World War II, the Florida Keys saw a further boom in population (see our Historical Evolution chapter), which spurred the construction of more churches. Unfortunately, the devastating hurricanes of 1935 and 1960 wiped out the physical church structures of the Middle and Upper Keys. None of these church buildings approach the age and stature of those of Key West, but vigorous and devout congregations welcome visitors and new parishioners.

Consult the Yellow Pages of the local telephone directory for times and locations of worship services. Some of the churches offer child care during selected services or prayer groups. If this is of interest to you, call the church directly to inquire about arrangements.

INSIDERS' TIP

The coral rock grotto built in 1922 at St. Mary Star of the Sea's Convent of Mary Immaculate in Key West holds a legend. A destructive hurricane passed over the island in 1919, leaving death and property damage strewn in its wake. Sister Louis Gabriel envisioned the grotto as a shrine dedicated to protecting Key West from hurricanes. Key West narrowly missed the hurricanes of 1935 and 1960 that hit the rest of the Keys but took a direct hit from Hurricane Georges in 1998.

St. Paul's Episcopal Church is a stately historic structure in Key West.

Key West

Earliest worship in Key West took place in the old courthouse in Jackson Square, where English-speaking persons would gather and hold nondenominational services. If a clergyman happened to be on the island for any reason, a service would be held and would be well attended by the devout of all faiths. When a group sharing the same beliefs became large enough, members splintered off and built a church of their own.

The first settlers to arrive were Bahamians who followed the Church of England's Anglican teachings. They were seafarers, descendants from the religious dissenters that left England more than 100 years before. They brought deeply religious convictions with them to the Keys. In March 1831, a movement started to bring a clergyman to the island of Key West on a permanent basis. It was stipulated, interestingly enough, that he would not be required to stay any portion of August or September that he found disagreeable. These happen to be hurricane-watch months in the Florida Keys.

From the Bahamian root of religious conviction sprang a proliferation of church denominations in Key West, some of which still meet for worship today. A number of churches in Key West are historically or architecturally significant: St. Paul's Episcopal Church, 401 Duval Street; First United Methodist (Old Stone) Church, 600 Eaton Street; St. Mary Star of the Sea, 1010 Windsor Lane; and Cornish Memorial A.M.E. (African Methodist Episcopal) Zion Church, 702 Whitehead Street.

For a complete listing of worship services in Key West each week, see the Friday edition of *The Key West Citizen*.

Index of Advertisers

Index

Symbols

N

O

P

Q

R